| Symbol | Definition | |
|---|---|---|
| $y^T$ | Real Transitory Income | Equation 9.10 |
| $R_{DEP}$ | Nominal Interest Rate on Bank Deposits | Equation 10.1 |
| $R_L$ | Nominal Interest Rate on Bank Loans | Equation 10.1 |
| EQ | Equity, in dollars | Table 10.4 |
| D | Debt, in dollars | Table 10.4 |
| q | Tobin's *q* | Equation 10.4 |
| m | M/P = Real Balances | Equation 11.2 |
| $m^d$ | Demand for Money | Equation 11.3 |
| n | Number of Transactions | Equation 11.5 |
| b | Transactions Costs | Equation 11.7 |
| V | Income Velocity of Circulation | Equation 11.12 |
| $R^B$ | Nominal Return on Bonds | Equation 11.14 |
| $R^E$ | Nominal Return on Equity | Equation 11.14 |
| $W_h$ | Human Wealth | Equation 11.14 |
| $W_n$ | Non-Human Wealth | Equation 11.14 |
| $E(\cdot\mid\cdot)$ | Expected Value of a Variable | Equation 12.1 |
| $S_t$ | Stock Price, at time t | Equation 12.1 |
| $d_t$ | Dividend Payment, at time t | Equation 12.7 |
| $V_S$ | Variance of Stock Prices | Equation 12.12 |
| $R_i^e$ | Expected Return, asset i | Table 13.3 |
| $pr_s$ | Probability of Occurrence in States of the World | Table 13.3 |
| $V_i$ | Variance of Returns, asset i | Table 13.3 |
| $\sum_s$ | Summation Symbol, over States of the World | Table 13.3 |
| $COV_{ij}$ | Covariance Between Returns on Asset i and Asset j | Table 13.4 |
| $CORR_{ij}$ | Correlation Coefficient Between Returns on Asset i and Asset j | Table 13.4 |
| $V_p$ | Variance of a Portfolio | Table 13.5 |
| $R^e$ | Expected Return | Table 13.5 |
| $R_p^e$ | Portfolio Expected Return | Table 13.5 |
| $SD_p$ | Standard Deviation of Portfolio Returns | Page 280 |
| $E^1$ | Expected Return on a 1-year Bond, 1 year from today | Equation 15.1 |
| $E_1^{n-1}$ | Expected Return on a 1-year bond, (n − 1) year from today | Equation 15.3 |
| $e^f$ | Forward Exchange Rate | Equation 15.7 |
| $R^f$ | Annual Yield on a Foreign-Dominated Asset | Equation 15.7 |
| L | Bank Loans | Table 16.1 |
| DEP | Bank Deposits | Table 16.1 |
| RES | Reserve Target (in dollars) | Table 16.1 |
| rr | Reserve Ratio | Following Equation 16.1 |
| TR | Total Bank Reserves | Equation 16.5 |
| er | Excess Reserves Ratio | Equation 16.8 |
| tr | Total Reserves Ratio | Equation 16.8 |
| $R_a$ | Nominal Return on Assets | Equation 16.13 |
| dur | Duration | Equation 16.19 |
| DD | Demand Deposits | Table 16.4 |
| TD | Time Deposits | Table 16.4 |
| GAP | Interest Sensitive Assets *less* Liabilities | Equation 16.18 |

# MONEY, BANKING, AND FINANCIAL INSTITUTIONS

## CANADA IN THE GLOBAL ENVIRONMENT

**SECOND EDITION**

# MONEY, BANKING, AND FINANCIAL INSTITUTIONS

## CANADA IN THE GLOBAL ENVIRONMENT

**SECOND EDITION**


**Pierre L. Siklos**

Wilfrid Laurier University



**McGraw-Hill Ryerson Limited**

Toronto Montreal New York Auckland Bogotá Caracas
Lisbon London Madrid Mexico Milan New Delhi
San Juan Singapore Sydney Tokyo

*McGraw-Hill*
*Ryerson Limited*

*A Subsidiary of The* ***McGraw-Hill*** *Companies*

**MONEY, BANKING, AND FINANCIAL INSTITUTIONS**
**Canada in the Global Environment**
Second Edition



ISBN: 0-07-552835-5

2 3 4 5 6 7 8 9 10 TCP 6 5 4 3 2 1 0 9 8

Printed and bound in Canada



Sponsoring Editor: Joan Langevin
Developmental Editor: Daphne Scriabin
Production Editor: Shirley Corriveau
Production Co-ordinator: Nicla Dattolico
Interior Design: Artplus Limited
Cover Design: Didier Fiszel Dessinateur Graphiste Inc.
Typesetter: Computer Composition of Canada
Printer: Best Book Manufacturers

**Canadian Cataloguing in Publication Data**

Siklos, Pierre L. (Pierre Leslie), 1955-
Money, banking and financial institutions: Canada in the global environment

2nd ed.
Includes index.
ISBN 0-07-552835-5

1. Money — Canada. 2. Banks and banking — Canada.
3. Financial institutions — Canada. 4. Money.
5. Financial institutions. 6. Securities. I. Title.

HG655.S55 1997 332.1'0971 C96-932098-1

To Nancy, Patrick, and James
for making life a lot of fun

To my mother for her constant support and love

and

To my late father, a wonderful source of
inspiration who is greatly missed

# Contents

# Preface

I was pleased by the reception given to the first edition of *Money, Banking, and Financial Institutions*, which has been used at virtually all major Canadian universities. This did not prevent several students, reviewers, and other users from making a number of useful criticisms and suggestions for changes. However, all those who commented appreciated and welcomed the textbook's overall organization. To be sure, while some would have liked to see, for example, more macroeconomic content here and there or some rearranging of a couple of chapters, there were no serious objections to the present order of chapters, which has been retained. Following the advice that "if it ain't broke don't fix it," and knowing from personal experience how annoying it is to use a new edition of a textbook that has been redesigned simply because of an author's whim, I chose instead to focus on improving the content and style of the existing chapters.

The philosophy of this edition is the same one as the previous edition, namely to ensure a clear and interesting description of the operations, functions, and historical development of the Canadian financial system and, more generally, the global financial system. However, in response to student and reviewers requests, the number of end-of-chapter questions has been doubled and more discussion-type questions have been added. In addition, this edition features several new focus boxes, a feature which previous users found to be a useful pedagogical device. As for chapter-by-chapter changes or improvements, only some highlights will be mentioned although every single chapter received thorough attention. Chapter 4, which describes financial instruments, has been revised to include recent changes in the Bank of Canada's operating procedures and instruments (e.g., Large Value Transfer System) and there is more extensive discussion of the Treasury bill market. Chapter 7 on the exchange rate now includes a discussion of the hysteresis concept in foreign exchange markets as well as trade-weighted exchange rates. Chapter 10, which deals with the financial and non-financial sectors of the economy, now has an illustrative example of the operation of the BIS capital-adequacy standards and the discussion of leverage has been simplified. Chapter 11, on the demand for money, now includes a brief description of money demand under hyperinflationary conditions. Chapter 12, which deals with stock prices, introduces material about stock price volatility and international linkages in stock prices. Discussion of the CAPM has been extended and improved in Chapter 13. Chapter 15 now incorporates a diagrammatic exposition of interest rate parity. Chapter 16 deals with the world of zero required reserves and contains a new section dealing with the so-called principal-agent problem. Chapter 17, which deals with the chartered banking system, has been thoroughly revised in light of the upcoming mid-term review of the 1991 Bank Act. Chapter 21, International Banking, sees the addition of material on the topic of central bank intervention in foreign exchange markets as well as a description of the so-called twin-deficits problem. Chapter 23, on International Financial Institutions, now covers the target zone exchange rate system and contains expanded coverage of the Maastricht Treaty and the European Monetary Union. Chapter 24, which discusses central banking and monetary policy, now incorporates sections dealing with the price stability objective of the Bank of Canada as well as the international experience with inflation targeting. Chapter 25, on the Art of Central Banking, now includes more extensive discussion of the recent debate over central bank independence. Finally, Chapter 26 deals in greater detail with the transmission mechanism of monetary policy and contains a new section on money and growth.

A text such as this one would not have been possible without the availability of economic data. Since the publication of the first edition of this text the advent of the World Wide Web has made it much easier to access information of the kind in this text. Below are some examples of Web sites that users may find interesting to visit. Some may, now or in the future, charge an access fee. In addition, McGraw-Hill Ryerson plans to launch a Web page for this text. At this site, updates, corrections, new suggestions for solutions, new questions, and the data may be accessed by users of the text.

| Web Site Address | Organization |
|---|---|
| www.bank-banque-canada.ca | Bank of Canada |
| www.statcan.ca | Statistics Canada |
| www.nytimes.com | New York Times |
| www.wsj.com | Wall Street Journal |
| www.theglobeandmail.ca | The Globe and Mail |
| www.fin.gc.ca | Department of Finance, Ottawa |
| www.cdhowe.org | CD Howe Institute. From this site you can access the home page of several large Canadian banks, the World Bank and the International Monetary Fund. |

# LEARNING AIDS

## CHAPTER INTRODUCTIONS

Each chapter begins with an introductory section that outlines what is to be accomplished in that chapter and links the chapter with the preceding and/or following chapters. In this fashion, students (and instructors) are constantly made aware of the continuity and context of the material being addressed.

## FOCUS BOXES

"Boxes" focusing on financial and economic matters appear regularly in most chapters. These boxes serve a number of functions. They instruct students in certain technical tasks such as reading the financial pages in newspapers. They stimulate further interest in a particular topic by summarizing existing research or by highlighting commonly held misconceptions about how the financial system operates. Occasionally, the aim of these boxes is to cast doubts on some of the theoretic propositions developed in the text. Many of the issues are illustrated by extensive references to articles in the financial press.

## ADVANCED MATERIAL

Whenever there is a section in a chapter that covers relatively advanced material the section begins with the asterisk symbol (*).

## END-OF-CHAPTER MATERIAL

### Summaries

All chapters conclude with a summary of the concepts and theories developed in the chapter.

### Important Terms

A list of important terms introduced in the chapter is presented at the end of each chapter accompanied by the page number where each term first appears in the body of the text and is in bold face print.

### GLOSSARY

A complete glossary of terms with page numbers for each term is included in the back of the book.

## INSTRUCTOR'S MATERIALS

To assist the instructor in making efficient and effective use of time, an instructor's manual is available with complete solutions to all the exercises in the text.

In addition, instructors who adopt the text will receive annually a newsletter outlining recent financial developments in Canada as well as international financial developments that have a bearing on Canada. Finally, instructors may choose to receive diskettes containing the data and figures presented in the text, thus allowing them to reproduce these data and figures or to create transparencies for overhead use. Please contact your McGraw-Hill Sales Representative to obtain diskettes.

## ACKNOWLEDGEMENTS

I owe a great debt to the many hundreds of students who have used this text and provided me with a great number of useful suggestions for improvements. I am grateful also to the many academic reviewers listed below whose criticisms and encouragement assisted me in the task of revision.

John Benson, *University of Guelph*
Dale Box, *University College of the Fraser Valley*
Patrick Crowley, *McGill University*
Chris Fader, *Acadia University*
Joel Fried, *University of Western Ontario*
Scott Lynch, *Memorial University*
Angela Redish, *University of British Columbia*
Apostolos Serletis, *University of Calgary*
two anonymous reviewers

Above all, however, I have to thank my family for understanding the magnitude of the task in revising a text and for providing a loving environment in which to complete this work. Any comments or suggestions are welcome by contacting me at the e-mail address below.

Pierre Siklos, 1997
e-mail address: banking@mach1.wlu.ca

## ALTERNATIVE PATHS THROUGH THE CHAPTERS OF THE BOOK

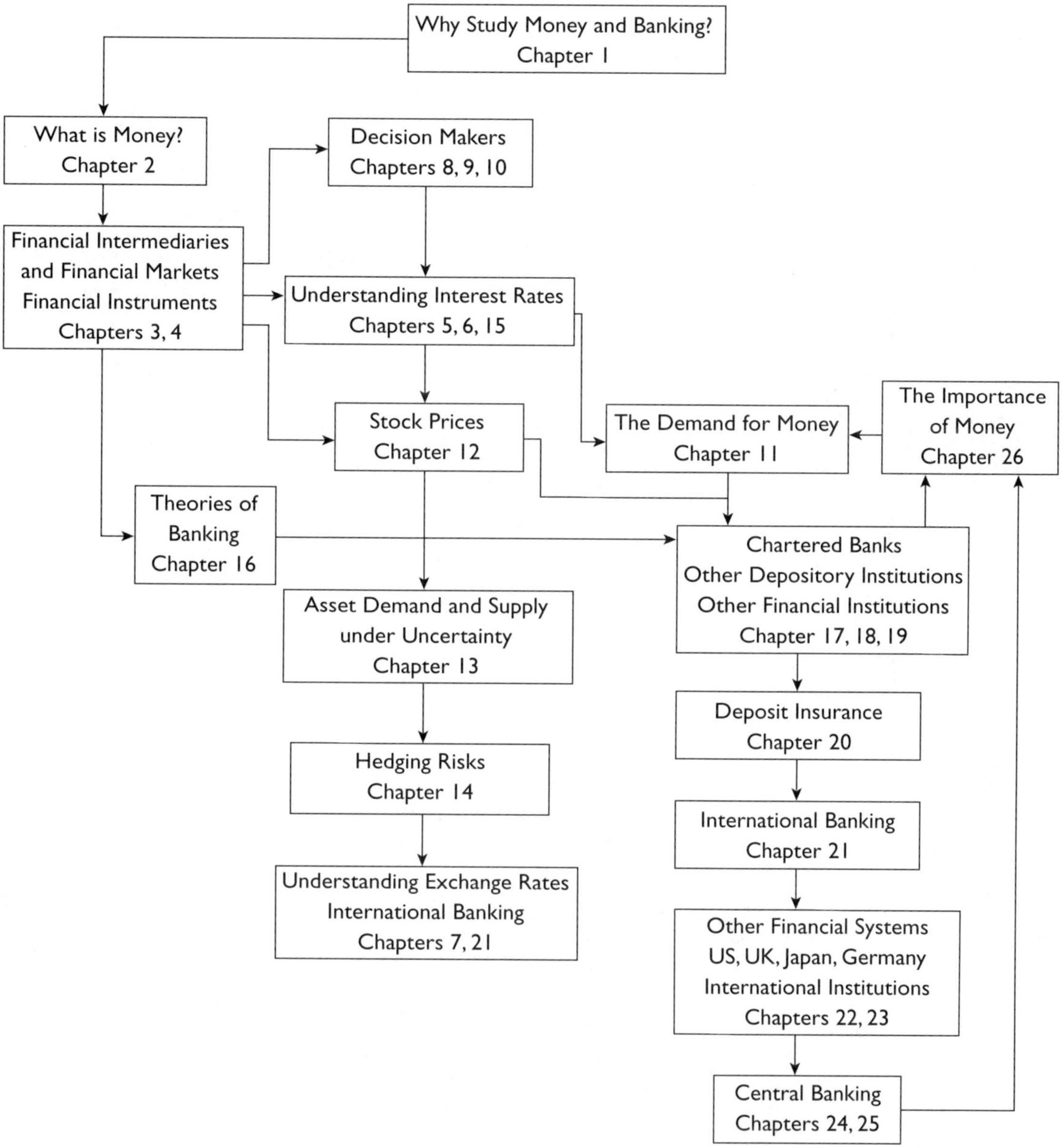

PART I

# OVERVIEW AND FUNDAMENTALS OF THE CANADIAN FINANCIAL SYSTEM

CHAPTER 1

# Why Study Money and Banking?

What is the study of money, banking, and financial markets? To answer such a far-reaching question will require this entire book. Chapter 1 seeks to whet your appetite with an overview of the subject and a glimpse of some of the fascinating issues in the field. By taking this approach you will finish the chapter with an idea of the major themes of the book, but you will also be left with more questions than answers. It is the task of the remaining chapters to answer these questions.

## THE ESSENCE OF MONEY AND BANKING

The study of money and banking is essentially the study of the role and function of monetary aggregates in the economy, and the study of financial markets—that is, the money, bond, and stock markets and their interrelationships. The effects of the financial system on the economy are determined by the instituted framework under which that system operates. Thus, the study of money and banking also requires an understanding of the organization, structure, and historical development of the various institutions that constitute the financial sector of the Canadian economy. One must know how government institutions and regulatory bodies influence the behaviour of financial institutions and financial market participants; one must understand the interplay among the financial system, the monetary authorities (that is, the Bank of Canada), and government economic policies, and their effects on economic activity as a whole. These topics are covered in this text.

Clearly, what takes place in the financial system affects the rest of the economy. The same might be said of other key sectors. What distinguishes financial markets from other key markets is the vital role played by *confidence* or *credibility.*

Credibility has two meanings here, both of which are essential to the financial system. First, individuals and firms entrust their funds to financial institutions in the confidence that these funds will be managed honestly and efficiently and will be available when promised. The sad truth is that financial systems, worldwide and throughout history, have not always been honest brokers of money. Scandals have plagued institutions from the United States to Japan in recent years. In Canada, too, individuals and groups have attempted to rig financial markets to their own advantage or abscond with funds entrusted to them.

The second meaning of credibility is "the extent to which the public believes a shift in policy has taken place when, indeed, such a shift has occurred."[1] Why is this confidence important? Whether the matter at hand concerns inflation, unemployment, or government policies in general, the public acts on the various announcements made by policymakers. If people guess incorrectly about how committed the government is to attaining a particular goal, the lack of synchronization between their actions and those of the government will have widespread consequences for interest rates and the rest of the financial system. A case in point is the recent debate over deficit cutting, about which we will say more later.

Thus, all people have ample reason to be interested in the arrangements and operations of their country's financial system.

## MONEY

When we say that the behaviour of monetary aggregates is one of our two principal topics, we are suggesting the crucial role of money in the analyses to follow. What is money? There are no easy answers to this question, as we will see. **Money** is, of course, an asset that embodies purchasing power in terms of goods, services, and other assets. One definition is the currency in circulation plus the deposits of the banking system. (We will discuss a more precise definition in the next chapter.)

Money is important in itself. It is also important because economists have developed explanations linking variations in the amount of money in circulation (caused by the process of monetary policy) to interest rates, stock prices, and economic activity in general. (Interest rate analysis plays a prominent role in the first two parts of this text). Thus, financial indicators such as interest rate changes and the yield curve may provide clues about future credit conditions—that is, the looseness or tightness of financial borrowing conditions.

For an idea of the central role that is played by money, interest rates, and inflation in this textbook, consider the various plots shown in Figures 1.1 to 1.3. Figure 1.1 displays the striking way the money supply and the price level seem

---

1 A. Cukierman, "Central Bank Behaviour and Credibility: Some Recent Theoretical Developments," *Review of the Federal Reserve Bank of St. Louis* 17 (May 1986): 6.

## ECONOMICS FOCUS 1.1 Reading the Monetary Tea Leaves

Central banks pay careful attention to a number of variables that are purported to track economic activity, interest rates, and inflation, to name just a few examples. Economists, on the other hand, are fond of attempting to guess what central banks' policies might be, since these instructions are prone to secrecy. One can find daily commentaries on the state of monetary policy in publications such as *The Globe and Mail* and *The Financial Post*. From time to time, think-tanks such as the C.D. Howe Institute publish monographs, intended for a fairly general audience about the Bank of Canada's policies.

Another contributor to the list of monetary tea-leaf readers is the Swiss Bank Julius Baer. In a report, the bank ranked the *tightness* of monetary policy according to changes in interest rates, the value of a country's money supply adjusted for changes in prices, the exchange rate, and the difference between interest rates on financial instruments maturing in 90 days and in 10 years or more (the yield curve).

We will see in this textbook how these variables may be indicative of future inflation rates. The tightness of monetary policy thus refers to how these variables influence the expected course of inflation. Generally, countries with tight monetary policies are prone to experience relatively less inflation than countries with loose monetary policies.

What did the Swiss bank conclude? Canada's policies, at least until early 1990, appear to have been neither tight nor loose, while West Germany (as it was called then) had the tightest monetary policy. (Indeed, Germany has acquired a formidable reputation as a country that will not tolerate much inflation.) The United States seemed to have the loosest policy of all the G-7 industrialized nations. Subsequently, it becomes difficult to tell countries' monetary policies apart. Almost in unison, they all embarked upon ambitious disinflation plans with Canada among the leaders in the drive to reduce inflation.

**Sources:**

"Bank Julius Baer," *The Economist*, 4 August 1990.

Peter Howitt, *Monetary Policy in Transition: A Study of Bank of Canada Policy* (Montreal: C.D. Howe Institute, 1986).

David E.W. Laidler and William P. Robson, *The Great Canadian Disinflation: The Economics and Politics of Monetary Policy in Canada, 1988–93* (Toronto: C.D. Howe Institute, 1993).

to have paralleled each other. Visual inspection of the two curves suggests a connection between money (or monetary policy) and price level movements that requires explanation.

Figure 1.2 shows the similar synchronous movements of the money supply and an aggregate measure of economic activity. Again, it appears that a link between the monetary and the real sides of the economy may exist.

A connection between money growth and inflation also follows from the suggested link between money and prices. Figure 1.3 suggests that a relationship between interest rates and inflation also exists. Thus, money, as it affects inflation, may also influence interest rates.

The apparent centrality of money, both for economic activity in general and for financial markets in particular, suggests that an understanding of the factors

**FIGURE 1.1** Money and Price Level Movements since 1913

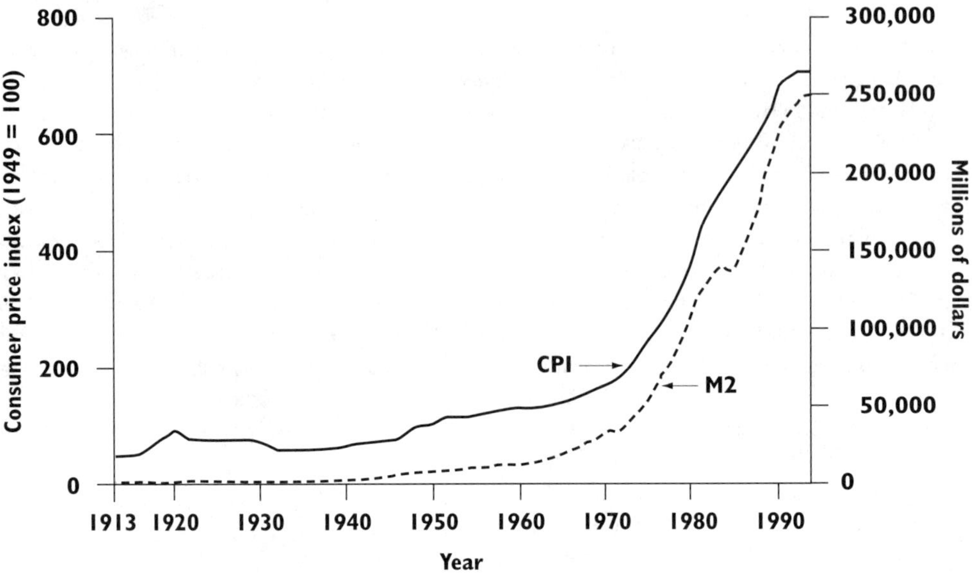


M2 is one of several official measures of the money supply.[a] The consumer price index (CPI) measures the price level (rises show inflation). The two data series appear to have moved in tandem for almost a century.

Source: P.L. Siklos, "Income Velocity and Institutional Change: Time Series Evidence from Five Industrialized Countries, 1870–1986," *Journal of Money, Credit and Banking* 25 (August 1993), with updates from the sources given therein.

[a] For the definition, see Chapter 2.

that determine its supply and demand must be a leading feature of the analysis to follow.

## THE TRANSMISSION MECHANISM

Economists have long been interested in how money and monetary policy influence individuals and economies as a whole. As usual, their views on the subject are not unanimous. Figure 1.4, however, illustrates a fairly well accepted *transmission mechanism*—that is, the means by which the money supply affects other aspects of the economy.

Starting from some equilibrium, that is, where none of the variables we are interested in show any tendency to change, sustained increases in the money supply imply positive money growth, which causes prices to change. Why? Because, as we'll shall see in Chapter 6, the market perceives that too much money

**FIGURE 1.2** Money and Real Income since 1913

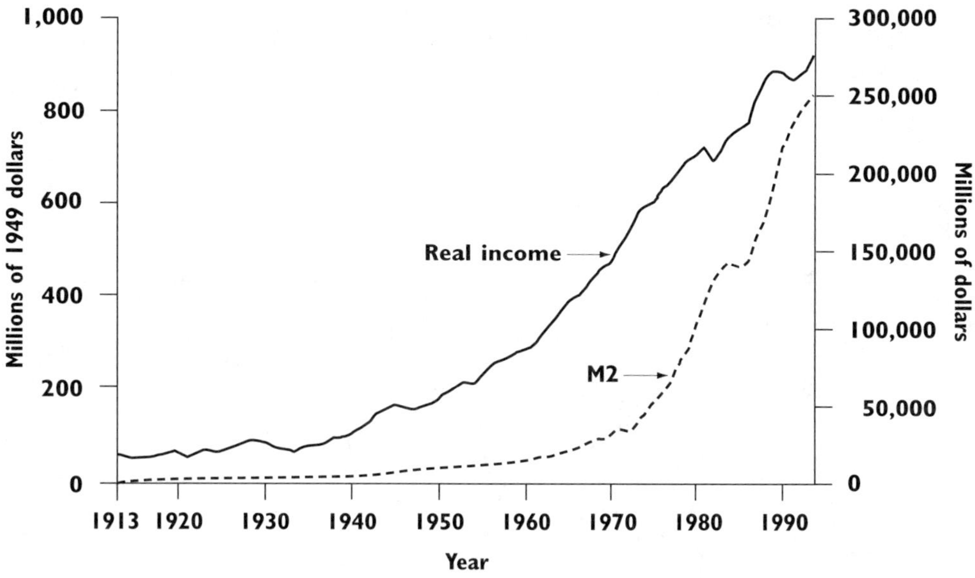


Real income, a measure of economic activity, is nominal national income divided by the price level. A common measure of real income is Gross Domestic Product or GDP. Like the money supply, real income seems to have moved in tandem with inflation for almost a century.

Source: P.L. Siklos, "Income Velocity and Institutional Change: Time Series Evidence from Five Industrialized Countries, 1870–1986," *Journal of Money, Credit and Banking* 25 (August 1993), with updates from the sources given therein.

is chasing too few goods. In an attempt to rid themselves of the "excess" money, prices for goods and services are bid upward. The result is **inflation**, which, by definition, is simply a measure of how quickly prices change over time.

Notice that the figure has an arrow running from money growth to inflation but a question mark on the arrow running from inflation to money growth. Economists generally believe that inflation must originate with money growth; as Milton Friedman has said, "Inflation is always and everywhere a monetary phenomenon."[2] Nevertheless, inflation erodes the purchasing power of money,

2 This is a famous quote that was repeated most recently in M. Friedman, *Money Mischief: Episodes in Monetary History* (New York: Harcourt, Brace, Jovanovich, 1992), xi. For many years, economists presumed inflationary expectations to be influenced solely by the past history of inflation. Recently, however, the profession has been greatly influenced by those who view individuals as forward-looking. In essence, these analysts believe that investors do not wait for inflation to happen before revising their views of the future; instead, they seek to anticipate its course by keeping track of indicators of future inflation, such as the money supply. This is why an arrow is drawn directly from money to expected inflation.

**FIGURE 1.3** Inflation and the Interest Rate since the End of World War II

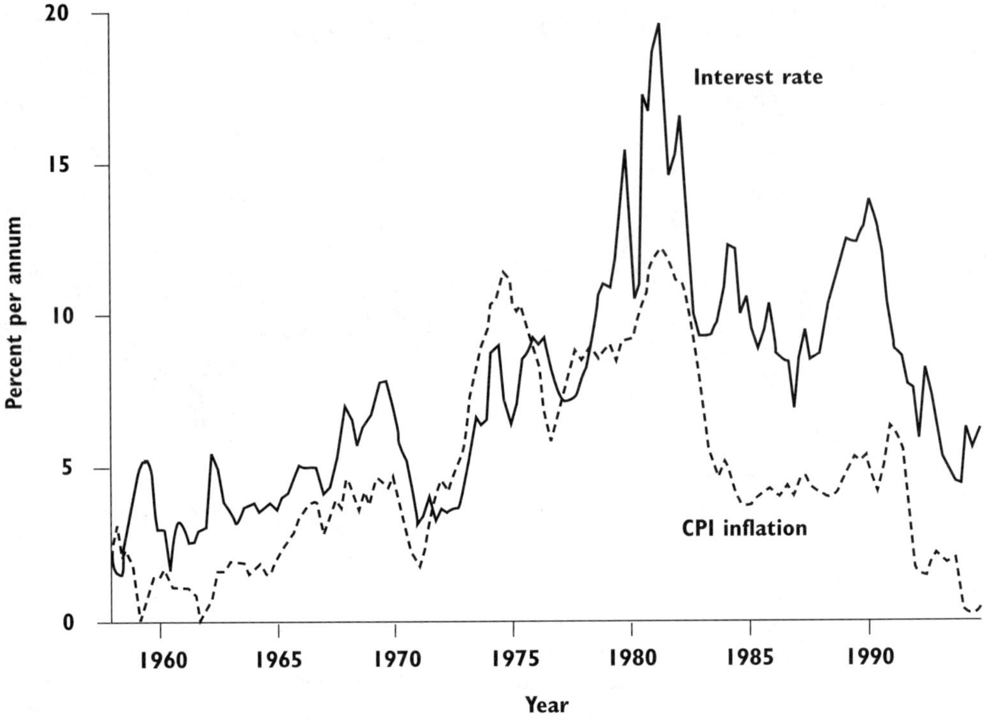


The inflation curve in each panel shows the rate of change in the level of prices. It is traced against the interest rate. (The interest rate is measured here by the yield on 3-month Government of Canada Treasury bills.)

Source: P.L. Siklos, "Income Velocity and Institutional Change: Time Series Evidence from Five Industrialized Countries, 1870–1986," *Journal of Money, Credit and Banking* 25 (August 1993) and updated from the sources given therein.

sometimes very badly as in *hyperinflation*, a situation in which the inflation rate exceeds 50% a month. Governments have been known to respond to sharp inflation by printing ever-increasing quantities of money. Therefore, although money growth usually causes inflation, there is the odd possibility that inflation may sometimes cause money growth.

Figure 1.4 also reflects the process by which interest rate change depends crucially on investors' beliefs about the anticipated course of inflation, which are called **expectations of inflation**. The reason, as we see later in greater detail, is that borrowing and lending activities are prompted in part by beliefs about the benefits and costs of purchasing goods and services today relative to the future. In other words, an interest rate exists because individuals enter into contracts

**FIGURE 1.4** A Possible Transmission Mechanism for the Influence of the Money Supply

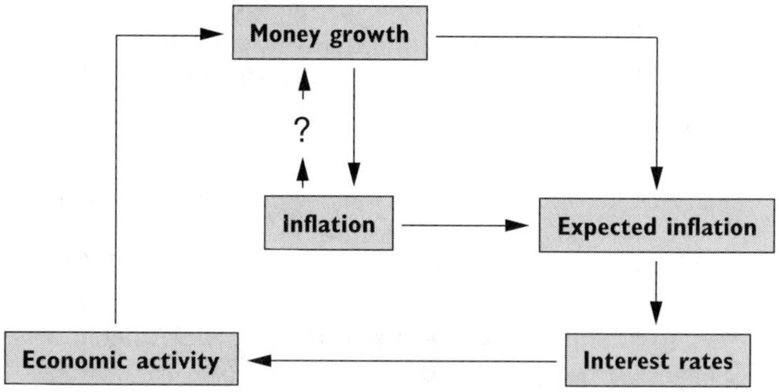


Starting at the top of the diagram, we see that growth in the money supply leads to changes in expected inflation. It likely also leads to changes in actual inflation (which may itself encourage money supply growth–see the text). Expected inflation affects interest rates and thus the level of economic activity.

either to defer spending or to enjoy more spending today. To postpone spending implies that people are concerned about the purchasing power of financial resources available only in the future, which will be affected by expectations of future inflation.

Finally, because spending is affected, economic activity is influenced by current interest rate levels. Economic activity, in turn, may have a bearing on the future course of money growth; whether it does or not depends in part on how the central bank and the government react to current economic performance, a topic of considerable interest to economists and others.

Where is the financial system in all this? The answer, as we begin to see in the next chapter, is that the links from money to economic activity are greatly influenced by the efficiency and innovations of the financial sector of the economy.

## WHY STUDY FINANCIAL MARKETS?

We should make clear that many different interest rates exist because financial markets offer a bewildering array of financial assets. To get some idea of this, consider Figure 1.5, which plots two different interest rate measures: one is called a short-term interest rate, because the asset in question matures in the not-too-distant future; the other is called a long-term interest rate, because the asset matures many years ahead. Notice that the two measures move more or less in tandem, but the short-term rate appears to be more volatile. An explanation of

**FIGURE 1.5** Short-Term and Long-Term Interest Rates since the End of World War II

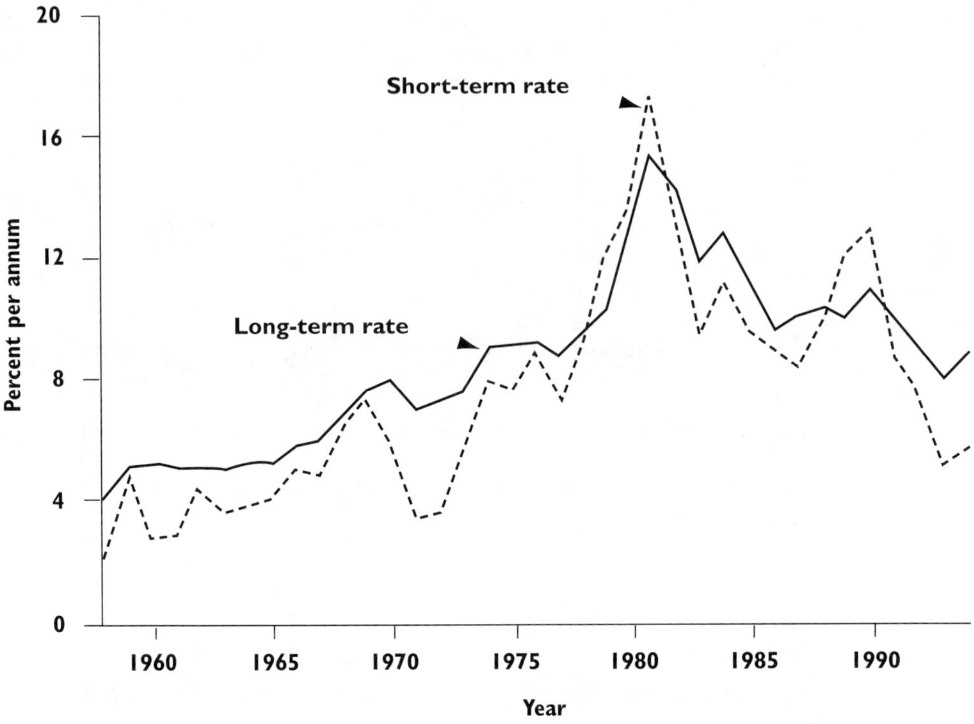


Short-term and long-term interest rates normally differ (the long-term rates are usually higher) but move in tandem.

Note: The long-term interest rate here is the yield on Government of Canada bonds with a term to maturity of 10 years and more. The short-term rate is the yield on 3-month Treasury bills.

Source: David R. Johnson and P.L. Siklos, "Political and Economic Determinants of Interest Rate Behavior: Are Central Banks Different?," *Economic Inquiry* (1996), with updates from sources given therein.

this phenomenon can provide clues about the future course of inflation and economic activity.

Another asset market that deserves close scrutiny is the market for stocks. Neither academics nor practitioners agree about explanations of stock price behaviour. Should one really laugh at the idea that the price of an individual stock represents the present discounted value of the future flow of dividends? Why do events such as the stock market crash of 1987 occur and how are they explained? Are stock prices forecastable, or do they simply randomly fluctuate around some value over time?

The clout of financial markets has increased dramatically in the last decade. A bad word here from a politician or a misstep there by some government official can send bond, stock, and foreign exchange markets into a tailspin. Financial markets trade 24 hours a day and events in Tokyo are no more distant to a trader in Toronto or New York than events in Ottawa or elsewhere.

## THE CANADIAN FINANCIAL SYSTEM

All this discussion about money, interest rates, inflation, and stock prices omits the fact that individuals and institutions are in the middle of all the action in the transmission mechanism. Yet, it is important to study and understand how financial institutions operate, how the economic environment influences decision making in financial institutions, and how the Canadian system compares with other prominent financial systems in the world.

One of the most significant developments in Canada (and in much of the rest of the world) in the last two decades has been the gradual reduction of the involvement of governments in financial systems. Because government intervention has usually taken the form of regulation, the simplification or elimination of regulations is called **deregulation**.

These developments have had a profound impact on the shape of the Canadian financial system. Its institutions used to fit neatly into four categories—chartered banks, trust companies and near-banks, insurance companies, and investment dealers—with government regulations precisely defining the role of each according to its specific functions. Since the 1960s, however, the divisions have been crumbling under the weight of two forces: the increased competition in the financial sector and regulatory reform, prompted in large part by financial innovation, the rapid development of computer technology, and the perception of increased volatility in the financial sector.

For example, it is becoming increasingly difficult to distinguish chartered banks from trust companies and credit unions. Nevertheless, all institutional change seems to have a common feature: it comes slowly. Although it is increasingly hard to tell the financial system's players apart, they still retain some distinct characteristics, as we will see. And the functions, permitted activities, and customs of Canada's financial institutions do not exactly match those of many other countries (they differ from each other too) nor those of international organizations, such as the International Monetary Fund.

## THE INTERNATIONAL DIMENSION

It is impossible today to explore our own financial system in isolation from events outside Canada. One reason is summed up in the catchword "globalization," that is, the growing integration of capital markets worldwide. The other is the nature of the Canadian economy: small (its gross domestic product—GDP—is only a small fraction of world GDP) and open (exports plus imports reached 65.9% of GDP in 1994.[3] Yet another reason is the rise in the reliance of the Canadian government (and the provinces) on foreigners to finance our deficits. For example, Canada's net indebtedness toward other countries grew an average of almost 22% in the period 1983–1993. Moreover, whereas 69% of our foreign obligations in 1983 were vis-à-vis the United States this share fell to just over 44% by 1993. A substantial portion of the change has been due to our growing indebtedness toward Japan.[4]

**Globalization** refers to the ability of investors to access foreign markets easily. For example, a Canadian-based firm can cross-list its stock on the London and New York stock exchanges. An investor in Canada can purchase financial assets that are sold from a foreign country.

The benefits of globalization are many. The ability to diversify is enhanced, as is the ability to access more markets. Markets become larger and more liquid, so they can absorb shifts in demand and supply with less impact on prices than can smaller markets. There are, however, some potential risks. For example, rules and regulations differ widely from one country to another; an uninformed investor can therefore incur different types of costs when investing abroad.

This text explores the phenomenon of globalization in three ways. First, whenever we discuss some important aspect of Canada's financial system or financial history, we mention lessons from abroad. Second, an entire chapter is devoted to brief surveys of financial systems in four countries that are among the main players in the global economy. Third, we spend some time exploring the role and functions of the most important international financial organizations.

To see why this international dimension is so crucial in a course about money and banking, consider the implications for a small, open economy such as Canada's.

International financial considerations loom large in influencing domestic financial conditions. The flow of funds from abroad, a means of financing both the public and the private sectors, is growing rapidly. Thus, such diverse issues as exchange rate systems and the international debt crisis are important topics for Canadian students.

International differences in economic performance further suggest the importance of the international dimension in financial markets. Inflation rates and interest rates all vary internationally, even among the leading countries of the industrialized West, such as the G-7 and G-10[5] (see Figures 1.6 and 1.7). Mean-

3 International Monetary Fund, *International Financial Statistics* (August 1995).

4 See "Canada's International Net Indebtedness," *Bank of Canada Review* (Summer 1994): 37–50.

5 The G-7 countries are Canada, France, Germany, Italy, Japan, the United Kingdom, and the United States.

**FIGURE 1.6** Inflation Rates in the G-7 Countries

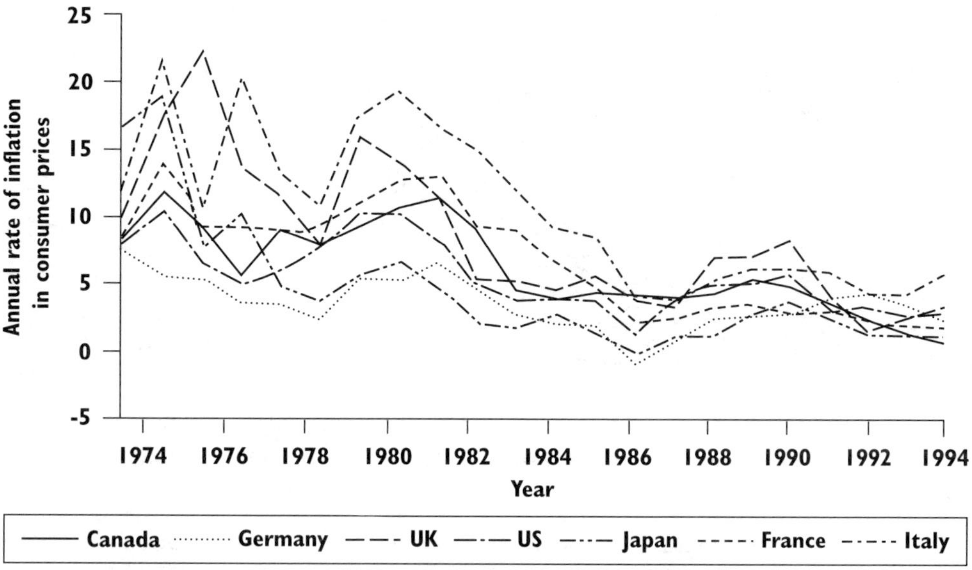


Although inflation rates were similar enough to make it difficult to distinguish one G-7 country's inflation curve from another's here, it is clear that the rate was more volatile (variable) in some countries than in others.

Source: Pierre L. Siklos and Mark E. Wohar, "Convergence in Interest Rates and Inflation Rates Over Countries and Across Time," *Review of International Economics* (1997 forthcoming).

while, the volatile nature of exchange rates in recent years (see Figure 1.8) has rekindled the issue of whether it is better to fix the exchange rate or instead continue to permit it to float. The large gyrations in the value of the Canadian dollar vis-à-vis the US dollar in the aftermath of Finance Minister Paul Martin's important 1995 budget are evident and reveal how quickly and strongly financial markets react to "news." Explaining the linkages and some of the reasons for the differences is part of the task of this book.

## A FINAL WORD

Students of money and banking must be conversant not only with the terms, facts, and concepts of the financial industry, but also with the analytical tools used to examine the relationships between sectors of the financial industry, and

The G-10 countries are the G-7 countries plus Belgium, the Netherlands, Sweden, and Switzerland. (Although there are 11 countries, the group is called the G-10 because Belgium and the Netherlands count as one.)

**FIGURE 1.7** Interest Rates in the G-7 Countries

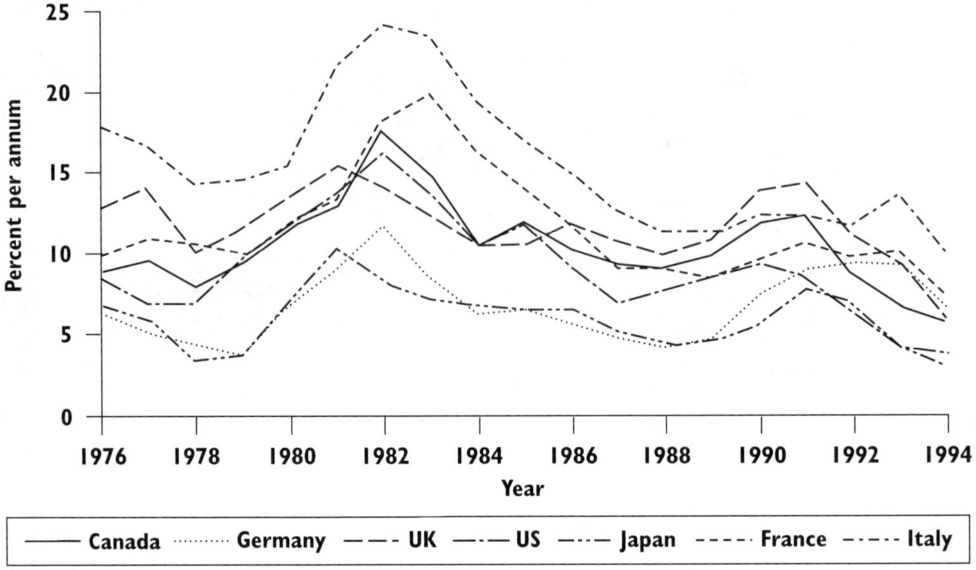


A financial instrument in a Eurocurrency is one denominated in a currency other than that of the country of issue. Here we see the annual yield on a Eurocurrency instrument denominated in each of the G-7 currencies. The interest rate movements are broadly similar, but there are differences in levels and volatility.

Source: Pierre L. Siklos and Mark E. Wohar, "Convergence in Interest Rates and Inflation Rates Over Countries and Across Time," *Review of International Economics* (1997 forthcoming).

the relationship between the financial sector and the rest of the economy. In turn, the ability to use these analytical tools to anticipate the future, and an understanding of the issues involved requires that we present theories, financial or economic in nature. Of course, theories require assumptions about how individuals and firms behave, and such assumptions are the source of many disagreements; but without theories, however imperfect they may be, we would be unable to explain the past and predict the future in a logical manner. We could only list a series of facts and figures without drawing any useful conclusion from them.

Lest you think that the subject is dull, consider the following quote from James Carville, a former strategist to the Democrats in the United States: "I used to think, if there was reincarnation, I wanted to come back as the President or Pope or a .400 baseball hitter. But now I want to come back as the bond market. You can intimidate everyone."[6]

6 As quoted in K. Phillips, "The Tyranny of Traders," *Report on Business* magazine (November 1994): 65.

**FIGURE 1.8** Exchange Rates: The Canadian Dollar against the US Dollar in 1995 (January – July)

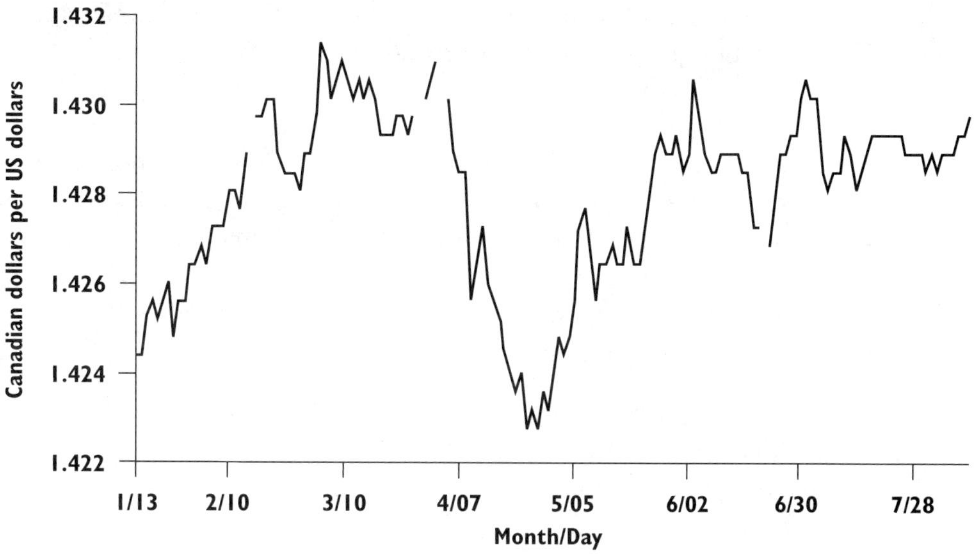


The curve shows the number of Canadian dollars needed to purchase one US dollar. The data are daily (noon rates) and the gaps are for holidays and weekends.

Source: Research Department, Bank of Canada.

The idea of studying such diverse and complex material may seem daunting. Take heart. No matter what your background, you have some knowledge of introductory economics. The discussions in this book make much use of the material you learned in the study of both microeconomics and macroeconomics (with relatively greater emphasis placed on microeconomic concepts). So, although the discussions in this book are complete in themselves, you may find that your introductory economics textbook is a useful supplementary roadmap.[7]

Enjoy your explorations in this fascinating subject.

## SUMMARY

- This chapter attempts to give a flavour of the things to come in this textbook. Specifically, it outlines the aspects of economics involved in studying money and banking.

7 See, for example, C.R. McConnell, S.L. Brue, and T.P. Barbiero, *Macroeconomics*, 7th Cdn. ed. (Toronto: McGraw-Hill Ryerson, 1996); and Michael Parkin, *Economics* (Reading, Mass: Addison-Wesley, 1994).

- Studying money refers to studying monetary aggregates and how these are linked to the rest of the economy via a transmission mechanism that involves inflation and interest rates.
- Studying the Canadian financial system involves more than learning a description of our own banking institutions. It involves studying the bond market and the stock market as well as international financial institutions.
- Because the Canadian economy is relatively small and open to international influences, discussion of the global dimension of economics is a vital part of the study of money and banking. Exchange rates and other international economic influences are important topics for analysis.

## IMPORTANT TERMS

| | |
|---|---|
| deregulation (p. 11) | inflation (p. 7) |
| expectations of inflation (p. 8) | money (p. 4) |
| globalization (p. 12) | price index (p. 6) |

## EXERCISES

1. See Figure 1.1. Did the change in the price level accelerate during the 1970s and 1980s relative to earlier periods?

2. During a recession there is usually a fall in real income. What events are associated with the dips in real income that occurred in 1929–33, 1973–74, 1981–82, and 1991–92?

3. Long-term interest rates are generally higher than short-term interest rates (see Figure 1.5). Why would this be the case?

4. Figure 1.7 suggests that the interest rate in Italy is generally higher than the interest rates in the other G-7 countries. Why would this be the case? (Hint: See Figure 1.6.)

5. Can you speculate why short-term rates tend to be more volatile than long-term rates?

6. Notice from Figures 1.6 and 1.7 that inflation rate and interest rate differences have become much smaller in the 1990s relative to the 1970s. Speculate on why this might be the case.

7. If you were a currency trader and could forecast exchange rates ahead of time

with a great deal of precision, when would it have been best to buy and then resell Canadian dollars ahead of time in the period covered by Figure 1.8?

## REFERENCES

Bordo, M.D., L. Jonung, and Pierre L. Siklos, "Institutional Change and the Velocity of Money," *Economic Inquiry* (1997 forthcoming).

Economic Council of Canada. *A New Frontier: Globalization and Canada's Financial Markets.* Ottawa, Ont.: Minister of Supply and Services, 1989: 17–19.

Goldstein, M., and M. Musa, "The Integration of World Capital Markets," IMF working paper 93–95 (December 1993).

International Monetary Fund. *International Financial Statistics* (various issues).

OECD. *Main Economic Indicators* (various issues).

Siklos, P.L. "Income Velocity and Institutional Change: Time Series Evidence from Five Industrialized Countries, 1870–1986." *Journal of Money, Credit and Banking* 25 (August 1993).

Statistics Canada, CANSIM database.

"Technical Note: A Weighted-Average Exchange Rate Index for the Canadian Dollar." *Bank of Canada Review* (September 1984): 19–24.

CHAPTER 2

# What Is Money?

What is money and how do we measure it? These questions are important because a variety of explanations about the behaviour of interest rates and economic activity, to name but two examples, depend crucially on how we define and measure money.

In discussing the asset that is called money, we consider various monetary standards of the past and present. We then turn to a description of the various ways in which the money supply in Canada can be measured.

The chapter ends with a discussion of the economic consequences of inflation. Since inflation affects the value of money, however defined, government policies that influence inflation also influence social welfare.

## WHY MONEY?

Economists rarely disagree that efficiency, and thus social welfare,[1] is improved by the introduction of an *asset* (something of value) called money. Notice our use of the phrase "called money." It is important to understand, even before we attempt official definitions, that money is not necessarily the bills people carry in their wallets. Rather, money is whatever people decide it is. In other words, there is a social agreement that some object (or objects) may fulfil the functions of money. Cattle, fish hooks, shells, hunks of stone, and beaver pelts have all been used as money.

### BARTER

The reason a money system improves social welfare is because the alternative is **barter**, the direct exchange of goods and services for other goods and services. Barter is probably as old as humanity, and it still persists even in highly indus-

1 Economists measure welfare in terms of utility, which refers to some quantifiable index of the satisfaction derived by individuals or society from, for example, the consumption of some good.

trialized modern economies.[2] You cut your roommate's hair and she drives you to Regina next week.

But what if your roommate has decided to let her hair grow? Or if you're headed for Halifax? The problem here is that barter requires a double coincidence of wants: the transaction the seller desires can take place only if the seller is able to find a purchaser who wishes to exchange for what the seller has and if the purchaser has something the seller wishes to obtain, or if the seller can arrange a series of transactions ending with possession of the desired good.

Several other problems arise in a barter system. The value of the asset the seller receives in exchange is probably variable. The two parties to each transaction have to negotiate its "price," a time-consuming process involving judgements of intrinsic value. And the sheer number of transactions required can be enormous.

To see the last point, consider a simplified example. Assume an economy has three goods, called 1, 2, and 3. A seller in a barter economy would face the following possible transactions:

| | | |
|---|---|---|
| — | $2 \longrightarrow 1$ | $3 \longrightarrow 1$ |
| $1 \longrightarrow 2$ | — | $3 \longrightarrow 2$ |
| $1 \longrightarrow 3$ | $2 \longrightarrow 3$ | — |

where the arrows indicate the direction of the transaction and the dashes mean no transaction can occur (we assume a good is never exchanged for itself). A total of six transactions are possible.

Now suppose this society elects to call good 1 "money." Any good can be purchased with money and then sold for money to obtain a different good, so there is no longer a need for goods 2 and 3 to be traded with each other. Therefore, a seller now faces only the following transactions:

| | | |
|---|---|---|
| — | $2 \longrightarrow 1$ | $3 \longrightarrow 1$ |
| $1 \longrightarrow 2$ | — | — |
| $1 \longrightarrow 3$ | — | — |

Having a monetary system has reduced the number of potential transactions to four—a more efficient situation. If the economy had more than three goods to exchange, the "savings" would be even greater.

Clearly, a monetary system can reduce transactions costs and simplify trades. Indeed, the bulk of our economy functions only because we use money and thus facilitate exchanges.

---

2 Indeed, some modern technologies, such as electronic bulletin boards, facilitate and thus encourage barter transactions.

## THE FUNCTIONS OF MONEY

If a monetary economy is more efficient than a barter economy, money must have special functions that cannot be easily duplicated by anything else. Money is thought to fulfil three basic functions.

1. **Medium of exchange**. Transactions can be settled through the use of the asset called money. This function, which is probably the most obvious one, eliminates the need for the double coincidence of wants and thereby separates sellers from buyers (you do not have to want to buy a good or service if you want to sell one). Money thus facilitates the division of labour, another aspect of an efficient economy.

2. **Medium of account**. The values of goods and services and other assets are denominated in terms of the asset called money. In other words, money provides a standardized way of measuring value in exchange—one that can be recorded for a variety of purposes, not least of which is debts and future payments.[3] The medium of account in Canada is the Canadian dollar.

3. **A store of value**. The asset called money enables individuals to hold their wealth and postpone purchases, or otherwise plan transactions as suits them best. One can store wealth in other assets (think of diamonds and land, as well as bank accounts and bonds), but their usefulness may vary with their **liquidity**, which means the ease and low cost with which they can be traded for the medium of exchange. If the asset storing wealth is itself the medium of exchange, that asset is said to be perfectly liquid.

Over the years, analysts have suggested various refinements or exceptions to this list of functions, meeting various degrees of agreement or objection from their peers. For example, some have suggested that money must be designated as legal tender—be specified by the government as something that must be accepted in settlement of transactions—if it is to fulfil the medium of exchange function. This corollary connection is incorrect for at least two reasons. First, a society seeking efficiency will eventually come up with a medium of exchange—one that everyone can identify easily and use confidently—no matter what the government does. Indeed, a government may not be able to enforce the use of an unsuitable medium. History is full of examples of people resorting to

---

3 The medium of account function is sometimes called the *unit of account* function. The former phrase is more correct because some physical item, be it gold, silver, or paper, has always served as money. Units of account do not exist, however. For example, the International Monetary Fund and the European Monetary System, respectively, express the values of some assets in the SDR (special drawing rights) and the ECU (European currency unit), even though no currency bearing either name circulates.

## ECONOMICS FOCUS 2.1 Russia and the US $100 Bill

In 1995 the US Government announced the introduction of a new $100 bill to replace the older version which was prone to counterfeiting. What should have been an innocuous annoucement sent panic-stricken Russians to their banks demanding to know whether the old bills would become worthless. Despite public pronouncements by the US Ambassador, the Federal Reserve in Washington and even the US Treasury assuring the Russian people of the validity of the old notes Russians, the Russian government, and even the Russian central bank were not satisfied. Why? Simply because Russians view the $100 bill in particular as a store of value, especially since inflation in Russia has often been in the double-digits per month! Indeed, the Russian central bank estimate that up to 80% of the US dollars held by Russians is in the form of $100 bills.

alternatives when their governments have so debased or devalued the legally defined medium of exchange as to render it virtually useless for transactions or caused a lack of confidence in it as a store of value.

A second problem with the legal tender view is the issue of **transactions costs**, which are the costs associated with converting one asset into another. People will use financial instruments that are not legal tender if doing so reduces transaction costs. For example, tourists often make purchases with traveller's cheques, which are accepted worldwide, reduce the potential cost of loss or theft, and may even provide some return when exchanged for other currencies. Table 2.1 shows how much a tourist in several foreign capitals can receive for $100 Canadian offered in various forms. A traveller's cheque or even a credit card may be a better transaction medium than cash.

Yet another issue is the relationship between the medium of exchange function and the store of value function. Some economists believe that the first need not imply the second. For example, "smart" credit cards and other computer-based devices could, in theory at least, overcome the need for money as a "temporary abode of purchasing power"[4] arising out of the lack of synchronization between sales and purchases.

Moreover, a wide range of assets generate interest income but are not generally accepted as a means of payment. Why should people treat cash and chequing accounts as stores of value when they could put their wealth in assets such as government bonds that produce a higher return? We are led once more to view the medium of exchange function as the primary one.

4 M. Friedman, "The Quantity Theory: A Restatement," in *Studies in the Quantity Theory of Money*, ed. M. Friedman (Chicago: University of Chicago Press, 1956), 3–21.

**TABLE 2.1** VALUE OF ONE HUNDRED CANADIAN DOLLARS IN VARIOUS FORMS

| City | Currency | Cash | Traveller's Cheques | Credit Card |
|---|---|---|---|---|
| London | Pound | 40.17 | 42.36 | 42.78 |
| Paris | Franc | 411.77 | 415.44 | 426.50 |
| Rome | Lira | 99,912 | 99,912 | 93,951 |
| Tokyo | Yen | —[a] | 9,916 | 9,912 |

[a] Tokyo offices do not pay yen for US dollars.

Source: *New York Times*, 25 August 1991, using exchange rates from the end of 1995. Original figures converted into Canadian dollars at an exchange rate of $1US = $1.36 Cdn.

## MONETARY STANDARDS

Given the inconvenience and lack of efficiency of barter, it is not surprising that all but the most unsophisticated societies have adopted some form of money. And once money exists, there will soon be rules, regulations, and customs regarding its issue and use.

A society's monetary standard is the basis of its monetary arrangements. Broadly speaking, history has produced two types of monetary standards:

1. A commodity standard, in which the monetary unit is some physical asset in a specified quantity and often quality. For example, the US dollar was once specified as "25.8 grains of gold nine-tenth fine." The *circulating medium*—what people actually use as money in exchanges—may be the physical commodity itself, perhaps marked in some special way. For example, metal may be minted into coins, which are called specie.

   In a more sophisticated arrangement, the circulating medium may be paper notes—evidence of a promise to pay—that have no intrinsic value but are backed by and convertible into the commodity. Notes and specie can and often have existed simultaneously.

2. A fiat-money standard, in which the circulating medium is notes (and perhaps coins with virtually no non-monetary uses) that are worth whatever the issuing agent—generally a government—says they are worth. (*Fiat* is the Latin word for "let it be done.") Under such a standard, which is also called a *paper money standard*, the value of the circulating currency is guaranteed not by some precious commodity but by the taxing and borrowing powers of the government.

Very roughly speaking, societies have moved from a pure commodity standard to fiat money. But the transitions have been neither smooth nor continuous. Paper-money standards existed in both Sweden and China many centuries ago.

No monetary standard is perfect, and many have led to bitter quarrels and serious economic difficulties. China may have experienced the world's first hyperinflation when it was using a paper-money standard in the eleventh and twelfth centuries. The main issue of the bitter US election of 1896 was whether silver should be part of the country's commodity standard. The issue of how to create a monetary standard has also resurfaced in the case of the former Republics of the Soviet Union, many of whom were anxious to introduce their own paper money. Issues such as the design, the size and number of denominations for what is, after all, a national symbol can become an emotional one.[5]

Myth is important in understanding how good or bad a monetary standard is. Ultimately, what dictates whether one standard is better than another is public confidence and, in the case of a commodity standard, the demand for and supply of the asset chosen. Nowhere are these points more clearly illustrated than in the case of monetary economists' favourite example, the stone money of Yap, as discussed in Economics Focus 2.2.

## THE GOLD STANDARD

Throughout recorded history, gold has probably been the commodity most often used as the basis of monetary systems. Gold is scarce but available, has an intrinsic value (that is, it is valued for use in ornaments, as well as in money), and is readily minted. Thus, many countries have used a **gold standard**, in which the market for gold dictates the value of money.

From the time of the Napoleonic Wars until 1914, much of the western world, including Canada, was on a stricter version of the gold standard. Each major nation specified the gold content of its currency, and anyone holding notes backed by that currency could redeem them on demand, receiving the face value in gold. In effect, this régime fixed the price of gold and, at least theoretically, held exchange rate fluctuations within narrow limits.[6]

---

5 On these questions, see the interesting article by Richard K. Abrams, "The Design and Printing of Bank Notes: Considerations when introducing a New Currency," International Monetary Fund working paper 95/26 (March 1995).

6 Exchange rates would have been fixed if international payments had actually been made in gold. To avoid shipping and insurance costs, the payments were usually made on paper, and exchange rates fluctuated. But if the premium or discount on exchange was greater than the shipping cost of gold, the metal itself was exported or imported.

## ECONOMICS FOCUS 2.2 Myth and Money

The natives of the Pacific Island of Yap in Micronesia are renowned for using as the medium of exchange large, circular stones, which are transported by inserting a tree trunk through a hole in their centre. Some of these stones measure as much as 12 feet in diameter.

The stones have been used for this purpose for almost 2,000 years. Since their denominations are quite large, the stones tend nowadays to be used mostly for large transactions such as the sale of land.

So powerful is the myth surrounding these stones that, for fear of breaking them, they are left largely untouched even though their ownership might change hands. Milton Friedman, in an interesting paper, relates how powerful the myth of stone money is on Yap. When Germany took control of the island from Spain at the end of the last century, the road network was in terrible shape, but the islanders could not be persuaded, even with threats, to rectify the situation—that is, until the Germans began to paint black crosses on the stones in order to claim them as payment to finance reconstruction work. This action had the desired effect: the roadways were repaired in short order.

**Sources:**

M. Friedman, "The Island of Stone Money," Hoover Institute Discussion Paper E-91-3 (1991).

This classical gold standard disappeared amid the chaos of World War I, although weaker versions were attempted afterward. Indeed, many economists long for such a classical standard today. The main attraction is the discipline it appears to impose on the price level. This rigour stems from the fact that, at least in theory, a pure gold standard—one in which circulating notes are backed 100% by gold—leaves no room for discretionary monetary policy of the kind practised by governments and central banks under an unbacked, paper-money standard. No country has enough gold to back all its currency, however, so the crucial question is the degree of backing. That amount can be manipulated by government backing, wherein lies one of the principal weaknesses of the gold standard. Indeed, it is the inflexibility of the strict rules of the gold standard which can exacerbate problems facing an economy when it experiences a recession. Add non-co-operation among countries participating in the gold standard, all of whom wish to escape the recession at the same time, and the result is a recipe for disaster.[7]

## BIMETALLISM

Western nations, including the United States in its earlier years, have also had considerable experience with another commodity standard: **bimetallism**, in which

7 For a fascinating and highly readable account of the final years of the gold standard, see Barry Eichengreen, *Golden Fetters* (New York: Oxford University Press, 1992).

the monetary system is based on not one metal but two—usually gold and silver with a fixed exchange rate between the two. Typically, gold is used for coins of larger denominations and silver is used for smaller ones. (Because gold is more valuable than silver, gold coins in small denominations would be too tiny to be practical.)

The problem with bimetallism is that the relative market values of the two metals may vary. The outcome may be an instance of **Gresham's Law**, whose general form is "Bad money drives out good" (that is, cheap money drives out more valuable money). For example, new discoveries of gold may increase the supply of the metal, thus lowering its market price. It may now be profitable to mint the now relatively cheaper gold, replace the gold-backed currency notes with silver-backed ones, and then melt down some silver and sell it as a metal, thereby removing it from the monetary system.

## CANADA'S EARLY PAPER MONEY

Canada had unhappy early experiences with monetary standards in which the circulating medium was something other than a metal. The persistent shortage of metals from the home countries of Great Britain and France forced local governments to issue various media of exchange ostensibly backed by anticipated shipments of gold or silver. During the French colonial period, for example, playing cards and later pieces of cardboard were authorized as temporary media of exchange. So long as these devices were fully backed by future redemptions[8] they proved successful. But the advent of the British colonial period and the debasing of card money ushered in an era during which people displayed a distinct preference for some metallic money standard. Although the War of 1812 meant the return to a paper standard, known as Army bills, they were eventually redeemed in full.

## FIAT MONEY AND CENTRAL BANKS

The widespread introduction of a fiat-money standard has characterized the industrialized world in the twentieth century.[9] The value of the medium of exchange is guaranteed only by the taxing and borrowing power of the government.

---

8 Meaning that when the actual currency was shipped in the future these would replace the temporary currency.

9 In fact, efforts to stay on or be tied to the gold standard lasted well into the century. The United States held to it until 1971. During much of the immediate post-World War II period, most other western countries tied their standard largely on the fortunes of the US dollar, as we see in Chapter 3.

## ECONOMICS FOCUS 2.3 Bimetallism and the Wizard of Oz

During much of the last century, the United States operated on a *free coinage* basis: that is, gold coins could be exchanged for silver coins and vice versa at a fixed exchange rate. The difficulty was that the price of silver became such that it was profitable to melt down gold and use only part of it to buy silver. The cheap silver dollar thus drove out gold, as Gresham's Law predicts.

Free coinage was suspended in 1873, and a 20-year battle over bimetallism ensued. One bimetallist was L. Frank Baum, whose best-known book. *The Wizard of Oz*, was published in 1900. Recently, Rockoff argues that the children's classic is actually an allegorical account of the battle for silver that reached its height during the Democratic convention of 1896. "Oz," he says, refers to an ounce of gold; the "Wicked Witch of the East" is President Grover Cleveland, a Democrat but an easterner and an ardent defender of the gold standard; the "yellow brick road" refers to gold and it leads to "Emerald City," which is really Washington, D.C.; and the silver (not ruby as in the movie) slippers that solve Dorothy's problems are an allusion to the silver component of a bimetallic standard.

The 1896 convention was primarily a battle between the pro-gold easterners and the pro-silver Populists (mostly westerners) led by William Jennings Bryan. The latter's famous speech, ending "You shall not press down upon the brow of labour this crown of thorns, you shall not crucify mankind upon a cross of gold," won him his party's nomination. Although he carried most of the west and the south, he lost the election to William McKinley, a supporter of the gold standard.

Unlike many contemporaries, who believed the bimetallists were cranks, the Populists actually had good reason to want to see a gold-and-silver standard—though by the time they attained political influence, it was too late.

**Sources:**

M. Friedman, "The Crime of 1873," *Journal of Political Economy* 98 (December 1990): 1159–94.

H. Rockoff, "The 'Wizard of Oz' as a Monetary Allegory," *Journal of Political Economy* 98 (August 1990): 739–60.

The increasing importance of the central banks has paralleled the adoption of fiat money. A **central bank** is a national bank responsible for the control and management of the country's money supply.[10] Canada's central bank is the **Bank of Canada**. The bills in your wallet are notes the Bank issues.

Central banks are usually (but not always) owned by the public sector and have a legally defined relationship with the government of the day. Their independence from political interference can be fragile, and sometimes it is open to complete subversion. For example, crises such as wars may lead a government to force its central bank to issue ever-larger quantities of money, resulting in hyperinflation.

10 As we discuss in several later chapters, a central bank may have other responsibilities, specific or implicit. Chapter 25 deals extensively with central banks, including their independence (or lack of independence) from governments.

# MEASURING THE MONEY SUPPLY

How much money is in Canada today? Or, to put the question another way, what is the Canadian money supply? The answer, which is not a simple one, raises many of the issues to be addressed in this text.

The **money supply**, often called the **money stock**,[11] is the amount of money in an economy that is easily available for use in payments (that is, to exchange for other assets, including money itself in some other form). Measuring that amount would be straightforward if it were only the Bank of Canada notes and coins in circulation. But in Canada, as in almost all countries, considerably more money is "easily available for use in payments." Consider what various financial institutions have in their tills and vaults; individuals' and firms' bank deposits (which are of many different types and some of which are denominated in foreign currency); Canada Savings Bonds; credit card balances; and so on and so on. The problem is knowing where to stop.

After pausing for a few definitions of terms, we list the empirical definitions of the money supply that are in general use. Then we touch briefly on a few theoretical views and objections.

## SOME HELPFUL CONCEPTS

Before we launch into a list of definitions of the money supply, it will be helpful to mention a few terms and concepts (most of which are covered in more detail later in the text).

### Types of Banks and Deposits

Canadian law used to differentiate between *chartered banks* (institutions such as the Bank of Montreal, the Royal Bank, and the Bank of Nova Scotia) and other financial institutions (trust companies, credit unions, and Quebec's caisses populaires). As we will see, although the distinctions have not completely disappeared, they still make a difference in calculating the money supply.

Both individuals and firms make deposits in banks. In essence, a depositor loans the money to the deposit-taking institution, which is responsible for re-

11 The term "stock" is useful here because it reminds us that we are dealing here with a *stock variable*—that is, the amount of money outstanding at a particular moment in time, such as December 31, 1996. Recall (from your principles of economics or business courses) that the opposite is a flow variable, which is a quantity measured over a period of time, such as your income last month or the economy's output during 1996. We use many flow variables in this textbook, but the money supply is not one of them.

paying it in the future with interest. Thus, deposits are assets to the makers and liabilities to the institution. (Similarly, a loan is an asset to the lender and a liability to the borrower.)

The variety of deposit accounts available seems limited only by the imagination of the banks' marketing staffs and the regulations imposed by law. Nevertheless, all deposits are one of three basic types:

1. **Demand deposits** must be repaid to the makers without their having given prior notice (that is, the funds must be returned "on demand"). Such accounts pay little or no interest but cheques can be written against them.

2. **Savings deposits** need be repaid only after the maker has given a stipulated amount of notice (although this legal requirement is often not enforced, especially for personal savings accounts). Such accounts pay more interest than demand accounts and need not be chequable (although many are).

3. **Term deposits** are made for a fixed term. Early withdrawal requires notice (often not enforceable) and normally means a significant loss of the fairly high interest the deposit would earn if left until maturity. Such accounts are not chequable.

Although the above deposit types apply to everyone statistics make a distinction between deposits which are "personal," that is, in the name of an individual or small group of individuals, and those which are non-personal such as corporate deposits.

## Cheques and Cheque-Clearing

A cheque is simply a written order for a bank to transfer a specific amount of funds from the writer's account to someone else.

If the economy had only a single bank, even one with many branches, sorting out cheques at the end of each day would be simple. Some of the recipients of cheques would have taken their payments in cash; others would have deposited the funds to their accounts, which would mean just bookkeeping entries for the bank. But Canada has many banks and trust companies that use cheques (and similar transfers) against accounts. Suppose your mother writes you a cheque on her account at a branch of the Canadian Imperial Bank of Commerce in St. John's, and you deposit it in your Ottawa branch of the Toronto-Dominion Bank then immediately write a cheque to your landlord who deposits it later in the day in an account at a Kingston branch of Canada Trust. Given that these sorts of transfers occur thousands of times every day, how do the financial institutions keep everyone's account straight?

The answer is a clearinghouse, which sorts out net interbank payments. All Canadian banks and trust companies belong to the **Canadian Payments Association**, which operates an automated cheque-clearing system.[12]

Computer technology has vastly increased the speed of cheque-clearing. Nevertheless, it does take time, and there are always some cheques in transit. Thus, a cheque that is drawn on an account at a branch in one bank and put into an account in a different bank may appear as funds deposited with the recipient bank before those funds have actually been withdrawn from the first bank. When the Bank of Canada tallies the portion of the money supply that is held by financial institutions, it would be easy to double count such amounts. To avoid that situation, an estimated amount called the *private sector float* is used to adjust the demand deposit figures.

## DEFINITIONS OF THE MONEY SUPPLY

Someone who studied money and banking a decade ago would have difficulty recognizing some of the money supply definitions in use today. A number of significant changes have taken place in the last few years in the reporting and presentation of monetary statistics. These are reflected in Table 2.2 which lists the definitions from narrowest to broadest. It also gives both seasonally adjusted and unadjusted figures for October 1995. (The difference between the two sets of figures will be explained at the end of this section.)

The definitions used in Canada are:

1. Currency in circulation. The narrowest possible definition of the money supply is the *currency in circulation*—that is, the currency that is outside the banking system. These Bank of Canada notes and coins represent, as already explained, a debt of the government accepted by the public. The actual amount is estimated by subtracting bank holdings of notes and coins from amounts reported outstanding by the Bank of Canada and the Royal Canadian Mint.[13]

2. M1. The currency in circulation plus current and personal chequing accounts (including chartered banks' demand deposits net of the private sector float) is called **M1**. This measure of the money supply was long popular in financial circles and economic studies of the impact of monetary policy because it

---

12 Cheque-clearing is the reason for the string of numerals at the bottom of a cheque. The last few digits identify a particular account. The first few indicate the institution, the branch, and what is called a transit (routing) number.

13 From the perspective of the Bank of Canada it can only control the so-called monetary base or high-powered money, which is the sum of currency in circulation and reserves of the banking system. The latter have fallen substantially with recent banking regulation reforms. In any event, obtaining data for the monetary base is not as straightforward as for the other aggregates discussed here.

**TABLE 2.2** THE CANADIAN MONEY SUPPLY—OCTOBER 1995

| Item | Seasonally Adjusted | Seasonally Unadjusted |
|---|---|---|
| Currency outside banks | 25,999 | 26,163 |
| Personal chequing accounts | 8,334 | 8,425 |
| Current accounts | 24,301 | 24,679 |
| Adjustments to M1[a] | −203 | −203 |
| Gross M1 | **58,434** | **59,065** |
| (Of which: Chartered bank demand deposits)[b] | 33,989 | 35,012 |
| (Net) M1 | **59,791** | **60,973** |
| Chartered bank non-personal notice deposits | —[c] | 27,834 |
| Chartered bank personal savings deposits | — | 292,914 |
| Adjustments to M2 | 474 | 474 |
| M2 | **381,896** | **382,195** |
| Deposits at trust and mortgage loan companies | 68,927[d] | 68,804[d] |
| Deposits at credit unions and caisses populaires | 87,127 | 86,938 |
| Life insurance companies annuities | — | 52,179[d] |
| Personal deposits at government savings institutions | — | 7,377 |
| Money market mutual funds | — | 19,227 |
| Adjustments to M2+ | −2,912[d] | −2,912[d] |
| M2+ | **610,852** | **611,582** |
| Chartered banks non-personal term deposits and foreign currency deposits booked by Canadian residents | — | 86,422 |
| Adjustments to M3 | −3,887 | −3,887 |
| M3 | **463,511** | **464,730** |

[a] Includes adjustments to ensure the continuity of the series, as well as for interbank deposits and, in the case of M2+, adjustments for government deposits at other than Chartered Banks.

[b] Net of estimated private sector float.

[c] Signifies that the Bank of Canada does not publish separate seasonally adjusted figures.

[d] Figure is for September 1995.

Source: *Bank of Canada Review* (December 1995).

appears to be the definition that most closely specifies money as it fulfils the medium of exchange function. It is still much used.

3. M2. If we add to M1, personal savings deposits (which are notice deposits but often have a variety of chequable features) and the notice deposits of firms (often called non-personal deposits) at chartered banks, we obtain the **M2** measure of the money supply. M2 captures the impact of financial innovations in the payment system better than M1 does. Indeed, the component of the Canadian money supply that is notice deposits—that is, M2 less M1—grew

dramatically in recent years (see Figure 2.1), indicating that innovations, permitting a combination of high interest rates and chequing privileges, had attracted depositors despite the relatively high inflation of the later 1970s and the 1980s. Thus, by 1989, some 85% of M2 was in notice deposits (see Table 2.2).

4. M2+. The increasing importance of financial institutions other than chartered banks led the Bank of Canada to start reporting a new monetary aggregate: **M2+**, which is M2 plus the deposits held by a variety of other financial institutions. The fact that M2+ is more than 60% larger than M2 has led the Bank to suggest that it prefers to monitor movement in the broader measure when it is carrying out its monetary policy. Indeed, the Bank looked even further; in early 1992, it began to include in M2+ *money market mutual funds*—funds invested in short-term instruments. M2+ now includes deposits at Alberta Treasury branches, deposits at Province of Ontario Savings offices and life insurance company individual annuities. It is easy to see the growing importance of M2+ which reflects the rapid growth of financial institutions other than chartered banks, particularly during the 1980s (see Chapters 18 and 19).

5. M3. The **M3** monetary aggregate is M2 with two additions: fixed-term deposits and the Canadian dollar value of chartered bank deposits denominated in foreign currencies (mostly US dollars) but owned by Canadian residents. This broader aggregate can be useful in understanding monetary policy and general economic activity. At one time, this measure was one of the broadest aggregates available until non-chartered banking institutions became important players in the financial system.

## Some Possible Refinements

Still broader measures could be constructed to reflect some highly liquid assets. Some people suggest including Canada Savings Bonds, which are cashable anytime at little cost and are thus sometimes used in lieu of bank deposits. Others suggest including the unused portion of credit card balances.[14] Still others like to look at consumer or residential mortgage credit. Unlike the monetary aggregates covered in this chapter, however, these are assets to the banking system, not liabilities.

A drawback of all the money supply definitions presented here is that each comprises what people perceive as qualitatively different assets. For example, most people view currency and daily interest accounts as distinct kinds of assets, yet

14 However, credit cards actually add to the volume of transactions, not to the monetary supply. Consider that a credit card purchase actually creates two debts: one between the card issuer and the merchant, and one between the card issuer and the individual holding the card.

**FIGURE 2.1** Major Canadian Money Supply Aggregates

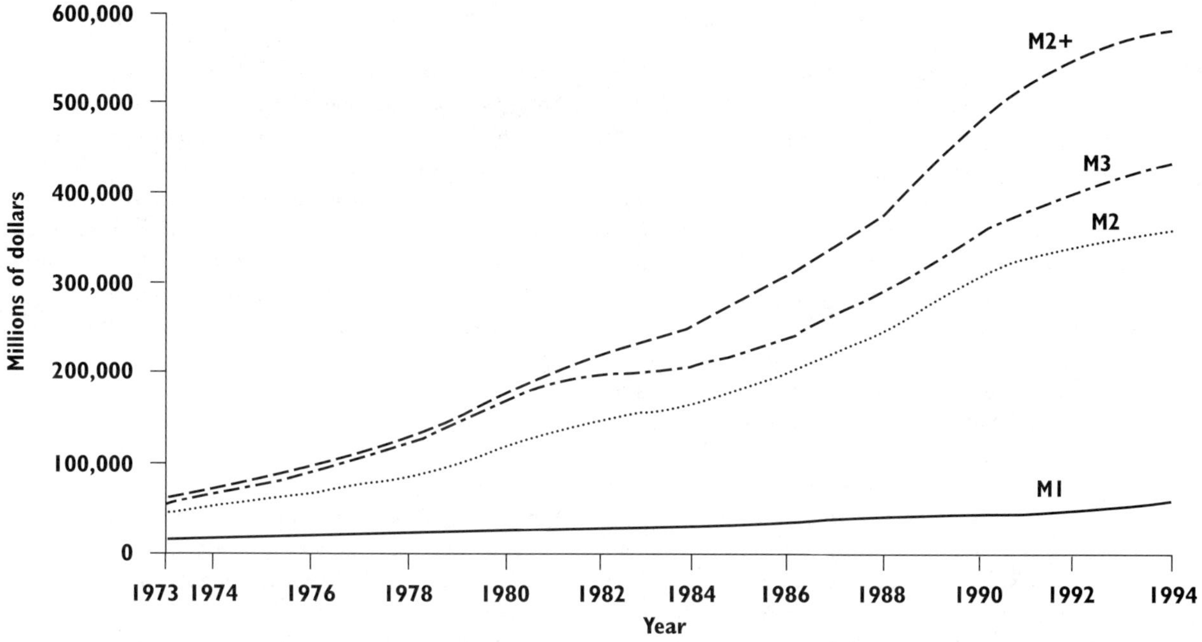


Economists are interested in the relationship of the size of the various components of the money supply over time. During the 1973–1994 period shown here M1 changed very little. The explosive growth was in term deposits and the deposits of financial institutions other than the chartered banks.

Note: All data are seasonally adjusted.

Source: *Bank of Canada Review* (Spring 1995).

the M2 measure adds them together. Partly as a response to such concerns, analysts have developed *divisia indexes*, which weigh the components of the various money supply measures according to the degree to which they provide liquidity. Such alternative measures have an obvious attraction, but they too have drawbacks.[15]

## Seasonal Adjustment

The public's demand for cash and use of chequing accounts is not evenly distributed over the course of a year. (It is, for example, always high at Christmas

15 Discussion of these problems would take us too far afield. See D.E.W. Laidler, *The Demand for Money: Theories, Evidence, and Problems* (New York: Harper & Row, 1985), 85. The Bank of Canada ceased publishing divisia monetary aggregates in 1990 due to the fact that they were expensive to produce and did not outperform the simple-sum aggregates in Table 2.2 as indicators of monetary policy. See David Longworth and Joseph Atta-Mensah, "The Canadian Experience with Weighted Monetary Aggregates," Bank of Canada working paper 95-10 (October 1995).

## ECONOMICS FOCUS 2.4 Money Supply Announcements

The text explains some of the issues in the measurement of the money supply, but there are many others. One is the problem of public announcements about the money supply and subsequent revisions to the data. Every week one can find in the daily press preliminary announcements about the amount of money that is expected to be injected into the economy and announcements about the rate of growth in GDP and the unemployment rate. A closer look at some important statistical publications, such as the *Bank of Canada Review*, confirms, however, that many preliminary figures are later revised (they are indicated by an "r" next to the statistics in question). If, as many economists believe, money supply announcements influence investors' and policymakers' decisions and therefore affect interest rates and stock prices, to name two obvious examples, then it is of some interest to consider how the revised and actual figures compare with each other. Although most of the work has been done on US data (see Siklos 1996 and references therein), it is likely that the results apply to the Canadian case as well.

Because data revisions may be thought of as unanticipated or unexpected money supply announcements, economic theory dictates that these should have real effects on the economy—unlike the announced figures, which, if treated as forecasts of the money supply, should be digested or discounted by the public. The difficulty is that the distinction between what the public expects and what it terms a "surprise" (unexpected monetary policy) is a subject of considerable controversy. The current state of the debate is mixed. There is some evidence that the preliminary announcements, if they are treated as if they were forecasts, could be improved. Therefore, information available to the monetary authorities could be, but is not, exploited by individuals.

**Sources:**

K.A. Mork, "Forecastable Money Growth Revisions: A Closer Look at the Data," *Canadian Journal of Economics* 23 (August 1990): 593–616. See also the references therein.

P.L. Siklos, "An Empirical Analysis of Revisions in U.S. Macroeconomic Aggregates," *Applied Financial Economics*, 6 (February 1996).

P.L. Siklos and J. Anusiewicz, "The Effect of Canadian and U.S. MI Announcements on Canadian Financial Markets: The Crow Years," manuscript (Wilfrid Laurier University).

time.) Data series are often *seasonally adjusted* to smooth some of the normal variations see Figure 2.2 as well as the two sets of figures in Table 2.2).

Notice, however, from Table 2.2 that the column for which there is most information is the seasonally unadjusted one. The reason is that when the Bank of Canada collects the information it is in raw form while it only tends to publish seasonally adjusted data for the main aggregates.

Seasonal adjustment is a useful device for many users of money supply data. It does, however, remove information that is useful to some analysts, such as those trying to make short-term forecasts that depend on the amount of cash or the volume of cheques written in the economy.[16] Luckily, seasonal adjustment

16 Some analysts claim that the regular use of seasonally adjusted data has led to omissions of important elements in our understanding of *business cycles* (fluctuations over time in economic activity). See R.B. Barksy and J.A. Miron, "The Seasonal Cycle and the Business Cycle," *Journal of Political Economy* 97 (June

**FIGURE 2.2** Currency in Circulation: Seasonally Adjusted or Unadjusted

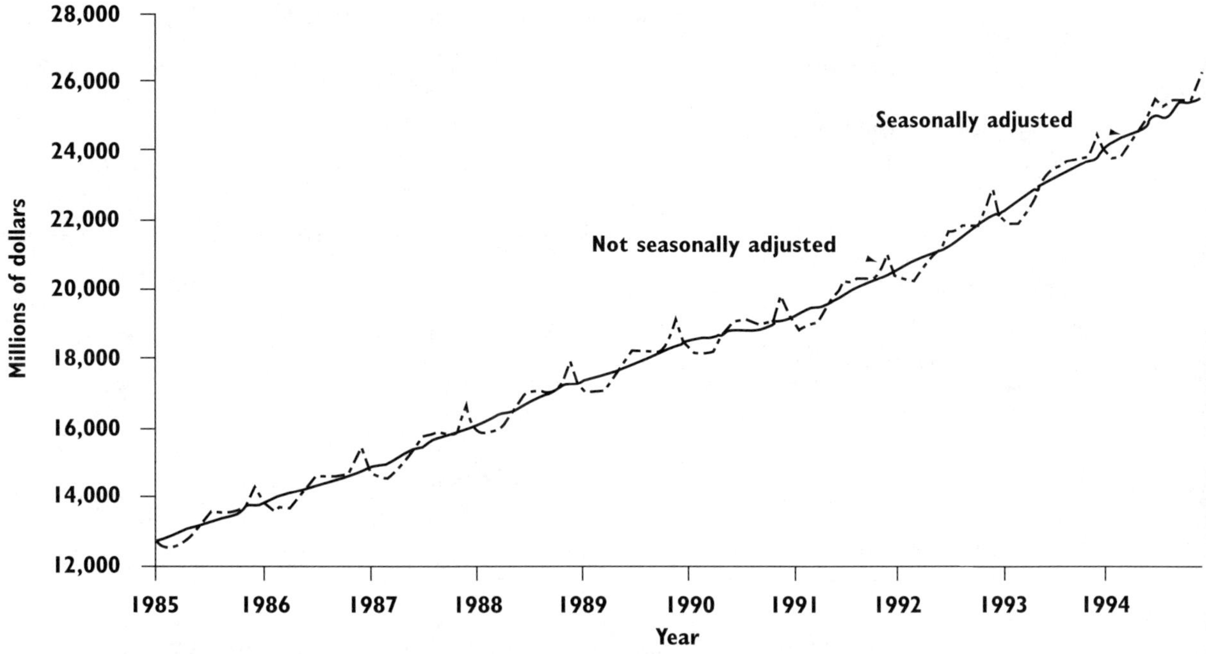


The seasonally adjusted data are smooth; the other series represents the raw data which always peaks at Christmas.

Source: *Bank of Canada Review* (Spring 1995).

becomes less drastic (and less necessary) as one moves from narrow to broad definitions of the money supply.

## *THEORETICAL ISSUES

The money supply measures we have described have been worked out empirically. Theoretical problems abound.

Consider Table 2.3, which shows highly simplified balance sheets[17] for the private sector and the public sector of the economy. Members of the private

1989): 53–34. The technique used to filter out seasonal influences is called X-11, a name coined by the US Census Bureau, and used worldwide. The Canadian contribution to seasonal modelling is an important one. See Estella Bee Dagum, *The X-11 ARIMA Seasonal Adjustment Method* (Ottawa: Statistics Canada, 1980). Unfortunately, applying X-11 does appear to do undesirable things to time series but most practitioners are not aware of the problem. See Eric Ghysels, Clive W.J. Granger and Pierre L. Siklos, "Is Seasonal Adjustment a Linear or Non-Linear Data Filtering Process?", *Journal of Business and Economic Statistics* (July 1996).

17 Recall that a *balance sheet* lists an individual's or a firm's assets and liabilities at a moment in time. By convention, assets are listed on the left and liabilities on the right.

**TABLE 2.3** INSIDE AND OUTSIDE MONEY

**(A) Consolidated Private Sector Balance Sheet**

| Assets | Liabilities |
|---|---|
| Currency | |
| Government bonds | Bank loans |
| Bank loans | Bank deposits |
| Bank deposits | Stocks |
| Stocks | |
| Net worth = Currency + Government bonds | |

**(B) Public Sector Balance Sheet**

| Assets | Liabilities |
|---|---|
| | Currency |
| | Government bonds |
| | Net worth = −(Currency + Government bonds) |

Note: The private sector here includes the banking sector and the public sector includes the central bank.

sector (individuals, firms, and financial institutions) hold currency and government bonds as assets. There are also banks loans (assets to the banks and liabilities to the individuals and firms that borrow), bank deposits (an asset to the deposit-makers and a liability to the deposit-takers), and corporate stocks (an asset to the holders and a liability to the issuing firms). Since bank deposits and loans, as well as corporate stocks, offset themselves as assets and liabilities, the *net worth* (assets minus liabilities) of the private sector is simply cash and government bonds.

We assume the public sector is separate (though a creation of the private sector). It has no assets in this simplified example, but it incurs liabilities by issuing currency (fiat money) and government bonds. Its net worth is clearly negative.[18]

Clearly, too, the existence of the public sector creates additional net worth—wealth that would not otherwise have existed—for the private sector.[19] This net worth consists entirely of currency and government bonds. Perhaps those two items should be our definition of money. For now, however, let us call them outside money.

18 This, of course, is because the public sector is assumed to have no assets. Clearly, things such as public roads, bridges, national parks, represent assets with some economic value. Most governments, however, do not construct balance sheets of the kind we are used to seeing for banks and other business firms. A notable exception is New Zealand which, by law, must publish a balance sheet following generally accepted accounting principles.

19 Such a result is consistent with our earlier finding that the introduction of a monetary economy improves social welfare.

What about bank deposits? As we have seen, the banking sector's assets and liabilities offset each other. They seem to create no additional net worth for the economy, so they can be called inside money.

This theoretical approach to defining money has at least two drawbacks. First, it leaves the banking sector no role in the economy except that of taking deposits and providing loans; yet most economists believe that banks and financial institutions in general do create additional net worth through a process known as *intermediation* (a subject of the next chapter). So perhaps inside money is not really "inside," and a definition of the money supply should contain some bank deposit component.

Second, the view that government bonds are net wealth suggests that deficit spending, which can occur via an increase in government bonds, can increase the private sector's net worth. A number of influential economists strongly disagree with this view.[20]

The inconclusive and unsatisfying nature of this theoretical approach to defining the money supply has led economists to seek an empirically oriented definition.

## INFLATION AND SOCIAL WELFARE

We have already mentioned inflation several times in this text, and will do so often again. What is this phenomenon and how does it affect social welfare?

*Inflation* is an increase in the general level of prices. To put the point another way, inflation reduces the *purchasing power* of money; when the price level rises, a given amount of money buys less than it did before.

Does inflation lessen social welfare? Yes, because it redistributes income, often in unanticipated and socially harmful ways.

1. Inflation can upset the debtor–creditor relationship. As we discuss later in this text, anyone who borrows or lends funds is making a guess about the future course of inflation. The less predictable future prices are, the more likely are negative consequences for lender or borrower.

2. Inflation means that individuals and firms must spend more money to obtain the things they need. So the government must create more money with a consequent increase in **seigniorage**, which is the government's profit from issuing money.[21] Government may spend these extra funds in ways different from the original holders of the money would have spent it.

20 See R.J. Barro, *Macroeconomics Policy* (Cambridge, Mass.: Harvard University Press, 1990), chap. 9.

21 The word dates from the days when kings and nobles minted coins. They often imposed a fee for turning

3. In response to inflation, individuals devote ever more resources to minimizing their cash holdings, which creates a deadweight loss for society (see Chapter 3). One estimate places the social cost of 10% inflation at almost 0.3% of the gross national product.[22] Other estimates are higher.

4. For the most part, our tax system is based on the *nominal* magnitudes of income and expenses, which by definition do not reflect inflation.[23] Although the system has some adjustments for large increases in inflation, tax liabilities tend to rise over time, leading many people to devote valuable resources to minimizing them.

5. As inflation accelerates, firms find the need to change forms more often and this process has costs associated with them called "menu costs." The term is derived from the notion that it is expensive to print new menus at restaurants every time prices change (and more so the more frequent are price adjustments!).

6. Inflation poses problems for the accounting profession which typically records assets and liabilities at "historical costs" not at their current (inflated) value.

7. Higher inflation usually leads to more variable inflation which exacerbates the difficulties faced by households and firms in forecasting future cash needs.

8. Once inflation is deemed to be unacceptably high, there are potential unemployment or output costs of reducing inflation to a more tolerable level. Others have argued that lowering inflation from very high levels (say 100% to 10%) brings with it net gains in economy-wide output and productivity.[24] The debate is still unsettled particularly for economies with moderate to low inflation rates.[25]

Although the exact size of the social costs of inflation is debatable, society is clearly better off if inflation is small or perhaps if it is zero.

---

individuals' gold or silver into coins; they also got to keep the inevitable shavings, which could add up to a sizeable amount.

22 B.T. McCallum, *Monetary Economics: Theory and Policy* (New York: Macmillan, 1989), 128.

23 Suppose you earned $10 an hour last year and paid income taxes on that amount. Suppose too that inflation last year was 10%. If you receive a 10% raise, your *real* income (that is, the amount of goods your income will purchase) does not change at all. But this year you will pay taxes on $11 an hour.

24 See Michael Bruno and William Easterly, "Inflation Crises and Long-Run Growth," NBER working paper 5209 (August 1995).

25 For a tolerant view of steady (but low) inflation, see James Tobin, "Stabilization Policy Ten Years After," *Brooks Papers on Economic Activity* 1 (1990). For an opposite view, see Peter W. Howitt, "Zero Inflation as a Long-Term Target for Monetary Policy," in Richard G. Lipsey, ed., *Zero Inflation: The Goal of Price Stability*, Policy Study 8 (Toronto: C.D. Howe Institute, 1990).

## SUMMARY

- Money exists because it produces benefits that do not exist in a barter economy.
- Money is useful because it satisfies three functions: medium of account, medium of exchange, and store of value.
- There exist several empirical definitions of money. The narrowest is called M1 and consists of currency and demand deposits. One of the broadest is M3, which includes M1, savings deposits, fixed-term and foreign currency deposits at banks. Another broad measure of the money supply is M2+, which includes deposits at banks other than chartered banks.
- Monetary standards have evolved over time. The movement has essentially been from a commodity-based monetary system to a paper-based or fiat monetary system.
- The survival of a monetary standard is partly a function of whether money retains its purchasing power over time. Inflation reduces the purchasing power of money over time and imposes social costs on society. Consequently, some economists advocate that we aim for zero inflation.

## IMPORTANT TERMS

Bank of Canada (p. 27)
barter (p. 19)
bimetallism (p. 25)
Canadian Payments Association (p. 30)
central bank (p. 27)
demand deposit (p. 29)
gold standard (p. 24)
Gresham's Law (p. 26)
inside money (p. 36)
liquidity (p. 21)
M1 (p. 30)
M2 (p. 31)
M2 + (p. 32)
M3 (p. 32)
medium of account (p. 21)
medium of exchange (p. 21)
money supply (money stock) (p. 28)
outside money (p. 36)
savings deposit (p. 29)
seigniorage (p. 37)
store of value (p. 21)
term deposit (p. 29)
transactions costs (p. 22)

## EXERCISES

1. Suppose that all transactions are done by a national computerized network that records purchases and sales and is able to debit and credit the appropriate

bank accounts instantly. Individuals need only carry a card with which all transactions can be effected, and visitors from other countries can purchase credits on a card at the border in exchange for their own currency. All prices continue to be quoted in dollars.

(a) What is the economy's medium of account?

(b) What is its unit of account?

(c) Is this a monetary economy? What unresolved questions or problems would arise from such a system?

**2.** Suppose that in the balance sheet of Table 2.3, we added the value of public roads and buildings as assets in the economy. How would this change the amount of outside money? Why?

**3.** Suppose we allow banks in the private sector in Table 2.3 to hold some of the government bonds outstanding. Would this change the amount of inside money or outside money in this economy? Why?

**4.** Suppose you are given the following data:

| | |
|---|---|
| Currency in circulation | 1,000 |
| Demand deposits at chartered banks—Personal chequing accounts | 3,000 |
| Notice deposits at chartered banks—Current accounts | 10,000 |
| Non-personal notice and personal savings deposits at chartered banks | 12,000 |
| Deposits at banks other than chartered banks | 6,000 |
| Non-personal term and foreign currency deposits | 9,000 |

What are M1, M2, M2+, and M3? Assume adjustments to the various aggregates are zero.

**5.** Should a $50 bill stuffed in your mattresses be counted as M1? Why?

**6.** You read the following statement in the financial press: "Based on data for November, M1 declined by $5 million but M2 rose by $7 million." How could M1 have fallen while M2 rose? Why?

**7.** Current legislation has eliminated reserve requirements for chartered banks altogether. Will banks bother to keep reserves? Why?

**8.** During the 1970s and early 1980s both inflation and the pace of financial innovation were substantially greater than, for example, in the 1960s. Was this a coincidence? Why?

**9.** Would the annual rush to buy RRSPs be reflected in seasonally adjusted or unadjusted data? Which component of the money supply would likely be affected? What about a postal strike? Explain your answer.

10. In Table 2.2, the seasonally unadjusted currency and demand deposit figures are larger than the adjusted figures. Why?

11. Explain how the government can generate revenue from the creation of fiat money. Also, briefly discuss the benefits and costs of inflationary financing. Finally, explain how inflation can be viewed as a tax on money.

12. Give an example of how inflation redistributes income between generations.

13. An annual inflation rate of 5% reduces purchasing power by approximately a quarter in six years and by half in 14 years. Explain.

## REFERENCES

Alchian, A. "Why Money?" *Journal of Money, Credit and Banking* 2 (part 2, 1977): 133–40.

Bailey, M.J. "The Welfare Cost of Inflationary Finance." *Journal of Political Economy* 64 (April 156): 93–110.

*Bank of Canada Review* (various issues).

Barksy, R.B., and J.A. Miron. "The Seasonal Cycle and the Business Cycle." *Journal of Political Economy* 97 (June 1989): 503–34.

Boorstin, D.J. *The Discoverers.* New York: Random House, 1983, 502–4.

Bordo, M.D. "The Classical Gold Standard: Some Lessons for Today." *Review of the Federal Reserve Bank of St. Louis* 63 (May 1981): 2–18.

Bordo, M.D., and A.J. Schwartz. *A Retrospective on the Classical Gold Standard, 1821–1931.* Chicago: University of Chicago Press and NBER, 1984.

Carlson, J.B. "The Stability of Money Demand, Its Interest Sensitivity, and Some Implications for Money as a Policy Guide." Federal Reserve Bank of Cleveland, *Economic Review* 25 (Fall 1989): 2–13.

Clower, R.W., and P.W. Howitt. "The Transactions Theory of the Demand for Money: A Reconsideration." *Journal of Political Economy* 86 (June 1978): 449–76.

Dorn, J.A., and A.J. Schwartz. *The Search for Stable Money: Essays on Monetary Reform.* Chicago: University of Chicago Press, 1987.

Eichengreen, B., ed. *The Gold Standard in Theory and History.* New York: Methuen, 1985.

Fortin, Pierre. "The Unbearable Lightness of Zero-Inflation Optimism," *Canadian Business Economics* 1 (Spring): 3–18.

Friedman, B.H. "The Roles of Money and Credit in Macroeconomics Analysis." In *Macroeconomics Prices and Quantities,* edited by J. Tobin, 161–88. Oxford: Basil Blackwell, 1983.

Friedman, M. "The Quantity Theory: A Restatement." In *Studies in the Quantity Theory of Money,* edited by M. Friedman, 3–21. Chicago: University of Chicago Press, 1956.

Friedman, M., and A.J. Schwartz. *Monetary Trends in the United States and the United Kingdom.*

Chicago: University of Chicago Press and NBER, 1982.

Gurley, J.G., and E.S. Shaw. *Money in a Theory of Finance.* Washington, D.C.: The Brookings Institute, 1960.

Harris, L. *Monetary Theory.* New York: McGraw-Hill, 1981.

Konieczny, Jerzy D. "The Optimal Rate of Inflation: Competing Theories and Their Relevance to Canada," in *Economic Behaviour and Policy Choice Under Price Stability* (Ottawa: Bank of Canada, 1994).

Laidler, D.E.W. *The Demand for Money: Theories, Evidence, and Problems.* New York; Harper & Row, 1985.

Laidler, D. "Presidential Address: Taking Money Seriously." *Canadian Journal of Economics* 21 (November 1988): 687–713.

Lucas, R.E., Jr. *Models of Business Cycles.* Oxford: Basil Blackwell, 1987.

Martin, P. *Inside the Bank of Canada's Weekly Financial Statistics: A Technical Guide,* 2d ed. Vancouver, B.C.: The Fraser Institute, 1989.

McCallum, B.T. *Monetary Economics: Theory and Policy.* New York: Macmillan, 1989.

McConnell, C.R., S.L. Brue, and T.P. Barbiero. *Macroeconomics,* 7th Cdn. ed. Toronto: McGraw-Hill Ryerson, 1996.

———. *Microeconomics,* 7th Cdn. ed. Toronto: McGraw-Hill Ryerson, 1996.

McCulloch, J. Huston. *Money and Inflation: A Monetarist Approach,* 2d ed. New York: Academic Press, 1982.

McIvor, R.C. *Canadian Monetary, Banking, and Fiscal Development.* Toronto: Macmillan, 1958.

Rich, G. *The Cross of Gold: Money and the Canadian Business Cycle.* Ottawa, Ont.: Carleton University Press, 1988.

Schumpter, J.A. *History of Economic Analysis.* New York: Oxford University Press, 1954.

Siklos, P.L. *War Finance, Reconstruction, Hyperinflation and Stabilization in Hungary, 1938–48.* London and New York: Macmillan and St. Martin's Press, 1991.

———. *Great Inflations of the Twentieth Century: Theories, Policies and Evidence* (Brookfield, VT: Edward Elgar, 1995).

Smith, G. *Money and Banking: Financial Markets and Institutions.* Reading, Mass.: Addison-Wesley, 1982.

CHAPTER 3

# Financial Intermediaries and Financial Markets

When asked what banks do, most students reply that they take in deposits and make loans. That response is partly correct, but it ignores the principal *economic* role of all financial institutions: their role as **intermediaries**. Indeed, the wave of deregulation and technological innovations sweeping the financial world has greatly reduced the traditional role of deposit-taking and lending in the banking world. Banks, in particular, now underwrite, provide financial advice, manage portfolios, and make available various forms of insurance. More than ever before, financial institutions act as go-betweens. This chapter opens, therefore, by explaining the intermediation function.

We proceed with a brief description of the principal types of intermediaries in Canada. (The structure of Canadian intermediaries is not unique, but it is by no means the only one possible. Later chapters in this book will consider the intermediaries of several major countries.) Next, we outline various ways in which financial markets can be classified. (This classification will serve as a starting point for the next chapter, which describes the major financial instruments traded in the Canadian financial system.)

Finally, we consider the financial system in the Canadian economy. How vital a role does it play? How important is intermediation? How does one even begin to consider whether the system is an efficient one?

## INTERMEDIATION

What does a firm do? In economic terms, it takes inputs and through a production function turns them into outputs. Thus, General Motors produces cars, The Bay produces retail sales of consumer goods, and your neighbourhood barber produces haircuts. But what does a financial institution produce? Think of a bank. One can view it in several ways. Loans can be seen as its output and deposits as its principal input. Alternatively, one can conceive of a bank as producing deposits, which then represent its output and are the result of making loans. Or, one can see a bank's output as the difference between the return on its assets (for example, its loans) and the cost of its debts (for example, its deposits).[1] Thus, one can speak of the banking firm's output as a set of services. Such a set of services can be termed **intermediation**, which can be thought of as facilitating the transformation of liabilities (that is, deposits) into assets (that is, loans).

An intermediary is a go-between. A financial intermediary is someone (more likely, some institution) that goes between individuals and firms that have excess cash, and individuals and firms that need funds.

This service is enormously useful in a society that uses money. The people who have extra money (the "savers") could, of course, stash it under their mattresses. But they would face problems of safety and convenience. Perhaps worse, their assets wouldn't be doing them any good. Most people want to put their assets to work earning more funds (interest or income).

Without intermediary institutions, the savers themselves would have to find users of their funds ("borrowers"). An individual who wanted to make a car loan would have to find someone who wanted to fund the purchase of a car, ascertain the person's creditworthiness, and work out arrangements for repayment. An individual who wanted to lend to a real estate developer would have to seek one out. And so on. The situation would be almost as complex as barter. Financial intermediaries make life much simpler for savers and borrowers.

## THE FUNCTIONS OF INTERMEDIATION

Intermediation between borrowers and lenders can improve economic efficiency—that is, channel resources to their most effective use—in four ways:

1. It facilitates the acquisition of and payment for goods and services. The chequing services provided by the banking system improve economic efficiency. Even though a cheque does not completely settle a transaction, it is a generally accepted form of payment. In later chapters we discuss some of the other financial instruments that facilitate purchases, some as simple as traveller's cheques or debit cards and some as complex as forward contracts for foreign exchange.

2. It facilitates the creation of a **portfolio** (a collection of assets) with all its attendant benefits. The financial system provides what economists call *economies of scale and scope*.[2] Through intermediation individuals can spread their

---

1 Recall from the previous chapter that to the client of a bank, a deposit is an asset and a loan is a debt. But to the bank itself, a deposit is a debt (the client has lent money to the institution) and a loan is an asset. This slippery point will appear over and over in this text.

2 Economies of scale are obtained when the unit cost of an operation decreases as more and more of it is done. Economies of scope are cost savings that stem from engaging in complementary activities.

*wealth* across a variety of assets in a way they could not accomplish through direct contacts. For example, many investors could not purchase certain types of government bonds directly because the amounts are too large (say, $1 million) to be affordable to any individual investors, but the financial system can pool the funds of many investors and purchase the security. As we will see, financial institutions provide such pooling arrangements in a variety of ways.

Economies also arise because a financial institution can offer a large variety of services to its customers at a cost far smaller than if they purchased them directly. For example, someone with a chequing account may have access to services from overdraft privileges to safety deposit box and to easy purchase of stocks for a relatively small flat fee.

Finally, markets are structured to accommodate *asymmetric information.* That is, financial institutions are in a better position than individuals to obtain information about borrowers and lenders, credit market conditions, and the inherent risks of the large variety of assets available. In other words, there are economies of scale in the collection of financial market information.

**3.** It eases the liquidity constraint of households and firms, which arises because the liquidity (think cash) required for certain purchases (such as a house or a factory) is grossly at variance with the immediate flow of income available. Recall the movie *It's a Wonderful Life*, which pits Banker Potter, who insists that the funds for purchasing a house must be paid up front, against Mr. Bailey, who pools the funds of investors at his savings and loan company and is able to advance the money so that families can buy housing immediately instead of waiting for years. The protagonists represent a long-ago battle that led to the creation of mortgage loan companies and credit unions. The ability to influence the allocation of consumption and investment is perhaps the single most important service that arises from intermediation.

**4.** It provides a measure of financial security from unexpected or unforeseen events, such as ill health or property damage. The existence of intermediation provides a host of services that reduce or shift risk. We discuss risk in detail in future chapters. Suffice it to say here that *risk* arises essentially because the future cannot be known with complete certainty. Financial institutions influence the riskiness of financial transactions and arrangements in several ways. Lenders and borrowers deal with each other only *indirectly*: contracting and thus its costs are borne by the intermediary. The intermediary specifies all the contingencies required when a contract for, say, a loan is written to spread the costs over all customers in the event of default. Intermediaries also permit insurance, which specifically shifts a potential loss of wealth from individuals to institutions that willingly bear such risks.

5. The need for intermediation services arises because information is costly to obtain and to process. In addition, financial transactions are costly to complete. These costs exist because of **asymmetric information**. As a result, two problems emerge. For example, if an individual makes a direct loan to someone there is a good chance that the lender has incomplete information about the motives of the borrower. Before the transaction occurs there is every incentive for the borrower to put his or her best foot forward and to offer every assurance that interest and principal payments will be made on time and in full. Similarly, after the loan is agreed to and funds are exchanged there is little the lender can do to prevent the borrower from using the proceeds of the loan in a manner other than was promised before the loan was made. The first problem is called moral hazard while the second is referred to as **adverse selection**.[3] These types of behaviour are especially evident when deposits of the banking system are insured, as we see in Chapter 20. Banks can, via the process of intermediation, reduce the asymmetric information problem since these institutions have a comparative advantage in offering specialized services (for example, monitoring of borrowers activities, information about financial markets). However, as agents for the depositors, banks can also exploit the asymmetric information problem by taking on undue risks or through fraudulent behaviour. We will encounter many such examples throughout the text. Consequently, governments have felt the need to regulate the banking sector perhaps to a greater extent than other industries or sectors of the economy. This reaction also raises some concerns such as when governments decide to insure depositors against losses when banks fail. Again, we explore the ramifications of government regulations later in the text (in particular, Chapters 17–20).

## BROKERAGE

The Canadian financial system provides not only intermediation but also brokerage services. The two functions are similar in purpose but differ in the way they operate.

**Brokers** are agents who bring would-be buyers and sellers together so transactions can be made. Some Canadian financial institutions, such as stock brokers, specifically offer the brokerage function. Other institutions emphasize interme-

3 The problems of moral hazard and asymmetric information are commonplace as in, for example, the doctor–patient relationship, the relationship between health insurance providers and those covered by such insurance or the used-car market. Indeed, it was examples such as these that prompted the now classic study by the economist George Akerlof. Akerlof's paper dealt with the market for "lemons" where, because of asymmetric information, it is possible to pass off a lemon of a car, for example, as a trouble-free vehicle. See G. Akerlof, "The Market for Lemons," *Quarterly Journal of Economics*, 84 (1970): 485–500.

diation but also fulfil a brokerage role to some extent. Consider a bank's chequing services. In a way, they bring buyers and sellers "together," and they certainly facilitate transactions.

### EXTERNALITIES

The existence of a financial system creates these wonderful efficiencies, but it also entails some **externalities** (spillover effects whose cost to individuals and/or society is not compensated by the economic agent that causes them). The reason, as we will see, is that the incentives of the managers of a financial institution may conflict with those of its shareholders, its depositors, and/or society in general. For example, managers, through some combination of a desire to increase profits, or incompetence or dishonesty, may violate the confidence of depositors and be unable to return their funds to them as promised.

The mere possibility of this kind of externality, which can be socially disastrous, has been used to justify government intervention in the financial system, sometimes via very strict regulations.

## FINANCIAL INSTITUTIONS

What types of financial institutions exist in Canada today? We'll provide only a brief sketch here, leaving details to later chapters. Don't worry if you don't understand the exact differences among institutions or the reasons for them. These matters will become evident when we describe the history, regulation, and performance of each type of institution.

You should be clear about our focus, however. Here we concentrate on **financial intermediaries**—institutions that permit indirect lending, which today constitutes almost two-thirds of the debt outstanding in the Canadian economy. (The rest is lent directly thorough the bond market, through trade credit, or as equity—that is, corporate shares.)

### TYPES OF FINANCIAL INSTITUTIONS

Within the Canadian financial system today, there exist three broad categories of intermediaries: (1) deposit-taking institutions, (2) insurance companies and pension funds, and (3) investment dealers and investment funds. See Table 3.1.

#### Deposit-Taking Institutions

**Deposit-taking institutions** (also called *depository institutions*) accept and manage deposits and make loans. Because of a combination of historical developments and the regulatory environment (which stems partially from jurisdictional battles

**TABLE 3.1** FINANCIAL INSTITUTIONS BY SIZE, 1995 FOURTH QUARTER

| | Total assets (millions of dollars) |
|---|---|
| Deposit-taking institutions | |
| Chartered banks[a] | 685,759[a] |
| Other deposit-taking institutions | |
| Trust companies | 68,382 |
| Credit unions and caisses populaires | 124,423 |
| Insurance companies[b] | 219,219 |
| Other | |
| Investment funds[c] | 149,168 |
| Consumer and business financial intermediaries | 66,391 |
| Other[d] | 55,432 |

[a] Combines Schedule I and Schedule II banks.

[b] Combines life insurers, accident and sickness branches of life insurers, and property and casualty insurers but omits segregated funds.

[c] Combines closed-end funds, investment funds (mutual funds, and the segregated funds of investment companies).

[d] Includes investment dealers.

Sources: *Bank of Canada Review* (various tables) and *Statistics Canada Quarterly Financial Statistics for Enterprises* (No. 61–008–XPB), various tables. Reproduced by authority of the Ministry of Industry, 1996.

Readers wishing further information on data provided through the co-operation of Statistics Canada may obtain copies of related publications by mail from: Publications Sales, Statistics Canada, Ottawa, Ontario, K1A 0T6, by calling 1-613-951-7277 or toll-free 1-800-267-6677. Readers may also facsimile their order by dialing 1-613-951-1584.

between the federal and provincial governments), they are divided into two types: chartered banks and other deposit-taking institutions. *Chartered banks* are large, federally regulated institutions and have a close relationship with the Bank of Canada. Other types of *banks* now much resemble chartered banks, and they operate under a combination of federal and provincial regulations. With the passage of the Bank Act of 1992, the significance attached to the term *bank* is considerably lessened. Nevertheless, it remains convenient to retain a term such as *near-banks* because they still perform slightly different roles in the financial system than do chartered banks. The near-banks comprise:

1. *Trust companies*, which in addition to acting as deposit-taking institutions also operate as fiduciaries (administrators of estates and trusts); in the latter capacity, they do not own the assets but simply administer them in the interests of the owners.

2. *Mortgage loan companies*, which accept deposits but essentially permit investors

to invest in a portfolio of assets primarily invested in real estate. At present most are fully owned subsidiaries of chartered banks.

3. *Credit unions* (called *caisses populaires* in Quebec), which are member-owned; that is, the depositors are the shareholders.

## Insurance Companies and Pension Funds

*Insurance companies* provide a way of channelling savings to provide a cushion against unexpected expenses. By *pooling risks*, such a company can provide clients with protection against a variety of risks without incurring a considerable risk of failure for its owners.

Next are the institutions that cater to the management of pension plans or funds (data not shown). The various types reflect divisions created in large part by legislation governing how pensions are administered. Registered retirement savings plans (RRSPs) are individuals' tax-sheltered funds administered by the individual themselves or by a deposit-taking institution or an investment dealer on the individuals' behalf. *Registered pension plans* (RPPs) are the pooled retirement savings of a group of employees administered by the employer (or a labour union). Finally, there are *public pension plans*, which are the funds accumulated by the federal government and the government of Quebec through deductions from income and dispersed as pensions through the Canada Pension Plan (CPP) and the Quebec Pension Plan (QPP), respectively.

## Investment Dealers and Investment Funds

The list in Table 3.1 is rounded out with a catch-all of intermediaries whose asset size is relatively small but whose services are important in the Canadian economy. Essentially, the many types of *investment funds* pool funds for investment in a wide range of activities and instruments without fulfilling the other functions of a typical bank. *Sales, finance, and consumer loan companies*, also called consumer and business financial intermediaries, make credit available to finance a wide range of purchases, from household goods and services to inventories and capital equipment. *Investment dealers* primarily *underwrite* corporate and government securities: that is, they acquire newly issued securities and resell them to the public.

## Government Financial Institutions

The government itself also participates in the financial industry (although its institutions do not appear in Table 3.1). Sometimes it plays a deposit-taking role, as in the Province of Ontario and Alberta savings institutions. There are also myriad agencies that either channel funds from the public to the private sector, such as the Federal Business Development Bank, or protect private funds in the private financial system, such as the Canada Deposit Insurance Corporation (CDIC).

## THE FOUR PILLARS: SOME HISTORY

If you had been a student as recently as the 1960s, when you were taught the types of Canadian financial institutions, you would have been handed a list of what were called the **four pillars** of the financial system and told that each existed to fulfil one—and only one—financial function. The four pillars were

1. Chartered banks: commercial loans.
2. Trust companies and credit unions: fiduciary responsibilities and personal loans.
3. Insurance companies (subdivided into life insurers, and property and casualty insurers): underwriting insurance contracts.
4. Investment dealers: underwriting and brokering securities.

Regulations enforced the separation of the four pillars; companies in one category could not engage in the activities of another, and cross-ownership was largely forbidden. The rationale was that specialization made all the institutions less prone to bankruptcy, and thereby protected the public.

The separation of the four pillars was, however, never absolute (for example, credit unions long offered insurance to their members) and they began to crumble in the late 1960s, when the chartered banks were given permission to make mortgage loans and to issue *debentures.*

Since that time, regulatory reform—prompted in large part by innovations in financial instruments, by the rapid development of computer technology, and by a perception of increased volatility in the financial sector—and rising international competition have largely eroded the separation of the four pillars. The most recently passed federal legislation regulating banks will hasten its demise. Several provincial governments have also relaxed their restrictions on the services that may be provided by near-banks.

Thus, the differences between types of institutions are likely to become increasingly blurred over time. Indeed, economists long ago argued that, in a deregulated environment, the distinction between banks and other types of financial intermediaries would vanish.[4] Nevertheless, institutions will probably continue for a time to specialize in the areas they have served in the past.

---

4 Fisher Black, "Banks Fund management in an Efficient Market," *Journal of Financial Economics* (December

## REGULATION

As already suggested, Canadian financial institutions are governed by a potpourri of legislation.[5] One reason for the variety is the history of four-pillars separation. Different laws were written to cover different types of institutions.

Another reason is the federal–provincial sharing of powers. The federal government has sole jurisdiction over banking. Hence all chartered banks and other federally regulated financial institutions fall under the federal Bank Act, which is revised approximately every 10 years. The most recent revision was passed and proclaimed in 1992.[6]

Other types of financial institutions may be incorporated federally or provincially and are regulated accordingly. Many (not all) insurance companies and trust companies are federally regulated institutions. Most credit unions are supervised by the provinces.

# TYPES OF FINANCIAL MARKETS

Understanding the financial system requires an understanding not only of its institutions but also of the types of markets they serve. There are many market classifications. They can be described as based on

1. Type of transaction. We have already encountered this classification. It includes direct transactions, in which lender and borrower deal with each other directly (perhaps with the assistance of a broker or agent) and indirect transactions, which go through a financial intermediary.

2. Selling and reselling. A **primary market** is one in which assets are sold for the first time; the assets traded in the primary financial market are newly issued securities or shares. A **secondary market** is one in which the same assets are resold (often over and over again).

3. Duration. Is the asset being lent for a short term or a long term? The problem here is that there are no clear definitions for "short" and "long." Nevertheless, interest rates may vary with the duration of the loan, and one can even perceive separate markets for different types of duration.

   (a) *Term to maturity* (length of time until the loan must be repaid). One set

---

1995): 323–39; and Eugene Fama, "Banking in a Theory of Finance," *Journal of Monetary Economics* (January 1980): 39–57.

5 The regulation of the various financial institutions is described in more detail in Chapters 16 through 19.

6 The changes are outlined in Chapter 17. Those pertaining to reserve requirements are described in Chapter 16.

of definitions calls financial instruments that mature in one year or less short-term and those that mature in more than one year long-term. An alternative set adds another step; maturities of less than one year are short-term; maturities of one to five years are medium-term; and maturities of more than five years are long-term.

(b) *Markets.* The **money market** is for the trading of short-term instruments, those with maturities of less than a year. The **capital market** is for transactions in long-term instruments, those with maturities of more than a year. The *mortgage market* is also for long-term debt, but maturities are typically more than 10 years.

4. Size. Occasionally the financial press distinguishes according to the size of the financial transaction. Thus, transactions of less than, say, $100,000, involve the *retail* side of the market whereas those greater than $100,000 involve the *wholesale* side. One reason for such a distinction is that financial institutions market to the two sides quite separately. Also, the costs of providing services to them can be significantly different.
5. Style of transaction. Financial transactions carried out in an open market, such as an auction or stock exchange, are said to involve the public market. By contrast, transactions involving face-to-face negotiations between borrowers and lenders, albeit via a financial intermediary, take place in the private market.
6. Sectoral classification. The National Accounts divide the economy roughly into five broad sectors: households and unincorporated businesses, non-financial corporations, the financial sector, the government or public sector, and the rest of the world (the foreign sector). Some financial markets involve one sector, some two or more.

## THE FINANCIAL SYSTEM IN THE CANADIAN ECONOMY

How important is the financial system in the Canadian economy? Figures 3.1 through 3.3 show three different ways of arriving at an answer. Figure 3.1 tells us that approximately three-fifths of all assets in the Canadian economy are financial in nature. Corporate debt is the largest component, followed by currency and bank deposits, government bonds, mortgages, life insurance and pension funds, and bank loans. Figure 3.2 shows that approximately one-quarter of all assets in the Canadian economy are owned by the financial sector. This ratio has been steadily declining over the years. Finally, Figure 3.3 shows the proportionof all assets held in financial assets by the various sectors of the economy. For example, more than half of all assets held by individuals and almost one-third of those held by corporations are financial assets.

**FIGURE 3.1** The Relative Importance of Financial Assets

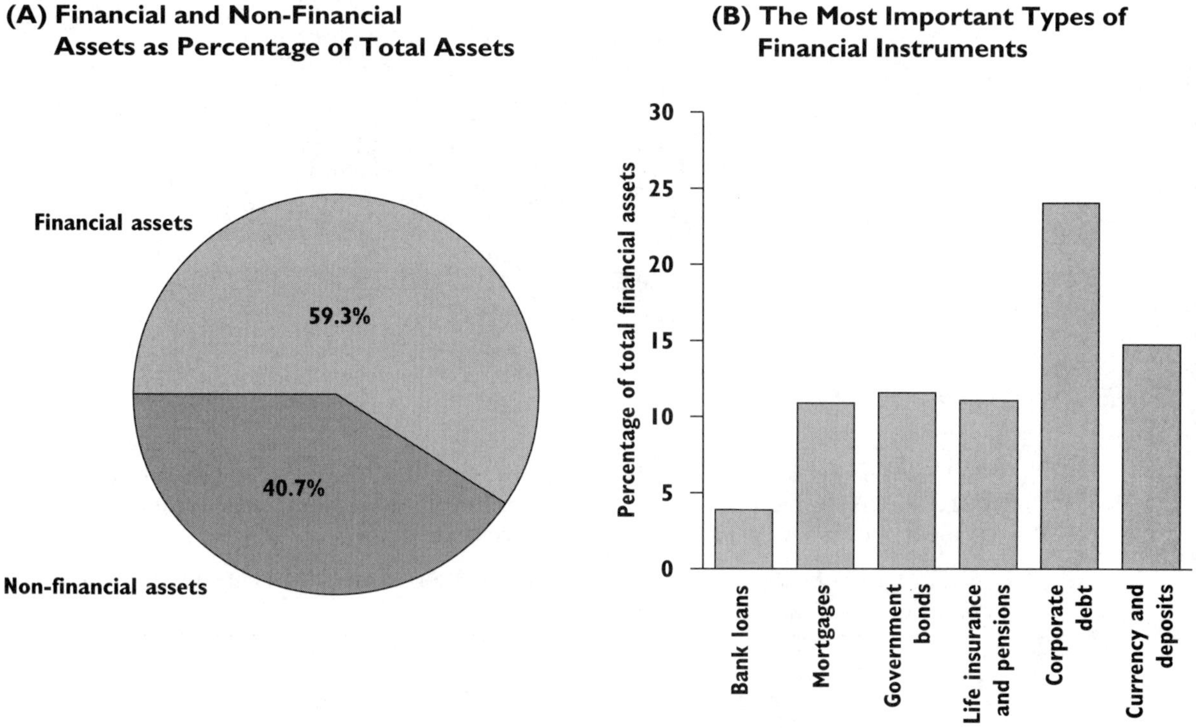


The pie chart in panel (A) shows that financial assets were almost three-fifths of all assets in Canada in 1993. Approximately three-quarters of those financial assets were in the form of six major instruments; their relative importance is shown in panel (B).

The data used here are from 1993, the most recent available as we write.

Note: Currency and deposits include deposits at chartered banks and other deposit-taking institutions. Government bonds include federal, provincial, and municipal bonds. Corporate debt includes shares issued by corporations.

Source: Statistics Canada, *Financial Flow and National Balance Sheet Accounts* (No. 13-214, 1993). Reproduced by authority of the Ministry of Industry, 1996.

Clearly, the short answer to our question is that the financial system plays an enormously important role in the Canadian economy. For more elaboration, let us consider the specific importance of financial intermediaries and the system's overall efficiency.

## INTERMEDIATION AND DISINTERMEDIATION

Measuring the financial development of an economy is difficult to do directly. One proxy is the change over time in the ratio of total bank financial assets to

**FIGURE 3.2** The Relative Importance of the Financial Sector

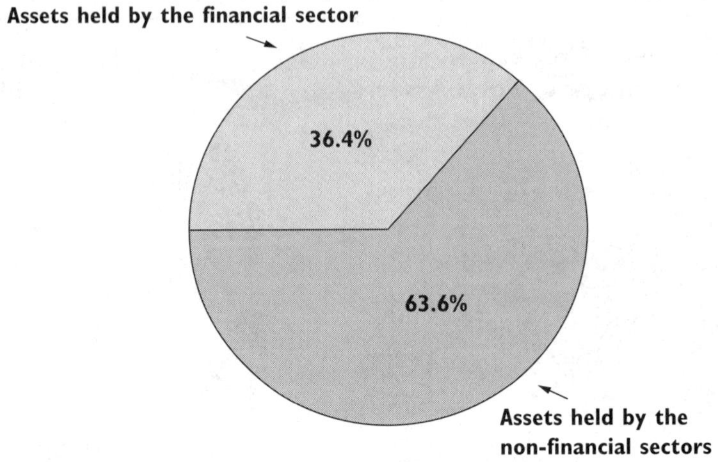


A large proportion of assets in the economy are held by the financial sector, which comprises the Bank of Canada, the chartered banks, the near-banks, insurance companies, pension funds, and various other private and public financial institutions.

Source: Statistics Canada, *Financial Flow and National Balance Sheet Accounts* (No. 13-214, 1993). Reproduced by authority of the Ministry of Industry, 1996.

total financial assets. If the ratio rises, the non-bank sector (that is, the general public) is holding an increasingly smaller share of the financial assets available in the economy. Presumably, this outcome is a reflection of growing financial development and sophistication.

Figure 3.4 plots this measure for Canada, the United Kingdom, and the United States from 1870 to 1986. A striking feature of the graph is the similarity of the patterns for the three countries. Such an observation suggests that the strong financial development that has occurred in the twentieth century is a fact in a variety of countries and that the speed of such development is common to several countries.[7]

The variations of the curves in Figure 3.4 can also tell us something about how inflation and other events affect the financial system. A fall in the total bank / total ratio means the banks are holding relatively fewer of the economy's financial assets. This fall, which is called *disintermediation*, is symptomatic of a financial

7 For a more formal presentation of this argument, see Lars Jonung, Michael Bordo and Pierre Siklos, "Institutional Change and the Velocity of Money: A Century of Evidence," *Economic Inquiry* (1997). Unfortunately, the data are extremely difficult to come by which is why the series ends in 1986.

**FIGURE 3.3** The Importance of Financial Assets by Sector of the Economy

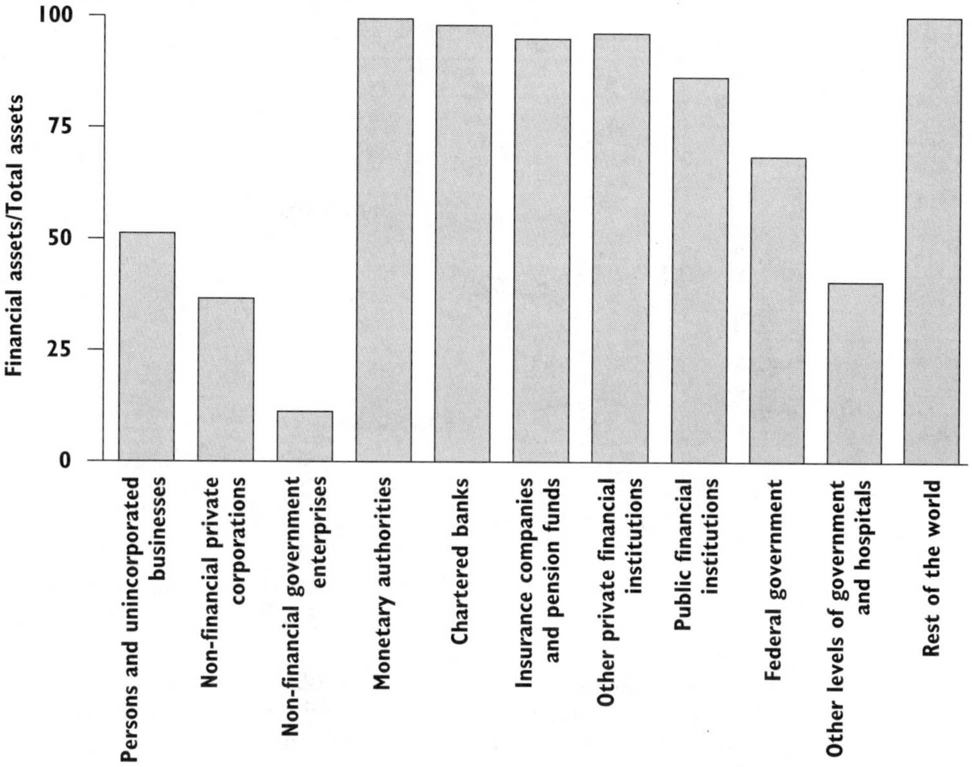


The various sectors of the Canadian economy differ considerably in the proportion of their assets that are financial assets. Not surprisingly, virtually all of the financial institutions' assets are financial in nature while assets held by foreigners (rest of the world) are overwhelmingly of a financial nature.

Source: Statistics Canada, *Financial Flow and National Balance Sheet Accounts* (No. 13-214, 1992). Reproduced by authority of the Ministry of Industry, 1996.

system shifting away from bank-intermediated transactions to direct borrowing and lending. A swing up from this state of affairs reflects *reintermediation*; the public again chooses to hold a larger share of the stock of existing assets.

As Figure 3.4 reveals, although the overall trend has been upward, there have also been some noticeable downturns. For example, during World War II, the financial systems ceased to function normally as government in each of the three countries took substantial control over financial activity. The trend turned sharply upward again following that war, but by the 1960s there was renewed reversal as regulations severely limiting the activity of financial institutions combined with

**FIGURE 3.4** Financial Development in Canada, the United States, and the United Kingdom since 1870

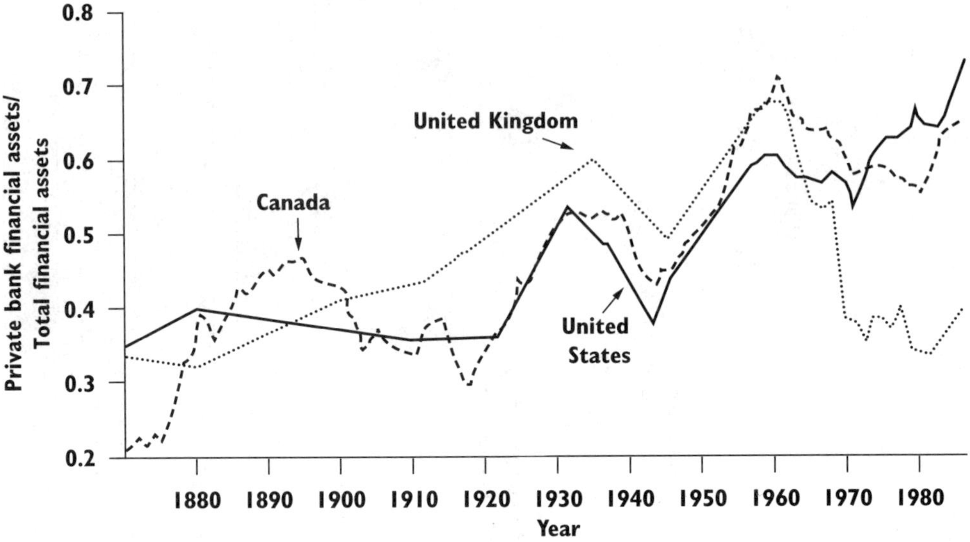


The plots show the ratio of private bank financial assets relative to total private financial assets. The trends in all three countries are similar and roughly simultaneous. Notice that the United Kingdom had the sharpest drop in the late 1960s and early 1970s. It also had the highest inflation during that period.

Source: M.D. Bordo and L.P. Jonung, "The Long-Run Behavior of Velocity: The Institutionalist Approach Revisited," *Journal of Policy Modelling* 12 (Summer 1990): 165–97.

the emergence of inflation to slow financial development and produce some disintermediation. In the 1980s, the onset of deregulation, disinflation, and the banks' introduction of a wide variety of new financial instruments reversed the ratio once again.

What can we expect in the future? Forecasting financial development is a particularly difficult exercise. But banks and brokers are worried by the mere fact that the costs of obtaining, processing, and acting on information continue to fall as computer technology becomes both cheaper and easier to use. Although the deposit-taking and loan-making functions of banks will probably always be needed in society, individual investors may soon be able to compete with the financial system in many financial markets. For example, firms may choose to buy and sell securities and stocks via direct access to computerized networks. Thus, technological developments may portend a new era of disintermediation.

# EFFICIENCY

Although the facts just discussed establish the vital role played by the financial system as a whole, they say nothing about whether it is efficient—whether the funds created by or flowing through that system have been channelled to their best use.

Efficiency can be measured along several dimensions. We'll look at two of them: the borrowing–lending rate differential, and the integration of financial markets.

## The Borrowing–Lending Rate Differential

One type of efficiency consideration stems from the financial intermediaries' attempts to earn a profit for their shareholders. They accomplish this, roughly speaking, by charging more on loans than they pay on their deposits. The efficiency problem is demonstrated in Figure 3.5, which shows a demand and a supply curve for a market that we call the market for *loanable funds* (the funds available in the economy for borrowing and lending).[8] The point of intersection marks the *equilibrium interest rate.* At this rate, $100 billion should be traded in the economy. However, because intermediaries charge more for loans than for deposits, the quantity of funds supplied may differ from that at equilibrium. Quantity supplied might actually be $90 billion for an interest rate of, say, 8%, but a quantity demanded of $90 billion would be consistent with an interest rate of, say, 11%. Thus, a wedge is introduced between the deposit rate—the interest rate on the funds supplied into the financial system—and the loan rate—the interest rate on funds required or demanded by borrowers. So what? Although the introduction of an interest rate differential means fewer funds are traded in the financial system than in an ideal world without frictions or costs of providing information or services, someone (the shareholders or the holders of the funds being lent out) benefits by earning a profit. One of the things which happens then is a redistribution of resources from one group in society to another. But as a result of this transfer, society as a whole has lost something. It is represented in Figure 3.5 by the triangular area *ABE*, which is called a deadweight loss to society. However, as pointed out earlier in this chapter, there are also gains from the existence of specialized institutions, that is, the intermediaries, which facilitate the borrowing and lending process.

---

8 You may treat the diagram in Figure 3.5 much like the many diagrams depicting markets you encountered in your principles of economics course. We develop the model, together with its underlying assumptions, more fully in later chapters, starting in Chapter 6.

**FIGURE 3.5** The Borrowing–Lending Rate Differential

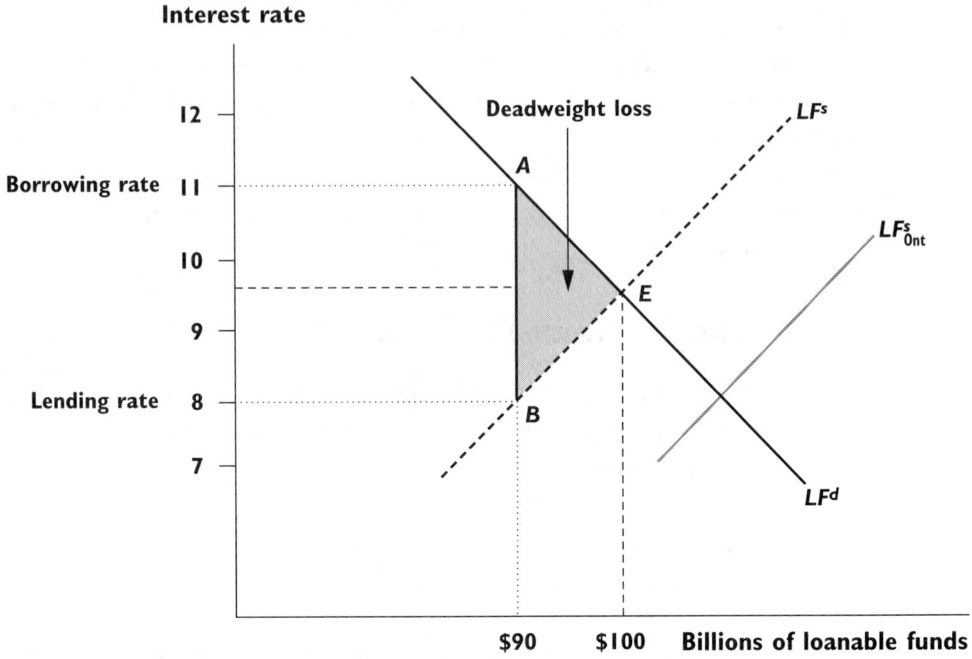


The vertical axis measures the interest rate and the horizontal axis measures the amount of funds available in the financial system (loanable funds). The supply curve is $LF^s$ and the demand curve is $LF^d$. Equilibrium is at point *E*, where $100 billion should be available. But since financial intermediaries wish to generate a profit, only $90 billion is available. This difference creates a wedge between borrowing and lending rates. The consequent loss to society is measured by the triangle *ABE*.

If regional fragmentation of the financial system were possible, the equilibrium interest rate in Ontario would be lower than that in Atlantic Canada. The reason is the relative scarcity of loanable funds supplied in Atlantic Canada ($LF^s$ compared to $LF^s_{Ont}$).

What is important is not the existence of such a loss but its size. One can imagine that the size of the borrowing–lending rate differential is a function of matters such as the ability of lenders to dictate interest rates. The study of efficiency therefore involves examination of the degree to which there is competition in the Canadian financial system because the extent to which competition is present in the economy partially dictates the size of the differential.

### Integration

One can also evaluate the efficiency of a financial system by exploring the advantages and disadvantages of a system in which individuals and institutions all have access to the same market. The process of *globalization* is an example of markets, previously defined on a national scale, becoming defined along international lines.

Alternatively, the question of access has been termed the problem of regional integration. For example, Canada's financial markets are fully integrated in the sense that interest rates are essentially the same in all parts of the country. Although such a situation may seem fair, it does not make everyone better off. For example, investors in Ontario could conceivably be made better off if their interest rates were lower than those in Atlantic Canada because, other things being equal, funds are relatively more plentiful in Ontario. In Figure 3.5, the supply of loanable funds in Ontario might be represented by the curve labelled $LF^s_{Ont}$ and the supply curve for Atlantic Canada by the original supply curve labelled $LF^s$. Although relatively lower interest rates in Ontario would doubtless please its residents, such differentials could not be enforced. Current technology, which permits dollars to be transferred electronically at very low cost, would enable Atlantic Canadians to obtain funds from Ontario at the lower rates. Then the total demand for funds would rise, eventually wiping out the interest rate differential.

Legal and economic barriers do, of course, create some differentials. For example, all provincial governments cannot borrow at the same interest rate. Despite calls from various parts of the country for policies attuned primarily to regional concerns (such as more regional representation in the conduct of the Bank of Canada), the increasingly strong push for worldwide integration of financial markets will make such policies increasingly difficult and thus costly to implement.

## SUMMARY

- Intermediation is what the financial system is all about. It represents the process by which the debts of one person or group become assets to others.

- In this chapter, we discuss the various types of financial institutions that perform the intermediation function in Canada.

- Banks are particularly adept at intermediation because they can perform the necessary functions more cheaply than most institutions. However, technological change and deregulation have narrowed the comparative advantage of banks.

## ECONOMICS FOCUS 3.1 The Problem of Economic Integration

In 1992, the European Union implemented a plan for full economic integration and began to work toward a single currency (referred to as EMU which stands for Economic and Monetary Union) for all members. At a meeting of the heads of state in December 1995, the leaders of the EU agreed to call this new currency the *Euro*, while at the same time reaffirming their desire to launch the new currency on 1 January 1999.

Yet even if the latter integration is achieved, the economic success of member countries will be dictated by how well each nation manages its own finances—that is, by its own fiscal policy. Credit ratings are not the same for all EC members. Germany has the highest and Greece, the lowest.

As a result, a thorny question for the EU is to decide which country will be financially and economically fit by 1999 (we explore these issues in greater detail in Chapter 23). This has led to the speculation that some EU countries will initially participate in EMU but others will not, thereby vastly complicating the prospects for full European integration.

The European example is one in which some fragmentation in the financial system may prove to be more efficient than an arrangement whereby, say, interest rates and monetary policy would be the same everywhere in the EU. It should be emphasized, however, that currently the richer EU states transfer various financial resources to the poorer ones to help create a level playing field in trade and other economic endeavours. In Canada, equalization payments compensate the have-not members of Confederation via transfers from the have provinces.

- The Canadian financial system can be classified according to types of financial markets. For example, markets can be divided according to when the asset or debt in question matures, or whether the sums involved are relatively large or small.

- To assess how well the financial system is performing it is important to determine how efficient it is. In this chapter, we look at two ways of measuring the efficiency of a financial system.

# IMPORTANT TERMS

adverse selection (p. 46)
asymmetric information (p. 46)
brokers (p. 46)
capital market (p. 52)
deposit-taking institutions (p. 47)
externality (p. 47)
financial intermediary (p. 47)
four pillars (p. 50)
intermediary (p. 43)
intermediation (p. 44)
money market (p. 52)
portfolio (p. 44)
primary market (p. 51)
secondary market (p. 51)

# EXERCISES

1. Can you think of a recent financial innovation that has implications for the efficiency of the financial system? That has influence on economies of scale? On economics of scope?

2. According to Figure 3.4, the ratio of non-bank financial assets to total financial assets peaked during the early 1930s and then fell in until the mid-1940s.What event or events could explain such a pattern? Explain.

3. Suppose that in Figure 3.5 the $LF^s$ and $LF^d$ curves represent the funds supplied and demanded when borrowing and lending activities are tax free. Now suppose lending is taxed while borrowing can be used to reduce investors' tax burdens. What would happen to the borrowing–lending rate differentials? To the deadweight loss? Use a diagram.

4. Is an issuer of traveller's cheques a financial intermediary? Why?

5. Investment funds, such as mutual funds, appear to intermediate just as banks do. How can the two institutions co-exist efficiently?

6. Why do issuers of stocks and bonds use an underwriter? (Hint: Explain in terms of efficiency.)

7. What is it about the housing market that makes mortgage lending a problem? Why do you think government intervention in this market has been necessary?

8. Approximately two-thirds of financial debt is held as assets by financial institutions. Why do you think this ratio has been fairly stable since 1980?

9. For a financial market to be efficient, it is necessary for all participants to be fully informed and up-to-date. Evaluate this statement.

10. Bankers actually dislike having to deal with cash. Why? In this respect, have automated teller machines made things better or worse for banks?

11. Why do you think that deregulation is eliminating the distinction between banks and other financial intermediaries?

12. According to two well-known economic theories, regulation and economic growth can act as spurs to financial innovations. Can you think why this might be the case?

# REFERENCES

Bordo, M.D., and L.P. Jonung. *The Long-Run Behaviour of the Velocity of Circulation.* Cambridge: Cambridge University Press, 1987.

Gertler, M. "Financial Structure and Aggregate Economic Activity." *Journal of Money, Credit and Banking* 20 (part 2, August 1988): 559–88.

International Monetary Fund. *International Financial Statistics Yearbook* (various issues).

Mayer, C. "Financial Systems, Corporate Finance, and Economic Development." In *Asymmetric Information, Corporate Finance, and Investment,* edited by R. Glenn Hubbard, 307–32. Chicago: University of Chicago Press, 1990.

McConnell, C.R., S.L. Brue, and T.P. Barbiero. *Microeconomics,* 7th Cdn. ed. Toronto: McGraw-Hill Ryerson, 1996.

Mishkin, F.S. "Asymmetric Information and Financial Crises: A Historical Perspective." NBER working paper no. 3400 (July 1990).

*Payment Systems in Eleven Developed Countries.* Basle: Bank for International Settlements (various issues).

CHAPTER 4

# Financial Instruments

We saw in the previous chapter that among the many ways to classify the financial system, a convenient and easy-to-remember way is by markets: the *money market*, for transactions in instruments with maturities of less than one year, and the *capital market*, for transactions in instruments with maturities that exceed one year. We use this division to examine the system's principal instruments.

An explanation of these instruments is important for at least three reasons. First, it provides an overview of how financial markets have developed over time to meet the needs of borrowers and lenders. Second, it provides an early glimpse of how the Bank of Canada can influence the financial system in order to fulfil some of its short-run interest rate and monetary policy objectives. Third, it helps to clarify how market efficiency is enhanced by the development of a vast array of instruments that facilitate the flow of funds from lenders to borrowers.

Before we begin our description of the characteristics and functions of the major financial instruments in the money and capital markets, two points are worth noting:

1. Even this minimum list includes both privately and publicly issued instruments. Figure 4.1 gives a picture of the division between the private and public sectors. Private sector borrowing generally has come to dominate while public sector borrowing has fallen to less than one-half of the total funds raised.[1]

2. At this stage we consider only brief descriptions of the most important instruments traded in the Canadian marketplace. In other words, the analysis presented in this chapter is neither exhaustive (if it were, it would be impossibly long) nor detailed (partly because we have yet to discuss how interest rates are determined). Therefore, you should think of what follows as a convenient compendium of financial instruments. Details on many of them may be found in later chapters.

---

1 The sharp reversals in 1993–96 may be partly due to definitional changes. Also, there was a sharp rise in provincial and municipal borrowing in 1993 which was reversed in 1994.

**FIGURE 4.1** Who Raises Funds in Canada?

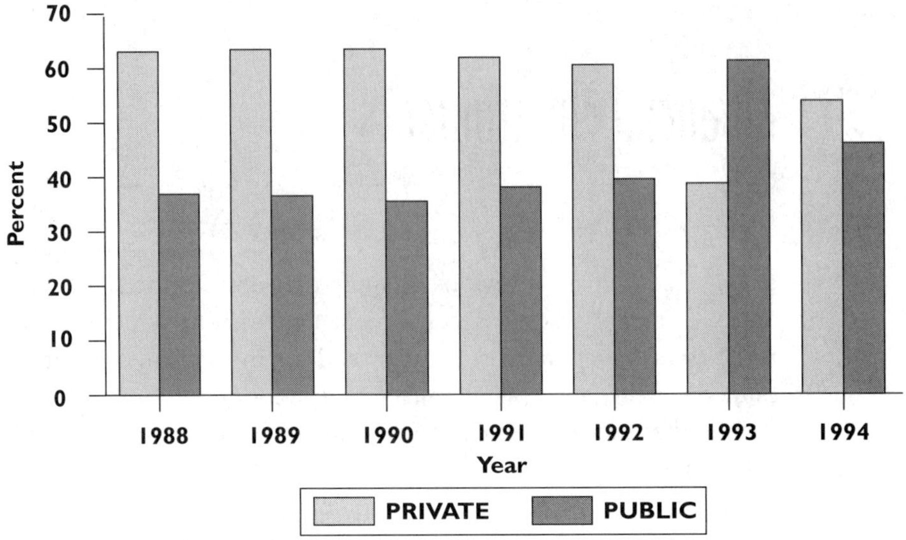


Except for 1993, a majority of funds were raised by the private sector. The data for 1993 probably reflect the impact of the recession of the early 1990s.

Source: Statistics Canada. *Financial Flow and National Balance Sheet Accounts* (13-214), various years, Analytical Table 4. Reproduced by authority of the Ministry of Industry, 1996.

# THE MONEY MARKET

Table 4.1 lists the principal money market instruments and indicates which sectors in the financial system rely on them to obtain funds and whether a significant secondary market exists. You should rely on this list for the essential points of the discussion that follows.

## TREASURY BILLS

A **Treasury bill (T-bill)** is a debt incurred by the government. Its issue price is determined in a weekly auction. There is no stated interest rate on this kind of debt. Rather, a Treasury bill is sold at a discount (deduction) relative to its **par value** (face value); the difference between the par value and the discounted price indicates the T-bill's return. Maturities range from 91 days to 1 year (the most commonly traded bills are for the 91-day maturity). Trading in T-bills accounts for well over one-half of the trading in the Canadian money market.

**TABLE 4.1** THE MONEY MARKET

| Instruments | Typical Maturities | Principal Borrowers | Secondary Market |
|---|---|---|---|
| Treasury bills | 91 to 365 days | Federal government | Yes |
| Provincial and municipal Treasury bills | 91 to 365 days | Provincial governments and municipalities | Yes |
| Government-backed funds | 91 to 365 days | Crown corporations | Yes |
| Bank of Canada advances | Few days | Chartered banks | None |
| Special purchase and resale agreements (SPRAs) | 1 business day | Money market dealers (jobbers) | None |
| Purchase and resale agreements (PRAs) | Up to 15 days | Money market dealers (jobbers) and chartered banks | None |
| Bankers' acceptances | 10 to 365 days | Chartered banks and money market dealers | Yes |
| Day-to-day loans | Callable at any time | Money market dealers | None |
| Special call loans | Overnight | Money market dealers | None |
| Certificates of deposit (CDs) | 30 days and longer | Chartered banks | None |
| Bearer deposit notes (BDNs) | 30 days to 1 year | Money market dealers | Yes |
| Interbank deposits | Few days | Chartered banks | None |
| Eurocurrency instruments | Overnight to 6 months or longer | Chartered banks | Yes |
| Corporate and finance company paper | 30 to 365 days | Business, and finance companies | Small |

Some of the instruments on this list are especially important either because they have wide-ranging effects on the entire financial system or because the volume of trade in these instruments dwarfs that of the others. The boxes here distinguish the items in this group.

The rate on Treasury bills has attracted considerable public attention since March 10, 1980, when it became linked to the **bank rate**, the rate at which the

Bank of Canada lends to chartered banks, as follows:[2]

$$\text{Bank rate} = \text{Treasury bill rate} + 0.25\%$$

In the large secondary market for T-bills, banks and investment dealers sell them to the general public in denominations starting at $1,000. By the early 1990s, however, the Bank of Canada began to develop a system which permitted same-day settlement of large value transactions. Accordingly, the Bank of Canada announced on 21 February 1996 that the bank rate would henceforth be set at the *upper limit* of the **band** for overnight financing (we deal with this type of transaction later in the chapter). In other words,

$$\text{Bank rate} = \textit{upper limit} \text{ of overnight rate band}$$

The band itself is +/− $\frac{1}{4}$ of 1 percent around the target overnight rate, that is, the spread between the upper and lower bands is $\frac{1}{2}$ of 1 percent or 50 **basis points**.

## The Treasury Bill Auctions

How is the influential T-bill rate determined? By the highest bidders in a weekly auction.

By 12:30 p.m. (all times are Eastern Standard Time) every Tuesday,[3] investment dealers and chartered banks electronically place bids for the purchase of T-bills with the Bank of Canada's Ottawa headquarters. Each bid specifies the dollar amount of T-bills the would-be buyer wishes to purchase as well as a yield.[4] Meanwhile the Bank of Canada puts in a reverse bid. For a purchaser, the lower the price, the greater the interest income that can be derived. The Bank of Canada, on the other hand, seeks the highest possible price since it translates into the lowest debt cost to the federal government, which is borrowing the money. Thus, the game played by the would-be buyers involves guessing the course of interest rates the Bank of Canada wishes to pursue though other factors, such as interest rates abroad (especially in the United States) and the amount of Treasury bills

2 This kind of link between the T-bill rate and the bank rate also existed between 1 November 1956 and 23 June 1962.

3 Until 24 November 1992, the auction was held on Thursdays. The auction was moved to Tuesdays in part because of the considerable turbulence in world foreign-exchange markets and also to allow auction participants more time to process and distribute each new issue. Another motivation might be the fact that the US Federal Reserve sets its key lending rate also on a Tuesday.

4 Before 11 April 1991, bids were expressed on the basis of a price. The yield (for a $1 million T-bill) is the average, weighted by volume, of all accepted bids.

## FINANCIAL FOCUS 4.1 Is This Any Way to Run a Market?

Until recently, the US federal government sold its debt through a small group of banks and investment dealers who bid in a weekly auction. Analysts such as Friedman suggested for a long time that this practice could lead to collusion, in which a handful of bidders could corner the market, with anti-competitive results.

The problem is less serious in Canada because all chartered banks may participate in the auction and may hold Treasury bills. Moreover, since the Bank of Canada places a reserve bid at every auction and monitors the activities, attempts to monopolize the purchase of newly issued government securities are unlikely.

Canada, the United States, and Japan also have active "when-issued" markets, in which dealers commit themselves to future sales and purchases prior to the auction. Because market participants can thus avoid the actual auction, the *Wall Street Journal* has said that attempts to solve problems with Treasury bill auctions are "bogus." Poitras suggests, however, that at least in the Canadian case, buyers and sellers in these advance markets do not predict future T-bill yields very well. As recent US experience attests, however, the current system for auctioning government securities does raise some important questions. Solomon Brothers was caught in 1990 and 1991 violating the US rule that stipulates that dealers can purchase no more than 35% of an issue. By purchasing large blocks of securities, the brokers could dictate the price at which these same securities were resold to other dealers, who often had had to promise price and quantity ahead of time to their own customers. The US Treasury solved the immediate problem by allowing all brokers to bid on government securities. But there might be better, more basic solutions.

Why not ask the dealers to specify the quantities they wish to buy at various prices and expect all purchasers to pay a single average price at the end of bidding, as in Switzerland? In this fashion the demand curve for the particular security is generated, but since no bidder knows the final price for the issue, there is less chance of collusion. Another option would be to open the market to all interested participants. Certainly computer technology offers the hope that this openness might be achieved someday if it is not already feasible to do so.

Ironically, just as the United States has begun to question its marketing practices, other countries, such as France, Belgium, and Italy have adopted a version of the US auction system.

**Sources:**

M. Friedman, "How to Sell Government Securities," *Wall Street Journal*, 28 August 1991.

G. Poitras, "The When-Issued Market for Government of Canada Treasury Bills," *Canadian Journal of Economics* 24 (August 1991): 604–23.

P. Thomas and J. Herman, "Treasury Sets Bidding Rules Aimed at Cleaning Up Troubled Auctions," *Wall Street Journal*, 23 October 1992.

maturing that week versus the quantity of new issues, also play a role in determining the T-bill price.

By 1:30 p.m. the Bank has ranked the bids from highest to lowest and announced the successful ones (in a 2 p.m. press release), which must be delivered by Thursday. The Bank of Canada also announces the amounts to be auctioned the following week.[5]

5 In the 1980s, cash management bills were used—they were introduced in 1968—which are T-bills with

## The Bank of Canada and Interest Rates

The weekly T-bill auction gives the Bank of Canada considerable influence over interest rates. Banks and money market dealers compete for Treasury bills because they are an attractive financial instrument: they are backed by the taxing and money-raising powers of the federal government, they are highly liquid, and there is a large secondary market for them. The acts of offering and bidding for T-bills thus influence the amount of reserves available in the financial system and, by implication, interest rates. Moreover, the Bank of Canada's reserve bid can lead to a T-bill rate that suits its policy at the time.[6]

The Bank of Canada can (and does) influence interest rates in three other ways. First, as the federal government's banker, it can manipulate the government's deposits. This action, in turn, influences the level of reserves.[7] Second, it can conduct **open market operations**, which involve the buying and selling of government securities (including T-bills) in regular markets. Third, it can manipulate the amount of deposits held by banks as it facilitates the cheque-clearing process and in its role as manager of government deposits in the banking system. This *drawdown and redeposit* technique has become an important tool of monetary policy as reserve requirements are phased out. Ever since the Bank of Canada and the federal government agreed on an inflation target (see Chapter 25), the bank has intervened in this fashion to influence the amount of liquidity in the so-called overnight market. Cash management techniques have been refined to such an extent that they permit financial institutions to keep cash on hand at a minimum. Nevertheless, cash needs do arise and banks, for example, frequently need to borrow very short-term to satisfy their liquidity needs as when, for example, the bank of Canada shifts funds of the government deposited in banks to its account at the Bank of Canada (we consider a detailed example of this phenomenon in Chapter 24). By manipulating the available liquidity in the overnight market the bank of Canada can influence the overnight rate and, consequently, send signals to the financial market. The Bank of Canada implements its drawdown or redeposit position by about 8:30 a.m. (EST) even though the decision is made at the closing of the previous business day. By supplying extra

---

maturities ranging from 8 to 50 days (the average is around 35 to 42 days) to finance government cash needs of $500 million or more on short notice (the amount is announced one day prior to the auction).

6 Although for the most part the Bank tries to stay neutral because it has, as we will see shortly, other instruments at its disposal.

7 This chapter has many references to *reserves* or *reserve requirements*, which are funds that banks hold readily available (in cash or at the Bank of Canada) to meet the demands of depositors. We deal with the subject in depth later. With deregulation, those requirements were phased out in 1994 (although banks will continue to want to hold reserves to meet their customers' needs).

cash into the system the overnight rate will fall as the banking system experiences excess reserves (remember the banks aim for zero reserves). The opposite, of course, is true when the Bank of Canada supplies fewer funds than the banks appear to demand and, consequently, the overnight rate will rise.

## LARGE VALUE TRANSFER SYSTEM (LVTS)

As noted above, the speed with which financial transactions take place means that the Bank of Canada has to focus on the overnight market. Since 1994, the Bank has set a target for the overnight rate and has specified a *band* around it (50 basis point spread between the highest and lowest rates). By changing the target the Bank sends signals about its monetary policy stance. By early 1996, the Bank of Canada had changed the band 21 times. This is accomplished via the Special Purchase and Resale Agreement (SPRA) or Purchase and Resale Agreement (PRA) instruments described below.

This method of conducting monetary policy is closely tied to the operations of the clearing mechanism. Although we look at a more detailed example in Chapter 24, it is sufficient for now to understand that, until recently, cheques were cleared overnight and settled retroactively. In early 1996, the Bank of Canada announced a new electronic system called the **Large Value Transfer System** or LVTS to be used by the Canadian Payments Association by 1997. This new system permits financial institutions to figure out their settlement balances on a daily basis thereby eliminating the uncertainty about settlement balances at the Bank of Canada.

Overdrafts would then be charged at the bank rate which, as pointed out earlier, have been set at the top of the overnight bands since February 1996. The rate earned on surplus balances is equal to the *bottom* of the overnight rate band, which means that a spread of 50 basis points exists between the penalty rate and the rate on excess settlement balances.[8]

## PROVINCIAL AND MUNICIPAL TREASURY BILLS

Provinces and municipalities also issue Treasury bills. They are similar to the federal government's T-bills, but there are no auctions to determine their rate. Instead, the return is based partly on the return on Government of Canada Treasury bills and partly on other factors such as the creditworthiness of the issuer.

---

8 For more details on the new operating procedures, see "A Proposed Framework for the Implementation of Monetary Policy in the Large Value Transfer System Environment," Discussion Paper I, 23 November 1995 (Ottawa: Bank of Canada) and Discussion Paper II, *Bank of Canada Review* (Spring 1996): 53–66.

## GOVERNMENT-BACKED FINANCIAL INSTRUMENTS

Federal and provincial Crown corporations and agencies also raise funds in the money market (and in the capital market as well). For example, the Canadian Wheat Board sells Treasury bills through investment dealers. Like provincial government T-bills, they are sold at a discount and, since they are ostensibly fully backed by the federal or provincial government responsible, there is little risk of default. Unlike the case for the federal government's T-bills, however, the secondary market for government-backed financial instruments is quite small, so they are relatively difficult to sell at a moment's notice.

## BANK OF CANADA ADVANCES

Central banks fulfil a vital function in today's economies: they are **lenders of last resort**—a source of funds for certain institutions (in Canada, primarily chartered banks, trust companies, and investment dealers)—when other sources of funds have essentially been exhausted.

**Bank of Canada advances** are one of the mechanisms by which the central bank fulfils this function. It advances funds to members of the Canadian Payments Association, generally for one business day, to meet emergency shortages of funds. The loan rate is equivalent to the bank rate. Like many central banks, the Bank of Canada is reluctant to lend funds to the financial institutions, viewing such action as a distinct sign of weakness in the system. It prefers that the institutions seek funds elsewhere; perhaps even more often in Canadian financial history, it has also encouraged mergers between weaker and stronger institutions.

Figure 4.2 chronicles the dollar amount of advances outstanding at the end of each year since 1977. Notice their relatively small size. The terms and conditions governing Bank of Canada advances have undergone significant changes over the years. Until the 1960s, the usual term for borrowing from the Bank of Canada was between one week and one month. This term has been substantially reduced. There are currently no specified limits on the size or the number of times a loan can be taken out. However, until 1991, there were strict limits based on a formula involving the amount of reserves a bank had on hand and the dollar amount of deposits, up to some maximum ($10 million at one time). Normally, banks could avail themselves of the line of credit at the Bank of Canada at most once or twice a month.

## SPECIAL PURCHASE AND RESALE AGREEMENTS

There are times when the Bank of Canada does not succeed in influencing overnight rates to its satisfaction. When this happens the Bank can intervene directly

**FIGURE 4.2** Bank of Canada Advances

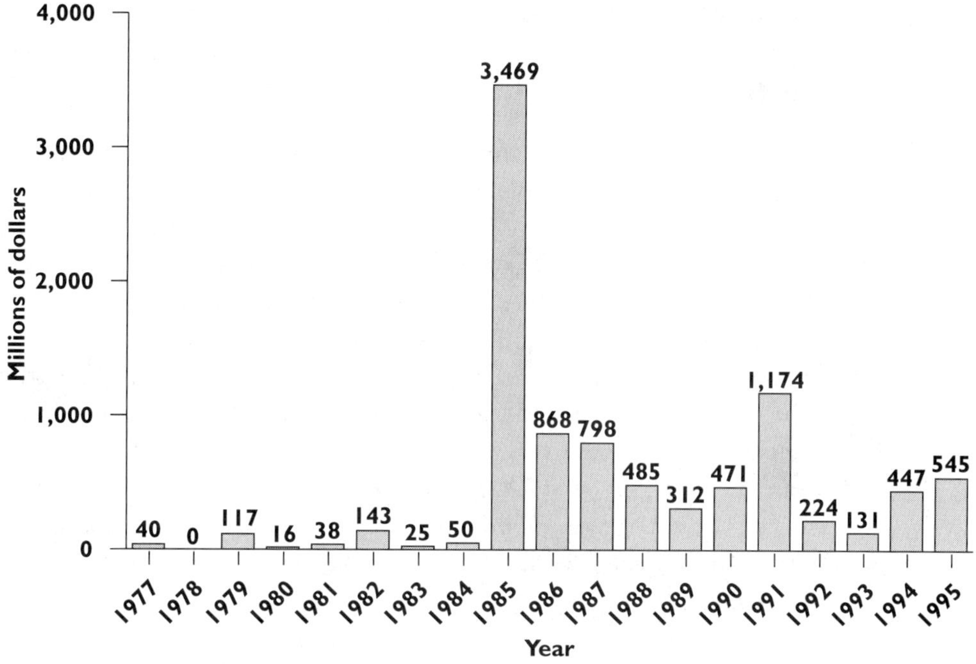


Even over the course of a year, Bank of Canada advances do not normally total huge sums. The overall increase in the mid-1980s is partly explained by changes in the cheque-clearing process following the Bank Act of 1980 that increased the number of institutions eligible for financial help from the Bank of Canada. But the sharp rise in advances in 1985 resulted largely from the collapse of the Canadian Commercial Bank.

Source: Statistics Canada, CANSIM database, series B210; and *Bank of Canada Review* (various issues), Table B1. The data are end-of-year figures. The figure for 1995 is the average for the months of January to November.

in financial markets. A **special purchase and resale agreement** (SPRA) is a two-step transaction between the Bank of Canada and a financial institution, usually an investment dealer. The Bank purchases short-term securities, such as Treasury bills, from the institution, which buys them back the following day. Thus liquidity is injected into the financial system, even if only temporarily. The Bank can also simply reverse the operation—that is, it sell securities one day and repurchase them on the next. To distinguish this sort of transaction from an SPRA, it is known as a *reverse PRA* (RPRA). Nevertheless, it is common to use the term *SPRA* to refer to both types of transactions.

The need for SPRAs arose during the 1980s, when financial institutions were experiencing one-day shortages of liquidity, which drove up interest rates or, at least, made them more volatile. Since the introduction of SPRAs, the Bank of Canada has also used them as a device to influence short-term interest rates.

The rate on SPRAs has lately been set at the bank rate.

## The Mechanics

Figure 4.3 uses balance sheets to show how an SPRA can be used to avert a temporary liquidity problem in the financial system. Suppose that the bank of Canada wishes to prevent an anticipated rise in the overnight rate. Perhaps this occurs because a bank expects a shortage of liquidity and plans to call in a loan from an investment dealer. If the Bank of Canada wished to temper the loss of liquidity to the investment dealer, and consequently influence short-term rates, it can offer to purchase an equivalent amount in Treasury bills from the dealer, who uses the proceeds to pay off the loan. The following day, the bank, finding itself with excess reserves, is likely to reverse the transaction and restore the call loan; meanwhile, the SPRA expires and the Bank of Canada is in the same balance sheet position it was in initially.[9] Such transactions can be arranged over the phone and signals to the money market take literally only minutes to spread throughout the market.

## The Use of SPRAs and RPRAs

The Bank of Canada's most notable use of SPRAs was after the stock market collapse of October 1987. Worried that the tremendous fall in stock prices would lead to a shortage of liquidity and a substantial reduction in the net worth of the money market, the Bank repeatedly made SPRAs available and drove short-term interest rates down by 0.75% in a couple of weeks. When the monetary authorities subsequently viewed the effects of the stock market crash as smaller than anticipated they reversed the Bank's earlier policy and offered RPRAs. By January 1988, overnight money market financing rates had risen to levels higher than they had been before the collapse.

The Bank of Canada used SPRAs more frequently than RPRAs in the 1985–1994 period, an indication of its policy in those years of generally attempting to keep interest rate levels up. By late 1995 the reverse was true as the Bank of Canada was putting downward pressure on interest rates.[10]

---

9 To prevent additional cash from entering the banking system through the rise in deposits at the Bank of Canada, the Bank could subsequently draw down these deposits. This action would be an example of the drawdown-redeposit technique mentioned earlier.

10 The data are published in the *Bank of Canada Review*, Table B3.

**FIGURE 4.3** Financing through an SPRA

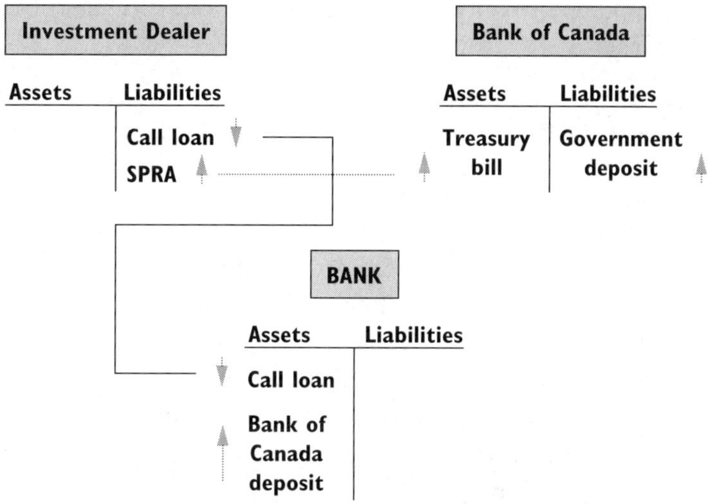


The arrows indicate the direction of changes in assets and liabilities. A bank calls in a loan from an investment dealer and the Bank of Canada offsets the drop in liquidity by offering an SPRA. The transaction is reversed the next day.

## PURCHASE AND RESALE AGREEMENTS

Purchase and resale agreements (PRAs) operate like SPRAs but are initiated by money market dealers.

PRAs first appeared in Canada in 1953 when the Bank of Canada extended its lending-of-last-resort facility to the emerging money market. Money market dealers can sell the Bank selected assets with an agreement to repurchase them within a 15-day period. (In fact, the repurchase usually takes place the following day.) The rate on PRAs has ranged from being equal to the Treasury bill rate minus 0.75% to the T-bill rate plus 0.25%.

PRAs are called "repos" and "reverse repos" in the United States, where they have had a long history as a tool of central bank intervention in the money market.

## BANKERS' ACCEPTANCES

A **banker's acceptance** is essentially a promise to pay at some future date. It is issued by a non-financial firm and guaranteed by a bank. The instrument is sold at a discount and is often rediscounted for the sizeable secondary market.

The term to maturity can be a few days or up to a year; the most common is the 30- to 90-day range. The denomination can be as much as $1 million; large acceptances are broken into smaller amounts (usually $100,000) for the secondary market.

## The Mechanics

The need for a financial instrument such as bankers' acceptances arose out of the risks inherent in international trade. Suppose a Canadian importer wants to purchase some items from a US manufacturer but, being short of cash, pays for them in three months after reselling them.

Will the bill ever be paid? The risk that it won't can be handled in several ways. The seller can assume it. Alternatively, the buyer can borrow the funds from a bank, but now there is the risk that the imports may not be sold successfully in Canada. Moreover, loans are expensive, particularly if the importer is only a small operation.

Another option is to use a banker's acceptance. Figure 4.4 provides a schematic representation of how it works. The importer asks the bank to prepare a **letter of credit**, which is a non-negotiable order, from one bank to another, authorizing payment to someone of a particular sum of money up to some maximum. The letter (or *draft*, as it is called), which is in the amount of the goods purchased, is intended for the exporter in the United States, which can then discount it, since it effectively implies that the funds exist and are at the exporter's disposal at its own bank. The transaction is completed when the exporter's bank stamps the original letter of credit as accepted, guaranteeing payment. The bank, of course, charges a stamping fee, which is equivalent to an interest rate of a fraction of a percent per annum.

## Use

Bankers' acceptances have existed for several centuries in the United Kingdom, and they made their appearance in the United States in the early 1900s. A secondary market emerged in Canada only in 1962, but since then bankers' acceptances have become one of the largest money market instruments in the country.

Indeed, although bankers' acceptances emerged to meet the needs of international trade and to cover the risk of delay between the purchase and subsequent resale of some manufactured good, Canada no longer restricts the type of transaction that can be covered. Since the 1980 Bank Act, bankers' acceptances can be issued to virtually any public or private borrower.

**FIGURE 4.4** Financing via a Banker's Acceptance

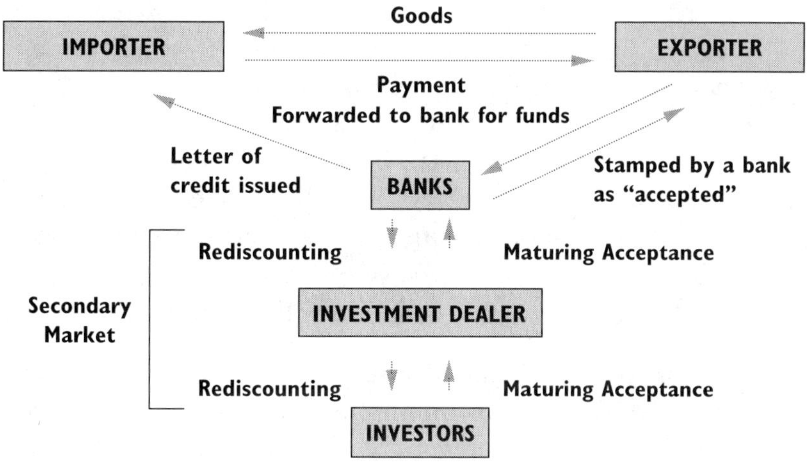


The arrows show the direction of the transactions.

## DAY-TO-DAY LOANS AND SPECIAL CALL LOANS

Day-to-day loans and special call loans represent the private overnight market. They were introduced in Canada in the 1950s and 1960s to increase liquidity for both the banks and investment dealers by providing very short-term instruments that could facilitate cash management.

Day-to-day loans (DTDLs) are made, primarily by chartered banks and other financial institutions, to money market dealers that have PRA facilities with the Bank of Canada. For these dealers, DTDLs represent a ready source of liquidity[11] although the collateral required is of the highest quality: Government of Canada bonds that mature in three years or less, Treasury bills, and bankers' acceptances. The minimum denominations for a DTDL is $100,000.

With the rise of interest rates and their increased volatility, DTDLs, which can be but were not originally overnight loans, are increasingly being replaced by special call loans (SCLs), which are overnight loans made by chartered banks to investment dealers. Unlike DTDLs, SCLs can be secured by commercial and finance company paper as well as by short-term notes issued by the provinces and financial institutions. Indeed, the overnight market has expanded to include

11 They can also be useful to the lenders. Until reserve requirements were completely phased out, DTDLs could be counted as part of chartered banks' secondary reserve requirements.

*offstreet lenders*, which include various financial and non-financial corporations as well as government agencies.

There is no organized market or exchange for such loans. Instead negotiation and trading take place over the telephone. Deals are completed fairly early in the day, when banks receive information about their cash reserve position and European rates on overnight loans are known.

Short-term instruments such as DTDLs and SCLs are important signals of the stance of monetary policy since the cash requirements of market participants drive the market and, consequently, influence short-term interest rates.

## OTHER CHARTERED BANK INSTRUMENTS

So far we have discussed instruments that mainly involve financial institutions of various kinds. In addition, the chartered banks have created a large variety of financial instruments that are used by individuals and other banks, as well as institutions. The brief list of "other instruments"[12] we consider here concentrates on the wholesale segment of the market (that is, they are issued in amounts of $100,000 or more).

### Certificates of Deposit

The bank deposit instruments that enter the money market are called **certificates of deposit** (CDs), which are issued for fairly sizeable time deposits at a fixed interest rate higher than that given for notice deposits. CDs emerged in the United States because legal restrictions on the maximum rate of interest banks could pay did not cover large deposits ($100,000 and up). In Canada, there was a ceiling on the rates banks could charge and thus, by implication, on what they could offer to customers. Deregulation has removed the ceiling, but with the high interest rates of the 1980s, CDs became an important source of funds.

### Bearer Deposit Notes

Introduced in 1964, bearer deposit notes (BDNs) are securities not registered in the owner's name (in contrast to CDs, which are). They are sold at a discount and mature at par; maturities range from 30 days to 1 year. BDNs are typically held by money market dealers who then resell them to their clients as buybacks: that is, the dealers arrange to rediscount them and then to repurchase them at a later date.

---

12 Notice that these "other bank instruments" are equivalent to the non-personal and notice deposits component of the Canadian money supply.

### Interbank Deposits

An **interbank deposit**, as the name implies, is a deposit one bank places in another. The chief advantage of interbank funds has been the opportunity they have provided banks to improve their management of cash reserves as the volume of cheques written on one bank and deposited into another has grown. The need has become particularly great with the increase in the number of foreign banks operating in Canada and the concomitant increase in trading between Canadian and foreign concerns via their respective home banks.

Although banks can deal with each other directly, brokers have emerged to facilitate interbank deposit transactions, particularly between the large institutions.

## EUROCURRENCY INSTRUMENTS

The **Eurocurrency** market is the market for financial instruments denominated in a currency other than that of the home country. Eurocurrencies are sometimes called *Eurodollars* because they originated after World War II with US-dollar deposits in European banks.[13] Today, however, they are not limited to Europe or to denomination in US dollars. Japanese banks hold Euromark deposits, Israeli banks issue CDs in Europounds, Germany offers bonds denominated in Swiss francs, and so on.

Not surprisingly, Canada has participated vigorously in the burgeoning Eurocurrency market. The importance of foreign-currency deposits booked by residents at Canadian banks grew significantly over the last decade. An important reason was, of course, our sizeable trading relationship with the United States.

## CORPORATE AND FINANCE COMPANY PAPER

Large firms with good credit ratings may borrow funds in the money market directly, rather than indirectly through financial institutions such as banks. So may finance companies.

**Corporate paper**, called *commercial paper* in the United States, is generally an unsecured promissory note for a specific amount to mature on a specific day. Given the usually short term, the issuers do not necessarily anticipate being able to have generated the income required to retire the debt when it matures. Rather, most paper is rolled over: that is, it is simply reissued and sold again (to the same investors or to new group).

By contrast, finance company paper is a note secured by instalment-debt contracts that have been sold to individuals or commercial concerns for durable consumer or industrial goods.

---

13 See Chapter 21 for more on Eurocurrency instruments, including the history of their development.

Both corporate and finance company paper are sold in denominations of $50,000.

# THE CAPITAL MARKET

The *capital market* is characterized by instruments that generally mature in more than one year.[14] Table 4.2 describes the principal capital market instruments. You should rely on this list for the essential points of the discussion that follows.

## BONDS

A **bond** is a certificate of long-term debt issued by a public entity or a corporation. Bonds are generally issued at par and return to the investor a *coupon rate* (a rate stated on the bond) one or more times a year. This rate can differ from the effective return because of price fluctuations in the relatively large secondary market for bonds.[15] Federal government bonds are a useful benchmark because they are considered default-risk free. The probability that other bond issuers will default is reported by the various services that provide *bond ratings.*

### Government of Canada Bonds

The federal government issues bonds with an array of maturities and in many denominations. They vary from the $100 Canada Savings Bonds familiar to many individuals to million-dollar bonds purchased by huge investors such as pension funds. Since April 1992 all such bonds have been sold at auctions.[16] The auction usually takes place on a Wednesday but since the *Notice of Call for Tenders* is issued earlier (about a week) the bonds trade on a "when-issued" basis at first. Each bid is for a minimum of $25,000 and a maximum of $3 million. The coupon rate is set to the ¼ of 1% nearest to the average yield of successful bidders.[17] In contrast, bidding on real return bonds is based on the principles of a "Dutch auction," that is, all successful bidders are alloted the highest real yield based on tenders.

---

14 All attempts to classify markets, including the one we are using, have drawbacks. It is not always possible to divide financial instruments neatly into mutually exclusive groups of assets that mature in less than one year and those that mature in one year or longer.

15 Exactly how the return on a bond is measured is the subject of the next chapter.

16 The general public comprises individuals, non-financial firms, near-banks, investment dealers, mutual funds, insurance companies, and provincial and municipal governments.

17 For example, if the average yield is 7.9% then the coupon rate is set at 6.75%.

**TABLE 4.2** THE CAPITAL MARKET

| Instruments | Typical Maturities | Principal Borrowers | Secondary Market |
|---|---|---|---|
| Government of Canada Bonds | Variable, from less than 3 years to 10 years and longer | Federal government | Yes |
| Provincial and municipal bonds | Variable, from 3 years or less to 10 years and longer | Provincial governments and municipalities | Yes |
| Corporate bonds | Variable, from 3 years or less to 10 years and longer | Corporations | Yes |
| Debentures | 2 to 20 years | Private corporations, public utilities | Yes |
| Stocks | Variable, depending on conditions | Corporations | Yes |
| Derivatives | | | |
| Futures | Contracts can mature in months or over 1 year | Chartered banks and money market dealers | Yes |
| Options | Exercise at strike price on or before expiration date | Chartered banks, near-banks, and money market dealers | Yes |
| Swaps | Exchange of interest streams over the lives of the underlying debt issue | Chartered banks, near-banks, and money market dealers | Yes |
| STRIPS | Can be semi-annual to over 10 years | Federal government | Yes |
| Forward rate agreements (FRAs) | Agreement on an interest rate to prevail in the future | Corporations | Yes |

As in Table 4.1, the boxes distinguish the items that are especially important either because they have wide-ranging effects on the entire financial system or because the volume of trade in them is huge.

Government of Canada bonds are held by four groups in society: The Bank of Canada, chartered banks, the general public,[18] and foreigners. Figure 4.5 shows

18 In January 1996, Finance Minister Paul Martin announced that compound interest Canada Savings bonds

**FIGURE 4.5** Holders of Canadian Government Debt

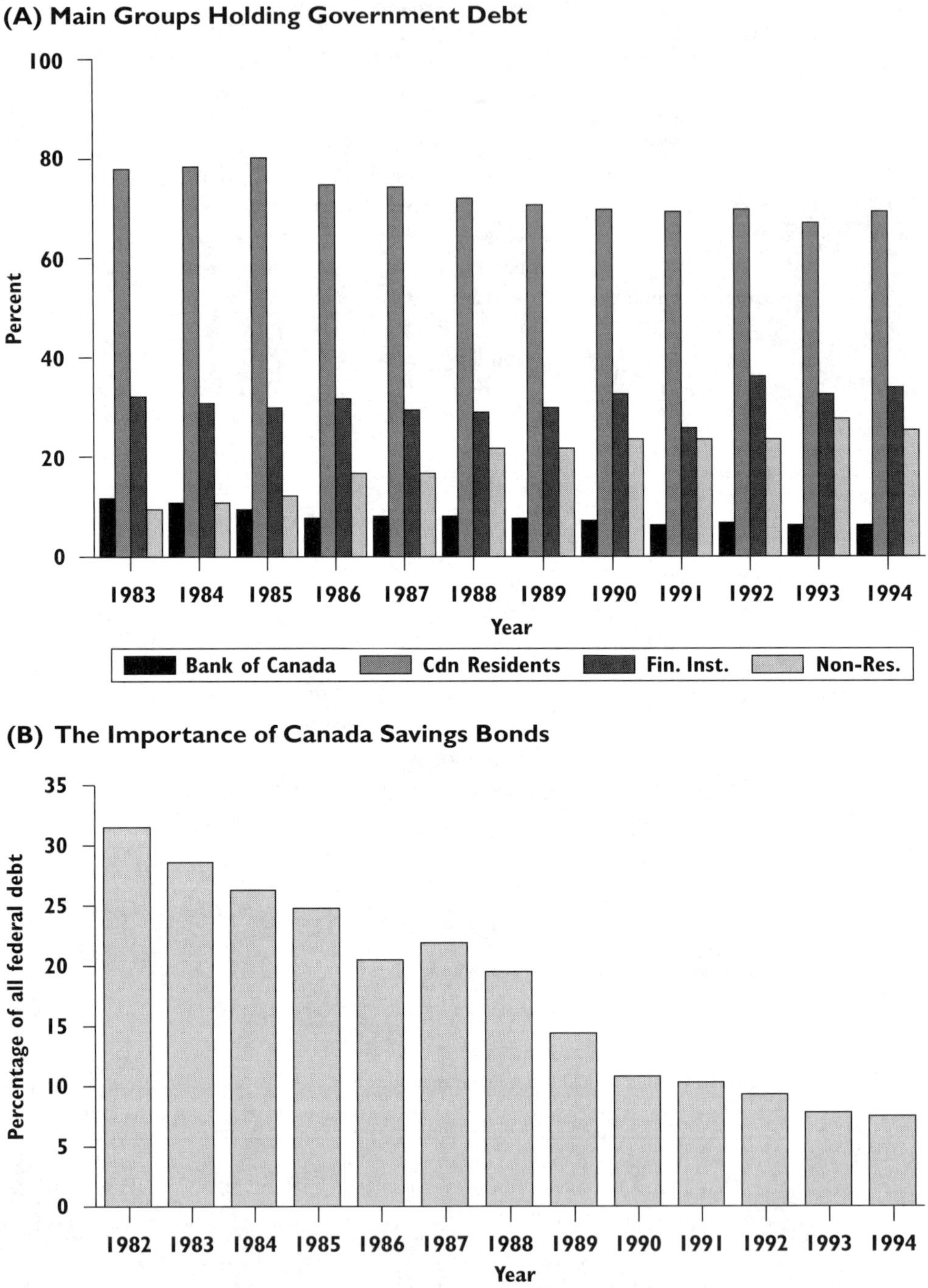


Sources: *Bank of Canada Review*, Tables G4 and G5. Groups excluded in Part (A) are provincial and municipal governments and funds held by the federal government at the Bank of Canada as well as (non-marketable) bonds held by the Canada Pension Plan.

the evolution of the Government of Canada's debt in the 1980s. The general public holds by far the largest share. Canada Savings Bonds have become an increasingly smaller source of federal financing. The proportion of the total held by foreigners rose steadily.

It is also interesting to note the average maturity of the Canadian government's debt. During the 1979–1989 period, it peaked at 7 years and 2 months in 1979 and fell to just under 5 years by the end of 1994.[19] Part of the reason for the change, as we will see in the next chapter, was changes in the *real* cost of the debt. Both the nominal return and inflation are factors here. In 1979, for example, the return on a Treasury bill was 11.57%, while inflation in consumer prices reached 7.90%. The difference, called the *real interest rate*, was 3.67%, which is quite close to the long-run historical value. By 1994, however, the real interest rate had risen to 5.41%, and it has remained relatively high through the 1990s. High real interest rates make short-term debt more attractive to lenders since they want to earn the high returns while possible (they assume interest rates will eventually fall to their average historical value).

The volatility of interest rates has produced so much uncertainty about the real return on long-term bonds that the Government of Canada introduced *real return (indexed) bonds* in fall 1991. Patterned after a similar instrument offered in the United Kingdom since 1981, they promise a specific real return—4.25% for the first issue—by adjustment of the semi-annual coupon rate as well as the principal according to changes in the consumer price index. If the real cost of borrowing is fixed, the government can better predict its borrowing costs and lenders receive a certain real return.

## Other Bonds

The list of bonds issued is rounded out by provincial, municipal, and corporate bonds. Apart from differences in risk and other characteristics, they are similar to Government of Canada bonds. Such bonds are less likely to be auctioned than Government of Canada bonds. Canada has the distinction of having one of the world's largest corporate bond markets.

Finally, debentures are a special kind of bond in that they are backed by the future sales or earning power of a corporation.

Bonds and debentures are generally sold to the public via an **underwriter** (often a syndicate of underwriters), which is an investment dealer that helps governments and corporations to raise capital by buying new securities (bonds

---

could be transferred to RRSP accounts. This will make CSBs more attractive and may well reverse the pattern evidenced in Table 4.5.

19 See *Bank of Canada Review*, Table G6.

or stocks) from the issuer at a discount and reselling them to investors. Until recently, commercial banks in Canada and the United States were prohibited from underwriting corporate debt. This regulation was the result of legislation, dating at least from the Great Depression of 1929–33, which separated the underwriting and commercial lending functions. Recent legislation in both countries has been proposed to do away with this legal separation in the financial system and there are several instances where the regulatory authorities have made exceptions under existing regulation.

## STOCKS

Private corporations also raise funds in the capital market through the issue of **stocks**, which are shares of ownership. Figure 4.6 reveals that corporations seeking to raise funds rely on both types of capital market instruments in roughly equal proportions though there is a tendency overall to prefer stocks, especially since 1991. Nevertheless, if one looks at the balance sheet of Canadian corporations, approximately half of their liabilities are in the form of equity, about 20% in the form of bank loans, and less than 8% in the form of bonds.

## DERIVATIVE PRODUCTS

As we have already emphasized, the increase in the volatility of interest rates and exchange rates that began in the 1970s has made future rates difficult to predict and increased the likelihood that investors will suffer losses. Consequently the value of products that can mitigate the effects of unpredictable changes in returns has been enhanced. Thus, the last few years have seen the development of many **derivative products**, new financial instruments created from existing ones.

### Futures and Forwards

A *futures contract* is a purchase contract stipulating that a particular asset is to be delivered at a predetermined future date. Because investors use financial futures to hedge against capital losses, delivery is generally not taken. There also exist *forward contracts*, particularly in foreign exchange; these agreements are similar to futures, but the investor actually takes delivery of the financial asset in question.

### Options

An *option* is the right, but not the obligation, to buy or sell an asset on or before a particular date. Investors use financial options as a device to protect themselves from higher- or lower-than-expected future prices. A call option gives the investor the opportunity to purchase a financial instrument at a specified price. A put option is an option to sell a financial instrument at a particular price.

**FIGURE 4.6** Net New Issues of Bonds and Stocks by the Corporate Sector

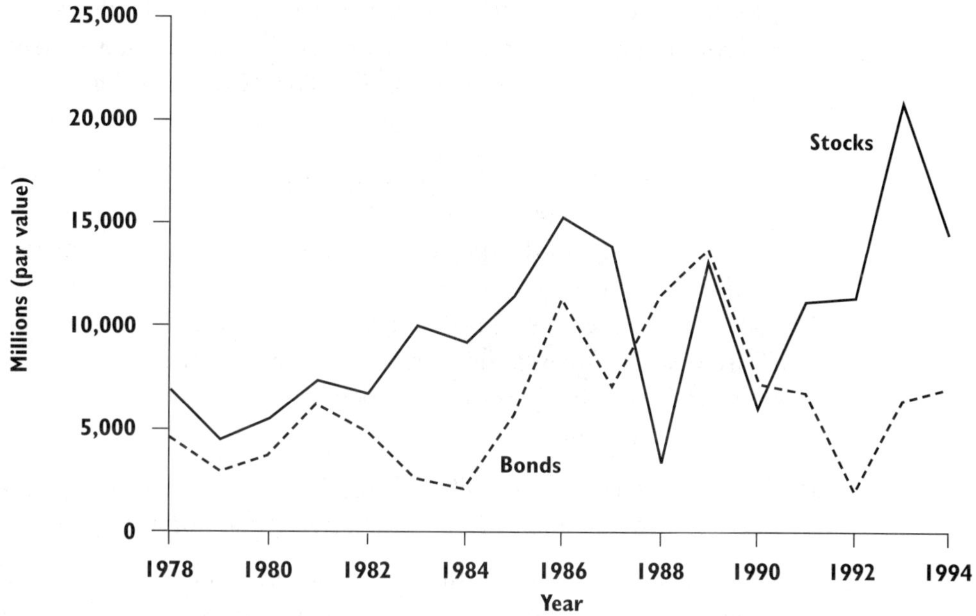


Notice the dramatic drop in new issues of stock in 1988. This phenomenon simply reflects the repercussions from the October 1987 stock market crash.

Source: *Bank of Canada Review* (various issues), Table K9.

# WHEN-ISSUED TREASURY BILLS

A fairly recent innovation, introduced in 1978, in the T-bill market is the possibility to engage in forward trading of T-bills. A **when-issued T-bill** is a contract to buy or sell, at an agreed-to price, a stated dollar amount of T-bills to be sold at the next weekly auction. Trading begins when the Bank of Canada announces the size of the following week's auction and ends just before the results of the auction are announced. The market is useful for the participants because it potentially acts as a gauge for determining future interest rates while the Bank of Canada uses the information generated by this market to assess market sentiments about the course of short-term interest rates.

## Other Derivative Products

More recent derivative products include:

1. Interest rate *swaps*, in which investors exchange interest payments.[20] They do

20 There are also foreign exchange swaps; see Chapter 24.

so because they have different expectations about the future. For example, suppose a financial officer with a corporation that holds long-term debt with a fixed interest rate believes that short-term interest rates are about to fall. His counterpart officer with a firm that holds short-term debt expects the opposite scenario for interest rates. The two firms have an incentive to exchange interest payments but not the debt.

2. *STRIPS* (Separate Trading of Registered Interest and Principal of Securities), which are zero-coupon instruments created by separating the principal from the coupons or interest payments (which are then sold separately). STRIPS bonds are sold at a discount. The return is paid at maturity so that the discounted price of stripped notes rises until then. The major attraction of STRIPS, which involve no periodic interest payments, is that their yield to maturity is certain (it does not depend on the return from interest payments reinvested over time).
3. *Forward rate agreements* (FRAs), in which an intermediary, typically a bank, agrees to provide funds at a specific interest rate for a specified period of time.
4. *Securitization* Some of the financial instruments covered in this chapter, such as bonds, are tradeable while others, for example, bank loans or mortgages, are not. However, by grouping or packaging outstanding bank loans or mortgages, banks have been able to create a secondary market for such instruments. This is called the process of **securitization** which has led to the creation of mortgage-backed securities and asset-backed securities.

## SUMMARY

- There exist a bewildering variety of financial instruments. This chapter defines some of the most important ones.
- A simple classification of financial instruments is into money market instruments, which have a maturity of a year or less, and capital market instruments, which have a maturity that usually exceeds a year.
- Tables 4.1 and 4.2 highlight the principal money market and financial market instruments surveyed in this chapter.

## IMPORTANT TERMS

Bank of Canada advances (p. 70)
bank rate (p. 65)
banker's acceptance (p. 73)
basis point (p. 66)

bonds (p. 78)
certificates of deposit (CDs) (p. 76)
corporate paper (p. 77)
derivative products (p. 82)
Eurocurrency (p. 77)
interbank deposit (p. 77)
Large Value Transfer System (LVTS) (p. 69)
lender of last resort (p. 70)
letter of credit (p. 74)
open market operations (p. 68)
overnight rate band (p. 66)
par value (p. 64)
securitization (p. 84)
special purchase and resale agreements (SPRAs) (p. 71)
stocks (p. 82)
T-bill auction (p. 66)
Treasury bills (T-bills) (p. 64)
underwriter (p. 81)
when-issued T-bills (p. 83)

## EXERCISES

1. One of the reasons the federal government has moved away from financing a large part of its expenditures with Canada Savings Bonds is the havoc the sale plays with monetary aggregates. Which monetary aggregates are affected and why is this a cause for concern at the Bank of Canada?

2. In both Canada and the United States, legislators have had an aversion to allowing banks to underwrite corporate debt. The Canadian banks have complained that this puts them at a disadvantage relative to near-banks, which have not faced the same restriction. What is it that legislators worry about?

3. Suppose the Bank of Canada feels that the prices being bid at its weekly Treasury bill auction are too high and places a reserve bid. Does this mean that the Bank wants higher or lower interest rates?

4. Explain how bank behaviour can make the interest rate on PRAs volatile.

5. Swaps and FRAs worry central banks because they fear loss of monetary control over the short run. Are their fears unfounded?

6. How would you explain the real interest rate? (Don't cheat by looking at Chapter 5!)

7. Will a higher real interest rate tend to shorten the average maturity of government bonds? Why?

8. According to Figure 4.6, corporations showed a distinct preference for issuing stocks rather than bonds in 1983. Can you think why?

9. Swaps were created because investors have opposite expectations about the

future course of interest rates. Is this possible? If so, develop a plausible scenario that would produce such a situation.

10. Why might the when-issued T-bill market provide information about *future* short-term interest rates?

11. The fall in the importance of Canada Savings Bonds (Figure 4.5(B)) might also reflect changing preferences of investors. Why?

12. Figure 4.6 shows two ways in which businesses raise funds. In fact, however, funds in the corporate sector are also raised from a third source. What is it?

13. Would you expect the spread of bids for the weekly T-bill auction to be large or small? Why? What are some of the factors determining the spread in bidding prices?

## REFERENCES


Bank of Canada. *Annual Report* (various issues).

*Bank of Canada Review* (various issues).

"Administrative Arrangements Regarding the Auction of Government of Canada Securities." *Bank of Canada Review* (Summer 1993): 71–76.

"Buy-Back Techniques in the Conduct of Monetary Policy." *Bank of Canada Review* (July 1989): 3–17.

"The Government of Canada Bond Market Since 1980." *Bank of Canada Review* (Autumn 1995): 3–22.

"The Government of Canada Treasury Bill Market and Its Role in Monetary Policy." *Bank of Canada Review* (Spring 1994): 35–53.

"The Interbank Deposit Market." *Bank of Canada Review* (February 1986): 3–12.

"Revisions to the Reserve Regulations: Introducing Weighted Averaging." *Bank of Canada Review* (September 1983): 17–20.

"The When-Issued Market for Government of Canada Treasury Bills: A Technical Note." *Bank of Canada Review* (November 1992): 3–22.

Martin, P. *Inside the Bank of Canada's Weekly Financial Statistics: A Technical Guide*, 2d ed. Vancouver, B.C.: The Fraser Institute, 1989.

Menlendyke, Ann-Marie. *U.S. Monetary Policy and Financial Markets.* New York: Federal Reserve Bank of New York, 1989.

Statistics Canada, CANSIM database.

Stigum, M. *The Repo and Reverse Markets.* Homewood, Ill.: Dow-Jones-Irwin, 1989.

Wilson, J.G. *The Money Market: The International Perspective.* London and New York: Routledge, 1993.

# PART II

# MODELS OF THE FINANCIAL SYSTEM

CHAPTER 5

# Understanding Interest Rates: Definitions and Concepts

Having introduced you to the principal institutions and instruments of the financial system, we are now ready to consider models of that system.

Because we are dealing with complex phenomena that involve a number of interrelated factors—interest rates, wealth, savings, inflation, risk, people's expectations to name but a few—selecting a beginning point is problematic. We're going to start—not quite at random—with interest rates, which are the primary prices of finance.

To see why, consider that financial markets, like all markets, result from the interaction of supply and demand, which sets a price. To put the point another way, assume that everyone's goal is the accumulation of *wealth*, which is defined as net assets minus net liabilities. Now consider that one person's financial debt is another's financial asset. The individual holding the financial asset forgoes some consumption of goods and services today in the hope of benefiting from more consumption in the future. Similarly, the individual holding the debt forgoes some future consumption in order to raise current consumption. The same logic applies to firms if one replaces "consumption" with "profit." In other words, the individual or firm makes a decision about the extent to which the future is *discounted.* The person lending money today discounts the future to a lesser extent than the one who borrows today. The more an individual discounts the future, the more he or she prefers consumption today. Current and future consumption can, in effect, be traded in a market because individuals differ in the degree to which they discount the future. Alternatively, they may have the same discount rate but expect different future income streams. Someone with surplus current income can seek to trade with someone else whose current income is insufficient to maintain a certain level of consumption.

In other words, individuals (and firms) differ in their *time preference*, which is the degree to which they value immediate consumption over deferred consumption. In effect then, debt is a futures contract for money. The debtor promises to pay the lender stipulated amounts—interest at a certain rate—on specific future dates; eventually, the debt instrument *matures* and the principal becomes due.

Words have to be used carefully here. People sometimes call interest rates the price of money. Such a statement is misleading. The price of money is the amount that money can buy—that is, the *purchasing power* of money. Interest is the price of *renting* money.

Defining the interest rate more exactly is complicated by several factors. First, there are various ways of paying a return on a financial asset. For example, some debts are to be repaid over time and others in a lump sum. Moreover, the financial sector has not yet agreed on a set of standards for reporting the return on a financial asset.

Because of these complexities, we discuss interest rates in two parts. In this chapter, we consider only definitions and the basic concepts of various interest rate measures. In the next, we examine how financial markets determine interest rate levels and changes.

Then, in later chapters in this part of the text, we turn to discussions of exchange rates, the decision makers in financial markets (households, firms, and the financial sector itself) and their reason for acting as they do, the demand for money, stock prices, and risk and uncertainty. By the end of this part, we consider the *structure of interest rates*—that is, how they differ by type of risk, by term to maturity, and across countries.

## THE PRESENT VALUE CONCEPT

Although the activities of borrowing and lending involve a futures contract the price of that contract must be set today (rather, at the time the loan is made). To understand how such a price is set requires a clear knowledge of the present value concept.

Suppose an individual borrows $X$ dollars at time $t$, denoted $X_t$, and promises to pay the lender \$100 one year from today. The difference between the amount to be repaid and the amount borrowed is the price of renting money; expressed as a percentage of the debt it is the **interest rate**. Letting $R_t$ denote the interest rate at time $t$ (today), we write

$$R_t = (\text{dollars to be paid back one year from today} - \text{dollars received today}) \div \text{dollars received today} \qquad (5.1)$$

or, in terms of our example,

$$R_t = (100 - X_t)/X_t \qquad (5.2)$$

We can also solve equation (5.2) in terms of the amount of the debt, $X_t$, to obtain

$$X_t = 100/(1 + R_t) \tag{5.3}$$

The last expression simply states the value today of $100 to be delivered one year from today. In other words, we are talking about the **present value** of an amount to be received at a particular time in the future.

Since $R_t$ is positive (renting money has a positive cost), the denominator in equation (5.3) must be greater than 1, so the right-hand side of the expression must be less than 100.

Such a result makes sense since a market for debt exists because the debtor is able to consume today but forgoes some consumption tomorrow. Hence, one dollar paid out a year from today is worth less than one dollar today.

Alternatively, one can rewrite equation (5.3) by multiplying both sides by (1 + $R_t$) to obtain

$$(1 + R_t)\, X_t = X_t + X_t R_t = 100 \tag{5.4}$$

$X_t$ is also called the *principal*, or the size, of the debt, and $X_t R_t$ is the *interest cost*.

Note, from either equation (5.4) or (5.3), that $R_t$ and $X_t$ are inversely related.

Consider a numerical example. Suppose the annual interest rate is 0.10 or 10%. If $100 is to be delivered one year from today, what is the size of the debt today? From equation (5.3),

$$X_t = 100/(1 + 0.10) = 90.91 \text{ or } \$90.91$$

Alternatively, one can ask, what is the annual rate of interest on a debt that is valued today at $90.91 and at $100 one year from today. To obtain the answer substitute today's value in equation (5.2):

$$\begin{aligned} R_t &= (100 - 90.91)/90.91 \\ &= 9.09/90.91 = 0.10 \text{ or } 10\% \end{aligned}$$

Thus, the present value of $100 at a 10% annual interest rate is $90.91. (Note that in this example $90.91 is the principal and $9.09 is the interest cost of the debt.)

One can easily generalize this one-year example to a case in which an amount borrowed today is to be delivered several years into the future. Since $R_t$ is the annual interest rate—by convention, interest is stated on an *annual* basis—a multiyear debt involves a compounding of interest. Thus, continuing with the previous example, $90.91 will be worth $110 after two years, or equivalently,

$$\begin{aligned} &\$90.91(1 + 0.10)(1 + 0.10) \\ &= \$90.91(1.1)(1.1) \\ &= \$90.91(1.1)^2 \end{aligned}$$

The *term* (duration) of the loan affects the number of times one multiplies the amount of the principal. To continue the example, the total amount due on maturity after $n$ years will be

$$100(1 + 0.10)^n$$

The present value of $100 received $n$ years in the future is, from equation (5.3),

$$X_t = \$100/(1 + 0.10)^n \tag{5.5}$$

The higher the value of $n$, the smaller the value of $X_t$.

To illustrate the effects these relationships create, Figure 5.1 shows the 1997 present value of $100 due between 1998 and 2008 for three interest rate levels. Notice that, for any interest rate, $100 due in 2008 is worth considerably less in 1997 than in, say, 2004.

Higher interest rates have the effect of reducing the present value of $100 regardless of when it is due.

Table 5.1(A) shows that at interest rates of less than 10%, the present value of $100 one year from today is greater than $90.91, and at interest rates of more than 10%, the present value falls to less than $90.91. Table 5.1(B) shows how present value is influenced by the term of a loan for a given interest rate. The longer the term to maturity, the larger the interest cost of the debt.

## YIELD TO MATURITY

In the simple 1-year loan we have been considering, the interest rate is the same as the **yield to maturity**, which is the actual rate of return from a stream of payments received when a debt is incurred today. Suppose the amount borrowed today is to be repaid by a single payment at some specified time in the future. By returning to Table 5.1(B), we see that, if the interest rate is 10% and the principal borrowed is $100, the interest cost for a debt repaid in one year's time is

$$\$110 - \$100 = \$10,$$

which represents a total yield of

$$\$10/100 = 0.10 \text{ or } 10\%$$

**FIGURE 5.1** 1993 Present Value of $100 Due in the Future

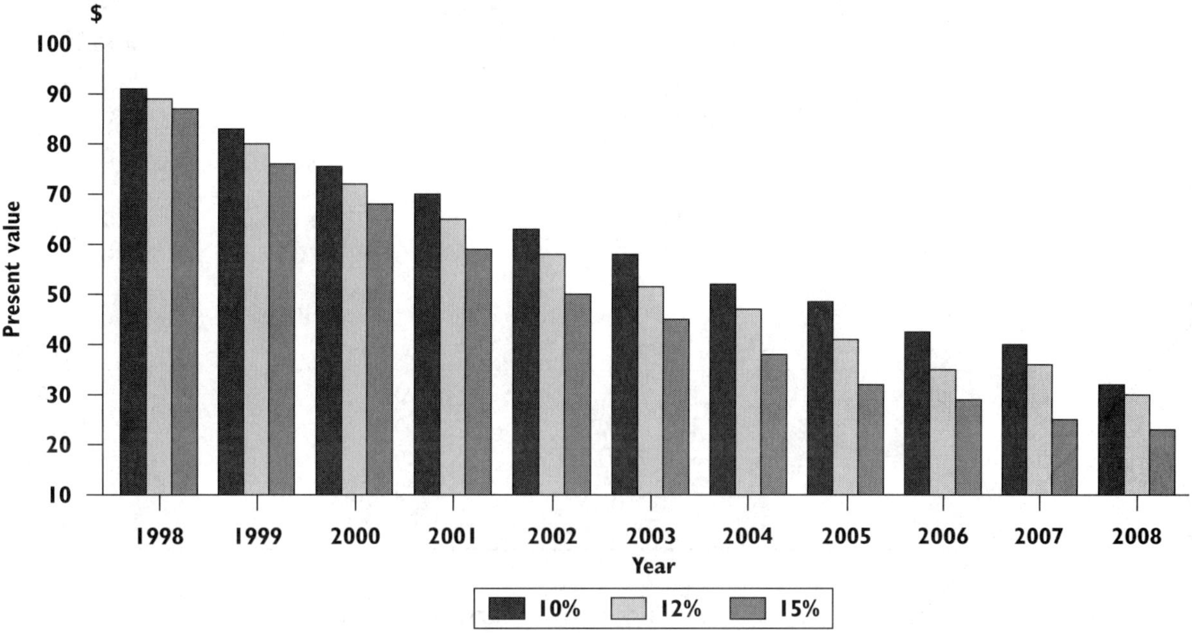


The present values were calculated by applying equation (5.5) for $n$ = 1 through $n$ = 11 and for interest rates of 10%, 12%, and 15%. Table 5.1 gives the actual dollar amounts. For example, $100 to be delivered in the year 2008 represents $35.05 in present value terms. Or $35.05 invested at 10% for 11 years (1997–2008) yields $100.

| | $R_t$ | | |
|---|---|---|---|
| | 10% | 12% | 15% |
| 1997 | 100.00 | 100.00 | 100.00 |
| 1998 | 90.91 | 89.29 | 86.96 |
| 1999 | 82.64 | 79.72 | 75.61 |
| 2000 | 75.13 | 71.18 | 65.75 |
| 2001 | 68.30 | 63.55 | 57.18 |
| 2002 | 62.09 | 56.74 | 49.72 |
| 2003 | 56.45 | 50.66 | 43.23 |
| 2004 | 51.32 | 45.23 | 37.59 |
| 2005 | 46.65 | 40.39 | 32.69 |
| 2006 | 42.41 | 36.06 | 28.43 |
| 2007 | 38.55 | 32.20 | 24.72 |
| 2008 | 35.05 | 28.75 | 21.49 |

**TABLE 5.1** PRESENT VALUES AT VARIOUS INTEREST RATES AND TERMS

**(A)** **One-Year Term**

| Present Value | Interest Rate (%) |
|---|---|
| $100.00 | 0 |
| $95.24 | 5 |
| $90.91 | 10 |
| 86.96 | 15 |
| $83.33 | 20 |
| $80.00 | 25 |

**(B)** **Annual Interest Rate of 10%**

| Term (years) | Present Value | $(1 + R_t)^n$ |
|---|---|---|
| 1 | $100.00 | 1.1000 |
| 2 | $100.00 | 1.2100 |
| 3 | $100.00 | 1.3310 |
| 4 | $100.00 | 1.4641 |
| 5 | $100.00 | 1.6105 |

For a loan repaid at the end of five years, the interest cost is

$$\$161.05 - \$100 = \$61.05,$$

which represents a total return of

$$\$61/\$100 = 0.6105 \text{ or } 61.05\%$$

That amount represents an *average annual rate* or *yield* of

$$61.05\%/5 \text{ years} = 12.21\%$$

even though the loan was taken out at an interest rate of 10%. The yield is 12.21% because of the effect of compounding.

Of course, not all financial instruments mature many years into the future. Indeed, some mature in less than one year. An annual percentage rate is often stated for such an instrument, but the annual yield will be somewhat higher. The reason is again compounding. For example, if a financial instrument is offered for a term of three months (one-quarter of a year) at 12% per year, the interest rate is equivalent to

$$\frac{12\%}{4} = 3\%$$

for three months. At the end of one year, however, each dollar invested at 3% each quarter will be worth

$$\$1 \times (1.03)^4 = 1.126$$

which translates into an annual yield of

$$12.6\%$$

These calculations explain the sometimes confusing bank advertisements that list two annual interest rates for the same financial instrument.

It is useful to have a simple formula for calculating the yield to maturity on a financial instrument. The yield to maturity is the value for $R_t$ obtained from

$$X_t = X_0/(1 + R_t/k)^{kn} \tag{5.6}$$

where $X_0$ is the principal of the loan and $k$ is the number of times a year interest is compounded. In the typical case considered in this text, $k$ is 1, so equation (5.6) becomes

$$X_t = X_0/(1 + R_t)^n$$

If the term of the loan is also one year, $n = 1$ and the expression simply becomes equation (5.3). At the other extreme, if \$100 is compounded daily at 10% for a 2-year period, then

$$X_t = \$100(1 + 0.10/365)^{365\,(2)} = \$122.14$$

which implies an average annual yield of 11.07%.

In general, the yield on a debt instrument need not be the same as the interest rate stipulated in the contract between the lender and the borrower. (It is the yield to maturity that is typically reported in the financial press.)

## MORE COMPLEX REPAYMENT SCHEMES

In the examples we have considered so far, we implicitly assumed that the lender would receive both principal and interest when the debt matured. Most debt contracts, however, specify other repayment schedules. These different schemes can, in a subtle manner, influence how we evaluate the yields on different financial instruments. Below, we consider three common types of debt repayment schemes.

### Fixed-Payment Loans

Some debt instruments involve a series of equal, fixed payments throughout the term of the debt so that the principal and the interest are both repaid by the end of the contract, a process called *amortization.* If you have had a course in finance or accounting, you have probably learned to call such a fixed-payment loan an *annuity*. Some pensions, also called *annuities*, are debts of this type (the individual loans an insurance company or other backer an amount that is repaid in a stream of constant payments for a specified number of years). Another example is the conventional home mortgage.

Suppose that a mortgage of $100,000 is to be repaid over 20 years at an interest rate of 12%. What are the annual payments? Finding the answer involves solving an equation much like equation (5.6). The flow of payments throughout the term of the loan is written as

$$\$\text{Debt} = \frac{\$FP}{(1 + R)} + \frac{\$FP}{(1 + R)^2} + \cdots + \frac{\$FP}{(1 + R)^n} \tag{5.7}$$

where $Debt is the size of the mortgage and *FP* is the fixed payment throughout the term. In our example, where $Debt = $100,000 and $R = 0.12$ or 12%.

$$\$100{,}000 = \frac{\$FP}{1.12} + \frac{\$FP}{(1.12)^2} + \cdots + \frac{\$FP}{(1.12)^{20}}$$

Solving for *FP* yields $13,387.96.

But *FP* is the annual amount and mortgage payments are typically made monthly. To compute the monthly payment, we need to recognize that 240 payments (12 payments per year for 20 years) will be made over the term of the loan and that a 12% annual interest rate is equivalent to a 1% monthly interest rate.[1] When we use these figures in equation (5.7), the monthly payment is $1,102.

In practice, the computation of an equation such as (5.7) often proceeds by assuming a value (or range of values) for the size of the debt, the prevailing interest rate, and the desired term for the loan to arrive at a value (or range of values) for *FP*. The reason is that the size of the debt will be a function of the individual's current and anticipated future income or the firm's expected profit stream.

Tables showing the monthly or annual payment necessary to amortize a loan are widely available. So are computer programs for the calculation. They are based on an expression such as equation (5.7).[2]

---

1 In Canada matters are additionally complicated because the number of years over which a mortgage is amortized almost always exceeds the number of years over which the interest rate is fixed. This fact does not affect the principles underlying equation (5.7), however, so we will not pursue the point further.

2 The present value of an annuity of *n* periods may be stated even more compactly as $X_t = (FP/R)(1 - [1/(1 + R^n)]$.

### ECONOMICS FOCUS 5.1 When Is a Million a Million?

Lottery winnings in many US states, unlike those in most Canadian provinces, are paid in instalments rather than a lump sum.

What is the difference? The instalment payments are an *annuity*—payment of equal instalments over a stipulated period of time—say $50,000 per year for 20 years ($1,000,000/20 instalments). Suppose the current interest rate is 12%. The present value of those amounts is considerably less than $1 million received today.

To put the point a little differently, consider the future value of $1 million received today and fully invested at 12% for 20 years. That amount is $9,646,300. By contrast, if $20,000 received each year over 20 years is completely reinvested at 12%, it will yield $1 million after 20 years.

## Coupon Bonds

A *coupon bond* is a debt instrument in which fixed interest payments are made throughout the life of the contract but the principal is repaid in a lump sum at the end of the term. The interest payment is called the *coupon payment* and the interest rate the **coupon rate**. Coupon interest provides a regular stream of income to lenders, and it is common for bonds to be sold in this fashion.[3]

The formula for the price or present value of such a bond is

$$PV^* = \frac{\$C}{(1+R)} + \frac{\$C}{(1+R)^2} + \cdots + \frac{\$C}{(1+R)^n} + \frac{\$FV}{(1+R)^n} \tag{5.8}$$

where

$C$ = annual coupon payment
$F$ = face value or par value
$n$ = years to maturity
$PV^*$ = present value or price of the bond.

Take the example of a $1,000 bond that promises to pay interest of $100 per year for five years, so that the coupon rate is 10% ($100/$1,000). The present value is the sum of the following payments stream:

3 Because the price of a financial asset is sometimes referred to as its capital value, the present value of an income stream is called the *capitalization* of the income stream.

$$PV^{*} = \frac{\$100}{(1 + 0.10)} + \frac{\$100}{(1 + 0.10)^2} + \frac{\$100}{(1 + 0.10)^3} + \frac{\$100}{(1 + 0.10)^4} + \frac{\$100}{(1 + 0.10)^5} + \frac{\$1{,}000}{(1 + 0.10)^5}$$
$$= \$1{,}000$$

Notice in our example that the present value of the bond is the same as its face value. Therefore, the coupon rate and the yield are identical. When bonds are traded in the marketplace, price and face value often diverge, however. If a particular bond trades at less than its face value, it is trading at a *discount.* One that trades at more than its face value is being traded at a *premium.*

What results in a bond's trading at a premium or a discount? Look carefully at equation (5.8). Since $C$ and $FV$ are given or fixed, a rise in $R$ will reduce $PV^{*}$ and a fall in $R$ will raise $PV^{*}$. This relationship is simply the inverse of the one between the price of a debt and its yield noted earlier. Indeed, one can obtain an approximate expression for the prevailing or **current yield**. $R_t^C$, on a coupon bond by evaluating

$$R_t^C = \frac{\$C}{PV_t^{*}} \tag{5.9}$$

where $\$C$ is the amount of the fixed coupon and $PV_t^{*}$ is the price of the bond at time $t$. The inverse relationship between bond price and yield is immediately clear.[4]

## Discounted Bonds or Bills

A **discounted bond** is a debt instrument that is issued at a discount and pays the face value at maturity. In other words, the face value represents the total of principal and interest. An example is the Government of Canada's Treasury bills.

To find the yield on such a debt instrument, we can employ the logic used previously: find the interest rate on an amount to be received one year from today with a known present value. In algebraic terms,

---

4 Another type of coupon bond, less well-known, is the perpetuity or consol bond. As its name implies, such a bond has a fixed coupon, $C, that is paid indefinitely into the future; the principal is never redeemed. Thus, in terms of equation (5.8), since $n$ tends to infinity, $PV^{*} = \frac{\$C}{(1 + R)} + \frac{\$C}{(1 + R)^2} \cdot \ldots$ With the help of some high school mathematics, it can be shown that the present value of a consol is $PV^{*} = \frac{\$C}{R}$. Thus, as interest rates rise, the price or present value of the perpetuity falls.

$$R = \frac{\$FV - \$PD}{\$PD} \tag{5.10}$$

where $PD$ is the discounted price.

Consider a discounted bond sold at a price of $975 today with a face value of $1,000 to be paid at maturity.

$$\$975 = \frac{1{,}000}{(1 + R)}$$

Solving for $R$ gives

$$R = \frac{1{,}000 - 975}{975} = 0.0256 \text{ or } 2.56\%$$

If the debt instrument in question is a Treasury bill, however, we should keep going. T-bills are typically issued for three months (approximately 90 days), but yields are conventionally quoted on an annual basis. We can convert the 90-day yield into an annual yield using the following expression:

$$R = \frac{\$FV - \$PD}{\$PD} \times \frac{360}{90} \tag{5.11}$$

where the year is taken to consist of 360 days.[5]

To continue the numerical example, the annual yield on a Treasury bill purchased for $975, with a face value of $1,000, 90 days from today, is

$$0.0256 \times \frac{360}{90} = 0.1026 \text{ or } 10.26\%$$

## STRIPS

In Chapter 4 we described the *STRIPS* instrument, a zero-coupon bond created by removing the coupons and trading them separately. The return to the investor from a STRIPS bond comes from increases in price until maturity when the face value is paid.

The rate of return on a STRIPS can be evaluated by using

5 Actual calculations use 365 in the numerator and 91 in the denominator. In the US, for example, 360 is used in the numerator.

$$X(1 + R)^n = FV \tag{5.12}$$

where $X$ is the amount invested today and all other terms have already been defined. For example, if a \$5,000 STRIPS bought today will return \$100,000 in 20 years, equation (5.12) becomes

$$\$5{,}000\ (1 + R)^{20} = \$100{,}000$$

or

$$(1 + R)^{20} = \frac{100{,}000}{5{,}000} = 20$$

Therefore,[6]

$$(1 + R) = (20)^{1/20}$$
$$(1 + R) = 1.16$$

so that

$$R = 0.16 \text{ or } 16\%$$

## THE CURRENT YIELD

Clearly, the return or yield and the coupon rate or interest rate on a particular debt instrument can differ considerably. Since the price of most forms of debt fluctuates over time while the yield to maturity can be evaluated with certainty, an individual may not wish to hold a debt until maturity, particularly when there exists a market in which it can be traded and when individuals gamble about the future course of interest rates. Therefore, an expression such as equation (5.9) is imprecise because it fails to consider **capital gains** or **losses**—that is, changes in the market value of debt instruments (or any assets) between the time they are purchased and the time they are sold. Yet such changes can certainly affect an investor's return on an asset. Indeed, the **holding period yield**—the return for the period of ownership—may be more relevant than the yield to maturity either because a financial instrument is not held until maturity or because it was not purchased at par or at the time of issue.

To illustrate, consider the return on a bond held for one year. The total return consists of (1) the current yield on the bond, found from equation (5.9), and

6 To find $(1 + R)$ from $(1 + R)^{20}$ we use the fact that $(1 + R)^{n/n} = (1 + R)$. Therefore, $(1 + R)^{20/20}$ implies that, for the right-hand side, we must evaluate $(20)^{1/20}$.

(2) the result of any change in the price of the bond—that is, a further gain or loss in return depending upon whether the price of the bond has risen or fallen. We can write

$$i = \frac{C}{PV_t} + \frac{\Delta PV_t}{PV_t} \tag{5.12}$$

where

$i$ = return from holding a bond from period $t$ to period $t + 1$

$\Delta PV_t$ = change in the price of a bond between period $t$ and $t + 1$ = $PV_{t+1} - PV_t$

The first part of the right-hand side of the equation is the current yield $R_t^C$ while the second part is the **capital gain/loss return rate**, which is more compactly denoted as $G$. Hence, equation (5.12) can be rewritten as

$$i = R_t^C + G \tag{5.13}$$

Notice that the return on a bond is a function of the current price (that is, today's price) relative to its future price. Clearly, no investor knows with certainty what that price will be. Therefore, the decision to hold the bond until maturity or to sell it is partly a function of some expectation of future bond prices or, what amounts to the same thing, partly a function of an expectation of future interest rates. We consider the important role of expectations later.

For the moment, let us consider the influence of interest rate changes on bond prices and their return. Suppose that today's interest rate is 10% and an investor purchases at face value a $1,000 bond that matures 20 years from today. The yield to maturity is 10%. Now suppose the interest rate rises to 15% sometime after the first year and remains at that level until the bond matures.[7] What is the effect of the interest rate change on the present value or price of the bond? We can use equation (5.8) to find out. The answer depends on when the change occurs. If the bond has 19 years left to maturity, its price is found by solving

$$PB_t = \frac{\$100}{(1.10)} + \frac{\$100}{(1.15)^2} + \cdots + \frac{\$100}{(1.15)^{18}} + \frac{\$100}{(1.15)^{19}} + \frac{\$100}{(1.15)^{20}} + \frac{\$1,000}{(1.15)^{20}}$$

$$= \$690.99$$

If, however, the bond has only one year left to maturity, its price becomes

7 The assumption of no further change in the interest rate is unrealistic but simplifying.

## FINANCIAL FOCUS 5.1 Reading the Financial News

Information about the bond market is published daily in tabular form in publications such as *The Globe and Mail* and *The Financial Post*. They classify the issuers in four types:

Government of Canada

Provincial governments

Municipal governments

Corporations and public utilities

A listing looks like this:

| (1) | (2) | (3) | (4) | (5) | (6) |
|---|---|---|---|---|---|
| Canada | 10.25 | 15 Mar 14 | 92.250 | 11.183 | −0.375 |

The first column identifies the issuer of the bond, the Government of Canada in this example. The second column gives the coupon rate in percent, 10.25% here, while the third column informs the reader about when the bond matures which, in the present case, is March 15, 2014. Columns 4 and 5 give the current price (*PB* in the text's notation) and the current yield ($R^c_t$). Finally, column 6 shows the change in yield from the previous trading day.

$$PB_t = \frac{\$100}{(1.10)} + \frac{\$100}{(1.10)^2} + \cdots + \frac{\$100}{(1.10)^{20}} + \frac{\$1{,}000}{(1.15)^{20}}$$
$$= \$912.47$$

Table 5.2 presents the results of such calculations for a range of years to maturity. Notice that the longer the time to maturity, the larger the effect on the price of the bond (column 5) and thus on its return (column 7). An interest rate change with 19 years left to maturity produces a price fall of roughly 30% but a change with only 1 year to maturity results in a price fall of less than 10%.

In general, bond prices are relatively more volatile at longer terms to maturity than at shorter terms. (**Volatility** refers to some measure of the size of changes—here in the return and price of bonds.)

## THE DISTINCTION BETWEEN NOMINAL AND REAL INTEREST RATES

So far we have considered interest rates and yields without any consideration of the effects of inflation or of taxes. Although such an approach is simplifying and is thus the one used throughout this book unless otherwise stated, it is not realistic. Inflation and taxes are realities that everyone must deal with. Moreover, people's expectations about the speed and magnitude at which and the direction in which they might move have a considerable effect on interest rates.

**TABLE 5.2** INTEREST RATES, BOND PRICES, AND RETURNS

| (1) Maturity | (2) Initial to Maturity | (3) Actual to Maturity | (4) Initial (*FV*) | (5) Current ($PV_t^*$) | (6) Capital (= \$1,000 − $PV_t^*$) | (7) % Return ([=(2) − (6)/1,000] × 100) |
|---|---|---|---|---|---|---|
| 20 | 10% | 10% | \$1,000 | \$1,000.00 | \$ 0.00 | 10.00 |
| 19 | 10% | 15% | \$1,000 | 690.99 | 309.01 | −20.90 |
| 15 | 10% | 15% | \$1,000 | 730.90 | 269.10 | −16.91 |
| 10 | 10% | 15% | \$1,000 | 799.62 | 200.38 | −10.04 |
| 5 | 10% | 15% | \$1,000 | 862.91 | 137.09 | −3.71 |
| 1 | 10% | 15% | \$1,000 | 912.47 | 87.53 | −1.25 |

For this 20-year bond, $FV$ = \$1,000, $C$ = \$100, and $R$ is initially 10% but changes to 15% when anything from 19 years to 1 year remain to maturity.

Note: An interest rate change of 5 percentage points in a year may seem extreme. As we will see, however, sharp and rapid changes have not been uncommon, especially during the last few years.

## THE ROLE OF INFLATION EXPECTATIONS

Let us consider first how inflation—and expectations of inflation—influences the behaviour of borrowers and lenders. When the consumers or firm managers we encountered at the beginning of this chapter postpone consumption today in order to consume more tomorrow, it is with an implicit expectation that their purchasing power will increase at some time in the future. Otherwise, there is clearly no incentive to forgo current consumption.

"Consumption" here refers to a real magnitude—to the purchasing power of current income relative to future income. Unfortunately, the price level has long tended to rise year after year in a seemingly unrelenting manner. Since price rises represent a measure of purchasing power loss over time, lenders want to protect themselves from such losses when agreeing to a debt contract. How do they do so? They cannot do so perfectly—after all, a debt is a futures contract and the future cannot be known with certainty—but they can form an *expectation* about the rate of *inflation* and adjust the price of debt accordingly.

Therefore, the **nominal interest rate** stipulated in a debt contract—that is, the amount to be paid in *current* dollars—is in reality the sum of two components:

1. Compensation to the lender for postponing current consumption (equivalently, the loss of future consumption for more current consumption on the part of the borrower). This portion is the **real interest rate.**

2. Compensation for anticipated or expected loss of purchasing power.

## The Fisher Equation

The preceding argument can be translated into what is known as the **Fisher equation**, named after Irving Fisher, one of the great economists of the twentieth century. It states that the nominal interest rate, $R$, is the sum of the real interest rate, $\rho$, plus an expected inflation component, $\pi^e$, or

$$R = \rho + \pi^e \tag{5.14}$$

We can see from equation (5.14) that the real interest rate is simply the nominal interest rate less expected inflation,[8] or

$$\rho = R - \pi^e \tag{5.15}$$

Unfortunately, there is no universally agreed upon measure for $\pi^e$.

One can, of course, compute equation (5.15) by replacing expected inflation with a measure of actual inflation, $\pi$. Real interest calculations that use $\pi$ instead of $\pi^e$ yield the ex post real interest rate (from *ex post facto* or "after the fact") while computations of $\rho$ that use some proxy for $\pi^e$ result in the ex ante real interest rate ("before the fact").[9]

## Some Historical Data

Figure 5.2 plots an ex post real interest rate and an ex ante real interest rate measure for Canada over a 35-year span. By the preceding arguments, one might expect real interest rates always to be positive. During the 1970s, however, even ex ante real interest rates were occasionally negative, which implies a great incentive to borrow since, in real terms, the debt would be repaid in cheaper dollars.

Note also from Figure 5.2 that the ex ante and ex post real interest rates diverged from each other somewhat during the 1970s. Ex ante real interest rates are what matter in borrowing and lending decisions, but borrowers would have been much better off had they known that the ex post rates would be much lower than they anticipated. Unfortunately, judgements such as these depend upon how the expected inflation component in equation (5.14) is generated. If the model used

---

8 The point can be put more precisely. If an individual sacrifices \$1 of consumption today in order to consume, say, 3% more next year and no inflation is anticipated, that individual receives $(1 + \rho) = \$1.03$ one year from today. If, instead, inflation is expected to average 5% over the year, the nominal interest rate becomes $(1 + \rho)(1 + \pi^e) = (1.03)(1.05) = 1.0815$ so the lender can preserve the same purchasing power on the \$1 loan and the \$0.03 interest earned. Thus, $(1 + R) = (1 + \rho)(1 + \pi^e)$ or $R = \rho + \pi^e + \rho\pi^e$ which differs slightly from equation (5.14). For small values of $\rho$ and $\pi^e$, however, the omission of the last term is negligible and simplifies calculations.

9 Modern economics assumes that individuals forecast inflation "rationally," which means conditional on a wide variety of macroeconomic information likely to affect inflation in the future. But economists generally treat the information set as consisting of only a few variables. Individuals' formation of expectations of inflation is discussed in Chapter 26.

**FIGURE 5.2** Ex Ante and Ex Post Real Interest Rates

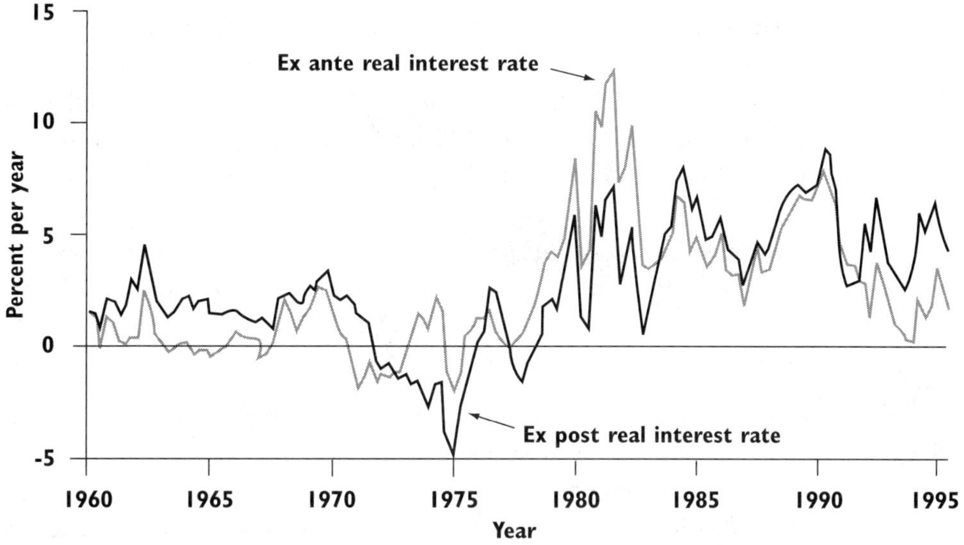


The divergence of ex ante and ex post real interest rates gives some idea of how accurately borrowers and lenders forecast inflation. Both interest rate measures here are based on the yield of 3-month Government of Canada Treasury bills.

Source: Pierre L. Siklos, "The Deficit-Interest Rate Link: Empirical Evidence for Canada," *Applied Economics* 20 (December 1988): 1563–78. The article explains how the ex ante real interest rate was computed. A simplified variant of the procedure in that study was used to generate the ex ante real interest rate here.

to derive expected inflation is correct, investors clearly expected far less inflation than was actually the case during much of the 1970s. One reason could have been that no one knew, until it was too late, about the inflationary consequences of the oil price shocks of the 1970s. (Alternatively, the model used to derive ex ante real interest rates may have omitted some important piece of economic information.)

By the early 1980s, real interest rates reversed sharply and became high relative to the historical average and remained so into the 1990s. The long-run average for ex post real interest rates is approximately 2.5%.

The recent experience with both positive and negative ex post real interest rates is nothing new. Real interest rates were quite volatile during the 1914–45 period because of a series of unusual events: the two world wars and the Great Depression. Otherwise, ex post real interest rates have been, on average, quite similar through history. They have, however, fluctuated more since the end of World War II than they did before the end of World War I. Some economists believe that this effect is a consequence of abandoning the gold standard and thereby producing more volatile and higher inflation

The link between inflation and interest rates is not confined to Canada. Figure 5.3 plots average interest rate levels and inflation rates for 11 industrialized countries from the late 1980s through the mid 1990s. According to the Fisher equation, the countries experiencing relatively higher inflation rates should also have higher nominal interest rates, and the graph shows clearly that this was the case for the countries in the sample.

It was evidence of this kind that led the Canadian federal government to argue in its 1992 budget that the road to lower interest rates is through lower inflation.[10]

### Empirical Evidence

The Fisher equation is a convenient device for describing the way expected inflation drives a wedge between nominal and real interest rates. It must be emphasized that other factors, such as the overall productivity of the economy, can also influence real interest rates in the long run. Discussion of these considerations would however, take us far afield, and so in what follows, we will retain the Fisher equation as the operational device to discuss real and nominal interest rate calculations. Nevertheless, it may be useful to point out that many empirical studies have found a negative relationship between ex post real interest rates and inflation.[11] Unfortunately, the exact cause of this relationship is unclear; the view that agents are able to detect permanent shifts in future inflation receives little empirical support.

## TAXES

The real interest rate calculations implicit in equation (5.14) are approximate because interest income in Canada is subject to income tax. The nominal interest rate after taxes is

$$R^* = R(1 - \tau) \tag{5.16}$$

where $\tau$ = income tax rate.

---

10 Note that the suggestion is that inflation must fall *before* lower interest rates prevail. This line of causality is also explicit from the way in which the Fisher equation is specified. Nevertheless, many analysts believe that causality runs from interest rates to inflation. (We discuss the question of causality in Chapter 26.)

11 M.D. Evans and K.K. Lewis, "Do Expected Shifts in Inflation Policy Affect Estimates of the Long-Run Fisher Relation?" *Journal of Finance* (March 1995): 225–53.

**FIGURE 5.3** Inflation and Nominal Interest Rates across Countries: 1988–95

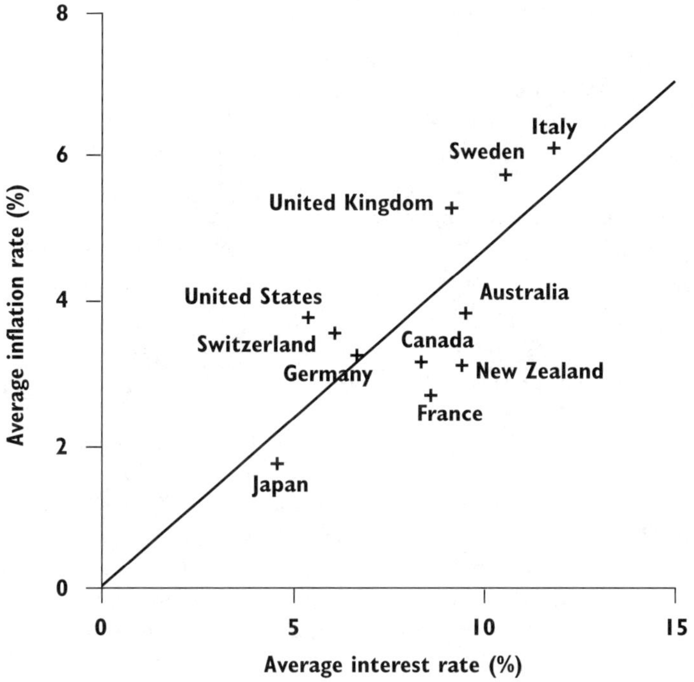


The graph plots inflation–interest rate combinations for major industrialized countries. A best fit straight line fits the scatter points well, suggesting that the Fisher equation held true: higher inflation rates accompanied higher nominal interest rates.

Source: International Monetary Fund. *International Financial Statistics Yearbook*. (Washington, D.C., various years). Annual data are from 1988 to 1995. The interest rate used is the Treasury bill rate, except for France and Japan, for which money market rates were used. Inflation is defined as the percentage change in consumer prices over the previous year. A simple average was used to arrive at the figures plotted.

The ex ante real interest rate after taxes becomes

$$R(1 - \tau) - \pi^e \tag{5.17}$$

For example, if the nominal interest rate is 14% and inflation is expected to be 7%, the ex ante real interest rate, according to equation (5.15), is

$$14\% - 7\% = 7\%$$

Suppose the income tax rate is 30%. The ex ante real after-tax interest rate is then

$$0.14(1 - 0.3) - 0.07 = 0.098 - 0.07 = 0.028 \text{ or } 2.8\%$$

## FINANCIAL FOCUS 5.2 Real Return Bonds

Most bonds have coupon payments that are fixed, so the purchasing power of their value is subject to erosion by inflation. As mentioned in Chapter 4, however, in 1991 the Canadian government introduced *indexed* or **real return bonds** in which the coupon and the principal are adjusted for inflation according to changes in the consumer price index (CPI).

To consider how such a bond would work in practice, suppose you purchased a real return bond on 20 January 1996. The CPI on that date was 126.64194. Now suppose that the same bond is sold 20 July 1996 or 6 months later. For the purposes of calculating the inflation rate during the time the bond is held, the government uses the CPI on what is called the *reference date* which is actually the CPI *three months earlier than the selling date.* Moreover, since CPI data are available only on a monthly basis one needs to do some *interpolation* to find a value for the CPI on a particular day. In the present example, this means that to find the CPI for April 20th ( 3 months before July 20th) one needs the CPI for the end of March, which is 129.9, and April 1996 which is 130.1 (CPI are for end-of-month prices; the data can be found in the *Bank of Canada Review*, Table H8, and represent consumer prices for all items).

$$\text{CPI 20 July 1996} = (130.1 - 129.9) \times (20/31) + 129.9 = 130.03333$$

Since July has 31 days, interpolation means that 20/31 of the CPI change between April and May is added to the April CPI to get the CPI for the 20th day of the month.

Since the CPI at purchase was 126.64194, inflation during the holding period was

$$(130.03333 - 126.64194)/126.64194 = 2.67794\%$$

Therefore, on a $100,000 real return bond, the investor would receive the following amounts:

A. $100,000 × 2.67794% = $102,677.94
B. 2.125% on $102,677.94 = $2,181.91
C. Total = $104,859.83

Part A adjusts the principal for inflation during the holding period; Part B pays interest (the annual rate is 4.25% or 2.125% on a 6-month basis) on the inflation-adjusted principal.

In 1993, securities dealers began to issue real return stripped bonds with a variety of maturities of up to 30 years. These bonds combine the features of STRIPS with those of real return bonds. For example, a $1,000 real return stripped bond maturing in 10 years with a real return of 3.9% and zero expected inflation over the term of the bond would fetch a price today of $682.09 ($1/(1.039)^{10} \times \$1{,}000$). If inflation in the CPI is expected to be 5% for each of the next 10 years the principal repayable at maturity would become $1,628.89 ($\$1{,}000 \times (1.05)^{10}$) which would compensate the investor for inflation.

Clearly, borrowing and savings decisions should be affected by after-tax considerations. However, because every individual does not face the same tax rate and because we want to simplify the subsequent discussion, henceforth the term real interest rate refers to the ex ante real interest rate computed from equation (5.15).

## ECONOMICS FOCUS 5.2 Lies the CPI Told Me

As we have seen, the calculation of real interest rates involves a measure of inflation. But how well is inflation measured? This is an important question for a number of reasons: Canada Pension Plan payments are partially indexed to inflation, the real return bond is also tied to inflation performance, wage claims are often tied to expected inflation, and our personal tax exemption only increases if inflation exceeds 3%. Concerns about measuring inflation have resurfaced both because central banks have targeted inflation performance (see Chapter 25) and because governments at all levels are seeking ways to save money.

So what's wrong with the CPI-based measure of inflation? Plenty, it seems. Many economists and government agencies now agree that there is a positive bias in reported CPI inflation, which means that inflation is lower than we think. Why? First, if one of the thousands of items surveyed in the construction of the CPI goes on sale it will leave a mark on the index when it returns to its normal price. Second, the CPI measures the spending habits of a "representative" consumer, whoever he or she is, based on a "basket" of purchases in a particular *base* year (1986 is the latest base year used by Statistics Canada). However, even if we believe in the representative individual, surely our spending habits would have changed since 1986 for example. Moreover, consumers, even the mythical representative one, do substitute items when their price changes. For example, when a frost or a drought drives up the price of a head of lettuce to over $2 a head, most consumers will give up on the leafy vegetable, at least for a time. In addition, the items surveyed in the CPI are based on prices in certain retail stores. This does not consider the impact of discount stores or warehouse type stores or the effect of "bulk-buying" by families. Also, consumers switch brands if the price is right and this too is not reflected properly in CPI calculations. Finally, there is no account taken of quality changes in the products we buy. For example, prices for VCRs today are probably lower, on average, than they were in, say, 1986 but the biggest change since then is the increase in the number of features VCRs are equipped with. None of this is directly reflected in CPI calculations. So what is the size of the bias we are talking about? Anywhere from 0.2% a year to 2%. Doesn't sound like much? Over a 10 year period, a 0.2 % bias implies a total overstatement of CPI inflation of approximately 2% while a 2% annual bias translates into a total overstatement of 21.9%!

## SUMMARY

- Debt is a futures contract.
- The price of debt is the interest rate.
- Present value is the discounted value of a stream of payments made in the future.
- There are many ways of repaying a debt:
  –lump sum in the future
  –fixed payments in the future

- There are many ways of paying interest:
  –fixed at specified intervals
  –compounded
- Interest rates are stated in nominal terms, but borrowers and lenders care about the real interest rate.
- Some key expressions related to interest calculations include:

Present value

$X_t = X_0/(1 + R)^n$

Fixed payment loan

$$\$Debt = \frac{\$FP}{(1 + R)} + \frac{\$FP}{(1 + R)^2} + \cdots + \frac{\$FP}{(1 + R)^n}$$

Coupon bond

$$PV_t^* = \frac{\$C}{(1 + R)} + \frac{\$C}{(1 + R)^2} + \cdots + \frac{\$C}{(1 + R)^n} + \frac{\$FV}{(1 + R)^n}$$

Discounted bill annual yield (90-day Treasury bill)

$$R = \frac{\$FV - \$PD}{\$PD} \times \frac{360}{90}$$

Current yield

$$R_t^C = \frac{C}{PV_t^*}$$

Fisher equation

$R = \rho + \pi^e$ (ex ante)

$R = \rho + \pi$ (ex post)

$R^* = R(1 - \tau)$ after-tax nominal interest rate

# IMPORTANT TERMS

capital gain/loss return rate (p. 101)
capital gain or loss (p. 100)
coupon rate (p. 97)
current yield (p. 98)
discounted bond (p. 98)
Fisher equation (p. 104)
holding period yield (p. 100)
interest rate (p. 90)
nominal interest rate (p. 103)
present value (p. 91)
real interest rate (p. 103)
real return bonds (p. 108)
volatility (p. 102)
yield to maturity (p. 92)

## EXERCISES

1. Assuming that an interest rate of 8% prevails, calculate the present value for the stream of income produced by the following assets.
   (a) A bond paying $50 in interest per year for two years, to be redeemed for $1,000 at the end of two years.
   (b) An asset that earns $75 per year for three years and then $150 per year forever.

2. If the interest rate is 10% per annum, what is the present value of a security that pays $1,100 next year, $1,200 the year after, and $1,400 the year after that?

3. If the asset in question 2 is sold for $3,000, is the yield to maturity more or less than 10%? Why?

4. A student obtains a government loan of $5,000 that requires repayment of $786 per year, which is equivalent to an interest cost of approximately 10%. Payment is to begin after graduation, which is expected four years from today. Is the effective yield to maturity greater or less than 10%?

5. The real rate of interest is 10% and investors expect 6% inflation in the coming year. What nominal rate of interest will they demand? Will the market necessarily generate it?

6. If the investor in question 5 is in a 30% tax bracket, what is the real after-tax interest rate?

7. Suppose that an investor requires a real after-tax return of 5% and inflation is expected to be 6% in the coming year. If a security with a nominal interest rate of 13% is purchased, what is the effective tax rate on the security based on the investor's expectations? If the after-tax real return is only 3%, what was the ex post rate of inflation, assuming a tax rate of 30%?

8. You are buying a car and are about to pay cash when the salesperson gives you the following advice: "Why borrow the $10,000 from the bank at 10% when I can lend you money at just 7%." The bank loan represents payments of $878.20 per month assuming the principal declines each month. However, you found out from the dealer that payments from her loan are based on the principal outstanding when the loan is taken out and that the principal declines only once a year. Is the loan from the car dealer a good deal?

9. The radio recently carried the following commercial: "Buy an appliance from

us and we will give you 50% of the price back in 10 years. Now there's a deal you can't beat!" If the typical appliance costs $500 and inflation is expected to average 5% per year, how much is the manufacturer's deal worth in current dollars?

10. If the tax rate is 30%, what additional nominal interest rate is required to leave after-tax yields constant if expected inflation rises by 20%?

11. Which $1,000 bond has the higher yield to maturity:
(a) A 20-year bond selling for $800 with a current yield of 15%
(b) A 1-year bond selling for $800 with a current yield of 5%?
Explain.

12. Which would you prefer to receive:
(a) $1 million today
(b) $1 million in instalments over 10 years?
Explain.

13. Explain why price changes for long-term bonds (term of 10 years or longer) can be greater than those for short-term bonds (term of 1 year or less).

14. Suppose that the current price of a $1,000 government bond is 98 and the coupon rate is 10%. If the price was 97 a year ago and the investor now chooses to sell the bond, what will the holding period return have been?

15. "Current yield is the illusion. Someone will snap up a bond if the broker tells him it yields 9% and reject one for 7% even though it may be the better deal," says one analyst (quoted in the Business Section of the *New York Times*, 10 November 1991). Comment.

16. "Short-term interest rates, in contrast, are less affected by inflation expectations. Investors here tend to have shorter planning horizons and, as a result, tend to be less concerned about the impact of inflation on real returns," says the *Royfund Report* (vol. 1, issue 1, 1991). How does this quote square with the theory and evidence presented in this chapter? Explain.

17. The average annual cost of attending a Canadian university in 1990–91 was $8,019. At present rates of growth, the annual cost is expected to rise by 2009 to $127,000 for a four-year program. What discount rate was used to arrive at this figure?

**18.** Suppose a Government of Canada STRIPS bond can be purchased for \$3,816.31 at the end of 1991. At maturity, in seven years, the investor receives \$6,987.50. What is the annual rate of return on the STRIPS?

**19.** "Short-term interest rates increased sharply during the latter part of 1992. Our investment strategy took advantage of this period by lengthening the term to maturity of the money market section from 91 days to 113 days at year end."
Does this strategy make sense? Why?

**20.** At 9%, a 48-month loan would result in a monthly payment of \$24.89 per \$1,000. Suppose you borrow \$17,192. What is the monthly payment?

**21.** Suppose you borrow \$23,000 (\$20,000 plus 15% taxes) to purchase a car. The total monthly payment is then \$742.21 (based on a 10% interest rate for a term of 36 months). If you could lease a car at the same interest rate with a buyback feature worth \$10,000, then the monthly payment is \$322.70. Is leasing a better deal in this case? Explain. (Ignore the discounting of the buyback.)

**22.** What do you think the main considerations are in lengthening or shortening the term to maturity of government debt? Explain.

**23.** Suppose you anticipate 3% inflation in the future. If you wish to generate the equivalent of \$10,000 in current dollars 10, 20, or 30 years into the future what amount of future dollars will you require? If you wish to accomplish the above objective via annual contributions instead *rank* the size of each contribution if you have 10, 20 or 30 years until you require the funds (Note: only a ranking is required for this part of the question, not an actual dollar value).

**24.** "I bought a 15-year Government of Canada bond yielding 7.4%. I expect the present inflation rate of 1.7% to continue throughout the 15-year term, yielding me a 5.48% real return. That's well above the 3.5% real rate on a real return bond." How was the 5.48% figure arrived at? Is the investor correct? Why? Why not?

**25.** Examine Figure 5.3. What can you say about real ex post interest rates during this period? Which country experienced the highest real ex post interest rate? Which country had the lowest?

## REFERENCES

*Bank of Canada Review*, various issues.

International Monetary Fund, *International Financial Statistics Yearbook.* Washington, D.C., various issues.

Siklos, P.L. "The Deficit-Interest Rate Link: Empirical Evidence for Canada." *Applied Economics* 20 (December 1988): 1563–78.

———. "Velocity and Institutional Change: Some New Time Series Evidence from Five Countries, 1870–1986." *Journal of Money, Credit and Banking* 25 (August 1993).

CHAPTER 6

# Understanding Interest Rates: Determination of Interest Rate Levels

In the previous chapter, we assumed the nominal interest rate to be given. In this chapter, however, we examine how interest rate levels are actually determined through the interaction of borrowers and lenders (generally operating via an intermediary) in a market. Also, in this chapter, we consider some of the factors that can cause interest rates to change over time.

We examine two theories of interest rate determination, each of which focuses on a different part of the financial system. The first is the loanable funds theory, which concentrates on developments in the bond market and on the *flow* of funds over a period of time. The second is the liquidity preference framework, which is concerned with the market for the quantity of money and is thus formulated in terms of demand for a *stock*.[1]

Each of these explanations focuses on a single interest rate, yet the models developed in this chapter suggest what accounts for movements in *any* interest rate. Clearly, several interest rates do exist in the economy simultaneously. Figure 6.1 plots the yields on three high-quality debt instruments since the 1950s. There have been differences at any given time, and some of the yields have been more volatile than others. Yet there is clearly a common trend.[2] Therefore, we need not be specific here about which particular interest rate is being described.

## THE LOANABLE FUNDS APPROACH

The loanable funds approach suggests that interest rate levels are determined by the forces of supply and demand for **loanable funds**—new funds available for investment. The interaction between the amount available for investment by

1 The two theories can be reconciled, as we show later in the chapter.

2 In Chapter 15 we discuss a simple explanation for this phenomenon.

**FIGURE 6.1** A Selection of Yields over Time

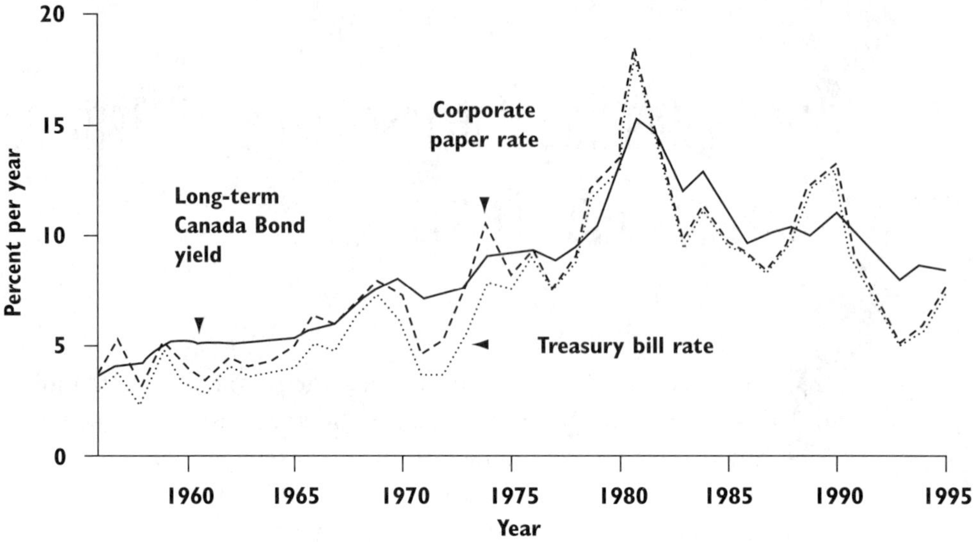


The maturities on the instruments involved were: long-term government bonds, 10 years or more; Treasury bills, 3 months; prime corporate paper, 90 days. Annual averages were used.

For the 1956–95 period, the correlation between yields on Treasury bills and Government of Canada long-term bonds is 93%; on Treasury bills and prime corporate paper, 99%; on prime corporate paper and long-term bonds, 91%. These high correlations indicate the strength of the linear relationships for the time series plotted.

Source: *Bank of Canada Review* (various issues).

lenders (the supply of loanable funds), and the quantity of bonds desired by borrowers (the demand for loanable funds) is assumed to generate a market-clearing price—that is, an **equilibrium interest rate** level.

As done in your principles of economics course, we analyze separately the determinants of supply and demand for loanable funds before we derive an equilibrium interest rate level. Since loanable funds are generally traded in the form of bonds, we focus on that market.

## BOND DEMAND AND SUPPLY

To make the analysis as simple as possible, we assume for now that individuals know with certainty the yield to maturity on bonds. If we further simplify the example by considering a 1-year discounted bond, then we can write

**FIGURE 6.2** The Supply of and Demand for Bonds

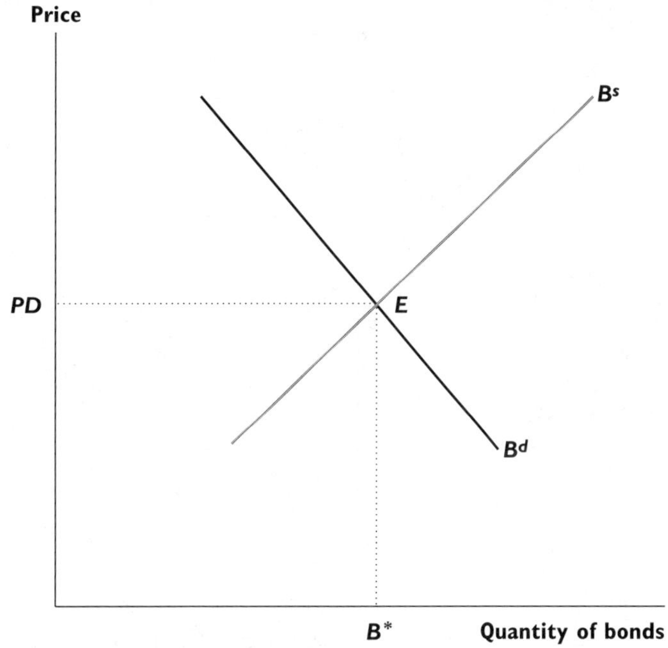


Bond demand is depicted by the curve $B^d$, which slopes downward to indicate the inverse relationship between the price of bonds and the quantity individuals desire to hold. Similarly, the bond supply curve, $B^s$, slopes upward since the higher the price of the bond, the lower its cost and consequently, the greater the desire to borrow.

$$R = \frac{\$FV - \$PD}{\$PD} \tag{6.1}$$

where

$R$ = the nominal interest rate[3]
$FV$ = face value of the bond, maturing in one year
$PD$ = discounted purchase price.

If $FV = \$1{,}000$, there exist unique combinations of $PD$ and $R$ that satisfy equation (6.1). Note that the relationship between $PD$ and $R$ is inverse. Clearly, the lower the price of new bonds—which is to say the greater the return—the

3 Recall that, unless otherwise stated, the interest rate we refer to in this book is the *nominal* interest rate.

**FIGURE 6.3** The Supply of and Demand for Bonds Again

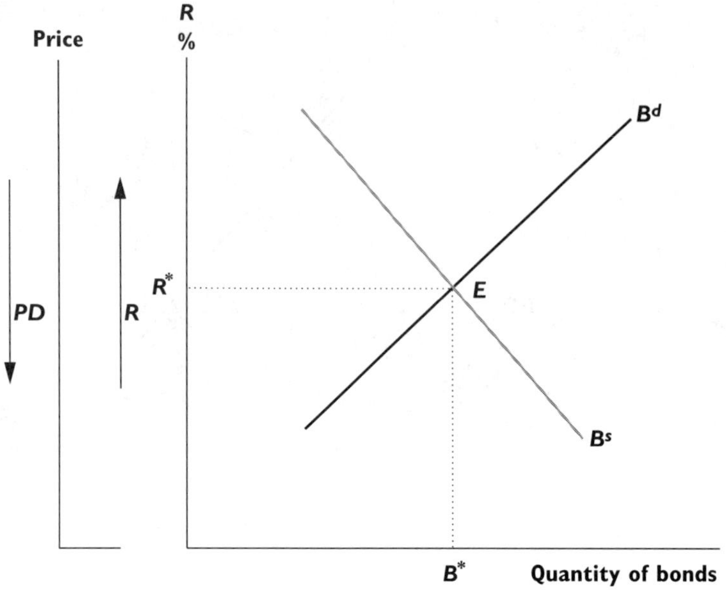


The bond demand and supply curves of Figure 6.2 are now reversed, so the vertical axis measures return, which is inversely related to price, as in equation (6.1). The vertical axis of Figure 6.2 is reproduced here to emphasize this inverse relationship.

more of them lenders will wish to hold. By contrast, the higher the price of the bond—which translates into a lower debt cost to the borrower—the larger the quantity prospective debtors will wish to issue. Thus, we can draw the bond demand and supply curves depicted in Figure 6.2. For simplicity, the demand and supply curves are straight lines, though, of course, nothing in the forgoing analysis suggests that this need be the case. All we know or need to know is that the curve for bond demand, $B^d$, is downward sloping whereas the curve for bond supply, $B^s$, is upward sloping. A lower price increases the quantity of bonds demanded but decreases the quantity of bonds supplied.

The subject of this chapter, however, is not bond prices but the determination of interest rate levels. Although there is a known relationship between bond price and return, as embodied in equation (6.1), it seems preferable to specify this relationship in terms of returns. We can do so easily by redrawing the supply–demand diagram with the percentage return measured on the vertical axis, as in Figure 6.3. Note, however, that the bond supply curve is now *downward* sloping and the bond demand curve is *upward* sloping. The reason for the reversal is that return is inversely related to bond price. The figure shows what we already

**FIGURE 6.4** The Supply of and Demand for Loanable Funds

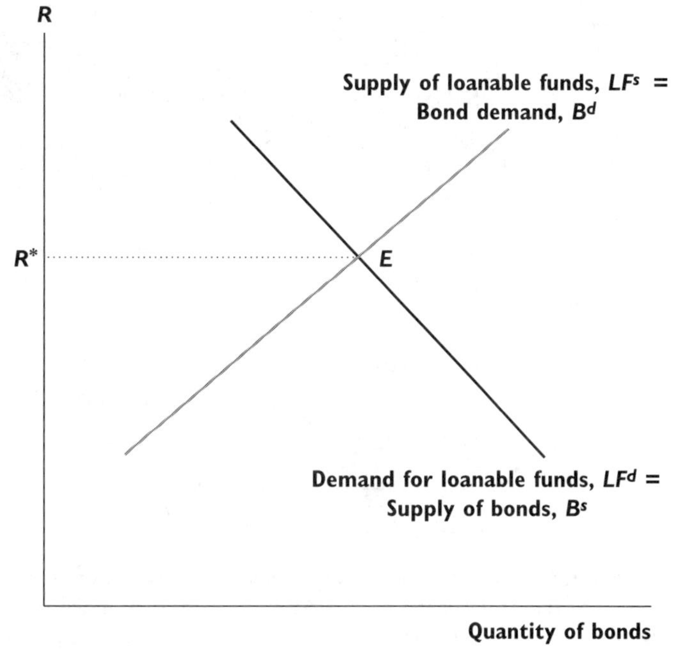


Since the purchasers of bonds provide loanable funds, the demand for bonds curve from Figure 6.3 is replaced by a supply of loanable funds curve. Similarly, since borrowers supply bonds into the market, they are, in effect, demanders of loanable funds. Thus, the supply of bonds curve of Figure 6.3 is replaced by a demand for loanable funds curve.

know: the larger the return, the greater the quantity of bonds demanded and, conversely, the smaller the quantity of bonds supplied in the market.

Figure 6.3 looks peculiar, however, because supply curves usually slope upward and demand curves downward. Can we make the bond market diagram more conventional? Yes, by recalling that one person's debt is another person's asset. A demand for new bonds reflects a desire to hold more funds than are being loaned out. Similarly, a supply of new bonds implies that new funds are being loaned out. Consequently, we may call bond demand the supply of loanable funds and bond supply the demand for loanable funds.[4]

If we redraw the diagram as the demand for and supply of loanable funds (Figure 6.4), the curves have their usual slopes.

4 Notice that the definition of loanable funds being used in the model is narrow—one type of new bond only. This assumption leads to no loss of generality, however. Clearly, the supply of and demand for loanable funds comes from all sectors of the economy. (See Chapter 8.)

**FIGURE 6.5** Market Equilibrium

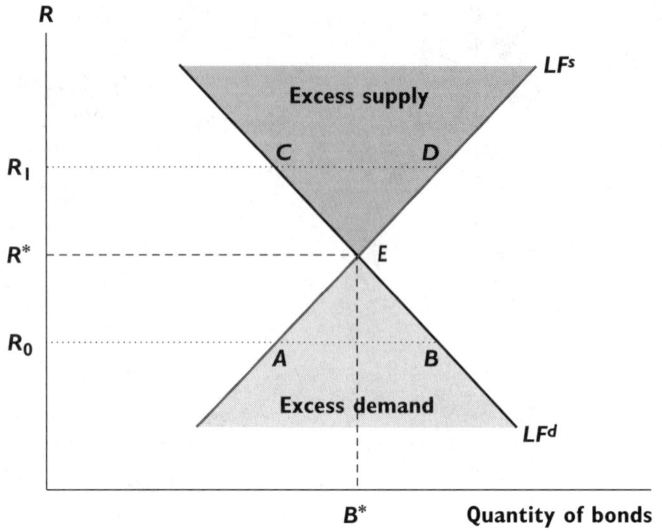


At point $E$, the quantity of loanable funds demanded equals the quantity of loanable funds supplied. $R^*$ is the equilibrium interest rate. At interest rates of more than $R^*$, such as $R_1$, there is excess supply of loanable funds since $LF^s > LF^d$. Conversely, when $R$ is less than $R^*$, $LF^d > LF^s$.

## MARKET EQUILIBRIUM

Point $E$ is obtained in Figures 6.2, 6.3, or 6.4 when the quantity of bonds or loanable funds demanded is equal to the quantity of bonds or loanable funds supplied—that is, when

$$B^d = B^s \quad \text{or} \quad LF^s = LF^d \tag{6.2}$$

Point $E$ is called an equilibrium because it is there that the supply and demand curves intersect, satisfying the conditions for equation (6.2). The point of equilibrium is important since the market gravitates toward it. In this series of figures, $R^*$ is the equilibrium interest rate, the rate that attains this balance of supply and demand. If the interest rate is lower than $R^*$, there is an excess demand for loanable funds. Thus, in Figure 6.5, when the interest rate is $R_0$, the quantity of loanable funds demanded is represented by point $B$, while the quantity of loanable funds supplied is given by point $A$. As in any market in which prices are allowed to move freely, excess demand pushes up price, which here is the interest rate.

Conversely, if the interest rate is $R_1$, it is now the quantity of loanable funds supplied (point $D$ in Figure 6.5) that exceeds the quantity of loanable funds

**FIGURE 6.6** Shifts in the Demand for and Supply of Loanable Funds

### (A) A Demand Shift

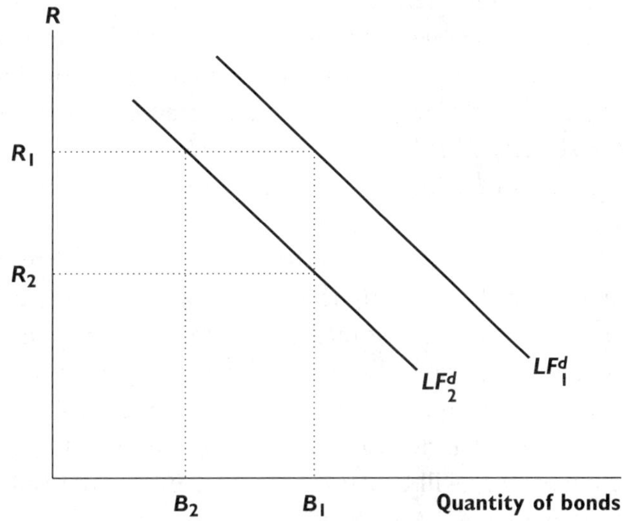


### (B) A Supply Shift

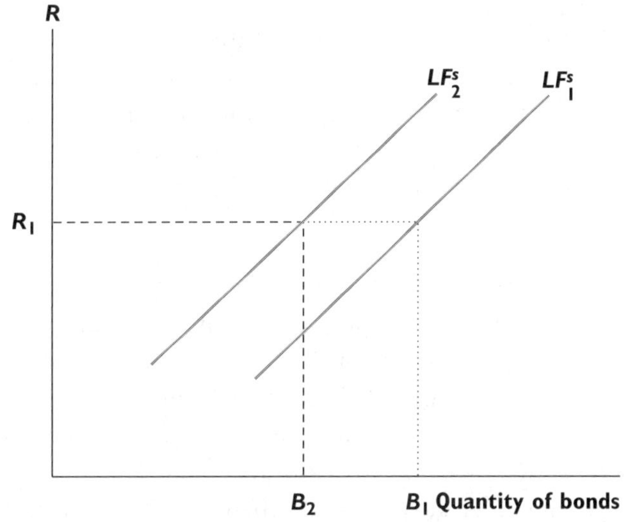


In panel (A), changes in the rate of return on investments, expected inflation, and government policies shift the demand for loanable funds. In panel (B), changes in wealth, relative returns, relative riskiness, and liquidity cause shifts in the supply of loanable funds.

demanded (point *C*). Since an excess supply leads to a rise in price, there is a tendency for the interest rate to fall until point *E* is reached once again.

Since equilibrium is the point at which an unfettered market will eventually settle, it is convenient to use it as the starting point for our analysis. Accordingly, in what follows, we examine how the equilibrium interest rate changes.

First, however, it is useful to emphasize the distinction between a *movement along* a demand or supply curve and a *shift* in these same curves. Changes in interest rates or in the quantity of bonds produce movements along the curves. Changes in other factors lead to shifts in the demand for or supply of loanable funds.

Consider first Figure 6.6(A), which shows a leftward shift in the demand for loanable funds. The implication is that the demand for loanable funds has decreased at *every* interest rate level. In other words, the demand for loanable funds has fallen. For example, consider an interest rate such as $R_1$. With a shift to the left in $LF^d$, the demand for loanable funds falls to $LF_2^d$ from $LF_1^d$; the desire to borrow funds has decreased at every interest rate level. To put the point differently, the quantity $B_1$ will be demanded only if the interest rate falls to $R_2$. If the interest rate remained at $R_1$, only $B_2$ would be demanded.

What are the factors that might cause a shift in borrowers' preferences? They include

1. Changes in the rate of return anticipated on investments. Investors (individuals and firms) typically increase or decrease their borrowing as they perceive profitable investment opportunities rising or falling. If they anticipate, say, a recession in the near future, they wish to restrict future borrowing. They reduce their demand for loanable funds, and so the $LF^d$ curve in Figure 6.6(A) shifts leftward from $LF_1^d$ to $LF_2^d$.

2. Government policies. Governments typically borrow more during recessions than during boom periods. During a recession, their tax revenue decreases but their spending on unemployment insurance and other social programs rises; the resulting deficit may have to be financed by heavy borrowing. Conversely, during a boom, general income levels rise and so do government revenues, whereas expenditures may fall, in part because of falling unemployment. A government deficit means an increase (shift to the right) in the demand for loanable funds while a government surplus implies a decrease in such demand.

3. Inflation expectations. Expectations of inflation also influence the desire to borrow and to lend. Thus, for example, if inflation is expected to fall, then, at prevailing nominal interest rates, the real interest rate rises so borrowing

costs, in terms of forgone future consumption, also rise. Therefore, with nominal interest rates expected to fall in the future, the current demand for loanable funds will fall.

Consider next the factors that can cause a shift in the supply of loanable funds. The desire to lend is influenced by changes in

1. Wealth. An increase in wealth means there are more funds available for lending. A reduction in wealth—perhaps caused by a recession—has the opposite effect.
2. Relative returns. An increase in bond returns relative to those earned on other assets leads investors to reallocate their asset holdings toward bonds, away from other assets.
3. Relative riskiness. If bonds become more or less risky than they have been, they become a more or less desirable asset, and wealth holders act accordingly.
4. Liquidity. An increase or decrease in liquidity also means that investors will increase or decrease their supply of loanable funds.
5. Expected Inflation. As noted above, expectations of inflation influence the desire to invest.

Any event, such as a recession, that makes bonds a less desirable asset reduces wealth holders' desire to supply loanable funds. In Figure 6.6(B), the loanable funds supply curve shifts from $LF_1^s$ to $LF_2^s$.

Conversely, any change that makes bonds a more desirable asset to hold increases the supply of loanable funds. Diagrammatically, the result is a rightward shift in the supply curve of loanable funds.

## EQUILIBRIUM INTEREST RATE CHANGES

The reason we are interested in shifts in either the demand or the supply curve is that they imply a change in the equilibrium interest rate level. We will consider two applications of shifts in the demand for and supply of loanable funds in order to illustrate some of the sources of equilibrium interest rate changes.

### The Fisher Effect

One of the important concepts introduced in Chapter 5 is the dichotomy between nominal and real interest rates. According to the Fisher equation, the nominal interest rate is the sum of the real interest rate and expected inflation:

$$R = \rho + \pi^e \tag{6.3}$$

(which is equation (5.14) reproduced here for convenience). The loanable funds framework lets us analyze how the Fisher effect operates.

Suppose that expected inflation is initially zero, so that $\pi^e = 0$. In that case the nominal and real interest rates are equivalent, or

$$R = \rho \tag{6.4}$$

Let the equilibrium nominal and real interest rates with zero expected inflation be denoted $R_0^*$ and $\rho_0^*$, respectively, as in Figure 6.7. Point $E$ then represents the equilibrium interest rates, nominal and real.

Now suppose that the market comes to believe that inflation will rise to 5% in the future. Our discussion of shifts in the demand for and supply of loanable funds suggests that expectations of inflation influence both sides of the market. Borrowers come to believe that the real cost of a bond will fall because, by equation (6.3) and holding the nominal interest rate constant, a rise in $\pi^e$ must mean a fall in $\rho$. Since the demand for borrowing is stimulated, the demand curve shifts from $LF_0^d$ to $LF_1^d$.

As borrowers display an increased desire to borrow because terms appear improved, lenders come to expect a lower real return. Consequently, the supply curve of loanable funds falls from $LF_0^s$ to $LF_1^s$. The new intersection between $LF_1^s$ and $LF_1^d$ establishes a new equilibrium at point $E'$.

Clearly, the interest rate has risen, but is it the real or the nominal rate that is affects? Since the real interest rate represents the sacrifice made by borrowers or the extra future consumption enjoyed by lenders, and since the only variable to have changed is expected inflation, the real rate must be unaffected. If it is unchanged in equilibrium, the nominal interest rate must have risen by the change in expected inflation, according to equation (6.3). In other words, the difference between the old and the new nominal interest rate is exactly equal to $\pi^e$, since

$$R_1^* - R_0^* = \rho_0^* + \pi^e - \rho_0^* - 0 = \pi^e$$

which is graphically represented by the distance EE' in Figure 6.7.

Look back at Figure 1.3(B), which plots inflation as measured by the consumer price index (CPI) as well as the yield on 3-month Treasury bills. The preceding discussion corroborates our visual impression of a positive correlation between inflation and the nominal interest rate.[5] Much research has gone into analyzing the significance of this relationship.

5 For the sample plotted in Figure 1.3(B), the correlation between the two series is approximately 50%.

**FIGURE 6.7** The Fisher Effect

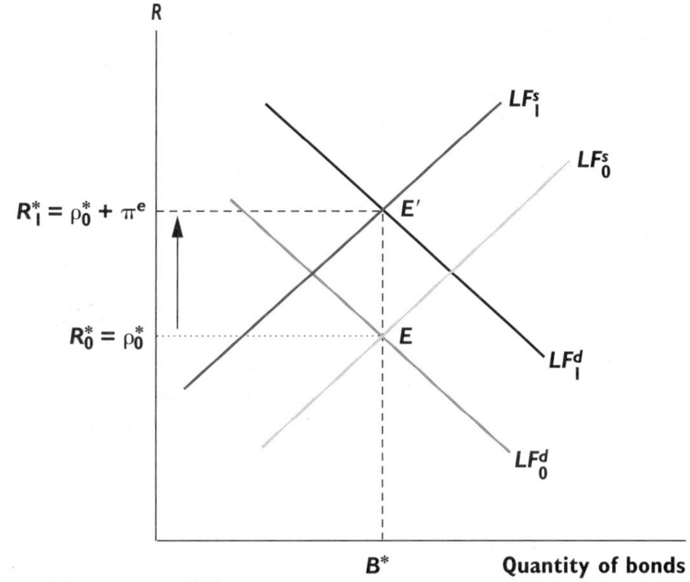


If expected inflation is zero, nominal and real interest rates are the same ($R_0^* = \rho_0^*$). Positive inflation expectations mean that the real cost of loans falls for borrowers. Consequently, the demand for loanable funds shifts from $LF_0^d$ to $LF_1^d$. If the real cost of borrowing falls, the real interest rate from lending also is expected to decrease. Therefore, the supply of loanable funds shifts from $LF_0^s$ to $LF_1^s$. At the new equilibrium, *E'*, the nominal interest rate rises by exactly the change in inflation expectations, thereby restoring the original real interest rate, $\rho_0^*$.

## Interest Rates and the Business Cycle

Now consider another important issue. We have suggested that factors such as wealth, relative returns, and liquidity may somehow be linked to fluctuations in the overall state of the economy, which economists refer to as the business cycle. Figure 6.8 illustrates the relationship among these factors since 1959 by plotting the yield on 3-month Treasury bills and the average growth rate in real gross domestic product (GDP). It appears that interest rates are roughly procyclical, meaning that they tend to rise and fall with increases and decreases in the average growth of real GDP. This is especially true of the two severe recessions of the early 1980s and 1990s. The figure also shows how real GDP growth plummeted in the aftermath of the two oil price stocks.

Figure 6.9 illustrates this possibility using the loanable funds framework. The equilibrium interest rate is initially $R_0^*$ where the original demand and supply curves, $LF_0^d$ and $LF_0^s$, intersect. Then, in anticipation of a recession, borrowers cut

**FIGURE 6.8** The Nominal Interest Rate and Economic Growth

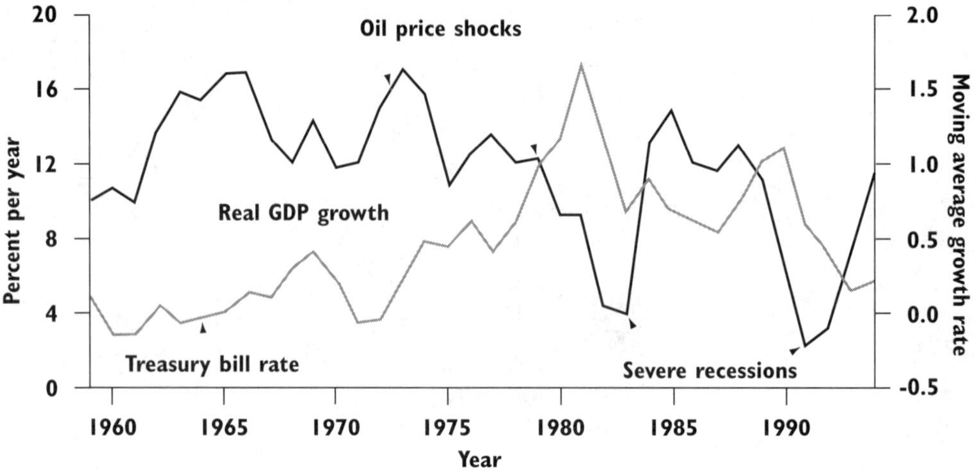


Here the business cycle is proxied by a 2-year moving average of the real GDP growth rate. (This is by no means the only possible proxy, but it is adequate for exploring the possible links between booms or recessions and interest rate level movements.) Generally, average real GDP growth is positive. Indeed, a recession is often defined as a time when real GDP growth is relatively low, as it was, for example, during the early 1980s and 1990s. The two oil price shocks occurred in 1973–74 and 1979–80.

Source: *OECD Main Economic Indicators* (various issues).

back their borrowing plans, so the demand for loanable funds falls to $LF_1^d$. At the same time, with a recession looming, incoming growth is expected to fall. It is reasonable to suppose that the supply of loanable funds will also fall, a phenomenon shown in Figure 6.9 by a shift in the supply curve to $LF_1^s$.

What is unclear is how large the shifts in the demand and supply curves will be relative to each other. This consideration is an important one since the relative size of the shifts will dictate whether the resulting equilibrium interest rate level will be higher or lower than the one before the recession began. Given the evidence presented in Figure 6.8, we conclude that interest rates fall in a recession. Thus we have constructed the figure with the new equilibrium interest rate at $R_1^*$, lower than $R_0^*$, the interest rate at the original equilibrium point.

An identical argument can, of course, be used to suggest that the equilibrium interest rate will rise when the business cycle booms. We leave working out the solution to you as an exercise.

**FIGURE 6.9** Interest Rates in a Recession

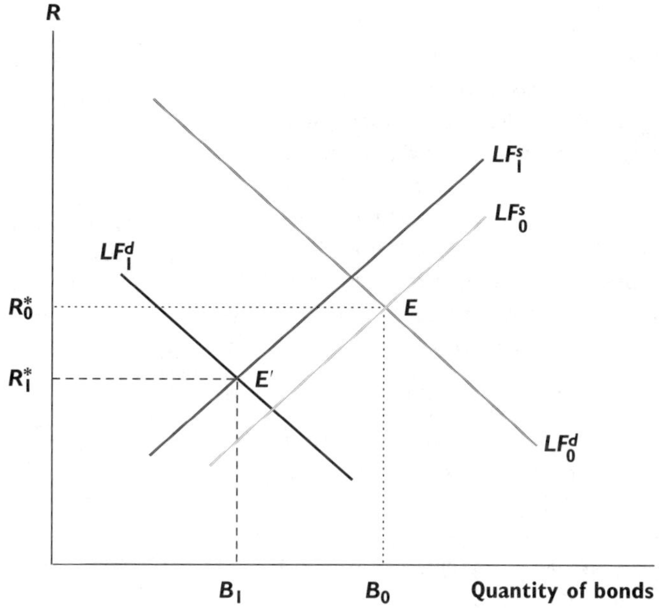


Interest rate level movements appear procyclical, rising and falling with business cycle booms and recessions. During a recession or in anticipation of one, the demand for loanable funds falls (from $LF_0^d$ to $LF_1^d$) as the desire to borrow drops. Similarly, since a recession indicates lower income growth, the supply falls off ($LF_0^s$ shifts to $LF_1^s$). The equilibrium interest rate level is now at point *E'*, which is lower than at point *E*.

## THE LIQUIDITY PREFERENCE APPROACH

**Liquidity preference** is the desire to hold wealth in the form of money rather than less liquid forms. It is, in other words, the demand for money.

What does this demand have to do with interest rates? Economists have long believed that interest rate level determination is primarily a *monetary* factor—one depending on the interaction of the demand for and the supply of money. The idea may seem odd at first since, as we saw in Chapter 5, the interest rate is an expression of the price of bonds. Assume that individuals' portfolios consist only of money and bonds. Linking the demand for and supply of money to the interest rate is sensible because, for a given level of wealth, any excess demand for bonds must imply an excess supply of money, and vice versa. If wealth is fixed, the forgoing assumption means we can write

$$W = M + B \tag{6.5}$$

## ECONOMICS FOCUS 6.1 Gibson's Paradox

It has long been known that a positive connection exists between interest rates and prices. For example, Thomas Tooke, an early pioneer in the use of statistical evidence to explain economic relationships, argued that as interest cost is part of production costs and the latter influences the price level: whenever one rises the other must follow in the same direction. Tooke's argument also leads, however, to the conclusion that interest rates cause rising prices, a theme used recently by opponents of the Bank of Canada's policy of relying on high interest rates to stem inflation.

The notion of a positive relationship between interest rates and prices is generally known to economists as *Gibson's paradox*. In two studies published in the 1920s, the English banker A.H. Gibson empirically established a positive correlation between commodity prices and the yield on consols (called perpetuities; see note 4, Chapter 5).

In 1930, John Maynard Keynes made Gibson's observation famous, saying

> For the extraordinary thing is that the 'Gibson's paradox'—as we may fairly call it—is one of the most completely established empirical facts within the whole field of quantitative economics, though theoretical economists have mostly ignored it (p. 198).

The figure below plots consumer prices (in logarithms) and a long-term interest rate measure for 120 years of annual Canadian data. A positive synchronous movement of the price level and the interest rate clearly emerges.

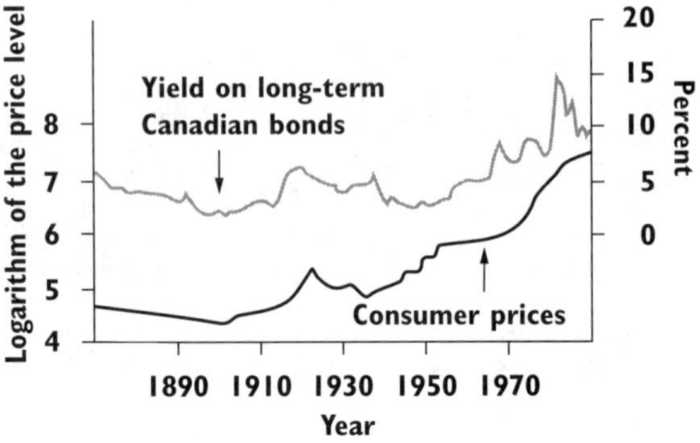


Source: P.L. Siklos, "Income Velocity and Institutional Change: Some New Time Series Evidence, 1870–1986," *Journal of Money, Credit and Banking* 25 (August 1993)

Gibson's findings are termed a paradox because microeconomic theory predicts that since interest is a cost of capital, which is taken as a fixed cost, output and, therefore, the price level will be unaffected by interest rate changes. Thus, interest rates and the price level are independent of each other.

Keynes suggested that the interest sensitivity of the supply of money may explain Gibson's findings. If aggregate demand for goods rises because of some innova-

---

where

$W$ = the fixed stock of wealth
$M$ = money stock
$B$ = stock of bonds.

Since $W$ does not change.

$$\Delta W = 0$$

where $\Delta$ refers to a change in a variable. We can, therefore, express equation (6.5) in terms of changes as

## ECONOMICS FOCUS 6.1 Gibson's Paradox (continued)

tion that creates investment opportunities, the subsequent rise in output causes a shift in the demand for money and, hence, raises the equilibrium interest rate. As this is happening, banks find that the opportunity cost of holding current reserves also rises, so they seek to expand loans and, hence, deposits, which ultimately implies an increase in the money supply. (The mechanism by which this is accomplished is discussed in Chapter 16.) Since a rise in the money supply leads to a price level increase, the positive link between interest rates and prices is thereby established. (Incidentally, the great Swedish economist Knut Wicksell came up with virtually the same explanation for Gibson's paradox many years earlier (1911) but Keynes was unaware of his work.)

The Fisher equation also suggests the Gibson phenomenon. (By equation (6.3), a rise in the price level is correlated with expected inflation.) However, since actual price changes are often used to proxy expected inflation, Fisher's equation is essentially only a restatement of the Gibson paradox rather than a theory to explain it.

One more recent theoretical explanation is that an interest-sensitive demand for money interacts with the velocity of circulation (see Chapter 11) to produce the Gibson paradox; Siegel and Shiller rely on the influence on portfolio reallocations (Chapter 13) of price changes that are unanticipated. Canadian empirical evidence favourable to the notion of a Gibson paradox may be found in Milne and Torous.

Recently, however, doubts have surfaced about whether past studies based their conclusions on statistical techniques that would tend to show a spurious correlation. Discussion of these issues is beyond the scope of this text; interested readers may wish to consult, Corbae and Ouliaris.

**Sources**:


D. Corbae and S. Ouiliaris, "A Random Walk Through the Gibson Paradox," *Journal of Applied Econometrics* 4 (1989): 295–303.

A.H. Gibson, "The Future Course of High Class Investment Values," *Banker's Magazine* 115 (January 1923): 15–34.

A.H. Gibson, "The Road to Economic Recovery," *Banker's Magazine* 122 (November 1926): 595–612.

J.M. Keynes, *A Treatise on Money* (New York: Macmillan, 1930).

W.J. Milne and W.N. Torous, "Long-Term Interest Rates and the Price Level: The Canadian Evidence on the Gibson Paradox," *Canadian Journal of Economics* 17 (May 1984): 327–39.

T.J. Sargent, "Interest Rates and Prices in the Long Run: A Study of the Gibson Paradox," *Journal of Money, Credit and Banking* 5 (1973): 385–449.

R.J. Shiller and J. Siegel, "The Gibson Paradox and Historical Movements in Real Interest Rates," *Journal of Political Economy* 85 (1977): 891–907.

K. Wicksell, *Lectures on Political Economy* (London: Routledge and Keegan Paul, 1911).


---

$$0 = \Delta M + \Delta B$$

or, finally,

$$-\Delta M = \Delta B \tag{6.6}$$

It is clear from equation (6.6) that any changes in the stock of bonds are exactly offset by changes in the money stock.

We can be more specific about this conclusion by considering that equilibrium is determined in both the money and bond markets by the point at which supply and demand are equated to each other. Moreover, if the bond market is in equilibrium, the money market must also be in equilibrium. We can, therefore, write

$$B^d + M^d = B^s + M^s \tag{6.7}$$

where $B^d$ and $B^s$ are bond demand and bond supply, and $M^d$ and $M^s$ are money demand and money supply.

Rearranging equation (6.7) to collect the terms in each market, we obtain

$$M^s - M^d \equiv B^s - B^d \tag{6.8}$$

which simply states that an excess demand ($M^s - M^d < 0$) or excess supply ($M^s - M^d > 0$) of money must be exactly equivalent to an excess supply ($B^s - B^d > 0$) or an excess demand ($B^s - B^d < 0$) for bonds.

In a sense then, the liquidity preference and the loanable funds frameworks are similar. In the liquidity preference framework, however, it is the demand for and supply of liquidity—money—a stock measure, that determines the interest rate.[6]

## THE DEMAND FOR MONEY

The desire to hold liquidity is a function of three factors: (1) the interest rate, (2) income, and (3) the price level.

According to the narrow definition of money, it is an asset that earns little or no interest. Thus, holders of liquidity incur the **opportunity cost**—the cost of the forgone action—of not holding an asset that could earn interest income.[7]

Does it make sense then for an individual to hold any money at all? Yes, because holding money is useful for three reasons:

1. **Transactions motive**. Money is useful as a means of settling transactions.

2. **Precautionary motive**. Money is useful as a precaution against unexpected expenditures.

3. **Speculative motive**. Money is held as an asset that can be used to purchase assets when a profitable opportunity arises.

---

6 This explanation reconciling the two approaches is deceptively simple. It took decades of intense debate to recognize how it could be achieved.

7 If we defined money more broadly to include some interest-earning assets, the opportunity cost of money would simply be the difference between the interest on bonds and that on money. For simplicity, we can retain our definition of the interest rate on bonds as the opportunity cost of holding money.

Most economists believe that the income level determines the amounts of money an individual wants to hold for transactions and precautionary purposes.[8] This relationship is depicted in the top part of Figure 6.10. The vertical axis measures income in current dollars, which is referred to as **nominal income.** Nominal income is affected by changes in its components. If we write

$$Y = Py$$

where $Y$ is nominal income and $P$ is the price level, then

$$y = \frac{Y}{P}$$

is **real income**—that is, the purchasing power commanded by nominal income $Y$.

The top part of Figure 6.10 also shows a particular level of transactions and precautionary demand for money, $M$, associated with a particular level of income. This demand changes with increases or decreases in $P$, in $y$, or in both.

The bottom part of Figure 6.10 plots the demand for money as an asset. Since money is assumed not to have any explicit yield, its opportunity cost is measured by the yield on a bond, $R$. If demand is held constant, the higher the yield on bonds, the greater the opportunity cost of holding money. Therefore, one would expect the quantity of money demanded to fall with higher bond yields. The resulting relationship is the **demand for money** or the demand for liquidity. The curve is marked $M^d$.

Note that, if income rises, the quantity of money held for transactions and precautionary purposes also rises, say from $M^*$ to $M^{**}$. In terms of the relationship depicted in Figure 6.10, such a change means that the demand for money curve has shifted to the right. There is now a new tradeoff between bond yields and the demand for money. In other words, price changes and real income changes shift the demand for money curve.

---

8 Of course, the precautionary demand for money involves uncertainty and, therefore, more than just income. We return to this issue in Chapter 11. Here, however, it is convenient and correct to make both the transactions and precautionary motives a function of income alone.

**FIGURE 6.10** The Transactions and the Precautionary Demand for Money

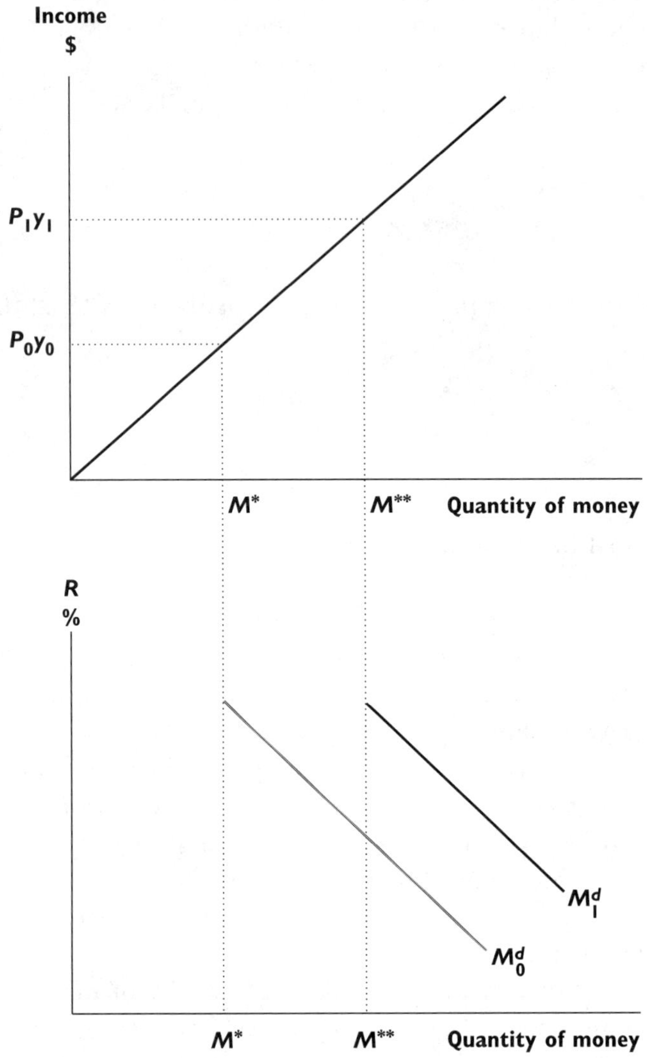


The top portion shows the positive relationship between income (the price level × real income) and the quantity of money demanded for transactions and precautionary purposes. The bottom portion depicts the demand for money as an asset that yields no explicit return. The opportunity cost of holding money is thus approximately the yield on a bond. Price changes and real income changes can shift the demand for money curve.

## ECONOMICS FOCUS 6.2 Measuring Real GDP

In your principles course you will have gone into some detail concerning the components of real GDP which proxies economy-wide income. This measure is called **current dollar GDP**. Because of inflation, however, we need to measure GDP in **constant** dollars called **real GDP** (or real income as the discussion of money demand in this chapter refers to it.) Since real GDP represents the constant dollar value of *all* goods and services in the economy it does not have some of the problems associated with the CPI (see *Economics Focus 5.2*). However, like the CPI, it is constructed from information collected in the *base* year. Recently, both the US and Canada introduced a *chain-weighted* index alongside the usual *fixed-weight* index on which the calculations of real GDP in this chapter are based (the new measure only goes back to 1986.) Is the *chain-index* better? In a sense the answer is yes since the new index takes into account the impact of changes in relative prices as well as changes in the composition of output over time. To see how real GDP calculations work under the old and new systems consider the following extraordinarily simplified example. Suppose the economy produces two goods and services only: haircuts and watches. The table below records the prices and quantities sold in the *base* year.

**Base year**

| | Expenditure | Quantities Consumed | Price per Unit |
|---|---|---|---|
| Haircuts | \$300 | 30 | \$10 |
| Watches | \$200 | 10 | \$20 |
| "GDP" | \$500 | | |

Nominal GDP in the base year is \$500. The table below gives the figures for the following year.

**Next year**

| | Expenditure | Quantities Consumed | Price per Unit |
|---|---|---|---|
| Haircuts | \$400 | 20 | \$20 |
| Watches | \$500 | 20 | \$25 |
| "GDP" | \$900 | | |

Nominal GDP is now \$900. Now lets see how real GDP would be calculated under the two weighting schemes. The results are shown below.

| Fixed-Weight (base year prices) | Fixed-Weight (current year prices) |
|---|---|
| [20 × \$10 + 20 × \$20]/ \$500 = \$600/\$500 | \$900/[30 × \$20 + 10 × \$25] = \$900/\$850 |
| 1.2 | 1.06 |
| Real GDP rose by 20% | Real GDP rose by 6% |

One way of calculating real GDP is to use the current year's quantities and the base year prices in the numerator and actual expenditure in the denominator. Another method begins by using the actual GDP in the numerator and base year quantities in the denominator. The difference in the two measures of real GDP growth is striking. One method reports a 20% increase while the other finds only a 6% increase. The chain-weighted index is the *geometric* average of the two evaluated as

$$\sqrt{(1.20)(1.06)} = 1.13$$

That is, the square root of the product of the two growth rates. Therefore, the chain-weighted index uses the weights from adjacent years to construct real GDP.

Are actual differences between the two methods significant for the Canadian economy? The table below shows they are.

| Year | GDP Growth (%) [fixed-weight] | GDP Growth (%) [chain-weighted] |
|---|---|---|
| 1987 | 4.2 | 4.2 |
| 1988 | 5.0 | 4.4 |
| 1989 | 2.4 | 2.8 |
| 1990 | −0.2 | 1.0 |
| 1991 | −1.8 | −1.9 |
| 1992 | 0.8 | 0.9 |
| 1993 | 2.2 | 1.2 |
| 1994 | 4.6 | 3.6 |

## THE SUPPLY OF MONEY

It is conventional to assume that the supply of money is entirely under the control of the central bank and that it is unresponsive or unrelated to interest rate levels. This simplistic assumption ignores the behaviour of banks and of the public. Banks, for example, hold reserves[9] against their deposits, and a portion of these reserves return no interest, some thereby incurring an opportunity cost.[10]

Banks can manage their reserves (RES). Despite the opportunity costs, they have sound reasons for holding RES from time to time (for example, during the Christmas season, when the demand for cash rises). Nevertheless, since banks presumably wish to maximize profits, they want to minimize RES. It is also reasonable to suppose that the higher the opportunity cost, the smaller the banks' reserve holdings will be. Money that would otherwise be held in reserves will be loaned out, so deposits in the banking system will rise. Recall that the money supply, by definition, includes some deposits. Therefore, a higher interest rate increases the quantity of money supplied.

The public too can influence the quantity of money supplied in the market. The public's holding of currency, another of the constituents of the money supply, is also presumably affected by interest rate levels.[11] Thus, the higher the interest rate, the higher the opportunity cost of holding currency and the more likely that individuals will economize on cash holdings. This translates into a larger money supply.[12]

The size of these effects is not clear. Nevertheless, the forgoing discussion suggests a positive relationship between the interest rate and the quantity of money supplied.

## EQUILIBRIUM IN THE MONEY MARKET

Having derived supply and demand in the money market, we can define the equilibrium. It is shown in Figure 6.11 by point $E$, which also defines the equilibrium interest rate level, $R^*$.

---

9 Recent legislation has phased out reserve requirements. Banks will still want, however, to hold some reserves.

10 Many countries, such as Germany and the US, still impose mandatory reserve requirements on the banking system. Strictly speaking, only the holding of currency incurs an opportunity cost. The new reserve management system introduced in Canada (see Chapter 4) does provide for the payment of interest on reserves at the Bank of Canada.

11 And by financial innovations, such as the introduction of automated teller machines.

12 If individuals hold relatively more of their money holdings in the form of bank deposits, their action swells the banks' reserves and thence the money supply because of the banks' desire to minimize such holdings.

**FIGURE 6.11** Money in Equilibrium

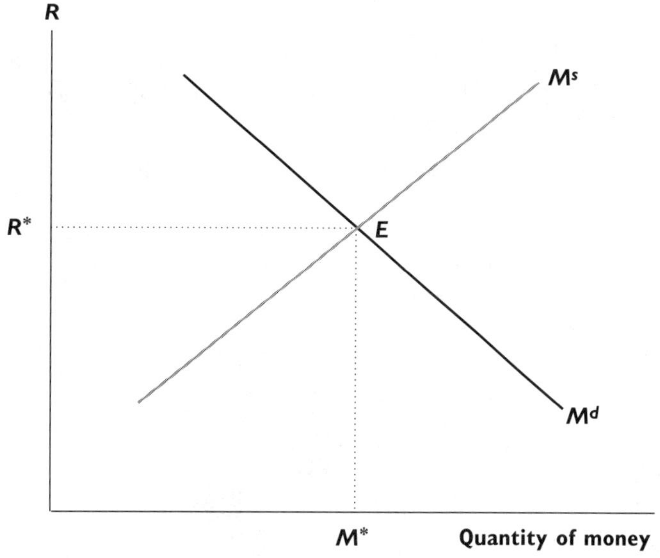


Equilibrium in the money market is at point *E*, the intersection of the demand for money and the supply of money curves. The result determines the equilibrium interest rate level, $R^*$.

## MONETARY POLICY AND INTEREST RATES

One of the most important uses of the liquidity preference framework is in exploring the influence of **monetary policy** on interest rates—that is, the money supply and credit policies of the Bank of Canada. A policy of increasing the money supply is called an **expansionary monetary policy**; a policy of decreasing the money supply is called a **contractionary monetary policy**.

To illustrate the potential impact of monetary policy on interest rate levels, we begin by considering how a reduction in the money supply changes the equilibrium interest rate. The decrease in the level of the money supply causes the money supply curve to shift to the left, from $M_0^s$ to $M_1^s$, as depicted in Figure 6.12. Assuming that the demand for money is held constant at $M_0^d$, the new equilibrium interest rate is $R_1^*$, which is higher than the original equilibrium rate of $R_0^*$. In other words, a contractionary monetary policy signals higher interest rates.

What is the connection between monetary policy and interest rates? In a dynamic economy, even if the demand for money remains fixed, the money supply rises or falls over time implying continual shifts in the money supply curve. Most discussions of the link between monetary policy and interest rates are generally expressed in terms of rates of change in the money supply, so it is useful here

**FIGURE 6.12** Contractionary Monetary Policy

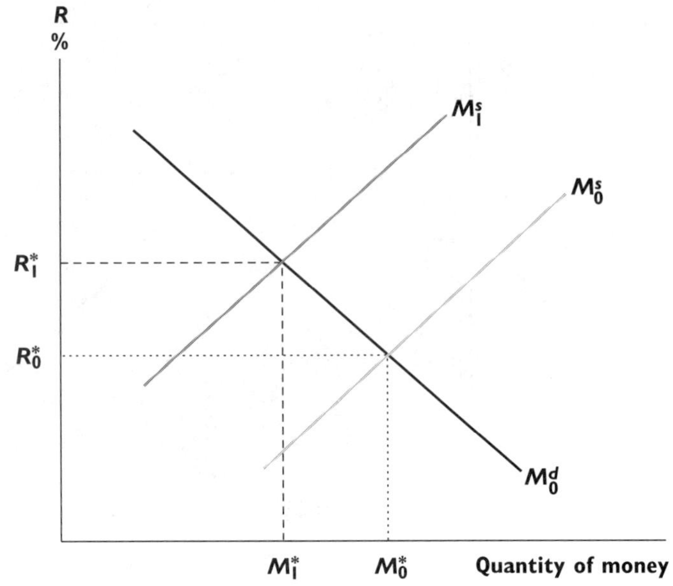


A reduction in the money supply shifts the money supply curve to the left, from $M_0^s$ to $M_1^s$. If the demand for money is held constant at $M_0^d$, the equilibrium interest rate rises to $R_1^*$ and equilibrium money holdings fall to $M_1^*$.

to emphasize the difference between *level changes* and *rates of changes.* Figure 6.13 will help fix some of the ideas.

In Figure 6.13(A), the money supply stays constant at $M_0^s$ until time $t_0$. Then it rises to $M_1^s$ once and for all. Note that given our assumption, the money supply levels remain constant before and after $t_0$. Therefore, there cannot be any growth in the money stock. For this reason, the *rate* of change in the money supply, labelled $g$ in the figure, is zero.

Figure 6.13(B) displays various growth rates over time. Until time $t_0$, the growth rate is $g_0$. Between $t_0$ and $t_1$, the growth rate is negative because the curve describing the evolution of the money supply over time is negatively sloped. By contrast, as the money supply rises between $t_1$ and $t_2$, the curve slopes in the other direction so we know the growth rate in the series is positive again. Finally, after time $t_2$, the money supply curve becomes flat, indicating zero money supply growth ($g_3 = 0$).

It should be clear by now that one way to measure the growth rate in the money supply is to examine the slope of the curve. In algebraic terms, one may compute the rate of change as

**FIGURE 6.13** Types of Changes in the Money Supply

**(A) A Level Change in the Money Supply**

**(B) Changes in Money Supply Growth Rates**

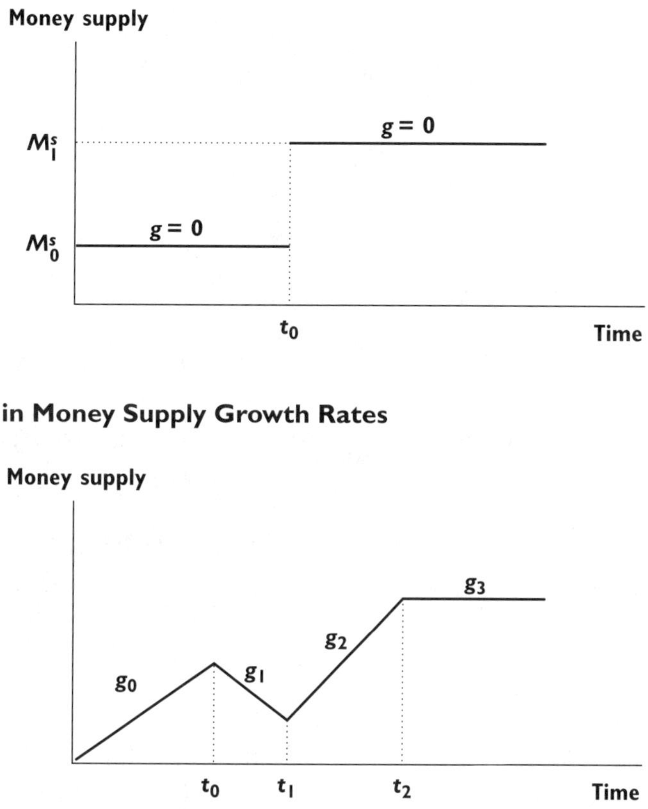


In panel (A), growth is zero ($g$ = 0), except at time $t_0$. In other words, the money supply stays constant over time except during its single jump upward, which is a change in *level* (assumed to be instantaneous). In contrast, panel (B) illustrates several *rates* of growth in the money supply. The rate depends on the slope of the line describing movements in $M_s$ over time.

$$\frac{M_t^s - M_{t-1}^s}{M_{t-1}^s} \times 100 = g \tag{6.9}$$

where $M_t^s$ is the current period's value for the money supply, and $M_{t-1}^s$ is last period's value.[13] Equation (6.9) simply evaluates the change in the money supply from one period to the next as a percent of last period's money supply.

13 An alternative to using equation (6.9) is to compute 100 times the first difference in the logarithm of

**FIGURE 6.14** Money Growth and Interest Rates

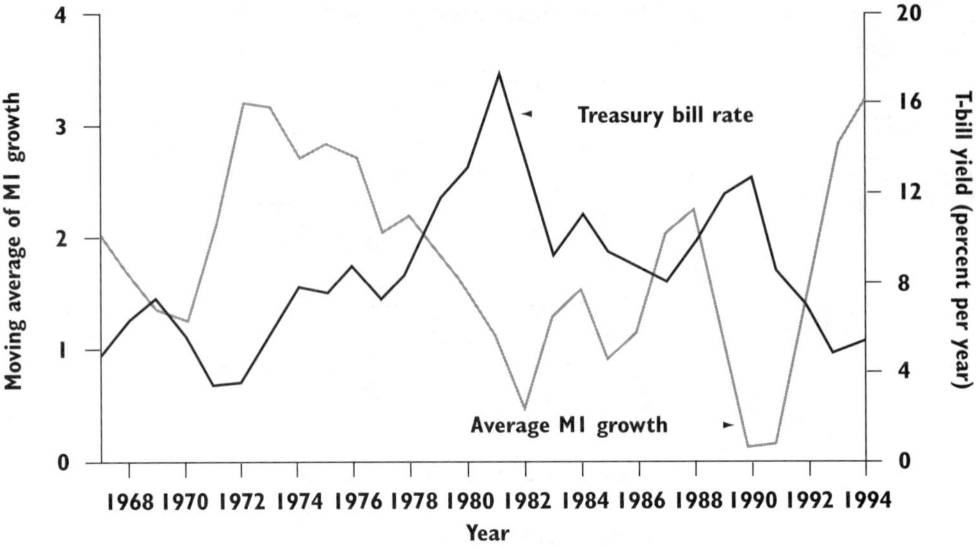


Money growth is measured as a four quarter moving average of the growth rate in M1.

Sources: OECD Main Economic Indicators (various issues) and *Bank of Canada Review* (various issues).

We can now recast our discussion of the link between monetary policy changes and interest rate levels by asking, what is the link between money growth and the interest rate? Figure 6.14 plots average values for money growth along with the yield on 3-month Treasury bills since the late 1960s. The relationship between money growth and interest rates appears to be inverse. When money growth falls, interest rates tend to rise and vice versa.

Let us now try taking our theoretical diagram a little further in Figure 6.15. Until time $t_0$, the money supply growth is zero, which is consistent with an equilibrium interest rate level of $R_0^*$. Now suppose, at time $t_0$, the Bank of Canada announces a policy to reduce the money supply growth from $g_0$ to $g_2$. Doing so requires a temporary negative growth rate, $g_1$, during the period $t_0$ to $t_1$, until the new money supply growth, $g_2$, is reached. According to the evidence in Figure 6.14, the prediction is that the equilibrium interest rate level, $R_1^*$, will be higher than $R_0^*$. And that is exactly what Figure 6.15 shows.

$M^s$—that is, to evaluate $g = \Delta \log M_t^s = \log M_t^s - \log M_{t-1}^s$. Economists tend to prefer this form for evaluating $g$ because there is a natural connection between the use of logarithms and the computation of an elasticity measure.

## FINANCIAL FOCUS 6.1 Why the Rise in Real Interest Rates?

High real interest rates have been a common occurrence in several countries for the last several years (see Figure 5.2). What accounts for the rise? The discussion in this chapter suggests many possible influences on real interest rates, including expected inflation, monetary and fiscal policy, and the business cycle. Two other explanations merit special attention. The first relies on the notion that monetary policy can influence real interest rates. The second involves the volatility of energy prices.

The figure below shows the growth rate of the money supply in Canada since 1955. (The plot is generated by applying equation (6.9) to actual data on the money supply measure M1.) It is clear that the *variability* of money growth (that is, the degree of variation in its fluctuations) has not been constant over time. For example, the standard deviation of money growth (a measure of volatility) is 2.05% for 1955 to 1987; the ex post real interest rate during those years averaged 1.92%. By contrast, the standard deviation of money growth was only 1.15% during 1960 to 1966 when the ex post real interest rate averaged 2.20%. Finally, during the 1980s, money growth variability rose to 2.33% and the average ex post real interest rate soared to 4.92%.

*Money Growth and the Real Interest Rates in Canada*

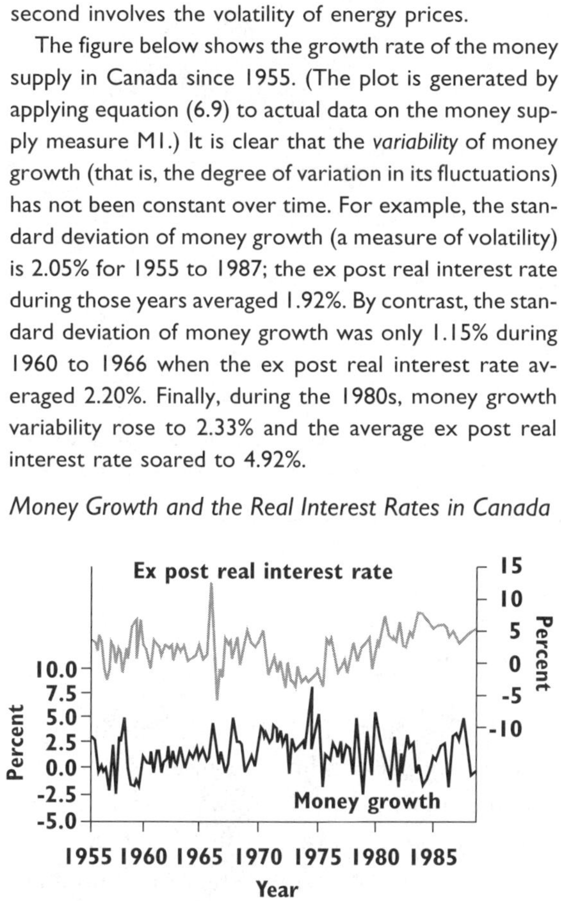


Sources: Pierre L. Siklos, "The Deficit–Interest Rate Link: Empirical Evidence for Canada, "*Applied Economics* 20 (December 1988): 1563–78; Statistics Canada, CANSIM database, as well as the author's calculations.

An increase in money growth variability implies greater shifts in the demand for money function (the $M^d$ curve developed in this chapter) and, consequently, greater uncertainty in expected future returns. The implication is a reduction in the supply of loanable funds (a shift to the left in the $LF^s$ curve as in Figure 6.6(B)) with a consequent rise in the equilibrium real interest rate.

Of course, risk-averse lenders might reduce their demand for loanable funds (as in Figure 6.6(A)) since they are more unsure about whether they can expect a constant positive real return. In that case, the rise in the real interest rate would fall. But Mascaro and Meltzer offer empirical evidence that the overall effect is positive.

Wilcox makes the case for another explanation of real interest rate changes, focusing on the impact of drastic fluctuations in the price of energy relative to other commodities. During the oil price shocks of 1973–74 and 1979, the price of energy rose sharply. Most other commodities require energy as an input to production, so the relatively higher energy prices would also lead to a lower expected return on investment. The results would be a leftward shift in $LF^d$ with a consequent lower real interest rate. The behaviour of real interest rates during the 1970s appears to lend support to the hypothesis.

One would expect the theory to work in reverse so that a falling relative price of energy, as experienced during the early part of the 1990s, would produce a higher real interest rate. Unfortunately, as Tatom points out, the empirical evidence on this account is weak. It is quite conceivable that, as the public became used to persistent inflation, the reversal of inflation expectations was a slow and difficult process.

The lack of symmetry in the prediction of the theory linking energy prices to real interest rate changes leads us to prefer the monetary policy explanation. Other factors may also have been at work.

**Sources:**

A. Mascaro and A.H. Meltzer, "Long- and Short-Term Interest Rates in a Risky World," *Journal of Monetary Economics* (November 1983): 485–518.

J.A. Tatom, "The Macroeconomic Effects of the Recent Fall in Oil Prices," *Review of the Federal Reserve Bank of St. Louis* 69 (June/July 1987): 34–45.

J.A. Wilcox, "Why Real Interest Rates Were So Low in the 1970s," *American Economic Review* 73 (March 1983): 44–54.

**FIGURE 6.15** The Link between Money Growth and the Interest Rate

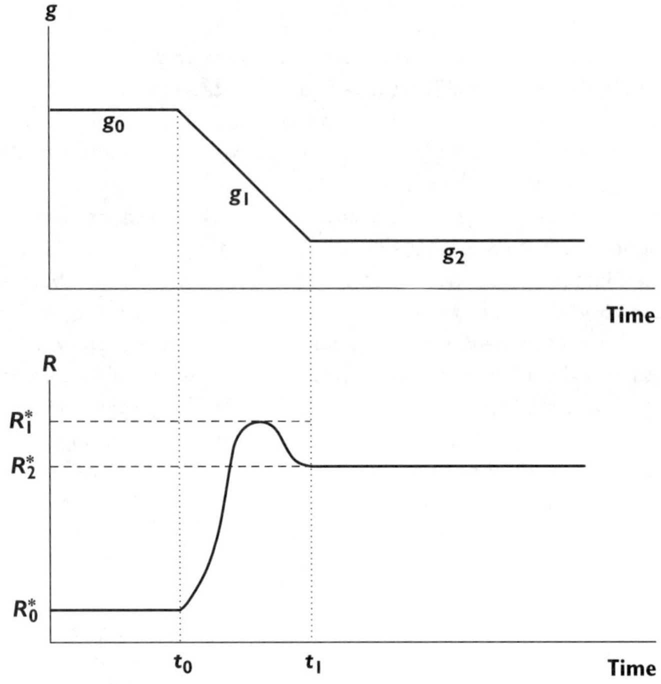


After money supply growth falls from $g_0$ to $g_2$, the interest rate evolves over time from $R_0^*$ to $R_2^*$. The equilibrium interest rate rises as long as we assume that the liquidity effect dominates. This need not always be the case.

Notice, however, that the figure also shows that the transition need not be smooth. What accounts for the humped response of the interest rate in the bottom part of Figure 6.15?

First, the leftward shift in the money supply curve in Figure 6.12 implies less liquidity in the economy. As long as the original equilibrium interest rate, $R_0^*$, holds, there is now excess demand for money, which puts upward pressure on the interest rate. Consequently, the interest rate rises to $R_1^*$. But the story does not end here. Eventually, the reduction in the money supply affects real income and the price level because, as we saw in Figure 6.10, a lower equilibrium money stock is associated with a lower level of income. As real income and the price level both fall, the demand for money curve also shifts to the left, potentially offsetting the initial increase in the interest rate level. Thus, in Figure 6.15, the equilibrium interest rate ends up at $R_2^*$, higher than it was originally but not quite as high as it rose at first. We have, therefore, assumed that the interest rate response to a change in money supply growth is dominated by the liquidity effect.

It must be emphasized, however, that it is possible for the real-income and price-level effects to dominate the liquidity effect.[14] In such a case, one would obtain a lower interest rate despite a fall in money supply growth.

The question, of course, is an empirical one. Nevertheless, it is important to realize that any link between money growth and the interest rate depends critically upon the central bank's ability to control the money supply, an ability that should not be taken for granted. (We'll discuss this point further in Chapter 24.)

## SUMMARY

- The determination of interest rate level can be understood in two ways:
  –The loanable funds approach examines the operation of the bond market.
  –The liquidity preference approach views individuals as deciding between holding bonds or money.

  In both approaches, it is the interactions of the demand for and supply of financial assets that determine the equilibrium interest rate.
- Some of the important factors that cause interest rates to change over time include liquidity, risk, expectations of future inflation, and government policies.
- Economists discern three reasons for individuals' holding money: the transactions motive, the precautionary motive, and the speculative motive.
- Monetary policy, as practised by the Bank of Canada, influences interest rates. Government actions in the bond market can also cause interest rates to change.

## IMPORTANT TERMS

constant (real) GDP (p. 133)
contractionary monetary policy (p. 135)
current dollar GDP (p. 133)
demand for money (p. 131)
equilibrium interest rate (p. 116)
expansionary monetary policy (p. 135)
liquidity preference (p. 127)
loanable funds (p. 115)
monetary policy (p. 135)
nominal income (p. 131)
opportunity cost (p. 130)
precautionary motive (p. 130)
real income (p. 131)
speculative motive (p. 130)
transactions motive (p. 130)

14 Some economists now believe that the liquidity effect no longer exists. See, for example, Y. Mehra, "Inflationary Expectations, Money Growth, and the Vanishing Liquidity Effect of Money on Interest: A Further Investigation," Federal Reserve Bank of Richmond, *Economic Review* 71 (March/April 1985): 23–35. An article by James D. Hamilton arrives at the opposite conclusion. See "Measuring the Liquidity Effect," working paper, University of California, San Diego (1995).

# EXERCISES

1. If the demand for loanable funds by the business sector decreases because of a recession but the demand for loanable funds by the government increases by an amount greater than the decreased demand, how is the equilibrium interest rate affected? Show the change on an appropriate diagram.

2. One way the Bank of Canada affects the money supply is by selling federal government bonds to the public. This is also known as an *open market operation.* Use the loanable funds framework to show the effect on the equilibrium interest rate.

3. How does the policy described in question 2 affect the Canadian money supply? Use the liquidity preference framework.

4. Suppose the Bank of Canada succeeds in persuading investors that inflation is expected to fall in the future. Trace the effects such a policy would have, based on the Fisher effect, on the nominal interest rate. Use the loanable funds diagram for your answer.

5. Under the new Bank Act (1992), required reserve requirements for chartered banks were phased out. Does this mean that banks will choose to hold no reserves? Why or why not? What will all such reserves be called when the policy is fully in place?

6. How would accelerating money growth affect the nominal interest rate? (Hint: Use a diagram such as Figure 6.15.)

7. What would be the impact of a sudden and immediate increase in money growth on the nominal interest rate? Would you qualify your answer? If so, how? (Hint: Again, use a diagram such as Figure 6.15.)

8. Using the loanable funds model, show graphically how taxes drive a wedge between nominal and real interest rates.

9. The Bank of Canada believes that slower money growth leads to higher interest rates and that these rates are necessary to fight inflation. Under what conditions will the Bank of Canada's policy work? Use the liquidity preference approach and explain your answer with a diagram.

10. Assume that the economy produces two goods A and B. The table below provides details of the prices and quantities consumed over a two-year period.

| Base Year | Quantities | Price |
|---|---|---|
| A | 20 | $40 |
| B | 30 | $20 |
| Following Year | | |
| A | 10 | $80 |
| B | 25 | $35 |

Find GDP and real GDP using both the fixed-weight and chain-weighted methods.

**11.** In Figure 6.1, changes in the long-term government bond yield appear less abrupt than changes in the Treasury bill rate. Can you think of a reason why?

**12.** Explain, using the loanable funds and liquidity preference frameworks, how an oil price shock might raise the nominal interest rate.

**13.** In Figure 6.8, the Treasury bill rate falls sharply after 1990, that is, since the Bank of Canada and the federal government agreed on a set of inflation targets. Is there a connection? Use the loanable funds framework for your answer.

# REFERENCES


Gapinski, J.H. *Macroeconomic Theory: Statics, Dynamics and Policy.* New York: McGraw-Hill, 1982, chapter 3.

Harris, L. *Monetary Theory.* New York: McGraw-Hill, 1981.

Keynes, J.M. *The General Theory of Employment, Interest and Money.* London: Macmillan, 1936.

Mehra, Y. "Inflationary Expectations, Money Growth, and the Vanishing Liquidity Effect of Money on Interest: A Further Investigation." Federal Reserve Bank of Richmond, *Economic Review* 71 (March/April 1985): 23–35.

Patinkin, D. *Money, Interest and Prices.* New York: Harper & Row, 1965.

Statistics Canada, CANSIM database.

CHAPTER 7

# Understanding Exchange Rates

So far we have concentrated on domestic financial instruments—that is, those denominated in Canadian dollars. Canadian investors can, however, purchase securities in different currencies, and foreigners can obtain financial instruments in Canadian dollars. These possibilities provide opportunities. They also pose an additional problem for investors, who must concern themselves with exchange rates—the prices at which they buy and sell different currencies.

Although exchange rates can be influenced by a number of factors, the principal ones are the flow of goods and services and the flow of funds (capital) across international borders. In this textbook we concentrate on the influence of capital flows, which is of particular interest in understanding financial systems.

Government policy aimed at regulating changes in the exchange rate is another important factor covered in a discussion of exchange rate régimes. We consider the role of exchange rates in interest rate determination, as well as how prices in different countries are related to each other through the exchange rate and how exchange rates are influenced by price developments in different countries. Knowing how exchange rates are determined is a vital first step in understanding the interrelationship of interest rates and inflation rates in different countries.

## EXCHANGE RATES

Because Canada is a small, open economy, most Canadian students are familiar with the idea of currency exchange. Nevertheless, some of the terminology and concepts involved are slippery, so we start our discussion of exchange rates with some definitions. Then we briefly consider how prices are linked internationally by exchange rates.

## DEFINITIONS

An **exchange rate** represents the price of one currency in terms of another. Table 7.1 provides the actual exchange rates that prevailed on a particular day in January 1996 between the Canadian dollar and six foreign currencies.

Notice that any exchange rate can be expressed in two ways:

1 unit of country A's currency = $x$ units of country B's currency

or

1 unit of country B's currency = $y$ units of country A's currency

Let us consider a couple of examples. Looking at the first column we see that

C\$1 = US\$ 0.72601

while examination of the first row reveals that

US\$1 = C\$ 1.3774

In other words, one Canadian dollar buys approximately 73 US cents or 1 US dollar is equivalent to about \$1.38 in Canadian currency. As a second example, by reading down the first column of Table 7.1, we find

C\$1 = DM1.0810

But by reading across, we find

DM1 = C\$0.92505

The point seems obvious (after all, 1.0810 = 1 ÷ 0.92505), but it often causes confusion in discussions. To avoid the problem, whenever we speak of the exchange rate in this textbook, we are referring to the price of one unit of a foreign currency in terms of Canadian dollars. In other words, the exchange rate, which is denoted by $e$, will be interpreted as

$e$ = Canadian dollars/1 unit of foreign currency

In Table 7.1, you can read the exchange rate for the Canadian dollar vis-à-vis the Japanese yen as 0.01284, which means that about 1.28¢ buys 1 Japanese yen.

### Cross-Rates

The data in the table also allow us to determine the value of any currency listed in relation to any other. For example, \$1 US is equivalent to 0.67159 deutschmark and \$1 US yields \$1.3774 Cdn. So we can calculate

**TABLE 7.1** A SELECTION OF EXCHANGE RATES

| Currency | C$ | US$ | DM | ¥ | £ | FFr | SFr |
|---|---|---|---|---|---|---|---|
| Canadian dollar, C$ | • | 1.3774 | 0.92505 | 0.01284 | 2.0737 | 0.26905 | 1.1325 |
| US Dollar, US$ | 0.72601 | • | 0.67159 | 0.00932 | 1.5055 | 0.19533 | 0.82223 |
| Deutschmark, DM | 1.0810 | 1.4890 | • | 0.01388 | 2.2417 | 0.29085 | 1.2243 |
| Japanese yen, ¥ | 77.879 | 107.27 | 72.042 | • | 161.49 | 20.953 | 88.201 |
| British pound, £ | 0.48224 | 0.66423 | 0.44609 | 0.00619 | • | 0.12975 | 0.54615 |
| French Franc, FFr | 3.7168 | 5.1195 | 3.4382 | 0.04773 | 7.7074 | • | 4.2094 |
| Swiss Franc, SFr | 0.88297 | 1.2162 | 0.81679 | 0.1134 | 1.8310 | 0.23756 | • |

Source: *The Financial Post*, 31 January 1996. The exchange rates published are those determined in the late afternoon of each business day.

$$\frac{\$\text{C in terms of the US\$}}{\text{DM in terms of the US\$}} = \frac{1.3774}{1.4890} = 0.92505$$
$$= 0.92505$$
$$= 1 \text{ C\$ in terms of the DM}$$

which is called computing the **cross-rate** between the Canadian dollar and the deutschmark. Our calculation agrees with the published rate shown in Table 7.1.

Knowing how to calculate cross-rates is useful because they are not published for all currencies (there is insufficient demand for many possible cross-rates). Suppose you wish to find the exchange rate of the Italian lira in terms of the Mexican peso. On 31 January 1996, one Canadian dollar could purchase 5.3652 Mexican pesos (or you needed .18639 C$ to buy one peso); on the same day one Canadian dollar was worth 1161.6 Italian lire (or you needed .00086 C$ to buy one lira). Therefore, one Mexican peso would buy

$$\frac{1{,}161.6}{5.3652} = 216.50637 \text{ lire}$$

## Changes in Rates

Another set of exchange rate definitions involve changes in currency values. When the market brings about changes in an exchange rate (which it does frequently), these changes inform us when a currency has **appreciated** (increased) or **depreciated** (decreased) in value. For example, in 1986 the exchange rate of the Canadian dollar vis-à-vis the US dollar averaged 1.3894. By 31 January 1996, the rate was 1.3774 (see Table 7.1). It cost fewer Canadian dollars to purchase one US dollar. The Canadian dollar had appreciated and the US dollar had depreciated.

In some cases a country's exchange rates are set by government regulation rather than the market (we'll examine how later in this chapter). A governmentdecreed increase in the value of one currency vis-à-vis another is termed a **revaluation** and a decrease is termed a **devaluation.**

## EFFECTIVE OR TRADE-WEIGHTED EXCHANGE RATES

Exchange rates are sometimes averaged over several currencies. A weighted average measure is used since the proportion of a country's trade with one country can be quite different from trade with another. For example, in the second quarter of 1995, 80.4% of merchandise exports went to the US. The next largest major export recipients were the European Union (EU; 5.6%) and Japan (4.9%). In the case of imports, we buy mainly from the US (66.5%), followed again by the EU (9.4%) and Japan (3.7%).[1] If the remaining trade is with the "rest of the world," then a trade-weighted exchange rate would be calculated as:

$$w_1 e_{\mathrm{US}} + w_2 e_{\mathrm{EU}} + w_3 e_{\mathrm{J}} + w_4 e_{\mathrm{ROW}}$$

where the $w$ represent the weights which, of course, add up to one, and $e$ is the exchange rate for the US, the EU, Japan and the rest of the world.[2]

## THE LAW OF ONE PRICE

Exchange rates provide a link between the prices prevailing in two countries. For example, suppose a bottle of California wine costs $10 in US currency. What is its price in Canadian dollars? If the exchange rate between two currencies is $1.14, the answer is

$$\$10 \times \$1.14 = \$11.40$$

More generally, the domestic price of an item produced abroad and imported can be written

$$P^f e = P \tag{7.1}$$

where

$P^f$ = the foreign price of the commodity
$e$ = the exchange rate
$P$ = the domestic or local price of the same commodity[3]

Thus, prices in Canada are linked to foreign prices via the exchange rate.

---

1 Data are from the *Bank of Canada Review* (Fall 1995), Table J2.

2 Of course, there is no such thing as an exchange rate for the EU or the rest of the world. These could, in principle, be separately calculated as trade-weighted exchange rates. Effective exchange rates are often published in index form. For example, in May 1995, the index for the C$ stood at 83.2 (1990 = 100) meaning that the Canadian dollar fell roughly 16.8% in value against the currencies of the countries it trades with. See *International Financial Statistics* (Washington, D.C.: International Monetary Fund).

3 Ordinarily, this is not the same as the prices discussed in earlier chapters (see note 4, this chapter). The approach followed here has the virtue, however, of avoiding the introduction of a new notation.

One way of understanding the relationship implied in equation (7.1) is to call it the **law of one price**. This law stipulates that the domestic price of a commodity should be equal to the foreign price converted into domestic terms through the exchange rate. That is, the price of a commodity should be the same in Canada as in the United States and in Australia and in Japan.

Few economists accept this law literally. Importing commodities creates a variety of costs, such as those for transportation as well as the transactions costs of converting foreign currencies into the domestic currency, to name but two complicating factors. Moreover, the law of one price can apply only to commodities that can be traded.[4]

By contrast, capital can flow from one country to the next at very low cost. Therefore, one would expect a kind of law of one price to apply to financial instruments. The difficulty is that investors who purchase securities denominated in a foreign currency have locked their funds into that currency even if only for a brief time. Hence, they must be concerned not only with today's exchange rate, which is called the **spot rate**, but also with the exchange rate that will prevail when the funds are converted back into the original currency. In other words, investors must make some sort of a guess about future or expected exchange rates (a question we develop in more detail in Chapter 15).

Nevertheless, for anyone who has doubted the importance of the law of one price, the recent experience of German reunification has illustrated the potentially devastating consequences of sidestepping exchange rate considerations.

## EXCHANGE RATE SYSTEMS

How are exchange rates determined? This depends first on the exchange rate system or régime a country has chosen. Most exchange rate systems can be classified as belonging to one of three categories:

1. A **fixed exchange rate system** in which the country's currency is pegged to another currency, such as the US dollar or the French franc. In the past, many currencies were pegged to gold.
2. A **flexible exchange rate system**, also called a *floating system*, in which market forces are allowed to determine the exchange level independently.
3. A **managed float system**, sometimes called a **"dirty" float**, in which some central authority, such as a central bank, intervenes in the market for foreign exchange to hold the rate at some desired level (usually a range of levels).

4 Labour, for example, is not generally considered a commodity tradable across international boundaries (the costs of commuting and of dealing regularly with customs officials would be prohibitive; moreover, immigration is generally regulated). Many services are also *non-traded commodities*; a taxicab ride in Montreal simply has no value to someone in Vermont.

## FINANCIAL FOCUS 7.1 Exchange Rates and Politics: The Case of German Reunification

When the former East Germany and West Germany were reunited on 30 June 1990, two price and currency systems had to be merged into one. One of the key economic questions was the exchange rate that would be used to convert East German ostmarks into deutschmarks. East Germans were wary of having to convert essentially worthless currency into a strong currency, fearing that their monetary wealth would be wiped out. Their leaders wanted a one-for-one exchange. By contrast, the German central bank, always mindful of the need to control inflation, proposed a 2-ostmark-for-1-deutschmark exchange. There was an uproar. The then president of the Bundesbank, Karl Otto Pöhl, resigned in July 1991. He later complained that the German politicians had made "impossibly costly promises" and that the exchange rates between the deutschmark and the ostmark was too generous for holders of the latter currency. What politicians were missing in this argument is that there are always winners and losers in the game of currency conversion. Clearly, individuals holding assets would be hurt by a two-for-one exchange rate but debtholders would be hurt by a one-for-one exchange rate.

Politics interfered and a compromise was reached. Below specific levels—4,000 ostmarks in general but 2,000 for those under 14 years of age and 6,000 for those over 59 years of age—individuals received one deutschmark for each ostmark deposited in the bank. Above these limits, the exchange rate was two for one. A total of 191 billion ostmarks were converted, 66 billions at the 1:1 rate and 125 billions at the 2:1 rate. The black market exchange rate at the time was 7:1.

Only nine months later, the president of the Bundesbank declared monetary union a disaster. Although the actual reasons for the disaster are complex, the law of one price is helpful in explaining an important source of the difficulties with the monetary union of two economically unequal states.

A survey reported in the *Wall Street Journal* shortly before monetary union gave then-current prices for four commodities likely to be comparable in quality.

| | Price in DMs | Price in Ostmarks |
|---|---|---|
| Loaf of rye bread | 3.17 | 0.52 |
| Potatoes (5 kg) | 4.94 | 0.85 |
| Electricity per kW•h | 0.42 | 0.08 |
| Coffee (1 kg) | 17.86 | 70.00 |

If the law of one price holds, the exchange rate to equilibrate the two sets of prices would be, according to equation (7.1).

| $e = P/P^f$ ($P$ = ostmark/ $P^f$ = DM) |
|---|
| 0.16 |
| 0.17 |
| 0.19 |
| 3.92 |

Clearly, the ratio of actual prices was not compatible with an exchange rate of one for one. Moreover, all the items on the list except coffee were highly subsidized by the East German state. With reunification, these subsidies disappeared, and with them any competitive advantage of the kind suggested in the table above. Thus, it is perhaps not surprising that the former East Germany experienced a depression of sorts with a fall in real GNP of at least 15% within months of the monetary union.

**Sources:**

G.A. Akerloff, A.K. Rose, J.L. Yellen, and H. Hessenius, "East Germany in from the Cold: The Economic Aftermath of Currency Union," *Brookings Papers on Economic Activity* 1 (1991): 1–106.

A. Fisher, "Pöhl Accuses Bonn of Risking D. Mark," *Financial Times of London*, 15 May 1992, p. 2.

T. Roth, "East German Winners in Election Now Seek Fast Monetary Union," *Wall Street Journal*, 20 March 1990.

Many countries do not have a pure form of any of the three systems. Table 7.2 gives the exchange rate arrangements of 31 countries as classified by the International Monetary Fund (IMF). Notice that that international body found it necessary to create a category for a system with flexibility limited by a co-operative agreement; it applies to the European Monetary System (EMS) currently used among countries of the European Community.

Notice too that the IMF classified Canada's system as of the independent floating variety. But the Bank of Canada (like the central banks of most countries) often does intervene in the market for foreign exchange. By manipulating official reserves of foreign exchange, it can influence the supply of foreign currencies (principally the US dollar) and thus the value of the Canadian dollar in relation to other currencies.[5]

## EXCHANGE RATE DETERMINATION

Now we are ready to consider the determination of exchange rates. To fix ideas, we consider the two extremes in régimes: purely flexible exchange rates and fixed exchange rates.

We can view the determination of the exchange rates in much the same way as the determination of the price of any commodity: as the result of the interaction of the forces of demand and supply. Figure 7.1 illustrates. The horizontal axes measure the quantity of foreign exchange (US dollars) demanded and supplied, while the vertical axes measure the price per Canadian dollar, which is the exchange rate.

Consider first the flexible exchange rate régime case depicted in Figure 7.1(A). The demand curve for foreign exchange, $D_0$, is downward sloping because a lower exchange rate implies that the Canadian dollar appreciates in value against the US dollar. Therefore, it becomes cheaper to buy US dollars. By contrast, a lower exchange rate means that holders of US dollars can now receive fewer Canadian dollars in exchange. These individuals thus supply the market for foreign exchange with smaller quantities of US dollars, so the supply curve, $S_0$, is upward sloping. Of course, transactions take place only when the market attains an equilibrium, which occurs at point $E_0$. We'll arbitrarily say the exchange rate it represents is $1.15.

In a floating exchange rate system, demand and supply are allowed to shift freely through time in reaction to other changes. For example, Canadian interest

5 The Bank of Canada argues that it attempts to reduce the volatility—see Chapter 12 for one definition of volatility—of exchange rates rather than seeking to target a particular exchange rate level. For example, see "Notes for remarks by J.W. Crow, Governor of the Bank of Canada," *Bank of Canada Review*, November 1992.

**TABLE 7.2** EXCHANGE RATE ARRANGEMENTS

| Pegged to: | | | | | | Limited Flexibility | | | More Flexible | |
|---|---|---|---|---|---|---|---|---|---|---|
| US Dollar | French Franc | Russian Ruble | Other | SDR[a] | Other Composite[b] | Single Currency[c] | Co-operative Arrangements[d] | Selected Indicators[e] | Managed Floating | Independent Floating |
| Barbados | Cameroon | Tajikistan | Estonia (DM) | Lybia | Iceland | Saudia Arabia | Austria | Chile | China, P.R. | Canada |
| Panama | Congo | | San Marino (Lira) | | Czech R. | | Belgium | Ecuador | Greece | Italy |
| | | | | | | | Denmark | | Hungary | United States |
| | | | | | | | France | | | United Kingdom |
| | | | | | | | Germany | | | Russian Federation |
| | | | | | | | Ireland | | | |
| | | | | | | | Luxembourg | | | |
| | | | | | | | Netherlands | | | |
| | | | | | | | Portugal | | | |
| | | | | | | | Spain | | | |

[a] Special Drawing Rights
[b] Basket of currencies of the country's choice
[c] Usually means limited flexibility via-à-vis the US dollar
[d] European Monetary System (EMS)
[e] Selected by individual countries but adjusted at frequent intervals

Source: International Monetary Fund, *International Financial Statistics* (August 1995): 8. As of 31 March 1995. The list of countries is incomplete.

rates might rise, increasing the attractiveness of domestic financial instruments relative to those denominated in US dollars.[6] Both the supply of and the demand for US dollars would change as investors attempted to take advantage of the higher rates in Canada. Similarly, changes in Canadian–US exports and imports of goods and services would shift the demand and supply curves for foreign exchange, respectively. These details are best left for macroeconomic texts so they are not pursued here. You could, however, explore the question of interest rate effects as an exercise.

Figure 7.1(B) depicts a market in which the exchange rate is *pegged* (fixed) at \$1.15 by government policy. The government guarantees to maintain the exchange rate at the stated figure. The Bank of Canada must, therefore, ensure that the quantity of US dollars supplied in the foreign exchange rate market is sufficient to be equal to the quantity demanded to create a market-clearing price of \$1.15 at all times.[7] Should the pegged rate be changed, the supply curve shifts—upward if the Canadian dollar is devalued and downward if it is revalued.

6 This assumption is made by abstracting from considerations of differences in risk, which we begin to address in Chapter 13.

7 In other words, the supply curve of foreign exchange is perfectly elastic.

**FIGURE 7.1** Exchange Rate Determination

### (A) Flexible Exchange Rates

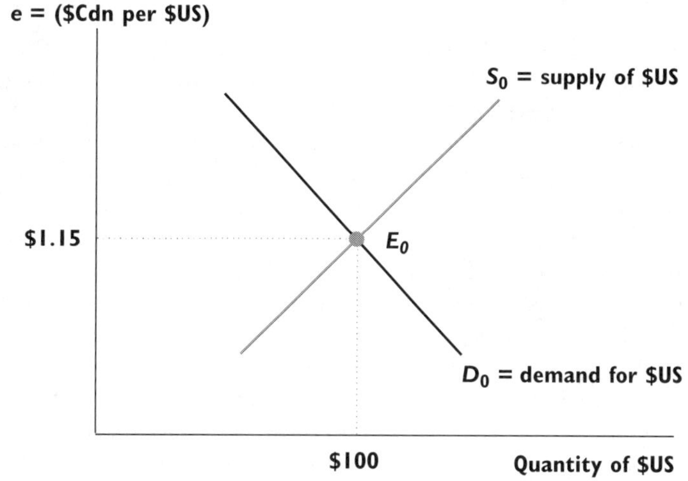


### (B) Fixed Exchange Rates

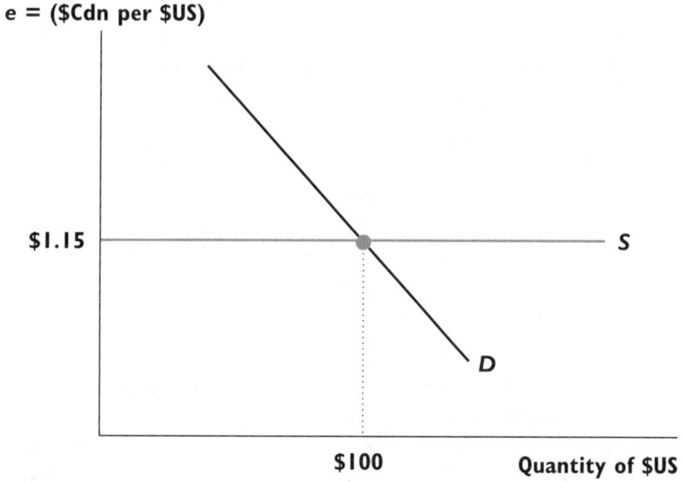


For clarity, we have set up both models here with an arbitrarily assumed exchange rate of $1.15 Cdn for $1 US. The difference between the two diagrams is how the exchange rate is determined. In panel (A), the driving force is the market. The supply curve for US dollars, labelled $S_0$, is upward sloping because a depreciation of the Canadian dollar makes it more attractive to supply US dollars to buy cheaper Canadian dollars. Since this also makes US dollars more expensive to buy, the quantity of them demanded falls, making the demand curve for foreign exchange, $D_0$, downward sloping. Equilibrium is the point at which $D_0$ intersects $S_0$.

In panel (B), the exchange rate is fixed by the government at $1.15. To guarantee this rate, the Bank of Canada has to supply sufficient quantities of US dollars to keep the supply curve, S, flat.

## FINANCIAL FOCUS 7.2 Peso Problems and the Pitfalls of Exchange Rate Management

Milton Friedman is apparently credited for coining the term "**peso problem**" in his analysis of the behaviour of the Mexican peso during the 1970s. This problem arises because, as we have seen, economic theory predicts that an exchange rate should be devalued if the domestic inflation rate exceeds inflation in other countries. However, in some instances, the decision to devalue may take many years more than most would expect and the Mexican peso is a case in point. Between April 1954 and August 1976 the exchange rate of the peso was fixed at .08 dollars per peso. During this time, consumer prices in Mexico more than tripled while the CPI only doubled in value in the US, Mexico's largest trading partner. It clearly took an inordinate amount of time for the peso to be devalued.

A similar event appears to have taken place in late 1994 when the Mexican government decided to allow the peso to float following a devaluation of 15% announced on 20 December 1994. The result was disastrous for the Mexican economy whose output fell by more than 20% in 1995 while the world's capital markets were shaken by the decision. For Mexico, the decision to float was supposed to be the crowning achievement of a struggle to relieve itself of previously acquired large foreign debts and was to be the culmination of a drive to modernize its political and economic system. But the devaluation and subsequent sharp depreciation of the peso reflected the markets' view that not all was well with the Mexican economy. Much of the capital inflows during the 1990–93 period was for short-term portfolio investment and not destined to finance infrastructure development or plant and equipment construction. Moreover, the Mexican banking system, largely state-owned, was financially weak. Finally, the rebellion in the Chiapas region of the country, the assassination of a presidential candidate, and political intrigue, meant that the new government of President Ernesto Zedillo, elected in August 1994, inspired little confidence inside or outside Mexico. The events in Mexico, on the heels of the passage of the North American Free Trade Agreement (NAFTA), produced a crisis in the US where politicians became concerned that, almost overnight, the US economy would become flooded with now suddenly cheap Mexican goods. The US government proposed a rescue package but the newly elected Republican Congress refused to go along with the plan and President Clinton was forced to use the country's Exchange Stabilization Fund to bail-out Mexico to the tune of $20 billion. Canada, Germany, and other countries and financial institutions were also somewhat reluctant participants in a deal which saw a total of $50 billion. The events which transpired in major capitals around the world in late 1994 and early 1995 is the stuff of intrigues found in suspense novels.

Other analysts of the Mexican crisis attributed the devaluation and subsequent crisis to balance-of-payments problems, a subject we will cover in Chapter 23.

**Sources:**

G. Graham, P. Norman, S. Fiddler, T. Bardacke, "Bitter Legacy of Battle to Bail-Out Mexico," *The Financial Times of London*, 16 February 1995.

*International Capital Markets: Developments, Prospects, and Policy Issues*, World Economic and Financial Surveys (Washington, D.C.: International Monetary Fund, 1995).

Martin D.D. Evans, "Peso Problems: Their Theoretical and Empirical Implications," *Handbook of Statistics*, Ed. By G.S. Maddala and C.R. Rao (1995).

G.A. Calvo and E.G. Mendoza, "Reflections on Mexico's Balance-of-Payments Crisis: A Chronicle of a death Foretold?", working paper, University of Maryland, 1995.

## ECONOMICS FOCUS 7.1 Longing for the Gold Standard

During the early 1980s there was a resurgence in interest in returning to the *gold standard*, a form of fixed exchange rates largely abandoned earlier this century. A country using a gold standard undertakes to fix the price of gold at some value and to ensure that its currency is freely convertible against it.

If most countries are on a gold standard, exchange rates are fixed and exchange rate risk is eliminated.

Another attraction of the gold standard is that it provides the inflationary discipline modern-day governments appear to lack. For example, when Canada was on the gold standard (from Confederation until World War I), it generally experienced deflation.

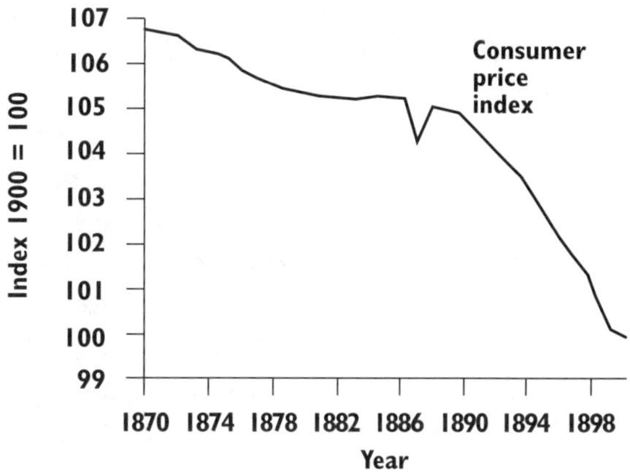


Given the roaring inflation of the 1970s and early 1980s, it is not surprising that many politicians and others yearned for a return to the gold standard in some form. Yet historically the gold standard in history failed largely for two reasons: governments were unwilling to maintain a fixed exchange rate in times of financial crisis or wars, and it prevents the flexibility of conducting policy, both monetary and fiscal, that voters expect politicians to be responsible for.

A pure gold standard is akin to a rigidly fixed exchange rate. Since it leaves no room for domestic fiscal and monetary policymakers to pursue economic policies independent of other countries', any policy to control the money supply has no significance. The loss of monetary control occurs because of what the classical economist David Hume best described as the price-specie-flow mechanism where specie is gold; essentially, a change in price causes inflows or outflows of gold, which, in turn, provide the focus that will equilibrate prices between countries in the manner described in the text.

**Sources:**

J.A. Dorn and A.J. Schwartz, *The Search for Stable Money: Essays on Monetary Reform* (Chicago: The University of Chicago Press, 1983).

B. Eichengreen, *The Gold Standard in Theory and History* (New York: Methuen, 1985).

G. Rich, *The Cross of Gold: Money and the Canadian Business Cycle, 1867–1913* (Ottawa: Carleton University Press, 1988).

# THE EXCHANGE RATE AND INTEREST RATE DETERMINATION

When we used the loanable funds framework to explain the determination of the equilibrium interest rate in Chapter 6, we implicitly assumed that all borrowing and lending occurred in a domestic market. What happens if the model reflects capital flows across international boundaries?[8] Consider Figure 7.2, which depicts the impact of international lending and borrowing on the Canadian economy. The curve labelled $LF^s$ is the supply of loanable funds ignoring international considerations. It is, in other words, the same as the supply curve we examined in Chapter 6. Now let us drop the assumption of restriction to the domestic economy and draw a new curve that reflects the supply of loanable funds from both Canadians and foreigners. We can label it $LF^s + LF^{sf}$.

Where will we put the new curve? We can assume that foreigners will be attracted to Canadian investments if, other things being equal, the rate on Canadian securities is relatively higher than that prevailing in other countries.[9] Suppose that the latter rate is 10%. At this rate, Canadian and foreign interest rates are equally attractive, so the total quantity of loanable funds supplied will be the same as if international considerations were ignored. That consideration gives us our first quantity, $B_0$, along the loanable funds supply curve $B^s + B^{sf}$. Now suppose that the interest rate on Canadian securities rises to more than 10%.[10] They become relatively more attractive, prompting an inflow of funds, which means an increase in the total quantity of funds supplied. The result is quantity $B_1$. Not surprisingly, when Canadian interest rates are lower than elsewhere, the opposite takes place: capital funds flow out of Canada, reducing the quantity supplied to $B_2$.

Notice the difference between slopes $LF^s$ and $LF^s + LF^{sf}$. The supply of loanable funds is more responsive to interest rate changes when foreign plus domestic funds are considered.[11] This is because when interest rates in Canada increase relative to those in the rest of the world, loanable funds supplied are increased by foreign lending, and Canadian interest rates that are low relative to those of the rest of the world turn foreigners into borrowers.

The effects of international borrowing and lending on the equilibrium interest rate are shown in Figure 7.2(B). When only domestic considerations matter, that rate is $R_0$, which is obtained at the intersection of $LF_0^d$ and $LF^s$. Introducing international borrowing and lending initially makes no difference since the demand for loanable funds, $LF_0^d$, intersects $LF^s + LF^{sf}$ also at $R_0$. But if the demand for loanable funds shifts to $LF_1^d$, then with international borrowing and lending

---

8 We could also use the liquidity preference framework to address the same question. But nothing of substance would be gained for the following discussion.

9 The rate for comparison need not be that of the United States alone, although it often is. We can view the comparison as between Canadian interest rates and some average of interest rates in, say, all industrialized countries.

10 Canadian interest rates might become relatively high for a variety of reasons. One is the risk involved in Canadian investments might be perceived as relatively high. We deal with perceptions of risk in Ch. 13.

11 That is, with international lending and borrowing, the supply of loanable funds becomes more elastic.

**FIGURE 7.2** Loanable Funds with International Borrowing and Lending

## (A) Total Supply of Loanable Funds

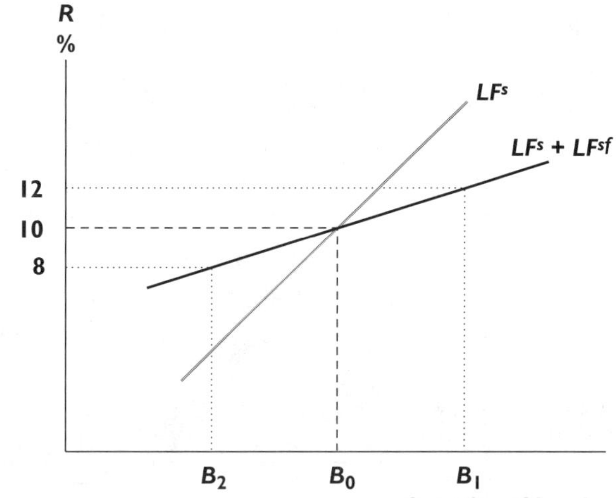


## (B) Equilibrium with International Lending and Borrowing

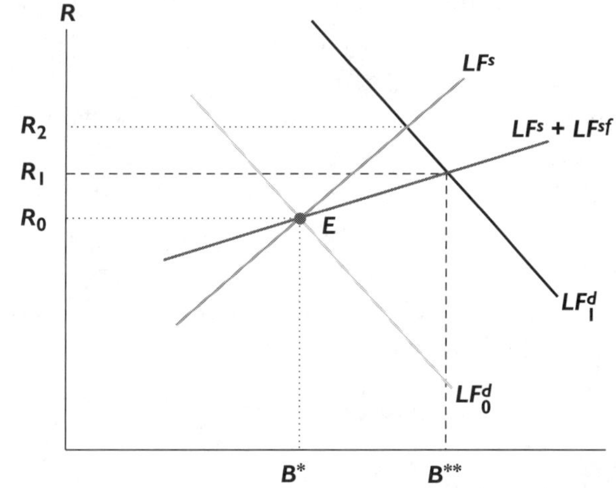


In panel (A), the domestic supply of loanable funds, $LF^s$, is supplemented by foreign funds, $LF^{sf}$, so long as the interest rate exceeds a certain rate (here assumed to be 10%). Below that rate, funds are invested abroad.

In panel (B), international lending and borrowing affect the equilibrium interest rate depending on the location of the demand for loanable funds. On $LF^d_0$, the effect is nil. But on $LF^d_1$, the equilibrium interest rate is $R_1$, which is lower than $R_2$, the equilibrium rate if international considerations are ignored.

the equilibrium interest rate is $R_1$. Note that this interest rate is lower than $R_2$, which is where the new equilibrium would be if international considerations were ignored. Of course, the opposite conclusion would hold if the demand curve for loanable funds shifted lower than $LF_0^d$. We leave the solution to this problem to you as an exercise.

In brief, the principles used to find the equilibrium interest rate are the same whether international considerations are ignored or not, but international considerations are likely to affect the actual level of the equilibrium interest rate because they make the quantity of loanable funds relatively more sensitive to interest rate changes. It is partly for this reason that Canadian policymakers, such as the Bank of Canada, must always consider domestic interest rates relative to those prevailing abroad.

## PURCHASING POWER PARITY

We can now summarize the relationship between exchange rates and prices by deriving an important proposition in economics. The purchasing power parity theory relates the domestic price level to the price level of another country, suggesting the relationship between the two is uniquely explained by the exchange rate.

**Purchasing power** is the amount of goods and services that one dollar or deutschmark or unit of any currency will buy. Hence, the **purchasing power parity (PPP)** hypothesis is that the exchange rate between two currencies is at equilibrium when their domestic purchasing powers are equivalent at that rate of exchange.

The PPP condition is reminiscent of the law of one price. More formally, the PPP hypothesis is that

$$e = \frac{P}{P^f} \tag{7.2}$$

All the terms are as defined previously, but $P$, domestic prices, and $P^f$, foreign prices, are measured in terms of an index of overall prices, such as the consumer price index (CPI) (not just the prices of traded goods as in the law of one price). Thus, equation (7.2), which is often called the *absolute form of PPP*, simply states that the exchange rate is a reflection of relative prices in two countries.

We can rewrite equation (7.2) in terms of rates of change in the variables:[12]

12 From equation (7.2) with $\log e_t = \log P_t - \log P_t^f$ where log is the logarithm of a variable and a time subscript ($t$) has been added. Then $\log e_t - \log e_{t-1} = (\log P_t - \log P_{t-1}) - (\log P_t^f - \log P_{t-1}^f)$. Using

$$\Delta e = \pi - \pi^f \qquad (7.3)$$

where

$\Delta e$ = rate of change in the exchange rate
$\pi$ = domestic rate of inflation
$\pi^f$ = foreign rate of inflation

Equation (7.3), which is called the *relative form of PPP*, states that exchange rate changes reflect differences in inflation rates between two countries.

Suppose, for example, that Canada's inflation rate is 1% while the US rate of inflation is 3%. According to equation (7.3),

$$\Delta e = 1\% - 3\% = -2\%$$

Remembering that a fall in the exchange rate means an appreciation of the Canadian dollar relative to other currencies, we see that this use of the relative form of PPP predicts that the Canadian dollar will rise in value over time.

Note that nothing has been said about whether the difference in inflation rates or the change in the exchange rate comes first. The direction of causality between the two sides of the equation makes no difference to the PPP hypothesis (though the issue of causality is an important one in practice).[13] Also, neither equation (7.2) nor (7.3) is specific about how long the adjustment process to a new equilibrium will be. Rather, these equations should be viewed as equilibrium conditions that hold in the long run.

So far our calculations have assumed a flexible exchange rate régime. What happens if the exchange rate is fixed? The relative form of the PPP equation (7.3) becomes

$$\Delta e = 0 = \pi - \pi^f \qquad (7.4)$$

which implies

$$\pi = \pi^f$$

In other words, if the Canadian–US exchange rate were fixed (as it was for most years between 1945 and 1970), US and Canadian inflation rates would be the same. If two or more countries set up a fixed exchange rate system at a time

---

previously introduced notation (see Chapter 6), this last equation becomes (dropping the time subscripts): $\Delta e = \pi - \pi^f$.

13 If causality goes from inflation to exchange rates, countries with high inflation need to reduce the value of their currencies to remain competitive. Alternatively, countries may try to remain competitive by attempting to reduce the value of their currency. But this course eventually has the effect of producing more inflation. These questions have important policy implications, but they are beyond the scope of this text.

when their inflation rates differ from each other, they could be expected to converge over time. (Arguments such as these have prompted many European countries to join the European Monetary System. In particular, by pegging their exchange rate to the deutschmark, they have implicitly committed themselves to eventual adoption of the German rate of inflation, traditionally one of the lowest among the industrialized countries.[14]

## WHAT'S THE EVIDENCE ON PPP?

Is there empirical data in favour of the relative form of PPP? Comparisons of the Canadian and US inflation rates yield mixed evidence, but careful analysis suggests that equation (7.3) is a valid expression of the equilibrium relationship.

Panel (A) of Figure 7.3 plots the consumer price index for Canada and the US since 1950. Panel (B) plots the exchange rate between the two currencies as defined at the beginning of the chapter. Finally, panel (C) implements a version of equation (7.2) to ascertain how well the absolute PPP hypothesis holds.

Recall from (7.1) that foreign prices expressed in domestic currency units should equal the domestic price level under the absolute PPP theory. Deviations from this equality is what is shown in panel (C) of Figure 7.3.[15]

If the absolute form of PPP holds, differences between the exchange rate and relative prices are plotted in Figure 7.3(C), which shows that although deviations from absolute PPP have persisted they have tended to return toward zero over time.

## REAL EXCHANGE RATES AND PPP

We can rewrite equation (7.2) as

$$\frac{1}{P^f} = \frac{e}{P} \tag{7.5}$$

Equation (7.5) says that under PPP, the reciprocal of the foreign price level, $1/P^f$, is equal to the exchange rate divided by the domestic price level. The re-

---

14 There is in fact some evidence that this has happened. See Pierre L. Siklos and Mark E. Wohar, "Convergence in Interest Rates and Inflation Rates Across Countries and Over Time" *Review of International Economics*, (1997).

15 For those with a statistics background, (7.1) in logarithms is written $\log(P^f e) = \log P$. To generate the values shown in panel (C) one has to estimate the regression $\log(P^f e) = \beta_0 + \beta_1 \log(P) + u_t$ where $\beta_0$ is the intercept and $\beta_1$ is the slope coefficient. Under absolute PPP, $\beta_0$ should be zero and the slope coefficient should be one while $u$ represents deviations from PPP. Estimates for the data shown in Figure 7.3 yielded the following results: $\log(P^f e) = -.061 + 1.068 \log(P)$. The intercept was found to be statistically insignificant but the slope was not different statistically from one confirming the validity of PPP as a *long-run* proposition. For more on related issues in this context, see Enders (1995).

**FIGURE 7.3** Absolute and Relative PPP between Canada and the United States

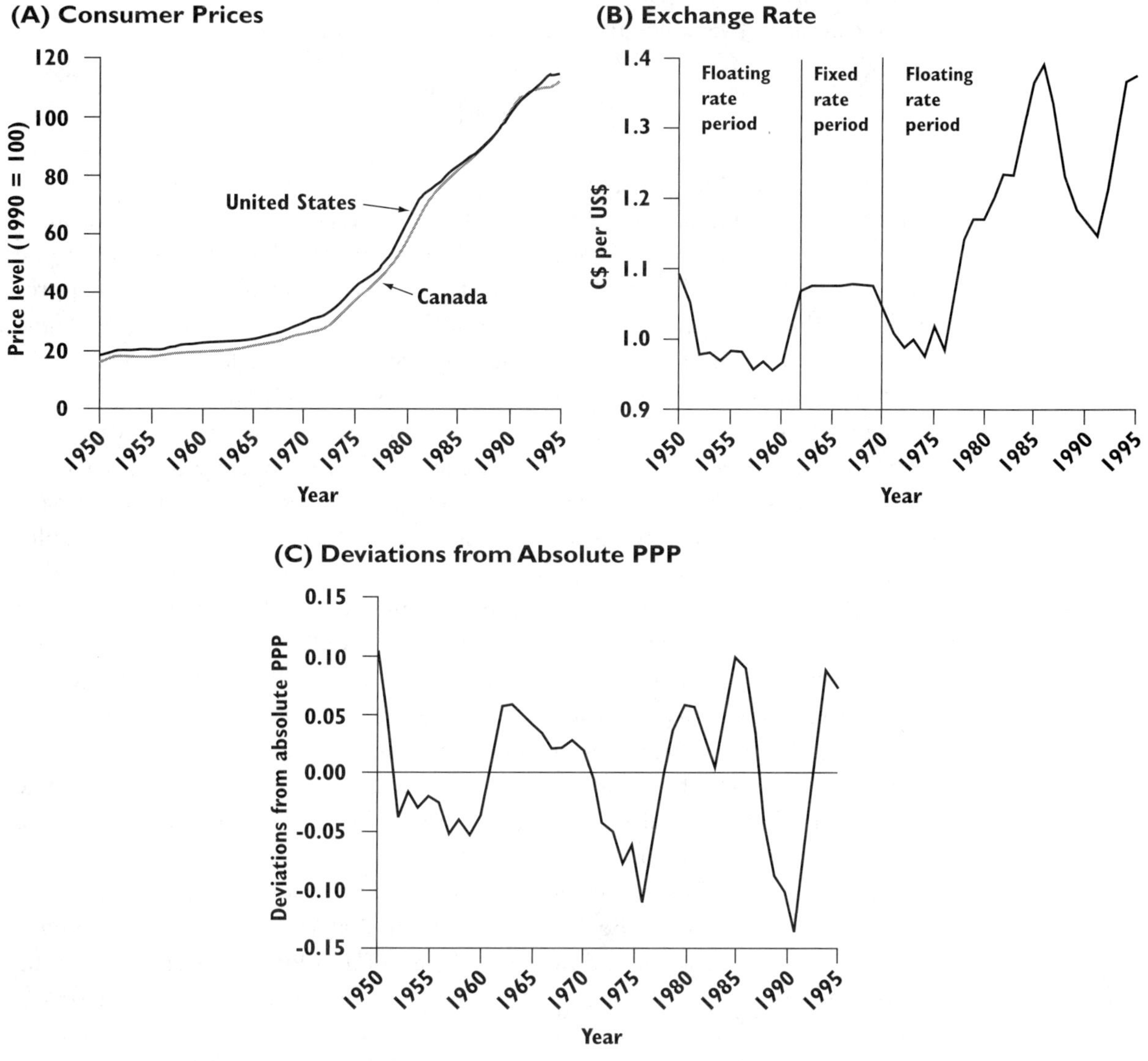


Panel (A) plots the price level for the United States and Canada since 1960, and panel (B) the Canadian–US exchange rate. Panel (C) reveals that deviations between the exchange rate and relative prices have tended to fluctuate around zero over time.

Note: In panel (A), the consumer price index was used to proxy $P^f$. The vertical lines in panel (B) separate the periods of fixed and flexible exchange rates between Canada and the United States. Panel (C) was created as explained in footnote 15.

Sources: *Bank of Canada Review*, Tables I1 and H8, *Survey of Current Business* (Washington, D.C.: US Dept. of Commerce), and *International Financial Statistics* (Washington, D.C.: International Monetary Fund).

ciprocal of the foreign price level simply represents the purchasing power of money in the foreign country.

We can also rewrite equation (7.2) as

$$\epsilon = e\left(\frac{P^f}{P}\right) \tag{7.6}$$

where $\epsilon$ = the **real exchange rate**—that is, the price of foreign goods relative to domestic goods. Equation (7.6) says $\epsilon$ is the product of the nominal exchange rate, $e$, and foreign prices divided by domestic prices. The real exchange rate concept has often been used as an indicator of competitiveness. Thus, an appreciation of the real exchange rate means $\epsilon$ *falls* or that domestic prices rise relative to foreign prices ($P^f/P$ *falls*) and so the country has become less competitive.[16]

Although equation (7.2) suggests $\epsilon$ should always be 1, we know that this is an equilibrium condition only. In the short run, there will be deviations away from equilibrium. If prices in Canada rise above those in other countries, so that $P^f/P$ falls, the nominal exchange rate, $e$, will rise. Higher prices in Canada have signalled a lower purchasing power; if a dollar is worth less, it should buy smaller quantities of foreign currencies. One implication of equation (7.6) then is that any inflationary monetary policy—that is, one that leads to higher domestic prices—will create a depreciation in the Canadian dollar.

The exchange rate may take some time to find its market-clearing value and it may overshoot its target for a while. The phenomenon of *overshooting*[17] is one of the ingredients contributing to the seemingly volatile exchange rates experienced since the Western industrialized nations returned to flexible exchange rates.[18] Therefore, the real exchange rate variable can be interpreted as a measure of departure from purchasing power parity.

Figure 7.4 provides some evidence. The plot of the real exchange rate of the Canadian dollar vis-à-vis the US dollar (Figure 7.4(A)) reveals that there have been some pronounced deviations from the absolute PPP condition. (Notice the steep rise in the late 1980s and again in the early 1990s which reflects the strong

---

16 Again, it matters very much how we measure the domestic and foreign price levels. If we wish to measure competitiveness between countries then the price index used should be for tradable goods only. Indeed, some analysts use a measure called the *terms of trade* which measures the (real) relationship between the prices of a country's imports and exports (*Bank of Canada Review* (Table J4) publishes just such an index). Other analysts prefer to look at labour costs in one country versus another as a gauge of competitiveness.

17 The process and pattern of overshooting is similar to what we saw, in Chapter 6, when we analyzed the effect on interest rates of a monetary policy aimed at reducing the growth rate of the money supply. The idea of overshooting was introduced by R. Dornbusch, "Expectations and Exchange Rate Dynamics," *Journal of Political Economy* 84 (December 1976): 1161–76.

18 From 1945 to 1971, most of the industrialized countries were on a quasi-fixed exchange rate system called the Bretton Woods System, which is explained in Chapter 23.

**FIGURE 7.4** Real Canadian–US Exchange Rates, 1975–90 (flexible exchange rates régime)

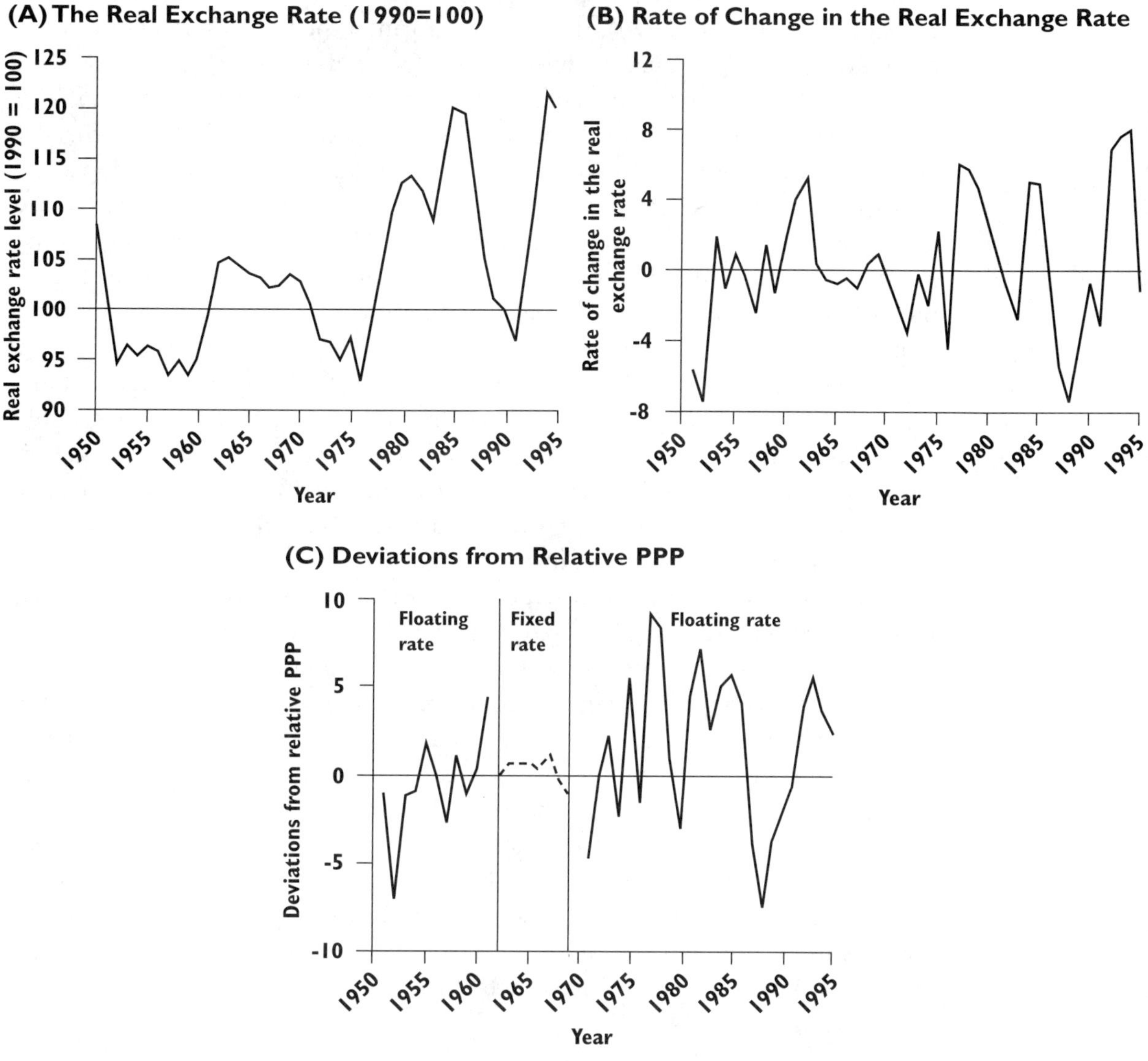


Panels (A) and (B) plot, respectively, the real Canadian–US exchange rate and its rate of change. The latter has tended to fluctuate around zero (with some exceptions), which suggests the presence of relative PPP. So does the picture of deviations from PPP in panel (C).

Note: The exchange rate measured on the vertical axis of panel (A) was converted to an index with 1990 as the base year. The curve in panel (C) reflects $\pi - \pi^f$ for the fixed exchange rate period and $\Delta e - (\pi - \pi^f)$ for the flexible exchange rate period. Because of differencing there are gaps between the lines through the various exchange rate regime periods.

Sources: *Bank of Canada Review*, Tables I1 and H8, *Survey of Current Business* (Washington, D.C.: US Dept. of Commerce), and *International Financial Statistics* (Washington, D.C.: International Monetary Fund).

real appreciation of the Canadian dollar relative to the US currency and therefore a loss of competitiveness.)[19] But notice the plot of the rate of change in the real exchange rate (Figure 7.4(B)). If the relative form of the PPP is correct, this series should display no particular pattern.[20] Thus, for example, a sustained increase in the real exchange rate would signal that the exchange rate was too low in view of the existing differential in domestic versus foreign rates of inflation, thereby violating the equilibrium condition of PPP. This translates into an undervalued Canadian dollar.[21] As Figure 7.4(B) reveals, although the rates of change in the real exchange rates have tended to hover around zero, there have been some notable and persistent departures—for example, in the late 1980s. By the beginning of the 1990s, the Canadian dollar had been consistently overvalued in PPP terms relative to the US dollar.

Consider finally Figure 7.5 which shows, for the 1984–94 period, the relationship between the rate at which currencies in the G-7 countries have appreciated (a negative value) or depreciated (a positive value) against the US dollar. Again, we see a positive relationship between the two magnitudes as predicted by relative PPP. It is too much to expect, however, that the link summarized in equation (7.3) holds exactly in a span of just 11 years.

So far our discussion has centred on the case of flexible exchange rates. What is the record for the period of fixed exchange rates? For relative PPP, we expect differences in inflation rates to be inconsequential under a fixed exchange rate system; under a flexible system, in contrast, inflation rates may differ and the exchange rate adjusts to reflect the differential. To put the point differently, relative PPP hypothesizes that the difference between exchange rate changes, $\Delta e$, and the differential in inflation rates, $\pi - \pi^f$, should be zero. In practice, because of time lags and overshoots, these deviations should wander randomly around zero. Figure 7.4(C) suggests that the relative PPP hypothesis is a reasonable approximation of what has happened. Notice, however, the relatively greater volatility of departures from PPP under the flexible exchange rates régime, which is a reflection of the volatility of exchange rates since 1970.

---

19 Incidentally, the *Main Economic Indicators* publication of the Organization for Economic Co-operation and Development began to publish comparative price levels for a country's output. These data show the number of US$ needed to buy the same representative bushel of goods and services in Canada costing $100 in the US. For Canada, the values for 1990, 1992 and 1993 were 112, 105 and 97, respectively. Our "competitive" position, therefore, improved by this measure which is based on GDP not just on the CPI.

20 This is because changes in the exchange rate over time should reflect differences in inflation between countries, plus random departures, which would be reflected in the real exchange rate.

21 In other words, when $\epsilon$ rises, other things being equal, foreign goods become relatively more expensive, which implies an improvement in competitiveness.

## ECONOMICS FOCUS 7.2 Big Mac Parity

*The Economist* magazine has developed an ingenious way to illustrate the application of purchasing power parity. From time to time it publishes a list of the price of a MacDonald's Big Mac in various countries around the world. For example,

| | Domestic Price | | | PPP | | | Actual e | | |
|---|---|---|---|---|---|---|---|---|---|
| | 1986(1) | 1990(2) | 1995(3) | 1986(4) | 1990(5) | 1995(6) | 1986(7) | 1990(8) | 1995(9) |
| Canada | 1.89 | 2.19 | 2.77 | — | — | — | — | — | — |
| United States | 1.60 | 2.20 | 2.32 | 1.18 | 1.00 | 1.19 | 1.39 | 1.16 | 1.39 |
| France | 16.40 | 17.70 | 18.50 | 0.12 | 0.12 | 0.15 | 0.18 | 0.21 | 0.29 |
| Japan | 370.00 | 370.00 | 391.00 | 0.005 | 0.006 | 0.0071 | 0.008 | 0.007 | 0.017 |
| Germany | 4.25 | 4.30 | 4.80 | 0.44 | 0.51 | 0.58 | 0.59 | 0.69 | 1.01 |

**Sources:** "Big Mac Currencies," *The Economist*, 18 April 1992; "On the Hamburger Standard," *The Economist*, 6 September 1986 and 5 May 1990, 15 April 1995.

Columns 1, 2, and 3 give the price for a Big Mac in the local currency. Columns 4, 5, and 6 are found by applying equation (7.2): that is, the exchange rate that would equate the relative prices shown. Columns 7, 8, and 9 give the actual values for the exchange rate at approximately the same time as the prices for Big Macs were sampled. In 1995, for example, the actual Canadian–US exchange rate was $1.39 so the actual price of a Big Mac in the United States was $3.22 Cdn. (2.32 × 1.39). In other words, Big Macs were relatively cheaper in Canada or relatively more expensive in the United States in 1995 when the US price is converted into its C$ equivalent. Thus, the Canadian dollar was undervalued in 1995 against all currencies listed in the table since it cost more Canadian dollars to buy a unit of a foreign currency than predicted by PPP. According to the Big Mac index, the situation has not changed since 1986 and the degree of undervaluation vis-à-vis the US$, for example, has changed little.

## HYSTERESIS

The previous section revealed that, at least in terms of PPP, an overvalued or an undervalued Canadian dollar can persist for some time. Recently, some economists[22] have found that the slow response of some economic variables appears to be a fairly pervasive phenomenon. In the present context, the problem, called *hysteresis*,[23] refers to an effect that does not disappear when the causes of the over- or undervaluation themselves fade away. One of the implications of the result is that it makes exchange rate forecasting that much more difficult. Hysteresis does *not* mean that deviations from PPP will never be corrected. Figure

22 A nice statement of the issues covered in this section is P.R. Krugman *Exchange Rate Instability* (Cambridge, Mass: The MIT Press, 1989).

23 The term was originally used in physics to describe the effect of the previous history of some phenomenon on its subsequent development.

**FIGURE 7.5** Inflation Versus Exchange Rate Changes

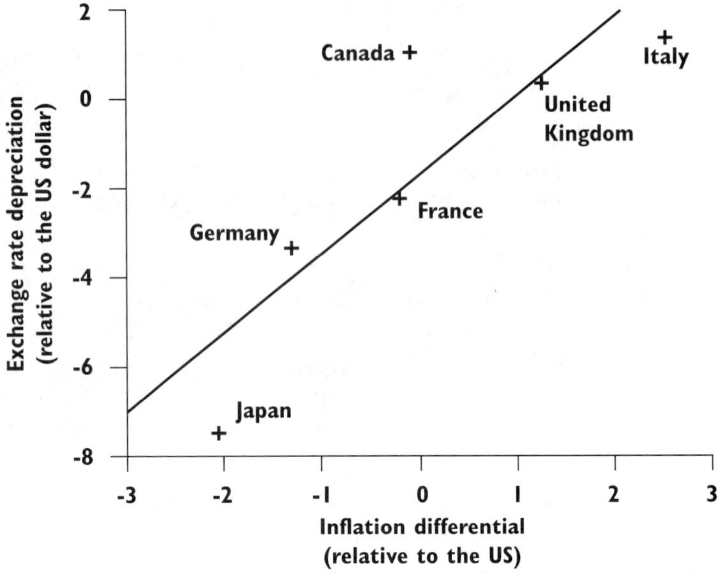


Inflation differential is a country's inflation rate relative to the US inflation rate. Exchange rate depreciation measures the percent change in a country's exchange rate defined in terms of the US dollar. Inflation is measured as the annual percentage change in the consumer price index. The exchange rate used is the average exchange rate during a particular year. The resulting inflation and exchange rate calculations were averaged over the 11-year period (1984–94) to produce the plot above.

Source: International Financial Statistics CD-ROM (International Monetary Fund).

7.4, for example, makes it clear that this is not so. What it does mean is that the length of time before equilibrium is restored is itself uncertain.

## SUMMARY

- An exchange rate expresses the relative price of two currencies.
- In the absence of transactions costs or other market positions, the prices of commodities should be the same in two countries. This relationship is known as the law of one price.
- There are two principal exchange rate systems: fixed exchange rates, which are set by government regulation, and flexible exchange rates, which are set by the demand for and supply of foreign exchange.

- Purchasing power parity (PPP) comes in two forms. Absolute PPP says that the exchange rate is simply the relative price of domestic versus foreign goods. Relative PPP says that exchange rate changes reflect differences in inflation rates between two countries.

## IMPORTANT TERMS

appreciation (p. 147)
cross-rate (p. 147)
depreciation (p. 147)
devaluation (p. 148)
exchange rate (p. 146)
fixed exchange rate system (p. 149)
flexible exchange rate system (p. 149)
law of one price (p. 149)
managed ("dirty") float system (p. 149)
peso problem (p. 153)
purchasing power (p. 158)
purchasing power parity (PPP) (p. 158)
real exchange rate (p. 162)
revaluation (p. 148)
spot rate (p. 149)

## EXERCISES

1. Assume the following exchange rates:

| Currency | Exchange Rate ($C per unit of the foreign currency) |
|---|---|
| United States | 1.1368 |
| United Kingdom | 2.0268 |
| France | 0.2076 |
| Germany | 0.7096 |
| Japan | 0.008 |

Calculate cross-rates for

(a) yen per deutschmark
(b) pounds per French franc
(c) deutschmark per US dollar

2. As noted in the **ECONOMICS FOCUS: Big Mac Parity**, *The Economist* publishes prices for a Big Mac in a variety of countries. In the 1990 survey a Big Mac that cost $2.19 Cdn cost 3,900 lire in Italy. The exchange rate between the lira and the Canadian dollar was 0.00098 (or 1,023.86 lire per $C). What was the price of a Big Mac in Canada in terms of lire? The Canadian price of a Big Mac in Italy? For absolute PPP to hold, should the dollar have appreciated or depreciated relative to the lira? Explain.

3. Below are some exchange rate data for three countries' currencies in US dollars.

| | 1988 | 1989 | 1990 |
|---|---|---|---|
| Canada | 0.813 | 0.845 | 0.857 |
| Denmark | 0.149 | 0.137 | 0.159 |
| Spain | 0.009 | 0.008 | 0.010 |

If relative PPP holds, which country had relatively higher inflation than the United States in 1989 and 1990? Explain your answer.

4. The Canadian consumer price index (using a base year of 1986 = 100) stood at 55.9 in 1978 and 119.5 in 1990. The US price index stood at 61.5 in 1978 and 122.0 in 1990, again at 1986 prices. The exchange rate against the US dollar similarly went from 1.1402 in 1978 to 1.1668 in 1990. If absolute PPP holds, was the Canadian dollar overvalued or undervalued relative to the US dollar in 1990? Had you known this would happen, would you have bought or sold Canadian dollars in the foreign exchange market? Explain your answer.

5. Show what would happen to the exchange rate if interest rates in Canada rose above US interest rates. Use a diagram like the one in Figure 7.1 to explain your answer.

6. Suppose that foreigners suddenly felt that it had become much riskier to invest in Canada. What would happen to the $LF^s + LF^{sf}$ curve depicted in Figure 7.2? To the equilibrium interest rate? Explain.

7. The 1993 version of *The Economist* Big Mac parity contest showed the following price and exchange rate data. Find the PPP exchange rate. Is the C$ over- or undervalued?

| Country | Domestic Price | Actual e |
|---|---|---|
| Canada | 2.76 | 1.26 |
| US | 2.28 | |
| France | 18.50 | 0.19 |
| Japan | 391.00 | 0.009 |
| Germany | 4.60 | 0.63 |

8. Calculate the percentage *over-* or *under*valuation of the exchange rates in Economics Focus 7.2 and in the question above.

9. According to the OECD, the following are the purchasing power parities for Canada vis-à-vis the United States for the years given in parentheses: 1.28(1985), 1.30(1990), 1.26(1992) and 1.25(1993). The following are the closing exchange rates for the same years, respectively: 1.40, 1.16, 1.27, 1.32. Was the C$ overvalued or undervalued for each of these years? Explain.

**10.** Use the exchange rate determination framework (Figure 7.1) to explain the consequences for Mexico's reserves of an overvalued exchange rate. Explain.

**11.** Use the loanable funds framework (Figure 7.2) to illustrate the consequences of Mexico's attempt to artificially keep interest rates high (given the fixed exchange rate) as well as the implications of the devaluation/depreciation for the demand for Mexican bonds. Explain.

**12.** Referring back to Figure 7.5, say a country's inflation rate is higher than the US inflation rate by 2% but its exchange rate has depreciated over the same period by only 1% against the US dollar. Has the country's competitive position improved? Explain. Does it matter over how many years such calculations are made? Why?

## REFERENCES

Copeland, L., *Exchange Rates and International Finance*, Second Edition. Wokingham, UK: Addison-Wesley, 1994.

Diebold, F.X., S. Husted, and M. Rush. "Real Exchange Rates under the Gold Standard." *Journal of Political Economy* 99 (December 1991): 1252–71.

Enders, W. *Applied Econometric Time Series.* New York: John Wiley, 1995.

Fisher, E., and J.T. Park. "Testing Purchasing Power Parity Under the Null Hypothesis of Co-Integration." *Economic Journal* 10 (November 1991): 1476–84.

Gibson, H.D. *International Finance.* London: Longman, 1996.

Gilli, V., and G. Kaminsky. "Nominal Exchange Rate Regimes and the Real Exchange Rate: Evidence from the United States and Great Britain, 1885–1986." *Journal of Monetary Economics* 27 (April 1991): 191–212.

Isard, P. *Exchange Rate Economics.* Cambridge: Cambridge University Press, 1995.

Johnson, D.R. "Cointegration, Error Correction, and Purchasing Power Parity," *Canadian Journal of Economics* 23 (November 1990): 839–55.

Mussa, M. "Exchange Rates in Theory and Reality." *Essays in International Finance*, no. 179 (December 1990), Princeton University.

CHAPTER 8

# Decision Makers: Introduction

This chapter is the first of several examining the economic behaviour of the principal participants in the Canadian financial system: the household, business, financial, government, and international sectors. It is the collective decisions of each sector—the sum of millions of decisions made by its economic agents, be they individuals, managers of firms, or bureaucrats—that shape an economy. In a macroeconomics course, the focus would be on this economy-wide behaviour. Here, however, we are more interested in the behaviour of the major participants in the operation of the financial system.

Before we can describe theories of consumer, firm, and bank behaviour, however, we need a device to organize the financial system in a manner that highlights the roles played by the major participants. Accordingly, this chapter opens with a review of some principles and conventions of the **System of National Accounts**, which is Statistics Canada's accounting for the entire economy. You are probably familiar with its short-term statements of economic activity, such as gross domestic product (GDP) and its components, which are analogous to a firm's income statements.[1] However, we are more interested here in examining the **national balance sheet accounts**, which are the set of balance sheets prepared for each group in the economy and for the economy as a whole, and the **financial flow accounts**, which report how funds are used in borrowing and lending activities. Such an analysis will allow us to determine, for example, which sectors of the economy tend to be borrowers or lenders over time as well as the financial relationship between sectors of the economy. After briefly defining a few basic accounting principles, we develop a flow of funds matrix for the entire Canadian economy and then analyze its behaviour over the last few years.

---

1 A. Blomqvist, P. Wonnacott, R. Wonnacott, and J. Fried, *Macroeconomics*, 4th ed. (Toronto, Ont.: McGraw-Hill Ryerson Ltd., 1994), ch. 6.

## SOME BASIC NATIONAL INCOME ACCOUNTING PRINCIPLES

The economy is divided into four major **sectors** (divisions that can be studied by themselves):

1. Households, formally called the persons and unincorporated firms sector.
2. Businesses, which are divided into non-financial private corporations and financial corporations. The latter are subdivided into (i) banks and near-banks, (ii) insurance companies and pension funds, and (iii) other private financial institutions.
3. Governments, of which the federal government is only one segment.
4. The foreign sector, often called the rest of the world.

Each sector generates revenues and incurs expenditures during a given period of time, say a year. The difference between the two determines whether the relevant sector experiences a surplus or is in a deficit position. Thus, for each sector, we can write

$$\text{Current Receipts} - \text{Current Expenditures} = \text{Surplus } (>0) \text{ or Deficit } (<0)$$

(Notice that the difference between expenditures and receipts is for the current period—the year in this case.) An expression such as this one is an **income statement** (if it were for a firm it might be called an earnings statement), but it is a form that can be integrated with a sector's **balance sheet,** which is a statement summarizing its **net worth**—that is, it is the value of assets and liabilities at a particular moment in time.[2]

Figure 8.1 shows how information from a sector's income statement feeds into its balance sheet. A surplus represents an addition to the sector's net worth, while a deficit represents a reduction. For an illustration, consider the government sector. In the 1995–96 fiscal year, which runs from April 1 to March 31, current receipts totalled $130,600 million. Current expenditures were $163,300 million. The difference of $32,700 million ($130,600 − $163,300) represents the budget deficit for that fiscal year. For fiscal 1994–95 the actual deficit was 37,500 million. It is useful to point out, at this stage, that while the National Income Accounts say that the deficit is a certain amount this is *not* the same as saying that the government needs to *borrow* an amount equivalent to the published deficit figure.

---

2 Following the usual accounting practice, these values reflect those at the time of purchase less some adjustment for depreciation (dictated by tax considerations). In general, balance sheets are not evaluated at current market values but at *historical cost,* which is the cost at the time of purchase.

**FIGURE 8.1** A Sectoral Income Statement and Balance Sheet

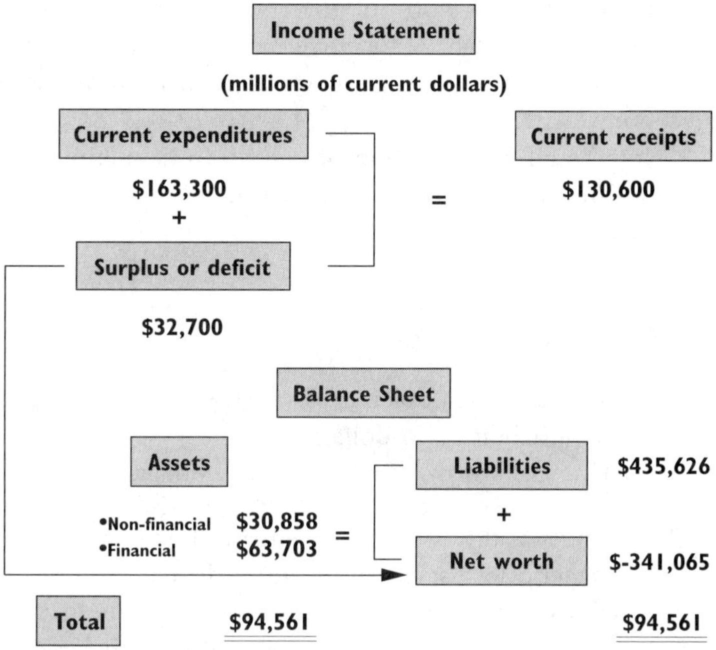


Sources: *Budget Chart Book 1996* (Ottawa: Department of Finance, March 1996); *Bank of Canada Review* (various issues), Table G1; Statistics Canada, *Guide to the Financial Flow and National Balance Sheet Accounts: Definitions, Concepts, Sources, and Methods* (No. 13-585E), Table P3-33; and National Balance Sheet Accounts, *Annual Estimates 1984–1993* (Ottawa: Statistics Canada, 1994). Because of the long delay in obtaining balance sheet data these figures are for 1993. The data for the income statement are the estimates for the 1995–96 fiscal year. Expenditures include interest on the debt and contingency reserves.

The reason is that there is an item referred to as *non-budgetary transactions* which, at least in the 1994–95 budget year, means that actual federal government borrowing was $25.8 billion.[3] Second, beginning with the 1996–97 budget year announced at the end of February 1996, the federal government added $2.5 to $3 billion as a "contingency reserve" in the event its assumptions about the future prospects for the economy turn out to be worse than expected. Obviously, this too will affect the actual size of the deficit and borrowing requirements.

Notice that the balance sheet divides assets and liabilities into two components. **Non-financial assets** are essentially physical assets, such as equipment, machinery, and land; they are also called *real assets.* **Financial assets** are, for the most part,

3 For example, when a government announces an infrastructure project the funds will be spent over several years even though they may be *budgeted* in a single fiscal year.

bank deposits, loans to various enterprises (including Crown corporations), and the public debt. By far the largest component of liabilities is financial in nature. Notice that the net worth of government is negative. It essentially represents the net accumulated debt of the government and it rises with every additional deficit incurred. (In later chapters we examine the balance sheets of other sectors of the economy as well.)

Now, recall the definition of net worth (sometimes called **net wealth**) as expressed in the basic accounting identity:

$$A - L = NW \tag{8.1}$$

where

$A$ = assets, in dollars
$L$ = liabilities, in dollars
$NW$ = net worth or net wealth, in dollars

That identity is the compact statement of any balance sheet.

The generic terms "surplus" and "deficit" accurately describe additions or subtractions to net worth, but they are usually applied to the government sector, and different terms are used for each of the other sectors of the economy. For example, surplus funds in the household sector are known as *savings.* In the business or firm sector they are often referred to as *retained earnings.*

The accounting identity makes it quite clear that changes in net worth will influence asset holdings, which can be non-financial assets (a house or a factory) or financial assets (money or bonds), as well as liabilities. It is also clear that one sector's activities cannot be analyzed in isolation from the others'. For example, tax payments are an important component of current expenditures for households and of current receipts for various levels of government. It is partly for this reason that we need to develop a matrix to represent the flow of funds between sectors of the economy.

Since the magnitudes in equation (8.1) are measured at a particular moment in time—say, December 31 of a particular year—they are known as **stock measures**. Since we are primarily interested in financial trends over time, we have to convert these stock measures into **flow measures**, which are measures of activity over time. By comparing successive balance sheets—say, between one year and the next—we can determine the change in the balance sheet position of a particular sector. All we need to do to convert stocks into flows is to determine the changes in equation (8.1) during the period in question:

$$\Delta A - \Delta L = \Delta NW \tag{8.2}$$

where $\Delta$ indicates the change during the period—say, from one year to the next. In other words,

$$\Delta A_t = A_t - A_{t-1}$$
$$\Delta L_t = L_t - L_{t-1}$$
$$\Delta NW_t = NW_t - NW_{t-1}$$

So the change in asset holdings, $\Delta A_t$, is simply the difference between the balance sheet value of assets at time $t$, which could be December 31, 1997, less their value at time $t - 1$, which could be December 31, 1996. The calculation of $\Delta L$ and $\Delta NW$ are interpreted in a similar fashion.

We can simplify the notion by agreeing that the symbol $\Delta$ refers to a year-over-year change. Then we can drop the time subscripts in the subsequent discussion.

## THE FINANCIAL SYSTEM IN THE FLOW OF FUNDS

What is the role of the financial system in the **flow of funds**? Finding the answer requires that we further analyze equation (8.2). We have already noted that liabilities tend to be mostly financial in nature, but assets may be financial or non-financial. We shall denote them as *FA* and *NFA*, respectively. So we can rewrite equation (8.2) as

$$\Delta NW = (\Delta FA + \Delta NFA) - \Delta L$$

Moreover, it will be convenient for our analysis to further subdivide financial assets into money, *M*, which, as we have seen, plays a central role in economic analysis, and other financial assets, *OFA*, such as bonds.

Thus, changes in financial assets, $\Delta FA$, represent the sum of changes in money holdings, $\Delta M$, and changes in other financial assets, $\Delta OFA$. Keeping the distinction between types of financial assets, we can further rewrite equation (8.2) as

$$\Delta NW = [(\Delta M + \Delta OFA) + \Delta NFA] - \Delta L \tag{8.3}$$

where

$$\Delta FA = \Delta M + \Delta OFA$$

Now consider that additions to other financial assets, *OFA*, stem from the particular sector's contribution to the financial system. They represent sources of funds or the amount of *lending* that takes place.[4] In contrast, changes in liabilities are an indication of the amount of additional *borrowing* by a particular sector—that is, the uses of funds.

We are now able to describe a flow of funds matrix, which describes the interlocking nature of the economic relationship among the principal sectors of the economy. Table 8.1 presents a simplified version of such a matrix. It provides a summary of the sources and uses of funds by sector and by type of economic activity, and lists some of the most important items that come under each heading. The plus signs indicate additions to net wealth while the minus sign indicates a reduction in net wealth. In other words, sources of funds add to net wealth while uses of funds reduce it. The percentages show the relative importance of each of the major components in the flow of funds. Notice that all the major sectors of the economy, except the non-financial private corporations sector, have by and large been acquiring financial assets rather than non-financial assets. Furthermore, bonds, stocks, and other interest-earning assets account for an overwhelming proportion of the financial assets acquired.

## THE FLOW OF FUNDS IN PRACTICE

Now that we have a structure with which we can analyze how funds flow through the economy, we can consider the relative importance of the various sectors of the Canadian economy and determine which are consistently net contributors to wealth and which are net borrowers.

The household and business sectors account for almost all the changes in currency and demand deposit holdings. This finding is not surprising since these are the sectors that use media of exchange most intensively for transactions purposes. For example, money holdings actually fell during 1982 and 1983. Now recall from Chapter 6 (see Figure 6.1) that interest rates in Canada hit their peaks in 1982 and 1983. One can hypothesize then that money holdings are quite sensitive to interest rate changes.[5]

Changes in the holdings of other financial assets, which include stocks and bonds of various kinds, are primarily accounted for by the private sector of the economy—that is, the household, business, financial, and foreign sectors. Periods of recession usually see the smallest overall annual change in holdings of other financial assets.

The bulk of changes in liabilities are incurred by the business and financial sectors. Note, however, one important difference between real assets and financial

4 Changes in money holdings are often called a *hoarding* activity because these funds are not made available for use by the financial system.

5 We develop this thesis in a more analytic fashion in Chapter 11.

**TABLE 8.1** A FLOW OF FUNDS MATRIX FOR THE CANADIAN ECONOMY

| Sources of Funds | Persons and Unincorporated Firms[a] | Financial Corporation[b] | Non-Financial Private Corporations | Federal Government | Non-Residents |
|---|---|---|---|---|---|
| Money | + 11% | + 1% | + 1% | + — | + 1% |
| Other Financial Assets | | | | | |
| • Bonds | + | + | + | + | + |
| • Stocks | + 41% | + 96% | + 37% | + 67% | + 99% |
| • Other | + | + | + | + | + |
| Non-Financial Assets | | | | | |
| • Land | + | + | + | + | + |
| • Machinery and Equipment | + | + | + | + | + |
| • Consumer Durables | + 48% | + 3% | + 61% | + 33% | + — |
| • Residential and Non-Residential Structures | + | + | + | + | + |
| • Other | + | + | + | + | + |
| Uses of Funds | | | | | |
| • Bank Loans | — | — | — | — | — |
| • Mortgages | — | — | — | — | — |
| • Other | — | — | — | — | — |

[a] Persons and Unincorporated Businesses according to Statistics Canada.

[b] Chartered banks, Near-banks, Life Insurance and pension funds and other financial institutions.

The numbers indicate the sources of funds by major category as percentages of the total sources of funds in 1993. A dash signifies not available or not recorded.

Source: The matrix uses the conventions and definitions of, as well as data from, Statistics Canada, *Financial Flow and National Balance Sheet Accounts 1984–1993*, (No. 13-214).

assets. A real asset appears only on the balance sheet of its owner.[6] In contrast, a financial asset, such as a government bond, is an asset to the individual holding

6 Of course, the asset may have been purchased via a loan, but the item itself does not appear on any other balance sheet.

the bond *and* a liability to the issuer, who undertakes to make regular interest payments and return the principal upon maturity of the financial instrument. Thus, when a business acquires a debt or a liability at an interest cost, it usually does so to gain funds to purchase an asset that also yields interest income. This practice of investing borrowed funds is known as *leverage*; we address this concept in greater detail in Chapter 10. Household debt, on the other hand, is financed through current and future labour income.

Finally, it is quite clear that households accumulate much of the economy's net worth and are thus the principal lenders in the economy. At the other end of the spectrum is the federal government, whose changes in net worth were consistently negative during the decade—a result of its policy of incurring substantial deficits over time.

In considering the kind of information in the National Balance Sheet Accounts, we should remain aware of several problems inherent in the way the data are kept and reported.

1. Government budget statistics, unlike those from households, businesses, and the financial sector, do not distinguish between spending on assets and current spending. Thus, government funds spent on roads or schools are treated as current spending, although these are assets from which society will benefit over a number of years.[7] This approach distorts government deficits (or surpluses), especially relative to those of the other sectors, but we cannot say by how much.

2. Financial institutions and, by and large, businesses report historical values, not market values, for their assets. This practice can lead to, for example, the over-reporting of net worth if the assets in question drop significantly in value over time (as happened in the late eighties in real estate).

3. All the measures introduced in this chapter have been expressed in nominal terms ("current dollars"). In theory they could also be expressed in real terms if we simply deflated the nominal values by the appropriate price index. Therein lies the problem: the relevant price index is often either unavailable or does not properly reflect the purchasing power of the goods and services of interest. Hence sectoral income statements and balance sheets are generally reported in current, not constant, dollars.

---

7 The United States publishes national accounts that properly distinguish current from capital expenditures. See "Balancing the Government's Books," *The Economist* 25 January 1992, p. 61; and K.M. Carlson, "The U.S. Balance Sheet: What Is It and What Does It Tell Us?" *Review of the Federal Reserve Bank of St. Louis* 73 (September/October 1991): 3–18.

## FINANCIAL FOCUS 8.1 A More Sensible Way of Accounting for Government Operations: The New Zealand Model

In 1994 the Parliament of New Zealand passed the Fiscal Responsibilities Act which is intended to ensure that governments practise prudent financial management. It forces the government not only to publish its fiscal forecasts but to explain why they might miss them, as well as how to get back on track. It also requires that the Minister of Finance issue a "Statement of Responsibility" in which he or she must accept "overall responsibility for the integrity of the disclosures" to the report required to be tabled in Parliament by the government. But equally important, it requires that the government publish a balance sheet according to generally accepted accounting principles or GAAP. This means that things such as public roads, bridges and national parks are to be given a dollar value and henceforth appear in the national balance sheet as assets. The Act also means that expenditures and receipts are recorded on an accrual basis which recognizes the fact that obligations voted on by the Parliament in one year bind fiscal policy throughout the expected stream of spending. For example, if the New Zealand government passes an infrastructure program costing say $ 6 billion over 5 years then rather than assuming that the money is all spent in the current year, as is the current practice in countries such as Canada, each budget over the next 5 years will have to account for the portion spent on the program each year the funds are spent. Therefore, in fiscal matters at least, "bygones are no longer bygones."

What are the implications of this approach to national income accounting? Well, for the first time, government sector net worth became positive in 1995–96 and was projected to be +$5.2 millions NZ$ for the fiscal year 1996–97. The table below gives a summary of the New Zealand government's balance sheet for 1994–95 (July 1 to June 30).

| Assets (millions) NZ$ | Fiscal 1994–95 | Liabilities | Fiscal 1994–95 |
|---|---|---|---|
| Market securities | 6,523 | Payables | 3,824 |
| Advances | 4,782 | Currency | 1,620 |
| State-owned enterprises | 16,420 | Borrowings | 44,096 |
| Physical assets | 13,432 | Pension Liabilities | 8,106 |
| State highways | 7,454 | | |
| Contingencies | — | | |
| Other | 5,876 | | |
| Total | 54,487 | Total | 57,646 |

**Source:** *Fiscal Update of December 1995* (Wellington: Department of the Treasury).

## SUMMARY

- This chapter explains how the national economy is subdivided by major sector groupings and how the size of each is measured.

- The major sectors are households, businesses, governments, and the foreign sector.
- A flow of funds matrix shows, for the entire economy, changes in the holdings of assets and liabilities by sector and asset type.

## IMPORTANT TERMS

balance sheet (p. 172)
financial assets (p. 173)
financial flow accounts (p. 171)
flow measures (p. 174)
flow of funds (p. 175)
income statement (p. 172)
national balance sheet accounts (p. 171)
net worth (net wealth) (pp. 172/174)
non-financial assets (p. 173)
sectors of the economy (p. 172)
stock measures (p. 174)
System of National Accounts (p. 171)

## EXERCISES

1. Table 8.1 does not list all the sectors of the Canadian economy. One of those omitted is the Bank of Canada, officially referred to as "the monetary authority." Now recall that money is the sum of currency and demand deposits. If we were to list currency separately in the flow of funds matrix as well as add the flow of funds from the Bank of Canada, what would be the change in net wealth for the economy as a whole? Explain. Does this result contradict the discussion in Chapter 2?

2. Why do all financial assets appear on two balance sheets but physical assets on only one?

3. Why are liability changes considered a source of funds? Explain your answer.

4. Suppose you are provided with the following flow of funds data for the household sector:

| Year | 1980 | 1981 | 1982 | 1983 | 1984 | 1985 | 1986 | 1987 | 1988 |
|---|---|---|---|---|---|---|---|---|---|
| $\Delta FA$ | 64,462 | 58,548 | 33,764 | 63,874 | 67,819 | 67,663 | 57,261 | 74,844 | 88,828 |
| $\Delta L$ | 17,464 | 8,914 | 2,569 | 13,411 | 9,641 | 23,918 | 28,076 | 38,900 | 42,690 |
| $\Delta NW$ | 112,195 | 104,421 | 61,595 | 82,679 | 88,321 | 84,525 | 92,725 | 109,611 | 124,932 |

Find the change in the holdings of non-financial assets.

5. Explain the difference between stocks and flows.

6. What are the advantages and drawbacks of the New Zealand system of balance sheet accounting.

7. Do you think government net worth is positive or negative? Explain.

## REFERENCES

*Bank of Canada Review* (various issues).

Blomqvist, A., P. Wonnacott, R. Wonnacott and J. Fried. *Macroeconomics*, 4th ed. Toronto, Ont.: McGraw-Hill Ryerson Ltd., 1994.

*Budget Chart Book*. Ottawa: Department of Finance, March 1996.

Canada, Department of Finance. *Quarterly Economic Review.*

Carlson, K.M. "The U.S. Balance Sheet: What is It and What Does It Tell Us?" *Review of the Federal Reserve Bank of St. Louis* 73 (September/October 1991): 3–18.

Chant, J., and S. Easton, "Development in Canadian Financial Markets: 1962–82." In *Postwar Macroeconomic Developments*, Collected Research Studies of the Royal Commission on the Economic Union and Development Prospects for Canada, vol. 20. Toronto: University of Toronto Press, 1986, chapter 7.

Statistics Canada. *Financial Flow and National Balance Sheet Accounts*, No. 13–214.

Statistics Canada. *Financial Flow Accounts —Preliminary Data, 1991*. No. 13–014.

Statistics Canada. *Guide to the Financial Flow and National Balance Sheet Accounts: Definitions, Concepts, Sources and Methods.* No. 13–585E.

CHAPTER 9

# Decision Makers: Household Sector

Households provide a major portion of the savings flow into the economy. The purpose of this chapter is to explore how a household determines its *savings rate* (the proportion of *disposable income*—after-tax income —devoted to saving rather than consumption). The topic is clearly important to households themselves. It is also a matter of concern to governments and firms, which need to ensure a steady flow of funds to finance their borrowing. Moreover, since the flow of savings provides the raw material necessary for the continued existence of financial intermediaries, it is important to understand some of the key elements of a theory of savings behaviour.[1]

Since savings represent a household's residual income—what is left after it pays for consumption spending and taxes—a theory of savings is also a theory of consumption. This is the approach traditionally taken in economic analysis, and we follow it here. This chapter is not, however, a survey of existing models of consumption or savings behaviour. Instead, we first build on the idea, introduced in Chapter 5, that savings is nothing more than consumption postponed and conversely, borrowing represents savings postponed. We also know that lenders and borrowers exchange funds at the equilibrium real interest rate. Now we explore how an individual's discount rate (the rate at which one values the future versus the present) interacts with existing interest rates to determine the amount of savings or borrowing for a given level of income.

To explain these phenomena, we use a simple model of consumption–savings behaviour. In it, we incorporate the element of time in the simplest possible fashion by assuming that we can express an individual's decision-making problem in two periods.

We conclude the chapter by examining briefly more sophisticated models of savings behaviour, those that consider that consumption and thus savings are a function of age and the type of income earned.

---

1 Scholars in the United States have recently focused much attention on household savings because that country's savings rates have reached historically low levels. In Canada savings rates are higher, but analysts watch them carefully.

## INTERTEMPORAL SAVINGS BEHAVIOUR

We begin by assuming that an individual earns a level of real income, denoted $y$, in each of two periods.[2] To avoid any element of uncertainty, we simplify by assuming that the flow of income over the individual's lifetime is known with certainty. In addition, we assume that this person or household has no wealth (from inheritance or from previous savings) and does not wish to bequeath anything to the next generation at the end of the second period. We also initially assume that the interest rate does not change.

To begin, we know from the discussion of Chapter 5 that the terms of trade between the present and the future are measured by the real interest rate. Thus, if the real interest rate is $\rho$, a \$1 investment will yield

$$1 + (1 \cdot \rho) \tag{9.1}$$

where $1 \cdot \rho$ represents the interest earned on \$1 one year later. Equation (9.1) can be rewritten as

$$1 + (1 \cdot \rho) = 1 + [1 \cdot (R - \pi^e)] \tag{9.2}$$

since the Fisher equation (again, see Chapter 5) equates the real interest rate with the nominal interest rate less expected inflation.

We now have at our disposal the two basic facts that determine consumption opportunities. We can combine them to define the budget constraint of the individual,[3] who can make one of several choices:

1. To keep each period's consumption spending even with its income.
2. To save at least part of the income in period 1 and then consume it in period 2 (along with the period 2 income).
3. To consume more than the income in period 1, financing the extra consumption by borrowing. The loan must, of course, be repaid from period 2 income.

Which course will the individual choose? As always in economic analysis, we assume it will be the one that provides **utility maximization**—that is, the one that provides the greatest satisfaction, which economists interpret as the most consumption.

---

2 A period can be a year, a month, a week, or a decade. The length of the period is not crucial for the discussion that follows. For the moment, income is the only constraint facing the individual.

3 Following the usual convention in microeconomics, all individuals are assumed to be alike.

To build our model, let $c_t$ represent real consumption spending in period $t$ and let $y_t$ measure the real income level again for period $t$. First we evaluate the present value of consumption spending and of income over the two periods:

$$c_1 + \frac{c_2}{1 + \rho}$$

$$y_1 + \frac{y_2}{1 + \rho}$$

Therefore, if we restrict individuals to spending no more than the present value of their lifetime (two-period) income, the budget constraint facing each of them can be written

$$c_1 + \frac{c_2}{1 + \rho} = y_1 + \frac{y_2}{1 + \rho} \tag{9.3}$$

We can now illustrate the situation in an intertemporal choice diagram often called a Fisher diagram (after the great economist Irving Fisher on whose analysis much of ours depends). Figure 9.1 provides the basic elements. Suppose that the individual chooses neither to save nor to borrow but simply to consume in each period exactly the income received in that period. In that case, $c_1 = y_1$ and $c_2 = y_2$.

Since the individual knows with certainty that income of $y_1$ and $y_2$ will be forthcoming in the two periods, selecting a consumption–income combination represented by the equalities above amounts to choosing to consume at point $E$ in Figure 9.1(A). It is called the *endowment point* because it reflects the income with which the individual is endowed.

The other two possibilities are, of course, saving in period 1 or borrowing in period 1. Given the endowment point, $E$, saving in period 1 occurs whenever $c_1 < y_1$ and borrowing takes place whenever $c_1 > y_1$. Notice, however, that the total consumption possibilities are limited by the interest income earned from savings in period 1 or the interest cost of a debt, which must be repaid in period 2. The consumption choices available to the consumer—called the set of **consumption possibilities**—are given by the triangle formed by the two axes in Figure 9.1 up to the limit imposed by the income availble in the two periods, which is called the consumer's **budget constraint** (the downward-sloping line $AB$).

The tradeoff is between current and future consumption. The slope of the tradeoff must, therefore, be determined by the real interest rate since that is what expresses the extent to which future consumption can be increased or decreased when a portion of current income is saved or sacrificed. Thus, the slope of the budget constraint is

$$-(1 + \rho)$$

**FIGURE 9.1** Fisher Diagrams

### (A) The Budget Constraint

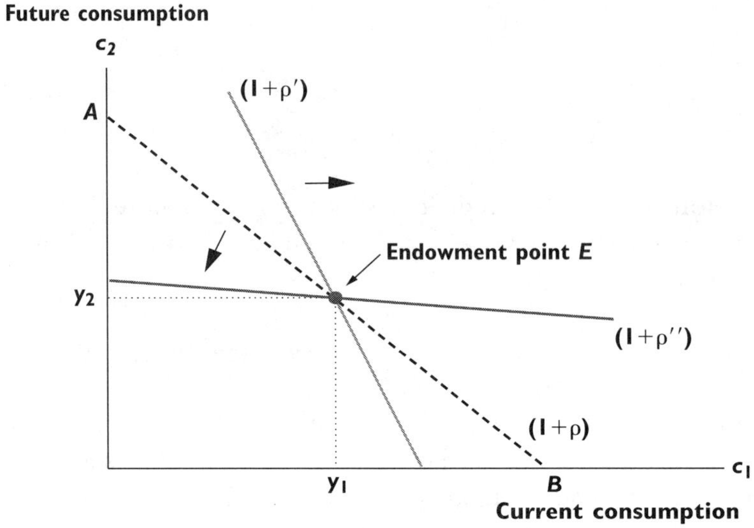


### (B) Indifference Curves

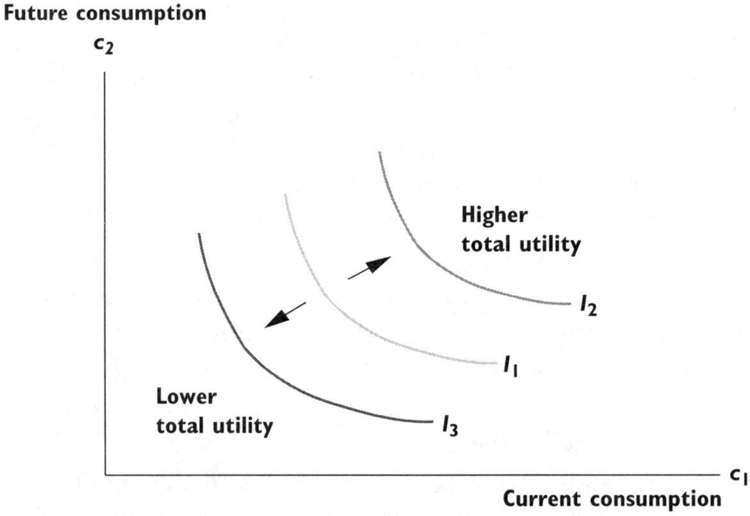


Panel (A) illustrates the endowment point, *E*, and how the real interest rate determines the slope of the budget constraint. Since the endowment (here $y_1, y_2$) is given, all consumption possibilities must pass through point *E*. A higher real interest rate signifies a steeper budget constraint.

Panel (B) illustrates an individual's preferences using indifference curves. They depict combinations of consumption in the two periods such that total utility is constant. Total utility along $I_2$ is higher than for $I_1$ while total utility is lowest along $I_3$.

Figure 9.1(A) also illustrates how different interest rates change the slope of the budget constraint. Recall that we have assumed that the income combination $y_1$ and $y_2$ is always available, no matter what the prevailing real interest rate. Therefore, all consumption possibilities or budget constraints must pass through the endowment point, *E*. The higher the real interest rate, the greater the future consumption possibilities for every dollar of real income saved in period 1. Hence, as shown in the figure, a higher real interest rate ($\rho' > \rho$) means a steeper budget constraint slope. Conversely, a lower real interest rate ($\rho'' < \rho$) signifies a flatter slope.

Next, we must incorporate the preferences of individuals. The utility an individual derives from consumption in this two-period case can be written

$$u = u(c_1, c_2) \tag{9.4}$$

where $u$ is the subjective utility that is a function of consumption spending in the two periods. Individuals are assumed to maximize equation (9.4) subject to the constraint of equation (9.3). The combinations of consumption (in both periods) that yield constant total utility are depicted by an *indifference* curve. Three such curves are shown in Figure 9.1(B). The slope of an indifference curve at a particular point is a measure of the rate of *time preference*—that is, of the relative preference for current over future consumption.[4] Recall that indifference curves cannot intersect. They can, however, shift with changing circumstances. As shown in Figure 9.1(B), a rightward shift signifies higher total utility since large combinations of consumption in *both* periods become possible.

We are now in a position to find the individual's optimal consumption pattern for the two periods. This is accomplished in Figure 9.2. Utility is maximized when the slope of an indifference curve is equated to the terms of trade between current and future consumption. Graphically, this equality occurs at the tangency between the indifference curve and the budget constraint. Such a tangency is depicted as point *O* (which stands for optimal) in Figure 9.2. The optimal consumption allocation for each period is given by $c_1^*$ and $c_2^*$, respectively.

In Figure 9.2(A), the individual is a saver. Optimal consumption in period 1 is less than income in that period so savings equal $y_1 - c_1^*$. Thus, consumption in period 2 is

$$(1 + \rho)(y_1 - c_1^*) + y_2 = c_2^*$$

Since the real interest rate, $\rho$, is positive, clearly $c_2^* > y_2$. In words, consumption in period 2 exceeds income in the same period.

4 Technically, the slope of an indifference curve is called the *marginal rate of substitution, MRS*. Algebraically, the MRS is the ratio of the marginal utilities of current and future consumption. The *marginal utility of consumption, MUC*, is simply an expression of the value of a change in consumption spending in utility terms.

**FIGURE 9.2** The Optimal Consumption Choice

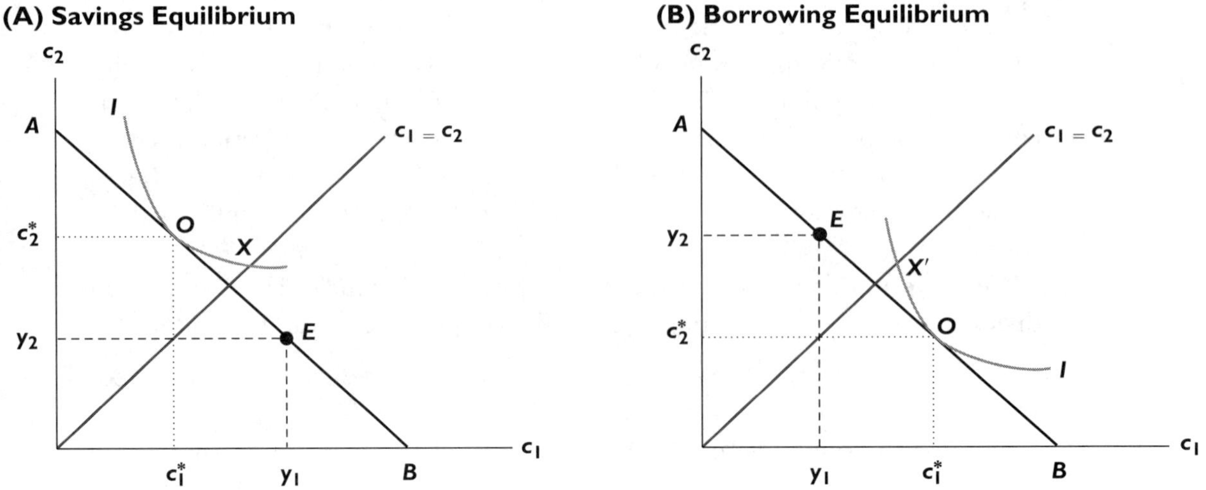


Point *O* is optimal because it represents the tangency between indifference curve *I* and the budget constraint *AB*. The optimal consumption allocation is $c^*_1$ and $c^*_2$ in periods 1 and 2, respectively. Since income in period 1 exceeds consumption in panel (A), a saver is depicted; consumption in period 2 can exceed income earned in period 1. The optimal consumption combination for a borrower is shown in panel (B).

A borrower, in contrast, will select the optimal consumption pattern illustrated in Figure 9.2(B). The individual chooses an optimum to the right of the endowment point, an indication of relatively greater consumption in period 1.

In using these Fisher diagrams to understand consumer behaviour, it is helpful to draw a 45° line emanating from the origin. All along this line, the consumption combinations in the two periods are equal to each other ($c_1 = c_2$). One way of expressing the time preference of an individual is to evaluate the slope of an indifference curve along the 45° line from the origin. The indifference curve for the saver (point *X* in Figure 9.2(A)) is flatter than that for the borrower (point *X'* in Figure 9.2(B)).

In other words, the saver finds consumption in period 1 relatively less valuable than consumption in period 2, and the opposite is true for the borrower.[5] Thus, the two are said to have different *discount rates*—to place different values on the

5 The mathematically inclined can suppose that equation (9.4) is written as

$$u(c_1, c_2) = u(c_1) + \frac{u(c_2)}{(1 + \rho)}$$

This expression assumes that total utility is time separable so that we can examine consumption choice in period 1 taking as given consumption in period 2. At the point where $c_1 = c_2$, it can be shown that the ratio of the marginal utilities for the saver is such that the discount rate or rate of time preference is lower than $\rho$. The opposite holds for the borrower.

present versus the future. Since the saver prefers future consumption over current consumption, such an individual tends to discount the future relatively less heavily than a borrower.

# THE DETERMINANTS OF INTERTEMPORAL SAVINGS BEHAVIOUR

The basic framework we have just established can be used to illustrate a number of interesting factors that influence savings behaviour. We will consider three examples.

## EFFECT OF AN INTEREST RATE CHANGE

If the real interest rate increases, what is the effect on the optimal consumption pattern chosen by a saver (Figure 9.3(A)) or a borrower (Figure 9.3(B))? Since the endowment point, *E*, in both diagrams is fixed (income in the two periods is given), any real interest rate change must cause the budget constraint to rotate about that point.

With an interest rate increase, \$1 saved today means greater future consumption opportunities than before; and \$1 borrowed has a higher interest cost, thereby reducing future consumption opportunities. Hence, the budget constraint rotates clockwise when the real interest rate rises, whether the individual's choice is to borrow or to save.

For the saver (Figure 9.3(A)), the initial optimal consumption pattern is $c_1^*$, $c_2^*$, since the tangency of the individual's indifference curve, $I_1$, and budget constraint, *AB*, occurs at point $O_1$. Thus, savings of $y_1 - c_1^*$ permit consumption $c_2^*$ in period 2, which exceeds that period's income by $c_2^* - y_2$. The difference, of course, is accounted for by period savings plus interest:

$$(y_1 - c_1^*)(1 + \rho) + y_2 = c_2^*$$

The opposite occurs in the case of a borrower (Figure 9.3(B)), whose initial optimal consumption pattern is given by $c_1'$, $c_2'$.

Evaluating the effect of an interest rate change on individual behaviour involves considering two factors. First, the rise in the real interest rate means that the price of current consumption rises relative to that of future consumption. The reason is that each dollar saved before the interest rate change now yields more future dollars and thus more future consumption than before. It is apparent from Figure 9.3(A) that if an individual decides to continue to consume $c_1^*$ in period 1, consumption opportunities in period 2 can now exceed $c_2^*$, the level of period 2 consumption chosen initially. This logic applies no matter what level of con-

**FIGURE 9.3** Effect of a Higher Real Interest Rate on Optimal Consumption

**(A) Savings Equilibrium**

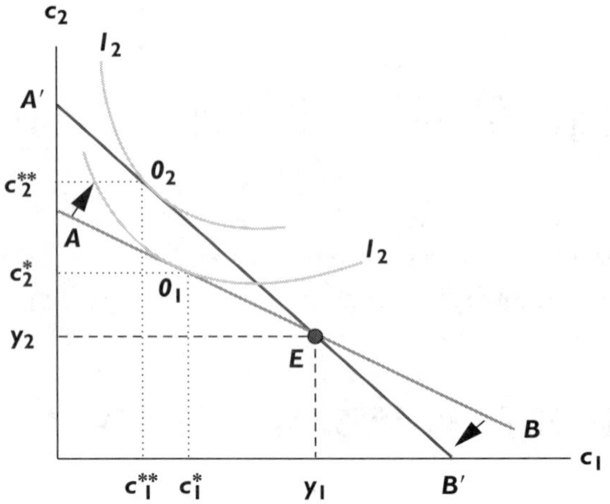


**(B) Borrowing Equilibrium**

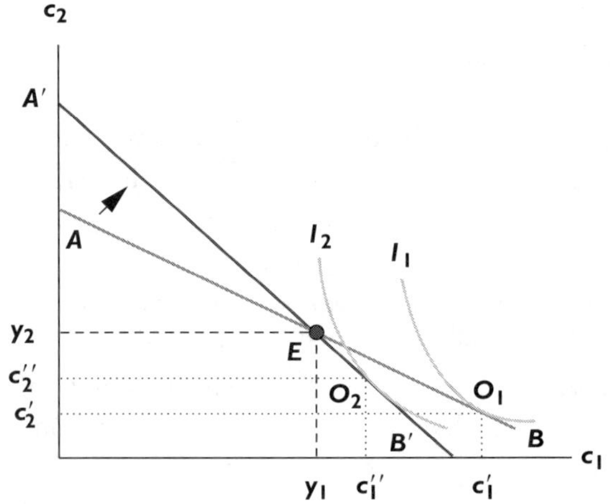


In panel (A), current income, $y_1$, exceeds current optimal consumption $c_1^*$ so a saver is depicted. A rise in the real interest rate results here in the selection of the optimal consumption pattern $c_1^{**}$, $c_2^{**}$. Preferences (the shape of the indifference curve) dictate whether current consumption rises or falls when the real interest rate rises.

In panel (B), current consumption, $c_1'$, exceeds current income, $y_1$, so a borrower is depicted. A rise in the real interest rate means lower current consumption since future consumption becomes relatively more expensive. The net effect on future consumption is ambiguous since it depends on the individual's preferences. Usually, however, one would expect lower current consumption and higher future consumption.

sumption is chosen for period 1, provided that the individual saves some portion of income in that period.

The same description applies to the borrower in reverse. Thus, a rise in the real interest rate means that the initial cost of the outstanding debt becomes higher than it was initially, prompting smaller period 2 consumption possibilities. Thus, for example, we see that consumption of $c'_1$ during period 1 is no longer possible for the borrower in Figure 9.3(B).

The upshot is that with the change in the terms of trade between present and future consumption, both a saver and a borrower will opt to reduce current consumption in favour of higher future consumption.[6]

The utility-maximizing individual must also contend with the fact that a change in the real interest rate affects total income over the two periods and consequently total consumption.[7] As already noted, if saving or borrowing are unchanged, the total available for consumption will be higher or lower, respectively, after the rise in the real interest rate.

What will the final response be? Some individuals will choose less current consumption and more future consumption, but the opposite is also possible. The answer depends on the preferences of the individual. Figure 9.3 reflects an individual who is relatively patient and sees a higher real interest rate primarily as a means of increasing future consumption at the expense of current consumption. However, someone who greatly discounts the future (that is, has a relatively higher marginal rate of time preference) will favour more current consumption over future consumption. The net effect is, therefore, uncertain although the results depicted in Figure 9.3 are the ones generally expected.

## EFFECT OF AN INCOME CHANGE

So far we have maintained the assumption of a fixed endowment: here, an equal amount of income in the two periods ($y_1 = y_2$). But suppose the individual has a windfall—for example, lottery winnings or a salary bonus—in one period. Figure 9.4 illustrates the effect of an increase in income during period 1. (Income in period 2 is assumed to be constant and remains, therefore, at $y_2$.) Clearly, if $y_1$ is increased, the original endowment point, $E$, is no longer the relevant starting point for the budget constraint. The new endowment point is $E'$, with the distance of $EE'$ representing the magnitude of the increase in income (that is, $y'_1 - y_1$). The increase in period 1 income implies a parallel rightward shift in the budget constraint since the endowment point also moves to the right. (The shift is a parallel one since the real interest rate is unchanged.)

---

6 Technically, this is known as the *substitution effect* of a higher interest rate.

7 This is known as the *income effect*.

**FIGURE 9.4** Effect of an Income Change

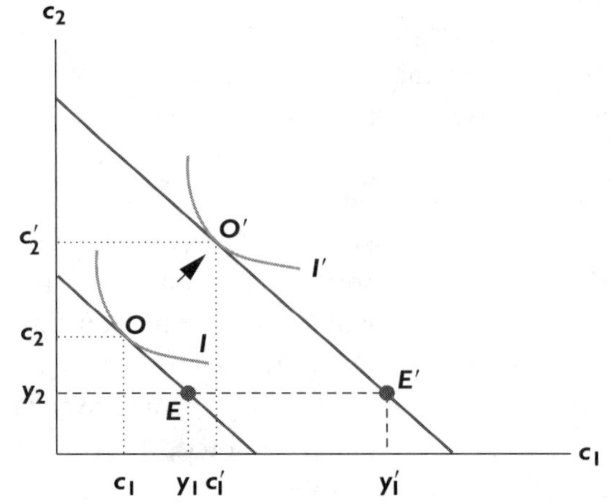


An increase in period 1 income ($y_1'$ instead of $y_1$) moves the endowment point from *E* to *E'*. Since consumption is believed to be positively related to income, optimal consumption is expected to rise in both periods, here from *O* to *O'*.

What is the effect on the optimal consumption pattern? An increase in period 1 income is usually believed to lead to more consumption in both the present and the future. The individual depicted in Figure 9.4 initially chose the optimal consumption pattern at point *O*; then, following the increase in income, point *O'* was chosen, which implies more consumption in both periods.[8]

## EFFECT OF A LIQUIDITY CONSTRAINT

So far we have assumed that preferences—technically, the marginal rate of time preference—dictate the choice between borrowing and saving as well as the amounts of debt incurred or assets accumulated. The only constraint is the budget constraint. But suppose the individual also faces a *liquidity constraint.* That is, the individual does not have sufficient liquidity to consume as much as desired in period 1 and cannot borrow (or cannot borrow enough) to finance consumption that is greater than that period's income even though the next period's is expected to be larger.

Figure 9.5 illustrates the situation. An individual is endowed with $y_1$ in period 1. It is sufficient to meet basic consumption needs, but no more. A considerable increase is expected for period 2 income ($y_2 > y_1$), but there is a liquidity constraint

8 Such an outcome is consistent with the notion that the *income elasticity of demand* can be presumed to be positive (that is, percentage changes in demand increase and decrease with percentage changes in income). One could, of course, depict a case in which period 1 consumption falls following an increase in period 1 income, but such an outcome would generally not accord with our everyday experience. Thus, consumption in both periods is presumably a *normal good* (the quantity demanded rises with increases in income).

**FIGURE 9.5** Effect of a Liquidity Constraint

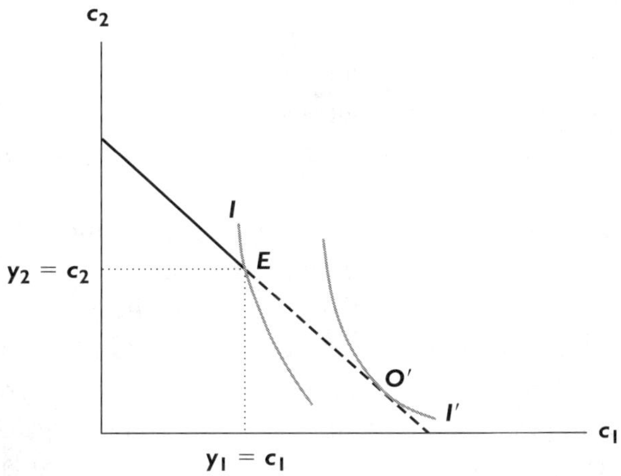


An individual with a liquidity constraint has a low period 1 income, so all of it is likely to be consumed in that period ($y_1 = c_1$). Such an individual is constrained to consume at point *E*. But there is relatively high period 2 consumption. In the absence of a liquidity constraint, the individual would have consumed at 0′.

in period 1. Consequently, the individual is likely to spend all of his or her meagre income in period 1 and not save anything. Although the individual would like to consume at point *O*′ along indifference curve *I*′, the constraint is binding, so point *E* is selected along a lower indifference curve, *I*. The kink in the opportunity set is the point likely to be chosen by the liquidity constrained individual.

This situation is not an unusual one. Consider the position of many students. Their income level is low, and the financial marketplace thinks the likelihood of default too high to grant them loans, even though they expect their education to yield them much higher income in the future.[9] The figure illustrates their liquidity constraint in the consumption–savings decision. This situation is the primary reason governments have found it necessary to intervene by providing loan guarantees, by directly subsidizing students through loans, and by providing subsidies to educational establishments.

## LIFECYCLE EXPLANATIONS OF CONSUMPTION BEHAVIOUR

The simple consumption–savings model we have developed can be useful in understanding the determinants of savings behaviour. Real interest rate changes,

9 Economists call education and skill *human capital.* A liquidity constraint arises in part because one can borrow against physical capital (such as a house or a car) but normally not against human capital.

temporary changes in income, liquidity constraints, and the extent to which an individual discounts the future are all factors influencing optimal consumption choice.

The difficulty with the two-period model is that an individual's optimum consumption choice is likely to be influenced primarily by the individual's age and by the nature of income changes over a lifetime (that is, are they short term—transitory—as modelled in Figure 9.4, or long term?). You are probably acquainted with economists' explanations about how consumption and savings behaviour is likely to be affected by what is known as the lifecycle. Such a discussion appears particularly important in light of Canada's ageing population. The age distribution in an economy may influence the flow of savings.

The great British economist John Maynard Keynes introduced the idea of the consumption function in the 1930s. According to his theory, consumption is largely determined by *disposable income*. The **consumption function** is the relationship between total consumer spending and total disposable income when all other determinants of that spending are held constant. A related concept is the **marginal propensity to consume (MPC)**, which is the ratio of a change in consumption to the change in disposable income that produces it, or $\Delta c/\Delta y$. The MPC measures the slope of the consumption function.

Several difficulties arise with the Keynesian theory because it neglects a variety of empirical facts that have come to light during research into the consumption function over the last 30 years. Figure 9.6 shows two scatter plots of consumption expenditure and personal disposable income, with both series expressed in real terms on a per capita basis.[10] Panel (A) shows the relationship between *levels* of consumption and income since 1947. Panel (B) plots changes in consumption and income. Added to each figure is the straight line that most closely fits the scatter points.[11]

Notice two things about these figures. First, the correlation between levels of income and levels of consumption is very high (Figure 9.6(A)), whereas changes in consumption are not so closely related to changes in income (Figure 9.6(B)). Second, the slope of the straight line fitted to the scatter plots is steeper in Figure 9.6(A) than in Figure 9.6(B).

We can call Figure 9.6(A) a model of a *long-run* consumption function because it shows the relationship between levels of consumption and income for the last 40 years or so of data, and Figure 9.6(B) a *short-run* consumption function because

10 That is, nominal consumption spending and income are deflated by an appropriate price index and by population. Thus, if the series $X$ is to be deflated by $P$ for price and $N$ for population, the real per capita value of $X = X/PN$.

11 This line is called the least squares fitted line. See any introductory statistics textbook for details.

**FIGURE 9.6** Consumption Spending versus Disposable Income

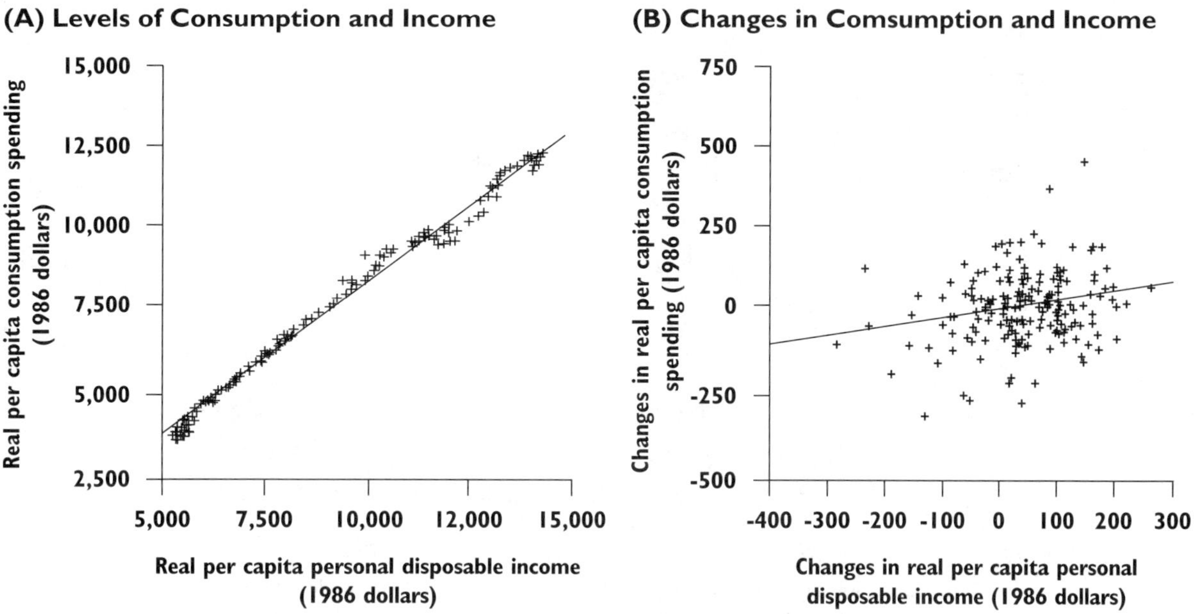


In panel (A) of these scatter plots, the long-run marginal propensity to consume is 0.81. In panel (B) the short-run marginal propensity to consume is 0.21. Thus, a $1 increase in disposable income raises consumption spending by 81¢ in the long run, but in the short run, consumption spending rises by only 21¢ for each $1 increase in disposable income.

Note: Consumption spending represents total consumption expenditures, seasonally adjusted, on a quarterly basis. Income is personal disposable income, also seasonally adjusted on a quarterly basis. Both series were deflated by population and prices (implicit price deflator for consumption expenditures and the implicit price deflator, both 1986 = 100).

Source: Statistics Canada, CANSIM database.

it shows how changes in consumption are influenced by changes in income. Then we can state that the long-run marginal propensity to consume is larger than the short-run marginal propensity to consume. The source of the difference lies in the fact that consumption spending evolves more smoothly over time than income (see Figure 9.7). As a result, temporary changes in income appear to have a relatively small influence on consumption, whereas over long periods of time changes in income and consumption seem to move more or less together.

The relative smoothness of consumption over time suggests either that individuals are influenced in their consumption behaviour by whether they expect an income change to be temporary or not or that individuals attempt to smooth their consumption spending over a lifetime even though their income varies considerably during that period. Figure 9.8(A) shows, in highly stylized form, how labour income evolves relative to consumption during an individual's life-

**FIGURE 9.7** Consumption Spending and Income over Time

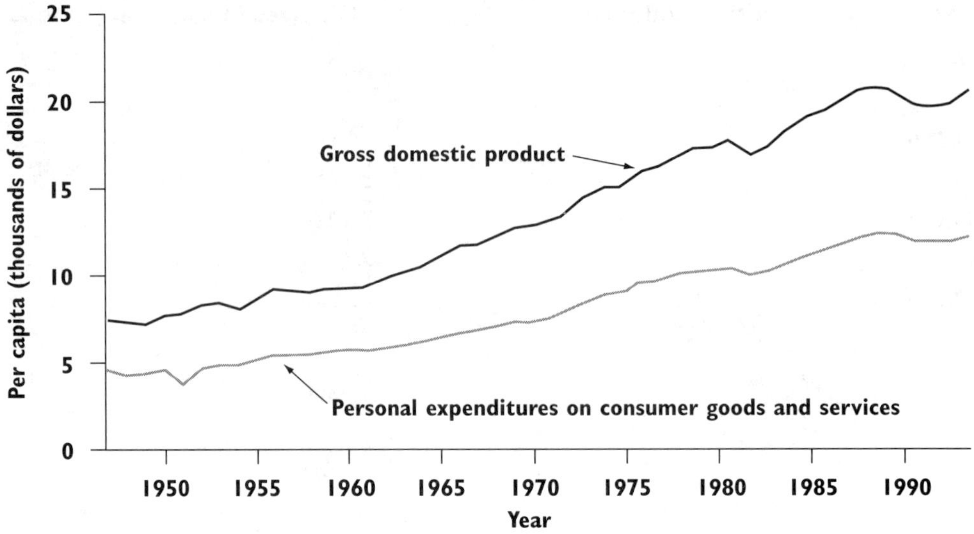


Income and consumption spending appear to move in tandem over the long term. But the former is more volatile than the latter in the short term.

Note: Consumption spending represents total consumption expenditures, seasonally adjusted, on a quarterly basis. Income is GDP, also seasonally adjusted on an annual basis. Both series were deflated by population and prices (implicit price deflator for consumption expenditures and the implicit price deflator, both 1986 = 100).

Source: Statistics Canada, National Income and Expenditure Accounts Catalogue No. 13-201, 1994. Reproduced by authority of the Ministry of Industry, 1996.

time. The individual depicted here is assumed to have a life expectancy of 85 years and to earn labour income from age 25 onward.[12] Labour income is assumed to grow with experience and seniority and to cease abruptly on retirement at age 65. One could make a number of other assumptions to increase the realism of the example but the essential conclusions of the analysis would be unaffected: individuals *dissave* (spend savings or take on debt) during the early and the latter stages of their lifecycle and accumulate wealth during much of their working lives. Figure 9.8(B), which is derived from Figure 9.8(A), shows lifetime accumulation of wealth.

The two ideas are known respectively as the permanent income hypothesis and the lifecycle theory of consumption. Both embody the notion that individuals are

12 Of course, the individual may also have acquired and accumulated assets in earlier years and/or plan lifetime consumption on the assumption that a bequest to the next generation will be made. These complications are ignored in the analysis.

**FIGURE 9.8** Lifetime Income, Consumption Spending and Wealth

**(A) Income and Consumption Spending (Saving and Dissaving)**

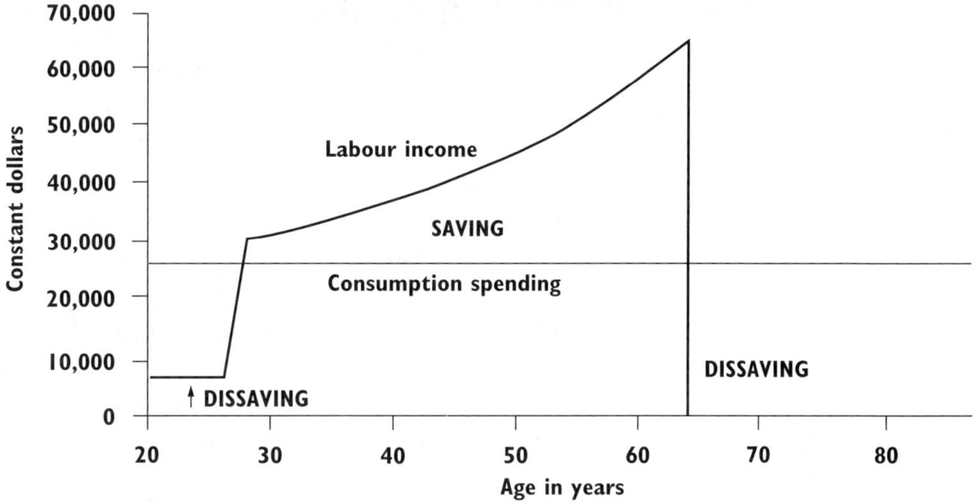


**(B) The Accumulation of Wealth**

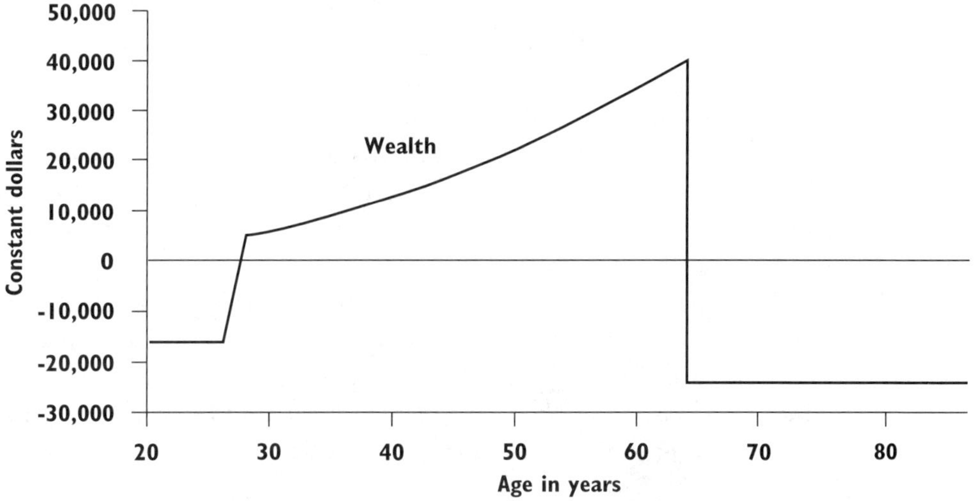


In this typical lifecycle, the individual has a very low income in young adulthood (presumably, student days). He or she enters the full-time labour force at age 25 and earns a steadily increasing income until retirement at age 65. Death occurs at age 85. The consumption level remains the same throughout the lifecycle. Thus, panel (A) shows that income exceeds consumption spending ($y > c$) from ages 25 to 65; the opposite is true before and after that period. Panel (B) shows the same lifetime pattern for the accumulation of wealth.

Note that the dollar amounts are stated in real terms: individuals care about purchasing power, not the nominal dollars earned or spent.

Source: Author's assumptions and calculations.

forward-looking in deciding their consumption spending levels. Both emerged at approximately the same time and are closely related.

## THE PERMANENT INCOME HYPOTHESIS

Milton Friedman, a Nobel laureate in economics, proposed the **permanent income hypothesis**, a theory that an individual consumes an amount equivalent to a stable income stream that would produce the same lifetime wealth as the one shown in Figure 9.8(B) if we had used actual labour income. Friedman calls this income measure permanent income. Since it is stable, consumption spending is also stable. Thus, in the long run, consumption is determined by permanent income. As Figure 9.9 shows, however, if we think of permanent income as proxied by the relatively smooth permanent income line, actual disposable income deviates from permanent income as shown in the bottom portion of the figure. If permanent income captures the long-run feature of consumption, the difference between actual and permanent values, called transitory income, captures its short-run aspects. Thus, we can write

$$y = y^P + y^T \tag{9.10}$$

where

$y$ = actual real income
$y^P$ = permanent income
$y^T$ = transitory income

Friedman hypothesized that the marginal propensity to consume out of permanent income (that is, the long-term MPC) is high, so that it captures the long-term behaviour of consumption, whereas the marginal propensity to consume out of transitory income is low.

The latter point corresponds with the empirical facts pertaining to short-run consumption behaviour described earlier. In Figure 9.9, notice that transitory income turned sharply negative during the 1982–83 recession. The magnitude of the drop was larger than any recorded before 1982—indeed, large enough for consumption spending to deviate somewhat from its smooth rise over time.

## THE LIFECYCLE THEORY OF CONSUMPTION

The **lifecycle hypothesis**, formed by Franco Modigliani, another Nobel laureate in economics, focuses on the relationship between consumption spending and how wealth is accumulated over an individual's lifetime. Consumption is determined by labour income as well as by the return on assets accumulated during the lifetime, so we can write

$$c = k_0 y + k_1 a \tag{9.11}$$

## ECONOMICS FOCUS 9.1 The Behaviour of Consumption Spending

How can one most accurately forecast levels of consumption spending? The graph below uses growth rates computed from the consumption series in Figure 9.7 since 1953. What is particularly striking is the way the plot fluctuates more or less randomly near or around the zero line. Also note the sharp drop in consumption growth in the 1982 and 1991–92 recessions. What does such a plot say about the behaviour of consumption?

A convenient way to calculate growth rates is to evaluate the first difference in the logarithm of a series. Thus, we write

$$c_t^* = \log c_t - \log c_{t-1}$$

where $c_t$ = level of real consumption spending. Now let us define randomness as a situation whereby the transformation of $c_t$ produces a series with a mean of zero and a constant variance. In other words,

$$c_t^* = e_t$$

where $e_t$ is random in the sense just described. Now note that we can summarize the above equations as

$$\log c_t = \log c_{t-1} + e_t$$

If this equation is used to forecast consumption, the striking result is that the best forecast for consumption spending next year is this year's value since the random element $e_t$ cannot, by definition, be forecast. This idea, first suggested by Robert Hall of Stanford, has stimulated much research into what is called the *random walk hypothesis of consumption*.

In what way does such an assumption make sense? If individuals attempt to smooth consumption during their lifetime in the manner described in Figure 9.8, then only an unpredictable event can influence consumption spending. Otherwise, this year's consumption spending should be the same as last year's. Therefore, the best-forecast for the next year's consumption is clearly this year's value.

Of course, not everyone agrees that consumption can merely be modelled as a random walk. Some researchers have found that wealth and interest rates, for example, also help us forecast consumption spending levels. Nevertheless, there is considerable empirical evidence that the random walk hypothesis of consumption is a reasonable empirical approximation.

**Sources:**

R.E. Hall, "Consumption," in *Modern Business Cycle Theory*, ed. R.J.Barro (Cambridge, Mass.: Harvard University Press, 1989): 153–77. Hall reviews the existing theories and empirical evidence in relation to the random walk hypothesis of consumption.

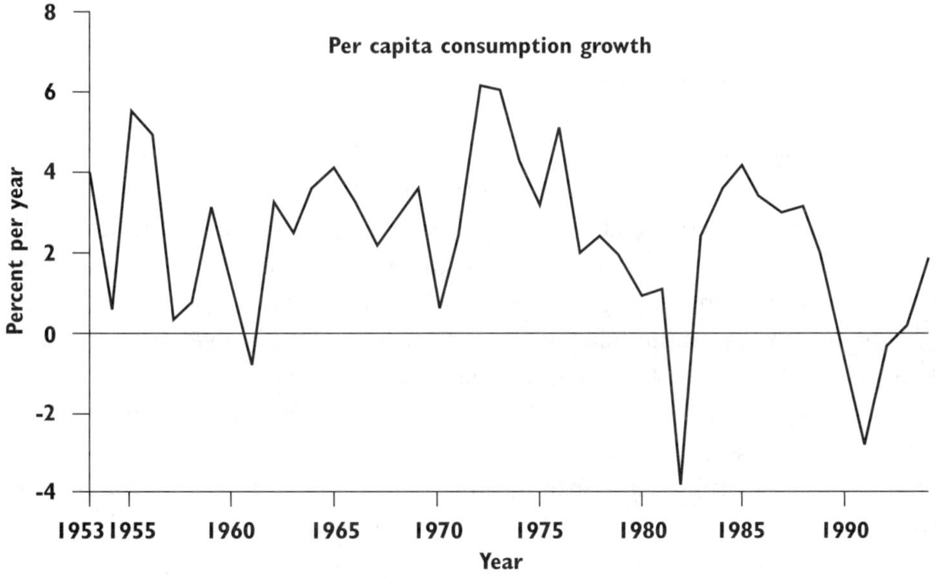

**FIGURE 9.9** Permanent and Transitory Income

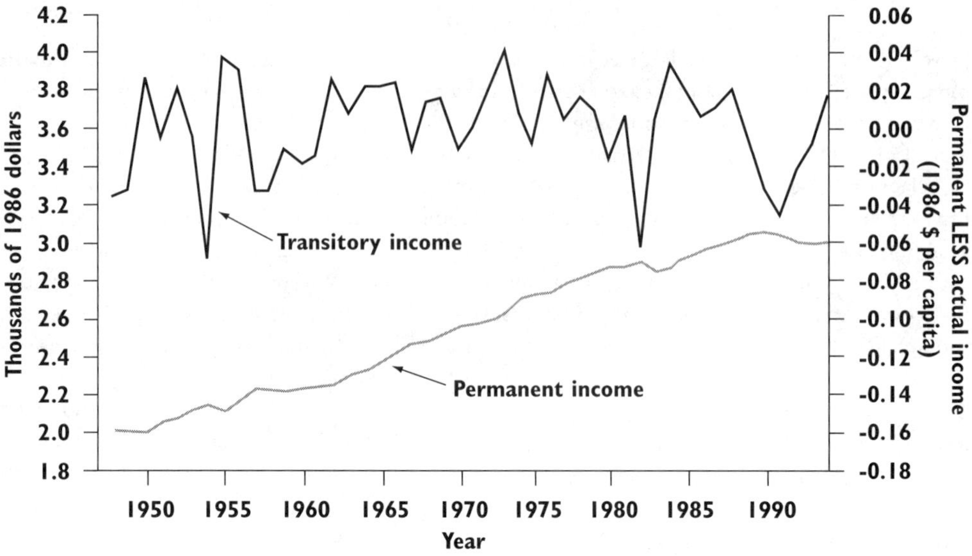


The upper curve is a proxy for permanent income; notice that it is relatively smooth. In contrast, transitory income (the bottom curve) fluctuates considerably. If the graph included actual income (permanent income plus transitory income), its curve would closely parallel that of permanent income.

Source: Statistics Canada, CANSIM database. Permanent income is proxied by a first-order autoregression fitted to the data on per capital real GDP.

where

$y$ = real disposable income
$a$ = real assets
$k_0$ = marginal propensity to consume out of disposable income
$k_1$ = marginal propensity to consume out of assets

The distinction between the short-run and long-run consumption functions is explained here by the high value of $k_0$ relative to that of $k_1$. Since wealth is accumulated over a long period, a transitory change in its value (perhaps because of a temporary change in the value of one of the assets in the individual's portfolio, such as stocks), is unlikely to have more than a temporary effect on consumption. By contrast, a change in $y$ is likely to have a much larger impact on consumption, for the reasons already elaborated.

Note that assets influence consumption in this model. Thus, a connection between interest rates and consumption is possible, although, as already noted, the net effect is an ambiguous one.

# THE ROLE OF GOVERNMENT AND TAXES

While we have been focusing on the connection between income and consumption we seem to have left government out of the equation. After all, much of the discussion above was in terms of *disposable* income, that is, income after taxes. But what about the impact of fiscal policy? How do government spending and taxes affect consumption? Governments have long used tax cuts or spending increases to indirectly boost consumption. Indeed, this was the original Keynesian policy prescription which has since fallen out of favour. Why? In part, because of the hypothesis called the **Ricardian equivalence theorem** coined by Harvard economist Robert Barro to describe the connection between deficits and economic activity. The general thrust of the Ricardian equivalence idea can be illustrated fairly easily.

Just as we can write a budget constraint for the representative consumer considered at the beginning of this chapter, so we can write a *government budget constraint* as follows

$$g_t + \rho\, b_{t-1} = \text{tax}_t + \Delta b_t \tag{9.12}$$

where $g$ represents government spending at time $t$, $\rho$ is the real interest rate as before, b represents the (real) value of government bonds outstanding, tax represents real tax revenues, again at time $t$, and $\Delta b$ represents the change in government bonds outstanding between $t$ and $t-1$ (i.e., $\Delta b_t = b_t - b_{t-1}$). Assume also, as we did for the consumer analyzed earlier, a two-period case.

Equation (9.12) says simply that government spending is made up of what it spends on goods and services as well as the interest cost of the debt outstanding. On the revenue side, the government earns income from taxes and from what it can raise in the bond market. The equality in (9.12) says that, in present value terms, the government must meet its budget constraint.[13]

Suppose now that we consider an example where, initially at least, $b_0 = 0$. Now let us suppose that in period 1 the government decides to finance a tax cut of \$1 (or \$1 billion if you prefer) by raising the funds in the bond market so that $b_1 = 1$. If equation (9.12) is to hold (and the government neither rolls over the debt nor incurs more deficit spending)[14] then the government must pay back the \$1 in principal as well as the interest cost on the debt which is $\rho \cdot \$1$ for a

13 Another way governments can raise revenues, as we have seen in Chapter 3, is via the printing of money. We return to this issue in Chapter 11.

14 All these complications can be accommodated by the theory without changing the flavour of the conclusions.

## FINANCIAL FOCUS 9.1 Is the Bequest Motive Important?

Do individuals have future generations in mind when they plan lifetime consumption decisions according to the intertemporal utility maximization discussed in this chapter? There is evidence that parents act as a "safety net" of sorts when their children fall on hard times and that consumption during recessions does not fall very much, as the lifecycle hypothesis might predict, because of parental transfers to children. The question has attracted considerable attention in economics lately because the answer affects one's view of whether interest rates and government deficits are linked to each other.

The Keynesian approach suggests that a deficit financed by a tax cut raises disposable income and consumption through a change in the real interest rate. Future generations do not play an important role. If, however, one examines the deficit question in the light of a model much like the one considered in this chapter, one in which the individual's utility is determined not only by lifetime consumption and savings but also by the utility to be derived by future generations from decisions made now and passed on via bequests, then a deficit today is merely a tax increase postponed. Hence, current consumption should be unaffected by a current deficit. Instead, savings will increase to finance future generations' higher tax liability. This theory has, perhaps inappropriately, been named the *Ricardian equivalence theorem* (after the great economist of the nineteenth century, David Ricardo).

The most prominent economist to advance the idea of Ricardian equivalence is Robert Barro of Harvard University. Bernheim (and others) have, however, attacked the theorem, which assumes that individuals behave altruistically. This assumption and others, they say, appear to be unrealistic or falsified through empirical observation. Some have argued that parents leave bequests as a way of controlling their children's lives (one study found that children of wealthy parents visit them more often than children of poorer parents).

Nevertheless, Barro, Evans, and Siklos have produced a significant body of empirical evidence suggesting that deficits and interest rates are independent of each other in a variety of countries. It is unclear, however, whether such a result arises strictly from Ricardian equivalence effects or from other, more complex considerations. This is an area of fairly intensive disagreement among economists.

**Sources:**

R.J. Barro, "The Ricardian Approach to Budget Deficits." *Journal of Economic Perspectives* 3 (Spring 1989): 37–54.

B.D. Bernheim, "Ricardian Equivalence: An Evaluation of Theory and Evidence," in *NBER Macroeconomics Annual 1987*, ed. S. Fischer (Cambridge, Mass.: The MIT Press, 1987). 263–303.

B.D. Bernheim, A. Schleifer, and L.H. Summers, "The Strategic Bequest Motive," *Journal of Political Economy* 93 (1985): 1045–1076.

P. Evans, "Do Budget Deficits Raise Nominal Interest Rates? Evidence from Six Industrialized Countries," *Journal of Monetary Economics* 20 (September 1987): 281–300.

G.P. O'Driscoll, "The Ricardian Non-equivalence Theorem," *Journal of Political Economy* 85 (1977): 207–10.

P.L. Siklos, "The Deficit-Interest Rate Link: Empirical Evidence for Canada," *Applied Economics* 20 (December 1988): 1563–78.

G.P. Zachary, "Parents' Gifts to Adult Children Studied," *Wall Street Journal* (February 9, 1995): A2.

total of $\$(1+\rho)$ in period 2. But, in present value terms, this last amount translates into

$$(1+\rho)/(1+\rho) = \$1$$

Therefore, the decrease in period 1 taxes of \$1 is completely neutralized in present value terms by a \$1 increase in taxes in period 2 to finance the retirement of the debt. More realistically, as the permanent income hypothesis would have predicted, a temporary tax decrease (or increase in disposable income) should have little or no effect on current consumption. Part of the debate then revolves around questions such as whether current generations selfishly consume their tax cut leaving future generations to incur the costs (see Financial Focus 9.1).

## SUMMARY

- Consumption spending by individuals can be thought of as being spread out over a lifetime.
- A simple model assumes that consumption choices are confined to two periods with the interest rate and income being the factors that determine whether the borrowing or savings take place.
- More elaborate and elegant explanations of lifetime consumption behaviour are the permanent income and lifecycle theories of consumption.
- The permanent income hypothesis says that consumption is more stable than income because individuals prefer to keep their consumption spending more or less a constant fraction of their expected lifetime income (permanent income).
- The lifecycle hypothesis says that in the face of variable income, individuals keep consumption spending stable by adding or subtracting from their wealth over their lifetime.

## IMPORTANT TERMS

budget constraint (p. 185)
consumption function (p. 194)
consumption possibilities (p. 185)
lifecycle hypothesis (p. 198)
marginal propensity to consumer (MPC) (p. 194)
permanent income hypothesis (p. 198)
Ricardian equivalence theorem (p. 201)
utility maximization (p. 184)

## EXERCISES

1. Using a two-period income–consumption diagram, show the impact on current savings of a fall in the interest rate. Assume that the individual saved part of her income in period 1.

2. Using a two-period income–consumption diagram, show the impact on current savings of a transitory fall in income. Assume the individual borrowed part of his income in period 1.

3. Using a two-period income–consumption diagram, show the impact on current savings of a permanent rise in income. If the individual is a saver in period 1, what is the likely effect on savings? (Hint: What does the permanent income hypothesis predict?)

4. Can the lifecycle concept of consumption explain why middle-aged individuals spend a smaller fraction of their income than do the young or the elderly? (Hint: Examine Figure 9.8.)

5. Using a two-period income–consumption diagram, show the impact of a rise in the interest rate assuming the household borrows in period 1.

6. What does the permanent income hypothesis say about the role of income in influencing consumption spending?

7. In terms of the permanent income hypothesis, contrast the effect on consumption of a temporary versus a permanent tax cut.

8. Why is it difficult to borrow against human capital in financial markets?

9. Suppose the liquidity constraint in Figure 9.5 could be eased but only by permitting loans at a premium over market interest rates. Show a possible optimum in such a case. How does time preference matter?

10. An alternative way of explaining the idea of the random walk hypothesis of consumption is to say that differences between consumption and income are transitory. Explain.

11. Explain how $k_0$ and $k_1$ are both a function of age in the lifecycle hypothesis.

12. What does the permanent income hypothesis predict would happen to consumption in the event someone wins a lottery? If someone is temporarily laid off? Explain.

# REFERENCES


Ando, A., and F. Modigliani, "The 'Life Cycle' Hypothesis of Savings: Aggregate Implications and Tests." *American Economic Review* 53 (March 1963): 55–84.

Fisher, I. *The Rate of Interest.* New York: Macmillan, 1907.

Friedman, M. *A Theory of the Consumption Function.* Princeton, N.J.: Princeton University Press, 1957.

Hall, R.E., John B. Taylor, and Jeremy Rudin. *Macroeconomics: The Canadian Economy.* Second Edition. New York: W.W. Norton and Co., 1995.

Harris, L. *Monetary Theory.* New York: McGraw-Hill, 1981.

Johnson, D.R., "Ricardian Equivalence: Assessing the Evidence for Canada," in W. Robson and W. Scarth, editors. *Debt and Deficits.* Toronto: C.D. Howe Institute, 1994.

Keynes, J.M. *The General Theory of Employment, Interest and Money,* Vol. VII of *The Collected Writings of John Maynard Keynes.* London and Basingstoke: Macmillan for the Royal Economic Society, 1973, Book III.

Modigliani, F., and R.E. Brumberg. "Utility Analysis and the Consumption Function: An Interpretation of Cross-Section Data." In *Post-Keynesian Economics,* edited by K.K. Kurihana, 388–436. New Brunswick, N.J.: Rutgers University Press, 1957.

Statistics Canada, CANSIM database.

CHAPTER 10

# Decision Makers: The Financial and the Non-Financial Sectors

In this chapter, we continue to develop models of the participants in financial markets by considering the case of business firms, which, as we saw in Chapter 8, may be either financial or non-financial. Firms exist, for the most part, because they borrow to invest or create assets that they hope will earn more than their borrowing costs. What differentiates firms from households is the *production process.* That is, firms use inputs to produce outputs, which are often physical in nature but can be non-physical commodities such as those produced by the service sector of the economy.

When households borrow and lend, the amount of utility they derive is determined primarily by their income, which the previous chapter took largely as given. By contrast, firms, financial and non-financial, derive income from the sale of the commodities they produce. Financial firms, in particular, derive income primarily from the spread between borrowing and lending rates,[1] a phenomenon ignored in the analysis of the previous chapter. This concept of leverage is basic to the financial firms with which we are primarily interested. We add it, therefore, to our analysis of consumption decisions. (The framework can also be used to explain the behaviour of non-financial firms.)

The chapter also considers other interesting questions related to firms' behaviour, such as whether they should borrow by issuing bonds or by selling shares. Surprisingly perhaps, the choice does not matter under some very special (and probably unrealistic) circumstances.

Finally, in this chapter we look at the association of stock prices with future economic performance. Observers often make this connection in the media. Is such a view warranted? As we will see, it has some validity.

1 Financial firms also derive income from various fees, but for the sake of simplicity we focus only on the spread in this chapter.

# THE CONCEPT OF LEVERAGE

**Leverage** refers to the practice of making investments or buying assets with borrowed funds with the object of profiting from the difference between the yield or return on the investments or assets and the cost of borrowed funds. One of the important ways in which a bank borrows is by taking deposits from clients. If a bank is able to borrow at an average rate of $R_{DEP}$ while simultaneously lending at a rate of $R_L$, we would expect

$$R_L > R_{DEP} \tag{10.1}$$

to hold. In other words, the **spread** (difference) between the borrowing and lending rates must be positive in order for the financial institution to make a profit.

To see why the spread is so important to a financial institution and its owners, the shareholders, consider the balance sheets in Table 10.1. The opening balance sheet in Table 10.1(A) is typical for a bank. Its assets consist of bonds and its liabilities comprise deposits and equity. Presumably it uses the deposits to invest in the bonds. Suppose that the assets are valued at market value (not at book value, which is the normal accounting practice). Now suppose that interest rates rise by 3%. Since bond prices are inversely related to interest rates, the market value of these bonds falls.[2] Although we know that the maturity structure of the assets will influence the size of the fall, assume for simplicity that a 3% rise in the interest rate results in a 3% fall in the market value of the assets. Now look at the balance sheet in Table 10.1(B). The impact of a seemingly small change in interest rates is to practically wipe out equity!

One way of ascertaining the impact of an interest rate change is to examine the **leverage ratio**, which is defined as

$$\frac{\text{Debt}}{\text{Equity}} = \text{Leverage ratio} \tag{10.2}$$

Since deposits represent the bank's debt in Table 10.1, the leverage ratio on the date of the opening balance sheet is

$$\frac{\$50 \text{ million}}{\$2 \text{ million}} = 25$$

2 See the discussion in Chapter 5.

## ECONOMICS FOCUS 10.1 The Spread

The model in this chapter, like most economic models, assumes that the spread between borrowing and lending rates is positive. But is it always so in the real world? The answer is usually but not always yes.

The rather volatile nature of interest rates has caused the spread between the borrowing and lending rates to become volatile too. The figure below illustrates by plotting the chartered banks' prime rate—the rate at which they lend to their most creditworthy clients—and the interest rate on non-chequable or savings deposits. The spread is usually positive, indicating that equation (10.1) is satisfied while a negative number, of course, points to the opposite results.

Given the data used in the figure, the assumption of a positive spread is a reasonable one. Indeed, notice that beginning in the mid-1980s, the spread increased considerably compared to that of earlier years. We leave it to you as an exercise to explain why this may have happened.

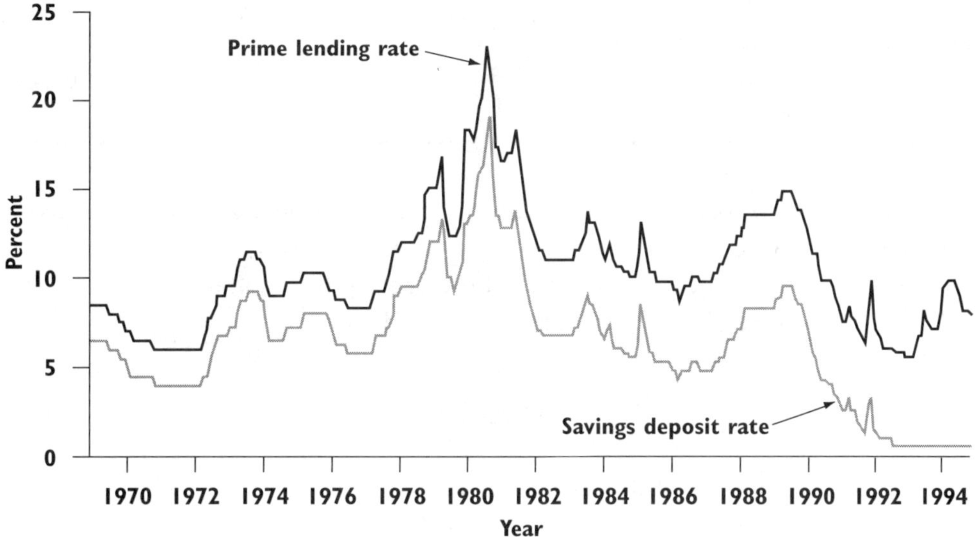


Source: Statistics Canada, The Spread from CANSIM database, reproduced by authority of the Ministry of Industry, 1996; and *Bank of Canada Review*, Table F1.

---

After the interest rate rise, the leverage ratio has more than quadrupled to

$$\frac{\$50.00 \text{ million}}{\$0.49 \text{ million}} = 102$$

Notice that the greater the proportion of assets financed through debt, the higher the leverage ratio. In the opening balance sheet, some 96% ($50 million/$52 million) of assets are financial through deposits or debt. After the interest rate

**TABLE 10.1** LEVERAGE AND THE INFLUENCE OF INTEREST RATE VOLATILITY

**(A) Opening Balance Sheet**

| Assets (millions) | | Liabilities (million) | |
|---|---|---|---|
| Bonds | \$52.00 | Deposits | \$50.00 |
| | | Equity | 2.00 |
| Total | \$52.00 | | \$52.00 |

Leverage ratio = \$50/2 = 25

**(B) Balance Sheet after a 3% Rise in Interest Rates**

| Assets (millions) | | Liabilities (millions) | |
|---|---|---|---|
| Bonds | \$50.49 | Deposits | \$50.00 |
| (52/1.03 = 50.49) | | Equity | 0.49 |
| Total | \$50.49 | | \$50.49 |

Leverage ratio = \$50/0.49 = 102

rise, the figure is more than 99%. Thus, a rise in the leverage ratio signals a greater reliance on debt to finance asset purchases.

Some people prefer to evaluate the ratio of equity (or capital) to assets as an indicator of leverage. The **capital–asset ratio** is defined as

$$\frac{\text{Equity}}{\text{Assets}} = \text{Capital–asset ratio} \tag{10.3}$$

For the balance sheets in Table 10.1, they are

**Opening**

$$\frac{\text{Equity}}{\text{Assets}} = \frac{\$2.00 \text{ million}}{\$52.00 \text{ million}} = 3.8\%$$

**After the Interest Rate Rise**

$$\frac{\text{Equity}}{\text{Assets}} = \frac{\$0.49 \text{ million}}{\$50.49 \text{ million}} = 1.0\%$$

After the interest rate rise, only 1% of assets are covered by equity, a fall of almost a quarter from the level before the interest rate changed.

Notice that the lower the capital–asset ratio, the more leveraged the firm. A fall in the capital–asset ratio gives the same signal as a rise in the leverage ratio: a bank that is less sound following the rise in interest rates.

## FINANCIAL FOCUS 10.1 The BIS Capital Convergence Requirements

The difficulties that faced banks worldwide during the 1980s have resulted in considerable attention being paid to capital–asset ratios. One development was the 1987 adoption of regulations relative to capital standards by the *Bank for International Settlements (BIS)*, an international central bank for central banks. (Its work is discussed in Chapter 21.)

The new BIS capital standards, called the *capital convergence requirements* were phased in during the early 1990s and were developed to prevent one country from taking advantage of lower capital–asset ratio requirements in another.

The target for the capital–asset ratio is 8%. This was supposed to have been attained by the end of 1992; by and large, banks met this goal. Equally important, the assets are risk-weighted: that is, the riskiness of an asset affects its value for the purposes of calculating the ratio. Table A gives an idea of the risk weights to be applied against specific assets. The lower the risk weight, the smaller the inherent risk of the asset in question. Individuals and institutions can thus re-evaluate intermediaries' balance sheets using these ratios to obtain a more realistic picture of the intermediaries' financial health.

What about off-balance-sheet items? For these increasingly important sources of business for many intermediaries, the BIS adopted conversion factors. Banks are to multiply the currency equivalent amount of such an item by the conversion factor to obtain an amount equivalent to the cost of capital should the instrument fall in value. Table B provides a list. The lower the conversion factor, the smaller the drain on capital should a loss occur.

Although the standards rely on the book value of assets, not their market value, they are significantly higher than the standards previously allowed in many countries. The rules are still full of loopholes, especially in defining capital. Nevertheless, the onset of a world-wide recession in 1990–91 combined with the implementation of the BIS rules has produced, according to some analysts, a severe "credit crunch," at least in the United States.

**Sources:**

R.C. Breeden and W.M. Isaac, "Thank Basel for Credit Crunch," *Wall Street Journal*, 4 November 1992, p. A10.

D.S. Bizer, "Examiners Credit Crunch," *Wall Street Journal*, 1 March 1993, p. A12.

Heather D. Whyte, "Canada's Bank Rules Tougher," *The Financial Post*, 3 July 1991, p. 2.

"A Survey of International Banking," *The Economist*, 7 April 1990, p. 65.

How realistic are the capital–asset ratios of Table 10.1? For many chartered banks, they range from 3.7% to 5.88% and they have typically risen over the last few years. For the reason underlying the change, recall that during the late 1960s and early 1970s Canadian interest rates were fairly stable, fluctuating only within a narrow range; by 1981, however, volatility had increased substantially. The lesson of Table 10.1 that increased interest rate volatility tends to raise the leverage ratio provides at least a partial explanation for the sharp rise in the chartered banks' resort to borrowed funds for purchasing assets during the 1980s.

Although banks throughout the world faced the same interest rate effects (see Chapter 1), Table 10.2 reveals that capital–asset ratios vary considerably world-

## FINANCIAL FOCUS 10.1 The BIS Capital Convergence Requirements (continued)

**TABLE A**

RISK WEIGHTS FOR BALANCE SHEET ASSETS

**Risk Weight = 0**

- Cash
- Reserves at the central bank
- Government-guaranteed claims
- Gold buillion

**Risk Weight = 0.2**

- Float or cash items in transit
- Claims guaranteed by banks
- Claims with maturities of less than one year by non-OECD banks
- Claims on local governments in OECD countries
- Claims on official multilateral lending institutions or regional development banks
- Claims that have as collateral cash or OECD government securities or securities of official multilateral institutions
- Shares in funds holding only securities with weights of 0 or 0.2

**Risk Weight = 0.5**

- Loans secured by residential real estate
- Revenue bonds
- Credit-equivalent amounts of interest rate and foreign exchange contracts not falling into risk weights 0 or 0.2

**Risk Weight = 1.0**

- Other private claims
- Other claims on non-OECD governments and banks
- Fixed assets and real estate
- Claims on state enterprises

**Table B**

OFF-BALANCE-SHEET CONVERSION FACTORS

**Conversion Factor = 1 or 100%**

- Standby letters of credit
- Sales and repurchase agreements
- Forward agreements representing commitments with certain drawdown

**Conversion Factor = 0.5 or 50%**

- Performance bonds, warrants, and standby letters of credit for non-financial obligations
- Revolving underwriting agreements and note issue facilities

**Conversion Factor = 0.2 or 20%**

- Short-term self-liquidating contingencies that are trade-related, such as commercial letters of credit

**Conversion Factor = 0 or 0%**

- Unused portions of commitments under one year that can be cancelled unconditionally

**Conversion of interest rate and foreign exchange contracts**

The replacement (market-to-market) cost *plus*

| Maturity | Interest rate contracts | Exchange rate contracts |
|---|---|---|
| < 1 year | 0.5% | 2.0% |
| 1 to 2 years | 1.0% | 5.0% |
| each additional year | 1.0% | 3.0% |

**Source:**
BIS.

wide.[3] The table gives an idea of the range of such ratios. The best banks have ratios of between 20% and 50% while the worst banks have ratios of approximately 1% or less. But as we have seen there is a big difference between the conventional capital–asset ratio and the risk-adjusted one. Part (B) of Table 10.2 shows that

3 To understand why differences in capital–asset ratios exist, we need to delve more deeply into the distinguishing characteristics of other countries' financial systems, a task we take up in Chapter 22.

**TABLE 10.2** SELECTED CAPITAL–ASSET RATIOS

**(A) The Best and Worst Capital–Asset Ratio Performers**

| *Bank Name* | *Capital–Asset Ratio (%)* |
|---|---|
| United Gulf Bank | 56.20 |
| Banque de Depôt | 49.24 |
| Invest Corp. | 29.12 |
| Pan Asia Bank | 24.04 |
| Far Eastern International | 19.24 |
| Security Capital | 19.17 |
| Deutsche Girozentrale | 1.56 |
| Taiwan Cooperative Bank | 1.14 |
| Rasheed Bank | 0.49 |

**(B) The Best Risk-Adjusted Capital–Asset Ratios**

| *Bank Name* | *Risk-Adjusted Capital-Asset Ratio (%)* |
|---|---|
| Chemical Financial Corp. | 27.16 |
| Asia Pacific Bank | 25.86 |
| Bank Julius Baer | 25.00 |
| Union Bank of Taiwan | 24.24 |
| Allied Banking Corp. | 23.18 |
| Northwest Bank Corp. | 22.98 |

Source: *The Banker* (July 1995), pp. 117–118, 120.

none of the banks with the highest risk-adjusted capital–asset ratios are the same ones with the highest such ratio calculated the usual way. Of course, capital–asset ratios and leverage ratios are not the sole indicators of bank soundness or performance, as we will see. Moreover, the figures given in Table 10.2 are based on book values, not the market values assumed in Table 10.1.

As we will see in Chapter 12, not all items in a firm's balance sheet are equal. Holding some assets, such as corporate bonds, entails greater risk of an unfavourable price change than the holding of cash or government bonds.

Unfortunately, some banks, in their pursuit of profit and market share put their shareholders at great risk of insolvency. Among these were the Herstatt Bank in Germany in 1974 and the Franklin National Bank in 1977 (see Chapter 22). Canadian banks are no exception, as we will see (Chapter 17). An international effort to give regulators worldwide a better idea of the risks that their banks were facing led to the formulation of risk-based capital standards (see Financial Focus 10.1).

To illustrate the implementation of these standards, consider the simple balance sheet in Table 10.3.

**TABLE 10.3** HYPOTHETICAL ASSETS OF A BANK

(A) Basic Financial Information

| *Balance Sheet Assets* | *Dollars* |
|---|---|
| Cash | 1,000 |
| Government bonds | 10,000 |
| Loans to corporations | 5,000 |
| Mortgage loans | 8,000 |
| Total | 24,000 |
| *Off-Balance-Sheet Items* (OBS) | |
| Standby letter of credit | 2,000 |
| Commercial letter of credit | 4,000 |
| Total | 6,000 |
| Equity: 5,000 | Capital–Asset Ratio: $5,000/$24,000=20.8% |

(B) Risk-adjusted Assets and OBS

| *Category* | *Actual (1) (Dollars)* | *Conversion Factor (2)* | *Risk-adjusted (1) × (2)* |
|---|---|---|---|
| Cash | 1,000 | 0 | 0 |
| Government bonds | 10,000 | 0 | 0 |
| Loans to corporations | 5,000 | 1 | 5,000 |
| Mortgage loans | 8,000 | .5 | 4,000 |
| Total | 24,000 | | 9,000 |
| *OBS* | | | |
| Standby letters of credit | 2,000 | 1 | 2,000 |
| Commercial letters of credit | 4,000 | .2 | 800 |
| Total | 6,000 | | 2,800 |
| Risk-adjusted capital–asset ratio | $5,000/$9,000 = 55.56% | | |

The actual values are organized according to whether the assets are balance sheet or off-balance-sheet (OBS) items, as shown in Part (A) of Table 10.2.[4] Next, one has to multiply the asset values by a conversion factor (again, see Financial Focus 10.1) to obtain what is called a risk-adjusted value. This is shown in Part (B) of the table. We see that since there is no perceived risk to holding cash or government bonds these assets receive a zero weighting. The impact of the BIS standards has been to *reduce the risk-adjusted* total assets and total OBS items relative to their originally recorded balance sheet values. If the capital–asset ratio was assumed to be 20.8% in the absence of risk-weighting, application of the BIS standards raises the capital–asset ratio to 55.51%. Therefore, banks which engage

4 These OBS items are typically derivative products you were introduced to in Chapter 4. We explore them in more detail in Chapter 14.

in risky activities relative to other banks are more easily identified using the risk-weighted method. In the present case, because the hypothetical bank has almost half of its assets zero-weighted, its risk-weighted capital–asset ratio means that it is "safer" than by the standards of the traditional capital-asset ratio measure.

## *THE PRODUCTION–INVESTMENT DECISION AND THE SPREAD BETWEEN BORROWING AND LENDING RATES

Clearly, firms do engage in leverage. We consider in this section why the process of intermediation creates a divergence between borrowing and lending rates, why leverage increases the welfare of financial institutions,[5] and what the optimal amount of leverage may be. We use a framework reminiscent of that described in Chapter 9. Recall that, in that chapter, we described the consumption decision of the consumer who is endowed with a certain income. For the firm, it is a little more complicated since its owners must also decide how much to produce as well as how much to consume. To keep matters simple, we begin by describing the production decision a firm faces.

### THE PRODUCTION POSSIBILITIES FRONTIER

Consider a firm that produces some output over time. If the firm is a financial institution, we label this output intermediation. (If the firm is a non-financial one, the output is a physical product or a service.) Suppose this idealized firm has no borrowing or lending opportunities and can decide only how much output to produce this period (the current period or period 1) and the next one (the future period or period 2).

We graph its choice in Figure 10.1, where $Q$ stands for the amount of production (which might be the volume of financial transactions generated or the number of units produced).

We assume that the firm can shift production between the two periods.[6] It can decide on any combination of $Q_1$, $Q_2$. It can even produce all its output during the current period, at $Q_1'$, or all during the future period, at $Q_2'$. The **production possibilities** frontier, the curve describing the set of tradeoffs between production in the current period and production in the next, is thus $Q_1'Q_2'$.

Note the concave (bowed outward) shape of the curve. The reason is the presence of **diminishing marginal returns** in production. If the firm decides to

5 Although our focus is on the behaviour of financial institutions, our discussion also applies to non-financial firms since they too borrow funds to invest in assets.

6 We include here the assumption that technology does not change during the two periods.

**FIGURE 10.1** The Production Possibilities Curve and Optimal Production

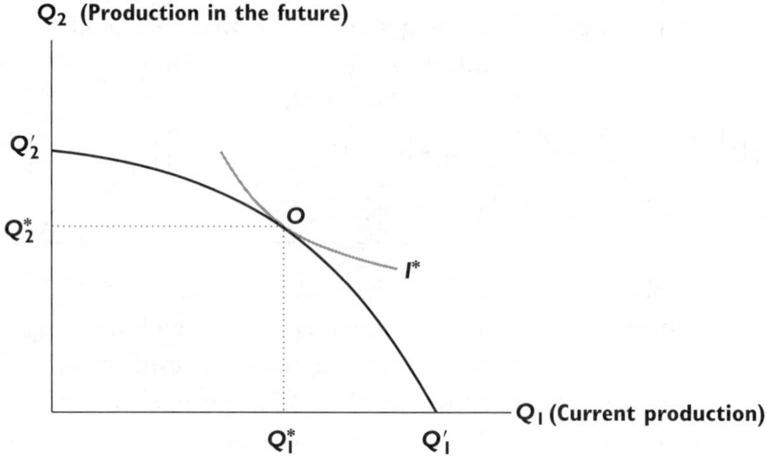


$Q'_1 Q'_2$ is the production possibilities curve. $I^*$ is an indifference curve. Utility is maximized at point $O$, where the production possibilities curve is tangent to the indifference curve.

produce at $Q'_1$, it will be accomplishing two periods' worth of production within the time of one period— a considerable amount of effort. The inputs into the production process, such as labour and machinery, might be used more efficiently if the production was spread out over two periods instead of one. In other words, sacrificing one unit of output in the current period can actually increase output in the next period by more than one unit. The same may be true of two or three or even a hundred units. But as production is shifted more and more away from the current to the future period, problems of congestion and overuse of the factors of production arise again. Thus, although postponing some production now produces some efficiencies, the rate at which these efficiencies raise production diminishes as too much production is relegated to the future. In other words, the returns "diminish."

With the production possibilities curve in place in Figure 10.1, we now add an indifference curve, labelled $I^*$. We obtain an optimum at, say, point $O$, at which the production possibilities curve and the indifference curve are tangent to each other. Here output is $Q^*_1$ in the current period and $Q^*_2$ in the future period. Just as with the consumer, a firm's (its owners really) rate of time preference will dictate whether it will prefer relatively more production today versus future production.

## THE PRODUCTION–INVESTMENT DECISION

So far our firm can only make intertemporal shifts of production. It cannot borrow or lend. What happens if we relax that assumption and allow it to invest with borrowed funds? Its opportunities are enhanced, as illustrated in Figure 10.2.

For convenience, we reproduce the findings of Figure 10.1. Notice that both production ($Q$) and consumption are measured on the horizontal and vertical axes because the firm must make the joint decision about production and consumption. In the absence of any borrowing or lending opportunities, the firm is limited to consume what it produces. It selects the highest indifference curve tangent to the production possibilities curve $FQ'G$. Utility is maximized at the optimum point $O$ on indifference curve $I^*$.

Suppose, however, that the firm can invest current savings or borrow or both at the real rate of interest $\rho$. What are the implications of engaging in such leverage? Can the firm increase its consumption possibilities? Line $AB$ in Figure 10.2 is the consumption possibilities constraint derived in Chapter 9 when the real interest rate is $\rho$[7] in periods 1 and 2. Given a borrowing rate of $\rho$, the firm will wish to produce at $Q'$, the point at which the production possibilities curve $FQ'G$ is tangent to the consumption possibilities curve $AB$. Why? Because the firm is bound to produce no more than its production possibilities and the decision about how much to produce in the current period ($Q_1$) versus the future period ($Q_2$) is dependent on market opportunities to save or invest at the prevailing interest rate ($\rho$). Now that consumption possibilities have expanded beyond $FQ'G$ (the no-leverage case) to $AB$, the next decision consists in finding the optimum level of consumption in the two periods. The firm maximizes utility at $O'$, where indifference curve $I^{**}$ is tangent to the consumption possibilities constraint.

Notice that optimum $O'$ is along indifference curve $I^{**}$, which is higher than $I^*$, the indifference curve when borrowing and lending opportunities did not exist. The firm is able to consume more than it produces in the current period by borrowing $Q_1^{**}Q_1'$ which it will repay out of the income generated from future production. Therefore, leverage improves welfare by raising the opportunity set available to the firm and, as a result, total utility.

Let us now pause to consider what is happening to the economy as a whole, rather than what is happening just to a single firm. The fact that not all investment is financed through savings implies that some people in society must be saving more than their investment. In the aggregate, however, savings must equal in-

7 Again, recall that firms in this set-up are thought of as producing as well as consuming. Think of the firm's owners (that is, its shareholders) as the ones consuming.

**FIGURE 10.2** Leverage

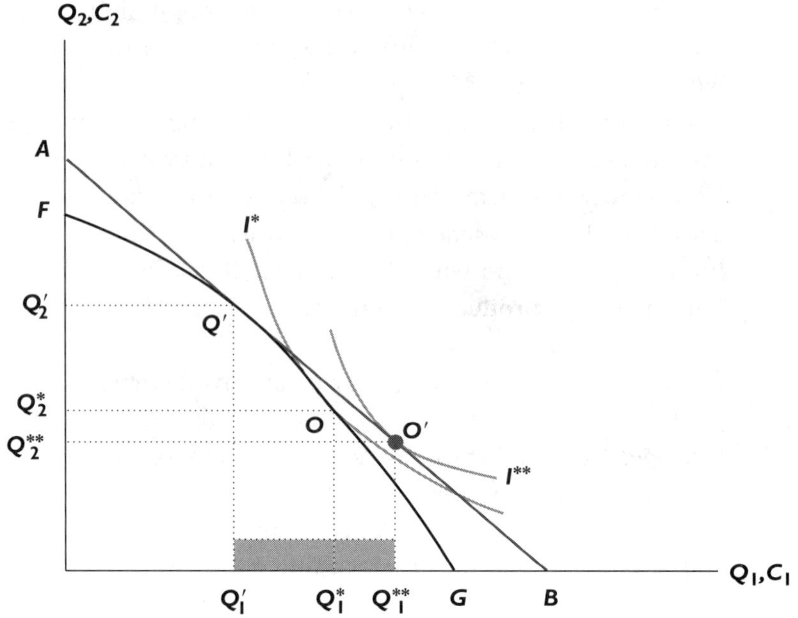


In the absence of borrowing and lending opportunities, the firm would reach an optimum of *O* along the indifference curve *I**. By borrowing, the firm can end up at the optimum *O*', which is along the higher indifference curve *I***. Thus, leverage opportunities increase total utility by expanding the available opportunity set.

vestment.[8] How is this the case if the interest rate is ρ for everyone? The answer is that everyone does not obtain the same return on investment (that is, the lending rate) or face the same borrowing rate. Risk characteristics differ and so does the desired term to maturity for both borrowers and lenders. Setting aside the question of how these features are reflected in interest rates,[9] we can examine the implications of divergent borrowing and lending rates. Figure 10.3 provides a simplified illustration. As before *FG* represents the production possibilities curve facing the firm. The curves *AZ'* and *ZB* are consumption possibilities constraints. *AZ'* is flatter than *ZB* because the real interest rate is lower in the former case than in the latter as we saw in Chapter 9. Suppose that an indifference curve (not shown) were tangent to the consumption possibilities line somewhere along *AZ'*. Depending on the shape of the indifference curve there could be a tangency

8 See Chapter 8, where we derive essentially the same condition in terms of the sources and uses of funds.
9 We consider this question in Chapter 15.

**FIGURE 10.3** Divergent Borrowing and Lending Rates

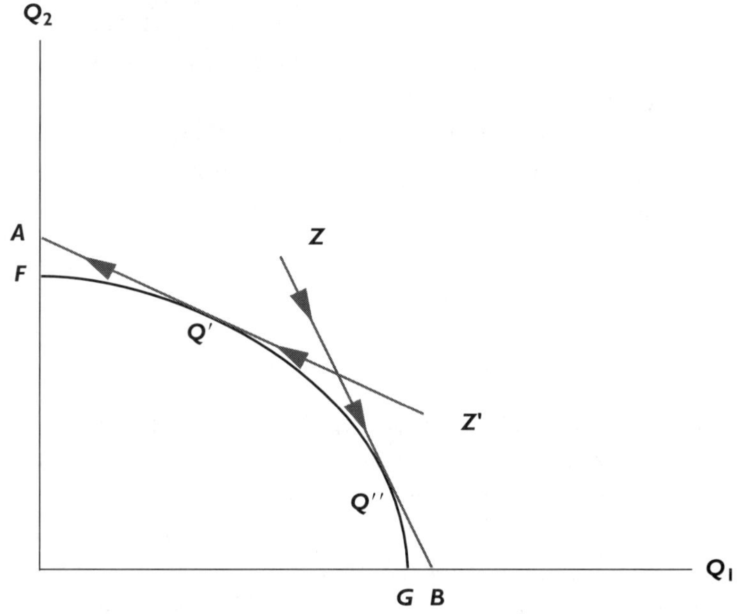


The production possibilities curve is *FQ'Q"G*. Borrowers face a higher interest rate than lenders. Consequently, borrowers' consumption possibilities lie along the relatively steeper curve *Z'B*. Lenders consume along *AZ'*. The arrows show the direction that borrowers or lenders will take in deciding their optimum consumption levels. The production level is *Q'* for lenders and *Q"* for borrowers.

anywhere between AQ'. Similarly, along ZB, a tangency could occur anywhere between Q"B. A tangency along Q'Q" simply means that the firm is not better off, given the prevailing interest rates, whether it borrows or lends (the case depicted in Figure 10.1). Borrowers, therefore, choose to consume along Q"B and produce Q"; lenders consume along AQ' and produce at Q'.

For example, if we think of the firm depicted in Figure 10.3 as a bank, it will borrow at a lower rate than that at which it lends, which is consistent with equation (10.1).[10] Individuals and non-financial firms that borrow usually have an optimum along *Q"B*, while a bank's optimum lies along *AQ'*. Changes in the spread between borrowing and lending rates will, of course, also influence consumption and production decisions.

10 Although equation (10.1) is formulated on the basis of nominal interest rates, the result holds for the real interest rate if both borrowers and lenders have the same expectations about inflation.

How can we determine which firms will be borrowers and which lenders? As we have seen, all economic decisions are governed by considerations of present value. A particular investment or loan will yield its return in the form of a stream of income generated over time. Similarly, borrowing will entail interest costs over time. If we assume, for simplicity, that the borrowing and lending rates are fixed, as they are in Figure 10.3, the firm will invest and borrow funds—engage in leverage—so long as the yield on an additional dollar invested (that is, the marginal return) exceeds the borrowing rate. Presumably, the number of such profitable investments will be limited.

## THE IRRELEVANCE PROPOSITION

The previous section focused on the choice of the optimal proportion of leverage, not on what the firm uses for leverage. Does it make any difference whether a firm (financial or non-financial) opts to raise funds by selling shares, by obtaining loans, or by turning to the myriad of other sources of funds?

The point here is not the relative merits of the variety of financial instruments in today's financial markets. It is rather the choice between financing with the sale of stock and financing with bonds (or any kind of loan). An influential theory in economics suggests that, under particular conditions, the choice between bond and stock financing is irrelevant. This theory is known as the **Modigliani–Miller (MM) theorem**, named after two economists who were awarded the Nobel Prize in economics, or as the irrelevance proposition. The essence of the MM theorem is that the value of a firm, defined as the anticipated stream of income generated by the firm, is independent of the debt–equity mix. What ultimately matters is the net return on the firm's investment, not how that investment is financed.

Let us consider an example, keeping in mind the accounting identity.

$$\text{Assets} = \text{Debt} + \text{Equity}$$

Recall that the reason the right-hand side of the equation provides a proxy for the value of a firm is that the value of debt (for example, bonds) is presumably determined by the discounted value of the future income stream that the firm will generate to pay off the debt. Similarly, the value of equity also reflects anticipated future income that, in turn, will generate the dividends the shareholders expect.[11] Consider the example given in Table 10.4, which contrasts two firms. Firm A has no debt and has raised all its funds in the form of equity, in the amount $\$EQ_1$. Firm B, in contrast, has financed part of its asset purchases via

11 See Chapter 12 for more about this issue.

**TABLE 10.4** AN ILLUSTRATION OF THE MODIGLIANI–MILLER THEOREM

| | Firm A (No leverage) | Firm B (Leverage) |
|---|---|---|
| Equity | $\$EQ_1$ | $\$EQ_2$ |
| Debt | $\$0$ | $\$D_2$ |
| Value | $\$EQ_1$ | $\$EQ_2 + \$D_2$ |

equities in an amount $\$EQ_2$ and the rest via debt valued at $\$D_2$. The firm's value is thus $\$EQ_2 + \$D_2$. In all other respects, however, we assume the two firms are alike. They can borrow and lend at the same rate, $\rho$. And both are expected to generate the same future income streams. All the income earned by firm A accrues to its shareholders, while income generated by firm B is shared by its shareholders and its debtholders.

Consider now two scenarios.

1. Suppose an individual can purchase $k\%$ of firm A's shares. The cost is $\$kEQ_1$. Alternatively, the same individual can buy $k\%$ of firm B's shares and debt at the cost of $\$kEQ_2 + \$kD_2$. Then $\$kEQ_1 = \$kEQ_2 + \$kD_2$. That is, the values of the two firms are the same. Otherwise, no rational investor would buy into the firm that is relatively less valuable.

2. An individual borrows $\$kD_2$, and simultaneously purchases $\$kEQ_1$ of shares in firm A. The net cost of this transaction is $\$kEQ_1 - \$kD_2$. Alternatively, the same individual may purchase $k\%$ of shares in firm B at a cost of $\$kEQ_2$. No one would invest in a less valuable firm, so $\$kEQ_1 - \$kD_2 = \$kEQ_2$ must hold. This expression can be rewritten as $\$kEQ_1 = \$kEQ_2 + \$kD_2$ which was the result obtained under the first scenario.

The conclusions are unmistakable: the leveraged firm's value is no higher than that of the unleveraged firm.

But, you must say, surely firms are not indifferent between holding either stocks or bonds at any given moment. Consider some of the crucial assumptions behind the MM proposition. It assumes that dividends (the earnings of shareholders) and interest payments (the earnings of debtholders) are the same. This is clearly not the case. Tax treatments of debt and equity, for example, have tended to favour the former form of financing.[12] Moreover, the managers of Firm A must answer only to the shareholders of that firm. By contrast, managers in

12 Mainly because interest payments are tax deductible for firms while dividend payments are not. (On the other hand, for the individuals providing the financing, interest income is taxable but equity holdings offer the possibility of capital gains, which receive favourable tax treatments.)

Firm B must deal with the preferences of shareholders and bondholders which, of course, need not be the same. Also, the transactions costs of bond financing need not be the same. It may, at times, be cheaper to raise money in the stock market than in the bond market. Firms clearly weigh all these factors in making decisions about financing. Finally, there is the presumption that shareholders and bondholders are equally knowledgeable about the firm's activities. As we saw in Chapter 3, there is asymmetric information in financial markets.

Despite all the indications that the MM theory is wrong in reality, it endures in economics, in part because of the controversies Modigliani and Miller's arguments engendered.

## TOBIN'S *q*

In the previous section we considered the problem firms have about whether to incur debts in the form of stocks or of bonds. Many choose to issue stocks, and the daily gyrations in stock prices, for individual firms as well as groups of them, are often viewed as a portent of the future for each company and for the economy as a whole. There is some justification for this view: the purchase of assets with borrowed funds is, of course, a form of investment. James Tobin, a Nobel laureate in economics, has proposed an investment decision rule based on the performance of a company's shares in the stock market. Presumably, a higher share price reflects the market's belief that the firm offers profitable investment opportunities. In other words, share prices reflect incentives to invest in the stock of a particular company. Tobin suggested a measure of these incentives, since called **Tobin's *q*.**

The measure $q$ is simply the ratio of the value of a firm's capital (assets), as perceived in the stock market, to the current cost of replacing the same capital. In other words,

$$q = \frac{\text{Market Value of a Firm's Capital}}{\text{Replacement Cost of a Firm's Capital}} \tag{10.4}$$

When $q$ is one this means that the stock market values \$1 worth of assets at exactly \$1. Market value reflects investors' view of the present (discounted) value of the current and future profits of the firm. Thus, if investors value the firm more than the sum of the cost of its assets, they must be anticipating relative profitability, and $q > 1$. As long as that condition holds, the firm's managers have an incentive to try to raise the market value of the firm's shares by purchasing more capital, which, of course, involves more borrowing. The opposite argument holds if $q < 1$. The firm has no incentive to replace capital because the market apparently believes that such investment will not generate a larger stream of income in the future.

For firms eyeing other firms, a low $q$ means that a firm can be purchased more cheaply than its replacement cost. So a merger-and-acquisitions boom is to be expected. A low $q$ also means that stock prices should rise since an investor in effect purchases a portion of a company at less than the replacement cost of the assets of that company. Similarly, stock prices should fall when $q$ is high. The evidence on how useful $q$ is as a forecasting tool is mixed. For example, $q$ in the US reached a historical peak at the end of 1995 at 1.5 (the measure has been calculated as far back as 1945) but there was no sign well into 1996 that stock prices reversed their rise to record levels.[13]

Thus, lower anticipated income signals lower investment and eventually lower output, and higher anticipated income signals the reverse. It is for this reason that investment and business cycles are related to each other and the stock market is closely watched as an indicator of future economic activity.

## SUMMARY

- Firms borrow to invest. This is the process of leverage.
- Measures such as the leverage ratio and the capital–asset ratio tell us about the firm's level of indebtedness and the likelihood of failure.
- There are many ways of incurring debt. Typically, a firm sells bonds or issues stock. Does it matter which form of debt is incurred? According to the Modigliani–Miller theorem, the choice is irrelevant. But the MM theorem holds only under very special circumstances.
- Many firms issue stock and many watch stock prices. Do stock prices tell us about the future state of the economy? The answer is, to some extent, yes since the decision to incur some debt is an indication of a firm's future earning potential. A measurement based on this idea is known is Tobin's $q$.

## IMPORTANT TERMS

capital–asset ratio (p. 210)
diminishing marginal returns (p. 215)
leverage (p. 208)
leverage ratio (p. 208)
Modigliani–Miller theorem (p. 220)
production possibilities (p. 215)
spread (p. 208)
Tobin's $q$ (p. 222)

13 See A. Ramirez "Cue for Q ratio: Dow is Too High," *New York Times* (26 November 1995), Money and Business section.

# EXERCISES

1. In explaining the spread, suppose we had used the rate on government bonds with a 5-year term to maturity instead of the rate on savings deposits. Would the spread have been larger or smaller? Why? (Assume the prime rate is still used as a measure of the borrowing rate.)

2. Redo Table 10.1 assuming that interest rates *fall* by 3%. What are the leverage and capital–asset ratios for the opening and eventual balance sheets?

3. What would happen to the production possibilities curve in Figure 10.1 if a technological improvement were introduced? Explain your answer.

4. What kind of preferences would lead the firm depicted in Figure 10.2 to become a lender instead of a borrower? (Hint: Look at Chapter 9 again.)

5. In Figure 10.3, what would the optimum level of production and consumption be if the firm elects to be on the $Q'Q''$ portion of the production possibilities curve?

6. Would the Modigliani–Miller theorem hold if borrowing and lending rates differ? Explain your answer.

7. "Debt financing is cheaper than equity financing, because investors take on less risk when purchasing debt, and thus require a lower return," said an analyst in *The Economist* (8 December 1990, p. 81). Explain why this might be the case. If the statement is true, how does it affect a firm's leverage ratio?

8. Using a diagram, explain why a financial institution benefits in utility terms from engaging in leverage.

9. Why do you think the spread pictured in Economics Focus 10.1 became larger during the 1980s and 1990s?

10. Explain why the Modigliani–Miller proposition fails when transactions costs, asymmetric information, or conflicts arise between the preferences of bond-holders and shareholders.

11. Explain whether the risk-adjusted capital–asset ratio in the following situations would be higher or lower than the unadjusted ratio.
    (a) 80% of assets are other than cash or government bonds
    (b) OBS activities amount to 100% of total assets
    (c) 90% of assets are in the form of residential mortgages

(d) 90% of assets are in the form of cash or government bonds

12. Why is Tobin's *q* likely to be an imperfect predictor of future stock prices?

13. Explain how a low *q* might lead to an increase in mergers and acquisitions.

## REFERENCES


*Bank Act of Canada: Orders and Regulations with guidelines, interpretation bulletins and other regulatory documents*, 3d ed. Don Mills, Ont.: DeBoo Publishers, 1989.

Bank for International Settlements, *Annual Reports* (various years), Basel: Switzerland.

*Bank Profits*, Report of the Standing Committee on Finance, Trade and Economic Affairs. Ottawa, Ont.: Supply and Services Canada, 1987.

Becker, G.S. *Economic Theory.* New York: Alfred A. Knopf, 1980.

Blomqvist, A., P. Wonnacott, R. Wonnacott, and J. Fried. *Macroeconomics*, 4th ed. Toronto, Ont.: McGraw-Hill Ryerson, 1994.

*Book of Vital World Statistics.* London: The Economist Books, Ltd., 1990.

Eng, M.V., F.A. Lees, and L.J. Mauer *Global Finance.* New York: HarperCollins, 1995.

Fama, E.F. "Stock Returns, Expected Returns, and Real Activity." *Journal of Finance* 45 (September 1990): 1089–1108.

Hirshleifer, J. *Investment, Interest and Capital.* Englewood Cliffs, N.J.: Prentice-Hall, 1970. Chapter 7.

———. *Price Theory and Applications*, 2d ed. Englewood Cliffs, N.J.: Prentice-Hall, 1980. Chapter 16.

Miller, M. "Debt and Taxes." *Journal of Finance* 32 (May 1977): 261–75.

Miller, M.H. "Leverage: Nobel Memorial Prize Lecture." *Journal of Finance* 46 (June 1991): 479–88.

Modigliani, F., and M. Miller. "The Cost of Capital, Corporation Finance and the Theory of Investment." *American Economic Review* 48 (June 1958): 261–97.

Ross, S.A. "The Determination of Financial Structure: The Incentive Signalling Approach." *Bell Journal of Economics* 8 (1977): 23–40.

Statistics Canada, CANSIM database.

CHAPTER 11

# The Demand for Money

It should be apparent by now that money plays a central role in any economic analysis of the financial system. We saw in Chapter 6 that money is one of several financial assets that individuals and firms hold in their portfolios. In this chapter, we specifically explore the demand for money as a separate asset.

We begin by sketching what governs the demand for money, a relatively straightforward task since previous chapters have laid the foundations. Next we explore two different ways of understanding the demand for money: one treats money much like an inventory of commodities that are costly to hold and must be managed efficiently, and the other treats money as it fits into a model in which individuals hold a variety of different assets.

After these theoretical discussions, we briefly outline what the demand for money might look like for the Canadian economy.

The chapter concludes with an explanation of the velocity of circulation. Such a discussion can be viewed as nothing more than another analysis of the demand for money, but there are, as we will see, valuable insights to be gained from exploring the subject separately.

How do we define the money supply in these discussions? In Chapter 2, we discussed various measures and concluded that although there is no widespread agreement on which is "best," the narrow definition of money—*M1*, which consists of currency and coins in circulation and demand deposits in the chartered banks—will do for our purposes. We therefore depend on it throughout this chapter, except where the data available require the use of M2.

Much of the modern thinking about money demand is not new but has only been formalized and popularized during the last three or four decades. The writings of Sir William Petty in the 1660s made clear his understanding of the connection between velocity and income. By the early 1800s such notable economists as Henry Thornton, Jean-Baptiste Say, and Nassau Senior understood that money demand was also influenced by the opportunity cost of money and expectations of inflation. Therefore, theories of the demand for money have a long and venerable history.[1]

## THE MICROFOUNDATIONS OF THE DEMAND FOR MONEY: A SKETCH

Let us review a few principles, developed in earlier chapters, that will allow us to derive relationships explaining the quantity of money demanded.

First, the foremost reason for holding money is the *transaction motive.* Money has convenience in use and, therefore, permits an individual to economize on time spent shopping. Presumably, the time saved in making trips to the bank translates into the benefit of more leisure time. On the other hand, since the return on M1 barely exceeds 0% (most of its components are non-interest-bearing) the more money an individual holds the more interest that is foregone. This *opportunity cost* limits the quantity of money that an individual will hold.[2]

Second, we know from our analysis of the household sector that the optimal consumption choice is an intertemporal decision problem. In deciding how much to save today, individuals must weigh how much they wish to consume now relative to the future. Moreover, since part of savings is normally in the form of money, the allocation of consumption over time significantly influences the demand for money.

Finally, individuals making decisions about consumption and savings are interested in the *real* values of that consumption or savings. To put the point differently, what matters to individuals is the *purchasing power* of money held. The *purchasing power* of money—what money can buy—can be given as

$$\text{purchasing power of money} = \frac{1}{P} \tag{11.1}$$

where $P$ represents the price level.

Prices are usually expressed in index form. For example, the consumer price index (CPI) may be arbitrarily set at 100 in 1986, so that prices in the past and in the future can be compared with those prevailing in 1986. Equation (11.1) makes it clear that if the CPI rises, the purchasing power of money falls. Therefore, discussions of the demand for money refer to a demand for the purchasing power of money or what economists call **real balances:**

1 See T.M. Humphrey, "The Origins of Velocity Functions," *Economic Quarterly of the Federal Reserve Bank of Richmond* 79 (Fall 1993): 1–17.

2 This concept is developed in greater detail in Chapter 6.

$$\text{demand for money} = \text{demand for } \frac{M}{P} = \text{real balances}^3$$

where $M$ = the (nominal) money stock.

We now have all the necessary information at our disposal to sketch a behavioural relationship that describes the demand for money.

Individuals face an income constraint on the total of what is to be consumed and saved. Preferences for consumption now versus the future, also known as a person's *discount rate*, dictate how consumption will be allocated over time. Once that choice is made, the individual must also decide whether to hold the savings in money, in bonds, or in other assets, financial or non-financial. Therefore, the demand for money during any particular period is influenced primarily by consumption and interest rates. For the moment let us assume only one interest rate is relevant to the consumer. In other words, a demand for money emerges from the principles of individual utility-maximizing behaviour. More formally, we can write a **demand for money function**, $f(c_t, R_t)$—the relationship of the relevant variables—as

$$\left(\frac{M}{P}\right)_t^d = m_t^d = f(c_t, R_t) \tag{11.2}$$

$$c \uparrow \rightarrow m^d \uparrow \ ; \ R \uparrow \rightarrow m^d \downarrow$$

where $m_t$ is the shorthand for real balances, $M/P$, and, as defined previously, $c$ denotes consumption spending and $R$ the *nominal* interest rate.[4] The flowchart below equation (11.2) shows how changes in each of the determinants of the demand for money change the quantity of money demand. Thus, a rise in consumption spending increases the desire to hold money, while a higher opportunity cost leads to a fall in the quantity of money demanded.

Although equation (11.2) appears to describe the demand for money adequately it looks somewhat different from the one alluded to in Chapter 6. The reason is that it uses consumption instead of income as a determinant of the demand for money. The discrepancy is readily reconciled, however. We saw in Chapter 9 that there is a fairly stable relationship between consumption planned over a lifetime

3 If the monetary authorities supply enough money to satisfy the quantity of money demanded, this expression is an equilibrium one.

4 Recall that although individuals make consumption–savings decisions based on what they believe the *real* interest is or will be, financial markets transact on the basis of nominal interest rates; it is thus this measure that should influence the demand for money.

and permanent income. Thus, we can rewrite equation (11.2), substituting real permanent income, $y^P$, for $c$ and obtain

$$m_t^d = f(y_t^P, R_t) \qquad (11.3)$$

The substitution of $y^P$ is straightforward, but there is the question of how to do it. It is common to use a measure of actual real income, $y_t$.[5] Then equation (11.3) can be rewritten as

$$m_t^d = f(y_t, R_t) \qquad (11.3a)$$

Equations (11.2) through (11.3a) have some interesting features. First recall that $R$, the nominal interest rate, can be defined as the sum of the real interest rate and expected inflation:

$$R = \rho + \pi^e$$

A rise in either expected inflation or the real interest rate means that individuals will reduce their holdings of money. If inflation soars, individuals reduce their holdings of cash and seek out assets that will yield sufficient return to cover the expected rise in the nominal price level.[6]

Another feature of the demand for money equation is that when $P$ increases, there should be no changes in the quantity of money demanded. In other words, the *price elasticity of money demand*—which measures the responsiveness of demand to change in price, or $\%\Delta M/\%\Delta P$—is 1 in this theory. A rise in the price level simply means that more money is required to buy the same quantity of goods. Therefore, the quantity of real balances will remain unchanged. One can see this result more clearly by rewriting equation (11.3a) as

$$M_t^d = M_t = P_t \cdot f(y_t, R_t) \qquad (11.4)$$

Notice that equation (11.4) is a demand for money function in *nominal* terms. In theory, it should translate easily enough to real terms. But what if people suffer from what is called **money illusion**—the belief that nominal values are not the same as real values—and hence do not understand that if prices rise by 10%, then 10% more cash is required to purchase the same quantity of goods? They simply do not think effectively about consumption or income or the demand for

5 Various proxies for permanent income have also been devised. We consider a very simple one later in this chapter when we examine some empirical data.

6 Alternatively, in what is known as the phenomenon of *currency substitution*, people may seek assets, financial or non-financial, denominated in a foreign currency that are more stable in value. For example, prices in several South American countries are as likely to be quoted in US dollars as in the home currency.

money in real terms. Thus, the actual price elasticity of money is an empirical question.

A final important question about any functional relationships such as the ones considered here is whether they are *stable*. How reliable is the relationship as a tool for analysis or forecasting? Nobel laureate Robert Lucas of the University of Chicago warned in 1976 of the dangers inherent in relying on a particular estimate of the relationship between a set of economic variables when changes in the economic environment could dictate different estimates for the same relationship over time. Economists had long believed that equations such as (11.3) and (11.3a) were invariant to changes in the economic environment caused by crises such as oil price shocks, but as the 1980s progressed, doubts began to surface about the predictability of the demand for money based on variables such as real income and an interest rate.[7]

## *THE BAUMOL–TOBIN MODEL: OPTIMAL CASH MANAGEMENT

The arguments just used to derive expressions describing the demand for money are fundamentally based on the notion that money's most important function is as a medium of exchange. There remains the problem of deciding how much money to hold since holding it incurs significant costs. One approach, called optimal cash management, provides a useful, if incomplete, way of thinking about the transactions demand for money.

The **optimal cash management approach**, also called the Baumol–Tobin inventory theory, applies a framework to the demand for money that firms have long found useful in considering inventory control.

William Baumol, formerly of Princeton, and Nobel Laureate James Tobin of Yale saw that firms and individuals face similar problems of income–expenditure gaps.[8] Because firms cannot synchronize their production and sales perfectly (a car must be made—and its components paid for—weeks or months before it is sold), they carry inventories of parts and finished goods. Similarly, individuals cannot synchronize their income and expenditure streams perfectly (the paycheque comes every other Friday, but the rent is due on the first of the month, the phone bill on the tenth, and grocery shopping is most convenient on Wednesdays), so they hold cash and chequing accounts.

7 See D. Laidler, *The Demand for Money: Theories, Evidence and Problems*, 4th Edition (New York: HarperCollins, 1993).

8 Baumol first made the point in 1952 and Tobin extended it in 1956. The two recently pointed out that Maurice Allais, a French economist and Nobel laureate, may have written about the same idea earlier.

## FUNDAMENTAL CONCEPTS

To see the basic concepts of inventory control as applied to the demand for money, consider Figure 11.1(A). Money is measured by M1, so it can be held in either notes and coins or in a chequing account. An individual is assumed to receive a paycheque monthly and to spend all of the income on a constant basis throughout the month.[9] The price level is initially assumed to be constant, so that changes in nominal money demanded are equivalent to changes in real balances.

The assumption of a constant rate of spending—as evidenced by the straight lines in Figure 11.1(A)—implies that average cash holdings during a particular month will be the simple average of the beginning cash balance (say, \$2,000) and the end-of-the-month cash balance (\$0). If the individual's monthly (nominal) income is \$2,000, the *average* amount of dollars held during any particular month is

$$M^d = \frac{\$2{,}000 + \$0}{2} = \$1{,}000$$

This kind of cash management gives rise to a sawtooth income–expenditure pattern.

One can think of a number of practical problems with the results so far. First, many individuals are paid twice each month or even more frequently. This difficulty is easily handled, as also shown in Figure 11.1(A). If the biweekly income is \$1,000 (it still totals \$2,000 during the month), the average monthly cash holding is

$$M^d = \frac{\$1{,}000 + \$0}{2} = \$500$$

which is simply one-half of the demand for cash of the individual paid monthly. This procedure can easily be extended when the frequency of payments is increased.

Second, many individuals often buy items using devices such as credit cards, thereby delaying the actual payment for purchases for several days or weeks. This situation is also easily handled in the model. Suppose that the individual who is paid monthly makes half of his or her expenditures with a credit card whose payments are due the first of each month. Since we have assumed that all of the \$2,000 is spent, the credit card bill is \$1,000. Figure 11.1(B) shows what happens. When the \$2,000 paycheque is received on the first of the month, \$1,000 is quickly

9 The assumption that all income is spent is a simplification that does not affect the conclusions of the analysis.

**FIGURE 11.1** Optimal Cash Management: An Inventory Approach

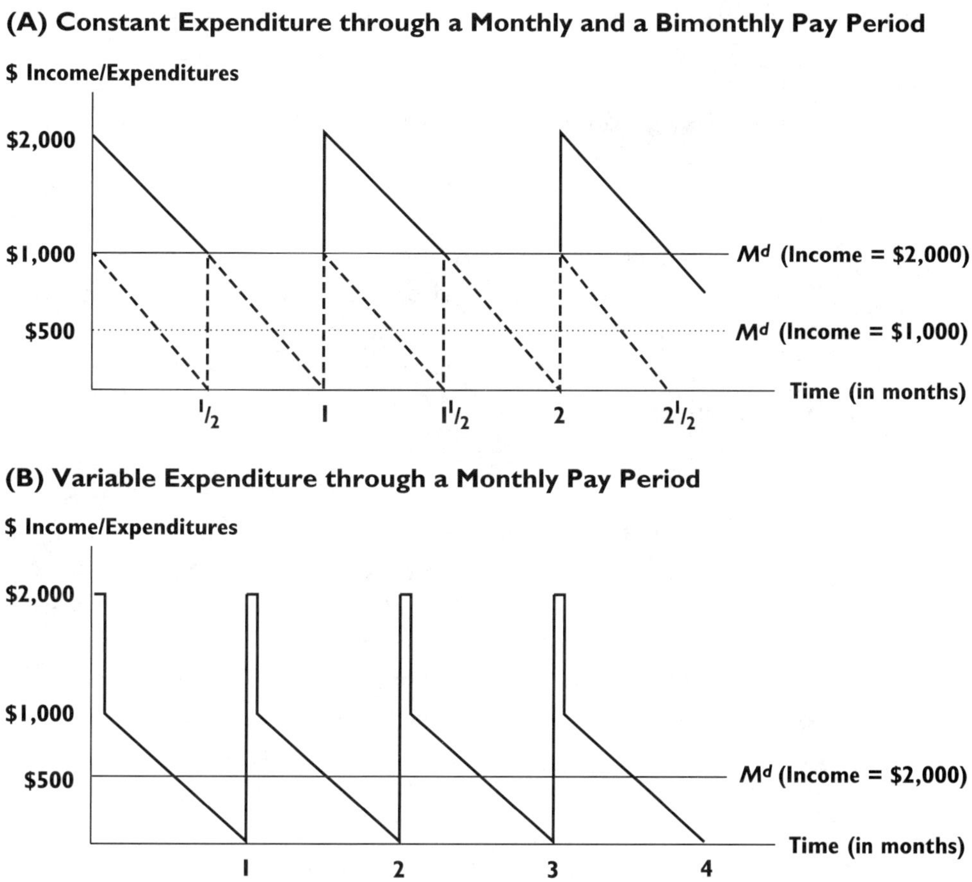


In panel (A), an individual who is paid \$2,000 once a month spends this income at a constant rate, giving rise to a sawtooth pattern of money holding (solid line). If the same individual is paid twice a month, the pattern is the same (dashed line), but the peaks (and average holdings) are half as high and occur twice as often.

In panel (B), the individual must pay off a number of debts after receiving each \$2,000 monthly paycheque; expenditures then proceed at a constant rate throughout the rest of the month.

paid to the credit card company, leaving the individual \$1,000 in cash or a chequing account. The average monthly demand for cash becomes

$$M^d = \frac{(\$1{,}000 + \$0)/2}{2} = \$500$$

which is half the amount demanded in the no-credit case. Thus, credit cards effectively permit individuals to economize on their cash and chequing account holdings. (The same result occurs if the individual transfers a sum of money from a savings to a chequing account at the beginning of the month. We leave the modelling of this solution to the reader as an exercise.)

## Optimal Cash Balance Holdings

With the help of a little bit of algebra, we can derive the optimal amount of cash for the individual to hold. What is meant by "optimal" here? It refers to the level of holdings that will minimize the opportunity costs of holding cash. Why is it important to know the optimal cash holdings? For one thing, that information will enable us to examine how the demand for money is affected by inflation. (We already touched upon this question earlier—see equation (11.3a)—in suggesting that a 1% increase in the price level increases the quantity of (nominal) cash held by 1%.)

We will find it helpful to have some notation. Let

$Y$ = nominal income = $Py$ = real income × price level
$b$ = transactions cost (cost each time a transfer is made in or out of cash)
$R$ = nominal interest rate, which is the opportunity cost of money
$n$ = number of transactions per period

The individual must decide how many transactions are optimal to minimize the costs of holding money. Since each transaction costs \$$b$, the number of transactions should increase until one more \$$b$ is greater than the additional amount that could have been earned had the funds been left in some interest-bearing account or asset.

To measure this opportunity cost, we need to know how much cash the individual would hold on average. By our previous calculations, the answer is

$$M^d = \frac{Y}{2n} \tag{11.5}$$

Y is the amount of funds available at the beginning of the month so $(Y/2)$ is the average amount of cash held during the month. Since there are $n$ transactions (or withdrawals) during the month, $(Y/2)/n$ or $(Y/2n)$ is the average amount of cash held by the individual adjusted for the number of transactions in a month. The interest lost on \$$(Y/2n)$ held in cash is

$$R\left(\frac{Y}{2n}\right)$$

since each dollar could have earned $R$ interest monthly.[10] Consider now what would happen if the individual contemplated $(n + 1)$ transactions instead of $n$. What are the consequences of this *marginal* transaction? The interest forgone in making $(n + 1)$ transactions instead of $n$ transactions is simply

$$\frac{RY}{2n} - \frac{RY}{2(n + 1)} = \frac{RY}{(2n(n + 1))} \tag{11.6}$$

Hence, when

$$b > \frac{RY}{2} \tag{11.7}$$

the transactions costs exceed the interest that could have been earned had the cash been invested in an interest-earning asset. The optimal number of transactions is thus the value of $n$ that equates the marginal cost of holding money to the marginal revenue of holding money. This condition can be written

$$b = \frac{RY}{2n^2} \tag{11.8}$$

where $RY/2n^2$ is the additional interest earned.[11] Solving equation (11.8) for $n$, we find

$$n^2 = \frac{RY}{2b}$$

$$n = \sqrt{\frac{RY}{2b}} \tag{11.9}$$

Finally, by substituting equation (11.9) into (11.5), we can find the optimal demand for money,

---

10 The interest rate here is defined on a monthly basis to render the analysis compatible with the numerical example considered.

11 Recall that $b$ is the cost of making an additional transaction and it stays constant regardless of the size of $n$ (again this assumption can be relaxed without changing the principles of cash management as outlined here). The opportunity cost *over the month totals* $(RY/2n)$. For the technically inclined, the marginal revenue or benefit of keeping more money in the bank by reducing the number of transactions by one (i.e, of reducing the average amount of cash help during the month) is $\partial(RY/2n)/\partial n$, that is, the partial derivative of $(RY/2n)$ with respect to $n$, since this measures the change in $(RY/2n)$ for a given change in $n$. $\partial(RY/2n)/\partial n = (2RY)/4n^2$ which is equation (11.8).

$$M^d = \frac{Y}{2n} = \frac{Y}{2\sqrt{RY/2b}}$$

which can be simplified considerably[12] to

$$M^d = \left(\frac{b}{2}\right)^{0.5} \cdot Y^{0.5} \cdot R^{-0.5} \qquad (11.10)$$

(Note that the exponent 0.5 denotes square root.)

Finally, since $Y = Py$, we can rewrite equation (11.10) as

$$M^d = \left(\frac{b}{2}\right)^{0.5} \cdot P^{0.5} \cdot y^{0.5} \cdot R^{-0.5} \qquad (11.11)$$

Equation (11.11) can be interpreted as indicating that a 1% increase in either the price level or real income increases the demand for money in nominal terms by the square root of 1%. By contrast, a 1% increase in the opportunity cost of money reduces the demand for cash by the square root of 1%. The implication is that in the face of inflation, the price elasticity of the demand for money is less than 1.[13] As prices rise, the demand for real balances falls.

## THE ROLE OF INFLATION

Using the optimal cash management model, we have just concluded that inflation—a sustained rise in the price level—does affect the demand for money. But earlier, when we discussed the demand for money function in nominal terms (equations (11.3) and 11.4)), we said that a rising price level should not change the quantity of money demanded. Have we managed to contradict ourselves?

The answer is no. In deriving the earlier equations, we assumed that the opportunity cost of holding money remained constant. The optimal cash management model uses no such assumption. Indeed, it treats money like an inventory of commodities, and inflation will clearly increase the cost of keeping it idle. The frequency of payment increases, so as we saw in Figure 11.1(A), average cash

---

12 As follows:

$$\begin{aligned} M^d &= (Y/2)/[R^{0.5} \cdot Y^{0.5} \cdot (2b)^{0.5}] \\ &= (b/2)^{0.5} \cdot YY^{-0.5} \cdot R^{-0.5} \\ &= (b/2)^{0.5} \cdot Y^{0.5} \cdot R^{-0.5} \end{aligned}$$

13 If we rewrite equation (11.11) in logarithms we obtain $\log M^d = \text{constant} + 0.5 \log P$ (since all the other terms in the equation are constant by assumption). If we then take changes on both sides of the equation, we get $\Delta\log M^d = 0.5\ \Delta\log P$ (since, by definition, $\Delta$ constant $= 0$). Finally, we can write $\Delta\log M^d/\Delta\log P = 0.5$. Since $\Delta\log M^d/\Delta\log P$ is approximately the same as $\%\ \Delta M^d/\%\Delta P$, which is the elasticity measure, we conclude that the price elasticity is 0.5.

holdings will fall. The individual must make more trips to the bank, which means greater transactions costs (a look at equation (11.7) will make this point clear).

The conclusion that real balances will fall as inflation accelerates is borne out by the experience of economies that have suffered **hyperinflation**, a condition in which price rises accelerate very quickly and very sharply (usually by 50% a month or more); money becomes worthless and the financial system collapses. To take just one example, when inflation skyrocketed in Hungary after World War II, real balances fell to almost zero in the space of just one year.

What about more normal experiences with inflation? We will see in the next section that the predictions contained in equation (11.11) are not entirely accurate. The inventory approach does not tell us the whole story about the demand for money.

# A MORE COMPLETE MODEL OF MONEY DEMAND

Another approach to estimating the demand for money rests on the fact that since money is a medium of exchange, some money changes hands whenever a transaction occurs. Variables of interest include the quantity of money in circulation—that is, the size of the money supply—and the **velocity of circulation**, which is the number of times a given quantity of money turns over to produce a given level of spending.

## QUANTITY THEORY

The **quantity theory** is very old. In its simplest form, it links the real and monetary sides of an economy in the following relationship:

$$M^s V = Py \quad (11.12)$$

where

$M^s$ = the quantity of money in circulation
$V$ = the velocity of circulation
$P$ = the price level (for example, as expressed by a consumer price index)
$y$ = the economy's *real* income (that is, real GDP or GNP)[14]

The equation is actually an identity. A given stock of money circulating in the economy changes hands a number of times, as measured by velocity. The dollar value of the stock of money multiplied by its rate of turnover. $V$, should equal the value of the goods and services purchased during a given period. For example,

14 Early versions of the quantity theory related the quantity of money to the volume of transactions. Problems of measurement led analysts to proxy transactions with aggregate output or income.

## ECONOMICS FOCUS 11.1 When Prices Go Wild

Economists have long been fascinated with episodes of hyperinflation since these are viewed as near laboratory-type situations in which to study money demand. Hungary has the distinction not only of having the highest inflation rate on record but of experiencing hyperinflation twice in one century (1920s and 1940s) each time after the end of a major war.

Under conditions of hyperinflation, prices rise so quickly that the impact of income changes on money demand are trivial (hyperinflation also tends to last for a short time). Moreover, the real interest rate is so small relative to inflation that it too can be ignored. What dominates money demand then are expectations of inflation. This led Philip Cagan, in a now classic article, to suggest that a money demand function under hyperinflationary conditions can be written as $m^d = f(\pi^e)$ which is a highly simplified version of equation (11.3a). Cagan used a version of the above equation to study money demand for a number of episodes of European hyperinflations. Hyperinflation was defined as occurring whenever the inflation rate exceeded 50% per month. Equally fascinating is the study of policies needed to end a hyperinflation. Ends of hyperinflations tend to occur rather abruptly. The study of hyperinflations proved to be especially useful to policymakers in Latin and South America during the 1970s and 1980s when they too had to grapple with high or hyperinflation. Hyperinflations are not a thing of the past. Most recently, the former Yugoslavia, Russia and the Ukraine, all remnants of the now dissolved Soviet Union, have experienced runaway inflation.

**Sources:**

Siklos, P.L. *Great Inflations of the Twentieth Century* (Aldershot: Edward Elgar, 1995).

Cagan, P., "The Monetary Dynamics of Hyperinflation," in *Studies in the Quantity Theory of Money*, edited by Milton Friedman (Chicago: University of Chicago Press, 1956), pp. 25–117.

if the stock of money was \$100 billion in 1990 and changed hands four times during the year, then $4 \times \$100 = \$400$ billion worth of purchases were generated.

If one assumes that the market for money is in equilibrium, so that $M^s = M^d$, equation (11.12) then becomes

$$M^dV = Py$$

or, by rearranging the terms,

$$M^d = \left(\frac{1}{V}\right)Py \qquad (11.13)$$

Thus, the quantity theory becomes a theory of the demand for money.

Early quantity theorists treated the reciprocal of velocity, $1/V$, as a constant. Some wished to focus on the direct and predictable relationship between money and income. Some felt that features of the financial system that could influence velocity, such as the payments system and technology, changed slowly or infrequently.

In the 1930s, John Maynard Keynes noted that the nominal interest rate could affect velocity. But the point was little emphasized in his exposition and that of his followers. They focused on a stable consumption function, relegating the role of money in the economy to the sidelines.

## FRIEDMAN'S MONETARY THEORY

The Keynesians reigned in academic economics until midcentury when Nobel laureate Milton Friedman, then of the University of Chicago, offered a model of the demand for money that incorporated a restatement of the quantity theory. The work of Friedman and his followers led to a revival of the view that money is the central macroeconomic variable.[15]

Friedman began with his *permanent income* hypothesis in which money is an asset in a portfolio of many assets and thus the desire to hold money is a function of the rate of return on a variety of alternative assets. Specifically, Friedman's version of the demand for money function is a genealized version of (11.3a) which can be expressed as[16]

$$\frac{M^d}{P} = f(\underset{-}{R^B}, \underset{-}{R^E}, \underset{-}{\pi}, \underset{+}{W_h/W_n}, \underset{+}{y}, \underset{?}{u}) \tag{11.14}$$

where

$M^d$ = desired demand for money
$P$ = nominal price level
$R^B$ = nominal return on bonds
$R^E$ = nominal return on stocks or equities
$\pi$ = return on money as measured by the rate of inflation
$W_h$ = human wealth
$W_n$ = non-human wealth
$y$ = real income
$u$ = other factors omitted in the functional relationship that can influence the demand for money

The signs below each variable in equation (11.14) denote how a change in a particular term of the function changes the quantity of real balances demanded.

Note that equation (11.14) is like equation (11.3a) in the sense that it specifies the demand for money as a demand for real balances. The first three terms in the functional relationship are various measures of the opportunity cost of holding money. Increases in the nominal return on bonds, on stocks or equities, or on goods (measured as the inflation rate) produce a fall in the quantity of real balances demanded.

---

15 For more on this view, see Chapter 26.

16 The differences between equation (11.3) and the one derived by Friedman are inconsequential for our purposes.

One of the novelties of Friedman's approach to the demand for money is that it allows for the influence of *all* forms of wealth, as represented by the variable $W_h/W_n$. Thus, in contrast with the definition given earlier, wealth here includes both non-human wealth—physical and financial assets, which we earlier called *net wealth*—as well as human wealth—essentially the present discounted value of earnings, which will be influenced by, for example, an individual's level of education. Because the human component of wealth is not easily marketable (see the example considered in Chapter 8), its "return" does not directly enter the formulation in equation (11.14). (However, individuals who accumulate relatively more human wealth also tend to acquire more non-human wealth in the future, assuming income and human wealth are positively related to each other.)

The term $y$ represents real income, which influences the demand for money in the manner already described.

Finally, the residual, $u$, reflects various factors, such as an individual's tastes and preferences, that may influence the demand for money but are not easily captured by the other variables in the equation. The relationship between $u$ and the demand for money is unclear, however, so a question mark appears below this variable in equation (11.14).

Since, as we saw in Chapter 9, permanent income is related to individuals' wealth constraint, it is influenced indirectly by alternative returns on assets, which affect the amount of wealth accumulated over a lifetime. Like the liquidity preference framework, Friedman's model shows that a rising interest rate reduces the quantity of money demanded, *other things being equal.* But, Friedman argued, other things are *not* equal. In particular, when bond yields increase, the return on money (proxied by the inflation rate) does not remain constant. Why? Say the yields on bonds rise. With bonds becoming a relatively more attractive asset and people considering the transfer of an increasing share of their wealth to bonds from money, the banks, eager to protect the aggregate size of their deposits (a major component of the money supply) are likely to raise the return paid on money (that is deposits). Thus, the quantity of money demanded may not change after all.

These insights enabled Friedman to suggest that equation (11.14) can be greatly simplified as

$$\frac{M^d}{P} = g(y^P) \qquad (11.15)$$

where $y^P$ = permanent income and all other terms are as already defined. This equation simply says that the demand for money is a function of $g(y^P)$ permanent income. It contains no interest rate variable. Friedman believed some early empirical evidence that the demand for money is insensitive to interest rate changes. The overwhelming bulk of modern empirical evidence from several countries suggests, however, that interest rates do influence the demand for money. With correction for that fact, Friedman's framework becomes equation (11.3a).

## DEMAND FOR MONEY FUNCTIONS: EMPIRICAL ESTIMATES

The demand for money that most economists rely on is a demand for real balances, which assumes that the price elasticity is 1. How accurate is such a view? Figure 11.2(A) shows the money supply *M2*[17] plotted against the consumer price index for annual Canadian data since 1913. The relationship is positive as expected, but while very close it is not equal to 1.[18]

Figure 11.2 (B) shows the relationship between real balances and real income, again since 1913. Once again, as the theory would predict, and as summarized by the straight line, the relationship is a positive one. Finally, Figure 11.2 (C) shows a plot of real balances against the nominal interest rate (here proxied by the yield on long-term government bonds). Unlike the hypothesized relationships with the other two variables, the relationship depicted here is quite different in the pre- and post-World War II periods. In the prewar period, the link is as hypothesized in equation (11.2), that is negative, but it then turns positive in the postwar era. Is there something wrong then with the theory? Not really. It is just that M2 after World War II becomes a more interest-bearing asset in competition with other assets and the positive relationship in Figure 11.2 (D) is a reflection of the relatively attractive rate of return on M2. But the change in the relationship before and after World War II also suggests that our story about what determines money demand over long periods of time is perhaps incomplete. The next section will help clarify the apparent contradiction by pointing out the importance of financial innovations and development in understanding money demand.

## VELOCITY OF CIRCULATION

So far we have largely ignored the behaviour of the velocity of circulation, treating this variable essentially as a constant. Is this assumption too strong?

17 Although we have been using M1 as our working definition of the money supply, the long sample of data considered in this section is available only for M2.

18 Using regression analysis of

$$\text{logarithm M2} = \text{constant} + \text{coeff(1)} \cdot \text{Trend} + \text{coeff(2)} \cdot \text{logarithm price}$$

resulted in the following estimates:

$$\underset{}{\text{logarithm M2}} = \underset{(0.12)}{1.33} + \underset{(0.001)}{0.034}\ \text{Trend} + \underset{(0.04)}{0.95}\ \text{logarithm}\ P$$

where 0.95 is the price elasticity and the standard errors (used to gauge the statistical significance of the coefficients) are in parentheses. All the coefficients are statistically significant.

**FIGURE 11.2** The Determinants of Money Demand, 1913–94

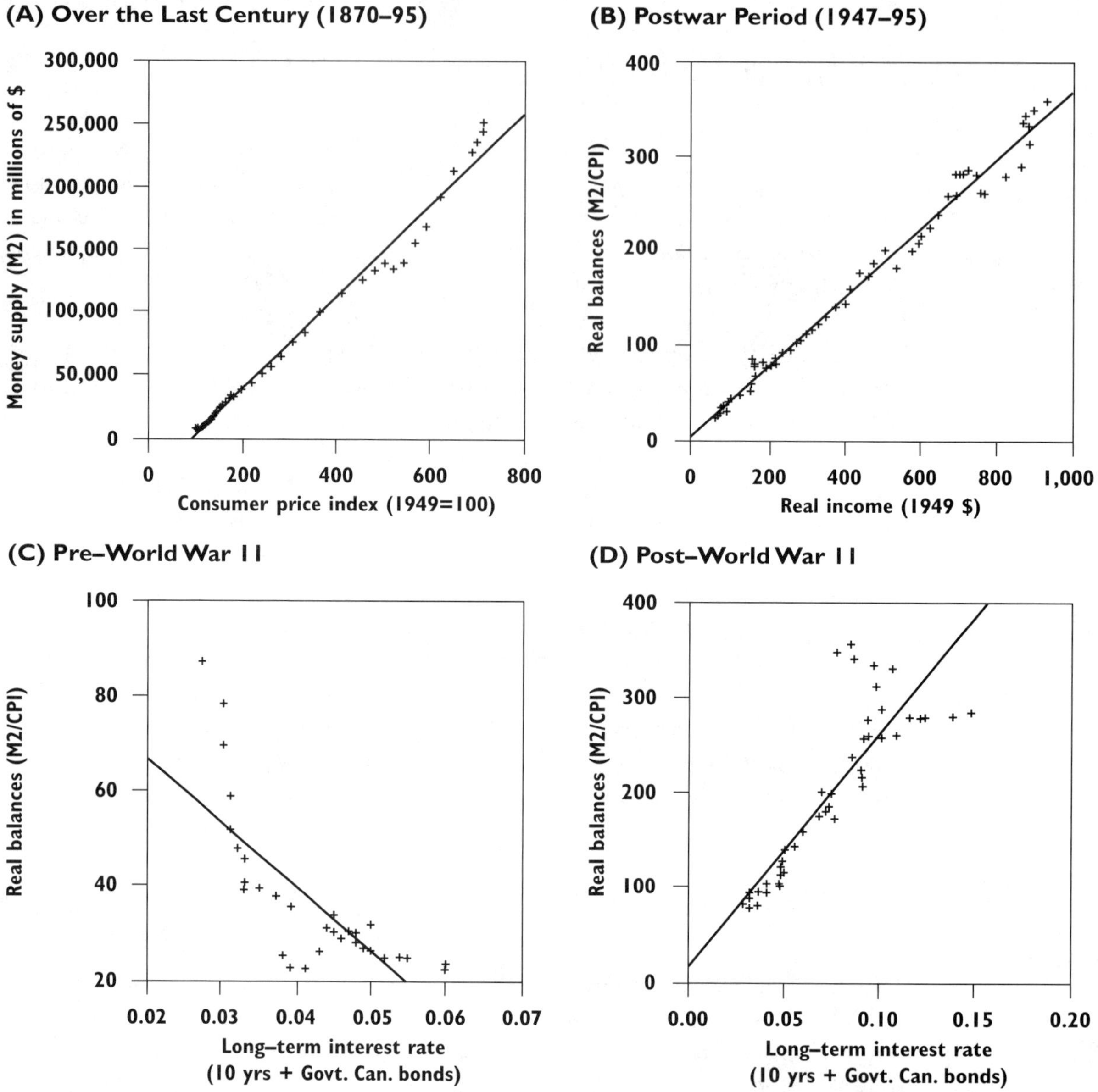


More than a century of data suggest the existence of a fairly strong link between M2 and the price level and real M2 and real income. The relationship between real balances and the nominal interest rates is, however, quite different after World War II. The reason is financial innovations.

Sources: M.D. Bordo and L. Jonung, *The Long-Run Behavior of the Velocity of Circulation* (New York: Cambridge University Press, 1987); and R.C.K. Burdekin and P.L. Siklos, "The Phillips Curve, The Persistence of Inflation, and the Lucas Critique: Further Evidence," manuscript, Wilfrid Laurier University.

Recall that the quantity theory is central to the understanding of the demand for money (see equation (11.12)). Thus, the demand for money, $M^d$, is a function of (real) income multiplied by the reciprocal of the velocity of circulation, or, as denoted in equation (11.13),

$$M^d = \left(\frac{1}{V}\right) Py \qquad (11.13)$$

Suppose now that velocity is a constant. Then, the demand for money is a function of real income alone, which is, in essence, Friedman's theory of the demand for money.

But how realistic is the assumption of a constant velocity? Figure 11.3 plots velocity for Canada for more than a century of data. We see that velocity is far from being a constant. It seems then that, at least for long periods, it is not appropriate to treat velocity as a constant in the demand for money function. (This result is indirect confirmation of the apparent lack of stability found in the estimated demand for money functions reported in the previous section.)

Notice that the curve in Figure 11.3 is a rough U-shape. Why? Some analysts suggest that the shape reflects the timing of **monetization** and financial innovation. During the early twentieth century, the Canadian and US economies were becoming more monetized: the use of cash and cheques was becoming increasingly common. As a consequence, the growth of money exceeded that of income during the pre-war period. The 1930s and 1940s saw a change in the direction of velocity. The Great Depression and World War II produced forces that promoted financial innovation and sophistication. We will be discussing several examples in subsequent chapters but two obvious examples come immediately to mind: credit cards and automatic teller machines. Both innovations permit individuals to keep some of their financial wealth in interest earning assets longer than would otherwise be the case. Over time, these events shifted the economy away from reliance on money for transactions purposes. This phenomenon, combined with the worldwide postwar boom in economic growth, resulted in a situation in which income grew faster than money, which explains the postwar tendency for velocity to rise over time. The theory which links velocity or money demand to financial development and innovations is known as the institutionalist hypothesis.[19] Moreover, the Canadian evidence is not unique; most other industrialized countries have had the same experience.[20]

---

19 A detailed description of these ideas can be found in M.D. Bordo and L. Jonung, *The Long-Run Behavior of the Velocity of Circulation* (New York: Cambridge University Press, 1987).

20 See M.D. Bordo, L. Jonung and P.L. Siklos, "Institutional Change and the Velocity of Money: A Century of Evidence," *Economic Inquiry* (forthcoming, 1997).

## ECONOMICS FOCUS 11.2 The Case of the Missing Money

In the 1960s, many economists thought they had settled on an approach to the demand for money function. A decade later, however, some of them, especially in the United States, were questioning its adequacy. The conventional demand for money function was regularly overpredicting actual money demand by the mid-1970s (Goldfeld called the difference between actual and predicted values "the missing money"), and underpredictions appeared just as regularly in the early 1980s. Various researchers (for example, Judd and Scadding, and Cooley and LeRoy) pointed out a number of flaws in the way analysts had estimated demand. But it was becoming apparent that the demand for money had an endemic lack of stability.

The most promising solution to the problem of finding a stable demand for money function may lie in explicitly incorporating the influence of financial innovation. On a more practical level, watching movements in velocity can be very useful. For example, during the recession of 1991–92, money growth was sluggish, providing evidence of the importance of money in influencing economic activity. Of course, sluggish money growth and recessions need not go hand in hand (for example, velocity may rise to offset slow growth, as it does in the simple quantity theory equation analysed in this chapter).

**Sources:**

T.F. Cooley and S.F. LeRoy, "Identification and Estimation of Money Demand," *American Economic Review* 71 (December 1981): 825–44.

S. Goldfeld, "The Case of the Missing Money," *Brookings Papers on Economic Activity* 3 (1976): 683–730.

J.P. Judd and J.L. Scadding, "The Search for a Stable Money Demand Function," *Journal of Economic Literature* 20 (September 1982): 993–1023.

P.L. Siklos, "Income Velocity and Institutional Change: Some New Time Series Evidence, 1870–1986," *Journal of Money, Credit and Banking* 25 (August 1993): 377–92.

## SUMMARY

- The demand for money represents a way of explaining how much cash (and bank deposits) individuals choose to hold.
- Income, interest rates, and prices are the principal determinants of the demand for money.
- Money illusion refers to the possibility that individuals do not realize that when prices increase, more cash has to be held to purchase the same quantity of goods.
- One way to think of the demand for money is as an inventory control problem. Individuals attempt to synchronize income with expenditures as well as possible and to minimize the opportunity costs of holding money. This is called the optimal cash management approach to the demand for money.

**FIGURE 11.3** Velocity of Circulation in Canada 1870–1994

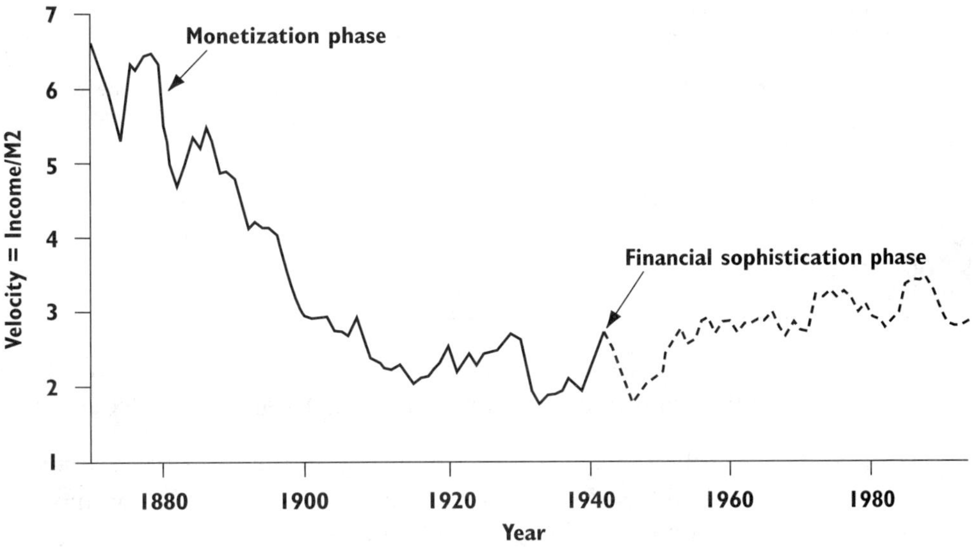


Note: Velocity is derived from equation (11.13) by rearranging its terms to produce $V = Y/M$.
Note that since $y = Y/P$, and $m = M/P$, $V = (Y/P)/(M/P) = Y/M$, where $Y$ is nominal GNP and $M$ is the stock of money, measured here as M2. Note too that $M^d$ was replaced with $M$ – that is, with actual values for the money supply. The implicit assumption is that the money market is in equilibrium.

Source: M.D. Bordo and L. Jonung, *The Long-Run Behavior of the Velocity of Circulation* (New York: Cambridge University Press, 1987), updated from data in *Federal Reserve Bulletin* and the *Bank of Canada Review*. Figures after 1986 are comparable with figures for earlier years but not identical due to definitional changes.

- The quantity theory expresses a relationship between the money supply and total spending. Interest rates play no direct role but can play an indirect role in this version of the demand for money.
- Friedman suggests a theory of the demand for money that essentially comes down to a restatement of the quantity theory.
- Empirical evidence suggests that the interest rate, prices, and income all play important roles in explaining the demand for money.
- Over long periods of time, the velocity of circulation is important in understanding the demand for money because it can reflect the influence of financial innovations.

## IMPORTANT TERMS

demand for money function (p. 229)
hyperinflation (p. 236)
monetization (p. 243)
money illusion (p. 230)
optimal cash management approach (p. 231)
quantity theory (p. 237)
real balances (p. 228)
velocity of circulation (p. 237)

## EXERCISES

1. According to the model of optimal cash management, would rich individuals differ from poor ones in their demand for money? Explain your answer.

2. Describe the effect of the following on the velocity of circulation:
   (a) Credit cards or debt cards become increasingly common in use.
   (b) All types of chequing accounts pay market interest rates.
   (c) Automatic teller machines become available in so many places that individuals can, at very little cost, obtain cash or transfer funds from one type of account to another.

3. Suppose that the total spending in an economy is \$200 billion and the money supply is \$5 billion. What is the value of velocity?

4. An economy has a money supply of \$50 billion, and the average price of goods and services being exchanged is \$50, and a billion transactions take place each week. On average, how long is a dollar held between transactions?

5. Suppose the Bank of Canada implements a policy of 3% annual growth in M2 in order to achieve zero inflation. Under what circumstances might zero inflation be attained? (Hint: Look at the quantity theory equation.)

6. Explain how one can associate strong growth in the money supply with either strong economic growth or weak economic growth. (Hint: Think about what must happen to velocity.)

7. Suppose that the demand for money is as given in equation (11.11). Assuming $b = 4$, answer the following:
   (a) If $Py = 2{,}000$ and $R = 0.10$, what is the demand for money?
   (b) If $b = 2$ and $Py$ and $R$ are as in (a) above, what is the demand for money?

8. The interest elasticity of the demand for M1 appears to have risen since the

end of World War II. What role may financial innovations have played in this trend?

9. The income elasticity of the demand for money appears to have fallen since the end of World War II. Can you explain why this might be the case?

10. Why is it that, under hyperinflation, one can ignore the effect of income and the real interest rate on money demand? Explain.

11. Would the case depicted in Figure 11.1(B) be the same if the bills were paid by a transfer of funds from a savings account? Explain.

12. Could the interest elasticity for the monetary aggregate M3, for example, be positive? Explain.

13. Suppose that transactions costs in the Baumol–Tobin framework were ($b/n$). What would be the marginal cost of an additional transaction? Would money demand be affected?

14. What is the institutionalist hypothesis of velocity? What does it explain that the quantity theory cannot? Explain.

15. According to the empirical estimates presented in the chapter, is there much evidence of money illusion? Do the results surprise you? Explain.

16. How would credit cards affect M1 and M2 velocity? Automatic teller machines? Explain.

## REFERENCES

Baumol, W.J. "The Transactions Demand for Cash: An Inventory Theoretic Approach." *Quarterly Journal of Economics* 66 (November 1952): 545–66.

Baumol, W.J., and J. Tobin. "The Optimal Cash Balance Proposition: Maurice Allais' Priority." *Journal of Economic Literature* 27 (September 1989): 1160–63.

Bordo, M.D., and L. Jonung. *The Long-Run Behavior of the Velocity of Circulation.* New York: Cambridge University Press, 1987.

Bordo, M.D., L. Jonung, and P.L. Siklos, "Institutional Change and the Velocity of Money: A Century of Evidence," *Economic Enquiry* (1997, forthcoming).

Dornbusch, R., S. Fisher, and G.R. Sparks. *Macroeconomics*, 2nd Cdn. ed. Toronto: McGraw-Hill Ryerson, 1985, 314.

Friedman, M. "The Demand for Money: Some Theoretical and Empirical Results." *Journal of Political Economy* 67 (August 1959): 327–51.

———. "The Quantity Theory of Money: A Restatement." In *Studies in the Quantity Theory of Money*, edited by M. Friedman. Chicago: The University of Chicago Press, 1956, 3–21.

Harris, L. *Monetary Theory.* New York: McGraw-Hill, 1981.

Judd, J.P., and J.L. Scadding. "The Search for a Stable Money Demand Function." *Journal of Economic Literature* 20 (June 1982): 993–1023.

Laidler, D.E.W. *The Demand for Money: Theoretical and Empirical Evidence*, 2d ed. New York: Dun-Donneley, 1977.

Leijonhufvd, A. *On Keynesian Economics and the Economics of Keynes: A Study in Monetary Theory.* New York: Oxford University Press, 1968.

Lucas, R.E., Jr. "Econometric Policy Evaluation: A Critique." In vol. 1, Carnegie-Rochester Conference Series on Public Policy, 19–46. Amsterdam: North-Holland, 1976.

———. "Money Demand in the United States: A Quantitative Review." In *Money, Cycles and Exchange Rates: Essays in Honor of Allan H. Meltzer*, vol. 29, Carenegie-Rochester Conference Series on Public Policy, edited by K. Brunner and A.H. Meltzer, 137–68. Amsterdam: North-Holland, 1988.

Miller, S.M. "Monetary Dynamics: An Application of Cointegration and Error Correction Modelling." *Journal of Money, Credit and Banking* 23 (May 1991): 139–54.

Ramanathan, R. *Introductory Econometrics.* San Diego, Calif.: Harcourt, Brace, and Jovanovich, 1989.

Siklos, P.L. *War Finance, Reconstruction, Hyperinflation and Stabilization in Hungary, 1938–48.* London and New York: Macmillan, and St. Martin's Press, 1991.

Tobin J. "The Interest-Elasticity of the Transactions Demand for Cash." *Review of Economics and Statistics* 38 August 1956: 241–42.

CHAPTER 12

# Stock Prices

Like bonds and money, stocks are a fascinating financial asset to analyse. Everyone seems to have an opinion abut the stock market and the future behaviour of stock prices. The proliferation of approaches—from that of chartists, who graph the past behaviour of stock prices in every conceivable fashion; technical analysts, who claim to make sense of the past and anticipated future performance of the stock market; contrarians, who deliberately go against the judgment of others—could make one think that stock prices can be predicted with some degree of accuracy.

Economists, in contrast, believe that the past is not a good guide to the future when it comes to stock prices. Yet their explanations face some considerable difficulties, particularly when it comes to attempting to understand large fluctuations in stock prices, such as those of 1987.

We take the same approach in this chapter as in previous chapters, beginning by exploring how stock prices should be determined at the level of the firm and then assuming that this model applies to all firms. We consider two approaches: (1) one, called the efficient market hypothesis, which views investors as rational forward-thinking individuals who process information quickly and efficiently, and (2) an alternative way of determining individual stock prices called the fundamentalist approach.

Each of these approaches can tell us only about how the level of stock prices is determined, not about volatility. On the latter subject, economists have considerably more diversity of opinion, and a satisfactory explanation seems to elude the profession. Nevertheless, it is interesting to consider some anomalies in stock price behaviour that seem consistent with the economists' basic model.

## THE MARKET FOR STOCKS

Some stocks are traded in brokers' informed **over-the-counter (OTC)** markets ("over the phone" or "over the fax" would be more accurate names today). In

Canada, the **Canadian Dealing Network**, also known in its previous incarnation as the Canadian Over-the-Counter Automated Trading System (COATS) and now referred to as CATS (Computer Assisted Trading Systems), quotes over 500 OTC stocks worth several billions of dollars. In the United States, the network that performs the same function is called the National Association of Securities Dealers Automated Quotations (NASDAQ). But many more stocks are traded on **stock exchanges**, which are organized markets, each of which sets its own rules for what corporations can list shares and how they are traded.[1]

Canada has four stock exchanges: the Montreal Stock Exchange, the Toronto Stock Exchange, the Alberta Stock Exchange, and the Vancouver Stock Exchange. Each is a non-profit institution in which membership is acquired by purchasing a seat on the exchange. Approximately 500 traders work on the floor of the Toronto Stock Exchange, the nation's largest. Many Canadian corporations also have their shares listed on one of the large US exchanges.

Modern technology is changing the way stock exchanges operate. Today's instant, worldwide communications, for example, mean that Canadian investors can easily use brokers who have seats on exchanges in Tokyo, London, or Paris. Computer technology is also modifying stock exchanges internally. Increasingly, buyers and sellers transmit their orders to a computer, and so do the brokers' traders in their exchange seats. The advent of Internet trading via Instinet, for example, is threatening the established exchanges.

Prices of individual stocks are published daily for the major Canadian, US, and overseas exchanges. Investors are also interested in the performance of the stock market as a whole, and a variety of **stock price indexes** are available. The best known Canadian index is the Toronto Stock Exchange 300 (TSE 300), which is an average of 300 stocks of 289 companies (some firms have more than one type or class of securities listed on the exchange). Like most indexes, it is based on the market value of the shares being traded (since the volume of shares traded is not the same for every company). Another index much reported in Canada is the Dow Jones Industrial Average, an average of the stock prices of 30 prominent companies traded on the New York Stock Exchange.

---

1 It is worth noting that this centralized-market approach, which relies heavily on the intermediation of brokers through a computerized network, is used in many industrialized countries besides Canada and the United States, but not in all of them. In Germany, for example, there is no independent clearinghouse. Rather, the stock exchange matches buyers and sellers and settlement is made through deposits. Thus, banks are directly involved in the stock market in Germany.

## FINANCIAL FOCUS 12.1 Stock Prices in the Financial Press

The financial press and many daily papers regularly present stock prices. On 16 April 1996, a typical line for an individual company read as the table below. In April 1996 Canadian stock exchanges fell in line with European and Asian exchanges by switching to the decimal system of reporting stock prices. A major advantage of the move is that stock prices would not be constrained by ⅛ changes in prices.

BCE is Bell Canada Enterprises. During 1995, the price of a share of its stock fluctuated between a high of $54.15 and a low of $41.25 a share. The difference between high and low prices is sometimes referred to as the bid–ask spread. In a competitive market the spread should be small. However, in an article that created quite a stir in US financial markets, Christie and Schultz found that collusion in the NASDAQ market meant that spreads were higher (and therefore dealer profits were higher) than necessary. A subsequent study concluded that spreads began to narrow right after the publication of the article!

*Div rate* is the size of the dividend payment, which may be quarterly or semi-annually (an "r" next to the stock in question would signify that dividends are in arrears).

The *High* and *Low* columns show the ranges of price the previous day; *Cls* is the price at the close of trading. *Net change* indicates the absolute change in the price of the stock between closing on the previous day and closing the day before that. *Vol 100s* shows the number of shares traded in hundreds. *Yield* and *P/E ratio* are measures of the stock's and the company's performance; yield is simply the dividend to stock price ratio at close converted into a percentage (that is, 2.72/50.15 × 100 = 5.4%), and the *P/E ratio* is the price of the stock divided by the company's earnings over a period of time (usually 12 months).

**Sources:**

W. Christie and P.H. Schultz, " Why do NASDAQ Market Makers Avoid Odd-Eighth Quotes," *Journal of Finance*, 50 (May 1995).

P. Harverson, "Study Makes New Claims of NADAQ Collusion," *Financial Times* 13 October 1996, p. 22.

| 52 Week | | | Div | | | Cls or | Net | Vol | Yield | P/E |
|---|---|---|---|---|---|---|---|---|---|---|
| High | Low | | Rate | High | Low | Latest | Change | 100s | % | Ratio |
| 54.15 | 41.25 | BCE Inc. | 2.72 | 50.20 | 49.45 | 50.15 | +.65 | 29.71 | 5.4 | 22.50 |

# STOCK PRICE DETERMINATION

Analysts have conceived two quite different approaches to understanding price determination in the stock market: the efficient markets hypothesis and the fundamentalist approach. On the surface they seem at variance with each other, but, as we will see, they are not necessarily contradictory.

## THE EFFICIENT MARKETS HYPOTHESIS

The **efficient markets hypothesis**, which economists favour, is that market participants use all available information efficiently in anticipating future prices; hence no one can earn an abnormal economic profit.

Economic efficiency includes the way in which individuals are assumed to obtain, use, and process relevant information in the determination of the price of any asset. The presence of efficiency in the stock market implies that the price of a stock reflects its inherent riskiness. No stock return can be excessive because it must reflect all information that might influence its price up to the time of trading.

Note that the proponents of this view do not say that the stock market offers no profitable opportunities. Rather, they imply, foreseeable events offer no special opportunities. For example, construction activity in Canada is at its lowest during the winter months and toy sales peak at Christmastime. Yet, stocks traded in these industries show no obvious seasonal patterns. Why not? Because these events are well known or fully anticipated. By contrast, events that are unanticipated can influence prices in an unexpected fashion, opening opportunities for profitable trades.

What are the implications of these principles? Answering that question requires distinguishing among three different versions of the efficient markets hypothesis.

### Weak Form

The weak form of the efficient markets hypothesis says that past stock prices contain no information useful in predicting the future course of prices. Let

$E$ = expected or anticipated value
$S$ = price of a stock
$t$ = time

Then we can write formally,

$$E(S_{t+1} \mid S_t, S_{t-1}, S_{t-2}, \ldots) \tag{12.1}$$

to mean the expected or anticipated value[2] of a stock at time $t + 1$, which is tomorrow, based only or conditional upon (the symbol $\mid$) the past performance of that stock ($S_{t-1}, S_{t-2}, \ldots$).[3]

---

2 There is a way of calculating such an expected value, otherwise known as a mathematical expectation. See the appendix to this chapter.

3 It is not necessary to specify how far in the past we need to go. The essentials of the story are unaffected whether we look back 10 days or a year.

The weak form of the efficient markets hypothesis then says that the anticipated *change* in the price between today and tomorrow cannot be predicted by anything that influenced that price in the past. Since the price of the stock today, $S_t$, is known and presumably reflects all information contained in the price previously, the best forecast of tomorrow's price is today's price, or

$$E(S_{t+1} \mid S_t, S_{t-1}, S_{t-2}, \ldots) = S_t \quad (12.2)$$

In the absence of new information, an investor would conclude that tomorrow's price is expected to be equal to today's price.

Of course, all sorts of *unpredictable* economics events, company-specific or economy-wide, can affect tomorrow's stock price. This would imply that the best forecast of tomorrow's stock price ($S_{t+1}$) is today's price ($S_t$) plus an unpredictable component ($U_t$). In other words, we can write

$$S_{t+1} = S_t + U_t \quad (12.3)$$

where $U_t$ represents the unpredictable component that explains stock price changes. Alternatively, note that (12.3) can be rewritten

$$S_{t+1} - S_t = \Delta S_{t+1} = U_t \quad (12.4)$$

which simply restates what has already been argued: that changes in stock prices are unpredictable.

If we now assume that, on average, the unpredictable component is zero, then from equation (12.3) we obtain[4]

$$\begin{aligned} E(S_{t+1}) &= S_t + E(U_t) \\ &= S_t \end{aligned} \quad (12.5)$$

This prediction is known as the **random walk**. If it is correct, one might as well pick stocks by throwing darts at a dartboard. Indeed, the *Wall Street Journal* has for several years run a contest between a group of expert stock pickers (who change from time to time) against a selection of common stocks picked by throwing darts at a list of stocks on the New York, American and NASDAQ exchanges. Research shows that the experts do not consistently outperform the "dartboard portfolio."[5]

4 Taking expectations of both sides of equation (12.3) we get $E(S_{t+1}) = E(S_t + U_t) = E(S_t) + E(U_t) = S_t$ because $S_t$ is known at the time a forecast is made and $U_t$ is expected to average zero.

5 See G.E. Metcalf and B.G. Malkiel, "The Wall Street Journal Contest: The Experts, the Darts and the Efficient Markets Hypothesis," *Applied Financial Economics* 4 (October 1994): 371–74.

Can such a possibility really be entertained? Consider Figure 12.1(A), which shows the performance of the TSE 300 since 1956. Despite several noticeable downturns, such as those in 1982 and 1987, the general price trend has been upward.[6] Does not such a clear trend imply that stock prices should be predictable? The answer is no because the apparent trend is a statistical illusion. In Figure 12.1(B), which shows percentage changes in stock prices over time, notice that the values hover around zero, leaving it in a seemingly random fashion (hence the term "random walk"). But also notice the sharp spikes in the curve. They indicate that a buy-and-hold strategy cannot produce excess returns over the long run and that losses are possible in the short run.[7]

## Semistrong Form

The semistrong version of the efficient markets hypothesis suggests that relevant information contained in the past behaviour of interest rates, inflation and even company performance is as irrelevant as past prices in forecasting future prices. Figure 12.2 shows for example, that no obvious link exists between changes in stock prices and either interest rate changes or changes in the growth of the money supply (which could be used as a proxy for inflation). Instead research suggests that sharp changes in individual stock prices are triggered by unexpected events and are very temporary. (Nevertheless, there are differences in opinions about what are sometimes referred to as large "corrections" in stock prices—sharp swings up or down.)

In going from the weak to the semistrong form of the efficient markets hypothesis, the idea is to expand the information set that might determine stock prices so that it includes other macroeconomic variables. Equation (12.1) could now be written

$$E(S_{t+1} \mid S_t, S_{t-1}, S_{t-2}, \ldots, R_t, R_{t-1}, R_{t-2}, \ldots, \pi_t, \pi_{t-1}, \pi_{t-2}, \ldots) \qquad (12.6)$$

where $R_t$ is the interest rate and $\pi$ is the rate of inflation. Other relevant macroeconomic information could also be included. The remainder of the analysis is unaffected, however, so we still conclude that

$$\Delta S_{t+1} = U_t$$

The only difference is that the possibility of forecasting errors is even more restricted because even less information can be profitably exploited.[8]

6 The same trend is apparent in stock prices on stock exchanges in several industrialized countries.

7 Not everyone agrees with the conclusion. For example, one study found that information from the distant past can indeed be used for forecasting stock prices. See Z. Ding, C.W.J. Granger and R.F. Engle, "A Long Memory Property of Stock Market Return and a New Model," *Journal of Empirical Finance* 1 (1994).

8 The accumulated body of evidence favours the weak or semistrong forms of the efficient markets hypothesis.

**FIGURE 12.1** The Random Walk of Stock Prices

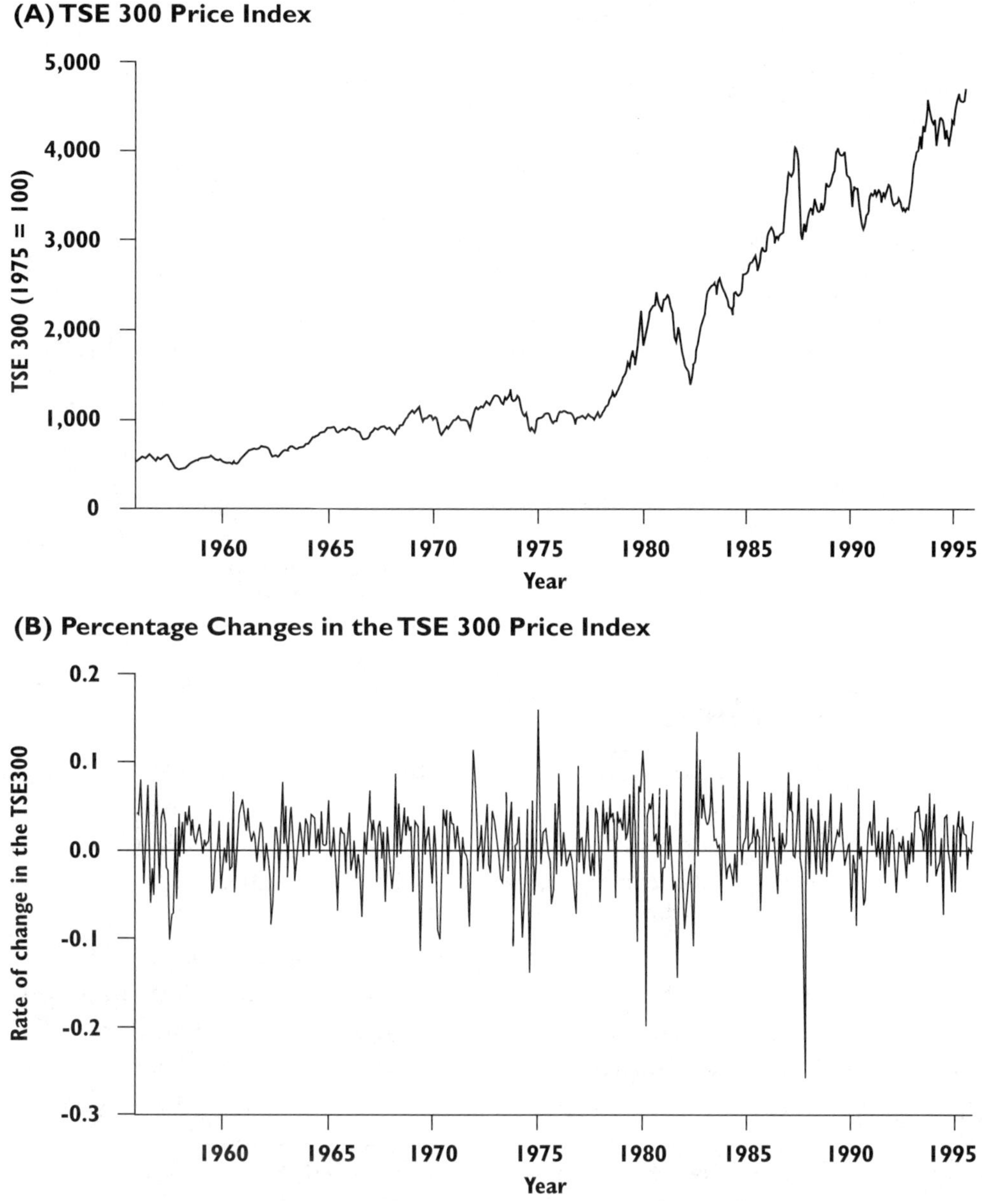


A graph of the level of the TSE 300 stock price index (panel (A)) shows a more-or-less steady rise since the mid-1950s. But a graph of the month-by-month percentage change in those price levels (panel (B)) reveals no discernible pattern. The latter phenomenon is referred to as a random walk.

Source: Statistics Canada, CANSIM database, reproduced by authority of the Ministry of Industry, 1996; and *Bank of Canada Review*.

**FIGURE 12.2** The TSE 300 and the Treasury Bill Rate, 1980–95

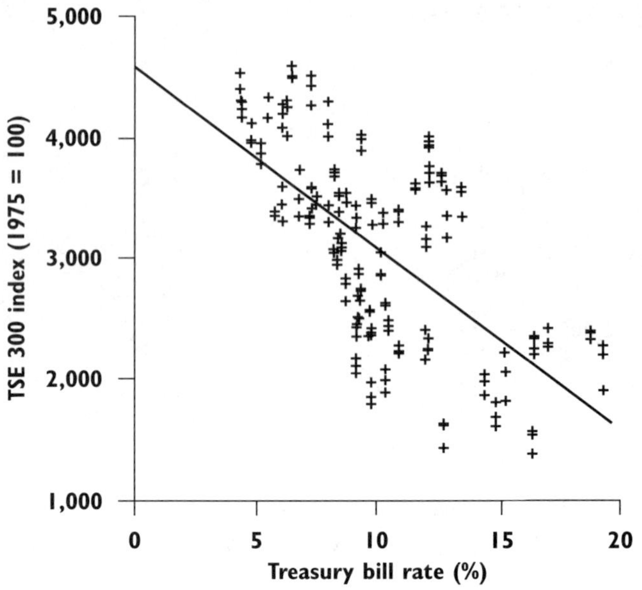


## Strong Form

There remains a final possibility: that there is no information whatsoever, public or private, that can be profitably exploited by an investor. This alternative is known as the strong form of the efficient markets hypothesis. Few economists believe in it literally because there are well-documented cases of profit from *insider* information (information available to a corporate officer, director, or major shareholder but not to all shareholders or the public at large).[9] It should be noted, however, that there is a difference between insider information, which cannot be acted on legally, and a rumour or gossip based on knowledge of a collection of events and information available publicly or privately. The distinction is not always clear.

More recent evidence favourable to the random walk hypothesis includes E.F. Fama and K.R. French, "Permanent and Temporary Components of Stock Prices," *Journal of Political Economy* 96 (1988): 246–73; J.M. Poterba and L.H. Summers, "Mean Reversion in Stock Prices: Evidence and Implications," *Journal of Financial Economics* 22 (1988): 27–59. A recent review of the literature is B.N. Lehmann, "Asset Pricing and Intrinsic Values: A Review Essay," *Journal of Monetary Economics* 28 (1991): 485–500.

9 Some years ago, Ivan Boesky of New York made (and subsequently lost) a fortune based on insider information. Similar instances occurred during the 1920s. And, during the spate of corporate takeovers and buyouts in the 1980s and 1990s, the volume of trading in shares of the companies involved sometimes rose during the few days preceding the official announcement.

## *THE FUNDAMENTALIST APPROACH

Although the efficient markets approach admits that a company-specific information may have impinged on the past performance of a firm's stock, it does not emphasize the connection. In contrast, the **fundamentalist approach** suggests that how well a firm performs over time determines the value of its earnings and thus the price of its stock.

Suppose, for simplicity, that a firm pays out all its profits in the form of dividends,[10] that it is expected to operate indefinitely into the future, and that suspension of dividends is not expected at any time.[11] Since dividends reflect the flow of profits to be generated now and into the future, they presumably should dictate the value of the firm and its stock as perceived by the market. It is for this reason that this approach to explaining stock price behaviour is known as the fundamentalist approach. As we have said repeatedly, a dollar paid today is not valued the same as a dollar paid in the future. Therefore, we must first discount the value of future dividend payments. Thus, we write

$$S = \frac{d_1}{(1 + R)} + \frac{d_2}{(1 + R)^2} + \cdots \tag{12.7}$$

where $d_1, d_2, \ldots$ represents the dividend payments paid out in years 1, 2, and so on, and $1/(1 + R), 1/(1 + R)^2, \ldots$ represents the discount factors.

So far nothing has been said about whether these dividend payments are fixed or not. Let us assume that as a firm grows, so do its dividends—say, at a rate of $g$ percent per year. In other words, if $d_1$ is the dividend paid in year 1, $d_2$, the dividend paid in year 2, is $d_1(1 + g)$. In this fashion, we can relate the dividends in any year to the dividends paid in the first year; that is,

$$d_n = d_1(1 + g)^{n-1} \tag{12.8}$$

where $d_n$ is the dividend paid out in the $n$th year, and $(1 + g)^{n-1}$ is the factor by which these dividends have grown over the $n$ years relative to the dividends in year 1. The net effect is that we can rewrite equation (12.7) as

$$S = \frac{d_1}{(1 + R)} + \frac{d_1(1 + g)}{(1 + R)^2} + \cdots \tag{12.9}$$

This equation has a fairly simple solution:[12]

10 We assume here that dividends are paid annually, even though they are typically paid quarterly.

11 These assumptions are certainly strong, but relaxing them would complicate only the final expression linking dividends and stock prices; it would not break the essence of the link between these two variables.

12 The proof is as follows. Multiply equation (12.9) by $(1 + R)/(1 + g)$ to obtain

$$S = \frac{d_1}{R - g} \tag{12.10}$$

Thus, the price of a stock, given a particular dividend, $d_1$, is determined by the interest rate in relation to the rate at which dividends grow. For a given interest rate, $R$, the faster dividends grow (that is, the higher is $g$) the higher is the price of a stock. Since dividends are presumably a function of a firm's performance, the better a company performs the higher the price of its stock. (See **FINANCIAL FOCUS: Trying to Explain the 1987 Stock Market Crash** for a practical implementation of equation (12.10).)

Notice also from equation 12.10 that an inverse relationship exists between stock returns and the interest rate. This establishes a link between bond market, discussed earlier, and the stock market. Figure 12.3 illustrates the link in terms of the loanable funds framework introduced in Chapter 6. The left-hand-side figure shows the usual loanable funds diagram. The interest rate fluctuates between $R_1$ and $R_2$ depending upon the position of the loanable funds demanded curve. According to equation (12.10) a rise in $R$, other things held constant, would reduce stock prices. This is illustrated in the right-hand-side diagram which clearly shows the negative relationship between $R$ and $S$. Figure 12.2 shows that, at least since 1980 there is a negative relationship between the TSE 300 index and the yield on Treasury bills.

## CAN THE TWO APPROACHES BE RECONCILED?

We appear to have two separate explanations for the behaviour of stock prices. In fact, under certain conditions, the fundamentalist and efficient markets approaches are consistent with each other. The technical details of the explanation are beyond the scope of this text, but it begins with the observation that a future stream of dividends, like any future event, cannot be known with certainty. It can only be forecast, and if we exclude the use of insider information, that forecast must be based on existing information known to all investors. The only information that could possibly alter the price of the stock is information on any

---

$$\left(\frac{1 + R}{1 + g}\right) S = \frac{d_1}{(1 + g)} + \frac{d_1}{(1 + R)} + \frac{d_1(1 + g)}{(1 + R)^2} + \cdots$$

From this equation, subtract equation (12.9) to get

$$\left(\frac{1 + R}{1 + g}\right) S - S = \frac{d_1}{(1 + g)}$$

which, when solved for $S$ yields equation (12.10). Since the price of a stock can never be negative, equation (12.10) holds so long as $R > g$.

## FINANCIAL FOCUS 12.2 Trying to Explain the 1987 Stock Market Crash

Stock market crashes appear to contradict the efficient markets hypothesis because the fall in prices seems out of proportion with any influence new information could possibly have on stock prices. We know that all markets have some inefficiency (without it there would be no incentive to search for information and exploit profitable opportunities at the expense of other investors). We also know the fundamentalist and efficient markets approaches can be viewed not as competing arguments but rather as different explanations of the information content used by investors to price stocks. Can any of these arguments be reconciled with the sharp fall in prices in the aftermath of Black Monday 1987?

The figure below shows what happened to stock prices and the Treasury bill rate during that year. Stock prices and interest rates rose sharply until October when both fell dramatically—but temporarily.

From the end of April to the end of September, the Treasury bill rate rose from 8.08% to 9.35%. The TSE 300 fell during October from 3902.37 to 2978.34, a drop of approximately 23.7%. Suppose that a typical firm's stock also fell by 23.7%. Moreover, suppose that this firm paid out annual dividends of $10 and that these dividends were expected to grow at an annual rate of 4%. At the end of April, according to equation (12.10), the present discounted value of the dividends and, therefore, the price of the stock were

$$S = \$245.10 = \frac{\$10.00}{8.08 - 4.00}$$

The same calculation for the end of September gives

$$S = \$186.92 = \frac{\$10.00}{9.35 - 4.00}$$

a drop of nearly 23.7%! Thus, relatively small changes in interest rates over a short time span can produce very large stock price changes.

Clearly, however, the forgoing calculations leave several unanswered questions. First, would the dividend rate and its growth stay the same after the crash? Second, why did stock prices not fall earlier? After all, it is clear that interest rates had risen sharply over a period of several months and yet stock prices kept climbing. In other words, why did investors allow stock prices to be overvalued for so long?

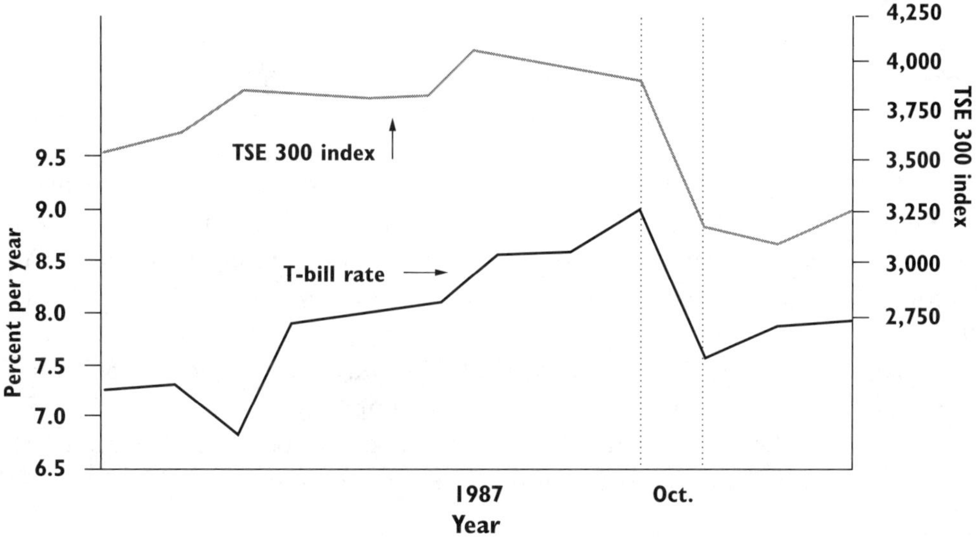

**FIGURE 12.3** Interest Rates and Stock Prices

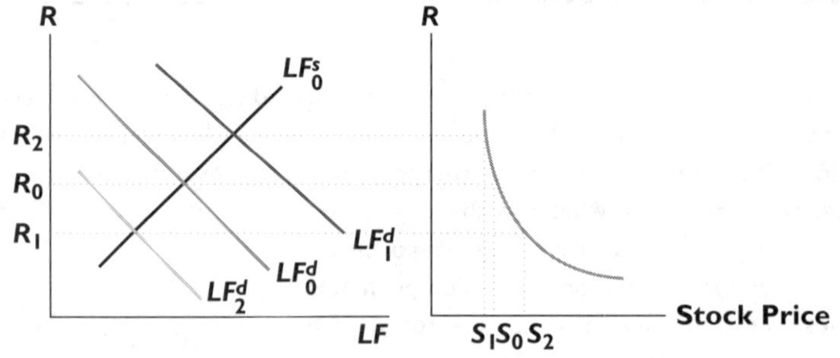


The diagram on the left shows the equilibrium interest rate as determined by the loanable funds model. The diagram on the right shows the connection between the interest rate and stock prices when dividends and dividend growth are constant in equation (12.10).

alteration of the projected flow of future dividends. By definition, that information cannot be anticipated. But this is just another way of saying that stock price exchanges are unpredictable. Thus, the fundamentalist and efficient markets approaches need not conflict.

## STOCK MARKET VOLATILITY

The *volatility* of the stock market can be defined in several ways. We examine a particular definition shortly; for the moment, just think of it as representing some measure of the size of the changes in stock prices.

Figure 12.1(B) shows this volatility. Although economists have not reached a broad consensus on this question of volatility, some do suggest explanations. One is based on the notion that the stock market has two types of participants:[13] "informed traders," who behave much as the efficient market hypothesis suggests, and "noisy traders," who follow fads and trends, jumping on or off particular bandwagons. Suppose that individuals attempt to forecast stock prices as in equation (12.10), but investors cannot evaluate the equation with certainty because information about the future behaviour of dividends is incomplete. Let $S^*$ represent the price of a stock evaluated with some imprecision and $S$ the price one would obtain if the indefinite future stream of dividends were completely known. We can write a relationship between these two prices as

13 A recent reference that stimulated much of this research is R.J. Schiller, *Market Volatility* (Cambridge, Mass.: The MIT Press, 1989), chapter 4.

## ECONOMICS FOCUS 12.1 The Latest in the Chartists' Toolkit

Yet another approach to stock market forecasting is that used by analysts who are called *chartists* (they prefer *technical analysts*) because they spend their days graphing the past behaviour of key stock market price indexes and looking for patterns. Such analysts consider information about company earnings or dividends irrelevant. Rather, they focus on what happens to the graphs, spotting particular events, such as the "triple witching hour" when stock-index futures, stock-index options, and options on individual stocks expire simultaneously.

One tool in the chartists' kit is a pattern called "three peaks and a domed house." Between 1989 and 1991 the Dow Jones Industrial Average (DJIA) in the United States went through three peaks: one in October 1989, a second in January 1990, and a third in July 1990. By early May 1991, the pattern appeared to reach the top of the "dome," and some analysts expected a plunge in the Dow Jones later that month. One did occur but it was a small interruption in a consistent rise in the DJIA.

The "three peaks and a dome" idea is one that seems to have appeared approximately a dozen times during the last 120 years. The difficulty is that the pattern does not appear to occur regularly. Nevertheless, many analysts are impressed with the idea.

Other chartists' ideas include the "plunging neckline" in which stocks tend to level off for a while (the left shoulder), rise sharply until a peak is reached (the head), then fall again (the right shoulder) before "plunging" below the neckline.

The efficient markets hypothesis implies that analysts who invest considerable resources in tracking the history of individual stock price or aggregate indexes are investing considerable resources in an activity that yields few benefits. Surveys and various pieces of research have consistently shown that neither stock market analysts nor mutual fund decision makers consistently outguess the market. However, one well-known study (LeBaron and Brock) found that some rules for stock pricing based on past performance do sometimes work.

Yet the search is always on for predictable patterns in stock prices. Some analysts have gone so far as to suggest that stock prices will be influenced by who wins in the Super Bowl, by whether a new Rambo or Rocky movie is released, or even whether a new skyscraper breaks the world height record.

**Sources:**

P. Bloomfield, "Beware the Plunging Neckline," *Financial Post*, 15 September 1993, p. 24.

"The Erection Index," *The Economist* 11 May 1996, p. 69.

B. LeBaron and W. Brock, "Simple Technical Trading Rules and the Stochastic Properties of Stock Returns," *Journal of Finance* (December 1992): 1731–64.

B.G. Malkiel, *A Random Walk Down Wall Street*, 3d ed. (New York: W.W. Norton, 1991).

$$S = S^* + U \tag{12.11}$$

where $U$ is the measure of the imprecision with which investors can evaluate equation (12.10).

Equation (12.11) is, however, only an expression about the *level* of stock prices. A statement about their volatility is more useful. If we measure volatility of stock prices as their variance, we can, under certain conditions,[14] rewrite equation (12.11) as

14 In Chapter 13, we explore these conditions and other aspects of this measure.

$$V_S = V_{S^*} + V_U \tag{12.12}$$

where $V_S$, $V_{S^*}$, and $V_U$ represent the volatilities of $S$, $S^*$, and $U$, respectively.[15]

The noisy investors can be viewed as raising $V_U$ for a given $V_S$. Because they are likely to react to information that is irrelevant to the fundamental value of a stock, the volatility of prices as measured by $V_{S^*}$ will become relatively less important in explaining actual volatility. In other words, if all stock market participants were informed traders, $V_S$ would be largely explained by $V_{S^*}$ since they presumably calculate the prices of stock on the basis of equation (12.10). By contrast, the uniformed investors who do not follow equation (12.10), are the ones who create noise, or $V_U$, and thus weaken the success which the efficient markets approach can explain the behaviour of stock prices.

Although this explanation may sound reasonable, it is not accepted by all economists. Indeed, many economists believe that the level and volatility of stock returns are linked to each other and have developed a number of statistical tools to explain this phenomenon (see Economic Focus 12.2).

## OTHER ANOMALIES

The volatility of prices is but one of many anomalies in stock price behaviour that economists have difficulty in explaining. Another is the market's failure to act on the well-documented evidence that stocks of companies with low price–equity (P/E) ratios outperform those of companies with high P/E ratios.[16] Presumably, the former are underpriced in the sense described in equation (12.10) and the latter overpriced. If so, stock market participants should be able to make regular profits by following a simple strategy based on information available to everyone. That they do not implies that something is wrong with the efficient markets hypothesis.

Another anomaly is called the "January effect." Stock returns are regularly higher in January than in December of the previous year. December and September are regularly the best and worst months, respectively, for the Dow Jones Industrial Average (DJIA). Low-priced stocks in the Standard and Poor's (S&P) index outperform the S&P 500 index some 93% of the time, according to one source.[17] But such regularities should be fully anticipated by market participants

15 Equation (12.12) is valid so long as the variances of $S^*$ and $U$ are independent of each other—that is, as long as they are uncorrelated. Correlation is a concept we define more formally in the next chapter.

16 Recent evidence continues to perpetuate this conclusion. See "Cheap and Cheerful," *The Economist*, 27 February 1993, p. 79.

17 *L. Rukeyser's Wall Street*, February 1993, p. 11.

## ECONOMICS FOCUS 12.2 ARCH, GARCH and Other Creatures

ARCH stands for *autoregressive conditional heteroskedasticity* and GARCH for *generalized ARCH*. The original concept was introduced by Robert Engle of the University of California, San Diego, and this modelling procedure has become widely used for financial time series. In terms of stock prices an ARCH model might be specified as follows. Recall that equation (12.3) says that the best forecast of tomorrow's price is today's price and an unpredictable component. This idea was summarized in equation (12.3). Clearly, this must have also been true for the forecast of yesterday's price so we can write

$$S_t = S_{t-1} + U_t \qquad (12.1A)$$

Now we can use regression analysis to estimate the nature of the link between stock prices today and yesterday. Using the TSE 300 index we find

$$S_t = .011 + .998\, S_{t-1}$$

(the actual estimates were generated by taking logarithms of the index because $S_t - S_{t-1}$ is a measure of the percent change in the index). Since the coefficient on yesterday's stock index is very close to one, $\Delta S_t$ is approximately $U_t$ plus a constant .011 which represents the average growth rate in the TSE 300 (1.1% since 1956). But, as we noted earlier, the variance of $U$ is not constant over time. What ARCH and GARCH models try to do is to explain the changing variance of stock prices over time. The simplest version of an ARCH model would be written

$$V_t^2 = \alpha_0 + \alpha_1\, U_{t-1}^2 \qquad (12.2A)$$

Equations (12.2A) says that the variance of stock prices today ($V_t$) depends on a constant ($\alpha_0$) and yesterday's variance in the unpredictable component or in the rate of change of stock prices ($U_{t-1}$). In the case where a GARCH model is estimated one would simply add the forecast of yesterday's variance in stock prices ($V_{t-1}^2$). Statistical techniques are then used to estimate equations (12.1A) and (12.2A) together. Again, using the TSE 300 data we found

$$V_t^2 = .0003 + .1066\, U_{t-1}^2 + .764\, V_{t-1}^2$$

---

and consequently disappear. Again, the efficient markets hypothesis stands contradicted.

Two other anomalies that have raised considerable interest in the study of stock prices are the behaviour of future prices and the possible role of mass psychology on price behaviour. A good example of anomalies in future prices is the case of the price of oranges in Florida. One would expect that adverse weather conditions, such as winter freezes, would affect the future size of the crop of oranges in Florida and that this information would be fully incorporated in future prices. Yet empirical evidence suggests that future prices for oranges are hardly influenced by variables such as weather.

Mention of the role of mass psychology conjures up famous episodes of explosive stock price behaviour, which economists call *bubbles*. The most famous is the South Sea Bubble. In 1720 the South Sea Company took over the British government's debt in exchange for exclusive trading privileges with Spain's American colonies. As individuals rushed to join this and similar ventures, the price of the South Sea stock rose phenomenally. During the five months from January 28 to June 22, 1720, it soared at an annual rate of approximately 5,000%. Then

## ECONOMICS FOCUS 12.2 ARCH, GARCH and Other Creatures (continued)

The plot below shows the plot of the GARCH term since 1956 and we see that major events such as the oil shock of 1973–74, the recession of 1981–82 and the 1987 stock market "crash" each contributed to raise the volatility of stock prices. Specifications like ARCH and GARCH make sense because investors make decisions about which stocks to hold based not only on the price of a stock but on the expected volatility of stock prices. Since the original ARCH and GARCH models were introduced, all sorts of exotic variants of (12.2A) have been proposed with names like ARCH-M, GARCH-M, EGARCH and TARCH, and so on, but these are beyond the scope of this text.

**Sources:**

R.F. Engle, "Autoregressive Conditional Heteroskedasticity with Estimates of the Variance of UK Inflation Rates," *Econometrica* 50 (1982): 987–1008.

T. Bollerslev, "Generalized Autoregressive Conditional Heteroskedasticity," *Journal of Econometrics* 31 (1986): 307–27.

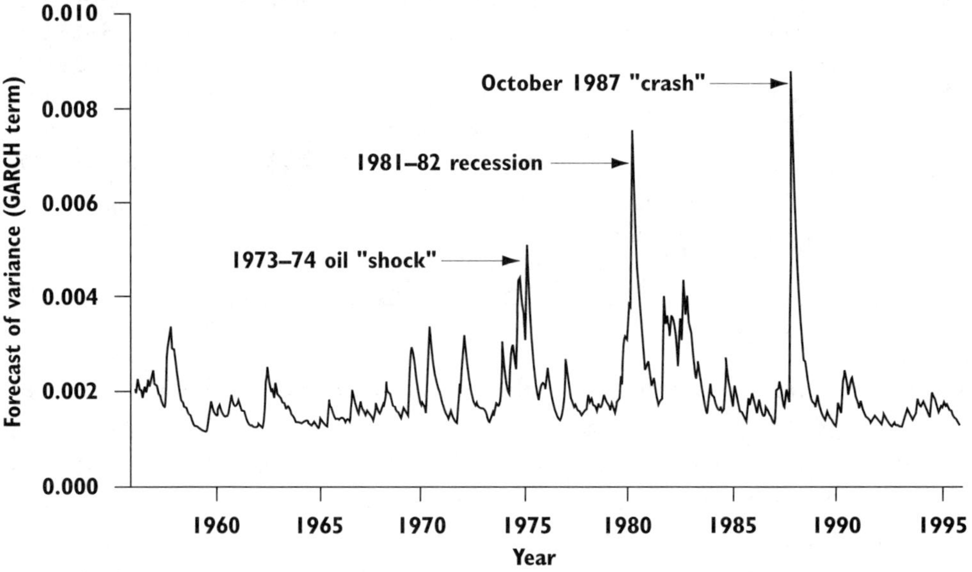


the South Sea bubble burst, and even the eminent Sir Isaac Newton was not spared from large losses. About a century earlier, Holland saw several years of wild speculation in tulip bulbs (1634–37). At the height of this "tulip mania," some bulbs sold for as much as $50,000 US.[18] Given that a tulip bulb is intrinsically worthless, the bubble eventually burst and many people lost fortunes.

Yet another famous example of a speculative bubble occurred closer to home during the early nineteenth century. The Mississippi Bubble arose when France

18 This calculation is based on gold valued at $450 US an ounce.

attempted to implement the economic ideas of John Law, a Scotsman who had become a financier in France. Law suggested that the government issue securities and use the proceeds to finance productive investments. The Regent of France, whose country's economy was depressed at the time, was attracted to Law's ideas and awarded him the monopoly right to develop Louisiana. Law refinanced France's entire national debt through the issue of stock in his company, the Compagnie des Indes formed in 1719. As he acquired more assets, by issuing ever-greater quantities of stocks, France's central bank, the Banque Royale, issued more currency to make loans to enable individuals to purchase that stock. The growing supply of shares eventually reduced the price of the stock. In March 1720, Law forced the Banque to exchange currency for shares at a fixed price (which he set). Since individuals expected the share price to fall because of the overissue, there was a rush to exchange the shares for currency. The result was a tremendous rise in the price level. The bubble burst when Law, realizing the consequences of his actions, ceased to convert shares into currency. The price of the Compagnie's shares collapsed to one-fifth of its peak value within a few months. Law fled France soon after.

Traditional explanations of such erratic ups and downs emphasize the "madness of crowds" or "speculative frenzy." More recent explanations, such as those of the 1987 stock market crash, emphasize that very large price changes can be justified by relatively small changes in fundamentals that govern stock price behaviour. For reasons that are beyond the scope of this text, however, economists have difficulty empirically distinguishing between a process that indicates explosive behaviour and one that has a more "rational" explanation.

## INTERNATIONAL LINKAGES IN STOCK PRICES

The globalization of financial markets has meant that investors have opportunities to purchase equities in many countries. Canadians, of course, have long been interested in US stocks and several Canadian companies have their stocks traded on both the Canadian and US stock exchanges. Indeed, anyone doing research comparing US and Canadian stock prices has to be careful to make corrections for the **inter-listing** of stocks in US and Canadian exchanges. However, unlike bond markets, where cross-border trading developed quickly as exchange controls and other regulations affecting international capital flows were gradually removed, the same has not occurred in the market for stocks. Figure 12.4 shows industrial stock price indexes for the US, the UK, Japan, Germany, and Canada. Since the indexes are based on the 1990 base year they are comparable. Notice, in particular, that stock price changes after 1990 are vastly different between the US and Canada,

## ECONOMICS FOCUS 12.3 The Equity Premium Puzzle

Stocks and bonds compete with each other in thousands of portfolios. Yet, if we look a the annual return of common stocks versus the annual return of, say, long-term bonds, stocks usually seem like the best bet in terms of return. The table below illustrates this point using some US data.

| Year | Dow Jones Industrial Average Annual return | Annual Yield on 10-year US Treasury bonds |
|---|---|---|
| 1992 | 4.2 | 7.01 |
| 1993 | 13.7 | 5.87 |
| 1994 | 2.1 | 7.09 |
| 1995 | 24.9 | 5.93 |
| Average | 11.25 | 6.48 |

**Sources:**

*Bank of Canada Review* and *Federal Reserve Bulletin*. For stocks the return is calculated on a December to December basis, except for 1995 which is for the December 1994 to October 1995 period. For the Treasury bond the data are annual averages, except for the 1995 figure which is for November 1995.

While the return on the DJIA has clearly been more volative, the mean return is almost double that of the long-term bond. Apparently, the above table summarizes a feature of the data present for over 200 years and has been termed the **equity premium puzzle.** But then, is it not the case that the higher return is at the expense of more risk? The answer is a partial yes but many studies have argued that even if we adjust for the higher risk of holding equities, stock returns appear to be "excessively" high. Can the puzzle be explained in any way? There are no definitive answers yet, but some argue that stocks command a premium because they are held by individuals who have very short-term horizons and demand extra compensation for holding stocks. An interesting explanation comes from the fact that, with the exception of the New York and London stock exchanges, all other stock exchanges are recent phenomena. Precisely because these are the only two markets to have survived for so long they are not typical of all stock markets or of all stock market returns.

All of this suggests that one must be careful in concluding that stocks necessarily outperform other financial instruments.

**Sources:**

S. Brown, W. Goetzmann and S. Ross "Survival," *Journal of Finance* (July 1995).

J. Siegel, *Stocks for the Long-Run* (Burr Ridge, Ill: Irwin Professional Press, 1994).

R. Thaler "Myopic Loss and the Equity Premium Puzzle," *Quarterly Journal of Economics* 110 (February 1995): 73–92.

on the one hand, and Japan, for example, on the other. Clearly, investors looking for positive stock returns would have been well advised to stay away from Japanese (and German) stock markets since 1990. Yet, a look at portfolios of domestic investors apparently suggests that they hold too few foreign stocks relative to what would be optimal in terms of the gains from diversification explained in the previous chapter.[19] Unfortunately, research has not yet pinpointed exactly why the internationalization of stock markets has not proceeded with the speed that might have been expected. One explanation might be that the transactions

19 For example, current rules governing registered retirement savings plans (RRSPs, see Chapter 19) limit the foreign asset content to 20% of the total investment.

**FIGURE 12.4** International Stock Price Behaviour

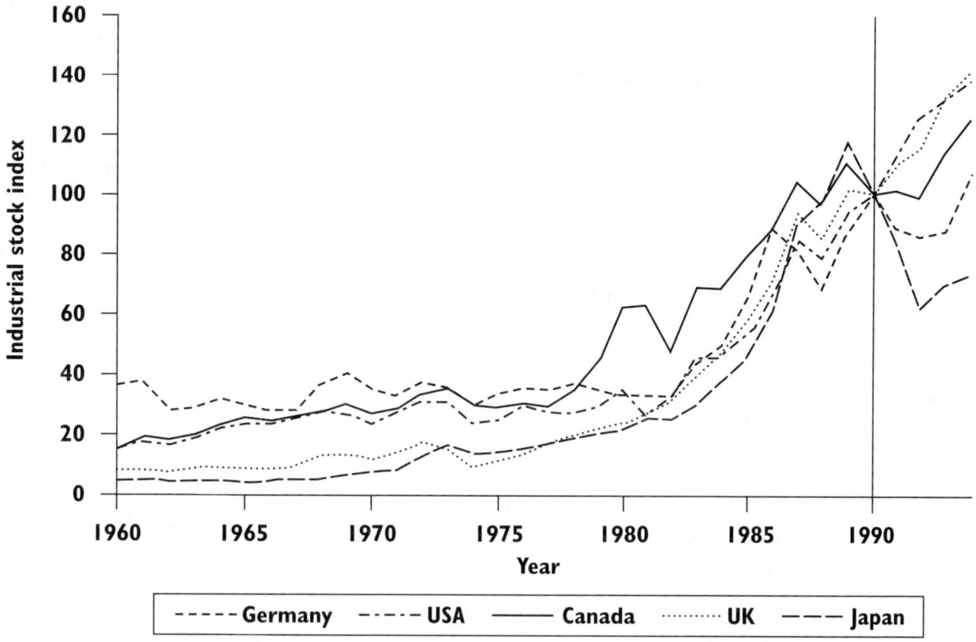


Source: International Financial Statistics CD-Rom (Washington, D.C.: International Monetary Fund).

costs of monitoring foreign stocks are high because it is relatively more difficult to keep track of what foreign companies do than what domestic companies do. Of course, as computer technology facilitates such monitoring (for example, via the World Wide Web) these costs should fall. Another possibility is that a lingering from past capital controls still persists.[20] Still another reason is the complex mix of tax treatments which might deter investors from taking advantage of apparently higher returns in other countries. It will be interesting to see, with time, how the freedom of movement of capital combined with the falling cost of providing and disseminating information will impact the attempt at diversification by investors around the globe.

# SUMMARY

- Stock markets are where stock prices are determined. Some of these markets are organized in exchanges; others operate electronically.

20 Recent papers on the subject include the one by Karen Lewis, "Consumption, Stock Returns and the Gains from International Risk Sharing," NBER working paper no. 5410 (January 1996) and "What Can Explain the Apparent Lack of International Risk Sharing? *Journal of Political Economy* (April 1996).

- There are two main views about stock price determination. The efficient markets hypothesis argues that stock prices behave like a random walk—that changes in them display no predictable pattern over time. The alternative fundamentalist view is that future company fortunes, as represented by dividends, should explain the current price of a stock.
- The two approaches to stock price determination may appear to contradict each other but they can be reconciled under certain conditions.
- Despite the popularity of the random walk hypothesis, it cannot explain a number of anomalies in the behaviour of stock prices. To name but two, stock prices are too volatile, and they seem to reach incredible highs and lows, called bubbles.

## IMPORTANT TERMS

Canadian Dealing Network (p. 250)
efficient markets hypothesis (p. 252)
- weak form (p. 252)
- semistrong form (p. 254)
- strong form (p. 256)

equity premium puzzle (p. 266)
fundamentalist approach (p. 257)
inter-listing of stocks (p. 265)
over-the-counter (OTC) trading (p. 249)
random walk (p. 253)
stock exchanges (p. 250)
stock price index (p. 250)

## EXERCISES

1. You feel so enlightened by your courses in economics that upon becoming a very wealthy business person, you decide to endow your alma mater with a chair (in economics, of course). If the university's financial officer tells you that your money can earn 10% a year, how large must your donation be in order to generate $150,000 a year forever? To avoid problems with inflation, you wish your endowment to rise by 6% a year. (Hint: Look at the equation determining stock prices according to the fundamentalist approach.)
2. Suppose a particular stock is expected to generate dividends of $5 a share annually. What is the price of the stock if
   (a) Dividends are constant and the opportunity cost is 10%?
   (b) Dividends are expected to grow by 3% annually and the opportunity cost is 8%?
   (c) The dividend growth rate is 3% and opportunity cost is 12%?
3. An investment advisor says: "Since we know stocks are going to fall as well

as rise, we might as well get a little traffic out of them. A man who buys stock at 10 and sells it at 20 makes 100 percent. But a man who buys stock at 10, sells it at 14½, buys it back at 12 and sells it at 18, buys it back at 15, and sells it at 20 makes 188 percent." How would you evaluate this advice?

4. Comment on the statements below, indicating whether they invalidate the weak form of the efficient markets hypothesis.
   (a) Money placed in a mutual fund that invests in stocks only consistently earns a positive return.
   (b) When the stock market goes down in January, it usually goes down during the following 11 months.
   (c) Whenever a New Democratic Party government is elected, the stock market goes down.

5. Can you detect any relationship between the average return in the portfolios listed below (ranked by size) and their P/E ratios? If so, does this result represent an anomaly in stock price behaviour?

| Portfolio Size | Mean Return | Mean P/E |
|---|---|---|
| Smallest | 1.79 | 0.84 |
| 2nd | 1.53 | 0.90 |
| 5th | 1.25 | 0.85 |
| 9th | 1.03 | 0.63 |
| Largest | 0.99 | 0.63 |

6. Does the random walk hypothesis of stock prices imply that an investor could just as well pick stocks by throwing darts against a dartboard? Explain.

7. The *Wall Street Journal* regularly holds a stock-picking contest. In its 8 November 1991 issue, it summarized the following results:

| | % change in stock prices: 2 May – 31 Oct. 1991 |
|---|---|
| Experts as a group | + 12.4% |
| Dartboard portfolio (4 stocks) | + 38.0% |
| Dow Jones Industrial Average | +4.4% |

   Are the above results evidence in favour of the random walk hypothesis? Comment.

8. In 1993, the Royal Bank of Canada issued preferred shares in Canadian dollars yielding 7.1% in dividends per year. The same bank also issued preferred shares in US dollars, yielding 6.3%. Ignoring transactions costs and taxes, why would an investor buy the lower-yielding US-dollar-denominated shares?

9. If the stock market were truly efficient, the probability that the darts portfolio would beat the experts would be 0.5. Is this true? Explain.

10. Because of the prominence given the *Wall Street Journal* stock-picking contest, one might expect the prices of selected stocks to rise on the day of publication. Is this possible? Explain.

11. The following table shows the return on the S & P 500 in January as well as over a 12-month period. Is there a January effect?

| Year | January Return | 12-Month Return |
|---|---|---|
| 1939 | −6.9 | −5.4 |
| 1941 | −4.8 | −17.9 |
| 1943 | 7.2 | 19.4 |
| 1945 | 1.4 | 30.7 |
| 1947 | 2.4 | 0 |
| 1949 | 0.1 | 10.3 |
| 1951 | 6.1 | 16.5 |
| 1953 | 0.7 | −6.9 |
| 1955 | 1.8 | 26.4 |
| 1957 | −4.2 | −14.3 |
| 1959 | 0.4 | 8.5 |
| 1961 | 6.3 | 23.1 |
| 1963 | 4.9 | 18.9 |
| 1965 | 3.3 | 9.1 |
| 1967 | 7.8 | 20.1 |
| 1969 | −0.8 | −11.4 |
| 1971 | 4.0 | 10.8 |
| 1973 | −1.7 | −17.4 |
| 1975 | 12.3 | 31.5 |
| 1977 | −5.1 | −11.5 |
| 1979 | 4.0 | 12.3 |
| 1981 | −4.6 | −9.7 |
| 1983 | 3.3 | 17.3 |
| 1985 | 7.4 | 26.3 |
| 1987 | 13.2 | 2.0 |
| 1989 | 7.1 | 27.3 |
| 1991 | 4.2 | 26.3 |

Source: *Louis Rukeyser's Wall Street*, February 1993.

12. Would anyone purchase a stock which gave out no dividends? Explain.

13. Suppose a firm has earnings of $10 million which it pays out in the form of dividends to its 5 million stockholders. Assuming an interest rate of 5%
(a) what is the price of the stock?
(b) what is the dividend yield?

(c) if earnings grow 1% per year, what is the price of the stock?

# APPENDIX 12.A

## MATHEMATICAL EXPECTATIONS: SOME BASICS

The concept of mathematical expectations is a useful one for the arguments of this chapter and for material presented later in the book. Here is a succinct and generally non-technical introduction.[1]

Suppose that the outcomes of some economic variables over time, such as stock prices, are labelled

$$x_1, x_2, x_3, \ldots, x_n$$

These numerical variables together are termed a *random variable*. Suppose also that $f(x_j)$ denotes the probability that the random variable $X$ will take on some value, such as $x_1$, $x_2$, and so on. The probabilities must sum to 1. In other words,

$$\sum_{j=1}^{n} f(x_j) = 1$$

where $\Sigma$ is the summation symbol for $f(\cdot)$ from 1 to $n$. If we compute the average or mean value of $X$ weighted by the probabilities, we obtain

$$\mu = \Sigma x f(x)$$

where $\mu$ denotes the mean of $X$. Thus, $\mu$ is a measure of what is called the *central tendency* of the probability distribution.

In general, however, we need not know what the probabilities are. Suppose that $\theta(X)$ represents another random variable of possible outcomes of $x$. The central tendency measure can thus be written more generally as

$$E[\theta(x)] = \Sigma\theta(X)f(x)$$

where $E[\cdot]$ is called the *mathematical expectation* of the random variable $\theta(X)$. This expression is identical to $\mu$ when $\theta(X) = X$ and so is more general than the expression for $\mu$.

A few observations about mathematical expectations are useful.

1 Any statistics textbook can provide further details, though they are unnecessary for any of the material covered in this book.

1. If we denote $k$ a constant, then

$$E[k\theta(X)] = kE[\theta(X)]$$

2. If there are two random variables, $\theta_1\ (X)$ and $\theta_2(X)$, then

$$E[\theta_1(X) + \theta_2(X)] = E[\theta_1(X)] + E[\theta_2(X)]$$

If $\theta_1(X)$ is completely unrelated to $\theta_2(X)$—that is, the two are independent of each other—then

$$E[\theta_1(X) \cdot \theta_2(X)] = E[\theta_1(X)] \cdot E[\theta_2(X)]$$

3. One way of measuring the spread is to ascertain departures from the mean of $\theta(X)$. If $\theta(X) = X$, the spread for any $x$, say $x_j$, belonging to $X$ is

$$x_j - \mu$$

A standard measure of the spread of a probability distribution is the *variance*, which is calculated as

$$\sigma^2 = \Sigma(x - \mu)^2 f(x)$$

We have seen that exchange rates and stock prices behave like a random walk, and we will see that many other assets behave in a similar fashion. Unfortunately, the variance of a random walk process is unbounded, which means that it is potentially infinitely large. Yet the volatility of asset prices, although large at times, is certainly not infinitely large. This is something of a problem since economists rely heavily on the random walk hypothesis. Unfortunately, economists have difficulty distinguishing between the random walk process considered in this chapter and a process that is nearly but not exactly a random walk.[2]

---

2 These issues and related questions are beyond the scope of this text. Interested readers may wish to consult J.Y. Campbell and P. Perron, "Pitfalls and Opportunities: What Macroeconomics Should Know About Unit Roots," in *NBER Macroeconomics Annual*, 1991 (Cambridge, Mass.: The MIT Press, 1991) or any intermediate econometrics textbook.

# REFERENCES


Campbell, J.Y., and P. Perron. "Pitfalls and Opportunities: What Macroeconomists Should Know About Unit Roots." In *NBER Macroeconomics Annual, 1991.* Cambridge, Mass.: The MIT Press, 1991.

Chernow, R. *The House of Morgan.* New York; Simon and Schuster, 1990.

Critchley, B. "A Look Inside the TSE." *The Financial Post.* 4 November 1992. p. 5.

Fama, E.F. "Stock Returns, Expected Returns, and Real Activity." *Journal of Finance* 45 (September 1990): 1089–1108.

———. "Efficient Capital Markets: A Review of Theory and Empirical Work," *Journal of Finance* 25 (May 1970): 383–416.

Fama, E.F., and K.R. French, "Permanent and Temporary Components of Stock Prices." *Journal of Political Economy* 96 (1988): 246–73.

Garber, P.M. "Famous First Bubbles." *Journal of Economic Perspectives* 4 (Spring 1990): 35–54.

———. "Tulipmania." *Journal of Political Economy* 97 (June 1989): 535–60.

Granger, C.W.J. "Forecasting Stock Market Prices—Lessons for Forecasters." *International Journal of Forecasting* 8 (1992): 3–13.

Huang, R.D., and H.R. Stoll. "Major World Equity Markets: Current Structure and Prospects for Change." Solomon Center Monograph Series in Finance and Economics, 1991–93.

Kasa, K. "Common Stochastic Trends in International Stock Markets." *Journal of Monetary Economics* 29 (February 1992): 95–124.

Kelley, D. "How the CDN Works." *The Financial Post.* 23 January 1993, p. 13.

Kim, M.J., C.R. Nelson, and R. Startz. "Mean Revision in Stock Prices? A Reappraisal of the Evidence." *Review of Financial Studies* 4 (1991): 515–28.

Kindleberger, C.P. *Manias, Panics, and Crashes,* rev. ed. New York: Basic Books, 1989.

Lakonishok, J., A. Schleifer, and R.W. Vishny. "Do Institutional Investors Destabilize Stock Prices? Evidence on Herding and Feedback Trading." NBER working paper no. 3846 (September 1991).

Lehmann, B.N. "Asset Pricing and Intrinsic Values: A Review Essay." *Journal of Monetary Economics* 28 (1991): 485–500.

LeRoy, S.F. "Efficient Capital Markets and Martingales." *Journal of Economic Literature* 27 (December 1989): 1583–1621.

Poterba, J.M., and L.H. Summers. "Mean Reversion in Stock Prices: Evidence and Implications." *Journal of Financial Economics* 22 (1988): 27–59.

Scott, L.D. "Financial Market Volatility." *IMF Staff Papers* 38 (September 1991): 582–625.

Schiller, R.J. *Market Volatility.* Cambridge, Mass.: The MIT Press, 1989. Chapter 4.

Stewart, J.B. *Den of Thieves.* New York: Simon and Schuster, 1991.

Statistics Canada, CANSIM database.

CHAPTER 13

# Asset Demand and Supply under Uncertainty

In analysing the consumption, saving, and borrowing choices faced by the private sector, we omitted incorporating an important feature, namely the role risk plays in these decisions. Can one measure risk as it pertains to the demand for assets or the supply of debt?

Since the answer seems to be yes, the individual's attitude toward risk is an important element in the portfolio balance decision.

Accordingly, we begin this chapter by defining risk, listing its sources, and exploring the implications of different attitudes toward it. Next, we investigate the portfolio balance decision by examining the choices facing an individual who must allocate his or her wealth among risky assets. In the following chapter, we consider how some people attempt to mitigate risk through what is known as *hedging* behaviour.

## RISK AND ATTITUDES TOWARD IT: DEFINITIONS

Generally, **risk** is the possibility of potential loss against which insurance is provided. In this chapter, however, we are more specific and identify risk as the kind of potential loss on investments against which borrowers provide a higher return than they would otherwise.

When risk is present, the number of possible future events exceeds the number of actual events that will occur, and some measure of probability can be attached to those possibilities.

Notice that risk does not mean uncertainty. Uncertainty reflects an ignorance about the future. Risk, on the other hand, is a fact of life. People can make informed decisions even in the face of risk because they can assess and rank the chances of experiencing a particular eventuality in the future.

## SOURCES OF RISK

Risk originates from a variety of sources and is often named according to them.

1. Default. **Default risk** represents the likelihood that a borrower will evade his or her financial obligations with respect to interest, principal, or both. Various services exist to evaluate the degree of default risk. For example, **bond rating** schemes, such as those displayed in Table 13.1, attempt to rank the chances that the issuer of a particular bond will or will not default.

2. Liquidity. Lenders face the possibility that they will require funds earlier than planned. If there is a large market in which the investor can sell a particular financial asset quickly, its liquidity is enhanced. By contrast, if the instrument is not easily convertible, the prospect of being short of funds at some time in the future is increased and so is **liquidity risk**. (This notion is sometimes referred to as the "marketability" of an asset.)

3. Market Risk. Unless an asset is held until maturity, its price may fluctuate over time.[1] Since the timing of the sale of an asset is not always known in advance, there is an inherent **market risk**: the possibility of a future change in price with a consequent loss of return.

4. Systematic Risk. Some risk is system-wide—that is, it is caused by a factor or factors common to all or most assets in the financial system. Price fluctuations can result from external factors arising out of political, legal, or aggregate domestic or international changes in economic conditions, each one of which can influence **systematic risk**. Prices and asset returns vary systematically with such events.

5. Foreign Exchange Risk. Investors dealing in assets denominated in a foreign currency face an additional market risk—that the exchange rate between that currency and the domestic currency may fluctuate in an unanticipated direction or to an unanticipated degree. Such risk is called **foreign exchange risk**.

6. Income Risk. Since borrowing is, to some extent, a function of the anticipated future earning power of an individual or a firm, any change in the stream of income or profits will influence the ability to pay the interest and principal on a loan. The possibility of unexpected fluctuations in income, therefore, produces **income risk**.

7. Inflation Risk. Lenders and borrowers have an incentive to accurately predict inflation, especially in the case of a debt instrument whose nominal interest

1 Of course, the asset need not be a bond. The price of many fixed assets, such as housing, also fluctuate over time.

**Table 13.1** CANADIAN BOND RATING SCHEMES

| | Dominion Bond Rating | | Canadian Bond Rating |
|---|---|---|---|
| AAA | Highest quality | A++ | Highest quality |
| AA | Superior quality | A+ | Very good quality |
| A | Upper medium grade | A | Good quality |
| BBB | Medium grade | B++ | Medium grade |
| BB | Lower medium grade | B+ | Lower medium quality |
| B | Middle speculative | B | Poor quality |
| CCC | Highly speculative | C | Speculative quality |
| CC | In default | D | Default |
| NR | Not rated | RATING SUSPENDED (uncertainty about company's future) | |

The two Canadian bond rating services consider Government of Canada bonds to be of the highest quality (possess the least risk) simply because the federal government is always able either to print money to pay interest and principal or borrow from abroad, if necessary, to meet its financial obligations. Next in line are other levels of government, usually beginning with the provincial governments. Corporate bonds are ranked according to the issuer's size, profitability, expectations about future success, and so on.

Of course, any country's ability to borrow is hampered by expectations of its future growth. Accordingly, Moody's and Standard and Poor's, both of which also publish bond rating schemes, evaluate credit ratings across countries.

rate is fixed.[2] An underestimate of future inflation benefits the borrower and penalizes the lender, and an overestimate has the opposite effect. Consequently, investors face **inflation risk**.

8. Changes in the tax treatment of interest income, registered retirement savings plans and capital gains, influences the after-tax returns of investors (see Chapter 5 for a numerical example). This type of risk is called **tax risk**. As governments in the 1990s began to try to cope with the impact of mounting deficits, changes in tax rates and coverage occurred more frequently with important consequences for investors.

## THE MEASUREMENT AND CONSEQUENCE OF RISK

By definition, risk can be quantified. In order to do so, we borrow from statistical methods.

### Variations in an Asset's Return

Risk stems from variation in returns over time. These variations are influenced by any or a combination of default, liquidity, market, income, and inflation risk.

2 Even bonds or pensions indexed to inflation are subject to some inflation risk to the extent that inflation cannot usually be forecast precisely. Even the Canadian tax system is not fully indexed.

To keep the discussion simple, let us focus on only one set of future prospects or "states of the world"—namely the business cycle, whose swings can be assigned the subjective probabilities listed in Table 13.2. We assume that the world has three assets, whose rates of return vary with the business cycle, as shown in the table. The diagrams at the bottom of Table 13.2 display the presumed relationship between probabilities and returns for the three available assets; this relationship is known as the *probability distribution of returns.*

Finally, let us assume that individuals choose to hold no more than two assets simultaneously. In other words, they may hold any one of the following six portfolios:

1. Asset I only.
2. Assets I and II.
3. Assets I and III.
4. Asset II only.
5. Assets II and III.
6. Asset III only.

An obvious way of characterizing the riskiness of an asset is to evaluate its range of returns. For the assets in Table 13.2, for example, the returns for asset I range from 6% to 15%, and those for asset II from 5% to 11%; the returns on asset III are constant, so its range is zero. The difficulty with the concept of range is that it makes no allowance for the fact that one asset may yield a consistently higher return than another. Thus, in the example in Table 13.2, the return on asset III is clearly inferior to the return on either asset I or II. Yet because asset III displays no variation, it is *risk-free* or *riskless* in relation to the state of the market. By contrast, asset II generally displays lower returns than asset I, and the distribution of its returns is narrower.

A common way of measuring risk, borrowed from the science of statistics, is to evaluate two statistics (or *moments*, as they are called) which can be used to characterize a probability distribution: (1) the average of mean return, and (2) a measure of the spread of variability of returns called the variance of returns. Table 13.3 provides the general formula for each of these two measures, as well as sample calculations for asset I. The *mean return* is simply the return weighted by the probability of occurrence of each state of the world. Because the probabilities measure potential variation in future returns, mean return is often called the **expected return.**[3] The **variance of returns** is simply the weighted average of

3 Technically speaking, the expected return is a mathematical expectation. See the appendix to Chapter 12.

**Table 13.2** STATES OF THE WORLD AND RETURNS

| State of the World | Probability of Occurrence | Asset Returns | | |
|---|---|---|---|---|
| | | I | II | III |
| Severe Recession | 0.10 | 6 | 11 | 4 |
| Mild Recession | 0.20 | 9 | 9 | 4 |
| Normal | 0.40 | 12 | 8 | 4 |
| Mild Expansion | 0.20 | 14 | 7 | 4 |
| Strong Expansion | 0.10 | 15 | 5 | 4 |

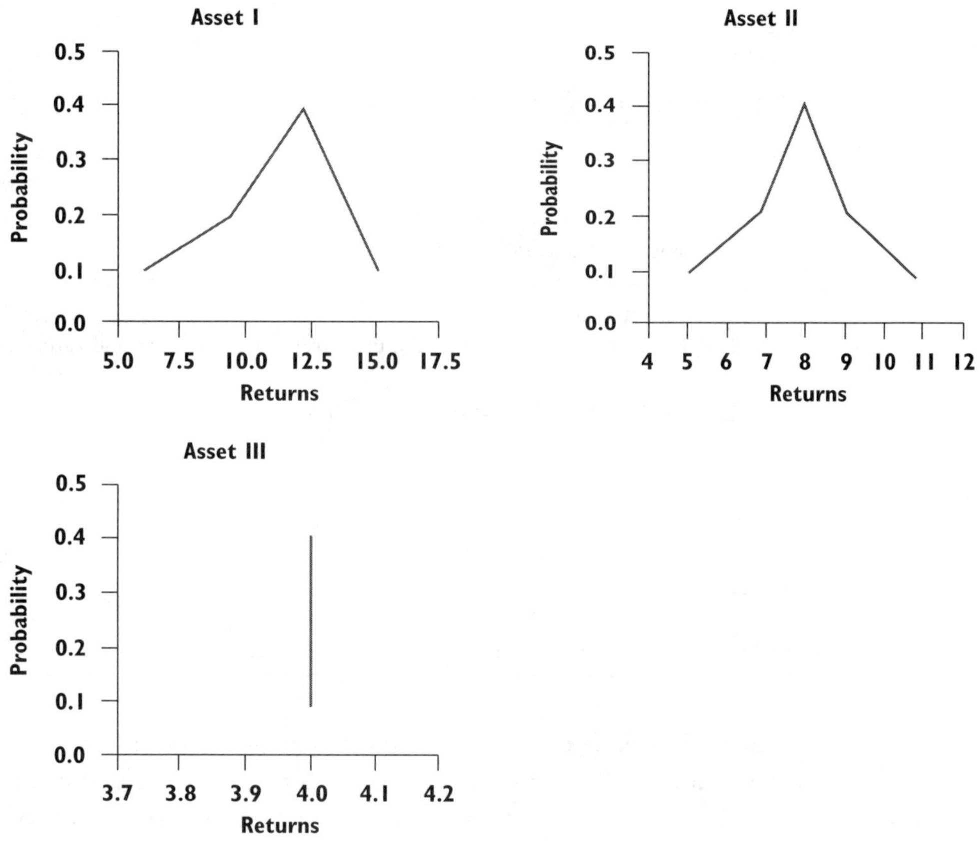


We assume that a business cycle has five stages, ranging from a severe recession to a strong expansion and that a subjective probability can be associated with each. For example, the normal state of the world (the economy is operating at, say, its historical growth rate), is assumed to occur 40% of the time. The diagrams plot how the returns for each of the assets vary according to the probability of the economy being in a particular stage of the business cycle. The information in such probability distributions helps us define risk.

**TABLE 13.3**

EXPECTED RETURNS AND VARIANCES

| Asset | Expected Return | Variance |
|---|---|---|
| I | 11.5 | 6.85 |
| II | 8.0 | 2.20 |
| III | 4.0 | 0.00 |

Formulae

- Expected Return $= R_i^e = \sum_s pr_s R_i^s$
- Variance of Returns $= V_i = \sum_s pr_s (R_i^s - R_i^e)^2$

where $R_i^e$ = Expected return, asset $i$
$s$ = state of the world
$pr_s$ = probability of occurrence for each state
$R_i^s$ = return in state $s$, asset $i$
$pr_s R_i^s$ = product, for each state, of the probability of occurrence and return for asset $i$
$V_i$ = variance of returns, asset $i$
$\sum_s$ = summation symbol over states of theworld

Example of Calculation for Asset I

$R_I^e = 0.1(6) + 0.2(9) + 0.4(12) + 0.2(14) + 0.1(15) = 11.5\%$
$V_I = 0.1(6 - 11.5)^2 + 0.2(9 - 11.5)^2 + 0.4(12 - 11.5)^2 + 0.2(14 - 11.5)^2 + 0.1(15 - 11.5)^2$
$= 6.85$

Note: Data on probability and asset returns are from Table 13.2.

the squared deviations[4] from the expected returns. (Some prefer to express risk as the **standard deviation of returns**, which is the square root of the variance of returns. Using the standard deviation enables interpretation of risk in percentage terms, whereas variance is an absolute measure of risk.)[5]

4 The squaring is performed for two reasons. One is because absolute deviations from expected return sum to zero (verify this on your own). Also, the larger the deviations from the mean, the faster variance rises. Thus, wider probability distributions signal riskier assets than narrower ones which is consistent with our intuition about risk.

5 Variance is not the only possible measure of risk but simply one that is in common usage. You could, for example, measure risk in terms of market size (i.e., its liquidity), which, as noted earlier, is often an important consideration for investors. Another measure of risk could be the absolute value of deviations in mean returns.

The results in Table 13.3 confirm what we suspected all along: asset I has the highest average return and it is a riskier proposition than asset II, which has a smaller expected return. Asset III has by far the lowest expected return, but it is also riskless since its variance is zero.[6]

## Correlation of Returns

Once we start to examine the risk inherent in a portfolio of assets, we must consider the possibility of an additional complication: fluctuations in the returns of one asset may be influenced by fluctuations in the returns of alternative assets. There is a degree to which assets fluctuate *systematically* with each other; that is, some components of the returns of several assets may fluctuate with each other. Concomitantly, the return of an asset has components specific to it (or to the particular firm, industry, or market) that vary over time or states of the world *unsystematically.*

Once again statistics are available to quantify the extent to which fluctuation in asset returns are common. The covariance and the correlation express the degree of linear association between asset returns across states of the world. The **covariance** measure provides an absolute value for the degree to which asset returns move together or in opposite directions; the **correlation statistic** provides a relative measure of association. Table 13.4 provides the relevant formulae, as well as calculations for two of the assets we have been considering.

Table 13.4 also shows a plot of returns across states of the world with the appropriate adjacent points connected to each other. What is clear is that returns of assets I and II move in opposite directions. Therefore, the returns for these two assets are negatively correlated (inversely related), which explains the negative values for the covariance and correlation between assets I and II found at the bottom of Table 13.4. The calculations for the other two pairs of assets—I and III, and II and III—are not made because the returns of asset III display no variance whatsoever. Hence, the covariance between these pairs is zero.

Correlation has no particular advantage over covariance except that the former provides a measure that is easily interpretable. In the case of assets I and II for example, the correlation is—0.95, which signifies that a 1% rise in the return on asset I implies a .95% fall in the return on asset II. In other words, the correlation statistic is a quickly interpreted measure of the degree to which two returns vary systematically with each other.

---

6 Strictly speaking, no asset is riskless. Money, for example, is riskless in the sense that it can always be used to purchase commodities. (In some countries, however, high inflation produces a risk of a currency's becoming essentially worthless!) In addition, there is the risk that governments, normally assumed to be default-risk-free, will renege on their debts.

**TABLE 13.4**

COVARIANCES AND CORRELATIONS

| Pairs of Assets | Covariance | Correlation |
|---|---|---|
| I and II | −3.70 | −0.95 |
| I and III | 0.00 | 0.00 |
| II and III | 0.00 | 0.00 |

Formulae

- Covariance: $COV_{ij} = \Sigma pr_s(R_i^s - R_i^e)(R_j^s - R_j^e)$
- Correlation: $CORR_{ij} = \dfrac{COV_{ij}}{\sqrt{v_i}\sqrt{v_j}}$

where $i$ and $j$ are two different assets and $\sqrt{v_i}$ and $\sqrt{v_j}$ are the square root of their respective variances, that is, the standard deviations of asset returns.

Example of Calculation for Asset I and II

$$COV_{I,II} = 0.1(6 - 11.5)(11 - 8) + 0.2(9 - 11.5)(9 - 8) + 0.4(12 - 11.5)(8 - 8)$$
$$+ 0.2(14 - 11.5)(7 - 8) + 0.1(15 - 11.5)(5 - 8) = -3.70$$

$$CORR_{I,II} = \frac{-3.70}{(2.62)(1.48)} = -0.95$$

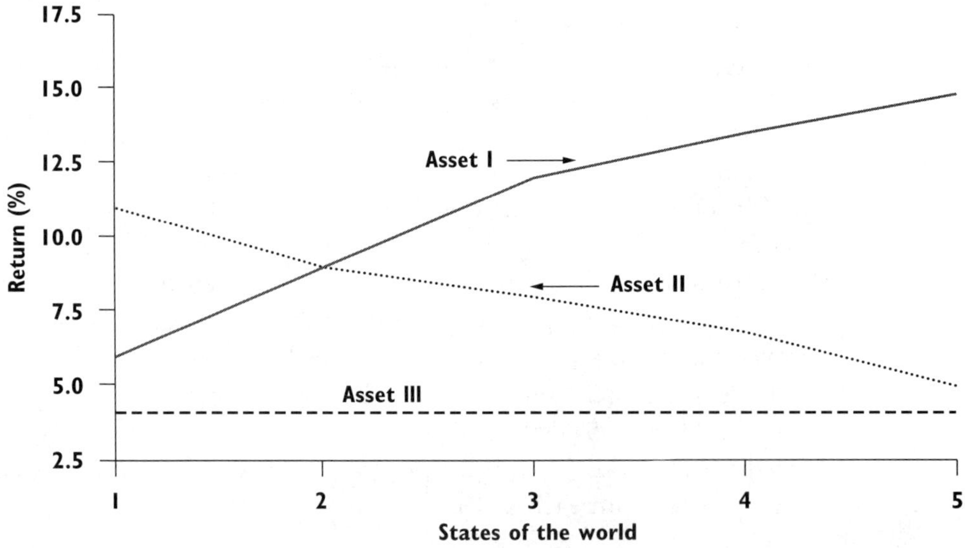


The diagram shows the variation in asset returns as a function of the state of the world. The returns on assets I and II are inversely related and so are negatively correlated (see the chart above). Asset III returns are constant and unrelated to the returns of either asset I or asset II; the result is a zero correlation between the returns of assets I and II and assets II and III.

## Risk in a Portfolio

We are now in a position to determine the overall risk of a portfolio of assets. For our example, we'll continue with the three assets we've been using, as evaluated in Tables 13.3 and 13.4, and maintain the simplifying assumption that a portfolio can contain one or two but not all three of them.

Table 13.5 lists 15 of the many possible portfolios and evaluates for each the variance, which is influenced by the covariance or correlation of any pairs of assets in it,[7] and the portfolio return, which is influenced by the proportion invested in each asset. The investor selecting a portfolio faces tradeoffs, of course. The table shows that investing a greater proportion of wealth in asset III—a riskless asset—reduces portfolio risk, but at the expense of a lower return. Similarly, for a portfolio comprising assets I and II, investing a greater proportion in asset II reduces portfolio risk (since the riskiness of asset II is relatively lower than that of asset I), but the investor is clearly worse off investing only in asset II since the riskiness of such a portfolio is greater and the return is lower than if, say, half the available funds were invested in asset I and the other half in asset II.

Plotting the 15 combinations, as in Figure 13.1, gives the *feasible set*, which is like the opportunity set facing the consumer or firm. Some combinations are superior in the sense that they produce the highest return for any given level of portfolio risk. These combinations are defined by the line *ABCD*, which describes the **efficient frontier**.[8] As we will see, under fairly general conditions, individuals will always select a portfolio on the efficient frontier.

Note that the efficient frontier in Figure 13.1 results from portfolios made up of assets I and II. What drives this result is the negative correlation or covariance between the two assets. Thus, diversification reduces portfolio risk so long as the assets within the portfolio are negatively correlated (this is demonstrated more formally in Appendix 13.A).[9] Indeed, we have now arrived at a precise definition

---

7 The expression for portfolio variance is derived from the expression

$$V_p = [k_i\sum_s(R_i - R_i^e) + k_j\sum_s(R_j - R_j^e)]^2$$

which is the expression for the variance of a sum of two assets. If we expand that expression, we obtain

$$V_p = k_i^2\sum_s(R_i - R_i^e)^2 + k_j^2\sum_s(R_j - R_j^e)^2 + 2k_ik_j\sum_s(R_i - R^e_i)(R_j - R_j^e)$$

$$V_p = k_i^2V_i + k_j^2V_j + 2k_ik_jCOV_{ij}$$

which is the expression that appears at the bottom of Table 13.5.

8 The envelope of efficient portfolios—that is, the portfolios that lie on the efficient frontier—is also called the *Markowitz frontier*. Harry Markowitz did the pioneering work in establishing and evaluating such frontiers and shared the Nobel prize in economics in 1990 for his work.

9 It must be added, however, that this conclusion is the result of combining two assets to construct a portfolio.

**TABLE 13.5**

PORTFOLIO RETURN AND RISK

| | Proportion (%) Invested in: | | Expected Return (%) | Variance or Risk |
|---|---|---|---|---|
| | **Assets I and II** | | | |
| Portfolio No. | I | II | | |
| 1 | 100 | 0 | 11.50 | 6.85 |
| 2 | 75 | 25 | 10.63 | 2.60 |
| 3 | 50 | 50 | 9.75 | 0.41 |
| 4 | 25 | 75 | 8.88 | 0.28 |
| 5 | 0 | 100 | 8.00 | 2.20 |
| | **Assets I and III** | | | |
| | I | III | | |
| 6 | 100 | 0 | 11.50 | 6.85 |
| 7 | 75 | 25 | 9.63 | 3.84 |
| 8 | 50 | 50 | 7.75 | 1.71 |
| 9 | 25 | 75 | 5.88 | 0.41 |
| 10 | 0 | 100 | 4.00 | 0.00 |
| | **Assets II and III** | | | |
| | II | III | | |
| 11 | 100 | 0 | 8.00 | 2.20 |
| 12 | 75 | 25 | 7.00 | 1.23 |
| 13 | 50 | 50 | 6.00 | 0.55 |
| 14 | 25 | 75 | 5.00 | 0.13 |
| 15 | 0 | 100 | 4.00 | 0.00 |

Formulae

- Portfolio Expected Return: $R_p^e = k_i R_i^e + k_j R_j^e$

  Portfolio Variance or Risk: $V_p = k_i^2 V_i + k_j^2 V_j + 2k_i k_j COV_{ij}$

  where $R_p^e$ = portfolio expected return

  $V_p$ = variance or risk of portfolio

  $V_i, V_j$ = variance or risk of assets $i$, $j$, and $i \neq j$

  $COV_{ij}$ = covariance between assets $i$ and $j$

  $k_i, k_j$ = proportion invested in asset $i$ or $j$

Example of Calculation: Portfolio No. 2

$R_p^e = 0.75(11.5) + 0.25(8) = 10.63$

$V_p = (0.75)^2(6.85) + (0.25)^2(2.20) + 2(0.75)(0.25)(-3.70) = 2.60$

**FIGURE 13.1** Deriving the Efficient Frontier

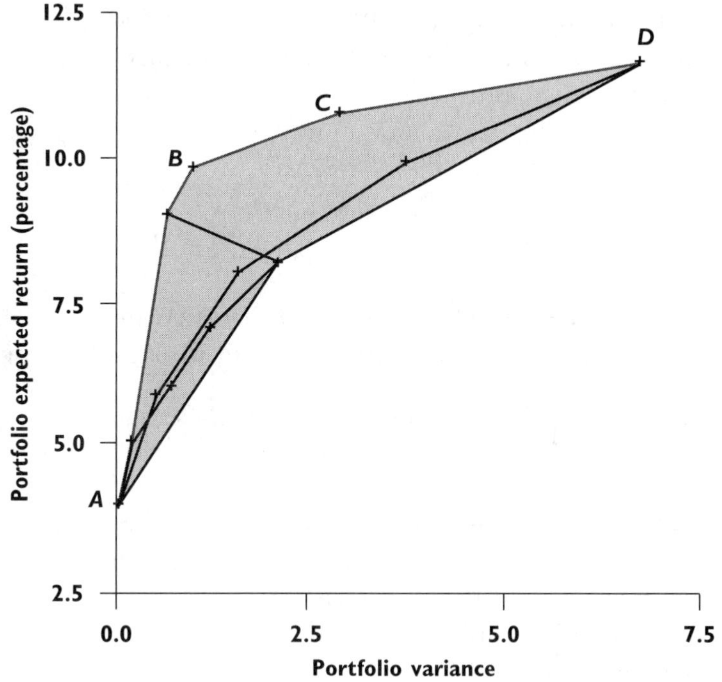


This figure continues the model set up in Table 13.5. The feasible set (the entire triangular area) includes all the combinations of risk and return available to the investor. *ABCD* is the efficient frontier; it marks the highest return for every level of risk. Point *A* is equivalent to portfolios 10 or 15 in Table 13.5; point *B* is portfolio 3; point *C* is portfolio 2; and point *D* is equivalent to portfolios 1 or 6.

Source: Table 13.5.

of the term **diversification**: this activity implies constructing a portfolio that reduces total portfolio risk.

Unfortunately, many people think diversification means increasing the number of assets in a portfolio. But that meaning applies only in a special and generally unrealistic case. Suppose, for simplicity, that the individual invests in equal proportions in a variety of assets:

$$k = 1/n$$

Indeed, as we will see in Figure 13.4, if we combine risky assets with riskless assets—in effect creating a portfolio of three assets—one can reduce portfolio risk even if some of the asset returns are positively correlated.

where $k$ represents the portfolio share, which is assumed to be same for each of the $n$ assets in the portfolio. Moreover, suppose that these assets are uncorrelated with each other so that $COV_{ij} = CORR_{ij} = 0$.[10] We have now imposed a sufficient number of conditions that the variance of such a portfolio is simply the sum of the individual asset risks, or

$$\begin{aligned} V_p &= k_1^2 V_1 + k_2^2 V_2 + \dots + k_n^2 V_n \\ &= \Sigma\, k_i^2 V_i \\ &= \Sigma\, (1/n)^2 V_i \\ &= n(1/n)^2 V_i = (1/n) V_i \end{aligned}$$

Thus, unless we believe that all of the assets in a portfolio are uncorrelated, an unlikely event,[11] diversification does not work the way some people think it does.

## PREFERENCES AND THE EQUILIBRIUM PORTFOLIO

How does an individual select from among the portfolios on his or her efficient frontier? Before we can answer the question, we need to develop an understanding of preferences in the face of risk.

Attitudes toward risk are generally explained as ranging among three alternatives:

1. Risk Aversion. The **risk-averse** individual is one who is willing to sacrifice either return or wealth to reduce risk. Such an individual is, for example, willing to accept a lower expected return if the probability distribution of returns is narrowed as a result. The extent of the sacrifice the individual is willing to make depends upon the degree of risk aversion. One extreme example would be preferring a portfolio consisting only of asset III; although it yields the lowest return, it is also risk-free.

2. Risk Neutrality. An intermediate case is **risk neutrality**. As the term implies, an individual with this attitude is neutral with respect to the riskiness of a portfolio and instead focuses on maximizing return. Such an individual will select the portfolio with the highest return irrespective of portfolio risk.

3. Risk-seeking. A final possibility is **risk-seeking**. The risk-seeker is an individual who prefers risk over return. Although we think we encounter few such individuals, many people seem to have at least an element of risk-loving—consider, for example, the purchase of lottery tickets.

10 Lack of correlation is imposed here primarily to simplify the calculations. The assumption is relaxed in Appendix 13.A.

11 To see why this case is unlikely, see Figure 6.1, which plots yields on assets that individuals are likely to hold. The returns have a high positive correlation.

Despite the gamblers we all know, most people tend to be cautious about wealth-building portfolios, both in the types of assets included and in the riskiness of the individual assets. Consequently, in what follows, we restrict ourselves to the risk-aversion case only.

## CHOOSING AMONG RISKY ASSETS

Figure 13.2 illustrates the essentials of optimal portfolio choice under risk aversion. The arguments rely on the kind of indifference curve analysis we already used to describe the optimal consumption stream for an individual in a two-period setting. Here we amend the utility introduced in Chapter 9 so that

$$U = U(c, V_p) \tag{13.1}$$

where $U$ is total utility, $c$ is consumption, and $V_p$ is portfolio risk.

Since combinations of expected portfolio return and portfolio risk determine total utility, we can rewrite equation (13.1) as

$$U = U(R_p^e, V_p) \tag{13.2}$$

The individual is now assumed to maximize (13.2) subject to the constraint imposed by the efficient frontier. Note that the marginal utility of a higher portfolio return is positive, but the marginal utility of an increase in portfolio variance is negative since the risk-averse individual wishes, by definition, to reduce portfolio risk.

The point is made graphically in Figure 13.2, where the vertical axis plots expected portfolio return and the horizontal axis plots portfolio risk. Indifference curves for the risk-averse individual recognize the explicit tradeoff between expected return and risk. Combinations of expected return and risk that leave total utility unchanged represent an individual's indifference curve; it is upward sloping, as shown in Figure 13.2(A). For any given level of risk, a risk-averse individual will choose a portfolio yielding the highest expected return, so the indifference curves yield higher total utility as they shift leftward. Thus, $I_1$ produces the highest total utility and $I_3$ the lowest.

Figure 13.2(B) displays the optimal portfolio choice in the present framework. As in the optimal consumption model considered in Chapter 9, the point of tangency between the individual's indifference curve and the efficient frontier produces the optimal portfolio. Given detailed knowledge of the various return–risk combinations that produced the results of Table 13.5, we could evaluate the proportions of assets I and II that would be selected by the individual depicted.

It is useful to consider how risk aversion will affect the location of the optimal point, $O$. As shown by the arrows in Figure 13.2(B), individuals whose aversion to risk is less than that of the individual who selected the portfolio $(R_p^*, V_p^*)$ will

## ECONOMICS FOCUS 13.1 Utility and Attitudes Toward Risk

One way to understand the concept of risk aversion is to first understand that individuals prefer certainty over uncertainty. They are willing, therefore, to forgo some part of their wealth to increase certainty. The amount an individual will forgo depends on the degree of the individual's aversion to risk.

In a classic work on game theory, John von Neumann and Oskar Morgenstern worked out what has become known as the Von Neumann–Morgenstern utility theory. It states that one can construct a utility function such that a level of utility is associated with each level of wealth. Total utility is assumed to rise with wealth but at a diminishing rate, which is indicated by the fact that the utility of wealth curve becomes flatter as wealth rises. (This is the result of the standard assumption of *diminishing marginal utility* in microeconomic analysis.) Consider then the situation depicted in the figure below where utility, a subjective measure of satisfaction or enjoyment, is measured on the vertical axis while different levels of wealth are measured on the horizontal axis.

The straight line *AB* describes the expected utility of wealth for levels of wealth. If there were no uncertainty, one could simply evaluate the total utility associated with each level of wealth. Unfortunately, uncertainty is a fact of life. Wealth may be either \$900 or \$100 depending on whether events, such as illness or a fire, occur. The *expected* level of utility depends on the probabilities of occurrence of the events that lead to a wealth level of \$100 or of \$900. In general, expected utility is evaluated according to

$$U^e = \Sigma pr_i U_j$$

where $U^e$ represents expected utility, *pr* is the probability associated with event *i*, and $U_j$ is the utility associated with wealth level *j*.

The expected utility function is a linear combination or weighted average of different levels of wealth where the weights are the respective probabilities of various events. Thus, in the present example, there are probabilities such that

$$pr(W = \$100)\$100 + [1 - pr(W = \$100)]\$900 = U^e(500)$$

where $pr\ (W = \$100)$ is the probability that $W = \$100$. Since probabilities must sum to *l*, the probability of $W = \$900$ is simply $1 - pr(W = \$100)$.

Notice in the model that the utility associated with \$500 with certainty, *U*(500), is greater than the expected utility of \$500, $U^e(500)$. The latter is a combination of the utility of \$100 and \$900 weighted by the probabilities associated with each level of wealth. The

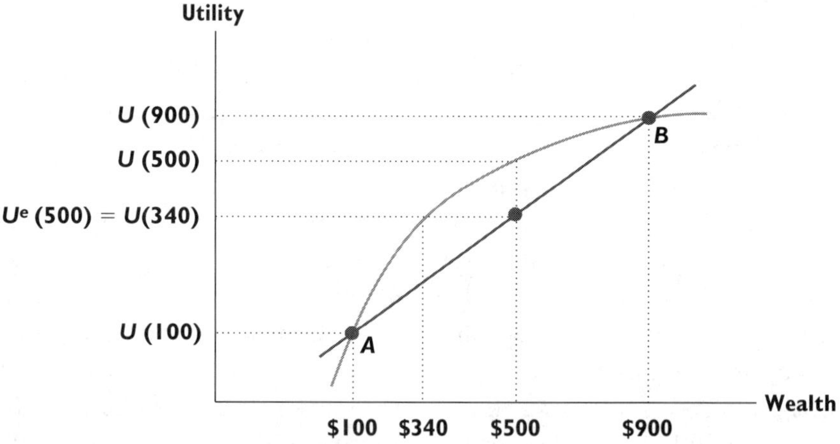

## ECONOMICS FOCUS 13.1 Utility and Attitudes Toward Risk (continued)

$$U(500) - U^e(500)$$

difference measures the loss of utility resulting from the existence of uncertainty. The utility function depicted here is obviously that of someone who dislikes uncertainty, a risk-averse individual. One can express the extent of this person's dislike of uncertainty by noting that he or she is indifferent between an expected utility level associated with \$500 in wealth with uncertainty and, say, \$340 in wealth with certainty. In other words,

$$U^e(500) = U(340)$$

Presumably this risk-averse individual would be willing to forgo up to \$160 in wealth to obtain $U(340)$ with certainty. (This explains why markets for various forms of insurance arise.)

Although the preceding analysis seems convincing, it has serious deficiencies. It does not explain why most people will accept very risky propositions under certain circumstances. For example, many will purchase lottery tickets, which involves gambling a small portion of wealth for a very slight probability of obtaining a large return. In these circumstances the individual appears to behave like a risk-seeker, not the risk-averter depicted in the figure. Friedman and Savage suggested that the utility of wealth may not be a smooth line but a function with an initial segment displaying the characteristics of risk aversion and another segment consistent with risk taking.

**Source:**

M. Friedman and L.J. Savage, "The Utility Analysis of Choices Involving Risk," *Journal of Political Economy* 56 (1948): 279–304.

---

choose portfolios yielding higher expected returns *and* higher risk. By contrast, individuals with even more aversion to risk will opt for portfolios that have lower risk and consequently lower returns.

## THE CASE OF A RISK-FREE ASSET

Another interesting case is the one in which the portfolio is made up of two assets, one of which is risk free. For convenience, assume the two are money (the archetype riskless asset), which earns a zero nominal return,[12] and corporate bonds, whose return is the opportunity cost of holding money.

The expected return on such a portfolio is

$$R_p^e = k_m R_m + k_b R_b = k_b R_b$$

where $R_m$ is the yield on money, assumed here to be zero, $R_b$ is the return on the risky bond, and $k_m$ and $k_b$ are the portfolio shares. Portfolio variance is, therefore (see footnote 7)

$$V_p = k_m^2 V_m + k_b^2 V_b + k_m k_b COV_{mb} = k_b^2 V_b$$

12 Technically, holding money *does* involve inflation risk, a point we ignore here for the sake of simplicity.

**FIGURE 13.2** Optimal Portfolio Choice under Risk Aversion

**(A) Indifference Curves**

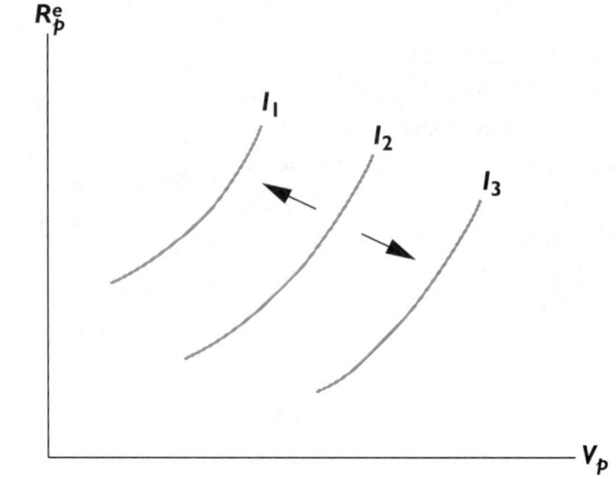


**(B) The Optimal Portfolio**

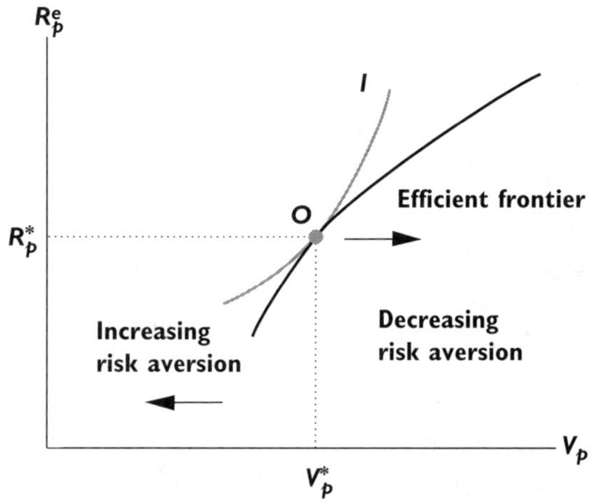


Because the risk-averse individual dislikes risk, total utility can be held constant when portfolio risk rises only if expected portfolio return also rises. For this reason, the indifference curve slopes upward. In panel (B), the optimal portfolio is at *O*, the tangency of the efficient frontier and the risk-averse individual's indifference curve, *I*. Individuals who are relatively more risk averse than the individual depicted will select an optimal portfolio to the left of *O* while those who are relatively less averse to risk will pick a point of tangency to the right of *O*.

where $V_m$ is the risk associated with money, and $V_b$ is bond risk. Since, by assumption, $V_m = 0$, $COV_{mb} = O$ also. Hence, portfolio variance is a function of bond risk alone. If we now take the square root of the portfolio variance equation, we obtain

$$SD_p = k_b SD_b$$

where $SD$ ($= \sqrt{V}$) represents the standard deviation, which, as we have seen, is an alternative measure of risk. It is convenient here to use the standard deviation measure because it makes portfolio risk a linear function of bond risk. In other words, the efficient frontier becomes a straight line.

Figure 13.3 illustrates the risk–return combination in this example. It also illustrates how uncertainty about the future combined with money's role as a liquid asset can produce a demand for money.[13] To see why, consider the bottom half of the figure, where the combinations range from the origin, defined as a portfolio consisting only of money ($k_m = 1$, $k_b = 0$), to the point at which the entire portfolio consists of bonds ($k_m = 0$, $k_b = 1$). Given moderate risk aversion, an equilibrium will be somewhere along the efficient frontier $R_m R_b$. The risk-averse individual will always choose to hold some money; at the equilibrium $E^{**}$, $k_b^{**} = 1 - k_m^{**}$ is held in the form of bonds. Now suppose the return on bonds falls from $R'_b$ to $R_b$. The implications are a flatter efficient frontier and, since the opportunity cost of holding money has fallen, a greater desire to hold money. Consequently, equilibrium is attained in a new position, such as point $E^*$, whereby the portfolio shares become $k_m^*$ ($> k_m^{**}$) and $k_b^*$ ($< k_b^{**}$). If we continue along these lines, we can trace out the quantity of money held for each level of bond return. We can conclude that even though bonds are a risky asset, the quantity of money demanded is negatively related to interest rate changes, just as we concluded in Chapter 6 when we first encountered the demand for money concept.

Figure 13.3 also makes clear that money, despite being a riskless asset with a relatively lower expected return, is nevertheless held in a portfolio that includes risky assets.

## *TOBIN'S SEPARATION THEOREM

Tobin's separation theorem shows that individuals allocate their wealth in two stages: first they choose the optimal mix of risky assets, and then they combine the risky portfolio with riskless assets to maximize total utility. This insight is especially useful in analysing cases that involve both borrowing and lending.

Most individuals and firms do not only own assets; they also incur debts. If they consider risk in the selection of the optimal portfolio, one expects similar considerations in the problem of debt choice or the degree of leverage (see Chapter 10). Indeed, the essentials of the analysis we just completed carry over to the case in which borrowing is allowed. So we do not consider it here in great detail except to note one important result.

---

13 This model was introduced by Nobel laureate James Tobin of Yale University.

**FIGURE 13.3** Liquidity Preference and Risk

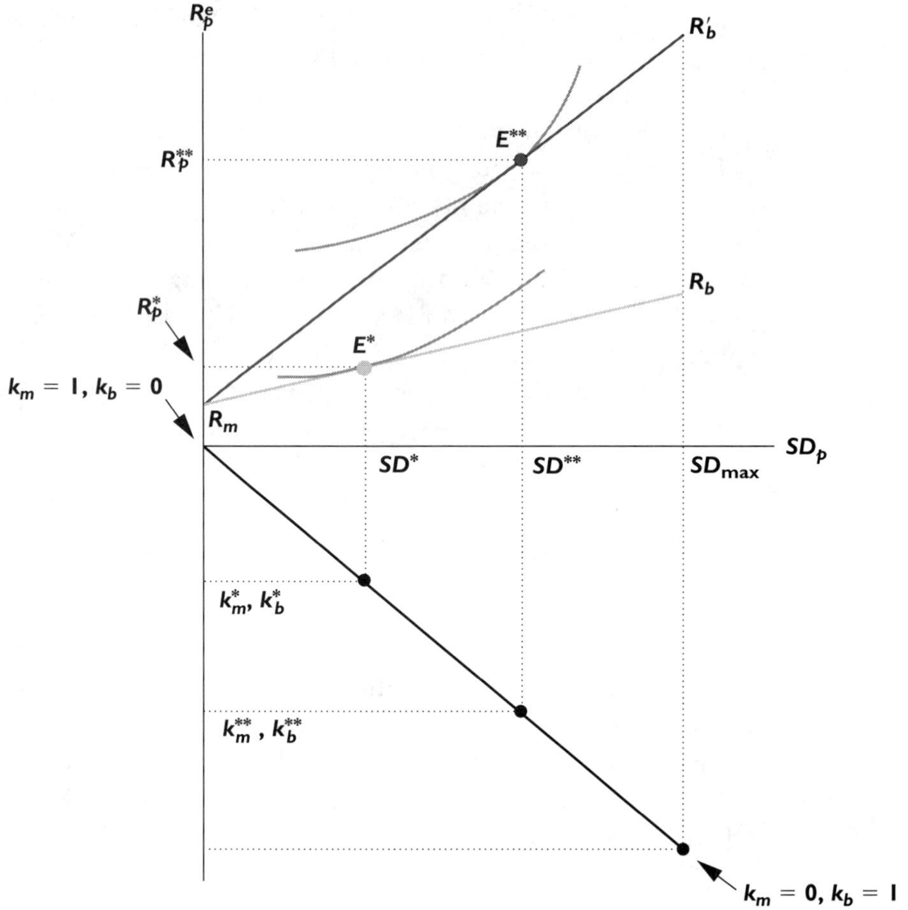


The top half of the figure shows the risk–return combinations of a portfolio consisting of a risk-free asset (money) and a risky asset (bonds). Because such a portfolio's risk is a function of bond risk alone, the efficient frontier is a straight line such as $R_mR_b$. The initial equilibrium is $E^{**}$, which results in a portfolio that is $k_m^{**}$ percent money and $1 - k_m^{**} = k_b^{**}$ percent bonds, as shown in the lower half of the diagram. A lower interest rate reduces the opportunity cost of money and raises the quantity of money held in the portfolio from $k_m^{**}$ to $k_m^*$.

In deriving the efficient frontier, we have used various portfolios made up of risky assets. We also discussed the possibility of taking a risk-free asset and combining it with risky assets. Consider then the situation depicted in Figure 13.4. The curve *AOC* represents an efficient frontier for a portfolio of risky assets while the straight line $R_0OD$ is an efficient frontier for a portfolio made up of the riskless asset and risky assets. Indeed, this efficient frontier dominates all other

**FIGURE 13.4** Tobin's Separation Theorem

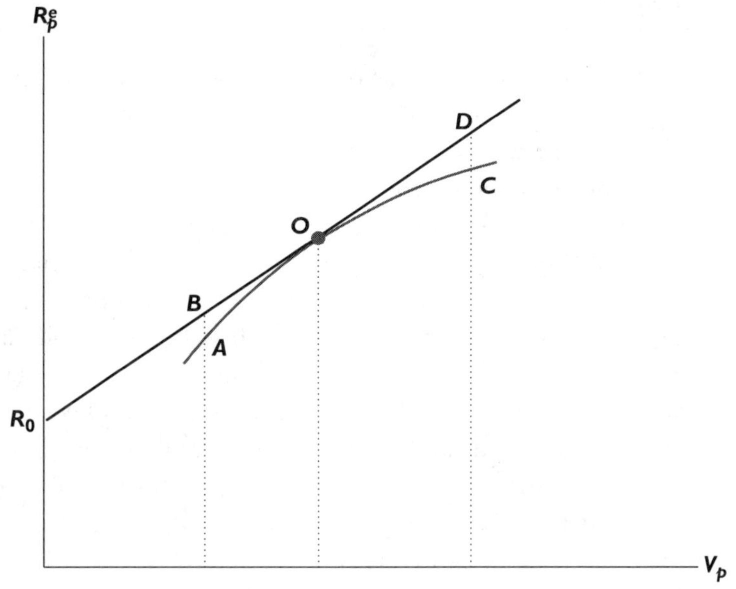


The efficient frontier is the curve *AOC*. A risk-averse individual might select portfolio *O*. The line $R_0O$ represents combinations of a safe asset and a risky portfolio *O*, as in Figure 13.3. If an investor can lend or borrow risklessly at $R_0$, he or she can move to portfolios such as *B* or *D*, which are preferred to *A* or *C* respectively. Thus, the selection of the optimal portfolio can be separated from the level of risk in the portfolio. Conversely, total utility is increased by combining risky assets to select point *A* and then adding riskless assets to reach point *B*. The reason for this result is that the investor *first* selects the optimal mix of risky assets and then maximizes utility, according to his or her degree of aversion to risk, to select the mix between risky and riskless assets.

efficient frontiers resulting from the combination of a riskless asset with risky assets. Why? $R_0OD$ is the line that produces the highest expected return for every level of risk. Lines steeper than $R_0OD$ would not be attainable since they would lie above the efficient frontier from which portfolios with risky assets are chosen.

The investor could choose portfolio *O* in which case such a portfolio is made up of risky assets only. Alternatively, the investor could select point *B* which combines the riskless asset with risky assets. This could be accomplished by lending at the risk-free rate $R_0$ and investing the rest in the risky portfolio. The investor sacrifices some return but portfolio risk is also lower. Instead, the investor can choose point *D* which again is clearly superior to any point along *AOC*. But to obtain the higher return (and risk), the investor must borrow, again at the risk-free rate $R_0$, and invest the proceeds in the risky portfolio.

## MATCHING ASSETS AND DEBTS

Neither individuals nor businesses can borrow risk-free since both groups choose a type of debt that suits their anticipated income or sales flows as well as their interest rate expectations. The question arises then as to whether they manage assets and debt separately or jointly.

Economic agents with income that is steady (at least when averaged over some period of time such as a lifetime) presumably try to match return on assets with debt costs. Not doing so would affect the return of their wealth, which, recall, is the difference between assets and debts. If asset yields are perfectly correlated with debt costs, the spread between them will be constant, thereby ensuring a constant return on wealth. This happy state is unlikely, but a positive correlation between asset yields and debt costs ensures a positive net return on wealth. And clearly, the smoother the pattern of net returns, the smoother the anticipated pattern of future consumption for the households or dividends for the firm.

Unless households or firms are so risk averse that they wish to minimize the variability of net returns, however, they will act on the understanding that a tradeoff exists between the expected return on wealth and the variance of consumption or equity. A positive correlation between asset returns and debt costs reduces the variance of consumption or equity because net returns become less variable.

## SUMMARY

- This chapter explains how return and risk can be quantified. Doing so is necessary because economic agents have to make informal decisions about the future, which is unknown.
- Average return on an asset is measured by its expected return, which is a weighted average of the various possible returns expected in the future.
- Risk of an asset is measured as the variance of expected returns.
- A portfolio of assets is the various assets that an economic agent combines in allocating wealth. Portfolio risk is akin to the risk of an individual asset except that the former is also influenced by correlation of returns, the common fluctuations in the returns to the assets in the portfolio.

## FINANCIAL FOCUS 13.1 A Simpler Approach to Portfolio Analysis: The Capital Asset Pricing Model (CAPM)

For an investor holding large diversified portfolios, the evaluation of the efficient frontier according to the mean-variance analysis developed in this chapter is not especially practical. If the portfolio consists of 1,000 assets, for example, it is necessary to compute almost 500,000 covariances! Nevertheless, our analysis has taught us some useful rules. For example, if asset returns are positively correlated, portfolio variance is raised, while asset returns that are negatively correlated reduce portfolio risk. We can formalize that idea in a simple equation analysed by William Sharpe, who shared a recent Nobel Prize in economics for his research in this area. Let

$$R_i = \alpha_i + \beta_i R_m + e_i \qquad (1)$$

where $R_i$ = return on asset *i*, $R_m$ = return on all assets in the market or the asset return on a market portfolio, $\alpha_i$ and $\beta_i$ are constants, and $e_i$ is a catch-all term to capture influences other than the market's return on the return on asset *i*.

The central ideal behind equation (1), usually called the *characteristic equation* or *Sharpe's model*, is that since interest rates tend to move together and stocks tend to be affected by common influences, one can predict asset *i*'s return on the basis of how strongly it is related to average returns in the rest of the market, $R_m$. The strength of the relationship is measured by $\beta_i$, which is called the beta of an asset. Thus, if $\beta_i = 0$ the asset's return is uncorrelated with the market return, while if $\beta_i > 0$, asset *i*'s return will move in the same direction as the market, and if $\beta_i < 0$, the correlation is negative. The error term, $e_i$, covers other factors that may influence asset *i*'s return independently (that is, uncorrelated with the influence of the market portfolio); they could be firm-specific factors, such as technological change, strikes, and so on.

Since an investor chooses a portfolio of assets, it is perhaps preferable to replace $R_i$ with $R_p$ for portfolio return. But notice that, as the number of assets used to compute $R_p$ increases, the value of $R_p$ approaches that of $R_m$. By contrast, as the number of assets in a portfolio approaches the market portfolio, the influence of the unpredictable component, $e_i$, would be expected to become smaller. These considerations allow us to explain the *risk premium* associated with the holding of an asset I (or a portfolio of assets) and the risk-free return. Using the argument summarized in (1), we can then write

$$R_i - R_F = \beta_i (R_m - R_F) + V_i \qquad (2)$$

where $\beta_i$ is the "beta" of asset *i*, $R_m - R_F$ is the difference between the market return and the risk-free return, and $v_i$ represents other factors which can influence the risk premium.[1] According to CAPM, on average, factors other than the "beta" of an asset should have no effect on the risk premium so that

$$E(R_i - R_F) = \beta_i (R_m - R_F)$$

Therefore, if $\beta_i = 0$, the risk premium is also expected to be zero. There is then no systematic risk. If $\beta_i = 1.0$, then asset *i* has the same systematic risk as the market portfolio and, consequently, the same risk premium. The implications of the ideas contained in (2) for portfolio risk are summarized in the diagram below.

The vertical axis measures total portfolio risk, $V_p$, while the horizontal axis measures the number of assets in a portfolio, *n*. As *n* increases, approaching the market portfolio, the *diversifiable* component of $V_p$, whose source is e, falls. The part that is *non-diversified* rises because some part of portfolio risk varies systematically with that of the market portfolio and is constant (because $\beta_i$ is assumed to be constant).

---

- Diversification does not mean buying more assets. It means including in a portfolio assets whose returns are either uncorrelated or negatively correlated with each other.

## FINANCIAL FOCUS 13.1 A Simpler Approach to Portfolio Analysis: The Capital Asset Pricing Model (CAPM) (continued)

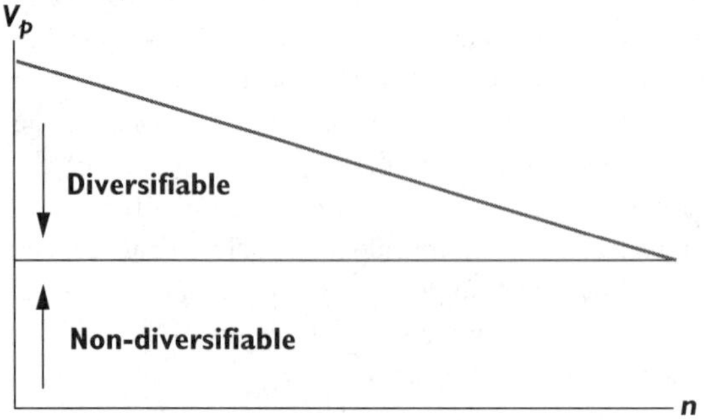


In terms of portfolio risk, it can be shown that

$$\beta_i = \frac{COV_{im}}{V_m}$$

where $COV_{im}$ is the covariance between the return on asset *i* and the return on the market portfolio. This is the conclusion of the capital asset pricing model (CAPM), which, despite its rather strong assumptions, has proven to be extremely useful for managers of large diversified portfolios, especially in the securities industry. (Any finance textbook will provide students with all the details of CAPM.)

Since the CAPM model says that the cost of capital is a linear function of the risk-free rate and the beta of a project, it is not surprising that this model has been extensively used by corporate managers in managing risk. An influential paper by Fama and French (1992) found, however, that CAPM was useless. The technical details as well as the criticisms raised against Fama and French are beyond the scope of this text. However, Jagannathan and McGrattan (1995) have concluded that CAPM is alive and well.[2]

It is fair to ask if all risk can be diversified as shown above. An alternative view, called the **arbitrage pricing theory (APT)** suggests that other factors (summarized in $V_i$ in (2) but essentially ignored by CAPM), such as the overall state of the economy, can influence the "beta" of an asset. One way of dealing with other factors is simply to include other relevant variables on the right-hand side of (2) which are believed to be relevant to the determination of the risk premium. Still others have pointed out that CAPM is flawed because of expected return changes over time, a feature also ignored in the above description of CAPM. Finally, how to define $R_m$? Should we use US data only or, in keeping with the globalization of markets, do we also include stocks in major industrialized countries? One study found that diversifiable risk is greater when investors buy equities across countries as opposed to a single country. This too seems to matter in how well CAPM works.

[1] One could add an intercept, lets call it *alpha*, which would represent the excess return on stock *i* when excess market return is zero. It is not added here because, in theory, alpha is expected to be zero.

[2] R. Jagannathan and E.R. McGrattan, " The CAPM Debate," *Quarterly Review* of the Federal Reserve Bank of Minneapolis (Fall 1995), 2–17.

**Sources:**

E.F. Brigham, A.L. Kahl, W.R. Rentz, and L.C. Gapenski, *Canadian Financial Management*, 3d ed. (Toronto: Holt, Rinehart and Winston, 1991), chapter 6.

J.Y. Campbell, "Understanding Risk and Return," NBER working paper 4554 (1993).

E. Fama and K. French, "The Cross-Section of Expected Stock Returns," *Journal of Finance* 47 (June 1992): 11.

J. Frankel (ed.), *The Internationalisation of Equity Markets* (Chicago, Ill: University of Chicago Press, 1994).

S. Heston and G. Rouwenhoust, "Does Industrial Structure Explain the Benefits of International Diversification?," *Journal of Financial Economics* (August 1994).

S.A. Ross, "Artbitrage Theory of Capital Asset Pricing," *Journal of Economic Theory* 13 (1976): 341–60.

W.F. Sharpe, "Capital Asset Prices: A Theory of Market Equilibrium under Conditions of Risk," *Journal of Finance* 19 (September 1964): 425–42.

"What Price Risk?" *The Economist*, 6 February 1993, p. 81.

## FINANCIAL FOCUS 13.2 The Perfect Portfolio?

Since 1989 *The Economist* has polled investment managers annually on how they divide their portfolios among equities, bonds, and cash. Not surprisingly, given the stock market's recent performance, the respondents revealed a distinct and significant bias toward equities. The table below shows what an average portfolio looked like from early 1990 to early 1995. (The portfolio is a simple average of holdings of equities, bonds, and cash, across nine investment managers.)

| | March 31 1990 | Sept. 29 1991 | Jan. 3 1992 | Jan. 15 1994 | Jan. 7 1995 |
|---|---|---|---|---|---|
| Equities | 70% | 51% | 56% | 52.2% | 50.0% |
| Bonds | 17% | 21% | 35% | 39.7% | 42.3% |
| Cash | 13% | 24% | 9% | 7.6% | 7.7% |

**Source:**
*The Economist*, various issues.

- The optimal portfolio is the one that gives the highest expected portfolio return for a given level of portfolio risk. Utility is maximized at this optimal point.
- Economic agents typically have assets as well as liabilities. To minimize the risk to their net wealth, they try to match the asset returns with liability costs so that the two are positively correlated with each other.

## IMPORTANT TERMS

arbitrage pricing theory (p. 296)
bond ratings (p. 276)
capital asset pricing model (CAPM) (p. 295)
correlation statistic (p. 281)
covariance (p. 281)
default risk (p. 276)
diversification (p. 285)
efficient frontier (p. 283)
expected return (p. 278)
foreign exchange risk (p. 276)
income risk (p. 276)
inflation risk (p. 277)
liquidity risk (p. 276)
market risk (p. 276)
risk (p. 275)
risk averse (p. 286)
risk neutrality (p. 286)
risk-seeking (p. 286)
standard deviation of returns (p. 280)
systematic risk (p. 276)
tax risk (p. 277)
variance of returns (p. 278)

## EXERCISES

1. Consider investments A and B, given the following information:

| State of the World | Probability of Occurrence | Rates of Return (%) | |
|---|---|---|---|
| | | A | B |
| 1 | 0.15 | 3.00 | 10.00 |
| 2 | 0.20 | 7.00 | 7.00 |
| 3 | 0.35 | 8.00 | 8.50 |
| 4 | 0.20 | 13.00 | 12.25 |
| 5 | 0.10 | 17.00 | 4.75 |

(a) Calculate the following:
  (i) Expected returns
  (ii) Variances and standard deviations of returns
  (iii) Covariance and correlation between A and B.

(b) Compute the risk–return combinations achieved by combining assets A and B in the proportions given below.

| Proportion in A | Proportion in B |
|---|---|
| 100% | 0% |
| 75 | 25 |
| 50 | 50 |
| 25 | 75 |
| 0 | 100 |

2. Suppose an investor can choose among three assets; the entire portfolio may be invested into any one of them or split equally between any two. Also suppose that the states of the world are all equally likely (that is, probability of each state is 25%).

| State of the World | Rate of Return (%) | | |
|---|---|---|---|
| | A | B | C |
| 1 | 10 | 90 | 5 |
| 2 | 30 | 70 | 25 |
| 3 | 70 | 30 | 85 |
| 4 | 90 | 10 | 105 |

Which portfolio would be selected by the highly risk-averse investor? (Hint: Look at the pattern of rates of return.)

3. An investor must allocate her wealth between cash, which earns no interest, and a corporate bond, which earns a positive rate of return. Soon after her choice is made, inflation suddenly rises. How is the investor's portfolio likely to be affected?

4. Using the liquidity preference under risk framework (see Figure 13.3) trace

the effect of an increase in wealth. All other factors should be held constant. Does the allocation of wealth between money and bonds change?

5. Suppose the following rates of return on an asset traded in the market and on an index covering the entire market are observed.

| | | Rate of Return (%) | | | |
|---|---|---|---|---|---|
| Year | Asset | Market Index | Year | Asset | Market Index |
| 1991 | 15 | 7 | 1995 | 8 | 15 |
| 1992 | 30 | 9 | 1996 | 22 | −5 |
| 1993 | 5 | 3 | 1997 | 10 | 10 |
| 1994 | −10 | −7 | | | |

Compute the beta for the above asset. (See **FINANCIAL FOCUS 13.1: A Simpler Approach to Portfolio Analysis**, which discusses the CAPM model).

6. Look at Figure 13.4. In the presence of riskless borrowing at $R_0$, why will an investor select portfolio D instead of C?

7. **FINANCIAL FOCUS 13.2: The Perfect Portfolio?** described a sharp movement away from equities into cash and bonds between 1990 and 1991. What reasons can you give for the shift?

8. List and briefly define three types of risk.

9. Is each of the following statements true or false? Explain your answer.
   (a) When constructing a portfolio of assets it is useful, in terms of total portfolio risk, for the assets to be highly correlated with each other.
   (b) Systematic risk between asset returns and debt costs increases equity risk (or risk of net worth).
   (c) No one who is risk averse will ever buy a security that has a lower expected yield, has more risk, or is less liquid than another security.

10. Using Tobin's liquidity preference theory, show graphically what happens to money demand when bond yields fall. Explain.

11. "Portfolio diversification always reduces risk." Comment.

12. Show graphically why a rise-averse individual is willing to pay insurance to avoid risk.

13. Why is the efficient frontier the only relevant part of the feasible set? Explain.

14. Define the concepts of diversifiable and non-diversifiable risks. Illustrate them graphically. (See **FINANCIAL FOCUS 13.1: A Simpler Approach to Portfolio Analysis**.)

15. Suppose you observe the following rates of return on an asset traded in the stock market and on an index of the performance of the entire market. (See **FINANCIAL FOCUS 13.1: A Simpler Approach to Portfolio Analysis.**)

| Year | 1991 | 1992 | 1993 | 1994 | 1995 | 1996 | 1997 |
|---|---|---|---|---|---|---|---|
| Asset (%) | 15 | 30 | 5 | −10 | 8 | −22 | 10 |
| Market (%) | 7 | 9 | 3 | −7 | 15 | −5 | 10 |

(a) Compute the beta for this asset. Explain your result.

(b) Given the value for beta, is the rate of return, on the asset in question in 1997 above or below the one predicted by the CAPM? Explain.

**16.** Consider investments, given the following information:

| State of the World | | 1 | 2 | 3 | 4 | 5 |
|---|---|---|---|---|---|---|
| Probability | | 0.1 | 0.2 | 0.4 | 0.2 | 0.1 |
| Rates of Return | −A | 0.0 | 5.0 | 8.0 | 10.0 | 15.0 |
| | −B | −12.0 | 5.0 | 9.0 | 12.0 | 24.0 |

(a) Compute the expected return, variance, and standard deviation for the returns of each of the two investments. Compute the correlation coefficient and covariance for the two investments.

(b) Plot the risk–return combination achieved by combining the two assets in the following proportions: 0:100%, 25:75%, 50:50%, 75:25%, 100:0%.

**17.** Using Tobin's liquidity preference model, illustrate graphically the effect of an increase in the return on the safe or risk-free asset. Explain.

**18.** The CAPM model (see **FINANCIAL FOCUS 13.1: A Simpler Approach to Portfolio Analysis**) suggests that diversifiable risk can be eliminated by buying the entire market portfolio. Do you think this is, strictly speaking, necessary? Why or why not?

**19.** If a stock's return falls by 6% but the return on a market portfolio rises by 12%, what is the "beta" for this stock?

**20.** Explain the advantages and problems with the CAPM model.

**21.** Is buying stocks in different sports organizations likely to produce results consistent with the notion of diversification? Explain.

**22.** Does a risk-neutral investor care about the variance of returns? Explain.

**23.** What is the difference between risk and uncertainty? Explain.

# *APPENDIX 13.A

## THE ALGEBRA OF PORTFOLIO SELECTION

The discussion in the chapter concentrated on cases in which the assets in a portfolio are uncorrelated. Such an assumption simplifies some of the necessary calculations. Nevertheless, it is unrealistic.

It can be shown that the expression for portfolio risk for two assets may be written

$$V_p = k_1^2 V_1 + k_2^2 V_2 + 2k_1 k_2 CORR_{12} SD_1 SD_2$$

where $CORR_{12}$ is the correlation between the returns on assets 1 and 2 and *SD* refers to the *standard deviation of asset returns*, which is simply the square root of the *variance of returns* ($= \sqrt{V}$).[1] By definition, the correlation measure ranges between $-1$ and $+1$ so that

$$-1 \leqslant CORR_{12} \leqslant +1$$

Thus, when $CORR_{12} = +1$, asset returns are perfectly positively correlated; at the other extreme, a value of $-1$ for $CORR_{12}$ implies perfectly negatively correlated asset returns. Uncorrelated assets have a $CORR_{12}$ value of 0.

Consider then what happens to the expression for $V_p$ under the following three cases:

$$CORR_{12} = 0 \rightarrow V_p = k_1^2 V_1 + k_2^2 V_2 \quad (13A.1)$$

$$CORR_{12} = +1 \rightarrow V_p = k_1^2 V_1 + k_2^2 V^2 + 2k_1 k_2 SD_1 SD_2 \quad (13A.2)$$

$$V_p = (k_1 SD_1 + k_2 SD_2)^2$$

$$CORR_{12} = -1 \rightarrow V_p = k_1^2 V_1 + k_2^2 V_2 - 2k_1 k_2 SD_1 SD_2$$

$$V_p = (k_1 SD_1 - k_2 SD_2)^2 \quad (13A.3)$$

Note that when asset returns are perfectly positively correlated, portfolio risk is a linear combination of the risks on each asset since, from equation (13A.2)

$$\sqrt{V_p} = SD_p = k_1 SD_1 + k_2 SD_2$$

Hence, all our investor can do is to average the risk on the two assets in the portfolio. In other words, there is no possibility of diversification in the sense of reduction portfolio risk through the purchase of additional assets.

Consider now the case in which asset returns are perfectly negatively correlated. Note from equation (13A.3) that it is possible to select a portfolio such that portfolio risk is reduced to zero. To see how, if you take the square root of $V_p$ in the equation:

---

1 As noted in the text, some analysts prefer to use standard deviation over variance as a measure of risk, although it makes no difference whether that statistic or variance is used.

$$\sqrt{V_p} = SD_p = k_1SD_1 - k_2SD_2$$

Setting $SD_p = 0$, you get

$$k_1\ SD_1 - k_2SD_2 = 0$$

or

$$k_1/k_2 = SD_2/SD_1$$

Thus, when the relative portfolio shares are equal to the reciprocal of the ratio of their standard deviation, portfolio risk is eliminated.

# REFERENCES


Laidler, D.E.W. *The Demand for Money: Theories, Evidence, and Problems*, 3d ed. New York: Harper & Row, 1985.

Markowitz, H. *Portfolio Selection.* New York: Wiley, 1959.

Statistics Canada, CANSIM database.

Tobin, J. "Liquidity Preference as Behavior Towards Risk." *Review of Economic Studies* 25 (February 1958), 65–86.

Van Horne, J.C. *Financial Management and Policy*, Tenth Edition. New York: Prentice-Hall, 1995.

CHAPTER 14

# Hedging Risks: Futures, Forwards, and Options

The world is a risky place. Since most economic agents are risk-averse, they naturally attempt to eliminate risk or at least shift it to other agents. This chapter explores some *derivative products* that attempt to shift the risk of holding various assets.

To understand the popularity of these hedging devices, recall the tradeoff between risk and return. They rise and fall together. Thus, if someone introduces a financial innovation that reduces risk to one party in a transaction, it will not be long before a market for that innovation begins to thrive.

The last quarter century has seen a large number of such innovations. One driving force has been the tremendous fall in the cost of computing and the concomitant rise in the volume of calculations that computers can handle. This technological revolution has made possible some new financial instruments and greatly widened the use of others. It has also increased the volume of available information about financial markets and the economy as a whole—increased it so much that diverse but widely held views about the future are common. These differences in expectations are also a stimulus for the development of financial instruments that enable shifting of risk. Other factors include the globalization of financial markets and competition among bonds and securities dealers who have responded by creating new financial products. Finally, the recent volatility of interest rates has made current decisions riskier than in the past—and the parties to a transaction have yet another incentive to shift some risk elsewhere.

In this chapter, we examine several types of increasingly important financial instruments: financial futures, forward markets, and options. Students should also recall another form of hedging risk: the use of **swaps** of interest payments or of foreign exchange (see **ECONOMICS FOCUS 14.2: Hedging and Monetary Policy: Swaps** on page 323.)

A word of caution is in order. What follows in only an introduction to an enormous subject. The literature on futures and options has grown tremendously over the last decade. Entire texts are devoted to their bewildering diversity and complexity. Indeed, it is the mystery of derivatives and the peculiar jargon used by market participants which has made politicians and the public suspicious of these financial instruments.

## DEFINITIONS

Our discussion can be made clearer with some definitions.

**Hedging** is a process of protecting oneself against future price changes by shifting some or all of the risk to someone else. The individual who desires to shift risk away from him- or herself is often called a *hedger* while the one who accepts greater risks is referred to as a **speculator**.

Hedgers typically have a *position* to protect: they either already own the commodity or financial instrument in question or they expect to do so sometime in the future. By contrast, speculators take no position; rather, they bet on price changes in the hope of making a profit.

Does the existence of speculators mean that some market participants are risk-seekers, not risk-averters? Not necessarily. The speculator foresees a very high return from a relatively small investment made by *purchasing on margin.*

**Margin**, which is the amount of cash put up by the investor, is a fraction of the value of the asset. The remainder is a loan from the broker handling the sale, and it must be backed by collateral. Buying on margin is regulated, and the amount of the loan cannot exceed a set percentage of the value of the instrument. Hence, if the price falls, the broker must make a *margin call* and obtain more funds from the investor.[1]

## FINANCIAL FUTURES

Futures markets trade **futures contracts**, which are agreements to accept or make delivery of an asset on a particular future date at a price struck today.[2] In contrast, an exchange of assets that occurs at the same time the price is agreed on is said to be a trade in the **spot market**, sometimes called the *cash market.*

A futures contract may be for a commodity (such as pork bellies or wheat) or for a financial asset (such as foreign exchange or an instrument linked to specified stock prices). Here we concentrate on financial futures, but it is worth knowing that commodity futures are much older. As early as the twelfth century, trading fairs in Europe gave producers of agricultural commodities an opportunity to make contracts for the future delivery of their products. Modern futures markets

1 Alternatively, the investor can sell the asset and take the loss.

2 Thus, one requirement for the existence of a futures market is that the commodity in question be durable and able to be stored.

can probably be said to have originated in the nineteenth-century United States. The Chicago Board of Trade began organizing a futures market in 1848 as a means of correcting some inefficiencies in the market for grain. Technological changes during the same period, such as the invention of the telegraph and improvements in rail transportation, doubtless improved the chances of establishing viable futures markets for there are inherent instabilities and uncertainties about producing agricultural commodities today to be sold and delivered sometime in the future. The principal form of uncertainty, of course, lay in the future price of the crop.[3]

Financial futures markets are a phenomenon of recent decades. When the post-war system of fixed exchange rates ended in 1971, the variability of exchange rates became a problem in financial circles. Soon after, many countries began what has become a worldwide movement toward deregulation of financial systems. One result was increased volatility in the prices of all financial assets. It was not long before financial futures appeared on the scene.

Table 14.1 provides some general information about the financial futures and options markets in Canada.[4] Activity centres in the Toronto and Montreal exchanges. There is also trading in Vancouver.

## FORWARD MARKETS

Before proceeding with a description of how participants can hedge in with futures contracts, it is important to be clear about **forward contracts**.

### Forward and Futures Markets Compared

Forward and futures markets are alike in many ways. Both deal in durable, storable products; both can be used for hedging; both require estimates of the future from participants.

There are also differences. The most obvious is the buyer in a forward market transaction generally intends to take future delivery of the asset or commodity in question. By contrast, futures market participants rarely plan to take or make delivery.[5] Typically, they intend **offset transactions**—that is, a purchase is to be offset by a subsequent sale.

---

3 For additional historical details, see W.W. Libeck, "The Origins of Futures Markets," in *The Handbook of Financial Futures*, ed. N.H. Rothstein (New York: McGraw-Hill, 1984), 9–22.

4 Canada has generally been somewhat slow to adopt financial futures trading. In at least one case, however, it has been the innovator in the futures field. In September 1990, the Montreal Stock Exchange launched futures on Canadian government bonds with 10 years to maturity. In 1992, the Chicago Board of Trade decided to offer a similar product.

5 For example, during the period 1 October 1988 to 30 September 1989, only 0.62% of financial futures and 1.48% of currency futures in the United States were settled in delivery or cash settlement. See R.W. Kolb, *Understanding Futures Markets*, 3d ed. (Miami, Fl.: Kolb Publishing Co., 1991), 16, Table 1.3.

**TABLE 14.1** LOCATION AND ACTIVITIES OF SELECTED CANADIAN FUTURES AND OPTIONS MARKETS

| Instrument | Contract Months | Trading Hours (a.m.–p.m.) | Contract Size | Minimum Price Fluctuation | Daily Limit |
|---|---|---|---|---|---|
| | | **Montreal Exchange** | | | |
| Bankers' Acceptances (futures) | Mar/June Sept/Dec over 2 years | 8:20–3:00 | $1,000,000 (face value) | 0.01 = $10 | 5,000 contracts |
| Government of Canada Bonds, 10 years (futures) | Mar/June Sept/Dec | 8:20–3:00 | $100,000 | 0.01 = $10 | 3 pts |
| Government of Canada Bonds (options) | Next 3 months + 2 on Mar cycle | 8:20–3:00 | $25,000 (face value) | $0.01 per contract | 4,000 contracts |
| | | **Toronto Futures Exchange** | | | |
| Bonds, 15 years (futures) | Mar/June Sept/Dec | 9:30–3:15 | $100,000 | 1/32 pt = $31.25 | 2 pt = $2,000 |
| Treasury bills, 13 weeks (futures) | Mar/June Sept/Dec | 9:30–3:15 | $1,000,000 | 0.01 pt = $24 | 0.60 pt = $1,440 |
| TSE 100 Spot (options) | Daily | 9:20–4:10 | $100 × index | 1 pt. = $10 | — |
| TSE 35 (futures) | 3 consecutive months plus 6 months | 9:30–4:15 | 500 × index | 0.02 pt = $10 | 13.5 pt = $6,750 |

Note: The terminology used in this table is explained later in this chapter.

Sources: *Futures* 1989 (supplement), pp. 7–8, and *The Fitzroy–Dearborn Directory of the World's Futures and Options Markets (N. Battley, ed.), Chicago, Ill.: Fitzroy–Dearborn, 1994.*

Another difference is in the relationship between buyer and seller. In a forward transaction, the two are usually directly responsible to each other for ensuring that the terms of the agreement are fulfilled. In a futures market transaction, however, an intermediary, which can be a bank but is often an organized exchange, ensures that payment (or, less often, delivery) is made. The bilateral nature of trading in forward markets makes it difficult for participants to change positions; there is considerably more flexibility in futures market trading as evidenced by the ability to offset transactions.[6]

In addition, futures markets operate in an auction setting while forward transactions are generally concluded over the phone. Items traded in futures markets are standardized so that the only decision variable of interest to investors is price.[7] Finally, as will become clear later in the chapters, expectations of future prices are better reflected in forward markets than in futures markets.

**FINANCIAL FOCUS 14.1: Forward Prices in the Financial Press** on page 309 shows how forward and spot rates are reported in the financial press, while Table 14.2 summarizes some of the major differences between futures and forward markets.

## The Forward Market in Operation

Perhaps the best way to explain the operation of the forward market is to use an example. Because forward transactions in foreign exchange are common, we base our example on this type of transaction.

Table 14.3 sets out the highlights. A Canadian importer expects delivery three months hence of widgets valued at $2,000,000 US. Today's spot exchange rate is $1.30 Cdn = $1 US, so the current Canadian value of the shipment is $2,600,000 Cdn ($2,000,000 US × $1.30).

Now assume the importer believes that the Canadian dollar will depreciate in the coming months. That means he anticipates that his cost for the imports will rise. If, for example, the exchange falls to $1 US = $1.40 Cdn, the Canadian dollar cost of the imports will rise by

$$(\$2{,}000{,}000 \times 1.40) - (\$2{,}000{,}000 \times 1.30) = \$200{,}000$$

To avoid this foreign exchange risk, the importer can fix the Canadian dollar price of products to be delivered in the future. He does so by arranging with a bank to deliver in 90 days $2,000,000 US at today's prevailing 3-month forward rate—say, $1 US = $1.35 Cdn. Upon acceptance of the forward contract, the cost of the imports is fixed at $2,700,000 Cdn ($2,000,000 US × $1.35), and

6 Indeed, the number of steps required to complete a futures or an options transaction is surprisingly large. See, for example, P.S. Rose, *Money and Capital Markets*, 4th ed. (Homewood, Ill.: Irwin, 1992), 861, Exhibit 12-11.

7 For example, in the case of commodities such as oil, a futures contract would operate for a specific grade only, such as light sweet crude oil. In the case of financial futures, standardization is less problematical.

**TABLE 14.2** FORWARD VERSUS FUTURES MARKETS

**Differences**

| Forward | Futures |
|---|---|
| 1. Delivery likely. | 1. Offset likely. |
| 2. Product may or may not be standardized. | 2. Standardized product; price is the only variable of interest. |
| 3. Transaction is bilateral in nature. | 3. Intermediary involved. |
| 4. Trading generally by phone. | 4. Trading in an auction setting. |
| 5. Self-regulated. | 5. Even if conditions 1 to 4 are not met, will exist if forward markets break down. |
| | 6. Regulated by agencies. |

**Similarities**

1. Can be used for hedging or speculating.
2. Products are durable and storable.
3. Product price variations are large.
4. Have large numbers of suppliers and demanders and are competitive.

**TABLE 14.3** A TRANSACTION IN THE FORWARD MARKET

| | Spot Exchange Rate: $1.30 | | Forward Exchange Rate: $1.35 |
|---|---|---|---|
| Current cost of imports | $2,000,000 × 1.30 | = | $2,600,000 |
| Anticipated future cost of imports in the spot market | $2,000,000 × 1.40 | = | $2,800,000 |
| Cost of imports at forward rate foreign exchange delivered in the future | $2,000,000 × 1.35 | = | $2,700,000 |
| Savings relative to future anticipated spot exchange rate | $2,800,000 − $2,700,000 | = | $100,000 |

The current spot exchange rate is $1.30 Cdn = $1 US. The exchange rate is expected to depreciate in value to $1.40 Cdn = $1 US. The importer, however, can arrange to have $2,000,000 US delivered three months hence at a rate of $1.35 Cdn = $1 US today. If the importer's exchange rate prediction is correct, the savings will amount to $100,000 Cdn.

## FINANCIAL FOCUS 14.1 Forward Prices in the Financial Press

Forward market prices for foreign exchange are regularly reported in the financial press. The listings are easy to read.

**Midmarket rates in Toronto at noon, August 17, 1996.**

| | $1 US in Cdn $ = | $1 Cdn in US $= |
|---|---|---|
| US/Canada spot | 1.3738 | 0.7279 |
| 1 month forward | 1.3724 | 0.7287 |
| 2 months forward | 1.3709 | 0.7294 |
| 3 months forward | 1.3697 | 0.7301 |
| 6 months forward | 1.3653 | 0.7324 |
| 12 months forward | 1.3591 | 0.7358 |
| 3 years forward | 1.3608 | 0.7349 |
| 5 years forward | 1.3838 | 0.7226 |
| 7 years forward | 1.4048 | 0.7118 |
| 10 years forward | 1.4331 | 0.6978 |
| Canadian dollars in 1990: | | |
| High | 1.3515 | 0.7399 |
| Low | 1.3685 | 0.7212 |
| Average | 1.3682 | 0.7309 |

| Country/Currency | Cdn $ per unit | US $ per unit |
|---|---|---|
| Britain/Pound | 2.1257 | 1.5473 |
| 1 month forward | 2.1228 | 1.5468 |
| 2 months forward | 2.1198 | 1.5463 |
| 3 months forward | 2.1177 | 1.5461 |
| 6 months forward | 2.1108 | 1.5460 |
| 12 months forward | 2.1001 | 1.5452 |
| Germany/Deutschmark | 0.9199 | 0.6696 |
| 1 month forward | 0.9206 | 0.6708 |
| 3 months forward | 0.9222 | 0.6733 |
| 6 months forward | 0.9250 | 0.6775 |
| 12 months forward | 0.9321 | 0.6858 |
| Japan/Yen | 0.012720 | 0.009259 |
| 1 months forward | 0.012761 | 0.009299 |
| 3 months forward | 0.012844 | 0.009372 |
| 6 months forward | 0.012967 | 0.009497 |
| 12 months forward | 0.013226 | 0.009731 |

The first column gives the name of the foreign currency as well as the horizon over which forward transactions can be made. Only in the case of the US dollar can one actually buy up to 10 years ahead of time. Generally, the longest horizon for forward transactions is 12 months and only for a few currencies between countries where a considerable amount of trade takes place. The next two columns give the exchange rate at which forward transactions can be made either in terms of the Canadian dollar or in terms of the foreign currency.

decisions about profit margins, among other things, can also be made today with certainty. Delivery is fully anticipated by both parties to the transaction.[8]

## THE WORKINGS OF FUTURES MARKETS

To understand how the market for financial futures operates, it is necessary to understand how participating in it enables investors to hedge against risk.

An individual who expects that prices for some asset will *rise* is said to take a **long position**. By contrast, someone who expects asset prices to *fall* is said to take a **short position**.[9]

Hedging takes place through the purchase of a futures contract, which specifies today both the delivery date and the price at which the asset will be acquired. Therefore, it involves taking one position in the cash market and an *opposite* one in the futures market. Trading also requires, of course, that there be someone who takes a long position and another individual who takes a short position.

A relationship exists between spot and futures prices. The differential between the spot price and the futures price is known as the **basis**.[10]

At time $t$ then we have

$$F_{\tau}(t) - S(t) = \text{basis} \tag{14.1}$$

where $F_{\tau}(t)$ = futures contract price purchased at time $t$ for delivery date $\tau$ and $S(t)$ = spot price at time $t$.

Futures contracts are **marked-to-market**, which means that gains and losses are settled at the close of trading each day, *not* at the end of the contract. If the price falls below the currently prescribed minimum margin, the buyer must deposit an amount equivalent to the change in price into the seller's account in order to maintain the margin. Thus, a change in the price of the futures contract affects the position of the buyer and seller in opposite ways.[11]

**FINANCIAL FOCUS 14.2: Futures Prices in the Financial Press** on page 312 shows how futures prices are quoted in the financial press. It is important to

---

8 Note also that this example ignores two considerations. First, it does not take account of discounting, since we know that \$1 today is not the same as \$1 in the future (even 90 days in the future). Second, the importer has the option of purchasing US dollars today and buying a 90-day financial instrument denominated in US dollars. The choice will depend primarily on the difference between US and Canadian yields (a consideration that will be discussed in Chapter 15). Finally, we have ignored transactions costs which may or may not be reflected in the forward rate being offered.

9 An often heard expression is *short selling* (or *selling short*). An investor sells an asset at one price with the intention of buying it back at a lower price. The investor usually does not own the asset. Rather, he or she borrows it, usually from a broker's inventory of assets.

10 Not to be confused with the "basis point" that means 1/100th of a percentage point.

11 By contrast, in forward markets gains and losses are not settled daily. Moreover, marked-to-market contracts and margins are negotiable.

understand that the reporting of financial futures differs from that of the spot market. Consider the \$100,000 Government of Canada bond in the example. The prices listed are not percentages of face value. Rather, they are points of 100 percent. Thus, the settlement (closing price) of 90.15 means an implied discount yield of

$$100.00 - 90.15 = 9.85\% \text{ per year}$$

This is equivalent to a delivery price of

$$100\left(1 - \frac{90(0.0985)}{360}\right) = 97.54$$

per \$100 of face value. This translates into a settlement price of \$97,538. Notice the term in parentheses, which is the adjustment factor required because the discount is expressed in annual terms. For a 90-day maturity period, an annual discount of 9.85% represents

$$9.85 \times \left(\frac{90}{360}\right) = 2.46\%$$

The brisk trade in futures means that their market price changes almost constantly. Recall from Table 14.1, however, that there are limits on how much the price of an instrument can vary during any one day. This is to ensure that margin accounts do not get wiped out by large price changes and that brokers (who must make up losses on defaulting customers) have time to make margin calls.

Stock index futures are sold in multiples of the prevailing index. In the example in Financial Focus 14.2, an investor can purchase \$500 times the index of the Toronto Futures Exchange 35. Thus, if the 35-stock index is 200, one could purchase \$500 × 200 = \$100,000 worth of the portfolio.

Finally, the "open interest" column reports the number of futures contracts not yet delivered or offset. This information is a measure of the size of the futures market on any particular day. It can also be used to evaluate the future direction of prices.

## A Long Hedge

We are now in a position to illustrate how interest rate risk can be hedged through the use of financial futures. Will the investor hedge long or short? It depends on circumstances and the individual's expectations about the future.

Suppose interest rates are currently high but the investor expects them to fall. Suppose too that this investor expects to obtain \$100,000 three months hence. If interest rates do fall before then, the yield on the \$100,000 asset the investor purchases will be less than the same asset would produce today. Some potential

## FINANCIAL FOCUS 14.2 Futures Prices in the Financial Press

Most financial newspapers publish futures prices. Two examples are shown here: one for Government of Canada bonds (Cdn Govt Bonds) with a face value of $100,000 and one for an index called the Toronto Stock Exchange 35.

ME is the Montreal Exchange and TFE is the Toronto Futures Exchange. The listing gives the month of delivery, the season's and the trading day's opening, high, and the low prices for a contract, the settlement price ("Settle") at the close of the trading day, and the previous opening interest ("Prev Op Int"), which is the number of contracts outstanding for trading. These represent contracts that have not yet been off-set by opposite futures transactions.

The prices listed are not dollars but points of 100 percent of face value. Thus, the government bond's closing (settlement) price of 90.15 means an implied yield of 100.00%—90.15% = 9.85% per year. (See text for more information.)

The notation "0.01 = $10 per contract" is the margin requirement; for the $100,000 bond, it is 0.01 × $100,000 = $1000. Alternatively, it is referred to as the price of a tick or .0001 × $100,000 = $10 where .0001 is 1/100 of 1%.

| Season | | | | | | | Net | Prev |
|---|---|---|---|---|---|---|---|---|
| **High** | **Low** | **Month** | **Open** | **High** | **Low** | **Settle** | **Chge** | **Opt Int** |
| **Cdn Gov't Bonds 9% (ME) $100,000 (points of 100%; 0.01 = $10 per contract)** | | | | | | | | |
| 95.52 | 84.12 | Sep 90 | 90.00 | 90.24 | 89.95 | 90.15 | +0.20 | 2,316 |
| **Toronto 35 (TFE) 500× index (0.02 pt = $10 per contract)** | | | | | | | | |
| 202.48 | 192.40 | Feb 92 | 195.10 | 195.80 | 194.90 | 195.40 | +0.48 | 1,864 |

interest income will be lost. But the investor can lock into current interest rates by purchasing a futures contract today and selling it three months from today.

Table 14.4(A) describes the position facing the investor considering a long hedge. Believing on March 1 that interest rates have peaked, the investor purchases a futures contract for a $100,000 bond to mature June 1. Today in the spot market a 9% government bond currently yielding 10.51% is available at 87.35; the futures price is 89. If the investor's expectations are correct, spot prices and futures prices in the bond market will rise as interest rates fall. Thus, on June 1, just before the futures contract purchased March 1 matures, the investor sells the futures contract at 90. Meanwhile, in the spot market, bond prices have risen to 89. The investor purchases a bond. Had the investor had the cash on March 1, the bond could have been purchased at 87.35. In other words, the investor has a loss of 89 − 87.35 = 1.65 or $1,650. This loss, however, is largely offset by the profit of 90 − 89 = 1 or $1,000 earned in the futures market from rising prices.[12]

12 Notice that this numerical example and the next are idealized. They omit transactions costs and brokerage costs and assume the investor knows with certainty what bond prices will be three months in the future. Moreover, they assume that the *yield curve*, a curve describing yields on a bond maturing at different dates in the future, is flat. We discuss the yield curve concept in the next chapter.

**TABLE 14.4** HEDGING IN INTEREST RATE FUTURES

**(A) Long Hedge**

| Cash Market — Unhedged Position | | Futures Market — Hedged Position | |
|---|---|---|---|
| March 1: | Interest rates are believed to have peaked. Lock into current high rate. 9% Government of Canada bonds, currently yielding 10.51% and due March 1, 2011, are priced at 87.35 or $87,350. | March 1: | Buy the equivalent of a $100,000 bond in futures at a cash price of 89 worth $89,000. |
| June 1: | With the cash received today, buy a $100,000 Government of Canada 9% bond at 89, yielding 9%. | June 1: | Sell the futures contract at 90, worth $90,000. |
| Loss: | $89,000 − $87,350 = $1,650 | Gain: | $90,000 — $89,000 = $1,000 |
| NET DIFFERENCE = $1,650 − $1,000 = $650 | | | |

**(B) Short Hedge**

| Cash Market — Unhedged Position | | Futures Market — Hedged Position | |
|---|---|---|---|
| March 1: | Investor owns a $100,000 9% Government of Canada bond, due on March 1, 2011, currently yielding 10.51% and priced at 87.35. Investor expects rates to rise. | March 1: | Sell the equivalent of a $100,000 bond in futures at a cash price of 95 for $95,000. |
| June 1: | Sell $100,000 bond at 86.8. | June 1: | Buy a futures contract at a cash price of 94.50 for $94,500. |
| Loss: | $87,350 − $86,800 = $550 | Gain: | $95,000 − $94,500 = $500 |
| NET DIFFERENCE = $550 − $500 = $50 | | | |

Hence, hedging has made the investor better off than remaining in an unhedged position.

## A Short Hedge

Now consider an alternative scenario, in which the investor anticipates a rise in interest rates. In this case, the investor will want to engage in a short hedge.

Table 14.4(B) illustrates the features of a short hedge. Our investor owns a $100,000 9% Government of Canada bond due on March 1, 2011; it currently sells in the spot market at 87.35 and yields 10.51%. At the same time, a futures contract is sold at a cash price of 95. If the investor's expectations are correct, bond prices in the cash market will fall by June 1, say to 86.8, thus leading to a loss of $550 upon the sale of the $100,000 bond on that date. By contrast, since the futures price will also have fallen to 94.50, from 95 on March 1, the investor gains $500. In this example a net loss of $50 on the hedge is made instead of the $550 loss in the unhedged position.

## The Difficulty of Perfect Hedges

If a sequence of transactions in the futures market produces a gain exactly equal to the loss, the investor has what is called a *perfect hedge*. Such an outcome is unlikely for several reasons.

First, it is not always possible for an investor to buy and sell the same asset in the futures market. He or she may have to settle for a *cross-hedge*, which means buying futures for one asset—say, Government of Canada bonds—and selling them for another—say, bankers' acceptances. Such transactions involve so many variables that they are unlikely to balance exactly.

Second, spot and futures prices do not necessarily move in concert.

Finally, futures prices in both the spot and futures markets are uncertain. Indeed, any error in the wrong direction can have disastrous consequences on the net gain or loss from hedging. Therefore, hedging cannot eliminate risk entirely.

## Futures Prices and Spot Prices

As the delivery month approaches, the spot price for an asset converges to the futures price so that the basis essentially becomes zero. In the intervening period, however, the basis clearly differs from zero, which is what imparts some risk to hedging.

We can illustrate the connection between the futures price and the spot price with a simple expression. As before, let $F_\tau(t)$ denote the price in the futures market with delivery date and $s(t)_t$ the spot market price, both at time $t$. Then,

$$F_\tau(t) = S(t) + (R^S - R^L)\frac{\tau - t}{360} \cdot S(t) \tag{14.2}$$

Equation (14.2) states that the futures price, $F_\tau(t)$ is the spot price, $S(t)$ plus the **cost-of-carry**, which is the opportunity cost of carrying the contract until delivery as a proportion of the spot price.

The cost-of-carry can be measured, for example, as the difference between the yield on a short-term instrument, $R^S$, and a long-term instrument, $R^L$, adjusted for the term of the contract (the carryover period). Since $\tau$ is the date of the delivery, and $t$ is today's date, $\tau - t$ is simply the number of days the contract is carried while $(\tau - t)/360$ is the carryover period in a fraction of a year defined as 360 days in length. The reason for including the term $(R^S - R^L)$ in equation (14.1) is that difference between short-run and long-run interest rates provides a measure of the direction interest rates will take during the carryover period.[13]

Note that, as the delivery date approaches, $\tau - t$ approaches zero and so $F_\tau(t)$ approaches $S(t)$; the cost-of-carry becomes more and more irrelevant.[14]

## *Optimal Hedging

The **hedge ratio** is the number of futures contracts bought or sold per unit of the asset in the spot market. Recall from Chapter 13 that investors trade off expected return and risk and that, as a result, there is some portfolio that represents an optimal mix of expected return and risk. Similarly, one can speak of an optimal hedge ratio.

Consider, for example, the short hedge case illustrated previously. The investor owns an asset in the spot market. The risk is the expected change in the price of bonds (resulting from an anticipated rise in interest rates), which will adversely affect the investor's spot market position. By selling futures contracts, the risk stemming from expected price changes in the spot market falls but so does expected return since the price of lower risk is lower expected return.

This notion is illustrated in Figure 14.1. *UH* represents unhedged position—the combination of expected return and risk that would be obtained if the investor does not engage in any hedging whatsoever. When the investor hedges in the futures market, both expected return and risk fall. The optimal hedge ratio is attained at some point, labelled *OH* in the figure.[15] Beyond this amount of hedging, risk actually increases because too many contracts are sold in the futures market.

Now, if we draw indifference curves reflecting various amounts of aversion to risk, we can determine how the investor's preferences will influence the amount of hedging that he or she will engage in. One such example is given in Figure

---

13 An explanation of this result is the subject of Chapter 15, where the topic of the term structure of interest rates is explored.

14 In the case of stock index futures, equation (14.2) would be written

$$F_\tau(t) = S(t) + (R - Div)\frac{\tau - t}{360} \cdot S(t) \qquad (14.2A)$$

where *R* represents the interest cost of carrying the index portfolio, and *Div* is the dividend income earned by carrying the index portfolio. Equation (14.1A) is interpreted in the same manner as equation (14.1). Dividends are paid discontinuously, however, so $F_\tau(t)$ does not approach $S(t)$ as smoothly as in the case of interest rate futures.

15 One could, in principle, look at how futures prices change relative to spot prices to ascertain the optimum amount of hedging that actually takes place. There are problems with such an approach, but they are beyond the scope of this text.

**FIGURE 14.1** The Optimal Hedge Ratio

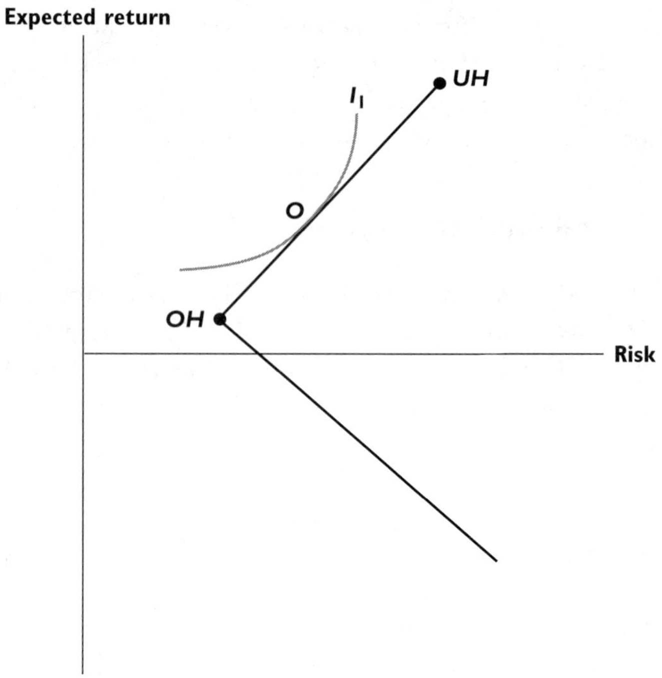


The tradeoff is between risk and expected return, which are measured on the axes. An investor who remains unhedged chooses point *UH*. With a short hedge, the investor can move to point *OH*, where risk is minimized by selling futures contracts. The optimal amount of hedging, however, depends on the investor's attitude toward risk. One optimum position is point *O*.

14.1. The investor with indifference curve $I_1$ chooses to sell enough futures contracts to reach point *O*.

## FINANCIAL OPTIONS

Like futures, options have a long history. Indeed, early forms of options trading apparently existed in ancient Rome and Greece. The Netherlands tulipmania described in Chapter 12 involved extensive trade in options.[16]

16 One of the difficulties of that episode was that because there was no enforcement mechanism to ensure that contractual obligations would be met, many options writers simply refused to honour their obligations when the extraordinarily high prices for tulip bulbs collapsed in the spot market.

## ECONOMICS FOCUS 14.1 Barings It All

The recent public exposure of derivatives and of their implications for the financial system was heightened by a series of spectacular financial losses incurred over the last few years by well-known institutions. Perhaps the best known of these was the collapse of the Barings Investment Bank which took place after a trader, Nick Leeson, who built up profitable positions in the Japanese futures and options market (the Nikkei) until the Kobe earthquake and concern over a recession in Japan turned to sharp losses, so much so that the margin calls exceeded the bank's entire capital! The reason? Instead of trading the normal 1,000 contracts or so, Leeson arranged to trade between 18,000 and 20,000 contracts to try to recoup earlier losses only to increase his losses when he made the wrong bet about the direction the market was taking. A Dutch bank (ING) was persuaded to purchase Barings and take on its losses for the grand sum of £1 (approximately $2.12 CDN).

Another notable incident was the huge losses incurred by the German firm Metalgesellshaft AG (MG) which lost over $1 billion US (approximately $1.38 billion CDN) in 1993 on what appeared to be a safe bet. The company sold gasoline, diesel and heating fuel at a fixed price to its customers for up to 10 years ahead of time (in effect arranging forward contracts with clients). To protect itself, the company hedged the full amount. If prices rose, for example, the company's costs would potentially rise above the receipts from the sale of fuels. So the company resorted to futures and swaps to hedge against the risk it faced. But oil prices fell and this led to large losses being sustained on its futures contracts. As we have seen, prices in futures move in the opposite direction of spot prices and are made for relatively short-terms unlike the long-term contracts with its customers. MG had fallen into the trap of mismatching its assets against its liabilities (see Chapter 13). Eventually, a group of German banks stepped in to rescue MG in 1994.

In the ensuing debate over the dangers posed by derivatives, some blamed these huge losses on a combination of bad luck and incompetence while others assumed that speculative-type behaviour was the culprit. In any event, central banks around the world have since tightened their supervision over such markets.

**Sources:**

J. Harding and C. Middelmann, "The Signs that Spell Danger," *Financial Times* (Derivatives), 16 November 1995, page 2.

*International Capital markets: Development, Prospects and Policy Issues* (Washington, D.C., International Monetary Fund, 1995).

R. Lapper, "Complex Jigsaw of Trade Emerging," *Financial Times*, 27 February 1995, page 2.

R. Lowenstein, "Is Corporate Hedging Really Speculative?" *Wall Street Journal*, 20 July 1995, page C1.

A. Steinherr, "Taming the Wild Beast of Derivatives," *Financial Times*, 16 December 1994, page 14.

An option is the right to buy or sell a given amount of a particular security in the cash or futures market at a particular price before a specified expiration date.[17] The right need not be exercised if the holder thinks it unprofitable to do so. The buyer of an option pays the seller for the *right* to exercise it; payment is not made until the exercise occurs. If the option is allowed to expire, the writer (seller) of the option realizes the original price, which is called the *premium.*

17 Such device is called an "American option." A "European option" permits the investor to exercise it only on the contract's expiration date.

The right to buy a financial asset is a **call option**. The specified price, known as the *call price*, includes the interest to maturity and hence is more than face value. For example, the right to buy a $1,000 bond paying 12% that matures one year from today will at least incorporate one year's interest. Hence, the call price for such a bond might be $1,000 + (0.12 × 1000) = $1120.[18]

By contrast, the right to sell a financial asset is known as a **put option**.

The price at which options are set is known as the **exercise** or **strike price**.

**FINANCIAL FOCUS 14.3: Options Prices in the Financial Press** on page 320 illustrates how options prices are presented in the financial press. The first column gives the strike price. For example, if the strike price on $1 million in Treasury bills is 9175—this implies $917,500 in terms of face value. The call option for September traded at 0.83 or 0.83% of the face value of the underlying bond.

If the asset itself trades at a strike price that is below the market price, it is said to be "in the money"—the strike price is favourable because the investor has the option of acquiring the asset below its current market value. Conversely, an option whose strike price is above the market price is said to be "out of the money"—the option is unfavourably priced for purchase. For put options, the arguments operate exactly in reverse.

A buyer of a call option is thus protected against unexpected price increases while buyers of put options are guarded against unanticipated price falls. In this way, options can be used to hedge against interest rate risk. For example, should interest rates rise significantly (implying a fall in bond prices), the lender can put the debt instrument and protect against opportunity cost. Similarly, if interest rates are expected to fall significantly, a borrower can call the bond and finance anew at a reduced interest cost. Of course, the change in the interest rate must be of a sufficient magnitude to offset the fact that options have transactions costs as well as the fact that the price of a call is above the face value of the financial asset.

Note that since a call feature works to the detriment of the lender while a put works to the advantage of the lender, the probability distribution of possible returns differs from that of an asset with no option feature. Figure 14.2 presents a hypothetical case for an option in stocks.

With no options, the probability distribution of returns for a particular stock is as portrayed by the probability distribution *OABC*. If a call option exists, the holder will exercise it whenever the spot price exceeds *z*; thus, the probability distribution of returns becomes *OGHz*. Similarly, a put option will be exercised wherever the spot price falls below *x*; thus, the probability distribution becomes *xIFC*. The probabilities at strike prices consistent with prices of *x* to *z* become

18 For simplicity, we ignore default risk in this example.

**FIGURE 14.2** Probability Distributions in the Presence of Options

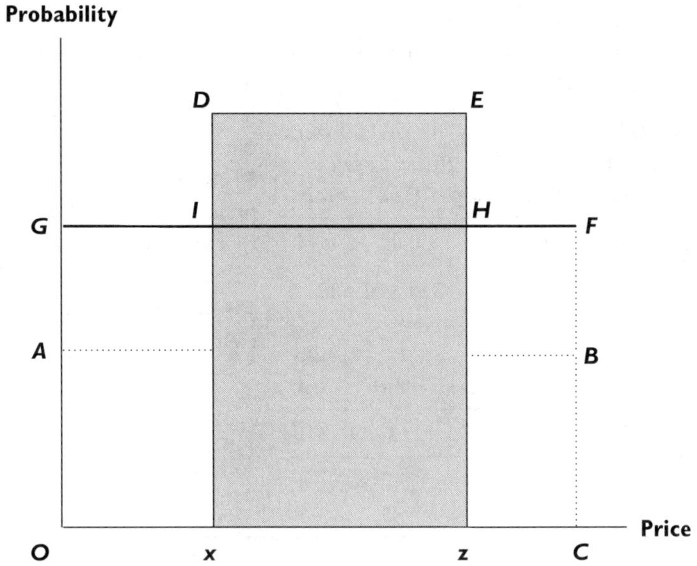


An option narrows an asset's distribution of returns and hence reduced interest rate risk. *OABC* is the probability distribution of a stock with no call or put features. If a call feature is present, any segment of the probability distribution above the strike price of z disappears. A similar effect obtains for the probability distribution of a stock with a put feature; anything below the strike price of *x* disappears. For a call, the probability distribution becomes *OGHz*, and for a put, *xIFC*.

Note: For simplicity of exposition, the probability distribution of returns is assumed to be uniform (equal probability for every price). This clearly is not the case in reality, but is done for the sake of simplicity only.

higher than they were when no options existed. Consequently, call and put options have the effect, among other things, of raising the likelihood of a price in the vicinity of the strike price. Note too, that if an investor purchases both a put and a call option simultaneously, the probability distribution becomes *xIHz*, guaranteeing a price of between *x* and *z*.[19]

19 This strategy is known as using *collars* or *range forwards*. It effectively permits investors to limit their gains and losses to some range. For example, in late 1991, many investors believed the risk of very high yields in the stock market was very small while there was more risk of yields falling below the bottom of the collar. At the end of the year, however, the return on the TSE 35 index and the Standard and Poor's 500 stock index had jumped well above the top of the collar. Investors who had not "donned the collar" did potentially very well.

## FINANCIAL FOCUS 14.3 Options Prices in the Financial Press

The financial press gives considerable information about options prices. For example,

**TREASURY BILLS — $1 million, pts of 100 pct**

| Strike | Calls: Last | | | Puts: Last | | |
|---|---|---|---|---|---|---|
| Price | Sep | Dec | Mar | Sep | Dec | Mar |
| 9175 | 0.83 | r | s | r | 0.02 | s |

**BOMBARDIER B c$15⅝ Opt vol 483**

| | Bid | Ask | Last | Vol | Op Int |
|---|---|---|---|---|---|
| Ap $12½ | 330 | 355 | 350 | 23 | 310 |

The months indicate the date of expiration of calls (right to buy) and puts (right to sell). "r" signifies that no options were traded while "s" means no options were offered. The strike price for a share of Bombardier is $12½. The stock closed ("c") at $15⅝ per share. The prices shown are for call options; prices bid and asked ranged from $3.30 to $3.55 with the last one bid at $3.50. Each option is for 100 shares so an investor would pay $350 for each contract. The contact expires in April ("Ap").

## *THE VALUE OF OPTIONS

The value of call and put options can be expressed in fairly simple terms. The value of a call at expiration can be written

$$\text{Call} = MAX\ \{0,\ S - E\} \tag{14.3}$$

where

$Call$ = value of the call at expiration
$MAX$ = maximum of the quantities in brackets
$S$ = spot price
$E$ = exercise price

The value of a call is simply the larger of the two numbers in the brackets. If the option is not exercised, its value is zero. Alternatively, if the difference between the spot and exercise prices is positive, then the option is exercised. In terms of Figure 14.2, if the spot price is greater than $z$ at expiration, the call will be exercised; otherwise, it will be allowed to expire.

The value of a put option can be expressed in a similar manner:

$$\text{Put} = MAX\ \{0,\ E - S\} \tag{14.4}$$

As described in Figure 14.2, whenever an asset's price falls below $x$ (that is, $S$ is less than $x$), $E - S$ has a positive value and the put should be exercised. Alternatively, when $E - S$ is negative the investor is better off letting the put option expire since a zero value is preferred to a negative value.

Note that equations (14.3) and (14.4) give no indication that the value of an option is a function of the particular financial health of the firm whose stock is being traded.[20] It turns out, however, that the value of an option is ultimately a function of the volatility of the stock with an available option feature.[21] (This point is perhaps obvious from the fact that the existence of an option and its value will be a function of the probability distribution of its returns, as shown in Figure 14.2.) Therefore, when investors trade in options, they are betting on the anticipated volatility of the stock.

## A NUMERICAL EXAMPLE

It is also relatively straightforward to illustrate the use of an option numerically. Consider a currency option. Suppose that a British company will require \$2,000,000 Cdn 90 days from today to pay for a shipment of goods, and that in the spot market for foreign exchange a Canadian dollar can be purchased for £0.465. Suppose too that the exercise price on a call 90 days from today is £0.50. Each option is for the purchase of \$100,000 Cdn, so the company must purchase 20 options. As we have seen, the call option will be purchased at a premium—say, £0.01 per Canadian dollar or £0.01 × 2,000,000 = £20,000. Thus, for £20,000 the UK importer in the United Kingdom can obtain \$2,000,000 Cdn 90 days from today at a cost of £1,000,000 if the option is exercised.

Clearly, the importer must be expecting the Canadian dollar to appreciate against the British pound since at the spot rate \$2,000,000 would cost only £930,000 (\$2,000,000 × £0.465). Indeed, so long as the spot rate 90 days from today is £0.50 or less, the option will not be exercised. At a £0.50 exchange rate, \$2,000,000 Cdn will cost

$$£0.50 \times \$2{,}000{,}000 = £1{,}000{,}000$$

Since the option costs £20,000, the total cost of a wait-and-see position is £1,020,000, which is what it would cost to exercise the option (\$2,000,000 × £0.50 = £1,000,000 + £20,000 = £1,020,000).[22]

---

20 It is beyond the scope of this text to consider the details.

21 It is, therefore, of considerable importance to determine the change in the value of an option when there is a small change in the value of the underlying asset in question. The resulting measure is known as the *delta* of an option or the hedge ratio.

22 In addition, of course, there is the opportunity cost of money, which we are ignoring for simplicity. Thus,

If the spot rate 90 days from today has risen to £0.55, the option will be exercised. We leave it as an exercise to complete the calculations to show why.

## OPTIONS AND FUTURES

The preceding pages have only touched upon some of the characteristics of futures and options. The variety of strategies and financial instruments covered by futures and options features is breathtaking, even though Canadian futures and options exchanges have yet to expand to the breadth of instruments offered in some US markets. Canadian options markets exist for a variety of financial assets—stock indexes, Eurodollars, foreign exchange, and precious metals, as well as commodities.

In all cases, these other options markets, although tailored to the needs and institutional arrangements of the asset or commodity concerned, essentially operate in the manner already described. The point to be emphasized is that any option requires differences in expectations about the future course of the price of an asset. Thus, an individual who believes that interest rates will rise in the future and decides to hedge against the resulting interest rate risk through a put option must encounter another investor who believes that rates will fall and is thus willing to trade away the upper end of the distribution of possible returns. Options represent a form of insurance against interest rate risk, so it is not especially surprising that they command a premium in the marketplace.

In addition, futures and options require that the underlying asset have enough price variability to provide the incentive to engage in hedging behaviour. Indeed, some people have lately questioned whether the mere existence of these instruments actually contributes to raising price volatility.

Note, finally, that options, unlike futures, leave the investor with potential for a gain while protecting against a loss. Such an advantage is obtained, however, at a considerably higher cost than the relatively small margin requirement in the futures market.

# THE IMPORTANCE OF HEDGING IN THE FINANCIAL SYSTEM

How important are hedging instruments for our financial system? It is a little difficult to measure the dollar value of futures and options since they appear as off-balance-sheet items in chartered banks' financial statements although one recent estimate put the value at \$2 trillion for Canada's financial institutions.[23]

---

if the interest rate is, say, 12%, then £20,000(0.12/4) = £20,000(0.03) = £600 is the interest cost of purchasing a 90-day option.

23 G. Ip,"Financial Firms Show \$2 Trillion on Books for Derivatives: Survey," *The Globe and Mail* (19 December 1995): p. B5.

## ECONOMICS FOCUS 14.2 Hedging and Monetary Policy: Swaps

The former Governor of the Bank of Canada, John Crow, argued that price stability—interpreted by most economists and others in the financial community as the zero inflation target—can be attained through an interest rate policy aimed at discouraging reliance on debt and thus on spending that would put pressure on prices through its impact on aggregate demand for goods and services.

It is becoming apparent, however, that in Canada and elsewhere the goals of monetary policy may be thwarted, to some extent, by the type of financial innovations described in this chapter. In the United Kingdom, the central government has, until recently, managed budget surpluses and was attempting to repay the national debt; yet it has one of the highest inflation rates in the industrialized West. Why? Some have argued the reason is that deregulation and innovation in the UK financial industry have not dampened the desire to accumulate debt despite very high interest rates.

Similar concerns were expressed in Canada. Between 1986 and 1992 the value of *swaps*, a financial instrument in which investors trade interest payments (but not debts) grew by an average of 46% per year. Similar growth has been experienced in the value of forward rate agreements (FRAs, 61% annual growth rate, again in the period 1986–92).

The mechanics of an interest rate swap can be illustrated as follows:

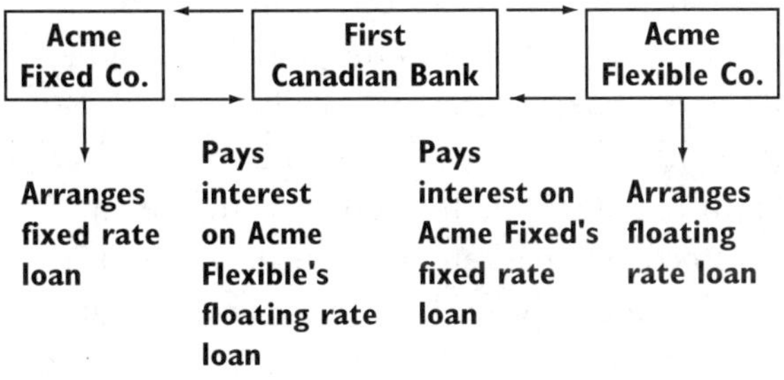


Acme Fixed Co. arranged a fixed rate loan while Acme Flexible Co. arranged for a flexible rate loan. If Acme Fixed believes interest rates will fall while Acme Flexible believes they will rise, the two firms can arrange through the First Canadian Bank to swap interest payments only. First Canadian, of course, charges a fee for arranging the swap.

Why, in the face of prime interest rates in the range of 14% to 15% during the summer of 1990, did hedged debt offset the Bank of Canada's strategy to stem spending through debt accumulation? According to an article in *The Globe and Mail*, 40% to 50% of the $210 billion outstanding short-term debt was hedged through a variety of instruments such as swaps and FRAs. Even the Bank of Canada, as the government's banker, hedged more than $4 billion of its debt.

The reasons for these developments as one person interviewed for *The Globe and Mail's* article put it, is that hedging techniques "have the effect of immunizing companies against rising rates." Nevertheless, hedging can work only for a limited time. Eventually, existing contracts expire, and if the Bank of Canada persists with higher interest rates long enough, all market participants will face high rates. Also, for every hedger there is a speculator. Consequently, for every institution or individual sheltered from interest rate risk, there is another institution or individual who is not. It is far from clear, therefore, that hedging has any lasting influence on the conduct of Canadian monetary policy insofar as it has highlighted the need for the Bank of Canada to follow a credible policy geared toward stable inflation.

**Sources:**

"The Development of Financial Derivatives Markets in Canada," *Bank of Canada Review* (Fall 1993), pp. 53–64.

"The Monetary Policy Implications of the Increasing Use of Derivative Financial Statements" Deutsche Bundsbank *Monthly Report* (November 1994), pp. 41–58.

"Rate Hedges Beginning to Worry Bank of Canada," *The Globe and Mail*, 22 May 1990.

## FINANCIAL FOCUS 14.4 Program Trading

The stock market crash of October 1987 has largely been associated with what is known as *program trading*. This is an electronic device by which investors can buy and sell blocks of stocks. In this fashion investors can build their own version of an index of stocks much like the one sold in the Toronto Futures Exchange. In the case of the 1987 episode, computers allowed investors to trade stock index futures and the stocks whose prices were incorporated into the index (for example, the TSE 35). One strategy was to sell index futures and buy the stocks in the TSE 35 when the price of the TSE index futures was sufficiently above the prices of the underlying stocks in the index.

One wonders whether this program trading really had that much influence. If stock prices reflect the market's assessment of the value of the stock, the same should be true of stock index futures. Although "noisy" traders can theoretically cause large price variations in order to take advantage of arbitrage opportunities, the reality seems doubtful since traders in futures tend to be well-informed market participants. Nevertheless, the 1987 collapse of stock prices was large enough to prompt the introduction of some restrictions in trading.

Nevertheless, the annual reports of some of Canada's largest chartered banks provide useful information (see Table 14.5). They suggest, for example, that the dollar value of hedging instruments in which banks are intermediaries is many times larger than the same banks' assets. The balance sheets of investment dealers (not shown) also reveal that hedging instruments have become an important part of our financial system. In the United States, where many of these instruments were developed, the value of hedging instruments is in the several trillions.

Banks are not the only entities that have become enamoured with derivatives. Large corporations and small businesses too have begun to use derivatives to hedge against adverse movements in interest rates and exchange rates.

Globally, the spread of hedging instruments has also been rapid. In its 1995 annual report, the Bank for International Settlements (see Chapter 21 for an analysis of this institution), estimated that by the end of 1994 the global derivatives market had risen to a combined value of approximately 12.38 trillion Cdn.[24] By 1993, 48% of derivatives instruments worldwide were traded in exchanges while the remainder were sold "over-the-counter" (OTC). Interest rate futures and options and interest rate swaps dominate these markets. By contrast, the OTC market has developed relatively faster in Canada.[25] Swaps have become so popular that in 1992 the Brazilian government agreed to swap land for $2.2 million of its debt to preserve a national park.[26]

24 See Bank for International Settlement, *65th Annual Report*, Basle, Switzerland (June 1995), pp. 184–85. The US dollar value reported was converted into Canadian dollars at $1.40C = $1 US.

25 "The Development of Financial Derivatives Markets in Canada," *Bank of Canada Review* (Fall 1993): 53–64.

26 As reported in the newspaper *The Independent*, 13 May 1992, p. 2

**TABLE 14.5** HEDGING INSTRUMENTS: THE CHARTERED BANKS IN 1995

| Interest Rate Contracts | Royal Bank (millions) | CIBC (millions) | Toronto-Dominion (millions) |
|---|---|---|---|
| Futures | 57,960 | 228,671 | 36,547 |
| Forward rate Agreements | 164,154 | 175,414 | 38,882 |
| Swaps | 334,235 | 273,442 | 159,001 |
| Options[a] | 56,928 | 129,968 | 74,302 |
| *Total* | 613,277 | 807,495 | 308,732 |
| Foreign Exchange Contracts | | | |
| Forward and futures | 537,147 | 274,425 | 3,598 |
| Swaps | 21,775 | 38,124 | 660 |
| Options | 69,577 | 51,746 | 173 |
| Equity and commodity contracts | 3,280 | 6,822 | 23 |
| *Total* | 631,779 | 371,117 | 4,454 |
| Total Derivatives | 1,245,056 | 1,178,612 | 313,186 |

[a] Purchased and written.
Sources: Annual Reports of chartered banks.

How dangerous are derivative products such as swaps to the financial system? Economists speak of "systemic risk," that is, of the risk that the credit markets and the payments system will break down if some of the parties to derivatives transactions default. A recent US study[27] suggests that there is relatively little systemic risk in the case of existing swaps because banks hedge their positions. In other words, banks avoid the risk of having to pay a fixed rate when rates are falling or floating rates when rates are rising by arranging offsetting swaps to hedge against the possibility of an adverse change in interest rates. Nevertheless, systemic risk could potentially remain a problem for other types of derivatives products. A difficulty with such products arises because the party entering into a derivative transaction is ordinarily an agent managing money for outside principals who cannot fully monitor the agent's behaviour leaving open the possibility of speculative behaviour. This type of behaviour, a reflection of the perennial problem of asymmetric information in financial markets, is especially evident in recent losses reported widely in the press (e.g., Metallgesellschaft, Orange Co. California).

27 G. Gorton and R. Rosen "Banks and Derivatives," working paper 95-07, The Wharton Financial Institutions Center (1995).

## SUMMARY

- Investors who are risk-averse wish to avoid risk. In recent decades many derivative products have been introduced to allow them to try either to shift risk or to avoid it entirely.
- Forward markets and futures markets trade financial instruments that are delivered at an agreed-upon price at an agreed-upon date in the future.
- The major difference between futures contracts and forward contracts is that investors in the former have little or no interest in taking delivery of the asset. By contrast, investors in forwards typically do wish to take delivery of the financial asset.
- Options are also a financial device for taking delivery of an asset in the future at a price determined today. The costs and benefits of holding options differ from those in either futures or forward markets.

## IMPORTANT TERMS

basis (p. 310)
call option (p. 318)
cost-of-carry (p. 314)
exercise or strike price (p. 318)
forward contracts (p. 305)
futures contracts (p. 304)
hedge ratio (p. 315)
hedging (p. 304)
long position (p. 310)
margin (p. 304)
marked-to-market (p. 310)
offset transaction (p. 305)
put option (p. 318)
short position (p. 310)
speculator (p. 304)
spot market (p. 304)
swaps (p. 303)

## EXERCISES

1. A Canadian asset holder can purchase a US security for $950 and sell it for $1,050 one year later.
   (a) What is the yield on the US security?
   (b) If the spot exchange rate is $1 today and $1.10 one year later, what will the effective yield be to the Canadian investor?
   (c) If the spot exchange rate is $1 today and $0.90 one year later, what will the effective yield be to the Canadian investor?

2. If you plan to take out a short-term loan a year from today and you expect interest rates to rise, how can you use financial futures to reduce interest rate risk?

3. Suppose that an investor will require $1 million US one year from today. The current spot exchange rate is $1.15 and the one-year forward exchange rate is $1.20. Is the Canadian dollar expected to appreciate or depreciate relative to the US dollar? Under what circumstances would it be advantageous for the investor to purchase $1 million today to be delivered one year from today?

4. In constructing Table 14.3, we ignored the role of discounting. How would interest rate considerations affect the calculation of the savings generated by buying currency in the forward market? Assume there is an interest rate of 10%.

5. An investor believes that interest rates have peaked but does not have the cash required to purchase a financial instrument today. Assuming that this investor is able to enter the futures market, would she engage in a long hedge or a short hedge?

6. Suppose the investor in question 5 is interested in a bond that sells for 71 today and for 79 two months from today in the cash market. In the futures market, a contract maturing in two months can be had for 72 today and sells for 78 in two months. If the investor buys this futures contract, what will be the gains and losses? What considerations have you ignored in making your calculations?

7. Show numerically why the currency option described on page 321 of this chapter will be exercised when the exchange rate is £0.55 for each Canadian dollar. Ignore the problem of discounting.

8. Suppose that the yield on a 90-day security is currently 10%, but you believe that it will fall to 7% in one year. Do you want to buy a call or a put option? Assume that one $1 million Treasury bill option costs $10,000 and ignore other discounting factors. Would you exercise the option if the actual yield one year from today is 8%?

9. Consider the following scenario: Current exchange rate $1.40 CDN = $1 US, current forward exchange rate $1.45 CDN = $1 US, and exchange rate forecast for spot rate one year ahead $1.43 CDN = $1 US. Now, assume that $100,000 US must be purchased by one year from today. What is the hedged cost of $100,000 US? Fill in the table below.

| After-the-fact spot exchange rate scenarios | Cost of purchasing US in the spot market | Gain or loss on forward contract |
|---|---|---|
| $1.30 | | |
| $1.40 | | |
| $1.45 | | |
| $1.50 | | |

**10.** In the example considered in Table 14.3, if interest rates on funds were 8% in Canada and 6% in the US would buying forward still make sense? Explain.

**11.** Suppose that silver sold for $8/oz in the spot market. Futures can be bought for $5.90/oz and sold for $8.45/oz. What would be the net cost of financing 10,000 oz? Explain.

**12.** Suppose that the settlement price for a Treasury bill option is 89. What is the implied yield and dollar delivery price for this instrument?

**13.** Explain how the fact that margins on derivatives are called in daily can lead to large losses.

**14.** What is the hedging ratio and why is the concept important?

**15.** Explain the logic behind equations (14.3) and (14.4).

**16.** What is the link between credibility of monetary policy and derivatives? Explain.

**17.** Explain, in broad terms, how the Barings and MG strategy in derivatives could have led to such large losses.

**18.** Explain Figure 14.2 assuming that bond return instead of stock price is measured on the horizontal axis.

**19.** The first edition of this text reported spot and forward prices for the Canadian dollar on 26 September 1990. The forward rate against US dollars to be delivered 17 September 1995 was 1.2999, the actual exchange rate was 1.3593. In hindsight, should investors have bought US dollars in 1990? Explain.

**20.** The following table gives call and put prices for some asset whose spot price is given in bold numbers.

| | 85 | 90 | 95 | 100 | 105 | 110 | 115 |
|---|---|---|---|---|---|---|---|
| Calls | 14.05 | 9.35 | 5.50 | 2.70 | 1.15 | .45 | .20 |
| Puts | .10 | .45 | 1.55 | 3.70 | 7.10 | 11.35 | 16.10 |

Suppose we believe the spot price will be 108 by expiration. What is the profit/loss for a call at 2.70 against the various spot prices given in the above table? Is the profit/loss the same if the investor is long or short? Explain.

## REFERENCES


Black, D.G. *Success and Failure of Futures Contracts: Theory and Empirical Evidence.* Solomon Brothers Center for the Study of Financial Institutions. Monograph series in Finance and Economics, no. 1. New York: Leonard N. Stern School of Business, New York University, 1986.

Black, F., and M. Scholes. "The Pricing of Options and Corporate Securities." *Journal of Political Economy* 81 (May 1973): 637–59.

Cecchetti, S.C., R.E. Cumby, and S. Figlewski. "Estimation of the Optimal Futures Hedge." *The Review of Economics and Statistics* (November 1988): 623–30.

Dubofsky, D.A. *Options and Financial Futures: Valuation and Uses.* New York: McGraw-Hill, 1992.

Edward, F.R., and C. Ma. *Futures and Options.* New York: McGraw-Hill, 1992.

Eng, M.V., F.A. Lee, and L.J. Mauer, *Global Finance.* New York: Harper Collins, 1995.

Figlewski, S., W.L. Silber, and M.G. Subrahmanyam, eds. *Financial Options: From Theory to Practice.* Homewood, Ill.: Business One Irwin, 1990.

Frankel, A.B., and J.D. Montgomery. "Financial Structure: An International Perspective." *Brookings Papers on Economic Activity* 1 (1991): 257–310.

International Monetary Fund. *International Financial Statistics, Supplement on Trade Statistics* (1988).

Isard, P. *Exchange Rate Economics.* Cambridge: Cambridge University Press, 1995.

Kolb, R.W. *Options: An Introduction.* Miami, Fl.: Kolb Publishing Co., 1991.

———. *Understanding Futures Markets*, 3d ed. Miami, Fl.: Kolb Publishing Co., 1991.

———. *Financial Derivatives,* Second Edition Cambridge, Mass.: Blackwell Business, 1996.

Leuthold, R.H., J.C. Junkers, and J.E. Cordier. *The Theory and Practice of Futures Markets.* Lexington, Mass.: Lexington Books, 1989.

Libeck, W.W. "The Origins of Futures Markets." In *The Handbook of Financial Futures*, edited by N.H. Rothstein, 9–22. New York: McGraw-Hill, 1984.

Miller, M.H. "The Last Twenty Years and the Next." *Journal of Financial and Quantitative Analysis* 2 (1986): 459–71.

Natenberg, S. *Option Volatility and Pricing* (Chicago, Ill.: Probus Publishing Co., 1994).

Ritchken, P. *Derivative Markets: Theory, Strategy and Implications.* New York: Harper Collins, 1996.

Van Horne, J.C. *Financial Market Rates and Flows,* 2d ed. Prentice-Hall: Englewood Cliffs, N.J., 1984.

Wood, J.H., and N.H. Wood. *Financial Markets.* San Diego: Harcourt, Brace, Jovanovich, 1985.

CHAPTER 15

# Understanding Interest Rates: The Structure of Interest Rates

We have considered various ways in which interest rates can be defined (Chapter 5) and have seen that returns rise with the level of risk (Chapter 13).[1] In this chapter, we reiterate the latter point by using the loanable funds framework to illustrate how risk can drive a wedge between assets that have the same maturity date. This process explains the existence of what is called the risk structure of interest rates.

Interest rates also differ with assets' term to maturity. In order to consider the role of maturity alone, we consider debt instruments that differ solely by term. What sets the term structure of interest rates? The answer has implications for whether one should believe that interest and inflation rates can be forecast.

Finally, we consider how interest rates may differ across countries. If the differentials are large enough, funds will flow across borders, giving rise to what are known as capital flows. Recent events have made international differences in interest rates an important topic for discussion.

## THE RISK STRUCTURE OF INTEREST RATES

The **risk structure of interest rates** refers to the relationship between risk and the rate of return on a financial asset. In this chapter we explore the interaction of the two factors, using, as before, a simple model of the demand for and supply of loanable funds.

Many kinds of risk exist. Rather than consider all forms of them, however, we can concentrate on one since, you will not be surprised to learn, any kind of risk influences the rate of return upward. A good and easily understood example of risk is *default risk*, which is the likelihood that the debtor will fail to pay interest,

1 Assuming one views people as generally risk-averse, a common-sense judgement.

the principal, or both by the stipulated maturity date. (The prominence of default risk in influencing rates of return stems in part from the notoriety of the once popular junk bonds; from the downturn in the fortunes of the real estate market during 1990 and 1991, which led mortgagors to foreclose on many properties; and from the spate of countries that have ceased, unilaterally in some cases, to pay interest and principal on outstanding debt.)

Since risk pushes the required rate of return upward, we expect the interest rate *spread* between a risky asset and a riskless asset to be positive and to rise with greater perceived risk. (In terms of the usual systems of bond ratings—see Table 13.1—the lower the bond rating, the greater the spread investors expect.)

A simple way to assess the inherent default risk in, say, Canadian corporate securities is to compare their yields with those of Government of Canada bonds, the latter being viewed as free from default risk.[2] Figure 15.1 plots the difference between the 90-day corporate paper rate and the yield on 90-day Treasury bills. With very few exceptions,[3] our proxy for default risk is positive as expected. Note, for example how default risk rose sharply during the two oil price shocks (1972–74, and 1978–79), as well as during the recession of 1981–82; those were the times when investors perceived corporations and their profit opportunities as being particularly weak.

Figure 15.2 illustrates how a spread arises in the market for loanable funds. We use two assets, labelled A and B, and, to make clear the relevant issues, we initially make the following simplifying assumptions: (1) wealth is constant, (2) investors can choose between two financial instruments that are both free from default risk, and (3) the demand for and supply of loanable funds are identical for the two.

Then initially, the two sets of supply and demand curves for loanable funds are identical, producing the same equilibrium interest rate for the two assets. In other words,

$$R_A = R_B$$

The reason, of course, is that we have assumed the two assets are identical in every way and that the respective demand and supply curves are also the same.

Now suppose we relax assumptions (2) and (3). Say that investors believe that the default risk for asset A has risen relative to that of asset B. Since we still assume that wealth is unchanged, we expect a portfolio reallocation to take place. Risk-averse investors will choose to hold relatively more of asset B and relatively less of asset A. The consequences of this action are shown in the right-hand side

---

2 Other forms of risk, most notably inflation risk, plague even government bonds. But the likelihood of the federal government's defaulting is almost nil—it can, after all, always print more money to pay its debts.

3 Remember, although default risk is an important variable here, it is not the only one.

## FINANCIAL FOCUS 15.1 Junk Bonds

One of the spectacular financial markets of the 1980s was the junk bonds market, whose growth and eventual disintegration was associated with the name of Michael Milken.

Junk bonds were not an innovation. They were simply low-rated bonds. Those graded are rated by a variety of services, and the so-called junk bonds are lower than BB+ by Standard and Poor's. The same bonds used to be called deep discount bonds because their price is significantly lower than for higher grade bonds; consequently, their yields are significantly higher.

What set Milken apart was his exploitation of an anomaly in the pricing of bonds. Using previous academic research, Milken exploited the apparent excessive yield on junk bonds in relation to their risk. To put the point differently, the market may have set the default rate on such bonds too high, giving rise to profitable opportunities. This apparent fact led to an explosion in the amount of debt during the 1980s, especially as a source of funds previously unavailable to many firms was now made possible.

More recent evidence about the behaviour of junk bonds also suggests that default rates do not stay constant over time. Rather, default rates peak in approximately 3 to 4 years for the lowest rated bonds (CCC according to the Dominion Bond Rating Service, see Table 13.1) and then decline thereafter. If a junk bond does not default after 10 years or so, the default rate in the United States for B-rated bonds is about half of that for C-rated bonds. The result has been called the "ticking time bomb" theory because it suggests that sometime in the future the market will be flooded with bond issues that have defaulted.

**Sources:**

C. Bruck, *The Predator's Ball: The Junk Bond Raiders and The Man Who Staked Them* (New York: Simon and Shuster, 1988).

D.B. Henriques, "Debunking the Junk 'Bomb' Theory," *New York Times*, 22 March 1992, Money section, p. 15.

of Figure 15.2: a leftward shift in the supply of loanable funds for asset A and a rightward shift in the supply of loanable funds for asset B. (Recall that the position of the supply curve for loanable funds reflects investors' desire to hold a particular financial instrument.) The net result is the creation of an interest rate *spread*, equal to $(R_A - R_B)$, so that the relatively higher return for asset A reflects compensation to investors for bearing default risk.

The greater the level of risk, the larger shifts in the supply curves and hence, the larger the spread.

# THE TERM STRUCTURE OF INTEREST RATES

Risk is not the only factor that varies among financial instruments. They also vary in their *term to maturity*, a fact that can give rise to the **term structure of interest rates**. Does it exist? Why?

Suppose we consider two securities that essentially differ only because they mature at different dates. Government of Canada bonds are good examples because they are all free from default risk and have the added advantage of being

**FIGURE 15.1** Default Risk

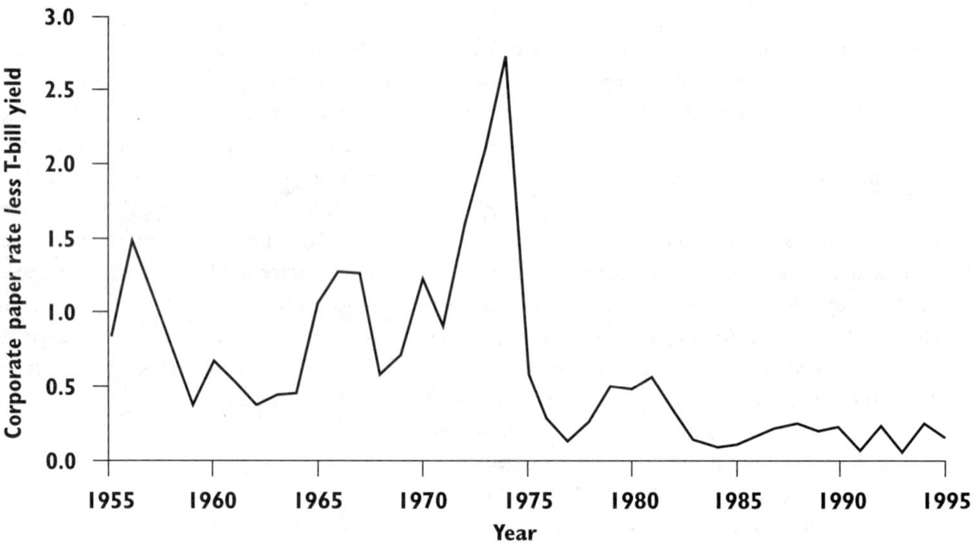


The graph traces the spread between corporate paper, which has some risk, and risk-free government securities of the same maturity. Not unexpectedly, the spread is usually positive. Notice the increase in its size during times of recession and the oil price shocks of the 1970s.

Note: Default risk is measured here as the differential between the 90-day corporate paper rate and the yield on 90-day Government of Canada Treasury bills. Annual averages were used.

Source: Statistics Canada, CANSIM database, reproduced by authority of the Ministry of Industry, 1996.

readily marketable (that is, they are *liquid*) since a large secondary market for them exists. Figure 15.3 plots the yield on two Government of Canada securities: short-term (90-day) Treasury bills and long-term (10-year or more) Government of Canada bonds. In general, the yield on the long-term bonds is higher than the yield on short-term bonds.

If instead of simply comparing the yields on two financial instruments, we plot their yields according to how many months or years in the future until maturity, we obtain what is called a **yield curve**, which is how the term structure is usually reported.

## THE EXPECTATIONS HYPOTHESIS

Why do long-term yields usually differ from short-term yields? The question is worth exploring both because it is an interesting one and because the answer can lead us to the expectations hypothesis, which many people believe to be useful in predicting interest rates, at least in the short term.

**FIGURE 15.2** The Risk Structure of Interest Rates

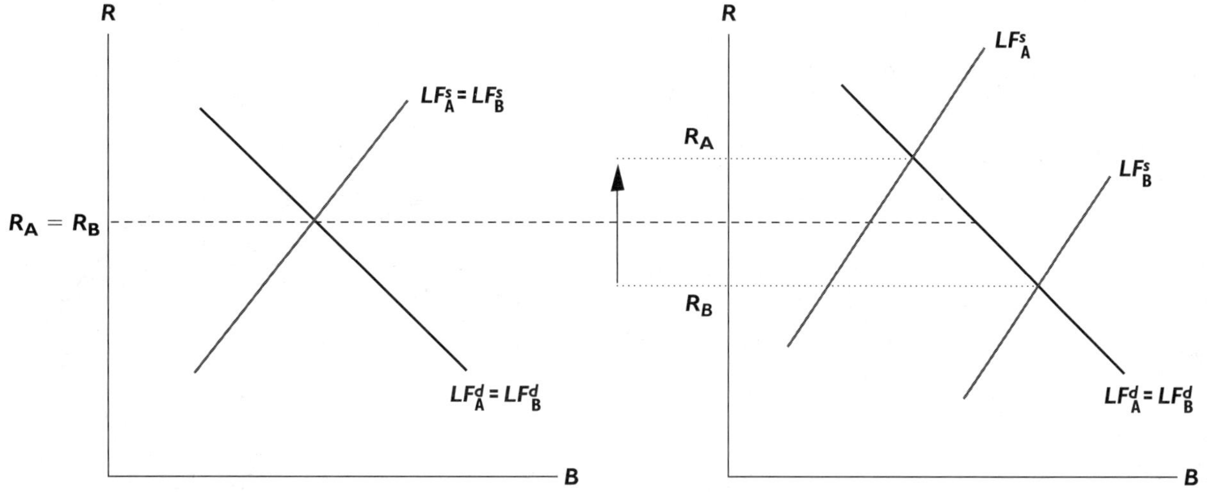


Initially (the left-hand side of the diagram), assets A and B are identical in all respects, so they produce the same equilibrium yield ($R_A = R_B$). Then the default risk for asset A rises relative to that of asset B. Risk-averse investors reallocate their portfolios so as to hold relatively more of asset B. Such a reallocation is shown in the right-hand side of the diagram as a leftward shift in the supply of loanable funds for A ($LF^s_A$) and a rightward shift in the supply of loanable funds for B ($LF^s_B$). The outcome is a spread equal to $R_A - R_B$, where $R_A > R_B$ to compensate holders of asset A for the extra risk they bear.

Since both long-term and short-term bonds are easily marketable, the choice of whether to hold one over the other does not really hinge on the question of liquidity. Rather, the investor presumably decides on the basis of which he or she expects to provide the greatest return. If the investor believes interest rates are peaking, he or she wants to hold a long-term bond because doing so will lock in funds at a high yield. Conversely, if the investor believes interest rates are bottoming out, the investor wants to hold a short-term instrument because buying a long-term one would result in being locked in at a low yield.[4]

In other words, choosing to go long or short hinges on the investor's expectations about future interest rates.[5]

4 Note that the yields being discussed are until maturity. What if the holding period differs from the term to maturity? Recall that yields move inversely with price. Although someone selling a long-term bond when interest rates are thought to have peaked out may be able to reinvest on the current wave of higher interest rates, a capital loss is incurred on the sale. Thus, if only for the ease of exposition, we deal strictly with a holding period equal to the term to maturity. It may be useful to go back to Chapter 5, Table 5.2, where a numerical example working out the connection between interest rates and prices is considered.

5 Hedging is, of course, an alternative way of dealing with the question of whether to go long or not (see Chapter 14).

**FIGURE 15.3** Long-Term and Short-Term Government of Canada Bond Yields

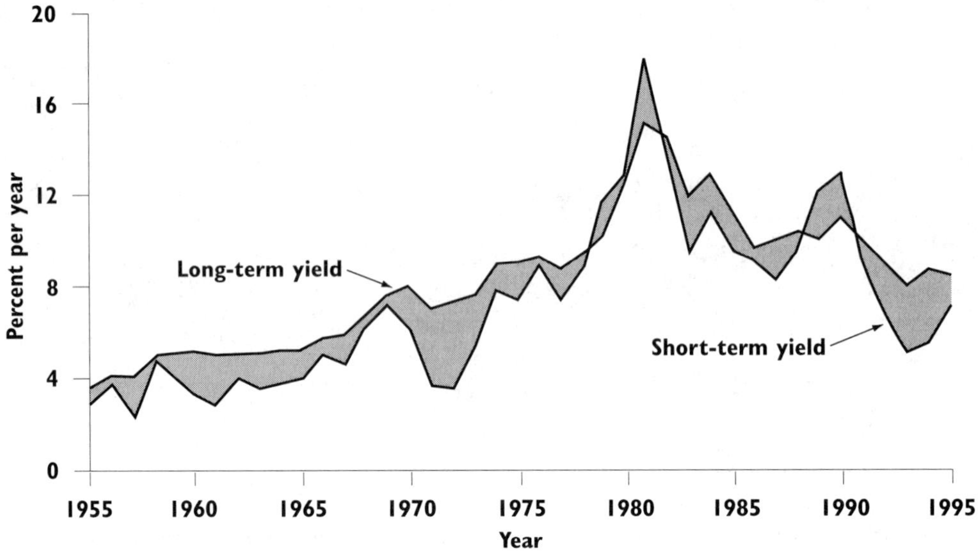


Note: The long-term interest rate is for Government of Canada bonds with a maturity of 10 years or more. The short-term interest rate is for 90-day Treasury bills. Annual averages were used.

Source: Statistics Canada, CANSIM database, reproduced by authority of the Ministry of Industry, 1996.

Before we examine the implications of this statement, let us introduce some notation to fix ideas. Let

$R_1$ = yield on a government bond maturing in 1 year
$R_2$ = yield on a government bond maturing in 2 years
$E_1^1$ = expected or anticipated yield on a 1-year government bond 1 year from today.

All yields are on an annual basis and are expressed in nominal terms.

Ignoring considerations other than term to maturity, the investor is presumably indifferent between the two 1-year bonds and the 2-year bond so long as the average yields are the same. In other words, investors are equally likely to go long as to go short if the following condition is satisfied:

$$R_1 + E_1^1 = 2R_2 \tag{15.1}$$

or, to rearrange the terms,

## FINANCIAL FOCUS 15.2 The Term Structure in the Press

*The Globe and Mail* and *The Financial Post* regularly publish the financial information necessary to construct a yield curve. Indeed, both newspapers regularly publish a plot of several yield curves. Generally, a yield curve for the most recent data is presented along with yield curves for data a month or a year ago. The *Financial Times of London* publishes yield curves for the major industrial countries.

The figures below illustrate how yield curves are constructed. The vertical axis measures yield to maturity while the horizontal axis measures the number of years to maturity. The points mark several such combinations that prevailed on 15 January 1991 and 23 February 1996. Connecting the points gives a precise idea of the link between yield and term to maturity. However, to ease interpretation, a straight line (or a curve) is usually fitted to the yield–term combinations, producing the downward-sloping line shown on the graph. Note that the yield curve between 1991 and 1996 went from being negatively sloped to displaying a positive slope.

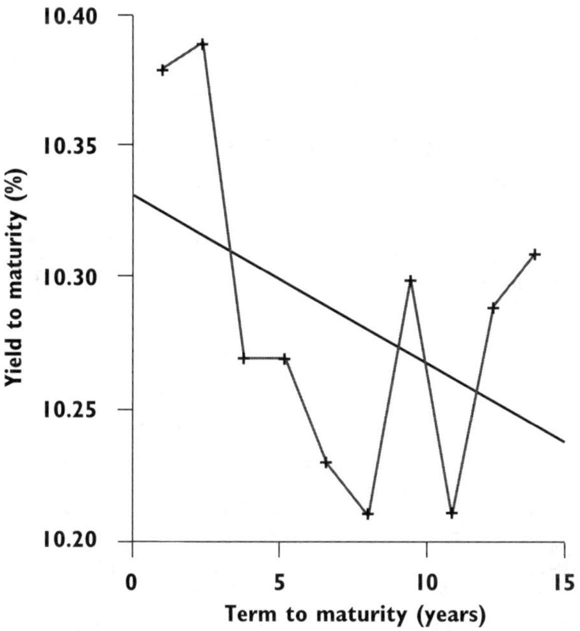


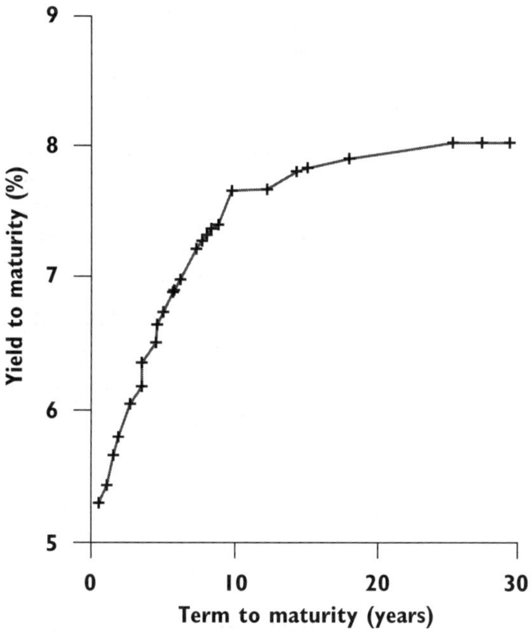


$$R_2 = \frac{R_1 + E_1^1}{2} \quad (15.2)$$

Equation (15.1) is obtained by noting that since the 2-year bond earns $\$R_2$ per year, $\$2R_2$ of interest will be earned in a 2-year period.[6] By analogy $\$(R_1 + E_1^1)$

6 To be more precise, equation (15.1) should be modified to reflect the fact that the investor who chooses to hold two 1-year bonds presumably reinvests the principal and interest after the first year. Indifference will obtain if, for each dollar invested, $(1 + R_1)(1 + E_1^1) = (1 + R_2)^2$, which, after some manipulation,

is the interest expected to be earned when the investor purchases two 1-year bonds. Consequently, an individual will be indifferent between holding the 2-year bond and two 1-year bonds if the annual return on a 2-year bond is equal to the average annual yield on two 1-year bonds.[7]

Generalization of equations (15.1) is straightforward. To keep things simple, we restrict the investor to choose either a bond with a term to maturity of $n$ years or $n$ 1-year bonds. Under these conditions, equations (15.1) can be rewritten to express the **expectations hypothesis**, which is the notion that investors are indifferent between long-term and short-term bonds so long as their average yields are the same. That is,

$$R_n = \frac{R_1 + E_1^1 + E_1^2 + \dots + E_1^{n-1}}{n} \tag{15.3}$$

where

$R_n$ = annual yield of an $n$-year government bond
$n$ = years to maturity
$E_1^2$ = expected yield on a 1-year government bond two years from today
$E_1^{n-1}$ = yield on a 1-year government bond $n - 1$ years from today.

and all other terms are as previously defined. Equation (15.3) simply states that an investor will be indifferent between going long or short so long as the annual yield on an $n$-year government bond is equal to the average of $n$ 1-year actual and expected yields.[8] Tables 15.1 and 15.2 give numerical examples of the application of equation (15.3).

What are the economic implications of equation (15.3)? If the expectations hypothesis is correct, the spread between the long-term and short-term interest

---

implies that $R_1 + E_1^1 + R_1E_1^1 = 2R_2 + R_2^2$. However, $R_1E_1^1$ and $R_2^2$ are small (for example, if $R_2 = 0.15$, $R_2^2 = 0.023$; if $R_1 = 0.12$ and $E_1^1 = 0.13$, $R_1E_1^1 = 0.016$). If we arbitrarily set both terms to zero, we obtain equation (15.2).

7 A possible objection is that although the 2-year yield is known with certainty, the average of the two 1-year yields is uncertain. We can assume away this problem by stipulating that investors are knowledgeable enough so that, on average, the expected 1-year yield is the correct forecast of future interest instruments. If one is not prepared to accept this assumption, equation (15.1)—and the entire expectations hypothesis—will not hold.

8 Restricting the investor to choosing either an $n$-year bond or $n$ 1-year bonds is done here for simplicity. Clearly, an investor could choose to hold, say, either an $n$-year bond yielding $R_n$ or an $(n - 1)$-year bond with yield of $R_{n-1}$ plus a 1-year bond with expected yield $E_1^{n-1}$. In this case, the expectations hypothesis would hold if

$$R_n = \frac{R_{n-1} + E_1^{n-1}}{2}$$

Numerous other combinations are also possible, but the central idea of the expectations hypothesis is unaffected.

**Table 15.1** THE EXPECTATIONS HYPOTHESIS: A NUMERICAL EXAMPLE

**Choose a 2-Year Bond or Two 1-Year Bonds**

| 0 | $R_2$ | 2 years |
|---|---|---|
| | Annual yield on a 2-year bond | |

| 0 | $R_1$ | 1 | $E^e_1$ | 2 years |
|---|---|---|---|---|
| | Yield on a 1-year bond | | Expected yield on a 1-year bond one year from today | |

%

| | |
|---|---|
| $R_2$ | 12 |
| $R_1$ | 10 |
| $E^e_1$ | 14 |

← By equation (15.2), (10 + 14)/2 = 12

Given an annual interest rate of 12% on a 2-year bond, an annual interest rate of 10% on a 1-year bond, and an expected annual interest rate of 14% on a 1-year bond, application of (15.2) yields an average interest rate of 12%.

rates gives investors a forecast of future short-term interest rates. For example, suppose that an investor has to decide between holding a 1-year bond and a 2-year bond. According to equation (15.2), the expectations hypothesis enables the investor to forecast the interest rate on a 1-year bond one year from today. The example in Table 15.2 shows that in the case of a choice between a 1-year and a 5-year bond, future 1-year interest rates are expected to fall one year to four years in the future.

This implicit forecasting is the reason that examining a yield curve provides such a powerful tool for investors who wish, at the very least, to find out the direction of change in short-term interest rates. Three possible yield curves are shown in Figure 15.4. Panel (A) is consistent with expectations of higher short-term interest rates because the yield curve is upward-sloping. Panel (B) indicates that investors anticipate falling short-term interest rates in the future. Panel (C) suggests short-term interest rates will remain unchanged.

## THE ROLE OF THE REAL INTEREST RATE

All the discussion so far has revolved around how nominal yields of interest rates are structured by term to maturity. Yet we know that investors should be primarily

**TABLE 15.2** THE EXPECTATIONS HYPOTHESIS: ANOTHER NUMERICAL EXAMPLE

**Choose a 5-Year Bond or Five 1-Year Bonds**

| 0 | $R_5$ | 5 years |
|---|---|---|

Annual yield on a 5-year bond

| $R_1$ | 1 | $E_1^1$ | 2 | $E_1^2$ | 3 | $E_1^3$ | 4 | $E_1^4$ | 5 years |
|---|---|---|---|---|---|---|---|---|---|
| Yield on a 1-year bond | | Expected yield on a 1-year bond one year from today | | Expected yield on a 1-year bond two years from today | | Expected yield on a 1-year bond three years from today | | Expected yield on a 1-year bond four years from today | |

| | % |
|---|---|
| $R_5$ | 12.6 |
| $R_1$ | 14 |
| $E_1^1$ | 13 |
| $E_1^2$ | 12.5 |
| $E_1^3$ | 12 |
| $E_1^4$ | 11.5 |

← By equation (15.3), $(14 + 13 + 12.5 + 12 + 11.5)/5 = 12.6$

| | % |
|---|---|
| $R_1$ | 14 |
| $E_1^1$ | 13 |
| $E_1^2$ | 12.5 |
| $E_1^3$ | 12 |
| $E_1^4$ | 11.5 |

→ By equation (15.3) →

| | % |
|---|---|
| $R_2$ | 13.5 |
| $R_3$ | 13.2 |
| $R_4$ | 12.9 |
| $R_5$ | 12.6 |

**Summary**

| Term to Maturity | 1 | 2 | 3 | 4 | 5 |
|---|---|---|---|---|---|
| Yield to Maturity | 14.0 | 13.5 | 13.2 | 12.9 | 12.6 |

In this table, equation (15.3) is applied. For example, if we are given annual interest rates on bonds maturing in one to five years ($R_1$, $R_2$, $R_3$, $R_4$, $R_5$) the equation allows us to solve for expected interest rates on 1-year bonds two to five years into the future.

**FIGURE 15.4** Hypothetical Yield Curves

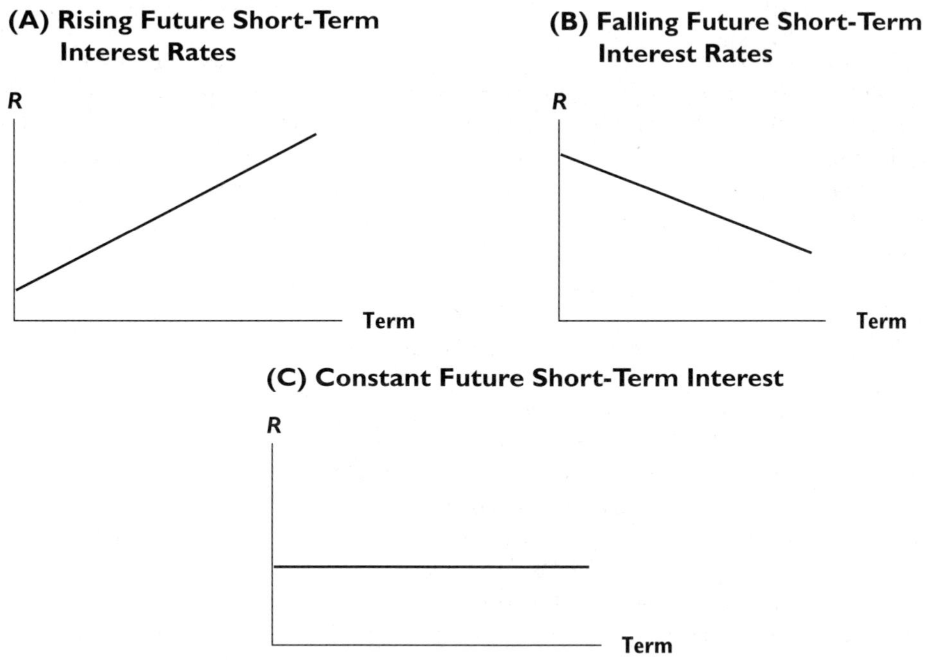


An upward-sloping yield curve (panel (A)) means that short-term interest rates are expected to rise, so the long-term interest rate will be higher than the short-term interest rate. The opposite is true for the yield curve in panel (B). Rates are expected to remain unchanged when the yield curve is flat (panel (C)).

influenced by the real interest rate. Does the expectations hypothesis have anything to say in this regard? The answer is a qualified yes. Recall the Fisher effect: the nominal interest rate, $R$, is the sum of the real interest rate, $\rho$, and expected inflation, $\pi^e$. That is,

$$R = \rho + \pi^e \tag{15.18}$$

which is reproduced here from Chapter 5 for convenience. If we now assume that the real interest rate is constant, we can rewrite it as

$$R = \overline{\rho} + \pi^e \tag{15.4}$$

where $\overline{\rho}$ = constant real interest rate. Since a constant, by definition, does not change, equation (15.4) says that any change in the nominal interest rate must be the result of a change in expected inflation. In other words, the change in the nominal interest rate equals the change in expected inflation:

$$\Delta R = \Delta\pi^e \tag{15.5}$$

## ECONOMICS FOCUS 15.1 How Accurate Is the Expectations Hypothesis?

Strictly speaking, most studies find little statistical evidence that yield spreads behave in the way predicted by the expectations hypothesis as developed in this chapter. Yet the expectations hypothesis remains an attractive theory because it is readily testable with actual data and because there are some features about the behaviour of the term structure that can be reasonably well understood within the expectations hypothesis framework.

First, recall that the discussion in this chapter abstracted from default risk. Yet even government bonds are plagued by other risks, such as those of liquidity and inflation. It has also been implicit in our discussion that investors form "rational" views about, say, future inflation—that is, they have all economic information available, process it effectively, and use it to form their forecasts of future inflation. Again, the expectations hypothesis may fail if expectations turn out to be less than rational. Finally, there may be "noise" in the relationship between short-term and long-term rates so that the links are not exact in a numerical sense, but rather show a tendency toward the results derived in this chapter.

The scenario depicted in Figure 15.5(B) stems, in part, from Fama's and Mishkin's recent evidence on the expectations hypothesis and the term structure. Mishkin finds that for the United States and several other countries, the term structure provides good forecasts about real interest rates for maturities of roughly six months or less and good forecasts of inflation for maturities of up to five years. These results do not, however, carry over to other countries, except perhaps Canada. Fama also uses US data and finds that for maturities of, say, longer than a year the term structure provides good forecast of nominal interest rates. At shorter maturities, the expectations hypothesis provides information about real interest rates but not nominal interest rates. Thus, attempts at manipulating the yield curve, as in Figure 15.5(B) should be viewed critically. Nevertheless, at least one study (Estrella and Hardouvelis) suggests that the slope of the yield curve can be a good predictor of future economic activity. Campbell, again using US data, finds that higher long-term rates are associated with rising short-term interest rates and points out that an understanding of the yield curve is vital in answering questions such as whether governments should borrow long or short. Nevertheless, he points out that, at times, yield curves seem too steep by the standards of the expectations hypothesis.

**Sources:**

J.Y. Campbell, "Some Lessons from the Yield Curve," *Journal of Economic Perspectives* 9 (Summer 1995): 129–52.

A. Estrella and G.A. Hardouvelis, "The Term Structure as a Predictor of Real Economic Activity," *Journal of Finance* 46 (June 1991): 555–76.

E.F. Fama, "Term-Structure Forecasts of Interest Rates, Inflation, and Real Returns," *Journal of Monetary Economics* 25 (1990):59–76.

A. Melino, "The Term Structure of Interest Rates: Evidence and Theory," *Journal of Economic Surveys* 2 (1988): 335–66.

F.S. Mishkin, "A Multi-Country Study of the Information in the Term Structure About Future Inflation," *Journal of International Money and Finance* 10 (1991): 2–22.

———, "What Does the Term Structure Tell Us About Future Inflation?" *Journal of Monetary Economics* 25 (1990): 77–95.

Now, suppose that, as before, the investor is considering buying a 1-year or a 2-year bond. In nominal terms, the spread between the two yields is

$$R_2 - R_1$$

In terms of equation (15.4), however, the spread could instead be written

$$(\bar{\rho} + \pi_2^e) - (\bar{\rho} + \pi^e{}_1) \tag{15.6}$$

where $\pi_1^e$ and $\pi_2^e$ are expected annual inflation rates over one- and two-year horizons, respectively. However, since the constant real interest rates cancel each other, equation (15.6) becomes

$$\pi_2^e - \pi_1^e = \Delta\pi^e \tag{15.6a}$$

Equation (15.6a) simply says that the term structure conveys information about changes in expected future inflation, $\Delta\pi^e$, by term to maturity.[9]

If the term structure provides information about the future course of inflation anticipated by investors, what are the implications? We consider two examples, both of which are illustrated in Figure 15.5.

What happens to the yield curve when there is a sudden and permanent increase in expected inflation? According to the Fisher effect (see also equation (15.5)), the nominal interest rate rises by the increase in expected inflation.[10] Moreover, since the expectations hypothesis links interest rates across the term structure, *all* yields rise by the change in expected inflation. Thus, the spread between long-term and short-term interest rates stays the same, but all nominal interest rates rise by the increase in expected inflation. Figure 15.5(A) illustrates this result with an upward shift in the yield curve from $YC^1$ to $YC^2$.

Now consider the scenario illustrated in Figure 15.5(B). Suppose the monetary authorities—here the Bank of Canada—believe that higher inflation is looming in the future (perhaps from world events beyond Canada's control). But investors appear unconvinced since they expect lower inflation in the future, given the downward-sloping yield curve $YC^1$. To ensure that investors' future inflation expectations are met, the Bank of Canada drives up short-term interest rates,[11] producing a kinked yield curve, $YC^2$, that eventually meets the original yield curve at some unspecified term to maturity. Since investors' expectations of inflation are unchanged, what must have happened? According to equation (5.16), if $\pi^e$ remains unchanged, the change in short-run nominal interest rates, $\Delta R$, can be explained only by a change in the real interest rate, $\Delta\rho$. Then, consumption

9 Note, however, that this result hinges on the assumption of a constant real interest rate. As we discussed in Chapter 5, this assumption may be a dubious one.

10 According to the discussion in Chapter 6, there will be a *temporary* change in the real interest rate. We return to this point below. For the moment, however, assume that the change in the nominal interest rate is instantaneous.

11 The most likely reason for the Bank to want to ensure that expectations are met is that it wishes to be perceived as credible, trustworthy, and clearly in charge of monetary policy.

**FIGURE 15.5** The Term Structure and Inflation: Two Examples

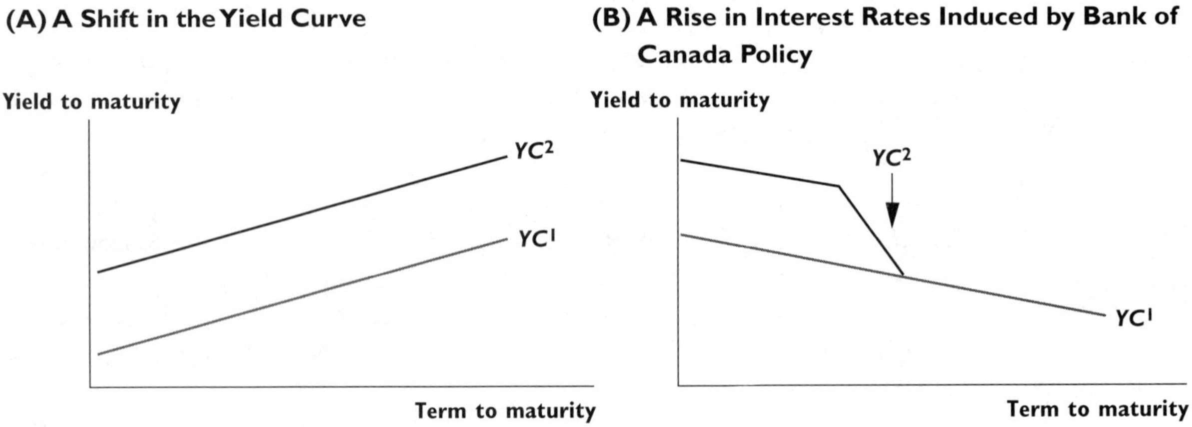


In panel (A), the Fisher effect operates to make all nominal yields rise with a permanent rise in expected inflation. The yield curve thus shifts from $YC^1$ to $YC^2$. In panel (B) short-term inflationary expectations remain unchanged, but the Bank of Canada is determined to dampen the possibility of higher future inflation. By raising short-term yields, it raises the real interest rate, again via the Fisher effect. The result is the kinked yield curve $YC^2$.

spending might fall, dampening the likelihood that inflation will be higher than future levels currently expected by investors.

A scenario of this kind has often been painted to explain the Bank of Canada's drive, particularly during 1990 and again in late 1994 and early 1995, toward attaining its zero-inflation goal.[12] Indeed, at times yield curves in the financial press closely resembled the ones shown in Figure 15.5(B).[13] By the summer of 1992, yield curves had become very steep and would remain that way for some time,[14] a reflection of the concern about future prospects for inflation in light of ballooning combined deficits at the federal and provincial levels and concerns

12 Success for the Bank's objectives requires meeting a number of other conditions, including (1) that its views are credible—that is, that the public believe in the Bank's objectives and in its ability to carry them out, and (2) that its policy is consistent with the federal government's fiscal policy. Clearly, if the federal government pursues an inflationary policy, Bank of Canada attempts to stem inflation in the future by raising real interest rates now are doomed to failure.

13 Alternatively, the kink in the yield curve depicted in the figure can be explained by a short-run spurt in anticipated inflation—for example, due to a temporary increase in oil prices—while longer-term inflation rates are expected to fall.

14 In the United States the spread between long-term and short-term rates reached historically high levels. See T.T. Vogel, Jr., "Steepest-Ever Yield Curve May Mean It's Time to Invest," *Wall Street Journal*, 20 July 1992, CI. A similar story applies to Canadian spreads.

over Canadian unity. These examples illustrate the usefulness and the uses of the yield curve as a tool of policy analysis.

## COMPETING VIEWS OF THE TERM STRUCTURE

Although the expectations hypothesis appears to provide a simple but powerful tool for forecasting future interest rates and inflation and for understanding some central bank policies, it faces several objections from academic studies that have attempted to gauge its empirical validity, as well as from competing theories of the term structure, which are illustrated in Figure 15.6.

### The Liquidity Premium Theory

Figure 15.6(A) illustrates the potential effect of a liquidity premium on the yield curve. The market for long-term bonds is "thinner"—that is, long-term bonds are likely to be less marketable—than that for short-term bonds. Therefore, investors who hold long-term bonds may expect a **liquidity premium**—an additional yield for accepting their relatively lower liquidity. If the degree of liquidity or marketability falls with a rise in the term to maturity, as shown by *LP* in Figure 15.6(A), the observed yield curve will provide incorrect information about investors' expectations of future interest rates. For example, the yield curve consistent with the expectations hypothesis may, in fact, be flat, implying that interest rates are expected to be constant in the future.

One difficulty with this explanation is that the link between the liquidity premium and the term to maturity may not be as depicted in Figure 15.6(A).

### Market Segmentation and Preferred Habitat Views

Another view about the relationship between short-term and long-term interest rates is shown in Figure 15.6(B), which depicts separate loanable funds diagrams for short-term and long-term bonds. In the "pure" **market segmentation** view of interest rate determination, the markets for short-term and long-term bonds are segregated, and there is no substitution between the two kinds of instruments. This separation of the markets may in part be explained by the fact that some investors show a distinct preference for short-term or for long-term bonds, perhaps because one type of risk (for example, inflation risk) is their sole determinant in choosing an asset, while another type of risk (for example, income risk) is all that matters to other investors. In other words, shifts in, say, the supply of loanable funds in one market have no impact on shifts in the supply of loanable funds in another market. Therefore, the spread between long-term and short-term interest rates reflects conditions purely local to a particular market.

**FIGURE 15.6** Other Views about the Term Structure

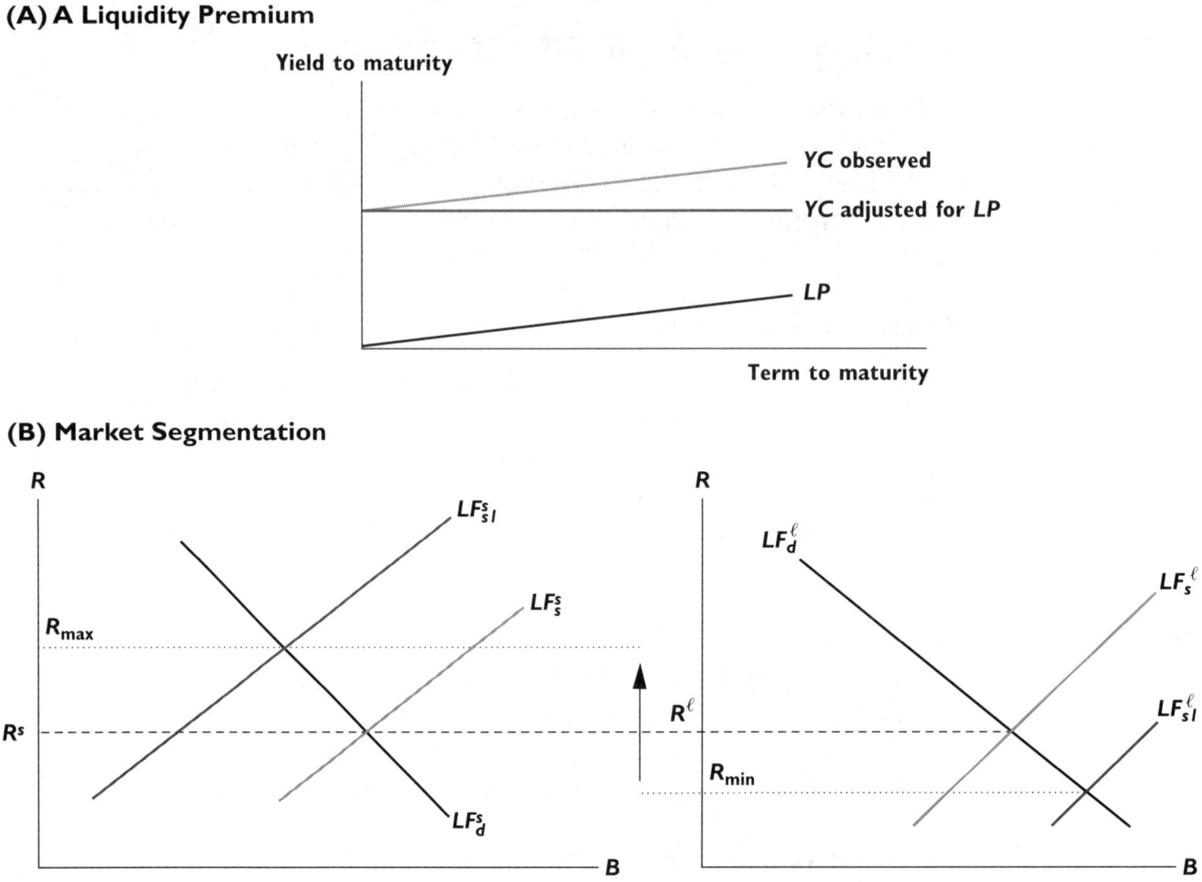


In panel (A), long-term bonds earn a liquidity premium, *LP*, because they are less marketable than short-term bonds. This gives rise to the distinction between an observed yield curve, "*YC* observed," and a yield curve that would obtain under the expectations hypothesis, "*YC* expected."

In panel (B), short-term and long-term bonds (labelled with the superscripts s and ℓ) are viewed as being distinct. In the extreme, there is no substitutability between the two. As the degree of substitutability increases, the spread between the short-term and long-term interest rates begins to reflect the movement of funds (here, from short-term to long-term). Overall, however, the spread has less significance in the market segmentation hypothesis than in the expectations hypothesis.

A similar but less rigid view is the **preferred habitat** view of the term structure. Its proponents see some substitutability between the long and short ends of the market but believe particular investors have a preference for certain maturities. The investors' willingness to leave their "preferred habitat" depends on the size of a term premium—an additional yield for accepting a less preferred term. If the term premium is large enough, investors who would otherwise prefer to go short will purchase long-term bonds. The relationship linking short-term and long-term rates is the same as under the expectations hypothesis except that a term premium is added.

The preferred habitat hypothesis might explain why yield curves are sometimes very steeply sloped at the short-term end of the maturity structure. At such times, a substantial term premium is required to induce investors to hold long-term bonds even if short-term yields are quite low. Figure 15.6(B) could then be viewed as illustrative of the potential term premium that would be observed if there was perfect substitutability between the two markets. Clearly, however, the objective of the preferred habitat view is to treat the short and long ends of the bond market as being somewhat but not completely distinct from each other.

## INTERNATIONAL LINKAGES IN THE TERM STRUCTURE

So far our analysis of risk and the term structure has been confined to *domestic securities*—debt instruments denominated in Canadian dollars—and hence it has been limited to the Canadian economy. That analysis would be sufficient if Canada existed in a world of its own. It is, however, a small, open economy in a world of increasing *globalization*. Capital funds can cross its borders freely, a phenomenon called **capital mobility**, which can influence and be influenced by international differences in exchange rates.

When investors purchase bonds and other financial instruments denominated in foreign currencies they open themselves to *foreign exchange* risk.

Consider then an investor who has to choose between investing in a 1-year Government of Canada bond or a 1-year US Treasury bill. The yield on the Canadian bond is 10% while the yield on the US security is 8%. Is the Canadian investment, with its higher interest rate, automatically the best one? The answer depends on the difference between the Canadian–US dollar exchange rate today versus the one that will prevail one year from today.[15] Alternatively, the answer depends on the difference between the Canadian–US dollar yield today and the foreign exchange rate bought forward one year (including any adjustments for transactions costs). Let us consider each strategy in turn.

If the investor buys either asset today and plans to wait until it matures and then put the proceeds into Canadian dollars, the investor must make a calculation

15 Throughout the following discussion, we will suppose that a system of perfectly flexible exchange rates prevails. Although this assumption is not entirely realistic (see Chapter 7), it allows us to focus on the link between exchange rates and interest rates.

about the implicit **forward exchange rate**, which is the future exchange rate that would make him or her indifferent between holding Canadian and US securities for that amount of time.[16]

Each dollar invested in Canada will yield \$1.10 one year from today since

$$\$1 \times (1 + R) = \$1 \times (1.10) = \$1.10$$

If the investor chooses the US-dollar-denominated investment, each dollar will yield \$1.08 one year later since

$$\$1 \times (1 + R) = \$1 \times (1.08) = \$1.08$$

But that return is still in US dollars. To compare the two returns, the investor has to apply exchange rates. The purchase will be at today's spot exchange rate. Suppose it stands at \$1.38. One Canadian dollar will buy roughly \$0.72 US (= \$1.00 Cdn/\$1.38). But the spot exchange rate for a year from today is not known, so the investor must calculate the implicit forward rate. The solution is obtained as follows:

| Return per Canadian Dollar after 1 Year | = | Return per Canadian Dollar after 1 Year Invested in the United States | × | Implicit Forward Exchange Rate |
|---|---|---|---|---|

$$\$1 \times (1.10) = \left(\frac{\$1}{\$1.38}\right)(1.08)(e^f)$$

The left-hand side of the equality is simply the Canadian-dollar return after one year invested at 10% in the Government of Canada bond. The first term in the right-hand side shows the amount of US dollars that can be purchased for each Canadian dollar at a spot exchange rate of \$1.38, and the second is simply the US return after one year. The only unknown is $e^f$ which represents the 1-year implicit forward exchange rate necessary to equate the yields on the Canadian and US investments.

Solving our equation for $e^f$, we obtain \$1.41 since

$$\left(\frac{\$1}{\$1.38}\right)(1.08) \times \$1.41 = \$1.10$$

Notice that if the Canadian dollar is expected to depreciate, what is lost in terms of the yield difference between the US and Canadian investments (10% − 8% = 2%) is recovered because more Canadian dollars will be obtained in the future for each US dollar held today. We can write this result more generally as

16 In what follows, we abstract from transactions costs.

$$\frac{(1 + R)}{(1 + R^f)} = \frac{e^f}{e^s} \tag{15.7}$$

where

$R$ = annual yield on a Canadian-dollar-denominated asset
$R^f$ = annual yield on a foreign-denominated asset
$e^f$ = 1-year implicit forward exchange rate
$e^s$ = spot exchange rate

Equation (15.7) allows one to compute any implicit forward exchange rate, one that makes the investor indifferent between holding an asset denominated in Canadian dollars and one denominated in any foreign currency. We can also rearrange equation (15.7) to solve for the implicit forward rate to obtain

$$e^f = \left[\frac{(1 + R)}{(1 + R^f)}\right] e^s \tag{15.8}$$

We have already seen (Chapter 14) that a forward transaction can be used to hedge against foreign exchange risk. By hedging foreign exchange risk and investing in a foreign currency, one is engaging in what is known as *covered interest arbitrage.* Quotes for forward exchange rates for a variety of maturities are readily available in the financial press. To continue our example, say the 1-year forward rate is \$1.39. What is the significance of the difference between this rate and the implicit forward exchange rate of \$1.41? It means that the 2% interest rate differential is not entirely covered by the differential between the spot and forward exchange rates since, by equation (15.7), we obtain

$$\frac{1.39}{1.38} < \frac{1.10}{1.08}$$

or

$$1.01 < 1.02$$

Therefore, *if the market is correct*, our US investment will yield less than the Canadian investment.

Conversely, if the actual implicit forward rate were, say, \$1.42, there would be added profit in the US investment since, again according to equation (15.7),

$$\frac{1.42}{1.38} > \frac{1.10}{1.08}$$

or

$$1.03 > 1.02$$

Presumably, the market will quickly notice any such profit opportunities and act on them until the differential is eliminated. But for those lucky investors who are able to benefit from such investment strategies, this is the essence of **covered interest arbitrage**, which means the purchase and sale of assets denominated in different currencies to generate a profit on potential changes in exchange rates.

The implication, however, is that the covered interest arbitrage is only a temporary phenomenon. Real-world data confirms the point. Ideally, the covered interest differential should be about zero or, at least, average close to zero over a period of time. Indeed, statistically speaking, the average has been close to zero since 1970, although there were persistent departures after 1978.[17]

If we regard the case in which arbitrage opportunities are no longer present as an equilibrium condition, this implies what is known as the **interest rate parity** condition. If the actual and implicit forward exchange rates provide the investor with information about what the market expects exchange rates to be in the future, and if this information is correct on average, the interest rate parity condition is simply

| | | | | |
|---|---|---|---|---|
| Canadian Dollar Interest Rate | = | Foreign Interest Rate | + | Expected Percentage Change in the Exchange Rate |

or, using the notation introduced earlier,

$$R = R^f + \left(\frac{e^{exp} - e^s}{e^s}\right) \tag{15.9}$$

where $e^f = e^{exp}$. That is, the forward exchange rate, $e^f$, proxies the expected exchange rate, $e^{exp}$, at maturity.

Equation (15.9) follows from equations (15.7) and (15.8). We can verify the point by using our hypothesized numerical values:

$$10\% = 8\% + \left(\frac{1.41 - 1.38}{1.38}\right)$$

$$10\% = 8\% + 2\%$$

Thus, in our numerical example, investors are indifferent between the US and Canadian investments so long as the Canadian dollar is expected to depreciate relative to the US dollar. While such an equality holds as an equilibrium condition, arbitrage is possible as the markets seek equilibrium. Empirical research suggests that equation (15.9) is a good approximation for Canadian and US data.[18]

---

17 Roughly speaking, after the Bank of Canada expressed public concern over exchange rate fluctuations and apparently began to try to manage them. See, for example, P. Howitt, *Monetary Policy in Transition: A Study of Bank of Canada Policy, 1982–85* (Montreal: C.D. Howe Institute, 1986), chapter 6.

18 See A.W. Gregory, "Testing Interest Rate Parity and Rational Expectations for Canada and the United

## ECONOMICS FOCUS 15.2 What Is Arbitrage?

*Arbitrage* comes from the French word "arbitre" (referee) and refers to the fact that markets act as a referee of sorts in influencing prices. Indeed, as explained in this chapter, market participants will, by their actions, quickly exploit profitable opportunities, whether they be available in one location or in different locations. In the examples considered in this chapter, arbitrage profits can arise from the sale and purchase of assets that match (that is, in term to maturity and risk characteristics) but are denominated in different currencies in order to obtain a profit until the interest rate parity condition takes hold.

Typically, arbitrage opportunities in the market for foreign exchange arise when the value of two currencies in relation to a third are inconsistent. For example, if the Canadian dollar is quoted at $1.38 in terms of the US dollar and $.0128 per Japanese yen, one would expect that a US dollar could be purchased for ¥107.27, ignoring transactions costs (see Chapter 7, Table 7.1). If this is not the case, profitable opportunities exist to sell one currency for another in order to buy a third currency.

The market for foreign exchange adjusts so quickly to any such discrepancies, however, that they are very difficult to detect and disappear quickly. This does not prevent the search for new ways to seek profit in foreign-exchange markets. Recent forecasting techniques rely on mathematical models of "chaos." These models try to find patterns in data that appear to behave in a chaotic fashion. But even if such models provide new arbitrage opportunities, they are far from perfect. Occasionally there is no substitute for a trader's experience in currency markets. Moreover, as we saw in Chapter 7, exchange rates are prone to "over-shooting"; that is, they change sharply when there is a change in the interest rate differential but fairly quickly return to equilibrium slowly. Various other inefficiencies have also been reported.

**Sources:**

R.L. Hudson, "Currency Traders' Computers Improve," *Wall Street Journal*, 25 September 1992, p. A5.

H. Riehl and R. Rodriguez, *Foreign Exchange and Money Markets: Managing Foreign and Domestic Currency Operations* (New York: McGraw-Hill, 1977), chapter 8.

"In Search of Inefficiency," *The Economist*, 5 September 1992, p. 81.

Table 15.3 also suggests that interest rate parity is a reasonable approximation of reality in many instances. The annual yields on 3-month Eurodeposit rates denominated in four different currencies, selected at random, are listed along with the relevant spot and 3-month forward exchange rates and the differential with the US yield. In every case, the expected appreciation of the US dollar is approximately the same as the differential.

Note too in the table that the US yield is less than the yields in the other currencies: the US dollar is expected to appreciate in value relative to the other currencies listed. Changes in interest rates quickly show up in the market for foreign exchange as an expected depreciation or appreciation of a particular

States," *Canadian Journal of Economics* 20 (May 1987): 289–305; P. Boothe, "Interest Parity, Cointegration, and the Term Structure in Canada and the United States," *Canadian Journal of Economics* 24 (August 1991): 595–603.

**Table 15.3** A CASE STUDY OF INTEREST RATE PARITY: EURODEPOSITS

| | (1) 3-Month Eurodeposit Rate | (2) Spot Exchange Rate | (3) 3-Month Forward Exchange Rate | (4) Interest Rate Differential | (5) Expected Appreciation US dollar |
|---|---|---|---|---|---|
| US dollar | 6.56 | — | — | — | — |
| Canadian dollar | 10.06 | 1.1600 | 1.1705 | −3.50 | 3.62 |
| Deutschmark | 9.00 | 1.4633 | 1.4702 | −2.44 | 2.42 |
| Japanese yen | 8.06 | 130.63 | 131.09 | −1.50 | 1.40 |

Note: The exchange rates (defined as the quantity of the foreign currency per US dollar) in columns (2) and (3) are vis-à-vis the US dollar, and column (4) is the difference between the US yield and that in other currencies. Column (5) is the percentage difference between columns (3) and (2) converted to an annual basis. For example, the expected appreciation of the Canadian dollar Eurodeposit is calculated as

$$\left[\frac{(1.1705 - 1.1600)}{1.1600}\right] \times 400 = 3.62$$

(Note that an appreciation of the US dollar is the same as a depreciation of the Canadian dollar relative to the US dollar. Note too that the conversion of a 90-day rate to a yearly rate is accomplished by multiplying the term in square brackets by 400.)

currency. Therefore, foreign interested rates need have no lasting influence on Canadian interest rates so long as: (1) exchange rates float freely, and (2) there is considerable capital mobility—which is also known as the condition of internationally integrated markets.

Clearly, both conditions are violated from time to time but apparently not in a systematic fashion. The illustrations suggest that the foreign exchange market is fairly efficient. It may also be helpful, by way of a summary, to graphically illustrate the connection between exchange rates and returns expressed in different currencies.

Figure 15.7(A) shows the relationship between relative returns and the exchange rate. For a given domestic interest rate ($R$), the foreign interest rate is inversely related to the exchange rate. Why? Because, according to equation (15.9), if we hold constant the left-hand side ($R$), then the two right-hand-side terms must be inversely related. When no exchange rate appreciation or depreciation is expected then interest rates in two countries should be the same ($R=R^f$ in terms of equation 15.9). This occurs at the intersection of the $R$ and $R^f$ curves. If the Canadian dollar is expected to depreciate vis-à-vis the US dollar then US interest rates can be lower than Canadian rates and still satisfy the interest rate parity equation (15.9). This occurs to the right of the intersection of the $R$ and $R^f$ curves.

**FIGURE 15.7** A Diagrammatic Exposition of Interest Rate Parity

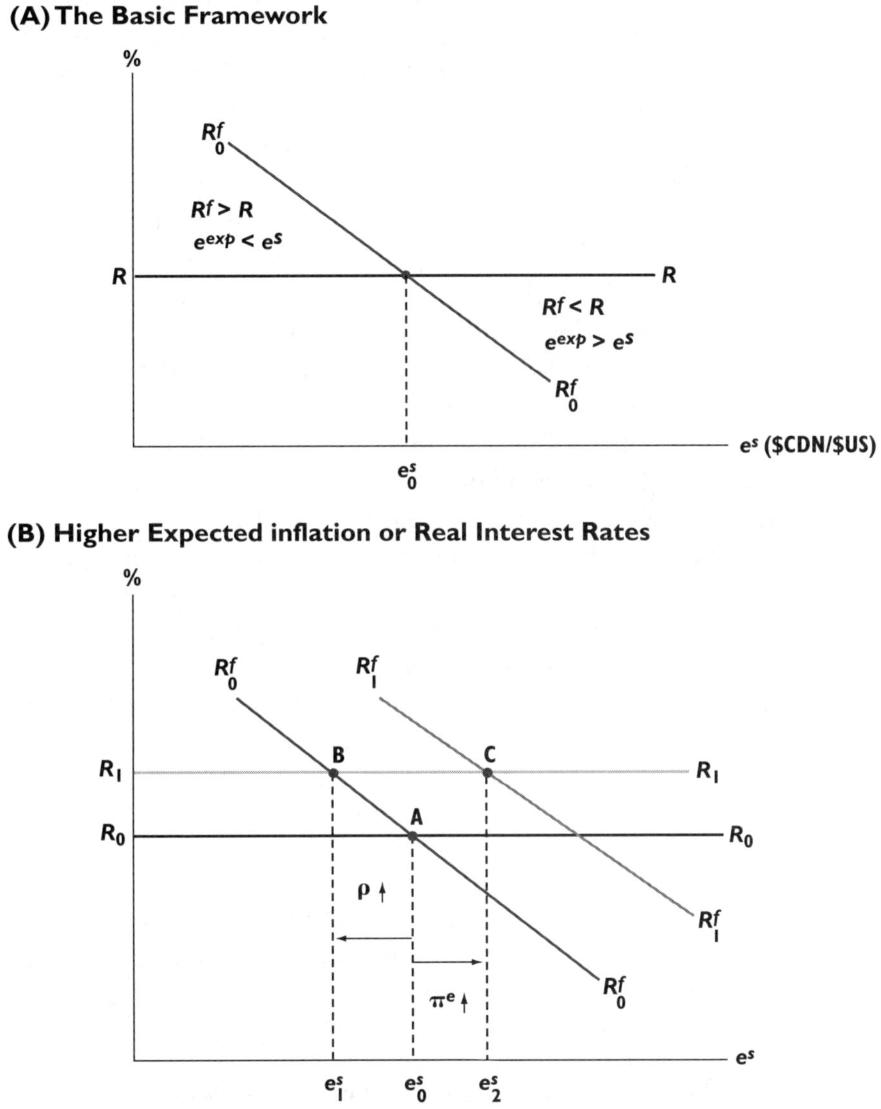


Panel (A) illustrates equation (15.9) in a diagrammatic fashion. For a given domestic interest rate, *R*, the foreign interest rate, *Rf*, is inversely related to the exchange rate. A depreciated exchange rate means that Canadian rates have to rise for foreign holders of Canadian dollars or to prevent outflows of Canadian investments to the US. Panel (B) illustrates what happens to the exchange rate when the Canadian real interest rate rises or when the Canadian expected inflation rate rises. In both cases, the Canadian nominal interest rate rises but with quite different implication for the exchange rate. A higher real interest rate leads to an appreciation of the Canadian dollar because Canadian investments are relatively more attractive while a rise in Canadian expected inflation has the opposite effect which leads, therefore, to a depreciation of the Canadian dollar.

Conversely, an expected appreciation will mean higher US interest rates relative to Canada. This framework is also useful because it can help us understand the impact of, say, an increase in expected inflation or the real interest rate. These cases are illustrated in Figure 15.7(B). Starting from the initial equilibrium position at point A, suppose that the real interest rate rises in Canada. This means, according to the Fisher equation (recall from Chapter 5: $R = \rho + \pi^e$, where $\rho$ is the real interest rate and $\pi^e$ is the expected inflation rate), that domestic nominal interest rates will rise. This is illustrated by the upward shift in the $R$ curve to $R_1$ from $R_0$. The result is an appreciation of the Canadian dollar as shown by point B. This should not be surprising since a higher Canadian real interest rate means that Canadian returns are more attractive than US investments. If, on the other hand, the rise in the Canadian nominal interest rate were due to higher expectations of inflation in Canada then, again according to the Fisher equation, this would translate into a *lower* real interest rate which would mean that capital would flow out of Canada into the US raising the foreign interest rate curve to $R_1^f$ from $R_0^f$. The new equilibrium, at point C, would imply a depreciation of the currency, again as predicted by equation (15.9).

Also note that, ignoring transactions costs, we have shown that there will always be the appearance of some arbitrage opportunities even though few will actually exist. Finally, it may be that if there are strong preferences for domestic financial instruments over foreign ones or if the risk of default differs across countries, what appear to be arbitrage opportunities are, in fact, a risk premium of the kind we explored in this chapter and in Chapter 13.

## SUMMARY

- Interest rates differ because the debts in question are not equally risky and, because debt matures at different times. In this chapter, we analyse the risk and term structure of interest rates.

- The risk structure of interest rates is such that the greater the risk of default on a debt, the higher the interest rate necessary to compensate the lender for undertaking the extra risk.

- The expectations hypothesis of the term structure says that long-term interest rates are averages of expected short-term interest rates. As a result, interest rates contain predictions about the future levels of interest rates and inflation.

- Another view of the term structure says that long-term interest rates contain a liquidity premium, which represents a payment to investors for agreeing to hold debt for a long period of time.

- The market segmentation hypothesis argues that the long and short ends of the maturity structure of interest rates are separate with little substitution between the two. As a result, interest rates contain no useful information about future interest rates or inflation.
- Interest rates can differ because of the currency in which the debt is denominated. The relationship between interest rates in different countries is explained by the interest rate parity condition: interest rates will differ between countries by the expected change in the exchange rate.

# IMPORTANT TERMS

capital mobility (p. 347)
covered interest arbitrage (p. 350)
expectations hypothesis (p. 338)
forward exchange rate (p. 347)
interest rate parity (p. 350)
liquidity premium (p. 345)
market segmentation (p. 345)
preferred habitat (p. 346)
risk structure of interest rates (p. 331)
term structure of interest rates (p. 333)
yield curve (p. 334)

# EXERCISES

1. What would you expect to happen to the spread between a risky asset and a riskless asset if the bond rating on the risky asset were downgraded? Illustrate by using a diagram of the loanable funds framework.

2. Suppose your newspaper gives the following hypothetical bond yields:

| Province of | Yield (%) |
|---|---|
| Quebec | 10.50 |
| Ontario | 10.25 |
| Newfoundland | 11.25 |

Name two risk characteristics that could explain the yield differences. Which one is likely to be most important?

3. Suppose the following interest rate structure was observed in 1996 and 1997.

| | 1996 | 1997 |
|---|---|---|
| | Yield (%) | |
| 3-month Treasury bill | 10.00 | 12.00 |
| 1-year government bond | 10.50 | 11.90 |
| 3-year government bond | 10.75 | 12.15 |
| 5-year government bond | 11.00 | 11.80 |
| 10-year government bond | 11.30 | 11.60 |

Plot the yield curves for 1996 and 1997. What does the yield curve say about future interest rates? What might explain the difference between the yield curve in 1996 and 1997?

4. Assume that the expectations hypothesis of the term structure is correct. You are given the following data:

| Yield | $R_1$ | $R_2$ | $R_3$ | $R_4$ | $R_5$ |
|---|---|---|---|---|---|
| % | 10 | 12 | 13 | 13.5 | 13.75 |

What are the 1-year expected interest rates predicted by the expectations hypothesis?

5. A forecaster of future interest rates provides you with the following data:

| Yield | $R_1$ | $E_1^1$ | $E_1^2$ | $E_1^3$ | $E_1^4$ |
|---|---|---|---|---|---|
| % | 8 | 12 | 11 | 10.5 | 10 |

What yield curve would result from these forecasts, assuming that they are consistent with the expectations hypothesis? Draw this curve.

6. Take the yield curve you have drawn for question 5. Now suppose that because of short-term inflation risk, investors start to show a distinct preference for long-term bonds. What happens to the yield curve? Use the loanable funds framework to illustrate what happens to the spread between short-term and long-term rates.

7. Suppose a professor asks her research assistant to produce a plot of the difference between the yield on 3-month Treasury bills (short) and the yield on government bonds that mature in 10 years (long). The research assistant produces the following plot for the period 1986–97.

**Long-Short Yields Differential**

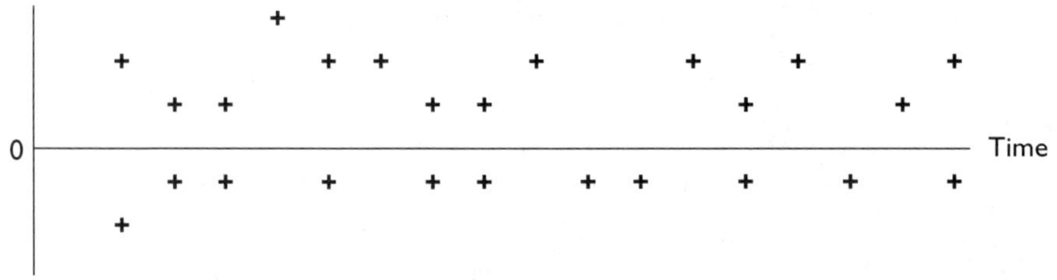


The professor says: "Well, the difference in yields appears to be randomly scattered around a mean of zero. That must mean that the expectations hypothesis holds." True or false? Explain.

8. The exchange rate is ¥120 per Canadian dollar (or 0.0083 Canadian dollars per yen). The 1-year interest rate is 10% in Canada and 6% in Japan. What is the implicit 1-year forward exchange rate?

9. Suppose you are given the following data:

| Country | Currency | Yield on 2-year Government Bonds |
|---|---|---|
| Canada | $ | 11 % |
| United States | $ | 7 % |
| Germany | DM | 6.5% |
| United Kingdom | £ | 12 % |

What is the annual expected appreciation or depreciation of the Canadian dollar relative to the other currencies in the table?

10. Suppose that the implicit forward rate is $2.00 per £ but the actual forward rate is $2.05 per £. Is there any profit to be made? If so, how?

11. Explain why government securities are usually graphed on yield curves.

12. Write out and explain the equilibrium condition for covered interest arbitrage.

13. Trace out the effect of the following using the framework developed to diagrammatically illustrate the interest parity concept (Figure 15.7):
(a) A fall in the Canadian real interest rate
(b) A rise in the Canadian money supply (Hint: go back to Chapter 6 and review the liquidity preference model)
(c) A rise in US interest rates
(d) A rise in the expected exchange rate

Use diagrams for your answer.

14. Assume that inflation is 3% in the UK, 2% in Japan, 4% in the United States, and 1% in Canada. What would you expect would happen to the exchange rate of the Canadian dollar against the currencies of these countries?

15. Suppose that the real return on investments in Canada is lower than in the United States. What impact would this have on the exchange rate?

16. Based on Figure 15.3, would you expect the yield curve to be upward sloping most of the time? Explain.

17. Explain the connection between interest rate parity and purchasing power parity (see Chapter 7) theories.

18. Why are yield curves of limited use under the liquidity premium and market segmentation hypotheses? Explain.

19. The following table was reported in an article from *The Globe and Mail.*

| Country | 1995 Return in Percent in Local Currency | In US Dollars |
|---|---|---|
| Canada | 20.4 | 23.3 |
| Spain | 20.0 | 30.7 |
| Australia | 19.4 | 15.0 |
| Netherlands | 18.5 | 28.5 |
| Italy | 18.0 | 21.4 |
| Belgium | 17.5 | 27.4 |
| Britain | 17.0 | 17.0 |
| United States | 16.9 | 16.9 |
| Germany | 16.9 | 26.6 |
| France | 16.8 | 27.7 |
| Japan | 13.9 | 10.5 |



Source: M. Stimson, "Foreigners Love Canadian Dollar Bonds," *The Globe and Mail*, 24 February 1996.

Answer the following questions based on the above table.

(a) Which countries' exchange rate appreciated or depreciated in 1995?

(b) Canada's return in local currency is the highest among this group of countries. Can risk considerations explain this result? Explain.

**20.** Compare the two yield curves in Figure 15.2. Could the Bank of Canada's policy of low inflation account for the change? Explain.

# REFERENCES

Boothe, P. "Interest Parity, Cointegration, and the Term Structure in Canada and the United States." *Canadian Journal of Economics* 24 (August 1991): 595–603.

Boothe, P., and D. Longworth. "Foreign Exchange Market Efficiency Tests: Implications of Recent Empirical Findings." *Journal of International Money and Finance* 5 (June 1986): 135–52.

Gregory, A.W. "Testing Interest Rate Parity and Rational Expectations for Canada and the United States." *Canadian Journal of Economics* 20 (May 1987): 289–305.

Harris, L. *Monetary Theory.* New York: McGraw-Hill, 1981.

Howitt, P. *Monetary Policy in Transition: A Study of Bank of Canada Policy, 1982–85.* Montreal: C.D. Howe Institute, 1986.

Kool, C.J.M., and J.A. Tatom. "International Linkages in the Term Structure of Interest Rates." *Review of the Federal Reserve Bank of St. Louis* 70 (July/August 1988): 30–42.

Statistics Canada, CANSIM database.

Van Horne, J.C. *Financial Market Rates and Flow.* Englewood Cliffs, N.J.: Prentice-Hall, 1984.

# PART III

# THE INSTITUTIONAL FRAMEWORK IN THE CANADIAN CONTEXT

CHAPTER 16

# Theories of Banking

Earlier in this text we broadly described what banks do and the functions they fulfil in the financial system. In this chapter, we examine more formally the processes by which banks create assets and liabilities. Finally, since the last Bank Act eliminated required reserves, special attention is given to the deposit creation process in the absence of formal reserve requirements. Obviously, the fact that banks are not *required* to hold reserves does not mean that no reserves will be held. On average, some reserves will always be held for seasonal needs of the public and to guard against unexpected cash withdrawals to give a couple of examples. It is therefore more accurate to state that banks will have *target* level of reserves even in a world of zero required reserves.

To get to the essence of their deposit-creating and lending functions, we make a few simplifying assumptions. Also, although we briefly describe how deposits are created when transactions take place between Canada's chartered banks and its other banks, we leave the institutional details about the different types of banks for subsequent chapters and concentrate here on the theory of banking.

Unfortunately, there is no single theory of banking. One branch of the literature stresses the loan-creation activities of banks. Accordingly, we begin this chapter with an analysis of the multiple expansion of deposits concept.

Another approach to the question of what banks do suggests that they behave like other profit-maximizing firms and so we can rely on the view that forms the backbone of microeconomic theory. Thus, we consider here a version of the familiar theory of the banking firm.

Finally, an older tradition in the finance literature views banks in a different light altogether. As a well-known article puts it:

> The concern with banks in macroeconomics centers on their role as portfolio managers, whereby they purchase securities from individuals and firms (and a loan is, after all, just a purchase of securities) which they then offer as portfolio holdings (deposits) to other individuals and firms.[1]

1 E. Fama, "What's Special about Banks?" *Journal of Monetary Economics* 15 (January 1985): 29–40.

To illustrate this view of bank behaviour, we use a very simple expression of the portfolio approach, inspired by concepts developed in Chapter 13.

These three approaches, it is worth pointing out, are complementary, not contradictory. They differ primarily in the aspects of banking on which they focus. The need for these different explanations, in part, stems from the fact that different countries have vastly different legislation governing this behaviour. Thus, for example, branch banking is severely limited in the United States, while in Germany banks raise relatively more funds via equity rather than through deposits.

It is also worth pointing out that understanding what banks do is of more than theoretical interest. Regulators in every major industrialized country debate the limits to the activities that banks should be permitted to engage in, and those limits have a direct effect on the workings of the economy and of firms in it.

## THE THEORY OF MULTIPLE EXPANSION OF DEPOSITS

Central to the understanding of any banking system is the notion of the multiple expansion of deposits, which is the process by which the system multiplies one dollar of reserves into many dollars of deposits, apparently creating money. As a well-known economist said years ago:

> The problem of the manner in which the banking system increases the total volume of the circulating medium, while at the same time the lending power of the individual banks is severely limited, has proved to be one of the most baffling for writers on banking.[2]

What puzzles students is the fact that although individual banks are restricted in the amount of deposits they can create, the banking system as a whole is able to expand deposits by a multiple. To see why this is the case, let us consider some simplified numerical examples. We'll start with a single bank (which can create a limited amount of deposits) and work up to a system.

The whole "secret" of deposit creation rests in public confidence. Only small children believe a bank keeps in its vaults every penny of every deposit it takes in. In fact, only a fractional reserve—a small percentage of total deposits—is kept to maintain liquidity and provide for depositors who want the use of some or all of their funds. The rest is used for money-making activities, of which the primary one is the making of loans.

2 From L. Mints, *A History of Banking Theory*, as quoted in T.H. Humphrey, "The Theory of Multiple Expansion of Deposits: What It Is and Whence It Came," Federal Reserve Bank of Richmond, *Economic Review* (March/April 1987): 3–11, 3.

## BANK RESERVES IN CANADA

A bank's **reserve ratio**—the proportion of total deposits to be held in reserve—may be set by law or by prudence and custom. With the implementations of the 1991 Bank Act (see Chapters 17 and 24) reserves are solely held for the sake of prudence. Legal restrictions establishing reserve ratios no longer exist. As a result, chartered banks have sharply reduced the amount of funds deposited at the Bank of Canada essentially to meet requirements for clearing purposes. Nevertheless, banks will continue to hold reserves and one way of understanding the process of deposit creation is via the analysis of a bank's balance sheet.[3]

## A SINGLE BANK

Let's start with the simplest possible example. Suppose an individual, call her Ms A, deposits $1,000 to her demand account at the Little Bank. For the sake of illustration, let us assume that the bank sets aside 5% of deposits as **reserves**. This figure may seem high but this is not the case, as we will see. To avoid confusion with cases where the reserve requirement is mandated by law, we will refer to the 5% figure as a **reserve target**. Reserves above this level can still be referred to as excess reserves, but where the excess is relative to the level of reserves the banks *wish* to hold as opposed to being *required* to hold.

What happens to the other $950? As long as it is simply sitting in the bank, it is an **excess reserve**—an amount of money that neither law nor prudence requires the bank to hold and that has an opportunity cost. So the bank wants to put it to work in the form of a loan.

Suppose the Little Bank lends the $950 to Mr B at 10% per year. This strategy will work nicely if the Little Bank is the only bank in the economy. Mr B will use the funds to pay his creditors, who will make deposits to their own accounts, from which they will pay their bills, and so on. All the money will flow in and out of the Little Bank, creating the multiple expansion process we detail in the next subsection.

*But* suppose the Little Bank exists in a more realistic economy, one with five or six or dozens of competitors. If it lends Mr B the $950, each of his creditors may patronize a different institution, and the funds may not flow back into the Little Bank. What will it use to pay Ms A next month when she wants her $1,000?

Unless Little Bank is a monopoly, most of that $950 is not really excess. To put the point another way, an individual bank that has competitors cannot safely lend (or otherwise tie up) any amount greater than the reserves it actually holds.

---

3 In chapter 24 we consider a more complete example of how the Bank of Canada will ensure that the banking system maintains sufficient reserves.

## A BANKING SYSTEM

The situation for a whole banking system is more like that of a monopoly bank, especially if, as is usual, the system has a clearinghouse operation.[4]

### A Simplified Balance Sheet

A simplified balance sheet will help to clarify our discussion of deposit expansion. Let's set one up (Table 16.1) for a system comprising two banks: the First Typical Canadian Bank (FTCB) and the Second Typical Canadian Bank (STCB). Both have the following assets and liabilities.

| **Assets** | **Liabilities** |
|---|---|
| Cash, *CUR*, to meet the daily withdrawal demand of depositors | Deposits, *DEP* |
| Reserve Target (*RES*) | Advances from Bank of Canada, *ADV* |
| Loans, *L* | Net worth (equity or capital) |
| Securities, *SEC* (bonds and other financial instruments) | |
| Physical assets (land and buildings) | |

Notice that we are making a few simplifying assumptions. For example, on the liability side, where a wide variety of deposits exist, we consider only demand deposits. Moreover, we concentrate on the behavior of the private sector—known as the *non-bank public*—ignoring other sources of deposit expansion.

To simplify matters still further, we also assume, (1) that banks always aim to minimize their excess reserve (*ER*) holdings (so that these are only temporary), (2) that once a deposit is made into the banking system there are no cash withdrawals while banks adjust to their new financial situation, and (3) that all banks have the same target reserves levels.

### The Effect of a Cash Deposit

Now suppose that Ms A makes her $1,000 deposit into the STCB. She makes it in cash (that is, currency). What is the effect on the economy's money supply? You can follow the answer through on Table 16.1.

---

4 The Canadian clearinghouse, an automated interbank settlements system operated by the Canadian Payments Association, is described in Chapter 2.

**TABLE 16.1** MULTIPLE DEPOSIT EXPANSION: THE BASICS

**Initial deposit (in cash)**

| First Typical Canadian Bank (FTCB) Assets | FTCB Liabilities | Second Typical Canadian Bank (STCB) Assets | STCB Liabilities |
|---|---|---|---|
| NO CHANGE | | + $1,000 *CUR* | + $1,000 *DEP* |
| | | of which<br>$50 *RES*<br>$950 *ER* | |
| | | $1,000 | |

**Cheque written on STCB**

| FTCB Assets | FTCB Liabilities | STCB Assets | STCB Liabilities |
|---|---|---|---|
| + $1,000 *CUR* | + $1,000 *DEP* ← | – $1,000 *CUR* | – $1,000 *DEP* |
| of which<br>$50 *RES*<br>$950 *ER* | | | |
| $1,000 | | | |

**New loans issued**

| FTCB Assets | FTCB Liabilities | STCB Assets | STCB Liabilities |
|---|---|---|---|
| + $950 *L* ← | + $950 *DEP* | NO CHANGE | |
| ⋮ | | ⋮ | |
| + $950 *CUR* | – $950 *DEP* | – $ 950 *CUR* | + $950 *DEP* |
| | | of which<br>$47.50 *RES*<br>$902.50 *ER* | |
| | | $950 | |

**The Creation of Deposits**

| | | |
|---|---|---|
| Initial cash desposit | $1,000 | |
| New Loans: STCB | $ 950 | = $1,000 – (5% of $1,000) |
| FTCB | $ 902.50 | = $950 – (5% of $950) |
| ⋮ | $ 857.38 | = $902.50 – (5% of $902.50) |
| | ⋮ | |
| Total Deposit Expansion | $1,000 + $950 + $902.50 + ... = $20,000 | |

Recall that *M1*, the narrow definition of the money supply, consists of currency circulating outside banks, *CUR*, and chartered bank demand deposit, *DEP*.[5] The transaction *initially* has no effect on the money supply since it represents simply a reallocation from currency to deposits. In algebraic terms, since

$$M1 = CUR + DEP$$

the initial effect on the money supply, as measured by the change in it, ΔM1, can be written

$$\begin{aligned} \Delta M1 &= -\Delta CUR + \Delta DEP \\ &= -\ \$1{,}000 + \$1{,}000 = \$0 \end{aligned}$$

What is the effect on the entire banking system? Ms A's $1,000 cash deposit requires, initially at least, that the cash reserves of the STCB rise by $1,000. To meet its reserve target on deposits, the bank allocates $50—5% of $1,000—to these reserves while the remainder ($1,000 − $50 = $950) becomes *excess* reserves in the sense described earlier.

Suppose now that Ms A writes a cheque for $1,000 to her landlord, Mr B, who deposits it in his account at the FTCB. If we ignore any time delay for cheque clearing, the first effect of this transaction is to eliminate the cash increase at the STCB. Its financial situation returns to where it was prior to the original deposit. The FTCB now, however, experiences a rise of $1,000 in deposits, which, as before, signals a rise of $50 in target reserves with the remainder, $950, representing excess reserves.

So long as there are no cash withdrawals, the banking system still has some excess reserves. Since these reserves incur an opportunity cost, the FTCB seeks to use them to make a commercial loan or purchase securities. Suppose the bank loans the $950 to Mr C, who uses it to pay a debt to Miss D. She deposits the proceeds, again in the form of a cheque, into her account at the STCB. The balance sheet of the FTCB first shows a rise in loans outstanding of $950 and then an withdrawal in the same amount, thereby eliminating all its excess reserves. Overall, the FTCB still has the original deposit increase of $1,000, necessitating a rise in target reserves of $50, but it is fully loaned up, meaning that it no longer has any excess reserves.

Since Mr C used his loan to pay Miss D, a depositor at the STCB, that bank now experiences a deposit increase of $950. It must add $47.50 (5% of $950) to its target reserves: the remainder ($950 − $47.50 = $902.50) now represents

---

5 In what follows, notations in capital letters refer to actual dollar amounts of the variable in question. Lower-case letters are used to denote fractions of some aggregate.

excess reserves. So far the original $1,000 deposit at the STCB has spawned an additional $1,852.50 ($950 + $902.50) in deposits at both banks.

The fundamentals of multiple deposit expansion should now be clear. The desire to eliminate excess reserves creates an opportunity for banks to expand deposits through the acquisition of assets in the form of loans. (We leave it as an exercise to determine whether the same result would be obtained if a bank chose to acquire securities instead of making new loans.)

## The Algebra of Deposit Expansion

Recall that we left the STCB with excess reserves. If its chooses to make further loans to the public, the deposit expansion process will continue. How long? The bottom of Table 16.1 shows the answer. It is easiest to reach it algebraically. (For convenience the argument—and assumptions—are summarized in Table 16.2).

Let's derive the equation. We know from our discussion above that target reserves, *RES* are a constant fraction, *rr*, of deposits, *DEP*. Therefore, we can write

$$RES = rr \cdot DEP \tag{16.1}$$

where *rr* is the reserve ratio. Since we wish to compute the total change in deposits, given an initial cash deposit of some amount and since the targeted reserve ratio is assumed to be fixed, equation (16.1) becomes

$$\Delta RES = rr \cdot \Delta DEP \tag{16.2}$$

where $\Delta RES$ represents the change in target reserves and $\Delta DEP$ represents the change in deposits. Returning to the numerical example in Table 16.1, we see that initially the cash deposit of $1,000 is equivalent to the change in target reserves. Therefore,

$$\$1{,}000 = 5\% \cdot \Delta DEP$$

from which we can conclude, using equation (16.2), that

$$\Delta DEP = \frac{1}{rr}\,\Delta RES \longrightarrow \Delta DEP = \frac{\$1{,}000}{5\%} = \$20{,}000 \tag{16.3}$$

Equation (16.3) shows that the initial rise of deposits and reserves of $1,000 is multiplied 20 times (= 1/0.05) in order to satisfy the requirement that there be no excess reserves, other than for the targeted amount, in the banking system. It comes as no surprise then that the term $1/rr$ is referred to as the **deposit multiplier**. Here,

**TABLE 16.2** THE CREATION OF DEPOSITS IN ALGEBRAIC FORM

$$
\begin{aligned}
\$\Delta DEP &= \$\Delta RES + (1 - rr)\$\Delta RES + (1 - rr)[(1 - rr)\$\Delta RES] + \ldots \\
&= \$\Delta RES + (1 - rr)\$\Delta RES + (1 - rr)^2\$\Delta RES + \ldots \\
&= \$\Delta RES[1 + (1 - rr) + (1 - rr)^2 + \ldots]
\end{aligned}
$$

•
•
•

$$\$\Delta DEP = \frac{\$\Delta RES}{rr}$$

**Assumptions**

1. Target ratio of 5%
2. No excess reserves
3. No currency drain

$$\frac{1}{rr} = \frac{1}{0.05} = 20 \tag{16.4}$$

What is the effect on the money supply? Recall that *initially*

$$
\begin{aligned}
\Delta M1 &= -\Delta CUR + \Delta DEP \\
&= -\ \$1{,}000 + \$1{,}000 = \$0
\end{aligned}
$$

Once we consider the effect of multiple deposit expansion, however, we see that the *final* impact on the money supply is

$$\Delta M1 = -\$1{,}000 + \$20{,}000 = +\$19{,}000$$

where $-\$1{,}000$ represents the original fall in the amount of currency in circulation while $+\$20{,}000$ is the total expansion in deposits. Clearly, then, the behaviour of the money supply is inextricably limited to the behaviour of banks.[6]

Two of the assumptions made in deriving equation (16.3) require a little further discussion. To the extent that either or both banks decide to hold some excess reserves, the deposit multiplier will be reduced. Since total reserves, *TR*, are simply the sum of target and excess reserves, we can write

$$TR = RES + ER \tag{16.5}$$

where $ER$ = excess over target reserves. Moreover, since by equation (16.1) we can express target reserves as a function of deposits, equation (16.5) becomes

6 We develop more precise behavioural relationships between the two in Chapter 24.

$$TR = rr \cdot DEP + ER \tag{16.6}$$

If we assume that banks want to hold no excess reserves, equation (16.5) is equivalent to equation (16.1). However, banks may want to hold some excess reserves. How much do they want to hold? The question is difficult, and the answer almost certainly varies from bank to bank. Different banks have different needs. For many, seasonal cash needs dominate their decisions on excess reserves. For others, it is conditions particular to the region in which they are located. We can, however, formulate a simple hypothesis based on observation of how excess reserves tend to fluctuate in the banking system as a whole. Assume that excess reserves depend on the nominal interest rate, the reasoning being that banks that have a targeted level of reserves are reluctant, given the opportunity costs,[7] to add to them. In other words, excess reserves would be negatively related to the opportunity cost of holding money. We can summarize this argument algebraically by rewriting equation (16.6) as

$$TR = rr \cdot DEP + ER(R) \tag{16.7}$$

Equation (16.7) differs from equation (16.6) in making excess reserves a function of the interest rate. Dividing both sides of equation (16.7) by *DEP*, we obtain

$$\frac{TR}{DEP} = \frac{rr \cdot DEP}{DEP} + \frac{ER(R)}{DEP}$$

which can be further simplified as

$$tr = rr + er(R) \tag{16.8}$$

where $tr$ is the total reserve ratio—that is, total reserves, $TR$, as a proportion of deposits, $DEP$. Note that in the numerical example outlined in Table 16.1, $er(R)$ was assumed to be zero. In that case,

$$tr = rr$$

Therefore, if we allow for excess reserves, the change in deposits becomes

$$\Delta DEP = \frac{1}{rr + er(R)} (\Delta RES) \tag{16.9}$$

where the term $1/(rr + er(R))$ represents the deposit multiplier. The only dif-

7 Before the introduction of the new reserve management system, all required reserves were subject to an opportunity cost. Under the new system only cash on hand incurs an opportunity cost because balances at the Bank of Canada earn interest if they are positive (in the case of a negative balance there is a penalty interest rate to be paid). Again, see Chapters 4 and 24.

ference between equation (16.9) and (16.3) is the addition of the $er(R)$ term in the denominator, which reflects the fact that if banks choose to hold excess reserves, they cannot expand deposits as much as they could if they choose to hold no excess at all. Algebraically, since $er(R)$ is positive,

$$\frac{1}{rr} > \frac{1}{rr + er(R)}$$

That is, $1/rr$ is larger than the deposit multiplier alone when there are positive excess reserves.

## A SYSTEM WITHOUT REQUIRED RESERVES

So far we have assumed that banks target a fraction of deposits as reserves. While this is certainly sensible, it was pointed out that this fraction might be close to zero. In fact, banks do keep a non-trivial fraction of some of their deposits at the Bank of Canada and in the form of notes and coins, although their levels have fallen since the passage of the 1991 Bank Act and the transition to zero required reserves. Table 16.3 shows the fraction of personal savings deposits (of the chequable and non-chequable variety) and demand deposits held at the Bank of Canada and in the form of notes and coins in 1994.

Note the strong seasonal component in reserves which rise substantially, and not surprisingly, during the month of December.

To deal with a system of new required reserves one could simply assume that all reserves are, in effect, a function of the need to maintain some minimum amount to satisfy regular cash needs such as those arising out of the use of ATMs (automatic teller machines) plus an adjustment for the calendar to deal with seasonal effects.

This would mean that we could rewrite equation (16.9) as follows:

$$\Delta DEP = [1/\ (k + seas_t)]\ \Delta RES$$

where $k$ = some minimum desired reserve-ratio level, and $seas_t$ fluctuates according to the calendar to capture seasonal effects. However, notice that the principles involved in deriving and using equation (16.9) are unaffected with the use of the above equation.

## THE EFFECT OF A CURRENCY DRAIN

A *currency drain*, also called a *cash drain*, means a cash withdrawal from the banking system. If we simply reverse the analysis of Table 16.1 and equation (16.10), we see that a currency drain implies a multiple contraction of deposits. Every bank experiences some currency drain every day when some depositors

**TABLE 16.3** RESERVES OF CHARTERED BANKS IN 1994

| Month | Fraction of Deposits (%) |
|---|---|
| January | 3.2 |
| February | 3.5 |
| March | 3.7 |
| April | 3.2 |
| May | 3.9 |
| June | 2.8 |
| July | 3.1 |
| August | 3.2 |
| September | 2.5 |
| October | 3.2 |
| November | 3.0 |
| December | 5.2 |

Note: Balances at the Bank of Canada, notes and coins, chequable and non-chequable personal savings deposit and gross demand deposits.

Source: Bank of Canada Review.

demand part or all of their funds in cash. Indeed, some individual banks end up with a net drain for a few days, even in the most expansionary monetary system.

The entire banking system can also experience a cash drain, perhaps for a considerable period. Such a contraction of deposits can have a variety of causes. One is a change in the public's desire to hold currency.[8] Public policies, such as actions by the Bank of Canada on its own account or as the federal government's banker, can also influence the quantity of cash and the reserves of the banking system.

## THE EFFECT OF A CHANGE IN THE COMPOSITION OF DEPOSITS

A limitation of the simplified balance sheet presented in Table 16.1 is that it lumps together different types of deposits. In particular, the distinction between demand and savings deposits is entirely ignored. This drawback is easily remedied. Consider Table 16.4 in which the liability side of the FTCB balance sheet is modified to show two types of deposits: demand deposits, *DD*, and time or fixed-term deposits, *TD*. The sudden withdrawal of funds from a time deposit usually involves a penalty of sorts.[9] As a result, the likelihood of sudden withdrawal is lower for time deposits than for demand deposits. Consequently, the portion of

8 As we'll see in Chapter 24, it is relatively straightforward to analyse the public's behaviour in this regard.

9 It may be implicit, as when interest income that would otherwise be earned is lost, or explicit, as when there is a monetary penalty for withdrawal if the term of the deposit was specified in advance.

**TABLE 16.4** DEPOSIT EXPANSION WHEN DEPOSIT COMPOSITION CHANGES

**First Typical Canadian Bank**
**Initial change from time to demand deposit**

| | |
|---|---|
| No Change | +\$1,000 *DD*<br>−\$1,000 *TD* |
| **Impact on reserves** | |
| $RES_d$ + \$40 (4% of +1000)<br>$RES_t$ − \$10 (1% of −1000)<br>net +\$30 | No Change |
| **Impact on assets** | |
| *RES* +\$30<br>*SEC* −\$30 | No Change |

reserves targeted against the possibility of withdrawals from fixed term deposits will also be much smaller than for demand deposits.

Table 16.4 assumes that this fraction is 1% while the fraction of deposits held as reserves against demand deposits is now assumed to be 4% so the total reserve ratio is still 5%.

Also suppose that a depositor of the First Typical Canadian Bank transfers a matured time deposit into her chequing account at the same bank. For simplicity, we assume no currency drain and no leakages to other banks. Initially, the FTCB experiences no changes in total deposits as the transaction simply represents a transfer from one type of deposit to another (see the first portion of Table 16.4). However, as a result of the transfer, the bank's overall reserve requirements do change. The reserves for demand deposits ($RES_d$) rise by \$40—4% of +\$1,000—while the reserves for time deposits fall by \$10—1% of \$1,000. In net terms, the FTCB requires \$40 − \$10 = \$30 of additional reserves. Consequently, it must change its portfolio to satisfy the new reserve requirement. One solution—there are others, which are left as an exercise—is to sell some of its holdings of securities, thereby reallocating its assets, leaving liabilities unchanged. (Of course, the sale of a security will have further effects of the kind considered previously.)

## TRANSFER OF DEPOSITS TO A NEAR-BANK

The near-banks, such as trust companies, do hold reserves against deposits, but they were never legally bound by specific reserve requirements.[10] Moreover, deposits in the near-banks are not counted as part of the monetary aggregates M1 and M2. Thus, if an individual transfers funds from, say, a demand deposit in the FTCB to a time deposit in a trust company, the chartered banks will experience a currency drain, necessitating the calling in of loans or the sale of securities. M1 and M2 will also be affected. Broader monetary aggregates, such as M2+, do include deposits in near-banks and so reflect any shifts in deposits between them and the chartered banks.[11]

Table 16.5 illustrates two scenarios involving transactions between a chartered bank and a near-bank. For the purposes of the illustration, we assume that both institutions hold the same reserves against time deposits and keep excess reserves to zero.

In the first case, the transfer of a demand deposit out of the chartered bank contracts those deposits according to the deposit multiplier, and the near-banks are able to expand their deposits, also by a multiple. If the transfer is made into a time deposit at a near-bank then, given the arguments outlined in Table 16.5, the shift means an overall expansion of deposits in the bank and near-bank sectors taken together. As far as the monetary aggregates are concerned, however, the direction of movement depends on which definition is used. M1 and M2 fall. The M2+ measure, in contrast, rises.

Two considerations should be kept in mind in assessing the effects of transactions between chartered banks and near-banks. First, most near-banks hold deposits at chartered banks.[12] Thus, in holding reserves against the new time deposit, the near-bank may choose to increase its deposits. If it does so, the drain of deposits from the chartered bank would be smaller than previously argued. Second, reserves held against time deposits need not be the same in the chartered banking and near banking sectors. Any difference can influence the size of changes in the money supply.

In the second scenario in Table 16.5, an individual switches a time deposit from a chartered bank to a near-bank (perhaps because the latter offers terms that the depositor perceives as more attractive). The chartered banks experience

---

10 Different regulations for different parts of the banking system is not restricted to Canada. Many other countries (such as those we survey in Chapter 22) have a myriad of rules that, broadly speaking, apply differently to commercial banks (Canadian chartered banks) and savings banks (Canadian near-banks).

11 As near-banks become more like chartered banks it is conceivable that the rather artificial distinction between M2 and M2+ will vanish. The existing distinctions are largely a matter of statistical expediency.

12 These deposits form part of Canada's large and active interbank market.

**TABLE 16.5** SHIFTS IN DEPOSITS BETWEEN A CHARTERED BANK AND A NEAR-BANK

**Scenario 1**

| Chartered Banks | Near-Banks |
|---|---|
| Lower *DD* | Higher *TD* |
| ↓ | ↓ |
| Impact on total deposits | Impact on total deposits |
| $\Delta DEP < 0$ | $\Delta DEP > 0$ |

**Net Effect of Both Changes**

| | |
|---|---|
| Reduction in M1 and M2 | Increase in M2+ |

**Scenario 2**

| Chartered Banks | Near-Banks |
|---|---|
| Lower *TD* | Higher *TD* |
| ↓ | ↓ |
| Impact on total deposits | Impact on total deposits |
| $\Delta DEP < 0$ | $\Delta DEP > 0$ |

**Net Effect of Both Changes**

Reduction in M2

M2+ can rise or fall depending on target reserve ratios at the chartered banks and near banks

a multiple contraction of deposits. The opposite holds for near-banks, which can now engage in a multiple expansion of deposits. The net effect on narrow monetary aggregates, such as M1 and M2, is negative. The impact on a broader measure of the money supply is a function of the reserves ratio for time deposits in the two segments of the banking sector. Whether the near-banks decide to raise their deposits in the chartered banks will also influence the size of the change in the various measures of the money supply.

## *A SIMPLE THEORY OF THE BANKING FIRM

Although the deposit multiplier model is useful in understanding how banks behave, it leaves out some important considerations, such as the degree of competition in the industry and the fact that the ability and willingness of a market to absorb, say, additional loans depends in part on prevailing interest rates. This section remedies these omissions by outlining a simple model of the financial firm.

This approach requires a bit of thought. When we defined what financial institutions do (Chapter 3), we faced the problem of putting it in terms of the conventional way in which economists view firms: that is, of having inputs and a physically definable output. The *intermediation* function is the one that distinguishes financial firms from others. Yet many observers of the industry associate banks primarily with their deposit-taking function. Indeed, it is convenient to view banks as *depository firms*—that is, firms that produce deposits.[13] Such an approach is convenient for it allows us to analyse banks as if they were like any other firm, guided as the economist assumes, by the principle of profit maximizing—that is, they attempt to reach the most profitable level of output by keeping costs per unit at the lowest level possible.

## THE MODEL

Let us set up a model, assuming the depository firm produces deposits as a function of several inputs such that

$$DEP = DEP(R_{DEP}, R_a, Y, W) \tag{16.13}$$

where

$R_{DEP}$ = deposit interest rate
$R_a$ = yield on alternative financial instruments
$Y$ = income
$W$ = wealth
$DEP$ = deposits

In other words, deposits are a function of the rate paid on them, of the yield paid on alternative financial assets, of income and of wealth. In what follows, we also ignore the effect of inflation. The cost of supplying deposits can be viewed as composed of two elements, one explicit and the other implicit. The explicit component is measured by the rate paid on deposits, $R_{DEP}$, and the implicit component reflects operation costs—salaries, maintenance of physical assets, and so on. Since more deposits may signal the need to hire more staff or expand banking operations, we can assume that the implicit costs are also a function of deposits. Therefore, to simplify the discussion we assume that costs are essentially captured by deposit costs, which are a function of deposits. In other words, we write

13 Alternatively, one could model that banking firm as one which "produces" loans but the essence of the model we are developing would remain unchanged.

$$R_{DEP}(DEP) \tag{16.14}$$

where

$$DEP \uparrow \rightarrow R_{DEP} \uparrow$$

Equation (16.14) is nothing other than the rising marginal cost rule.[14] Thus, as the bank seeks more deposits, it raises the rate paid on deposits. But these same deposit costs must rise at an increasing rate to attract additional deposits.

We assume, for the sake of exposition, that the firm offers only one type of deposit. Similarly, although several alternative assets exist, it seems preferable to let $R_a$ represent some financial asset that acts as a substitute for deposits.

In this setup, the banking firm books a certain volume of deposits (in an amount to be specified below), which are transformed, via the process of intermediation, into interest-earning assets that yield $R_a$. Now the average yield on assets likely depends on the amount of assets purchased, which, in turn, depends on the volume of deposits used to finance this purchase. Also, we know from previous discussions that some banks obtain lower yields than others because the Bank of Canada auctions off Treasury bills from the highest to the lowest price. Similarly, we can reasonably assume that all firms seek out the highest-yielding assets, and thus they purchase the better-yielding ones first and the lower-yielding ones only as necessary. Consequently, it seems reasonable to hypothesize that

$$R_a(DEP) \tag{16.15}$$

where

$$\text{DEP} \uparrow \rightarrow R_a \downarrow$$

Equation (16.15) encapsulates both the positive relationship between deposits and asset yields as well as the diminishing marginal revenue aspect of the function.[15]

The profit function of the firm is then simply

$$\text{Profit} = R_a(DEP) \cdot DEP - R_{DEP}(DEP) \cdot DEP \tag{16.16}$$

---

14 If you have forgotten this rule, consult an elementary economics textbook, such as A. Blomqvist, P. Wonnacott, R. Wonnacott, and J. Fried, *Macroeconomics*, 4th Cdn. ed. (Toronto: McGraw-Hill Ryerson Ltd., 1994), chapter 24.

15 Again a relationship introduced in all principles of economics courses. See for example J.E. Stiglitz, *Economics* (New York: W.W. Norton, 1993), chapter 13.

Equation (16.16) describes the fact that the banking firm earns revenues of ($R_a \cdot DEP$)—that is, an average yield or $R_a$% multiplied by the volume of outstanding deposits.[16] It faces costs of ($R_{DEP} \cdot DEP$)—the deposit interest rate multiplied by the volume of deposits—as well as the other costs of operating the firm.

Figure 16.1 illustrates the profit-maximization problem facing the banking firm. Its output, measured on the horizontal axis, is deposits. The vertical axis measures the various yields it faces. The curve labelled $AR_{DEP}$ represents average revenues, which, as we saw earlier, fall with increases in the volume of deposits. Consequently, marginal revenues, labelled $MR_{DEP}$, also fall. Note that the $MR_{DEP}$ curve is below the $AR_{DEP}$ curve (because marginal increases in the volume of deposits yield smaller and smaller revenue increments). On the cost side, the curve $AC_{DEP}$ represents average costs and $MC_{DEP}$ summarizes the marginal costs. The $MC_{DEP}$ curve lies above the $AC_{DEP}$ curve (because additional deposits increase the costs of providing them faster as more deposits are accepted).[17]

Now recall how one finds the profit-maximizing level of output for a firm. So long as marginal revenues are greater than marginal costs, profits rise (because additions to total revenues are larger than additions to total costs). They will cease to rise when marginal revenues are equal to marginal costs. After that point, as is clear in Figure 16.1, any additional deposits will add more to costs than to revenues (that is, $MC_{DEP} > MR_{DEP}$). Therefore, profits reach their maximum at the point at which the revenue from an additional dollar of deposits is exactly offset by the cost of providing that additional dollar of deposits. This profit-maximizing condition can be written in algebraic form as

$$MR_{DEP} = MC_{DEP} \tag{16.17}$$

According to Figure 16.1, the condition summarized in equation (16.17) yields deposits of $DEP^*$. With that volume of deposits, the banking firm earns an average asset yield of $R_a$ and incurs average costs of $R_{DEP}$. The spread between the two reflects the average profit per dollar of deposits.

---

16 For a variety of reasons, including the changes implemented in the management of bank reserves, banks increasingly rely on fees of all kinds to generate revenues. No doubt the rise in interest rate risk during the 1980s also contributed to this phenomenon. It would be preferable to model such fees separately; we can, however, continue to use equation (16.16) for exposition since *DEP* and perhaps $R_a$ both reflect the influence of such fees.

17 In a perfectly competitive environment the MC curve would be horizontal because if one bank tried to lower the interest rate offered on deposits it would receive none. We are therefore assuming that the typical bank portrayed in this analysis has some market power. Consequently, it must raise the interest rate to attract more deposits or lower the interest rate to attract more loans.

**FIGURE 16.1** Profit Maximization of the Banking Firm

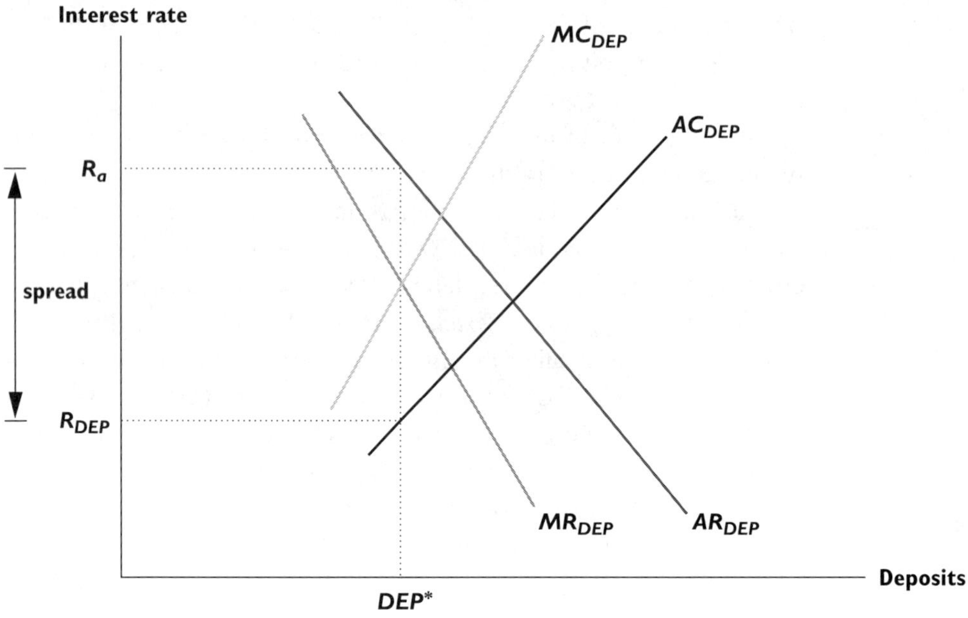


The banking firm faces falling average revenues, $AR_{DEP}$, and, consequently, diminishing marginal revenues, $MR_{DEP}$. Since total costs are a function of deposits, average costs, $AC_{DEP}$, rise with the volume of deposits. Therefore, marginal costs, $MC_{DEP}$, also rise with deposits. The optimum volume of deposits is $DEP^*$, the point that yields the profit-maximizing solution. The difference ($R_a$ - $R_{DEP}$) is the spread between average asset earnings and average costs.

Note: The functional form has been dropped here to save space and because both $R_a$ and $R_{DEP}$ are functions of deposits.

## Other Uses of the Model

The model illustrated by Figure 16.1 can be used to consider a variety of situations in the banking industry. For example, if we wish to explore the impact of a cost-saving technological improvement, we need only shift the marginal and average cost curves to the right.

Another change for consideration is a loosening of regulations, permitting banks to compete in an area in which they had previously been forbidden to do so.[18]

18 For example, Canadian banks becoming eligible to enter the mortgage-lending market in 1967.

The average and marginal revenue curves presumably shift to the right because enhanced market opportunities lead to higher average revenues.

The model can also be used to describe the effects of interest rate ceilings (caps on interest rates) and similar distortions caused by government regulations.[19] Figure 16.2 illustrates the outcome of a deposit rate ceiling of $R$, which is below the profit-maximizing deposit rate of $R_{DEP}$. Since the deposit rate is relatively less attractive to depositors the volume of deposits is lower. At this reduced volume, the banking firm now generates average revenues of $R_a$, which is higher than the profit-maximizing rate. Because there are fewer deposits, fewer assets are purchased. Given our assumption about the relationship between average revenues and deposits, average asset returns rise. Note too the spread between average asset returns for the banking firm and its average costs increases by *more* than the difference between the profit-maximizing rate and the deposit rate ceiling.

Even if there is a fall in market interest rates (those not subject to the ceilings), deposits will not necessarily expand. The banks may simply impose more fees on borrowers and lenders. Consequently, one can imagine how in the face of lower interest rates and an increased desire to borrow, banks might induce a *credit crunch*—a shortage of liquidity in the financial system. The financial innovations discussed in earlier chapters have, however, reduced the likelihood of such credit crunches.

## The Role of Competition

Finally, we can use the theory of the firm framework to discuss the role of competition in the financial industry. Imagine an average revenue curve that is perfectly flat (as illustrated in Figure 16.2 by the line labelled $MR\dagger_{DEP} = AR\dagger_{DEP}$). Under this scenario, which is the one faced by the perfectly competitive firm, the average and marginal revenue curves coincide. Each additional dollar of deposits always yields the same additional revenue because each firm is so small in relation to the entire industry that when additional deposits are turned into assets, they have only a trivial impact on asset returns. Consequently, the perfectly competitive firm can treat average and marginal revenues as constant. The profit-maximizing solution is now to set $MR\dagger_{DEP} = MC_{DEP}$, which yields a deposit volume of $DEP\dagger$ and average asset returns of $R_a^\dagger(DEP)$.

The consequence of perfect competition is to reduce the spread between average asset returns and the average deposit rate (to $R_a^\dagger$ $R\dagger_{DEP}$). Therefore, the slope or

---

19 Canada dropped interest rate ceilings in 1967. But consideration of the phenomenon is useful because regulatory distortions of various kinds persist around the world.

**FIGURE 16.2** The Impact of a Deposit Rate Ceiling on the Market for Deposits

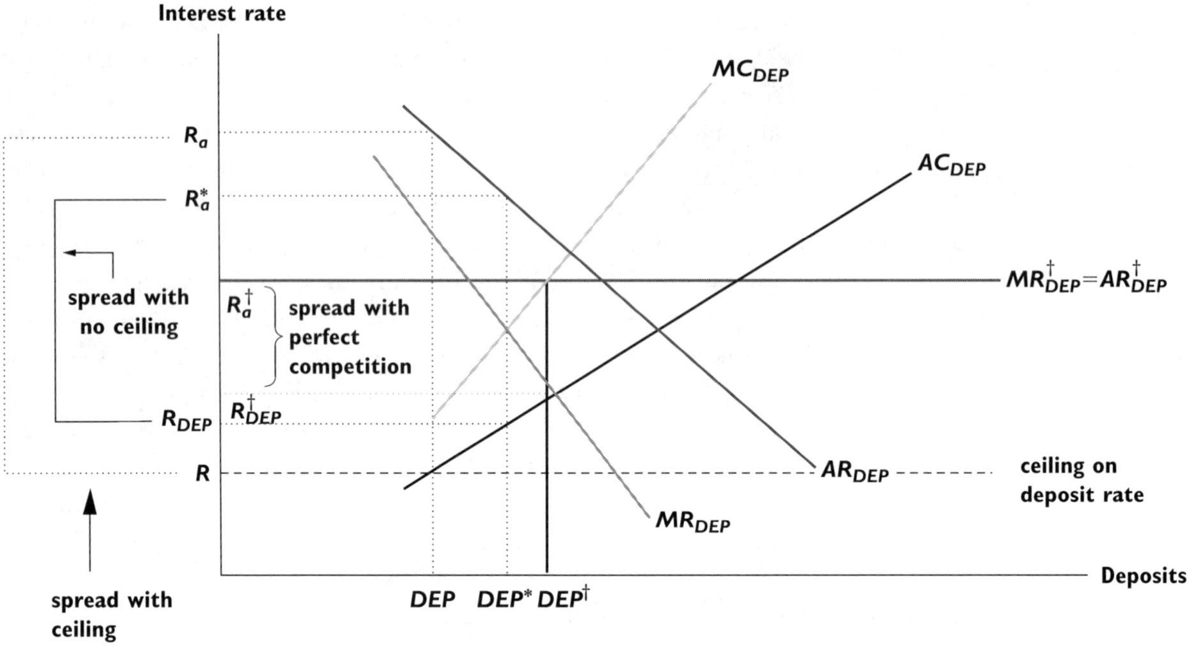


With no deposit rate ceiling, the profit-maximizing level of deposits is $DEP^*$, as in Figure 16.1. With a deposit rate ceiling of $R$, fewer deposits are booked at banks. As a result, fewer asset purchases can be made, so average asset revenues $R_a(DEP)$ rise. The result is a larger spread between asset returns and average costs. Notice that the spread rises by more than the difference between the profit-maximizing deposit rate and the ceiling. $MR_{DEP}^{\dagger} = AR_{DEP}^{\dagger}$ illustrates the case where the banking firm operates in a perfectly competitive industry. This scenario produced the smallest spread of all.

elasticity of the demand for deposits can be used as a gauge of the degree of competition in the banking industry.

## GAP ANALYSIS

Although the preceding analysis leads to much insight about the economic forces influencing the banking industry, it omits consideration of uncertainty or term to maturity, so we are still unable to measure banking performance adequately. What approach can we use?

We can safely assume that risk aversion leads banks, like individuals, to seek to reduce portfolio risk for a given portfolio return. They could use the kind of

## ECONOMICS FOCUS 16.1 Capping Credit Card Interest Rates

Nowhere is the impact of interest rate ceilings more dramatically revealed than in the recurring debate about capping interest rates on credit cards. Both Canadian and US politicians talk about forcing banks to reduce or cap the interest rates charged on credit card balances. So far, however, governments have generally avoided legislating interest rates on this kind of debt, preferring to resort to moral suasion to nudge interest rates lower.

Borrowers often fail to realize that credit card debt is unsecured. Also, as credit card purchases are increasingly replacing cash transactions, they provide convenience, which is a valuable commodity. The combination of these two factors—not a lack of competition in the credit card industry—explains the spread between credit card interest rates and other interest rates.

There are also a couple of additional reasons why ceilings on credit card interest rates could be catastrophic. First, credit card securitization is a large market. Card issuers package the amounts receivable from credit cards to back or finance the issue of bonds. In the United States alone, this represents a $60 billion market. The threat of a cap has the effect of raising the risk of this kind of debt. Second, the public appears to be ignorant about alternative ways to finance debt, and just plain lazy in paying off credit card balances. Moreover, those most financially strapped—and thus most at risk of defaulting—resort to this type of debt finance so that high credit card rates simply reflect the risks of default and the costs of not obtaining financial information.

**Sources:**

"Catastrophic Cap," *The Economist*, 23 November 1991, p. 81.

"Many Keep on Paying High Rates on Cards, Through Bad Planning," *Wall Street Journal*, 26 December 1991, p. A1.

"Solving the Credit Card Mystery," *Wall Street Journal*, 26 December 1991, p. A12.

portfolio analysis (matching debts and assets) that we examined earlier, but given the volume of debts and assets involved, it is doubtful that banks are willing to perform the necessary risk–return calculations. Fortunately, there exists a relatively simple alternative called gap analysis.

Essentially, **gap analysis** proceeds by subdividing a bank's assets and liabilities into components that are *rate sensitive*—that is, influenced by interest rate changes—and components that are not. Then the gap is calculated as

$$GAP = IRSA - IRSL \tag{16.18}$$

where

$$IRSA = \text{interest rate sensitive assets}$$
$$IRSL = \text{interest rate sensitive liabilities}$$

Assets that are sensitive to interest rates include variable-rate loans and T-bills, among other items. Liabilities in the same category are daily interest rate accounts.

Fixed-rate assets (such as long-term government bonds) and liabilities (such as long-term loans) count for little here.

Table 16.6 gives the breakdown for the First Typical Canadian Bank and the calculation of equation (16.18). The positive gap of \$2 million means an increase in interest rates of, say, 3% would increase the bank's revenues by 0.03 × \$20M = \$600,000. A positive gap may be a reflection of a bank's belief that interest rates will rise since its revenue (and, presumably, profit) picture will improve.

Unfortunately, any simple approach to measuring bank performance always has a catch. Recall that increases in interest rates adversely affect the market value or price of assets such as bonds. Since market values are not reflected in balance sheets, gap analysis ignores them. Yet a 3% rise in interest rates can substantially reduce the value of the fixed-rate assets. Indeed, depending upon the term to maturity of the long-term assets and whether the bonds need to be sold on the market, a 3% rise in interest rates can reduce the fixed-rate component of assets sufficiently to make net worth negative, thereby bankrupting the banking firm.

Despite this drawback, gap analysis is frequently used by banks in managing interest rate risk.

## DURATION ANALYSIS

A different approach to evaluating interest rate risk is to explicitly consider the length of time assets and liabilities of a bank yield a certain stream of income or interest expense. The first step involves calculating the so-called **duration** of a financial instrument which can essentially be defined as a weighted average of the maturities of the payment stream generated by assets or liabilities in question. This, of course, means that we have to resort to the present value concept first encountered in Chapter 5. If $PV_t$ is the present value of a stream of payments (principal and interest) at time t, then the value for all instruments (assets or liabilities) can be written as:

$$P = \sum_{i=1}^{N} PV_t$$

For example, if one asset yields $\$X$ at the end of year 1 and $\$Z$ at the end of the second year, then $\$X/(1+R)$ and $\$Z/(1+R)^2$ are the relevant present values and $P$ would simply be the sum of the two, that is, $\$X/(1+R) + \$Z/(1+R)^2$. Duration is then defined as the sum of these present values weighted by the time to maturity for each stream of payment, as a fraction of the market value of assets or liabilities, that is,

**TABLE 16.6** AN ILLUSTRATION OF GAP ANALYSIS

**First Typical Canadian Bank**

| Assets | | Liabilities | |
|---|---|---|---|
| Rate-sensitive | \$70M | Rate-sensitive | \$50M |
| Fixed-rate | \$30M | Fixed-rate | \$40M |
| | | Net worth | \$10M |

| | | | | |
|---|---|---|---|---|
| Rate-sensitive assets | − | Rate-sensitive liabilities | = | GAP |
| \$70 M | − | \$50M | = | \$20M |

$$dur = \sum_{i=1}^{N} t\,(PV_t/P) \tag{16.19}$$

where $t$ is the time until the payment is made (in the example above it would be 1 and 2) and $P$ is the definition for the value of a financial asset (see Chapter 5 again). It helps to see why the duration concept is important by evaluating the return on an asset or a liability which can be shown to be approximately

$$\Delta P/P \approx -dur\,(\Delta R/(1+R))$$

Therefore, if *dur* is large, the effect of an interest rate change is larger than when *dur* is small. But then this is essentially the result we arrived at in Chapter 5 when we considered the impact of interest rate changes on the price of bonds with different maturities. The only difference here is that the principle is applied to any asset or liability.

We can also evaluate the impact of the duration measure on a banking firm's balance sheet as follows. Recall that a firm's net worth is the difference between its assets and its liabilities, that is,

$$NW = A - L$$

Therefore, changes in net worth (see Chapter 8), are simply

$$\Delta NW = \Delta A - \Delta L = (\Delta A/A)A - (\Delta L/L)L$$

Now, if we define $dur_A$ and $dur_L$ as the duration of assets and liabilities, respectively, then the previous expression can be rewritten as

$$\Delta NW = -\,dur_A\,(\Delta R/(1+R))A + dur_L\,(\Delta L/L)L$$

or, finally,

$$\Delta NW = [\Delta R/(1+R)]\,(dur_A\,A - dur_L L) \tag{16.20}$$

We can then define the gap, measured in terms of duration, as

$$dur\ GAP = dur_A\ (A/L) - dur_L \tag{16.21}$$

# THE PRINCIPAL–AGENT MODEL

The approaches considered in this chapter focus, directly or indirectly, on the bank's bottom line, that is on the management of its balance sheet.

However, in the area of industrial organization, there has been much research done on the relationship between managers and CEOs (chief executive officers) and their shareholders or debtholders. In this framework, CEOs are viewed as the agents while the shareholders (and possibly other debtholders) are viewed as the principals.

The two groups may, however, be in conflict. We first saw this in Chapter 10 in the discussion of whether it makes any difference for a firm to borrow via equity issues or through the selling of bonds. The difficulty is that the agent may, at times, be more concerned with his or her own fortunes than with those of the owners. These concerns have led to much discussion about the "optimal" design of a contract to foster outcomes which satisfy both agents and principals (indeed, as we will see in Chapter 24, this has affected how central bank governors are appointed). The design of such contracts also involves issues of attitudes toward risk. Thus, for example, if the CEO is risk averse but the shareholders are risk neutral, there will be conflict since shareholders will want to maximize, say, dividends, regardless of risk while the CEO will trade off risk versus return in a manner previously described in Chapters 13 and 14. This means that in order to understand the principal–agent problem one has to make assumptions about the utility function of these two groups.

To illustrate some of the issues involved, consider the information in Table 16.7. The table gives the probability that the bank's CEO will generate profits of 5 or 15 depending upon the amount of effort expended (which might be a combination of hours worked and skills for the job). If effort equals 1, the expected profit will be $3/4(5) + 1/4(15) = 7.5$; under effort equals 2, the expected profit is $1/4(5) + 3/4(15) = 12.5$. Clearly, shareholders will prefer the latter outcome. But how to achieve this if the salary of the CEO is fixed? Perhaps by providing the CEO with extra perks such as a generous expense account. Alternatively, a contract could specify a small salary if profits turn out to be less than expected and a bonus tied to the level of profits if they end up higher than, say, 7.5 the expected profit when effort equals 1. Not surprisingly, many companies have shown interest in tying CEO's salaries to company performance.

**TABLE 16.7** A NUMERICAL EXAMPLE OF THE PRINCIPAL–AGENT MODEL

| | Profit | |
|---|---|---|
| Effort | 5 | 15 |
| 1 | 3/4 | 1/4 |
| 2 | 1/4 | 3/4 |

Note: The above table gives the level of profit earned by a bank as a function of the level of effort produced by the CEO. Each of the four possible outcomes has a probability attached to it.

At a fundamental level, the problems discussed above arise because it is not always possible or feasible for the principal to monitor the agent constantly. In addition, it is also possible that while shareholders take a long-term view of the firm's activities and prospects the managers may take a short-term view. This is another source of conflict between agent and principal that can produce a less than optimal outcome for the firm. These, and the other problems referred to above, are manifestations of the problem of asymmetric information whereby the managers possess perhaps relatively more information about the market the firm operates in than the shareholders.

## SUMMARY

- In this chapter, we examine the mechanics of deposit and loan creation in the banking system.
- One way of understanding what banks do is to consider the theory of multiple expansion of deposits. Because only a fraction of the funds deposited at banks need to be kept immediately available, banks can create additional deposits by some multiple.
- An alternative view of what banks do assumes that the banking firm maximizes profits. In doing so, it takes deposits and issues loans until it reaches the point at which marginal cost equals the marginal revenue of an additional dollar of deposits.
- Banks have to manage assets and liabilities simultaneously. A simple way of determining whether interest rate changes will enhance or reduce the bank's revenues is to calculate the gap: the difference between interest-rate-sensitive assets and interest-rate-sensitive liabilities.

# IMPORTANT TERMS

deposit multiplier (p. 367)
duration analysis (p. 382)
duration gap (p. 382)
excess reserves (p. 363)
gap analysis (p. 381)
reserves (p. 363)
target reserves (p. 363)

# EXERCISES

1. At one time, some economists argued that banks should hold 100% reserves against their deposits. How would the deposit multiplier process work then?

2. If the target reserves on deposits is set to zero, the deposit multiplier is infinitely high. Is this statement true, false, or uncertain? Explain your answer.

3. Assume a reserve requirement of 10%. If deposits fall throughout the entire banking system by $1,000 million and, thus, system-wide primary reserves decline by $100 million, necessitating loans of $900 million to be called in, will the deposit contraction process be completed? Use a balance sheet for your answer.

4. Suppose that in the example illustrated (Table 16.1), the Second Typical Canadian Bank decides not to lend out the extra $950 in reserves. How much deposit creation will take place in the banking system?

5. Show the impact of a cost-saving technological improvement on the banking firm model of Figure 16.1.

6. Suppose there are two types of deposits. Using Figure 16.1, describe the process by which the banking firm would select the profit-maximizing volume of deposits.

7. Suppose a bank's assets and liabilities have been reclassified into assets and liabilities that are rate sensitive and those that are not. The data are as follows:

| Assets | | Liabilities | |
|---|---|---|---|
| Rate-sensitive | $400M | Rate-sensitive | $200M |
| Fixed-rate | $200M | Fixed-rate | $400M |

Evaluate the gap for this bank. What is the effect on total revenues of a $2% fall in interest rates?

8. Perfect matching of assets and debts will result in a zero gap. In what sense is this statement true? Explain.

9. If a bank expects interest rates to fall, will it prefer a positive or a negative gap? Do you need to qualify your answer?

10. Suppose that in the example illustrated in Table 16.1, the STCB chooses to purchase securities instead of making loans. How much deposit creation will take place in the banking system?

11. Suppose that in the example considered in Table 16.4, the FTCB decides to call in loans instead of selling securities. Trace the impact on deposits for the banking system as a whole.

12. Suppose that in the example considered in Table 16.4, the transfer is from demand deposits to time deposits. Trace the impact on the deposits of the banking system.

13. Suppose that in the first scenario considered in Table 16.5, the near-bank decreases its time deposits at the chartered banks. What would happen to M1? M2? M2+? Explain your answers.

14. Suppose that in the second scenario in Table 16.5, the near-banks keep reserves (against the rise in their time deposits outstanding) in the form of demand deposits at the chartered banks. What happens to M1? To M2? Explain your answers.

15. Suppose that financial instruments generate the following stream of income: $1,000 in the first year, $1,500 in the second year and $2,000 in the third year. Assuming that market interest rates are 6%, calculate the duration. What would happen to the market value of these instruments if the market interest rate were to rise to 9%?

16. Assume that a bank has assets of $100 million with duration of 15, and liabilities of $95 million with duration of 9. Calculate the duration GAP.

17. Assume that a bank has assets of $75 million with duration of 6 and liabilities of $65 million with duration of 6. What is that duration GAP? What would happen to net worth if market interest rates rose by 2%? How would the bank reduce interest rate risk in the event of an interest rate increase?

18. Show, using a figure such as Figure 16.1, that the interest rate charged to a good customer (i.e, low risk of default) would differ from one charged a bad customer (i.e., high risk of default).

**19.** Compare, using the framework developed in Figure 16.1, the spread for a bank which happens to have more "dishonest" customers than another.

**20.** Does the growth of ATMs (automatic teller machines) increase or decrease the need for banks to keep cash reserves on hand?

## REFERENCES


*Bank of Canada Review* (various issues).

Blomqvist, A., P. Wonnacott, R. Wonnacott, and J. Fried. *Macroeconomics*, 4th Cdn. ed. Toronto: McGraw-Hill Ryerson Ltd., 1994.

Humphrey, T.M. "The Theory of Multiple Expansion of Deposits: What It Is and Whence It Came." Federal Reserve Bank of Richmond, *Economic Review* (March/April 1987): 3–11.

Martin, P. *Inside the Bank of Canada's Weekly Financial Statistics*, 2d ed. Vancouver: The Fraser Institute, 1989.

Mints, L. *A History of Banking Theory in Great Britain and the United States.* Chicago: University of Chicago Press, 1945.

Spellman, L.J. *The Depository Firm and Industry: Theory, History and Regulation.* New York: Academic Press, 1982.

CHAPTER 17

# Chartered Banks: History and Performance

Having broadly outlined various analytical approaches to understanding bank behaviour and performance, we can turn to a description of the Canadian banking system.

This subject is a large and fascinating one that could be tackled in many ways. We concentrate here on the chartered banks (we'll turn to other depository institutions, as well as the rest of the financial system, in subsequent chapters). In our focus on their regulation, we review the **Bank Act** and its revisions over the years and reflect on the process of financial innovation and its influence on regulation. Finally, we describe the actual performance of chartered banks since the end of World War II, paying particular attention to the way regulation and globalization have shaped their asset–liability management.

## THE EVOLUTION OF COMMERCIAL BANKING THOUGHT

When Canadians say "bank," they are usually referring to a **chartered bank**, which is a specific kind of private banking firm, federally chartered and regulated, that accepts deposits and makes loans.

The Canadian chartered banks can be called commercial banks, which is the term used in most countries over recent centuries for privately owned institutions in the business of borrowing funds by the issue of short-term deposits or bank notes and making short-term, self-liquidating loans to finance firms' inventories. (In the strict sense, a *self-liquidating loan* is one expected to generate funds for its own repayment.) Although custom as well as the inflation and deregulation of the 1970s and 1980s has fundamentally altered the way the chartered banks do business, they are, for the most part, still recognized by their commercial lending function.

Thus, our history of the chartered banks can be clarified by some discussion of the evolution of the way people think about how commercial banking should work.

## THE REAL BILLS DOCTRINE

In pre-Confederation Canada, as in many other parts of the world, banking emerged to satisfy the needs of trade. Indeed, an early theory of the role of banks in the economy sought to explain how changes in the money supply should be linked to the needs of trade. The **real bills doctrine** stipulated that money supply growth should be tied to output growth via the use of short-term credit, such as that provided by *commercial paper* (which used to mean private bank notes). In this fashion, the money supply would always be backed by the economy's existing production, thereby ensuring a stable price level. This theory, which is almost 300 years old, may have originated with the Scotsman John Law, who proposed that the volume of notes in circulation be in fixed proportion to the market value of land. Law put his theory into practice in eighteenth-century France, where it led to disastrous inflation. Why? Law and other early proponents of the doctrine failed to understand that prices are not independent of the quantity of money, as we have already seen.[1]

## FREE BANKING

We are used to thinking that social welfare demands that the banking industry be regulated to some extent.[2] The initial financial development of Canada was influenced by this view and by the cautious approach to banking taken in contemporary England. But it was also much influenced by the free banking experiments of Scotland and the United States in the first half of the nineteenth century. As the phrase suggests, **free banking** consists of a financial system that is largely unregulated and that can be entered easily without, for example, obtaining a charter or meeting huge capital requirements. Given the current trends toward financial deregulation around the world it is not surprising that the study of previous experiences with minimal state regulation in financial affairs has blossomed in recent years. The basic philosophical tenet of economic activity unfettered by regulation is that individuals or groups of individuals will tend, perhaps in an evolutionary fashion, to seek out institutional arrangements that minimize the costs of doing business. Competition does not produce financial instability (say, from banks' reckless behaviour to obtain and hold on to customers), as

1 A new version of the real bills doctrine has recently been popularized in the search for a way to end inflation or at least stabilize it at some low level. The rejuvenated view argues that government deficits financed from known or anticipated revenues are not inflationary since they are backed by financial resources that will be available in the future. Other excessive deficits, however, eventually force a government to resort to the issue of money, creating inflation. We will consider these issues in further detail in Chapter 26.

2 One reason is fear that the failure of one bank will become contagious, leading to additional failures. As we will see in Chapter 22, such *bank runs* have been common in the United States throughout that country's financial history.

critics contend; rather, it fosters stability. There is no need for a lender of last resort, such as a central bank. Competition leads to an economy with many banks, none of which monopolize the financial system. Thus, for example, Scotland had 19 banks by 1844 (after which free entry was no longer allowed). The four largest supplied almost half the notes in circulation.

Despite some controversy about the degree to which Scottish banks were actually unregulated (there were restrictions on the denominations of notes that private banks could issue, and some barriers to entry), the overall evidence on the success of free banks appears positive.

> The [Scottish] banking system made rapid strides in both stability and efficiency. Freedom to issue notes insured healthy competition and adequate banking services wherever they were in demand. The regular note exchanges made the banks watchdogs of one another and prevented any bank from getting seriously out of line with the general development of the economy. The notes exchanges were forerunners, in fact, of modern clearing houses. Scotland did not altogether avoid bank failures, but its record with respect to stability was much better than those of most countries in similar stages of development.[3]

The small geographical size of Scotland may also have played a role and the proximity of the Bank of England which could have, in principle, acted as a lender of last resort.

### LEGAL RESTRICTIONS

A different perspective on the evolution of banks is suggested by those proponents of the *legal restrictions view.* They claim that regulation has shaped our current financial institutions and specifically that only regulation forces the public to hold non-interest-bearing government debt (that is, currency). In a laissez-faire or free banking world, banks as intermediaries would, for example, offer interest-earning currency in small denominations suitable for transactions purposes. (It will come as no surprise that not everyone is so sanguine about the possibility for interest-earning money.)

## DEVELOPMENT OF COMMERCIAL BANKING IN CANADA

We think of banks as institutions that accept deposits and make loans. In the eighteenth and early nineteenth centuries, however, an equally important function

3 R. Cameron, *Banking in the Early Stages of Industrialization* (New York: Oxford University Press, 1967), 70. The United States' experience with free banking was apparently not so successful. See G. Gorton, "Banking Theory and Free Banking History," *Journal of Monetary Economics* 16 (1985): 267–76.

was issuing bank notes. Provided these notes could be easily converted into *specie* (not always true, as some found to their sorrow), they were "as good as gold" and far more convenient for transactions. But a government does not want its people (still less, its merchants, traders, and developers) exposed to the dangers of "money" that may suddenly become worthless.[4] So many countries began to regulate the issue of bank notes.

Another contemporary convention was the requirement that any joint-stock operation (what we would call a limited liability company or a corporation) obtain a charter from the appropriate legislature. Banking charters especially were not easy to obtain, particularly in the farflung colonies of Great Britain, which was developing a tradition of careful, conservative banking.

In 1792 and again in 1807 and 1808, groups of Montreal merchants formed banking ventures that failed because they could not obtain permission to issue notes. In 1817, another group applied for a charter and meanwhile opened its door as the Bank of Montreal. The application, caught in political battles and bureaucratic delay, was not granted until 1822. Meanwhile, the Bank of New Brunswick and the Bank of Upper Canada had been granted charters in 1820 and 1821, respectively.

All these early charters essentially authorized a bank organization to

1. Issue notes.
2. Lend for commercial purposes and incur an indebtedness up to a stipulated amount.
3. Open branches, usually.[5]
4. Report to the government on its financial activities from time to time.

This conservative, regulated pattern, based on a British model,[6] set the model for the Canadian banking system, one quite different from that already under way in the United States.[7]

---

4 A healthy amount of self-interest was also involved since, by monopolizing the note issue, governments also generate revenue for themselves (called seigniorage, as we saw in Chapter 2).

5 New Brunswick specifically forbade branches and Upper Canada authorized them. Lower Canada made no explicit provision either way, but given the absence of restrictions and subsequent history, one may assume they were permitted.

6 It had also been the model for the First and the Second Banks of the United States in 1792 and 1816, respectively. But the individualistic Americans distrusted "big money." Each bank was successful, but the US Congress would renew neither charter.

7 Yet the adoption of a nation-wide branch banking system was inspired by the writings of Alexander Hamilton, the first Secretary of the Treasury of the United States. See R.M. Breckinridge, *The History of Banking in Canada* (Washington, D.C.: United States Government Printing Office, 1910), 7–8. This volume was published as part of the US National Monetary Commission's report.

More Canadian banks were chartered during the next quarter century, all in growing urban areas. Although the country went through hard economic times in 1837–38 and again in 1847–50, few of these banks failed, perhaps because they were so few (some had near-monopolies in their areas).

Because bank charters were usually granted to men with the "right" socio-political ties, objections from populists were inevitable. They pleaded for free—unchartered—banking to establish small banks under local control with local funds, to ease the introduction of banking facilities in areas of smaller population, and to expand the effective market for government securities (which were becoming an important source of financing). The populists got their way in Upper Canada in 1850, when the legislature introduced a free banking statute, modelled on banking laws in place in New York State. This free banking was not, however, entirely unregulated. There were, for example, rules specifying the minimum start-up capital as well as a requirement that notes were to be redeemable in specie on demand. And charters were still available (the US states that adopted free banking laws simultaneously abolished chartering). Moreover, banks had emergency access to funds in markets in London and New York.

Free banking was not much of a success in Canada. Only five new banks were founded under the Free Banking Act; two failed and the others converted to legislative charters, which permitted branches and the issuing of bank notes. Since mortgages and personal loans were prohibited throughout this whole early period, banking was largely limited to commercial lending activities. By the 1860s, however, an important and a peculiarly Canadian provision widened the scope of banking activities. The banks were permitted to lend against goods still in the possession of the borrower. In other words, the collateral could be a bill of lading or a warehouse receipt—often for agricultural goods[8]—an arrangement that does not meet the strict definition of a self-liquidating loan. This famous rule, known as Section 88 or the "pledge section" was introduced in 1859. It gave the banks an important role in Canadian agriculture and mineral resource development. But the fact that the collateral had to be available when the loan was granted (as opposed to some expectation that it would be available sometime in the future) provided a severe restriction on the growth of economic activity in Canada.

## THE CANADIAN BANK ACTS

About the same time that commercial banking and other financial services were spreading throughout the infant Canada, government was beginning to intervene

8 Only a select group of agricultural commodities, such as grains, qualified initially.

in the emerging financial system more effectively and on a broader scale than in earlier periods. This raises the question of how one should view the government approach to regulation. Economists postulate a profit-maximizing motive for the individual banking firm. What then are the motives of a government? What principle should guide the formation and implementation of regulation? Economists generally view governments as attempting to maximize a *social welfare function.* It is akin to the individual utility function (see Chapter 9) except that it must incorporate the varied needs and pressures of society on government and its politicians.[9]

In Canada, perhaps the most important regulation of banks has taken the form of the federal Bank Acts throughout the years. Through them we can trace the development of banking since Confederation.

## THE FIRST BANK ACT

The Constitution Act, 1867, granted the newly formed federal government of Canada monopoly powers in all areas of banking and currency issue. Shortly thereafter Parliament enacted the **Bank Act** of 1871, the first of a series of statutes that would regulate the activities of all chartered banks.

Perhaps the most important break from the past was the gradual introduction of a state monopoly in the issue of currency. Initially, the government monopolized the issue of $1 and $2 notes, called Dominion notes. Private bank notes, although not legal tender, could be redeemed for specie or Dominion notes. (Private bank notes remained popular. For example, between 1873 and 1913, they represented approximately 95% of all notes and demand and notice deposits held at chartered banks.) One possible reason for monopolizing the low-denomination note issue was to protect the least sophisticated individuals from the effects of a bank failure. Assuming the least sophisticated (and likely the poorest) individuals held small denomination notes, a government monopoly in the issue of such notes would, in effect, represent a state guarantee that these notes could be redeemed for goods and services.

## THE BANK ACT OVER THE YEARS

The first Bank Act came into effect in 1871 (as noted above) and the legislation was to be revised every 10 years. Table 17.1 summarizes the Act's history by

9 The problems of trying to specify and actually find the optimal point for consumption in a social welfare function are complex and beyond the scope of this text. In the context of a financial system, considerations such as equity across regions and provinces, promoting growth across the country, maintaining the efficiency and integrity of the financial sector, and the maintenance of the safety net would all enter a social welfare function. For more on this point, see J. Chant, *Regulation of Financial Institutions: A Functional Analysis* (Ottawa: Bank of Canada, 1987).

## FINANCIAL FOCUS 17.1 Anatomy of a Bank Act

Because the Bank Act is revised approximately every 10 years, it may appear that legislators put aside concerns about the financial industry for a few years at least. Nothing is further from the truth.

Indeed, as this text is written, the government is entertaining submissions from interested parties (banks, insurance companies) about revising the Bank Act. A revision is permitted before the 10-year term of the current Act is up.

Shortly after a Bank Act receives royal assent, lobbying for changes or improvements begins. But the world of banking is a complex place, and many voices must be heard and weighed. Moreover, because the Canadian financial system is also subject to regulations at the provincial level, lawmakers must face the additional complication of provincial legislation conflicting with federal legislation.

Finally, events may overtake the law. For example, the Home Bank failed soon after a new Bank Act was introduced. The 1980 Bank Act was delayed in part because changes in the financial system occurred with such speed that legislators were unable to craft laws that would be suitable for the next 10 years.

The following list of events, which reflect only attempts to influence the direction of *federal* legislation, suggests why the regulatory process is an ongoing affair. It illustrates the long, drawnout process by which the latest Bank Act was revised.

| | **Proposal** |
|---|---|
| November 1984 | "A New Direction for Canada: An Agenda for Canada." Proposal for restructuring the financial sector. |
| April 1985 | "The Regulations of Canadian Financial Institutions: Proposals for Discussion," Green Paper. |
| June 1985 | The Wyman Report on reforming the Canada Deposit Insurance Corporation. |
| November 1985 | Report by the House of Commons Standing Committee on Finance and Economic Affairs on Canada's Financial Institutions. |
| May 1986 | "Towards a More Competitive Financial Environment." A Report by the Senate Standing Committee on Banking, Trade and Commerce. |
| October 1986 | An attempt is made, but subsequently withdrawn, to introduce Bill C-9 to amend the Bank Act. |
| December 1986 | "New Directions for the Financial Sector." White Paper outlining the government's proposals for the reform of the financial system. |
| July 1987 | "Bank Profits." Report of the Standing Committee on Finance, Trade and Economic Affairs. |
| 1989 | "A New Frontier: Globalization and Canada's Financial Markets." Statement is released by the Economic Council of Canada with recommendations for reform of the Canadian financial system. |
| September 1990 | The federal government introduces a new Bank Act as part of a package to reform the entire financial system. |
| December 1991 | New Bank Act is passed by Parliament. |
| June 1992 | New Bank Act takes effect. |

listing the years in which revisions were enacted and some of the most important characteristics of each. It is, of course, possible to discuss only some of the principal provisions of the legislation enacted over the last 120 years or so.

**Table 17.1** THE BANK ACT: A CHRONOLOGY

| Enacted | Principal Characteristics |
|---|---|
| 1871 | • Definition of a bank<br>• Decennial revision process<br>• Minimum denomination $4 |
| 1881 | • Scope of banking operations widened to increase commercial borrowing opportunities<br>• Provisions to enhance security of the financial system |
| 1891 | • Increased start-up capital (an entry barrier)<br>• Bank Circulation Redemption Fund introduced<br>• Notes to circulate at par |
| 1901 | • Increase in the number of products against which commercial concerns could borrow<br>• Canadian Bankers' Association given oversight powers over members |
| 1914 | • Provision for bank audits<br>• Provision for loans to be made in anticipation of sales (easing financial distress of farmers)<br>• Separate Finance Act: government lender of last resort |
| 1924 | • Changes in reporting financial transactions<br>• Continuance of the Finance Act, 1914<br>• Tightening of requirements for creation of banks (following the failure of the Home Bank) |
| 1935 | • Severe limits on private note issue in anticipation of the Bank of Canada<br>• Reserve requirements to be held with the Bank of Canada<br>• Permitted collateral for commercial loans expanded yet again |
| 1945 | • Bank financial statements to be made public<br>• Ban on further issue or re-issue of private bank notes<br>• Creation of the Industrial Development Bank (separate act) |
| 1954 | • Permission for banks to offer mortgages issued under the National Housing Act (Central Housing and Mortgage Corporation)<br>• Legal reserve ratio raised; control by the Bank of Canada<br>• Establishment of a money market<br>• Issuances of Bank of Canada Advances |
| 1967 | • Deposit insurance introduced<br>• Removal of interest rate ceiling<br>• Banks free to enter mortgage lending field<br>• Secondary reserve requirement introduced |
| 1981 | • Subsidiaries of foreign banks permitted charters in Canada (Schedule II)<br>• Changes in reserve requirements<br>• Conventional and residential mortgages capped to 10% of Canadian dollar deposits<br>• Banks permitted entry to new fields: financial leasing and data processing services<br>• Creation of the Canadian Payments Association |

**Table 17.1** THE BANK ACT: A CHRONOLOGY (Continued)

| Enacted | Principal Characteristics |
| --- | --- |
| 1980s (various interim measures) | • Increase in the limit on domestic assets of foreign banks (to 16% of industry-wide assets)<br>• Creation of position of superintendent of financial institutions<br>• Approval for banks to acquire discount brokerage firms |
| 1991 | • Comprehensive banking law<br>• Permission for chartered banks to own trust companies (but they continue to be barred from selling life insurance)<br>• Maintenance of rule that chartered banks must be widely held<br>• Trust companies permitted to offer commercial loans<br>• Chartered bank reserve requirements to be phased out<br>• Real estate holdings permitted for as much as 70% of capital |

Sources: A. Power and D.K. Varma, *The Touche Ross Guide to Financial Reporting for Canadian Banks* (Toronto: CCH Canadian Ltd., 1984); *Bank Act: Orders and Regulations with Guidelines, Interpretation Bulletins and Other Regulatory Documents*, 3d ed. (Don Mills, Ont.: Richard de Boo Publishers, 1989); *The Canadian Bank Act 1980* (Price Waterhouse Canada); J.W. O'Brien and G. Lermer, *Canadian Money and Banking*, 2d ed. (Toronto: McGraw-Hill, 1969); A.B. Jamieson, *Chartered Banking in Canada* (Toronto: Ryerson Press, 1953), "Restructuring The Canadian Financial Industry," *Bank of Canada Review* (Winter 1992–93): 21–45.

One can spot two overriding or summarizing themes: (1) widening of the scope of chartered banking operations, and (2) concern over bank safety. An example of the increasing of scope was the frequent broadening of the "pledge section." The types of commodities for use as collateral were redefined with the introduction of every Bank Act until after World War II, when restrictions were essentially lifted and banks allowed to stipulate their own collateral requirements.

The concern for bank safety was first met in 1891 with the creation of a Bank Circulation Redemption Fund to guard against the loss of funds when a note issue became valueless because a bank had failed. Further bank safety enforcement provisions over the years included the extension of auditing of bank activities, culminating in the creation of government supervision of the banking system, and the introduction of deposit insurance.[10]

In addition, many regulations were altered or dropped over the years because they proved unnecessary or inconsistent with the prevailing financial environment. For example, initially, all bank directors had to be British subjects. This restriction was later relaxed to apply only to a majority of directors and subsequently, it was dropped altogether.

10 Deposit insurance is discussed separately in Chapter 20.

The degree to which Bank Act revisions represented fundamental changes in the regulations governing chartered banks has varied considerably over time. The first two sets of regulatory changes were fairly minor. The first major overhaul of the financial system took place in 1891 with the introduction of more stringent start-up capital requirements and more extensive supervision over private note issue. During the first half of the twentieth century four important events shaped revisions of the Bank Act: the crisis of 1907, the Great Depression, the creation of the Bank of Canada, and the push for global markets. Of course, the two world wars also played a role in the timing of regulatory reforms.

## The Crisis of 1907

The crisis of 1907 originated, like many Canadian recessions, in the United States. Several bank failures there triggered bank runs. Part of the problem may have been that the relative importance of the agricultural sector in the activity of the US economy and the banks' heavy loans to farmers led to seasonal interest rate fluctuations that corresponded with seasonality in the demand for money. Similar difficulties faced western Canadian farmers, and a very poor crop in 1907 exacerbated the situation. The Canadian government stepped in to facilitate the provision of credit. Thereafter, the role of government in providing credit and in influencing the portfolios of chartered banks would become increasingly important.

The need to finance the war and the resulting disruption in the international payments flow led to the Finance Act, 1914, and effectively made the government the lender of last resort, by providing access to Dominion notes, until the Bank of Canada was formed in 1934. This also meant that Canada was effectively no longer under the Gold Standard. The Finance Act also heralded the introduction of a monetary market of sorts: the government advanced notes against its own securities without any constraint on expansion.

## The 1920s and 1930s

The failure of the Home Bank (1923), which a royal commission blamed on the misconduct of several officers, led to more stringent oversight of the chartered banks. And the government's role as lender of last resort was reinforced when it advanced grants to the Home's creditors.

This increasing regulation may have proved its value in the 1930s. The Great Depression brought a tremendous contraction to the US banking system but Canadian banks experienced no failures or runs during that period. Some analysts think that Canada's salvation was the stability provided by a banking system with few institutions and an extensive branch framework. An alternative view suggests that an effective government bailout saved a banking system that had become essentially insolvent. In any event, government involvement in the workings of the financial system increased and culminated in the creation of a central bank, the Bank of Canada.

## The Modern Period

The end of World War II heralded a period of strong economic growth and banks lived in a world of relative calm. It was shattered by the oil price shocks of the 1970s. Consequent inflation necessitated the introduction of new financial products; the prospect of financial innovations was encouraged by the uncertainty and volatility of interest rates during the 1970s, which made it difficult for banks to manage their assets and liabilities in a profitable manner.

In general, financial legislation after the 1970s was also meant to liberalize the regulations governing chartered bank behaviour. In a break with the past, Canada, like most governments around the world, began to *deregulate* in many areas—that is, to reduce its regulation of business activities, including approval for new investments and types of products. For the chartered banks, deregulation has meant gradual removal of impediments to the type of products offered and to restrictions on the kinds of firms eligible to apply for a charter. Thus, chartered banks were allowed to enter the residential mortgage lending field, to engage in financial leasing,[11] and to provide data processing services, among other financial services. By 1981, subsidiaries of foreign banks could obtain a bank charter; domestic Canadian banks became Schedule A (now called *Schedule I*) banks and foreign subsidiaries Schedule B (now *Schedule II*) banks. Permission for chartered banks to acquire brokerage firms led to a buying spree during the late 1980s and early 1990s. Thus, for example, the Bank of Montreal purchased Nesbitt Thomson in 1987 and Burns Fry in 1994, the Bank of Nova Scotia purchased McLeod, Young, Weir in 1988, while the Canadian Imperial Bank of Commerce bought Wood Gundy. During the same year the Royal Bank acquired Dominion Securities. Finally, in 1993, the Toronto-Dominion Bank purchased Marathon Brokerage.

The number of chartered banks had grown to 66 by January 1991. Restrictions remain on the overall size of the foreign segment of the chartered banking system, but they have not, so far, proved to be a constraint barrier to the growth of foreign banks in Canada.[12] Moreover, the government has made tentative steps

---

11 In a white paper on reforms for the banking sector to be considered in 1997, the federal government proposed that banks be permitted to offer auto and consumer goods leasing.

12 Nevertheless, foreign banks based in countries other than the United States have begun to complain that the Canada–US Free Trade Agreement leaves them at a competitive disadvantage. For example, Schedule

to ease the separation of commercial lending from securities underwriting. (Similar steps are being contemplated in the United States; other nations' financial systems have no such separation of financing functions.)

## The Bank Act of 1991

So rapid was the process of financial innovation and deregulation that the Bank Act of 1981 was outdated before it was passed. As a result, existing legislation, which did not provide for contingencies or activities outside the legislation, were forbidden territory (the legal term is *ultra vires*). For this reason, several stopgap reform measures (see Table 17.1) were introduced during the 1980s, and the Bank Act of 1991,[13] written in co-ordination with some other new financial legislation, offers many changes. Pressure also came from a number of provincial initiatives. For example, Quebec permitted financial institutions under its jurisdiction to offer a complete range of financial services as well as commercial-financial links.[14] Previously, we also saw how the federal and Ontario governments agreed to lift restrictions on ownership of securities dealers (see **FINANCIAL FOCUS 17.1: Anatomy of a Bank Act** on page 395). Thus, the need for a major overhaul of the financial sector became evident to all interested parties. One of the consequences of globalization is that the new Bank Act would permit an institution to engage in any financial activity unless it was specifically prohibited from doing so in the new Act.

The current regulatory environment favours the creation of equal or near-equal competition throughout the financial sector and thus the virtual elimination of the *four pillars approach* to financial institutions (see Chapter 3). Therefore, instead of legislating for one branch of the financial system in isolation from the others, the new Act introduces a comprehensive set of reforms for all types of financial institutions, especially chartered banks, trust companies, and insurance companies.

For example, the new Bank Act phased out required reserves,[15] levelling some terms of competition between near-banks, which had never had to meet the

---

II banks must operate as subsidiaries, not branches, of the home bank, so their lending is limited to the funds they have in Canada and they may not draw on the financial resources of the parent bank. One proposal, made in anticipation of the mid-term review of the Bank Act due in 1997, is to eliminate all restrictions on foreign banks as New Zealand and Australia have already done.

13 The Senate passed the new Bank Act on December 13, 1991. The statutes were proclaimed in June 1992.

14 See *Reform of Financial Institutions in Quebec: Objectives, Guiding Principles and Action Plan* (Government of Quebec: Associate Minister for Finance and Privatization, October 1987).

15 Implementation of the phase-out began in November 1991 and was completed before the July 1994 deadline. See "The Evolution of Routine Bank of Canada Advances to Direct Clearers," *Bank of Canada Review* (October 1992): 3–22.

requirements, and chartered banks, which had. This does not mean that banks will not hold reserves. Rather, the requirement is that banks should average, at a minimum, zero reserves over some specified period of time. However, as both the Bank of Canada and other central banks commonly refer to this as a state of zero reserve requirement we will follow their wording.[16]

Although reserve requirements have long been a cornerstone of bank regulation, they no longer seem necessary for ensuring the safety of the financial system. The ease with which liquidity is now available has considerably reduced the need for idle cash to be held as reserves, and the Bank of Canada possesses more effective means of controlling the amount of liquidity in the economy. Moreover, other countries, including Switzerland, have eliminated reserve requirements with no signs that the financial systems have become more unstable. Finally, the banking system itself has become more efficient, reducing the need for holding cash reserves. All financial institutions are now permitted to offer a much wider range of financial services within each branch, such as portfolio management and investment advice. Other services, such as trust services, can be "networked," that is, offered via subsidiaries or related institutions.

Another example of the Act's levelling of competition is the provision that allows chartered banks to pursue real estate development previously engaged in by trust and insurance companies. To get around previous restrictions on owning or erecting buildings not for their own use, several of Canada's largest chartered banks had created wholly owned realty subsidiaries. This brought banks into conflict with other private developers, who borrow from the same banks, and thus raised the question of the fairness of a market in which the lenders were competing with potential borrowers for the same contracts. Even as the legislation was being debated during 1991, several chartered banks began to purchase trust companies. Thus, in 1993 the Royal Bank acquired Royal Trust. In 1991 the Laurentian Bank purchased Standard Trust and in 1992 it purchased General Trust and Guardian Trust. During the same year, the Canadian Imperial Bank of Commerce purchased Morgan Trust, and the Toronto-Dominion Bank acquired Central Guarantee Trust. Moreover, a number of insurance companies already own trust companies, and further takeovers are imminent.

Perhaps one of the greatest difficulties facing the legislators in revising the Bank Act was the ownership rules because Schedule I banks were required to be widely held, while trust and mortgage loan companies were closely held institutions. The 1991 Bank Act produced a complex compromise. Essentially, trust, mortgage loan, and insurance companies can continue to be closely held. These institutions

16 We examine in detail, via a numerical example, the operation of the new reserve requirement rules in Chapter 24.

will now come under the Schedule II designation. However, federal institutions with capital of $750 million or more will be required to have at least 35% of shares widely held within five years.[17]

One major source of division left in the financial industry concerns whether banks should be permitted to sell insurance directly. As the mid-term assessment of the Bank Act draws near, there is much lobbying going on both sides of the issue. The chartered banks argue that the current Bank Act limits consumer choice and that non-banking institutions have been able to encroach on the traditional lending function of the chartered banks.[18] The insurance industry replies that allowing banks to sell insurance directly will lead to the effective disappearance of an independent insurance industry. They point to trusts and investment dealers who have been largely taken over by the chartered banks.[19]

## INNOVATION

As this text is being written, the pace of changes in the worldwide economy continues unabated, impinging on the financial system. Political and economic developments, from the crumbling of the Iron Curtain to the Canada–US Free Trade Agreement (FTA) and the North American Free Trade Agreement (NAFTA), will have a lasting impact on the Canadian financial sector. Several recently introduced innovations also seem likely to have a substantial impact in the years to come.

A theme common to many Bank Act revisions has been the desire to introduce financial innovations. Regulations that cause financial institutions to invest resources into areas either unlegislated or unforeseen in the existing legislation have also encouraged innovations. An example is provided by *automated teller machines (ATMs)*. They spread across the country at a remarkable pace, quickly becoming the method of choice for many individuals' transactions with a bank. Yet banking legislation did not foresee various associated problems (such as liability in the event of theft or fraud). Consequently, the legal system had to create precedents governing ATMs and their use. Table 17.2 provides some aggregate statistics which show the tremendous growth of ATMs.

Not all types of innovation are so well received at first. The *debit card*, the financial industry's latest development in channelling funds between individuals,

---

17 For more details on these and other changes, see "Restructuring the Canadian Financial Industry," *Bank of Canada Review* (Winter 1992–93): 21–46.

18 Canadian Bankers Association News, Press Release of 16 November 1995. In the 1996 Budget Speech, Finance Minister Paul Martin confirmed that banks will not be permitted to sell insurance directly.

19 Banks point out that the insurance industry fears competition in what they feel is an inefficient industry. G. Kelly and P.L. Siklos (1995) in "Evaluating Cost Economies in Canada's Property and Casualty Insurance Industry," manuscript, Wilfrid Laurier University, find evidence of relatively high efficiency in the P&C insurance industry.

## ECONOMICS FOCUS 17.1 Chartered Banks and Free Trade

In October 1987 the Canadian and US governments completed the Canada–US Free Trade Agreement (FTA), and during the summer of 1992, the governments of Canada, the United States, and Mexico reached agreement on a similar treaty called the North American Free Trade Agreement (NAFTA). The primary objectives of free trade is the eventual elimination of trade barriers and access for each country to the others' markets with a minimum of government interference.

The passage of these pieces of legislation has not led to a rush to buy banks in either Mexico or the United States although the Bank of Montreal, for example, has been acquiring interests in both US and Mexican banks. The peso crisis (see Chapter 7) and the Savings and Loan debacle (see Chapter 22) did not help make the US or Mexican banks terribly attractive to Canadian banks. It is interesting, however, to see what the agreement specifies for financial institutions. (The NAFTA provisions for the financial sector are similar.)

- US bank subsidiaries in Canada are exempted from the 16% ceiling on assets of foreign banks as a percentage of total domestic chartered bank assets.
- Canada drops its restrictions on US firms' purchases of stock in federally regulated insurance and trust companies.
- US firms seeking entry into Canadian financial markets are treated like Canadian applicants in the review process.
- Banks are permitted to underwrite and deal in debt securities fully backed by the federal government or the provinces.

Although the US financial system is far more fractionalized and regulated in some respects than the Canadian, the FTA ensures that any new federal regulations will apply to Canadian banks operating in the United States and vice versa. It is important to note, however, that provincial and state regulations of the financial sector are unaffected. Therefore, considerable limitation to US access is still possible, though the US federal government, in the wake of the savings and loan scandal, is taking a more active role than previously in regulating the entire financial system.

is essentially a means of settling transactions without cash or cheque via an electronic transfer of funds from, say, the purchaser's bank account to the merchant's bank account. Although such cards offer major advantages including lower transactions costs for the banking industry (less paper and fewer human operations are required to transfer funds between bank accounts) and increased security for bank customers (the risk of loss of cash is lowered), the public was slow at first to accept them despite banks' heralding the arrival of yet another revolution in the financial industry. The problem appeared to be competition between financial institutions, which is preventing them from charging merchants the true cost of writing and cashing cheques and thus virtually eliminating the cost advantages of the debit card system.

In any event, usage of debit cards has grown rapidly. For example, the number of items processed in 1992, 1993 and 1994 grew by 105%, 693% and 450%, respectively.[20]

20 See Canadian Bankers Association, *Bank Facts 1995: Looking Ahead.*

**Table 17.2 NUMBER OF ATM MACHINES IN CANADA**

| Year | Total | Number of Transactions (millions) |
|---|---|---|
| 1988 | 4,102 | n/a |
| 1989 | 5,590 | n/a |
| 1990 | 7,391 | n/a |
| 1991 | 9,714 | 700.4 |
| 1992 | 10,992 | 784.4 |
| 1993 | 11,765 | 834.6 |
| 1994 | 12,318 | 921.1 |

Note: The data are annual averages of quarterly data (Jan., April, July, October).

Source: Canadian Bankers Association Research and Data Service.

New instruments and tools continue to be offered as banks promise the cashless society. There are plans, for example, to introduce a card to take the place of money altogether. Such cards, occasionally referred to as "smart" cards, would work very much like phone cards currently in use in Canada with one notable exception, namely that once all the "money" on a card is used up, it can be "recharged" at a local bank (for a fee, of course).

But with innovations come concerns about security and confidentiality of funds stored in effect "electronically," prompting concerns among regulators about how to deal with new forms of theft, as Financial Focus 17.3 illustrates.

Perhaps even more revolutionary is E-money or the transfer of funds over the Internet. This would bypass completely the conventional deposit-taking institutions, unless they begin to provide a network or some framework to help facilitate financial transactions for their clients. Indeed, several banks are now on the World Wide Web (e.g., Royal, Bank of Montreal, Canada Trust, etc.). The overall implication is that the branch of the future is more likely to involve a PC screen at home than a line in front of a teller's window.[21]

## OTHER ISSUES

The other issues that Bank Acts and other Canadian financial legislation have attempted to address over the years include a variety of economic and social concerns. Two recurring points are market concentration and regional concerns.

21 One study which confirms what has been stated elsewhere in this text, namely that regulators will avoid the chance to implement much needed reforms in 1997 (i.e., the regulator as lagging indicator of institutional change), is J.L. Evans, "Technical Change and the Regulation of Financial Services," in J. Mints and J. Pesando, *Issues in the Reform of the Canadian Financial Services Industry* (Toronto: C.D. Howe Institute, 1996). This article also paints a picture of coming revolutionary changes in the financial sector.

## FINANCIAL FOCUS 17.2 Chartered Banks and the GST

As part of its economic strategy, the federal government implemented the goods and service tax (GST) on 1 January 1991. The new tax classifies all goods and services as either tax-free (no GST is applied throughout the production chain), or tax-exempt (the final sellers collect no tax but have incurred some GST costs throughout the production chain against which they are able to claim a credit), or taxable (the GST must be applied to the final sale).

Looking at the tax experience of other countries with GST-type taxes (often called value-added taxes or VATs), the federal government tried to classify financial services as tax-exempt. The implication is that financial institutions pay GST on their purchases of items such as stationery, equipment, and so on, but financial services are not taxable. This rule applies to chartered banks, trust and mortgage loan companies, and insurance companies. Other services such as safety deposit boxes are taxable.

The actual rules, however, are exceedingly complicated. For example, leasing is not considered a financial service so it is subject to the GST. Other complications arise because services imported from abroad are taxable, but financial institutions are required to tax them on a self-assessment basis (that is, on an honor system). Transactions in precious metals that exceed a particular level of purity are exempt. And so on and so on.

## Market Concentration

A concern sometimes expressed about the Canadian financial system is its apparently high **market concentration** (the extent to which a small number of firms in an industry account for a large proportion of its output, employment, profits, and/or assets). For example, the Economic Council of Canada estimated that the proportion of assets accounted for by the four largest financial institutions (all chartered banks) was 47.2% in 1987. But that ratio was down from 54.8% in 1979, and the proportion of deposits (booked by residents) as well as the share of personal and commercial loans accounted for by the same four largest banks also fell during the same years.[22] These figures may indicate an increase in the competition or economic efficiency of the financial system over time.

Nevertheless, the Canadian banking system is clearly dominated by a few large banks, so one can understand the popular belief that they collude in some fashion in order to generate monopoly profits. Yet there is little evidence that collusion or monopoly profits are a facet of the performance of the Canadian banking system. Moreover, chartered banks do not seem to be less competitive than trust or mortgage loan companies despite different ownership rules.[23]

22 Moreover, the number of financial institutions (all deposit-taking institutions and life insurance companies) that account for 80% of assets, deposits, and loans rose in the same period. See Economic Council of Canada, *A New Frontier: Globalization and Canada's Financial Markets* (Ottawa: Economic Council of Canada, 1989).

23 The Bank Act stipulates that Schedule I chartered banks must be *widely held*, which means that no single

## FINANCIAL FOCUS 17.3 PIN Money for Thieves

In 1992, Italian thieves glued a replica of an ATM onto an existing machine. Unsuspecting customers lost cards as the fake machine swallowed them up after revealing (unknowingly of course) their PIN or personal identification number to the thieves. After taking the cards the thieves spent the rest of the day withdrawing cash from real dispensers in as many locations as possible. They were eventually caught.

**Sources:**

J. Kerr, "Pin Money for Thieves," *The European*, 2 July 1992.

---

It must be remembered that although depository institutions have different ownership structures, a fact that may have an influence on the industry's competitiveness, they also aim to satisfy different segments of the financial market. For example, the chartered banks are heavily involved in international banking, which is highly competitive, while the other depository institutions are not. Moreover, the ability of chartered banks since the 1970s to compete in the market for residential mortgages has increased competition in an industry in which trust companies were historically dominant.

Nevertheless, there has been some concern that Canadian banks, in general, may be less competitive than they ought to be because ownership restrictions and financial barriers to starting up banks imply an absence of *contestability*. Contestability refers to the likely success of potential competitors to enter a particular industry. In the present context, this means that banks are barred from acquiring other banks and therefore this places a limit on the size of Canadian institutions. Canadian banks are well behind in size, at least by comparison with banks around the world. For example, the Royal Bank, Canada's largest bank. Ranks only 54th globally.[24] But there is another reason why contestability is important. If banks need not worry about the threat of a takeover, they may be less efficient than possible. It should be noted, however, that links between mergers and acquisitions and efficiency are not clear-cur and the topic is the subject of some controversy.

There are a number of other ways to measure how competitive a particular market is. Some studies have looked at bank profits (see the end of this chapter), others have looked at the reaction of banks to changes in costs while still others have examined how bank stocks react to regulatory changes. All in all, and despite

---

shareholder can own more than 10% of the outstanding shares. Schedule II chartered banks (foreign subsidiaries) and trust companies may be *closely held*, which means that one shareholder can own a majority or even all of the outstanding shares. At the other end of the scale are the credit unions and caisses populaires, which are owned by their many members.

24 Based on the rankings reported annually in the magazine *The Banker*.

the methodological difficulties involved in evaluating the state of competition in a market, Canadian banks appear to be operating in a fairly competitive market.[25]

## Regional Concerns

Several Banks Acts over the years have reflected the peculiarly Canadian attempt to maintain strong centralized institutions and regional interests. The industry's desire to concentrate financial centres in Montreal and Toronto became quite evident by the 1920s as institutions either moved to the centre of the country or merged with stronger banks whose activities were centred there.

Although this centralized development of the financial system may be said to be efficient in an aggregate sense, that view has not been shared by some of the regions, most notably the West and the Atlantic Provinces. Indeed, early Canadian financial history is full of cases in which the outlying regions felt wronged by the financial centres of central Canada. Although many changes in the Bank Act have been intended to mitigate some of the credit difficulties faced by producers in the West and Atlantic Canada, the perception that the centre has too much influence has persisted. Certainly a cursory examination of the distribution of the assets of chartered banks by region reinforces such an impression. For example, in 1995, the Atlantic Provinces (Newfoundland, Nova Scotia, Prince Edward Island, and New Brunswick) had 4.5% of chartered banks' total assets but 7.4% of Canada's labour force. Of total assets, 14.2% were located in Quebec; 37% in Ontario; 11.9% in the Prairie Provinces (Manitoba, Saskatchewan, and Alberta); and 11.8% in British Columbia. The labour force proportions were, respectively, 24.2%, 38.4%, 17%, and 12.9%. Thus, Ontario had a share of chartered bank assets similar to its share of the Canadian labour force, as did B.C., while this is not the case for the Prairie Provinces and Quebec.[26] Of course, chartered banks are not the only deposit-taking institutions, so these figures may be somewhat biased. Credit unions and caisses populaires are, for example, important financial institutions in the Prairies and Quebec, but chartered banks tend to be the only national institutions.

Mortgage lending interest rates across the country provide another illustration of the tensions between a centralized financial system and regional concerns. As recently as 1966, these interest rates showed significant differentials with rates approximately 1/4% above the Canadian average in the Atlantic Provinces.[27] Considerable care must be exercised in interpreting such figures. The mixture of

---

25 See L. Boothe, "Competition and Profitability in the Financial Services Industry," in J. Mintz and J. Pesando (eds.), *Issues in the Reform of the Canadian Financial Services Industry* (Toronto: C.D. Howe Institute, 1996).

26 Percentage calculated from data in *Bank of Canada Review* (November 1992): Tables C3 and H7.

27 By contrast, the regional distribution of bank branches is highly correlated with the regional distribution of the population and income.

federal and provincial legislation governing the behaviour of financial institutions doubtless plays a role in dictating interest rate differentials. So do various economic factors that are not biased against a particular region of the country.

The oil boom in the 1980s in western Canada only reinforced the desire of Westerners for their own share of financial or banking power. The first expression of this desire to shift the balance of banking power to the western part of the country came at the Western Economics Opportunities Conference in July 1973. This ultimately led to the formation of several Western banks, including the Canadian Commercial Bank (CCB), in July 1975, and the Northland Bank, in December 1975. Unfortunately, however, the banking practices of these newly formed banks in western Canada led to some of the most spectacular banking failures in Canadian financial history. These practices also spawned a royal commission to investigate the causes of the failures and to make some recommendations.[28]

Both banks were based in western Canada and both aimed to attune their operations to the financial needs of Westerners, although the CCB also had visions of becoming a large national bank, headquartered in western Canada.[29] The Northland Bank was, by contrast, a regional bank. It seemed doomed from the start, as evidenced by the lack of banking experience of its CEO and the high turnover rate of its senior staff.

The Northland Bank and the CCB each had a tendency to make bad loans, in part by lending large sums of money to relatively few borrowers and in part by excessively concentrating loans and other investments to a narrow geographical area, thereby avoiding some of the obvious benefits of diversification. Moreover, loans were often backed by the resource sectors or real estate at a time when expectations were for rising prices (and thus a rising ability to repay loans in the future) in all major sectors of western Canada's economy. The CCB also expanded into the growing California economy,[30] which was also experiencing a real estate boom of unprecedented proportions.

When the loans they had made turned out to be bad, both banks sought to avoid failure by refusing to recognize, in an accounting sense, the non-performance of the outstanding loans.[31] Moreover, by capitalizing—in effect, raising

---

28 W.Z. Estey, *Report of the Inquiry into the Collapse of the CCB and Northland Bank* (Ottawa: Minister of Supply and Services, August 1986).

29 The CCB was a national bank, but on a small scale to begin with. It later expanded into eastern Canada and California.

30 By purchasing a minority interest in Westland Bank, a bank heavily involved in the California real estate market.

31 As Estey's report makes clear, Alberta's recession during the early 1980s played a secondary role in influencing the financial health of both banks.

the size of loans outstanding—and accruing uncollected interest payments—pretending that the interest will be received at some time—both banks gave misleading pictures of their financial positions. While these accounting devices are common responses to good loans that later turn out to be bad loans, provisions are usually made to write off bad loans over time, as many chartered banks did during the 1980s when their foreign loans turned sour. Neither the CCB nor the Northland Bank made these provisions.

Despite advances by the Bank of Canada and several failed attempts by the Inspector General of Banks[32] to merge both banks with the National Bank, among others, both banks were liquidated in 1985, leaving the Canada Deposit Insurance Corporation with huge losses (see Chapter 20).

As the Estey Commission report makes clear, it was the Bank Act and the lax supervisory role of the then-Inspector General of Banks that allowed the situation to get out of hand. Proper supervision would not have permitted either bank to capitalize and accrue interest for as long as it did, and the public would have been warned about the banks' risky portfolio practices. Moreover, proper supervision would have prevented the Bank of Canada from having to bail out—unsuccessfully as it turned out—a failing bank due to its mismanagement. Finally, proper supervision of banking practices would have permitted the responsible agency to step in and take over a mismanaged institution *before* the financial situation became unsustainable. Thus, the Northland Bank and CCB failures are as much a story of regionalism in banking as they are about inadequate regulations and supervision in the financial industry.

Regional concerns can never be far from the minds of legislators in Canada, and these have in part shaped the structure of the financial system. The reliance on a branch banking system and the long-standing use of the pledge section in the Bank Act are examples of the importance given regional concerns. The tension between regional and national concerns will, however, continue to shape and influence chartered bank policy.

## LENDING TO SMALL AND MEDIUM BUSINESSES

During the elections which led to the return of the Liberals in late 1993, one of the campaign issues dealt with the belief that chartered banks deliberately avoid loans to small and medium-sized businesses. Even before the elections, changes were made to the Small Business Loans Act to encourage banks to increase their lending to these types of businesses. Banks have often viewed small businesses as far riskier loan candidates than large corporations. Moreover, transactions costs

32 The name of this office was subsequently changed to the Office of the Superintendent of Financial Institutions.

in monitoring and managing loans to small businesses are likely to be higher than for a loan to some large conglomerate. Since the last recession, however, banks have apparently had a change of heart because they see small and medium-sized businesses as having relatively greater potential for growth.[33] Moreover, the Bank of Canada (in the *Review*, Table C11) now publishes data from the Canadian Bankers Association giving the number of loans to small and medium-sized businesses (defined as lending in amounts of $5 million or less) which certainly means that banks are more aware of the significance of such loans from a public policy perspective.

# THE PERFORMANCE OF CHARTERED BANKS

How have the Canadian chartered banks performed over the years–say, since the end of World War II? Here we examine the composition and management of their portfolios (using the approaches whose theory we considered in the last chapter) as well as their size and profits.

## ASSET AND LIABILITY COMPOSITION

We begin with an overall examination of asset–liability management since the end of World War II. Tables 17.3 and 17.4 show the major asset and liability components of chartered bank balance sheets as percentages of total assets or liabilities at selected 10-year intervals.

We can see some unmistakable trends caused largely by two factors: government regulation and the dramatic rise in interest rates since the late 1970s.

On the asset side (Table 17.3) notice that reserves have been falling steadily and are now close to zero. This decline is a direct consequence of various relaxations in reserve requirements.

Overall holdings of Government of Canada bonds have also fallen substantially over the years, and the relative popularity of long- and short-term bonds was reversed in favour of the latter. Part of the explanation for these portfolio shifts was the substantial indebtedness of the Canadian government occasioned by the need to finance World War II. As the war debt matured during the late 1950s, the government first converted it into long-term debt and then switched its borrowing requirement toward the short-term end of the market. The relative desirability of short-term debt was heightened during the great inflation of the 1970s and early 1980s and the increased default risk of the 1980s. The high (real)

33 S. Thorn, "Banks Renew Interest in Small Businesses," *The Globe and Mail* (23 November 1993), p. C5.

**Table 17.3** PRINCIPAL ASSETS OF CHARTERED BANKS

| | 1950 | 1960 | 1970 | 1980 | 1990 | 1995 |
|---|---|---|---|---|---|---|
| Treasury bills | 1.5% | 13.3% | 6.6% | 3.0% | 3.1% | 4.1% |
| Foreign assets | 9.6% | 18.4% | 33.8% | 44.7% | 36.9% | 31.5% |
| General loans | 28.2% | 34.1% | 38.9% | 37.9% | 34.5% | 24.5% |
| Long-term government securities | 23.2% | 6.8% | 5.6% | 0.5% | 0.6% | 2.6% |
| Short-term government securities | 8.3% | 7.4% | 4.8% | 0.45% | 0.25% | 2.4% |
| Other securities | 19.6% | 6.8% | 2.4% | 3.1% | 3.5% | 4.1% |
| Reserves | 9.6% | 6.7% | 4.2% | 2.9% | 1.0% | 0.4% |
| Residential mortgages | 0.0% | 6.6% | 3.6% | 7.5% | 20.1% | 20.8% |

Sources: *Bank of Canada Review*, various issues; *Historical Statistics of Canada*, 2d ed., No. CSII-516E (Ottawa: Minister of Supply and Services, 1983). The data for 1995 are for July. Reserves represent Bank of Canada deposits, notes and coins. Other securities are provincial, municipal, and corporate securities. Short-term government securities mature in 3 years or under. General loans represent loans to persons and businesses.

interest rate policy of the early 1990s and the recession early during that decade reversed the trend as banks once again held more government securities.

Chartered banks have also become increasingly less important holders of provincial, municipal, and corporate securities. One reason is again the effects of inflation. Another is the tremendous growth in the number of financial system participants, especially foreigners, who have increasingly been inclined to hold debt issued in Canada.

An interesting illustration of the impact of financial regulation is the continuing rise in the share of residential mortgages held by chartered banks. Recall that the severe restrictions on their mortgage lending began to be lifted with the 1967 Bank Act. The relatively attractive returns on mortgage lending during the 1980s no doubt spurred the shift toward residential mortgages.

Finally, general loans, primarily of the commercial variety, continue to be the single largest domestic asset of chartered banks. Despite the deregulation of the 1970s and 1980s, chartered banks can still properly be labelled commercial banks. This suggests that, so far at least, chartered banks have retained a comparative advantage in the commercial lending market.

The liability side of the balance sheet (Table 17.4) has also had some noticeable changes. First, advances from the Bank of Canada, have tended to be negligible.[34]

It is also clear that financial innovations have made their mark. The removal of the deposit rate ceiling and the introduction of a variety of types of deposits have reduced the spread between rates on deposits and rates on a variety of

34 See Chapter 4 which does reveal that Bank of Canada advances rose during the 1980s as a result of the wave of failures discussed earlier.

**Table 17.4** PRINCIPAL LIABILITIES OF CHARTERED BANKS

| | 1950 | 1960 | 1970 | 1980 | 1990 | 1995 |
|---|---|---|---|---|---|---|
| Advances | 0.0% | 0.0% | 0.0% | 0.0% | 0.0% | .02% |
| Demand deposits | 33.4% | 27.3% | 16.4% | 6.2% | 4.4% | 3.9 % |
| Shareholders' equity | 4.0% | 6.3% | 3.7% | 2.7% | 3.5% | 2.6 % |
| Foreign liabilities | 9.7% | 16.9% | 31.3% | 45.3% | 39.3% | 33.8 % |
| Notice deposits | 4.4% | 3.7% | 10.3% | 13.7% | 12.7% | 10.3 % |
| Personal savings deposits | 48.5% | 45.8% | 38.4% | 32.1% | 40.1% | 33.9 % |

Sources: *Bank of Canada Review*, various issues; *Historical Statistics of Canada*, 2d ed., No. CSII-516E (Ottawa: Minister of Supply and Services, 1983). See note to Table 17.3.

alternative financial assets. Thus, the share of demand deposits plummeted while the share of notice deposits rose until lower (nominal) interest rates in the 1990s made bank deposits generally unattractive.

The globalization of the financial system has contributed to a growing reliance on the foreign sector for funds. Indeed, foreign currency liabilities were the largest liability item in 1980 and the second-largest in 1990 and again in 1995.

Finally, the share of equity has remained more or less stable over the years. It did, however, average slightly lower during the 1980s and 1990s than in the 1950s or 1960s, a reflection of the increase in leverage in chartered banks.

## ASSET AND LIABILITY MANAGEMENT

Table 17.5 shows in detail the balance sheet of all chartered banks. The essentials are summarized at the bottom of the table. A substantial proportion of assets and liabilities are fairly liquid and rate sensitive.

Almost a third of assets and liabilities are in foreign currencies. Almost half of Canadian dollar liabilities are classified as fixed term (though, thanks to financial innovations, these need not all be at a fixed rate of interest). By contrast, over 75% of assets (typically loans) are of the less liquid variety. Again, some of these may be of the fixed or floating variety (for example, as in the case of mortgages). More than 70% of the liabilities are fixed term; a similarly large percentage are in the form of long-term loans.

Overall, Table 17.5 tells us that chartered bank assets and liabilities are fairly well matched. The gap appears to be largely positive. We can obtain a better idea of the size of the gap by examining Table 17.6, which reports the gap for the Royal Bank of Canada at the end of its 1995 financial year. Recall that a positive gap is a signal that a bank anticipates a rise in interest rates and the opposite holds for a negative gap. The negative figures for terms of a month or less and

**Table 17.5** THE BALANCE SHEET OF CHARTERED BANKS (July 1995, millions of dollars)

| Assets | | Liabilities | |
|---|---|---|---|
| Bank of Canada deposits + notes | 3,799 | Deposits (Personal) | |
| Treasury Bills (Government of Canada) | 35,275 | Chequable | 47,459 |
| | | Non-chequable | 44,305 |
| Government of Canada Bonds[a] | 42,660 | Fixed-Term | 198,182 |
| Special call and short loans | 2,801 | Total | 289,946 |
| Total liquid assets | 84,535 | | |
| Loans to | | Non-Personal and Notice Deposits | |
| Federal government, provinces and municipalities | 1,835 | Notice | 28,939 |
| | | Fixed-term | 59,173 |
| General | 209,398 | Total | 88,112 |
| Residential mortgages | 177,525 | Demand deposits (gross) | 33,632 |
| Non-residential mortgages | 13,869 | Government of Canada | 3,916 |
| Leasing receivables | 1,763 | Total deposits | 415,605 |
| Securities | | | |
| Provincial + municipal | 9,961 | Bank of Canada advances | 217 |
| Corporate and Other[b] (corporations associated with banks) | 24,978 | Bankers' acceptances | 31,826 |
| | | Other liabilities[c] | 75,738 |
| Total less liquid assets | 439,329 | Appropriation for contingencies | 0 |
| Deposits with other banks | 10,275 | Shareholders' Equity | |
| Items in transit (net) | −666 | Common | 16,764 |
| Customers' liability under acceptances | 31,826 | Preferred | 5,354 |
| Other assets | 20,074 | Retained earnings | 20,724 |
| Total Canadian-dollar assets | 585,370 | Total Canadian-dollar liabilities | 566,229 |
| Total foreign currency assets | 269,409 | Total foreign currency liabilities | 288,549 |
| Total assets[d] | 854,778 | Total liabilities[d] | 854,778 |

**Summary**
**(as a percentage of total assets or liabilities)**

| | | | |
|---|---|---|---|
| Liquid assets | 9.9 | Personal deposits | 33.9 |
| Less liquid assets | 51.4 | Non-personal + other deposits | 14.7 |
| Foreign currency | 31.5 | Foreign currency | 33.8 |
| Total assets | 92.8 | Total liabilities | 82.4 |

[a] Approximately 52.5% are for bonds with a maturity of three years or more.

[b] Approximately 46.2% are invested in corporate shares.

[c] These include liabilities of subsidiaries other than deposits (5.2%), other liabilities (73.3%), minority interest in subsidiaries (1%), and bank debentures issued and outstanding (10.2%).

[d] Difference between total assets and liabilities results from rounding error. Also, asset and liability totals may not add up exactly due to rounding errors.

Source: *Bank of Canada Review* (Autumn 1995): Tables C3 and C4.

**Table 17.6** GAP ANALYSIS, ROYAL BANK OF CANADA (October 31, 1995, millions of dollars)

| | Term to maturity | | | |
|---|---|---|---|---|
| | ≤ 3 months | 3–6 months | 6–12 months | 1–5 years |
| Risk-sensitive assets | 84,626 | 15,539 | 15,689 | 44,967 |
| Risk-sensitive liabilities | 97,400 | 16,478 | 17,422 | 22,734 |
| Gap | −12,774 | −939 | −1,733 | +22,233 |
| Off-balance-sheet GAP | 5,420 | −1,261 | −653 | +4,144 |

Source: Royal Bank of Canada, *Annual Report, 1995*, Table 21.

three to six months suggest the Royal was anticipating a fall in interest rates toward the end of 1995. The longer-term gap figures put the bank at an advantage if rates were to rise over a year into the future or longer.[35]

It is worth emphasizing again some of the difficulties one faces in analysing bank behaviour by relying on balance sheet figures. First, classifying assets according to the degree of risk embodied in them is not always straightforward. The liquidity of the instruments is much more obvious. Second, balance sheets do not reflect items such as swaps, futures, and options; this omission can impart a strong bias to gap calculations. For this reason, the Royal Bank also publishes the gap in its off-balance-sheet items. These are also given in Table 17.6.

## SIZE

So far our description has focused only on the chartered banks in aggregate. It is also of some interest to consider how large some of these institutions are in relation to their industry as a whole. This information is useful in assessing how competitive the banking industry is and where the banks are regionally based, as well as how large the Canadian banks are in relation to some of the many foreign banks that now operate in Canada.

Table 17.7 lists some of the largest chartered banks (measured in terms of asset size). The top five are Schedule I, but several Schedule II banks are well up the list of the top 50. The ranking of the top five has not changed since at least 1990. Before 1980, no foreign-based bank was chartered in Canada; in only a decade, many have grown to be among the largest banks in the country.

35 In fact, interest rates fell during 1995, which benefited the banks in the short term. Indeed, Canadian chartered banks performed extremely well in 1995.

**Table 17.7** CANADA'S LARGEST CHARTERED BANKS

| Asset Size (billions) | Head Office | Name of Chartered Bank | Schedule |
|---|---|---|---|
| $173 | Montreal | Royal Bank of Canada | I |
| $151 | Toronto | Canadian Imperial Bank of Commerce | I |
| $138 | Montreal | Bank of Montreal | I |
| $133 | Halifax | Bank of Nova Scotia | I |
| $100 | Toronto | Toronto-Dominion Bank | I |
| $ 45 | Montreal | National Bank of Canada | I |
| $ 16 | Vancouver | Hongkong Bank of Canada | II |
| $ 4 | Toronto | Citibank Canada | II |
| $ 4 | Toronto | Crédit Suisse Canada | II |
| $ 2 | Montreal | Banque Nationale de Paris (Canada) | II |

Note: The asset figures are for 1994, rounded to the nearest billion.

Source: "The Top 1000," *Globe and Mail Report on Business*. Reprinted with permission from *The Globe and Mail* (July 1995), 145, 147.

Notice too that most chartered banks, Schedule I or Schedule II, continue to have their headquarters in Toronto or Montreal, although because of the restructuring of bank organization in recent years, it is unclear whether this translates into a reinforcing of the concentration of financial decisions in the centre of the country.

## PROFITS

Our description of the chartered banks has concentrated on the structure and size of balance sheets, which represent the stock of assets and liabilities that banks enjoy. But banks also accumulate wealth for their shareholders by earning profits. Indeed, few items in the financial news catch the public's attention as much as reports on bank profits.

A common misperception is that bank profits always rise with increases in interest rates. In fact, making precise statements about the relationship between interest rates and profits is difficult because estimates are based on the book values published by the banks, instead of the more informative market values. Nevertheless, as Table 17.8 suggests, bank profits are just as likely to rise as interest rates *fall*. Gap analysis teaches us that profits are a function of the management of assets and liabilities jointly. Thus, if a bank is able to lock in assets at relatively high interest rates and then borrow at lower rates, profits will rise. In other words, precisely because the gap can be negative, bank profits tend to be related to interest rate changes inversely, not positively as many people believe.

**Table 17.8** BANK PROFITS AND INTEREST RATES

| | Profits as a % of Assets | Treasury Bill Rate |
|---|---|---|
| 1980 | 0.52% | 12.67% |
| 1981 | 0.61 | 17.76 |
| 1982 | 0.35 | 13.81 |
| 1983 | 0.51 | 9.32 |
| 1984 | 0.27 | 11.11 |
| 1985 | 0.24 | 9.46 |
| 1986 | 0.30 | 8.99 |
| 1987 | 0.45 | 8.19 |
| 1988 | 0.79 | 9.42 |
| 1989 | 0.49 | 12.02 |
| 1990 | 0.59 | 12.80 |
| 1991 | 1.90 | 8.85 |
| 1992 | 0.50 | 6.50 |
| 1993 | 0.69 | 4.91 |
| 1994 | 1.20 | 5.42 |
| 1995 | 1.40 | 6.54 |

Note: The data for 1995 is for the third quarter.

## SUMMARY

- This chapter surveys the history and performance of the chartered banks in Canada.

- Intermediation can be thought of as the process of facilitating the process of turning liabilities (such as deposits) into assets (such as loans). An important financial intermediary in Canada is the chartered banks, which are private depository institutions that are federally chartered and regulated.

- Chartered banks are also called commercial banks because they have concentrated their expertise on loans for commercial purposes.

- Chartered banking in Canada began shortly after Confederation in 1867, when the federal government began to regulate the financial system.

- The centrepiece of financial legislation is the Bank Act, which is revised approximately every 10 years.

# IMPORTANT TERMS

Bank Act (p. 394)
chartered bank (p. 389)
free banking (p. 390)
market concentration (p. 405)
real bills doctrine (p. 390)

# EXERCISES

1. Based on the evidence in this chapter, is it your impression that financial regulations anticipate changes in the banking industry or vice versa? Why? Why not?

2. One argument against free banking is that the cost of monitoring all the various notes from individual banks would be too large. What does this statement mean?

3. Is it feasible to pay interest on currency? Why or why not?

4. Barriers to entry through regulation is an anti-competitive practice and one that induces wasteful activity. What does this statement mean?

5. That residential mortgage lending interest rates are higher in Atlantic Canada than elsewhere in the country proves that banks show a bias against eastern Canadian borrowers. True or false? Explain your answer.

6. Do you think it is appropriate to compare the share of chartered bank assets by region with the share of the labour force by region? If so, why? If not, why not?

7. The Estey Commission revealed how capitalization of interest can mislead shareholders into thinking a bank is financially healthy when it is not. Use a simplified balance sheet to illustrate why this might be the case. What other accounting practice considered in this text might also mislead shareholders about the true state of a bank's financial health. Why? (Hint: See Chapter 10).

8. What do you think of the argument that governments need to regulate banks in order to prevent money from becoming worthless?

9. "Governments are slow in adapting to financial innovations." Give an example from the history of chartered banking.

10. Why have the FTA and NAFTA not been a boon to Canadian chartered banks?
11. Try to estimate the GAP for all chartered banks based on the data in Table 17.5. How comparable are the results with those of the Royal Bank of Canada (Table 17.6)?
12. Examine the relationship between bank profits and interest rates in Table 17.8. Overall, is the relationship a positive one or a negative one?

# REFERENCES


*Bank Act: Orders and Regulations with Guidelines, Interpretation Bulletins and Other Regulatory Documents*, 3d ed. Don Mills, Ont.: Richard de Boo Publishers, 1989.

*Bank of Canada Review* (various issues).

*Bank Profits: A Report by the Standing Committee on Finance.* Ottawa: Supply and Services Canada, 1987.

Bordo, M., H. Rockoff and A. Redish, "The US Banking System from a Northern Exposure: Stability versus Efficiency" *Journal of Economic History* 54 (June 1994): 325–41.

Cameron, R. *Banking in the Early Stages of Industrialization.* New York: Oxford University Press, 1967.

"Canada's Largest Corporations." *The Financial Post Magazine*, Summer 1991.

*The Canadian Bank Act 1980.* Toronto: Price Waterhouse Canada.

Chant, J. *The Market for Financial Services: Deposit-Taking Institutions.* Vancouver: The Fraser Institute, 1988.

———. *Regulation of Financial Institutions: A Functional Analysis.* Ottawa: Bank of Canada, 1987.

———. "Reform and Soundness of the Financial System" *Policy Options* (June 1995): 11–16.

Chernow, R. *The House of Morgan.* New York: Simon and Schuster, 1990.

Cowen, T., and R. Kroszner. "Scottish Banking Before 1945: A Model of Laissez-Faire?" *Journal of Money, Credit and Banking* 21 (May 1989); 221–31.

Dow, S. *Financial Markets and Regional Economic Development.* Aldershot, UK: Avebury, 1990.

Gorton, G. "Banking Theory and Free Banking History." *Journal of Monetary Economics* 16 (1985): 267–76.

Granger, A. *Don't Bank On It.* Toronto: Doubleday, 1981.

*The Historical Atlas of Canada*, Vol. III, *Addressing the Twentieth Century.* Toronto: University of Toronto Press, 1990.

*Historical Statistics of Canada*, 2d ed., No. CSII-516E. Ottawa: Minister of Supply and Services, 1983.

Humphrey, T.M. "The Real Bills Doctrine." Federal Reserve Bank of Richmond, *Economic Review* 68 (September/October 1982): 3–13.

Jamieson, A.B. *Chartered Banking in Canada.* Toronto: Ryerson-Press, 1953.

Koutsoyiannis, A. *Modern Microeconomics*, 2d ed. London: Macmillan, 1979.

Mayrand, A. "Concentration in the Canadian Financial Sector: The Situation in 1987." Working paper no. 5. Economic Council of Canada (1990).

Nathan, A., and E.H. Neave. "Competition and Contestability in Canada's Financial System: Empirical Results." *Canadian Journal of Economics* 22 (August 1989): 576–94.

Naylor, T. *History of Canadian Business.* Toronto: University of Toronto Press, 1975.

Neave, E.H. "Canada's Approach to Financial Regulation." *Canadian Public Policy* 15 (1989): 1–11.

*A New Frontier: Globalization of Canada's Financial Markets.* Ottawa: Economic Council of Canada, 1989.

*1997 Review of Financial Sector Legislation: Proposals for Change.* Ottawa: Department of Finance, June 1996.

O'Brien, J.W., and G. Lermer. *Canadian Money and Banking,* 2d ed. Toronto: McGraw-Hill, 1969.

Power, A., and D.K. Varma. *The Touche Ross Guide to Financial Reporting for Canadian Banks.* Toronto: CCH Canadian Ltd., 1984.

Reddish, A. "Monetary Lessons from Canada: A Review Essay." *Journal of Monetary Economics* 26 (1990): 489–99.

Rich, G. *The Cross of Gold: Money and the Canadian Business Cycle, 1867–1913.* Ottawa: Carleton University Press, 1988.

Royal Bank of Canada, *Annual Report, 1990.*

Rudin, R. *Banking on François: The French Bank of Québec 1835–1925.* Toronto: University of Toronto Press, 1985.

Selgin, G.A., and L.H. White. "The Evolution of a Free Banking System." *Economic Inquiry* 25 (July 1987): 439–58.

Shaffer, S. "A Test of Competition in Canada." *Journal of Money, Credit and Banking* 23 (February 1993): 49–61.

Statistics Canada, CANSIM database.

Stewart, W. *Towers of Gold, Feet of Clay: The Canadian Banks.* Toronto: Collins, 1982.

Wallace, N. "A Legal Restrictions Theory of the Demand for 'Money' and the Role of Monetary Policy." Federal Reserve Bank of Minneapolis, *Quarterly Review* (Winter 1983): 1–7.

White, L.H. *Free Banking in Britain: Theory, Experience, and Debate, 1800–1845.* Cambridge: Cambridge University Press, 1984.

CHAPTER 18

# Other Depository Institutions

Although Canada's financial institutions are increasingly alike, there continue to be good reasons to distinguish among types of depository institutions. The country's depository institutions that are not chartered banks long satisfied a particular set of financial needs of the Canadian public, and they continue to do so. These institutions have traditionally been referred to as *near-banks* because although they appeared to offer many of the same services as the chartered banks, they were legally prevented from using the term "bank." The 1991 Bank Act removed this prohibition, as well as some restrictions on their activities. But tradition dies hard. Even if the barriers of the four-pillar financial system are no longer as effective as they once were, it will be some time before depository institutions become largely indistinguishable from each other. In any event, it is useful, for historical reasons alone, to examine these types of institutions separately.

Consequently, this chapter provides an overview of the history and activities of three types of depository institutions: trust and mortgage loan companies; credit unions (called caisse populaires in Quebec)[1]; and a few other minor depository institutions.

## THE SIZE OF THE NEAR-BANK SECTOR

During the 1980s, other depository institutions began to take away market share from the chartered banks. But with the passage of the 1991 Bank Act, chartered banks began to buy up existing trust companies. In the space of four years, the size of depository institutions, other than chartered banks, began to fall substantially from previous levels due to the restructuring of the financial industry in Canada. For example, if we combine the assets of chartered banks with those of trust, mortgage loan companies and credit unions, then the share of total assets controlled by chartered banks stood at 85.3% by the end of 1995. By comparison, the same figure was 66.2% in 1989.

1 Unless otherwise noted, we use "credit unions" to refer to credit unions and caisses populaires.

# TRUST AND MORTGAGE LOAN COMPANIES

A **trust company** is a depository institution that may also offer services as a corporate trustee. In other words, it has two distinct roles:

1. An intermediation function, by channelling deposits and making loans, primarily in the form of mortgages.
2. A fiduciary (trusteeship) function, by providing **estates, trusts, and agencies (ETA)** business—that is, by administering assets it does not own.

A **mortgage loan company (MLC)** also accepts deposits and makes mortgage loans, thus providing intermediation services. As we will see, there are several types of MLCs today, and some are owned by chartered banks.

Trust companies and mortgage loan companies arose as separate kinds of institutions. But because they both play such an important role in the mortgage market and because the most recent data on the financial sector lumps them together, it seems convenient to treat both of them here under one heading.

Another similarity is that both the federal and the provincial governments regulate these institutions. Most are federally regulated.

At the provincial level, Ontario, Quebec, Alberta, and British Columbia regulate the trusts in their jurisdictions, while Saskatchewan, Manitoba, and the Atlantic Provinces have chosen to delegate supervision to the federal Superintendent of Financial Institutions. Many trust companies must, however, answer to more than one regulator. The Canadian constitution assigns property and civil rights to the provinces. Thus the fiduciary component of trust companies' business is subject to provincial legislation, even if the institution is federally incorporated. This has led to duplication with the resulting inefficiencies since regulation is a costly activity.

## THE HISTORY OF TRUST COMPANIES

The first trust company in the country was the Trust and Loan Company of Canada, formed in 1843 in Kingston, Ontario. Chartered banks were not allowed to act as trustees, so a number of these separate institutions were created in the second half of the nineteenth century. Early in the 1900s, trust companies were authorized to accept deposits but not to issue cheques. They became true financial intermediaries in the 1920s when they started to borrow in their own names and engage in the process of asset transformation as opposed to acting purely as financial agents.

Today the ETA function continues to be the most important component of trust companies, although their role as depository institutions has grown rapidly.

As part of the ETA function, trust companies sponsor mutual funds of various kinds, act as trustees for various corporate bonds and stocks, serve as agents for real estate agencies, and perform the function of investment managers. A currently important area is their role as trustees for the pooled pension funds of large employers and unions.

Mortgages are also an important source of profit. And the Bank Act of 1991 has opened new business possibilities by permitting trust companies to make commercial loans. One expects it will be increasingly difficult to distinguish the trusts from chartered banks.[2] As of early 1996, however, these new areas of business still represent a relatively small fraction of their total business, at least as measured by asset share.

## THE HISTORY OF MORTGAGE LOAN COMPANIES

Historically, mortgage loan companies preceded trust companies. Chartered banks were long precluded from offering residential mortgages, and MLCs were founded to meet the need. The first were patterned after the building societies that still exist in the United Kingdom; they were known as terminating societies because an individual joined one only to borrow enough to purchase land or a house; once he or she had repaid the loan (in instalments) association with the society was terminated.

The activities of MLCs expanded after 1874, when they were allowed to raise funds by issuing debentures. By increasing the amount of funds they had available for lending, MLCs could increase their activities beyond the narrow geographical limits of building societies. They ceased to be terminating societies and became permanent societies.

Today there are three different types of MLCs.

1. Some are simply deposit-taking mortgage companies, operating under either the federal Loan Companies Act or similar provincial legislation.[3] Assets are limited to deposits and certain debt instruments such as debentures. Liabilities must primarily be invested in mortgages.

2. Since 1973, federally regulated MLCs have been permitted to create mortgage investment companies (MICs). MICs do not take deposits but rather allow investors to enjoy the benefits of portfolio diversification through investment

---

2 Chartered banks are now allowed to own trust companies as we saw in the previous chapter. One restriction on commercial loans by trust companies remains. Unless the company's capital exceeds $25 million, it can issue commercial loans only to a maximum of 5% of its assets.

3 This statement is actually a simplification. To avoid having to give too many details here, they are called savings certificate, investment certificate, or investment contract companies. These institutions, which operate under provincial regulation, differ from other MLCs not in their investment practices but in the nature of the savings investments they offer.

## ECONOMICS FOCUS 18.1 What Next?

It seems that it is not just the differences between deposit-taking institutions that is being blurred these days. Now supermarkets chains want customers to shop for financial services where they shop for food. A joint venture between Royal Trust and the Loblaws supermarket chain resulted in the opening in 1991 of President's Trust, providing a full-range of consumer banking services on the premises of a supermarket. Although many malls and stores already contained automated teller machines, offering a full range of financial services commercially linked with the supermarket itself was novel.

The goal of such a joint venture is to forge the kind of customer loyalty to a supermarket chain and a deposit-taking institution of the kind evident in the airline industry with its awards for frequent fliers. Or, as the managing partner for President's Trust said: "Use your debit card eight times and get a free turkey."

Free turkeys were obviously not good enough as the only branch of President's Trust closed down in 1992, perhaps more a victim of the recession than of poor financial innovation.

In the United States, by contrast, such joint ventures are thriving. For example, Wells Fargo bank in California has dozens of branches with full-service banking and each branch is usually staffed by a single individual.

**Source:**
"Use Your Debit Card Eight Times and Get a Free Turkey," *Wall Street Journal*, 25 November 1991, p. B1.

---

in mortgages, bonds, and equities.[4] In addition MLCs can raise funds through the sale of shares as well as debentures with a term of less than five years. (The latter are insured by the Canada Deposit Insurance Corporation.) There are also MLCs under provincial jurisdiction; they are similar to federally regulated ones except they raise funds primarily by issuing guaranteed investment certificates.

3. Institutions known as **real estate investment trusts (REITs)** exist primarily to finance mortgages. They differ from real estate developers in that they operate via a *declaration of trust*: that is, shares are issued and shareholders receive all net income in the form of annual dividends, which has tax advantages for them. Anyone affiliated with an REIT is limited to channelling funds solely through the trust, which can hire an agent or adviser to offer advice about how to invest its funds.

## ASSETS AND LIABILITIES

Figure 18.1 traces the recent development of trusts' and MLCs' principal assets and liabilities. Mortgages continue to dominate assets, a reflection of these institutions' traditional role. Despite the chartered banks' entry into residential

4 Primarily mortgages because of legal restrictions in the Loan Companies Act. But permission to invest in equities confers some tax benefits that conventional MLCs do not enjoy.

**FIGURE 18.1** Trust and Mortgage Loan Companies: Asset and Liability Composition

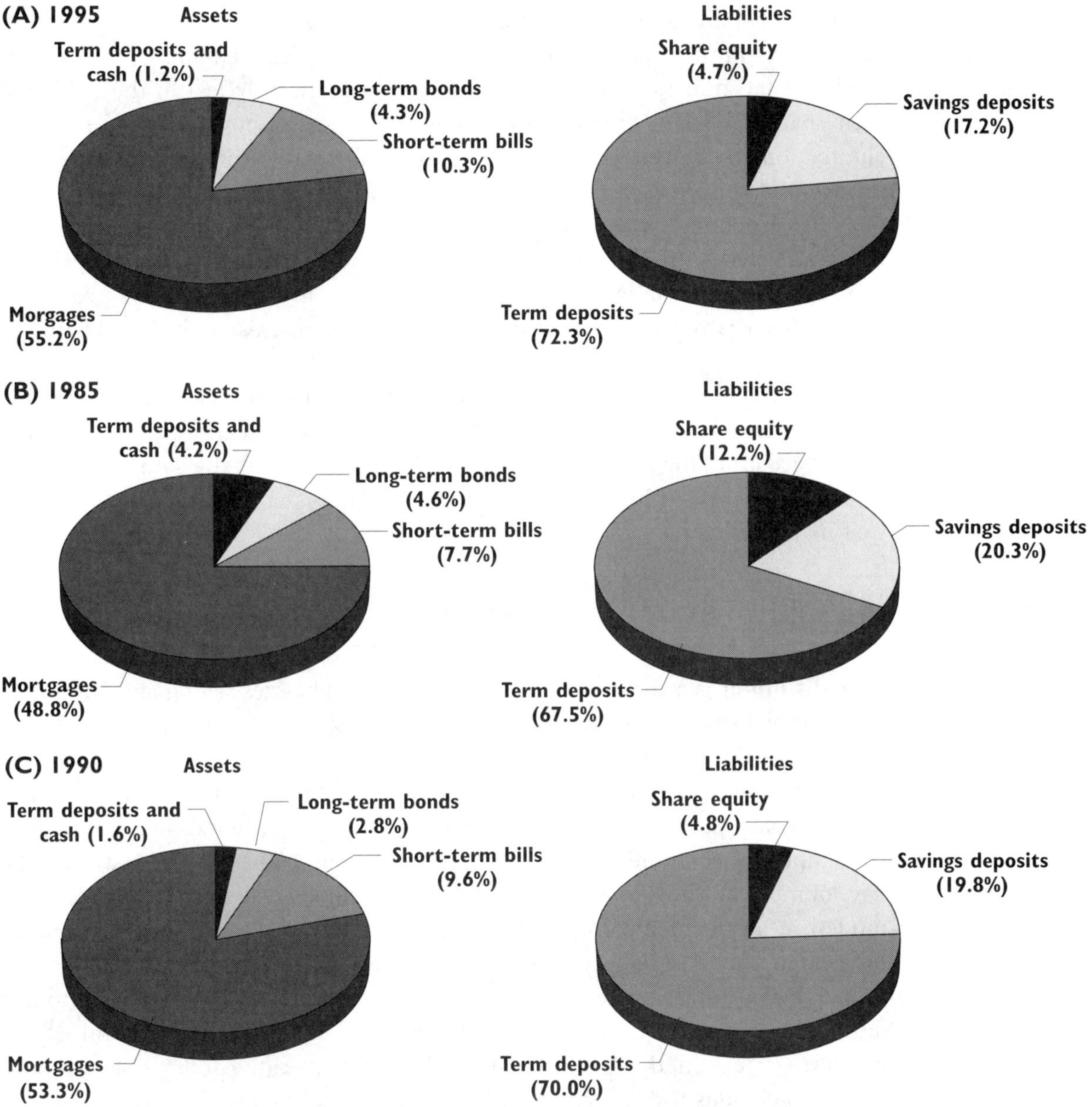


Note: The "deposits" shown as assets are the funds that trusts and MLCs have placed with other institutions. The "deposits" shown as liabilities are, of course, funds held for clients.

Source: *Bank of Canada Review*, Table D1. The figures for 1995 are for July and apply only to those trust companies not affiliated with the chartered banks. Sum of shares is less than 100% as not all assets or liability shares were calculated.

mortgage lending in the late 1960s, the trusts and MLCs still provide many of the mortgages in Canada.

On the liability side, term deposits, many in the form called *guaranteed investment certificates (GICs)*, dominate the balance sheet. Demand deposits, principally of the non-chequing variety, make up significantly less of the total, and their share has fallen dramatically owing to financial innovations and the 1967 elimination of deposit ceilings, which fostered greater competition. The only features not captured by Figure 18.1 are the impact of chartered bank purchases of trust companies since 1991. Although the asset and liability composition of trusts affiliated with chartered banks is very similar to that of the independent trust sector, the total assets of the latter group of institutions is now relatively smaller (over two-thirds of all trust assets are in the hands of chartered banks as of 1996).

Table 18.1 presents a detailed balance sheet for trusts and MLCs not affiliated with chartered banks. Mortgages and short-term assets, such as bankers' acceptances, accounts for the vast majority of all assets. About the same proportion of liabilities is issued in the form of term deposits. Assets and liabilities are fairly well matched.

## CREDIT UNIONS AND CAISSES POPULAIRES

A **credit union** is a depository institution that emphasizes saving and lending at a local level. Its shareholders are its own depositors and borrowers.[5] It is established as a non-profit organization, and these institutions are provincially regulated.[6]

Credit unions grew up because small investors and savers had little access to the financial system. The fact that Canada's early banks, like those of almost all contemporary economies, concentrated on commercial banking, spawned the development of "people's banks" whereby individuals and small businesses with modest means formed community-based financial institutions. This co-operative movement was especially prevalent in Germany, Great Britain, Italy, and the Scandinavian countries, among others, where it continues to be important to this day. Co-operative institutions were also part of the early development of the financial system in the United States, where they became today's savings and loans associations (S&Ls), credit unions, and mutual savings banks.

5 Today some credit unions do not limit borrowing to members.

6 The tax benefits of non-profit status have been eroded since 1972, when credit unions became liable for corporate taxes. Nevertheless, their members still reap some tax advantages; for example, they pay no income tax on the earnings distributed to them as rebates.

**Table 18.1** THE BALANCE SHEET OF TRUST AND MORTGAGE LOAN COMPANIES (July 1995, millions of dollars)

| Assets | | Liabilities | |
|---|---|---|---|
| Cash + demand and notice deposits | 558 | Chequable savings deposits[b] | 8,132 |
| Items in transit | 134 | Non-chequable deposits[c] | 5,146 |
| Term deposits[a] | 384 | Term deposits[d] | 55,976 |
| Government of Canada Treasury bills | 4,278 | Total deposits | 69,254 |
| Short-term paper and bankers' acceptances | 3,731 | Loans and overdrafts | 772 |
| Bonds | | Promissory notes + debentures | 1,164 |
| Government of Canada | 2,116 | Other liabilities | 2,557 |
| Provincial + municipal + corporate | 1,244 | Shareholders' equity | 3,664 |
| Residential mortgages | 42,764 | Total liabilities | 77,519 |
| Personal loans | 8,595 | | |
| Non-residential mortgages | 4,625 | | |
| Other loans | 3,320 | | |
| Leasing contracts | 848 | | |
| Canadian preferred + common shares | 1,906 | | |
| Other assets | 3,018 | | |
| Total assets | 77,519 | | |

[a] Of which 60.2% are in chartered banks.

[b] Of which 85.8% are in daily interest accounts.

[c] Of which 82.7% are in daily interest accounts.

[d] Of which 82.9% are for a term which exceeds one year.

Source: *Bank of Canada Review*, various issues, Table D1. Excludes bank mortgage loan company subsidiaries and trust companies affiliated with chartered banks. Assets and liabilities may not add up exactly due to rounding errors.

Perhaps the best known of the co-operative banks in Canada are the **caisses populaires** of Quebec. Alphonse Desjardins, inspired by the co-operative movements in Europe and the inability of farmers and individuals to obtain credit, founded the first in 1900 in Lévis, Quebec. The movement spread throughout the province, with individual caisses operated more or less as separate units but united under the leadership of Desjardins. By the 1920s, regional associations were formed, and, following the Great Depression, all the regional unions were brought together in a federation known today as the Confédération des Caisses Populaires et d'Économie Desjardins, or more simply, the Caisses Populaires Desjardins.

The credit union movement also became a feature elsewhere in Canada. It started in the French-speaking communities of New Brunswick, Ontario, and Manitoba, but in the 1930s, it spread to the Atlantic Provinces (the Antigonish movement) and then to the Prairies. In both eastern and western Canada, credit unions tended to serve rural communities, differing somewhat from the institutions of the Desjardins movement, many of which were based on urban parishes. The credit unions outside Quebec also often had relatively more flexible lending policies, like those of the US movement, which inspired their development.

A common feature in the development of all credit unions in Canada has been the formation of regional unions or *centrals* to facilitate cheque-clearing[7] and to act as lenders of last resort. Thus, centrals could confer some of the advantages of the vast branch networks established by the chartered banks, but centrals being creatures of individual credit unions, power could emanate from the grass roots, not from the centre.

Today there are provincial central credit unions regulated by provincial legislation. Since 1973, they have been authorized to accept deposits, make loans, and act as agents for their locals—powers much in line with those enjoyed by trust companies. Moreover, the CDIC can act as a lender of last resort to the provincial centrals.

These are also quasi-national bodies—in particular the Canadian Co-operative Credit Society (CCCS) and the Caisses Populaires Desjardins in Quebec—which, among other things, enable the transfer funds from one provincial central to another.[8] Reforms in Ontario during the early 1990s, for example, permitted credit unions to compete with banks in the area of lending to small businesses. However, it is too early to tell how successful these institutions will be in this market since the overall importance of loans of all types, as a percent of total assets, has been rather stable over the last decade (see Figure 18.2).

## ASSETS AND LIABILITIES

Figure 18.2 traces the recent development of the principal assets and liabilities of local credit unions. Cash loans to members and mortgages form the vast majority of assets. But in line with the credit union philosophy of conservative financial management, cash and demand deposits, primarily with centrals, also represent a significant proportion of total assets.

The distribution of liabilities is instructive. Share capital, originally a basic source of the funds credit unions raised is now a small fraction of total liabilities.

7 With the formation of the Canadian Payments Association (CPA) in 1980, local credit unions gained access to the nationwide cheque-clearing system on an equal basis with other deposit-taking institutions. Nevertheless, most have opted to rely on the CPA via the network of national centrals.

8 Unfortunately, the CCCS has been a financially weak institution since its inception in 1953.

**FIGURE 18.2** Local Credit Unions: Asset and Liability Composition

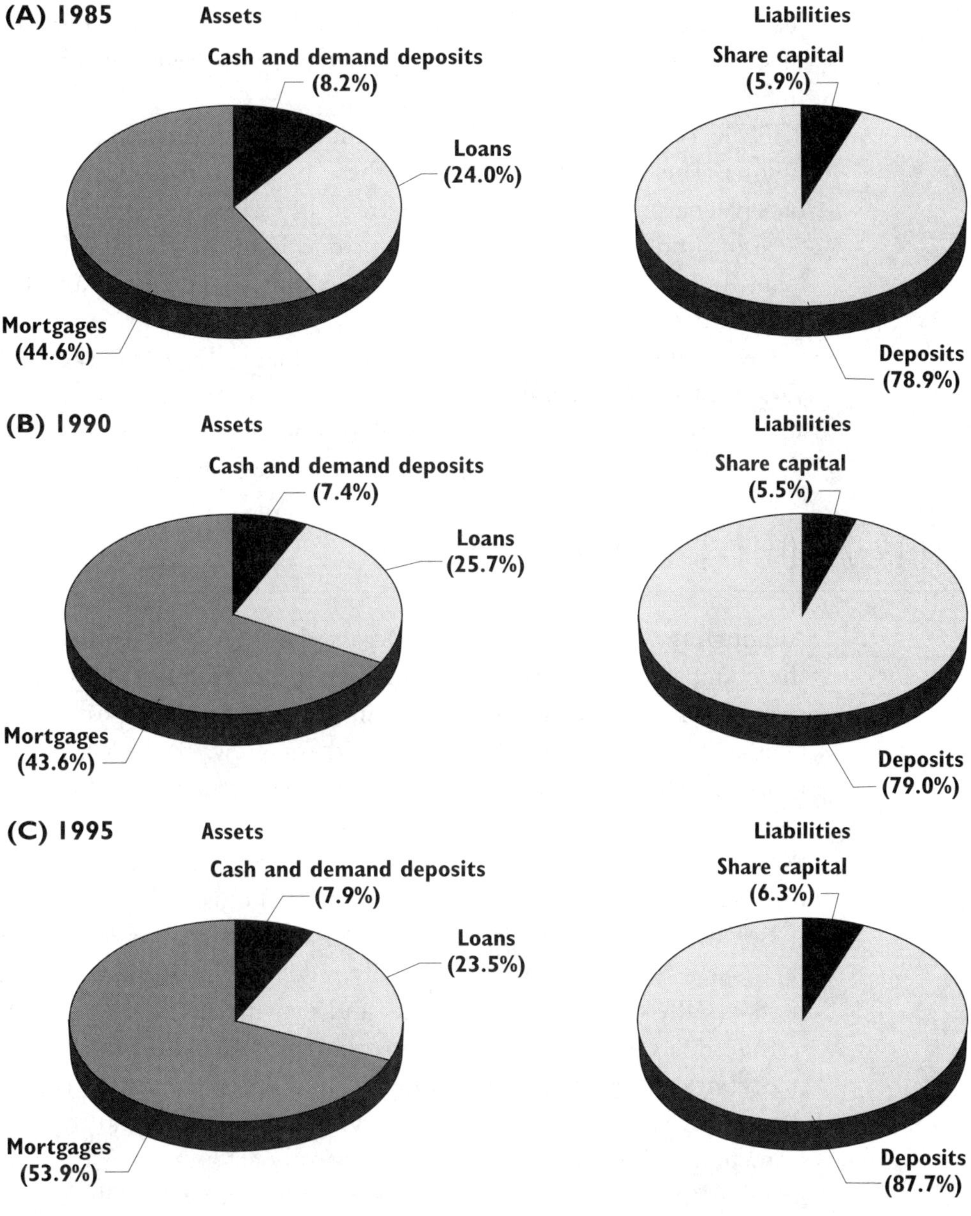


Note: The "deposits" shown as assets are the funds that credit unions have placed with other institutions. The "deposits" shown as liabilities are, of course, funds held for clients.

Source: *Historical Statistics of Canada*, 2d ed., No. CSII-516E (Ottawa: Minister of Supply and Services, 1983) and *Bank of Canada Review*, various issues, Table D3.

Deposits, primarily of the savings or term kind, are the principal source of funds. This development is explained by the fact that local credit unions are no longer institutions whose membership is narrowly defined along parish, occupational, or geographical lines and that they have begun to resemble other deposit-taking financial institutions.

Table 18.2 gives a more detailed picture of the balance sheet of local credit unions. The financial structure of these institutions is clearly simpler than that of, say, chartered banks (compare Table 17.5). Thus, deposits account for almost 80% of funds raised and assets are primarily in the form of mortgages and cash loans. In this respect, the asset composition of local credit unions has not changed much since 1970.

Credit unions have quietly evolved as financial supermarkets, offering a wide variety of services from personal loans, mortgages, and cheque-clearing, to insurance and travel-related services. This is precisely the type of financial institution that the other deposit-taking institutions seek to become.

## OTHER DEPOSIT-TAKING INSTITUTIONS

Although the Constitution Act 1867 gave the federal government jurisdiction over the country's whole financial system, its primary interest historically was commercial-type banks. As we have seen, however, other types of depository institutions arose as the public need for them grew. Some were trust companies, mortgage loan companies, and co-operatives. Others were savings banks, a type of deposit-taking institution present in most parts of the world (usually called a thrift in the United States) that specializes in holding individuals' savings, usually in time deposits, and making loans to households.

Because Canadian savings banks originated at local or regional levels, most of them, as a result, became provincially regulated institutions. A couple of exceptions are the Quebec savings banks and provincial government savings offices.

Indeed, a variety of provincial governments have, over the years, offered banking services, particularly in remote or rural areas. Currently, the only significant deposits are at the Province of Ontario Savings Offices and the Alberta Treasury Branches. Although these institutions mostly act as savings banks, they do make loans to small businesses and farmers, although a relatively large share of their funds are naturally invested in provincial securities.

For many years, the federal government did supervise some banks under the Quebec Savings Bank Act, which was originally quite restrictive, barring these savings banks from engaging in commercial lending and limiting their operations

**Table 18.2** THE BALANCE SHEET OF LOCAL CREDIT UNIONS AND CAISSES POPULAIRES (second quarter, 1995; millions of dollars)

| Assets | | Liabilities | |
|---|---|---|---|
| Cash on hand and demand deposits | 7,786 | Loans payable | 3,506 |
| Term deposits | 8,511 | Deposits[d] | 86,398 |
| Government of Canada securities | 715 | Other liabilities | 2,376 |
| Provincial + municipal securities | 347 | Members' equity share capital | 6,204 |
| Other securities | 868 | Total liabilities[c] | 98,484 |
| Shares in central credit unions | 500 | | |
| Loans[a] | 23,100 | | |
| Mortgages[b] | 53,095 | | |
| Other assets | 3,563 | | |
| Total assets[c] | 98,484 | | |

[a] Of which 57.3% are personal loans.

[b] Of which 86.7% are residential.

[c] Difference in total due to rounding error.

[d] Of which 27.6% are tax sheltered.

Source: *Bank of Canada Review*, various issues, Table D3.

first to a single branch (except in Montreal) and later to branches only in the province of Quebec. The Act expired in 1991 and was not renewed because it was no longer needed. Since 1969, the only institution falling under it had been the Montreal City and District Savings Bank, which, in 1987, became a Schedule II chartered bank operating under the name of Laurentian Group.

## SUMMARY

- This chapter surveys Canada's various depository institutions other than the chartered banks.

- The trust companies and the credit unions are the principal firms under the heading of "other depository institutions."

- Over the last decade or so, both trusts and credit unions have taken some market share from the chartered banks.

- These other depository institutions have tended to specialize in mortgages and other loans to households. But they are beginning to branch out into other activities as the differences between them and the chartered banks diminish.

# IMPORTANT TERMS

caisses populaires (p. 427)
credit unions (p. 426)
estate, trust, and agency (ETA) (p. 422)
mortgage loan companies (MLCs) (p. 422)
real estate investment trusts (REITs) (p. 424)
trust companies (p. 422)

# EXERCISES

1. Why do you think legislation barred chartered banks from engaging in estate, trust, and agency business?
2. Based on the balance sheet of trust companies (Table 18.1), estimate the gap and the leverage ratio of trust companies.
3. Do the same as in question 3 for the data in Table 18.2.
4. Explain why, historically, credit unions were created and why they may have played a relatively larger role in some areas of the country than in others.
5. Apart from banking-type services what other important functions are filled by trust companies?

# REFERENCES

*Bank of Canada Review* (various issues).

"Canada's Largest Corporations." *The Financial Post Magazine*, Summer 1991.

Chant, J.F. *The Market for Financial Services: Deposit-Taking Institutions.* Vancouver, B.C.: The Fraser Institute, 1988.

*Historical Statistics of Canada*, 2d ed., No. CSII-516E. Ottawa: Minister of Supply and Services, 1983.

Mercure, G. "Credit Unions and Caisses Populaires." Working paper prepared for the Royal Commission on Banking and Finance (November 1962).

*Reform of Federal Financial Institutions Legislation: Overview of Legislative Proposals.* Ottawa: Department of Finance, Fall 1990.

Statistics Canada. *Financial Flows and National Balance Sheet Accounts, 1988 and 1989*, No. 13-214.

———. *Financial Institutions: Financial Statistics*, No. 61-006.

*Trust and Loan Companies Act: Explanatory Notes.* Ottawa: Department of Finance, Fall 1990.

*Trust and Loan Companies and Co-operative Credit Associations: Industry Overview.* Ottawa: Minister of Supply and Services, 1989.

CHAPTER 19

# Other Financial Institutions

As a group, deposit-taking institutions are the largest financial intermediaries in Canada. However, a variety of other intermediaries—leasing and consumer finance companies, investment dealers, government financial institutions, insurance companies, mutual funds, and pension funds—also play an important role in the country's financial system.

In a sense, each of these kinds of institutions fulfils an intermediation function *in addition* to one or a few specialized functions. For example, insurance companies protect policyholders against unexpected and generally unwanted events, but they often couple insurance with ways for individuals to save for retirement or facilitate the leaving of bequests. Mutual funds and pension plans take advantage of the efficiencies inherent in the pooling of funds by a large number of contributors. Some combinations of services are precluded by government regulation. Deposit-taking institutions are barred from selling insurance, for example; banks are prevented from leasing cars, an area of specialization of some financial corporations. Government financial institutions, on the other hand, fill financing gaps in certain areas of the economy where the private sector is thought to have failed or where banks or other financial institutions would find it unprofitable to operate.

With the deregulation of the financial sector, banks and near-banks have soared ahead of the institutions covered in this chapter, at least as measured by asset size. Nevertheless, total assets of all the non-bank financial institutions still exceeds total assets of the chartered banks and near-banks.

## FINANCIAL AND LEASING CORPORATIONS

Firms in the finance company segment of the financial industry are essentially involved in the creation of debt with the funds used for purchasing specific goods and services at the corporate, wholesale, or retail levels. Credit is secured by mortgages or current and anticipated income or sales, and by the sale of debentures.

## TYPES OF INSTITUTIONS

Four major categories of institutions come under this heading.

1. Acceptance or sales finance companies make loans to consumers via retailers. For example, a car dealer takes a signed contract to buy an automobile to the finance company, which "accepts" it by purchasing the contract (for its face value plus a discount factor). The acceptance company is then the lienholder and collects regular payments. Not surprisingly, acceptance companies that finance the sale of automobiles are generally the largest in terms of asset size.

   Many acceptance companies are wholly owned subsidiaries of the manufacturers of products ranging from automobiles to dishwashers to computers. Having a more-or-less captive market for financing seems a good opportunity for large corporations, which have shown great interest in acting as intermediaries. But they have met with mixed success, especially during the 1980s when the predilection of such finance arms for also making real estate loans led to considerable losses for some. This diversification did not enhance returns primarily because it was done in areas in which these firms had little or no expertise.

   Acceptance companies may also finance inventories.

2. Consumer loan companies make cash advances to individuals for the purchase of goods and services and for debt consolidation. Since the chartered banks and near-banks have become increasingly competitive in the personal loans market, the consumer loan companies' market has shrunk and become concentrated on low-income customers, who are often high-risk borrowers.

3. **Financial leasing corporations** engage in leasing equipment, primarily to firms, which can then enjoy the benefits of the items without some of the risks of ownership. Leases are of two kinds. A *full-out financing lease* covers the anticipated life of the asset. The payments cover the cost of the equipment (perhaps at the wholesale level) as well as a margin for the lessor's costs of operation and a profit. But the lessee has acquired a debt without the costs of having to obtain the funds first and then negotiate a price for purchase. Alternatively, an *operating lease* does not cover the anticipated life of the asset. But, the lessee typically has the option, at the end of the lease, of purchasing the asset at a price stated by the lessor at the time the contract is signed. If

the lessee fails to purchase the asset, it can, of course, be leased (or sold) to someone else.

4. Business financing institutions serve primarily as an alternative to banks in their traditional commercial lending activities. Business financiers may also engage in other activities, such as the financing of inventories, *factoring* (the selling or discounting of accounts receivable to a specialist, who undertakes to collect the amounts owing), the financing of exports and of specific types of construction, and the provisions of working capital (the excess of current assets over current liabilities).

   They may also be involved in bridge financing—that is, supplying funds until longer-term financing arrangements can be worked out.

   In the past, merchant banks were included under the heading of business financiers but, since the 1980 Bank Act, many of them have become Schedule II banks. **Merchant banks**, in addition to arranging regular business loans, deal in *venture loans* (that is, loans to high-risk enterprises) and advise and assist clients who are seeking mergers or acquisitions. Venerable institutions such as J.P. Morgan, Morgan Stanley, and Rothchild's are called merchant banks. These types of institutions have grown rapidly during the 1980s in an attempt to capitalize on the financing needs of rapidly growing emerging markets in Asia, Latin and South America, and Eastern Europe. Another stimulus for growth has been the relative decrease in the role of banks in corporate financing. Large corporations with an international outlook need the financial services of institutions which can offer a complex set of financial arrangements and not simply just borrow or lend money.[1]

## ASSETS AND LIABILITIES

Table 19.1 presents a balance sheet for sales finance and consumer loans companies. The almost equal division of liabilities between long-term and short-term debt is a fairly recent occurrence.[2] The maturity structure of assets here is difficult to ascertain, but it seems safe to say that receivables and household credit are of a relatively short-term nature. Since these components represent almost three-quarters of the total, there is considerable mismatch between assets and liabilities.

---

1 See J. McNish, "Bankers' Brawl," *The Globe and Mail* Report on Business (January 1996), p. 82–5.

2 During much of the 1980s, relatively more of the debt was short term because long-term interest rates were higher than short-term rates during much of this period. By 1990, a reversal of sorts began with a downward-sloping yield curve, prompting a shift toward long-term borrowing. This shift accelerated into the mid-1990s as interest rates continued to fall.

**TABLE 19.1** THE BALANCE SHEET OF SALES FINANCE AND CONSUMER LOAN COMPANIES (November 1995, millions of dollars)

| Assets | | Liabilities | |
|---|---|---|---|
| Cash and deposits | 93 | Owed to parents + affiliates | 3,412 |
| Retail sales financing | 3,816 | Bank loans | 291 |
| Wholesale and business financing[a] | 4,279 | Short-term paper | |
| Household credit[b] | 8,246 | Canadian-dollar | 7,637 |
| Due on leasing + rentals | 5,031 | Foreign currency | 1,026 |
| Other receivables | 1,221 | Long-term debt | 11,458 |
| Allowance for doubtful receivables | −305 | Other liabilities | 929[c] |
| Investment and advances | 443 | Shareholders' equity | 3,424[c] |
| Investment in subsidiaries + | | Total liabilities | 28,177 |
| other assets | 5,348[c] | | |
| Total assets | 28,177 | | |

**Summary**
**(as percentage of total assets or liabilities)**

| | | | |
|---|---|---|---|
| Receivables | 22.2 | Short-term debt | 30.7 |
| Wholesale + business financing | 15.2 | Long-term debt | 40.7 |
| Household credit | 29.3 | Total liabilities | 71.4 |
| Total assets | 66.7 | | |

$$\text{Leverage Ratio} = \frac{20{,}412}{3{,}424} = 5.96$$

[a] Of which 91.4% is wholesale financing.

[b] Of which 89.9% is for personal loans.

[c] Estimate from September 1995, last available date.

Source: *Bank of Canada Review*, various issues, Table D3, and D4.

On the other hand, the sector's leverage ratio is small compared with that of deposit-taking institutions.

## INVESTMENT DEALERS

**Investment dealers** primarily *underwrite* securities, which involves purchasing newly issued debt from government or corporations and then reselling it in the secondary market. A select few, called *primary market dealers*, have privileged access to credit (from the chartered banks via day-to-day loans or the Bank of

Canada via special purchase and resale agreements if needed) and are designed to purchase federal government Treasury bills at the weekly auction.[3]

Until a few years ago, Canadian investment dealers were independent institutions. When 1989 changes to federal banking regulations[4] permitted banks to own brokerage houses, however, most investment dealers became wholly owned subsidiaries of banks. Others are subsidiaries of large foreign firms.

Unlike many other areas of the Canadian financial system, investment dealers are regulated by provincial bodies, usually called *securities commissions*, and the rules differ considerably across provinces. Nevertheless, in order to guarantee access to the Toronto Stock Exchange, most adopt rules set by the Ontario Securities Commission (OSC). In effect, these rules have become a quasi-national standard for securities dealers. Attempts during late 1990 to form a national body of sorts to regulate underwriting activities created a stir in the industry and were flatly rejected by several provincial bodies, including those of Quebec and British Columbia.

Unlike dealers, brokers act as agents for investors, that is, they are purely "middlemen." All investment brokers are members of the *Investment Dealers Association (IDA)*, an industry association that provides self-regulation. Nevertheless, because of recent and unhappy experiences in the United States, there is a growing concern about the degree to which this segment of the financial industry is unregulated by government. Overall, however, investment brokers' assets represent a relatively small fraction of the total financial sector.

## GOVERNMENT FINANCIAL INSTITUTIONS

The federal and provincial governments have for many years made credit available to the private sector directly or indirectly through Crown corporations. The list of these institutions is exceedingly long, but a few of the better known ones are worth mentioning.[5]

The *Canada Mortgage and Housing Corporation (CMHC)* assists specific types of residential construction, such as housing for individuals and families with low income. It also insures private mortgages issued by banks to individuals unable

3 See Chapter 4 for a discussion of this procedure, which essentially originated in the 1950s when the government wanted to ensure the presence of a ready market to absorb its debt.

4 Called Canada's "little bang" because it followed London's Big Bang (see Chapter 22).

5 Not included in this list are the Bank of Canada and the Canada Deposit Insurance Corporation, who provide implicit and explicit subsidiaries and other guarantees. These institutions are so important in their own right that they receive separate treatment in this book; see Chapters 20, 24, and 25.

to meet a minimum down payment, thus protecting those institutions against the default risk. The *Federal Business Development Bank* is a lender of last resort for firms unable to obtain financing through conventional means; most are interested in raising funds for fairly new high-risk ventures. The *Export Development Corporation* provides financing to foreign concerns for the purchase of Canadian exports. This assistance to Canadian producers mitigates some of the risk, such as credit risk, that cannot be eliminated through, say, bankers' acceptances because banks are unwilling to absorb the high level of risk involved in a particular transaction. The *Farm Credit Corporation* is one of a myriad of government financing arms meant to assist the agricultural sector. It provides the long-term credit required to finance, for example, the machinery and equipment used in farming.

Finally the government's financial intervention is also significant in its programs to facilitate regional economic expansion, its various incentives to reduce unemployment in regions where it is chronically high, and its bewildering array of other schemes whose objective is to "equalize" opportunities across provinces and regions.

## INSURANCE COMPANIES

**Insurance** is a contract to pay a premium in return for which the insurer provides financial compensation if a specified eventuality occurs. In effect, the insurance company pools the risk of many policyholders. If the group is large enough, actuaries can predict the incidence of most kinds of losses (but not the individuals to whom they will happen); thus, premiums can be calculated so that they total, on average, enough to pay claims, cover administrative costs, and give the company a profit.

In Canada, regulations originating in the last century have produced an industry that specializes in insurance. Recent reforms to the Bank Act will not result in significant changes in the near term. The industry will retain its oligopoly status over the sale of insurance to the public.[6] It may even expand.[7]

6 There are a few exceptions. Insurance has long been sold by credit unions, which qualify as "fraternal benefit societies," and chartered banks sell specific forms of insurance (health, car rental) through their credit card operations. Companies also work via banks to provide life insurance coverage for mortgage loans.

7 Bill C-28, which was tabled in June 1991 and later passed as part of the restructuring of the financial industry, forming the basis of the latest Bank Act, did away with many of the strict provisions that stipulate the activities insurers can engage in. Insurance companies are able to acquire deposit-taking institutions and so offer more banking services. Banks are also permitted to buy insurance companies (but not to sell insurance in their branches). Manulife Financial became the first insurer to directly purchase a bank. Manulife Bank of Canada was formed in 1992 with the merger of three small regional trust companies.

Nevertheless, it is a crowded industry with over 250 firms competing in the property and casualty area and over 100 firms selling life insurance. Moreover, unlike the banking sector, concentration levels are low.[8]

## KINDS OF ISSUERS

Insurance firms can be either joint stock companies, owned by shareholders, or mutual companies, owned by their policyholders. Most (about 95%) are incorporated and regulated federally, though a few are provincially regulated.[9]

Canada has three kinds of insurance companies, divided by the type of insurance they write: life; property and casualty; and accident and sickness.[10] Any firm that offers life insurance must maintain for it a **segregated fund**—that is, accounts separate from those for the rest of its activities.

Some property and casualty firms offer **reinsurance**. In a kind of secondary market, they assume a share of the insurer's liability in return for a share of the premiums. Risk is shifted. (Liability for payment to the policyholder who suffers a loss remains, however, with the insurer, not the reinsurer.)

Insurance companies may not take deposits or make many kinds of loans. But they have found mechanisms that enable them to offer equivalent services. Commercial loans are allowed if they are secured by property; personal loans are possible if backed by the cash value of a life insurance policy. And by selling annuities, payments from which are deferred into the future against periodic deposits, insurance companies effectively play the role of intermediaries.

Canada's insurance companies may not, however, participate in the Canada Deposit Insurance Corporation. Instead, they have set up their own contingency fund against defaults on policies. But unlike the case in the United States, where insurance activities are relatively unregulated, no insurance company in Canada failed between 1875 and 1990 (despite some near disasters during the nineteenth and early twentieth centuries). In 1991 two insurance companies, the Coopérants Mutual Life Insurance Society (which switched from federal to provincial jurisdiction in the 1980s) and the Sovereign Life Insurance Company (based in Calgary), failed. The most prominent failure in Canada, however, occurred fairly recently when Confederation Life (Confed) collapsed in 1994. Like many financial institutions, Confed had invested heavily into real estate. When the real estate market collapsed following the recession of 1991–92, its capital was insufficient to cover anticipated losses. Confed's capital–asset ratio (actually called the min-

---

8 See "Overcrowded," *The Economist* (31 October 1992), p. 67.

9 The regulations described here are federal. Provincial regulations are similar, though companies incorporated in Quebec are less restricted in investments and ownership.

10 Two or three kinds may, however, be wholly owned by a single holding company.

imum continuing capital and surplus ratio by the Office of the Superintendent of Financial Institutions which oversees the financial industry) looked acceptable, although it was below the industry average at the time. In reality, Confed's capital was grossly insufficient to meet its obligations.[11]

Attempts at merging with Great-West Life, one of the largest insurance companies (see Table 19.2) failed precisely because Great-West had concluded that Confed's balance sheet was worse than presented to regulators, ratings agencies and policyholders. Confed, a 123-year-old company, failed in August 1994 at which time federal regulators seized control of the company.[12]

A recent trend in Canada has been the incursion of insurance companies from other countries, in the main from Europe.[13] Foreign insurance companies are separately regulated by the federal government. They must, among other things, keep sufficient assets in the country to match their Canadian liabilities.

## TYPES OF INSURANCE CONTRACTS

Much of the insurance sold today is **term insurance**. The insurer contracts to cover a risk (death, fire, accident, and so on) for a set period. Premiums are collected from policyholders and claims paid to the relatively few who experience the eventuality.

Life insurance companies also offer two other types of contracts. One is permanent insurance, which combines life insurance with savings; if a policyholder has not died by a specified age (often 65), he or she receives a lump-sum payment.[14] The premiums are partly actuarily based; the excess is the savings.[15] By contrast, term insurance premiums are actuarially based and so these premiums rise with age.

Another kind of contract is an **annuity**, which provides a stream of payments, usually upon retirement, to an individual or his or her beneficiaries. A variety of such schemes exist. One of the best known is the **registered retirement income fund (RRIF)**, which promises a rising payment schedule until age 90. The pre-

11 Look back at Chapter 10 to see the difficulty with conventional accounting measures of the capital–asset ratio.

12 For a description of the sequence of events that led to Confed's collapse, see R. McQueen, "The Story Behind the Death of a Giant," *Financial Post* (24 September 1994), p. 10–11.

13 At the end of 1988, there were some 180 insurance companies operating in Canada, of which 96 would be classified as foreign.

14 These policies, also called *whole life policies*, are still available but are much less popular than they were in the past.

15 A type of whole life policy where the premiums were paid for a fixed term, called "vanishing premiums," was introduced in the 1980s, but, in some cases, the premium did not vanish. This led to court cases in the US which prevented insurance companies (in Canada too) from extracting premiums beyond the specified term.

mium is often paid as a lump sum, usually a rollover from a *registered retirement savings plan (RRSP)*.[16]

### ASSETS AND LIABILITIES

To meet their contractual obligations, insurance companies rely on premiums, investment income, and reserves. (Life insurance companies call this pool the *actuarial reserve.*) The insurance regulations are specific (and complicated) about what insurance companies can invest in and the overall size of their debt in relation to shareholders' equity.[17] Even more important is a regulation forbidding the raising of funds through the issuing of debt. All these restrictions have been justified by the need to ensure funds to meet liabilities, in particular the long-term liabilities of life insurance companies.

Not surprisingly in view of the existing legislation, these firms are less leveraged than other financial institutions. Moreover, claims of various types represent at least 80% of expenditures. Premiums, annuities, and interest earned on investment accounts for over 90% of revenues for life insurers, and premiums alone represent more than 80% of property and casualty insurers' revenues.

Assets and liabilities are well matched for life insurers; over three-quarters each of investments and claims are long term. The same is true for property and casualty insurers except that their investments and claims are primarily short term.

### SIZE

Table 19.2 on page 442 provides a list of some of the largest insurance companies in Canada by revenues generated. Despite the recent proliferation of foreign insurance companies, Canadian firms lead the industry.

## INVESTMENT FUNDS AND COMPANIES

One of the ways in which intermediaries improve the efficiency of the financial system is through the pooling of funds, thus diversifying risks to a greater extent than is possible for the typical individual investor. This is, in essence, what in-

16 RRSPs are discussed later in the chapter, with pensions. On reaching age 71 (reduced to 69 in the 1996 federal budget), holders of RRSPs must collapse these funds, paying the deferred tax or transferring them to an approved annuity scheme. Life insurance companies can themselves accept RRSP deposits.

17 For example, an insurance company can purchase no more than 30% of a corporation's shares (there are some exceptions); no more than 15% of its own assets can go into real estate; and no more than 7% of its assets can be invested in "speculative" securities.

**TABLE 19.2** THE LARGEST INSURANCE COMPANIES IN CANADA, 1995

| (A) Life Insurance | | (B) Property and Casualty Insurance | |
|---|---|---|---|
| Rank | Company | Rank | Company |
| 1 | Sun Life | 1 | Insurance Corporation of British Columbia |
| 2 | Manulife Financial | 2 | Co-operators Financial Services |
| 3 | Great-West Life Co. | 3 | General Accident Assurance |
| 4 | London Ins. | 4 | Zurich Canada |
| 5 | Canada Life | 5 | Roins Holding |

Note: Ranking based on total revenues.

Source: "The Top 1000 Companies," *Report on Business Magazine*, July 1995, 147. Reprinted with permission from *The Globe and Mail*.

vestment funds (**mutual funds**) and **investment companies** do.[18] They exist for the sole purpose of purchasing securities of other firms, financial or not. Participants own shares or "units" whose value is proportional to the value of the total pool of funds.

Anyone can set up investment funds, and they are not closely regulated. Some are established as trusts by other financial institutions (subsidiaries of banks and trust companies, for example). Others are separate companies, chartered provincially or federally. Many banks have entered the mutual funds market, in particular the money market and mortgage segments, but, as we briefly describe below, there exist a large variety of investment funds.[19]

## KINDS OF INVESTMENT FUNDS

For simplicity, investment funds can be categorized in two ways. One is according to how they are set up, which affects how they are sold. *Closed-end funds* have a fixed number of shares that cannot be redeemed on demand. After the original issue is sold, the shares are traded on the secondary market.[20] Alternatively, an

18 Technically the two differ. Investment funds are what are usually called mutual funds. Investment companies are legally defined as principally engaged in holding securities issued by other companies. Some investment companies are called holding companies because they have a controlling interest in one or more corporations. For most purposes here, we can ignore the difference.

19 A recent overview of this market is contained in "The Mutual Fund Market in Canada," *Bank of Canada Review* (Winter 1992–93): 57–69.

20 One use of such shares is to acquire control of other corporations, in which case the fund becomes a kind of *holding company* (a firm that owns a controlling interest in the shares of one or more other corporations and thus has the right to supervise its management).

investment fund can be an *open-end* mutual fund, which means there are no restrictions on the issue of shares to new subscribers and shares can be redeemed on demand at net asset value (the market value of all the fund's assets less any liabilities, divided by the number of shares).

The other way of classifying mutual funds is by the type or types of investments they make. A few are unspecialized. Many, termed equity funds, invest principally in common shares; some of those choose to concentrate on a particular sector of the economy, such as energy or pharmaceutical companies. Bonds funds allocate their resources to the purchase of government securities or corporate bonds. Mortgage funds invest in financial instruments, usually bonds, used to finance mortgage lending. Money-market funds invest in short-term bonds, such as Treasury bills and commercial paper.

Table 19.3 lists the larger mutual funds in Canada. Investors Group has retained its first place ranking since at least 1990 and the fund has grown a prodigious 57.4%, on average, annually. The popularity of mutual funds suggests that we explore some of the reasons behind their success. As financial wealth has risen, investors look to take advantage of the benefits of diversification. As we have seen, mutual funds can provide this as well as economies of scale and scope, especially to individual investors. The growing importance of having to plan for retirement in an ageing population also plays a role in the growth of mutual funds. Nevertheless, the particular appeal of *no-load* funds where investors pay no up-front brokerage fees (unlike load funds for which they do) raises the question about whether these perform better than other types of funds or better than if the investor were to construct a portfolio by himself or herself. One worry is that, in the absence of firm regulations concerning the disclosure of fees to fund managers, investors in no-load funds may in fact be worse off than under any alternative because the monitoring fees may be considerably higher than either with load funds or with the management of one's own portfolio.[21]

## PENSION FUNDS

Facilitating the reallocation of consumption over time is an important function of financial intermediation. The premier device for doing so is **pension funds**, which are arrangements for accumulating a portion of a worker's income tax-free until retirement and then paying out periodic benefits. We'll discuss private and public plans, which work quite differently. We'll also look quickly at registered

21 The whole question of mutual fund performance and its impact is the subject of a growing literature which is beyond the scope of this text.

**TABLE 19.3** THE LARGEST MUTUAL FUNDS IN CANADA (year end 1995)

| | | Assets (millions of dollars) |
|---|---|---|
| 1 | Investors Group | 19,830 |
| 2 | Trimark Investment | 13,799 |
| 3 | Royal Mutual Funds | 12,277 |
| 4 | MacKenzie Group | 11,277 |
| 5 | AGF Management | 7,655 |
| 6 | Templeton Management | 6,339 |
| 7 | Canadian Imperial Bank of Commerce Securities | 6,254 |
| 8 | Fidelity Inv. | 6,249 |
| 9 | TD Asset Mgmt | 6,231 |
| 10 | Altamira Inv. Services | 5,344 |

Source: *Financial Post* (16 January 1996), p. 1.

retirement savings plans, which are not truly pension plans but share some of their characteristics.

## PRIVATE PENSION PLANS

Private pension plans are pension plans established by private employers (or in some cases, by unions). They are regulated by the provincial governments. They are also registered with the federal government so that participants can obtain deferral of income tax on contributions until they are paid out as pensions.

Private pension plans exist in great variety. A plan may be *contributory* or *non-contributory* (the employer does or does not match the employee's contributions); compulsory or voluntary (the employee may or may not choose whether to join the plan); *trusteed* or *insured* (managed by a trust company or a committee of trustees, the contributors, or by an insurance company[22]).

Plans also vary according to when members are entitled to draw retirement benefits, and what sort of death benefits accrue to the survivors of a planholder who dies before retirement.[23]

Most important, private pension plans differ in the basis of which benefits are earned. In a *defined-benefit plan*, a policyholder who retires is guaranteed a specific benefit. It may be calculated in a variety of ways (perhaps $x$ dollars a month or $y$% of the individual's average earnings over some period) and it may be indexed

22 Insured pension plans are, in effect, group annuities. Although common, they tend to be used for relatively small groups. The large pension plans are usually trusteed.

23 A frequent provision is that survivors are entitled to the benefit's *commuted value*, which is the present value of the implicit income stream.

for inflation, but the amount is known. Since actuaries can predict with some accuracy the number of policyholders who will be collecting benefits at a given time in the future, they can say whether such a plan is fully funded (its current assets equal the present value of expected benefits).[24] For example, suppose a worker contributes $1,000 a year for 20 years. If the annual return is expected to be 8% per year, the value of the accumulated savings would be $45,762 after 20 years.[25] If the defined benefit plan pays less than $45,762 the plan is under-funded.

In a *defined-contribution plan* (also called a money-purchase plan), benefits are not known. They vary according to the amount of accumulated contributions and the return on the fund's investments.

What private pension plans have in common is provincial regulation. They are also registered with the federal government, however, so that income tax on contributions is deferred until they are paid out as pensions.

Are defined-benefit plans superior to defined-contribution plans? In the former, employers assume the risk since they (or their trustees) must take investment decisions and make up shortfalls in order to fully fund the plan. But, as we know, risk and return are positively related to each other. Therefore, although employees may think it advantageous to have someone else bear the risk, they may be doing so at the expense of lower return and, consequently, fewer funds at retirement age.[26]

## PUBLIC PENSION PLANS

A public pension plan is one operated by a government. The largest are the Canada Pension Plan (CPP) and Quebec Pension Plan (QPP), which, since 1966, have provided retirement benefits to all members of the Canadian labour force between the ages of 18 and 65 (or 70 depending on circumstances). Membership

---

24 Some provinces require that private pension plans be fully funded. This requirement arose because some companies were accused of deliberately diverting funds from pension plans which, in some cases, led to serious under-funding problems.

25 The future value of such an annuity can be calculated in one of two ways: (1) $\$1,000(1.08) + \$1,000(1.08)^2 + \ldots + \$1,000(1.08)^{20}$, where the last term is the value of $1,000 in 20 years and the first term is the value of $1,000 contributed in year 20 (remember from Chapter 5 that interest is earned at the *end* of a period, here a year); (2) application of the formula for the future value of an annuity of $1,000 a year for 20 years, namely $[(1.08)^{20} - 1]/.08$, which would yield the same answer.

26 The problem here, known as *moral hazard*, is perhaps best illustrated with the management of public funds. Instead of investing them at market rates, the government simply borrows what it needs for benefit at an interest rate it sets itself! To the extent that the public sector never has to worry about the government running out of money, no particularly serious problem is created. But if a private sector company behaves in essentially the same way—for example, by appropriating "surplus" pension funds—the outcome is usually not to the benefit of the employees.

in the funds is mandatory. Contributions are a fixed percentage of earnings, to a maximum, and are matched by the government. Benefits from these programs accounted for almost two-thirds of tax filers income who were 65 years or older in 1993. Not surprisingly, benefits were a relatively more important source of income for those earning $20,000 or less than for those earning more than $60,000 (less than 25%).

CPP contributions are invested in provincial non-marketable government bonds, but benefits are paid out of general revenues. The QPP operates in similar fashion, except that the accumulated funds are managed separately by the *Caisse de Dépôt et Placement*, which acts like an ordinary (but huge) pension fund.

Although CPP and QPP benefits are tied to contributions, the former are not fixed in any sense. Moreover, the ageing of the labour force during the past decade or so has resulted in benefits' exceeding the value of the accumulated contributions. The federal government has used several increases in contribution levels, but even these now seem unlikely to be sufficient to prevent the CPP fund from being extinguished sometime during the 1990s. The QPP shows fewer signs of running out of its accumulated funds, but it still seeks to operate on a pay-as-you-go basis.

The unsustainability of the current system came to a head in 1996 when finance minister, Paul Martin Jr., announced the phasing out of the current system with a new system, tentatively called Seniors Benefits, which would pay out tax-free pensions to seniors on a sliding scale, depending on their income. Under this plan, which would replace the current Canada Pension Plan and Old Age Security systems, "wealthy" seniors, that is, those who earn more than $52,000 (or a couple who earn more than $78,000) would no longer receive any benefits.[27]

Canada has a variety of public pension plans in addition to the CPP and QPP. Many public groups and Crown corporations—from the British Columbia Civil Service to Ontario Hydro—have plans for their employees. They generally resemble private plans, but the money flows through a public agency.

## REGISTERED RETIREMENT SAVINGS PLANS (RRSPs)

Many working Canadians are not covered by an employer's pension scheme, and others foresee that the retirement benefits from such a scheme will not be sufficient in their declining years. These people can place a certain amount of income in special trust accounts called **registered retirement savings plans (RRSPs)**. As with pension plan contributions, no tax is assessed (on this income or on its yield) as long as it remains in the tax-sheltered account. When the individual is

27 Interestingly, the threshold amounts seem to be fixed in nominal terms although pension payments will be fully indexed to inflation.

between ages 65 and 69, he or she must collapse the RRSP; if the proceeds are used to buy an annuity or RRIF, however, tax is due only on the benefits as they are paid out. Despite the tax-shelter status of RRSPs, only a third of the labour force makes contributions annually. Nevertheless, almost two-thirds of the labour force has some type of pension plan (RRSPs or registered pension plan).

Although there are regulations about the investments the trustees of an RRSP can make, no special form of intermediation is involved. Indeed, RRSPs are offered by banks, trust companies, life insurance companies, brokers, and mutual funds. Financial intermediaries compete hard for the funds because the market for RRSPs (as for RRIFs) is huge—worth several billion dollars annually. Recent changes in the Income Tax Act have made these tax-deferment plans the savings vehicle of choice. However, since the early 1990s these plans have become less advantageous for tax purposes as successive governments have not allowed caps on contributions to rise as originally promised.

## SUMMARY

- This chapter surveys financial institutions whose functions differ from those of deposit-taking institutions.
- These other financial institutions perform some intermediation functions but they also allow consumers to either shift risk or shift income from the present to the future.
- Leasing companies offer a specialized form of lending for the purpose of purchasing physical assets for the most part.
- Investment dealers underwrite securities. These dealers act as brokers rather than as intermediaries since they do not create new assets. Instead, they facilitate the transfer of funds from lenders to borrowers.
- Insurance companies allow individuals to reduce the costs of unforseen events. But because these companies also accept deposits for the purposes of deferring current income they also perform an intermediation function.
- Investment companies and funds invest a variety of assets, fractions of which can be purchased by individuals who are therefore able to cheaply acquire a diversified portfolio.
- Pension funds allow individuals to reallocate their income thus also facilitating the maintenance of consumption over a lifetime. Many funds are privately run but a government-run or public pension plan also has an important place in Canada.

## IMPORTANT TERMS

annuities (p. 440)
financial leasing corporation (p. 434)
insurance (p. 438)
investment company (p. 442)
investment dealer (p. 436)
merchant bank (p. 435)
mutual fund (p. 442)
pension fund (p. 443)
registered retirement income fund (RRIF) (p. 440)
registered retirement savings plan (RRSP) (p. 446)
reinsurance (p. 439)
segregated funds (p. 439)
term insurance (p. 440)

## EXERCISES

1. The table below shows the evolution since 1985 of the short-term and long-term debt of sales, finance, and consumer loan companies. Given the behaviour of short- and long-term interest rates during the same period (also shown below), did these institutions act in such a way as to minimize their debt costs? Discuss your answer.

| | 1985 | 1986 | 1987 | 1988 | 1989 | 1990 | 1991 | 1992 | 1993 | 1994 |
|---|---|---|---|---|---|---|---|---|---|---|
| Treasury bill rate | 9.44 | 8.99 | 8.19 | 9.42 | 12.02 | 12.80 | 8.85 | 6.50 | 4.91 | 5.42 |
| Long-term government bond rate | 1.11 | 9.54 | 9.95 | 10.23 | 9.92 | 10.81 | 9.82 | 8.77 | 7.86 | 8.60 |
| Short-term debt (millions of dollars) | 6,060 | 7,295 | 8,394 | 9,195 | 10,072 | 9,196 | 7,310 | 6,738 | 6,208 | 8,498 |
| Long-term debt (millions of dollars) | 4,125 | 5,352 | 6,893 | 8,180 | 8,475 | 9,376 | 9,723 | 8,952 | 8,873 | 9,474 |

Source: *Bank of Canada Review*, various issues, Tables A1 and D3, and D4.

2. Do investment dealers as a whole respond to risk–return considerations and suffer any consequences as outlined in this text? The following table shows the dollar holdings of three important assets as well as total assets held by investment dealers during 1987. Discuss how the financial events of 1987 may be reflected in the balancing sheet changes. (Recall that the stock market crash occurred during that year.)

| Assets | 1987 (thousands of dollars) Second Quarter | Third Quarter | Fourth Quarter |
|---|---|---|---|
| Corporation shares | 511,944 | 1,073,098 | 478,290 |
| Bankers' acceptance | 1,156,790 | 973,463 | 1,690,682 |
| Canada Treasury bills | 3,557,103 | 2,603,906 | 3,236,130 |
| Total assets | 18,370,826 | 17,905,143 | 14,731,906 |

3. A life insurance company operates an investment fund. The following table shows the hypothetical accumulated value of a single deposit of $10,000 at various years as a function of three different interest rate levels. The figures assume that an "acquisition fee" has been deducted to cover administration expenses. Calculate the dollar and percentage amount of the acquisition fee. Would you expect that fee to vary according to the size of the deposit?

| End of Year | Accumulated Value at 5% | 10% | 12½% |
|---|---|---|---|
| 5 | $12,154 | $ 15,345 | $ 17,164 |
| 10 | 15,516 | 24,708 | 30,928 |
| 15 | 19,802 | 39,786 | 55,740 |
| 20 | 25,270 | 64,084 | 100,441 |
| 30 | 41,167 | 166,201 | 326,165 |
| 40 | 67,056 | 431,093 | 1,059,741 |

4. The following table gives the 1-year, 5-year, and 10-year average return on a variety of assets, which are indexed according to their risk characteristics (specifically, default risk and income risk). Plot the risk–return combinations for the three periods separately. Are the results consistent with the analysis in the text? If so, why? If not, why not? Does the risk index make sense?

| Asset | Risk Index | 1-year | 5-years | 10-years |
|---|---|---|---|---|
| Savings account | 1 | 6.21 | 6.68 | 7.66 |
| 5-year term deposit | 2 | 10.00 | 7.84 | 11.85 |
| 5-year GIC | 2 | 11.25 | 10.01 | 13.19 |
| Canada Savings Bond | 0 | 10.87 | 9.69 | 11.03 |
| 3-month Treasury bill | 0 | 10.97 | 10.71 | 11.24 |
| TSE 300 at close | 3 | 11.58 | 6.20 | 10.04 |
| S&P 500 | 3 | 26.73 | 10.89 | 12.81 |
| Equity funds | 5 | 31.66 | 15.26 | 15.95 |
| Balanced funds | 3 | 24.39 | 10.56 | 15.53 |
| Consumer Price Index | — | 5.66 | 4.75 | 5.09 |

Source: *The Globe and Mail*, 17 October 1991, p. C2.

5. The Canadian population is ageing. Why does this put more pressure on the CPP and QPP? Does this also affect private pensions? Explain.

6. What kind of specialized service do finance and leasing companies perform that banks do not?

7. Why has the fixing of caps on RRSPs in nominal terms meant an effective reduction in the tax advantage provided by this kind of tax shelter?

8. Why did banks find it natural to take over much of the investment dealer industry?

9. What kind of gaps are filled by government-run or -backed financial institutions?

10. Why are mutual funds so popular? Why do some feel they are a "rip-off"?

## REFERENCES

*Bank of Canada Review* (various issues).

Brown, S.J., and W.N. Goetzmann, "Performance Persistence," *Journal of Finance*, 50 (June 1995): 679–98.

Bliss, M. *Northern Enterprise: Five Centuries of Canadian Business*. Toronto: McClelland and Stewart, 1987.

*Industry Overview: Life Insurance Companies and Fraternal Benefit Societies, 1989*. Ottawa: Office of the Superintendent of Financial Institutions, 1989.

Malkiel, B.G. "Returns from Investing in Mutual Funds," *Journal of Finance* 50 (June 1995): 549–72.

*Report of the Superintendent of Financial Institutions: Investment Companies*. Ottawa: Minister of Supply and Services, 1990.

*The Seniors Benefit: Securing the Future* (Ottawa: Dept. of Finance, March 1996).

Statistics Canada, CANSIM database.

———. *Financial Institutions*. No. 61-006.

———. *Pension Plans in Canada, 1988*. No. 74-401, Appendix III.

———. *Quarterly Estimates of Trusteed Pension Funds*. No. 74-001.

———. *Quarterly Financial Statistics for Enterprises*. No. 61-008.

———. *Trusteed Pension Funds*. No. 74-201. Ottawa: Minister of Supply and Services, April 1991.

CHAPTER 20

# Deposit Insurance

Insurance against losses from holding deposits, commonly referred to as deposit insurance, is a fairly recent development in Canada, having been introduced in 1967. But in view of the recent savings and loan fiasco in the United States and the Canadian federal and provincial governments' occasionally inconsistent attitudes and practices toward depositor protection, the subject has been receiving considerable public attention.

In this chapter, we examine the operation of deposit insurance in Canada and, more cursorily, in some other countries. Then we consider why deposit insurance is thought to be necessary. Next we turn to moral hazard and adverse selection, two problems that arise in all types of insurance but are especially troublesome in deposit insurance. We also discuss why government intervention in providing deposit insurance is controversial. The chapter concludes by asking how Canada's existing deposit insurance scheme could be improved.

## DEPOSIT INSURANCE IN CANADA

If a deposit-taking institution fails, what happens to the funds that have been deposited with it? The short answer is that they disappear,[1] leaving the depositors out of luck. The only existing protection against this risk is **deposit insurance**, which compensates depositors for at least some of their loss if an institution fails.

### THE MECHANICS

Canada provides deposit insurance through a Crown corporation called the **Canada Deposit Insurance Corporation** (CDIC). "The primary objective, of course, is to ensure the safety of small investors who are usually not in the position to

1 When the failed institution's affairs are wound up, there may be some funds to be divided among depositors and other creditors. But there will not be enough to cover everything (recall that *insolvency*, by definition, means that assets are less than liabilities). In some cases, depositors will be lucky to get back a few cents on the dollar.

judge for themselves the financial soundness of the institution to which they entrust their savings."[2] All federally chartered banks, trust companies, and mortgage loan companies must be members; provincially chartered institutions may also belong, and many do.[3]

As of 1995, the CDIC had 121 members of which 101 were federal institutions; the rest are provincially regulated institutions.[4] Each paid a flat premium of one-tenth of 1% of insurable deposits.[5] On 1 May 1993 premiums were raised by 25% (from $1 per $1,000 of insurable deposits to $1.25) and were raised again by a further 33.6% (to $1.67 per $1,000 insurable deposits) on 1 May 1994. Put a different way, the premiums represent one-sixth of 1% of insurable deposits. In return, all eligible deposits—Canadian-denominated savings and chequing accounts; term deposits (including GICs maturing in less than five years); money orders, drafts, and traveller's cheques issued by members; trust deposits; and deposits held in registered retirement savings plans (RRSPs) and registered retirement income funds (RRIFs)[6]—are insured to a maximum of $60,000 per deposit.

This limit can, however, be rendered inconsequential in a number of ways. First, since it applies to deposits held with a single member, an individual or firm can enjoy protection of $60,000 multiplied by the number of members it has deposits with. Second, since joint deposits, RRSPs, and RRIFs are insured separately, investments in these instruments can multiply coverage many times over. Moreover, public perception of what is and what is not insured is confused by several factors. First, some financial institutions are organized in such a way that a separate entity manages RRSPs and RRIFs; thus, investment in some of these plans may not be insured at all. Second, the depositor-protection agencies that some provinces operate (mainly for the benefit of credit union members) have rules that differ from the CDIC's; Alberta, for example, guarantees 100% of credit union deposits, and British Columbia covers deposits denominated in US dollars.

---

2 *Final Report of the Working Committee on the Canada Deposit Insurance Corporation* (Ottawa: Minister of Supply and Services, 24 April 1985), 3.

3 In fact, all the provinces except Quebec now require their trusts and mortgage loan companies to join the CDIC. These provinces insure their own credit unions' deposits, however, and some also provide insurance for deposits with trusts that is more extensive than that of the CDIC. Quebec has its own deposit insurance agency, the *Régie de l'assurance; dépôts du Québec (RADQ)*. Largely modelled on the CDIC, it covers all deposit-taking institutions in the province except the chartered banks.

4 A "member" includes all the branches of an institution. Thus the multibranch Canadian Imperial Bank of Commerce is one member; so is a single-branch trust company in New Brunswick. The year-end for the CDIC is March 31st.

5 There is a $5,000 minimum.

6 The CDIC provides no protection against losses in, for example, foreign-currency deposits, term deposits that mature in more than five years, debentures, Treasury bills, or funds invested in mortgages, stocks, and mutual funds.

The public often fails to understand distinctions among types of deposits, institutions, and deposit-protection agencies.

Third, the federal and provincial governments *sometimes* go well beyond the coverage of the relevant deposit-protection agency. When the Canadian Commercial Bank failed in 1985, for example, the federal government covered some $720 million of *uninsured* deposits (the CDIC paid out $352 million for insured deposits). Yet no such bailout occurs in some other instances.[7] For example, when the Calgary-based Tower Mortgage failed, uninsured depositors incurred sizeable losses. The discrepancy arises because governments have viewed some institutions as too big to fail. Depositors in large banks are treated as covered, whether they are or not, because regulators view such institutions as too costly or difficult to liquidate. By contrast, losses incurred by uninsured depositors at smaller banks are viewed as tolerable.

## THE CDIC

The CDIC is run by a board of directors whose members, significantly, include the Governor of the Bank of Canada, the Deputy Minister of Finance, and the Superintendent of Financial Institutions.[8] The chairperson is appointed for a five-year term.

The corporation's powers to intervene in the affairs of its members are quite broad, however. It can acquire assets from a member institution, make loans or deposits with members without any collateral if it wishes, borrow from the Canadian government or issue debt instruments to raise funds, act as a liquidator, and assume the costs of winding-up operations.

In the event of a failure, the CDIC can take one or more of the following options.

1. Payoff of the depositors and closure of the bank.
2. Merger with a solvent bank (sometimes referred to as purchase and assumption).
3. Transfers of the deposits to another institution, which receives funds necessary to assume the additional liabilities. The insolvent bank is then wound up.

---

7 L. White, *The S&L Debacle* (New York: Oxford University Press, 1991), 211. White points out that some uses of the term "bailout" are misleading because the word suggests financial relief to an undeserving group. This characterization is inappropriate since deposit insurance is an obligation the government has committed itself to. To the extent that *uninsured* deposits are redeemed, however, the relief is a form of subsidization.

8 This office was created in 1987 by merging the Office of the Inspector General of Banks and the Department of Insurance. The latter office had been responsible for supervising trust, mortgage loan, and insurance companies.

**4.** Bailout to permit the insolvent institution to continue operations.

Although these powers appear fairly wide, critics complain that the Bank of Canada's role in the process is unclear and that the CDIC cannot formally order the merger of weak banks with strong ones.[9]

In 1993 and 1994, the CDIC's functions were extensively re-examined in a government white paper entitled "Enhancing the Safety and Soundness of the Canadian Financial System." This review culminated with a clarification of the respective functions of the CDIC and the OSFI (Office of the Superintendent of Financial Institutions), as well as outlining the circumstances under which both institutions would have to co-ordinate their activities.[10] Essentially, the Corporation can force action only after a member institution has effectively become insolvent. Since it has extensive powers of inspection, the agency might be able to prevent some problems if it could step in *before* it is too late and an institution has to be wound up in some fashion.

Table 20.1 gives a snapshot of the recent performance of the CDIC. The list of member institutions that have resorted to its help is surprisingly long considering the Canadian history of avoiding bank failures. There were only 22 failures between 1867 and 1923, and none whatsoever from 1923, the date of the failure of the Home Bank, until 1966. From 1967 through 1989, the CDIC was called on to act in 23 instances. From 1984 on, there was a string of failures, and, as the table makes clear, the agency paid out considerably more than it was expected to recover.

The two largest failures occurred in 1991 and 1992. Standard Trust, the ninth-largest trust company in Canada, filed for bankruptcy in April 1991, when the holders of more than $100 million in debt contended that the institution was essentially insolvent. The following year Central Guaranty Trust Co. failed and the size of the rescue was the largest in the CDIC's history. The resulting losses, due to bad commercial real estate loans, might have been larger had the Toronto-Dominion Bank not agreed to take over Central Guaranty's branches and operations. One of the most celebrated cases may have been the failure of the Bank of Credit and Commerce International (BCCI). Among the charges were those that the offices operated a Ponzi (pyramid) scheme[11] in which money from new depositors was used to finance the needs of others, including illegal activities of

---

9 It must seek permission from the minister responsible (federal institutions minister). Historically, however, this has often been the outcome in the Canadian banking industry. See "Central Bank Role Urged in CDIC Act," *The Financial Post*, 11 March 1992, p.15.

10 See CDIC, *Annual Report 1994–1995* (Toronto: CDIC, 1995), appendix 2.

11 Named after Charles Ponzi, of Boston, Massachusetts, who operated such a scheme in the 1920s. It was not the first attempt at this kind of fraud. The South Sea Bubble (see Chapter 12) was an earlier version of a Ponzi scheme.

**Table 20.1** CANADA DEPOSIT INSURANCE CORPORATION OBLIGATIONS, 1995

| Member Institution | Year | Claim (millions of dollars) | Recoveries[b] |
|---|---|---|---|
| Crown Trust | 1983 | 930 | 100 |
| AMIC Mtge Inv. Trust | 1983 | 28 | 54 |
| Fidelity Trust | 1983 | 792 | 55 |
| Greymac Mortgage | 1983 | 174 | 53 |
| Greymac Trust | 1983 | 240 | 48 |
| Seaway Trust | 1983 | 420 | 86 |
| Canadian Commercial Bank | 1985 | 352 | 23 |
| Northland Bank | 1985 | 318 | 68 |
| CCB Mortgage Investment | 1985 | 123 | 90 |
| Pioneer Trust | 1985 | 201 | 88 |
| Principal Savings and Trust | 1987 | 116 | 119 |
| Settler's Savings | 1990 | 43 | 52 |
| Bank of Credit and Commerce | 1991 | 22 | 81 |
| Saskatchewan Trust | 1991 | 64 | 87 |
| Standard Loan | 1991 | 157 | 98 |
| Standard Trust | 1991 | 1,164 | 78 |
| Central Guaranty | 1992 | 1,684 | 90 |
| First City Trust | 1992 | 175 | 24 |
| Shoppers Trust | 1992 | 492 | 96 |
| Dominion Trust | 1993 | 431 | 84 |
| Prenor Trust | 1993 | 821 | 92 |
| Confederation Trust | 1994 | 679 | 100 |
| Monarch Trust | 1994 | 65 | 99 |
| Income Trust | 1995 | 194 | 73 |
| Total | | 9,685 | |

[a] The payment and recovery figures are the actual amounts cumulated from the time the institution failed through the end of 1990. It is often years until the final amounts, especially for recoveries, are known.

[b] As a percent of total plus expected before closure of estate.

Source: Canada Deposit Insurance Corporation, *Annual Report 1994–95* (Toronto: CDIC), Table 4.

all kinds. When the number of new investors was insufficient to cover the cash needs of earlier ones, the scheme collapsed.

## DEPOSIT INSURANCE IN OTHER COUNTRIES

Canada is not the only nation that offers deposit insurance. Indeed, it was far from being the first in this area of financial regulation (see Table 20.2). The first country to provide deposit insurance was the United States.

**Table 20.2** DEPOSIT INSURANCE IN SELECTED COUNTRIES

| Country | Introduced | Maximum Insured[a] | Type of Deposits Covered | Premium |
|---|---|---|---|---|
| Canada | 1967 | $60,000 | C$ only | 0.17% insured deposit |
| France | 1980 | FF400,000 ($110,000) | FF only | unfunded |
| Germany | 1966 | 30% of liable capital of bank, per depositor | all | 0.03% of all deposits |
| Italy | 1987 | 100% of first L200M, 75% of next L800M | all | unfunded |
| Japan | 1971 | ¥ 10,000,000 ($129,000) | ¥ only | 0.012% of covered deposits |
| Netherlands | 1979 | Dfl 35,000 ($28,200) | all | unfunded |
| Norway | 1961 | Unlimited | all | 0.015% of total assets |
| Switzerland | 1984 | SF300,000 ($34,750) | SF only | unfunded |
| United Kingdom | 1982 | 90% of protected deposits up to £20,000 ($43,090) | £ only | progressive but up to 0.3% of domestic £ deposits |
| United States | 1933 | $100,000 ($138,000) | all | 0.195% of domestic deposits |

[a] The amounts in parentheses are Canadian-dollar equivalents calculated at May 1996 exchange rates.

Sources: "International Banking Survey," *The Economist*, 7 April 1990, 65; *The Banker*, September 1991, 19, and "International Banking Survey," *The Economist* 27 April 1996, p. 18.

State-sponsored schemes can be traced back to the 1820s in New York, and national deposit insurance was introduced in the 1930s when the country's banking legislation was overhauled, following the financial excesses of the 1920s, which had been replete with fraudulent and imprudent banking practices.[12] The agency that handles deposit insurance is the Federal Deposit Insurance Corporation (FDIC for short), which maintains two separate funds, one for the country's commercial and savings banks and one for its savings and loan (S&L) institutions.[13] Like the CDIC, the FDIC is a government agency. Insurance is provided on deposits to a current maximum of $100,000,[14] but, as in Canada, there are

12 For an excellent account of this period in US financial history, see C. Calomiris, "Is Deposit Insurance Necessary?" *Journal of Economic History* 50 (June 1990): 283–96. Remember, however, that there is still much controversy about whether the many bank failures of that time were the consequence of bad monetary policy or of reckless behaviour by the private sector.

13 Until the recent S&L scandal, two separate agencies had handled deposit insurance for the two types of institutions.

14 Originally, the maximum insured deposit was set at $5,000. Maximum insured amounts have been raised five times since 1949.

ways to raise effective coverage many times over. The scheme is so popular that current US banking reform proposals seem unlikely to touch it, despite experts' widespread dissatisfaction with its current structure.[15]

Other industrialized countries also have the deposit insurance schemes; their generosity varies widely. What is interesting is that all the programs except those of Great Britain, the United States, and Canada are financed privately by the institutions themselves and administered by an association of members without the help of an officially sanctioned agency.

## THE REASONS FOR AND CONSEQUENCES OF DEPOSIT INSURANCE

The need for deposit insurance arises because the consequences of a bank failure differ from those of the failure of firms in other industries. The failure of a single bank can lead to fears of failure in other banks and thus creates the potential for a run on the banks or a banking panic.[16]

This contagion of fear has caused regulators and legislators to suggest deposit insurance as a means of preventing widespread banking crises.[17] They want to avoid the social costs of widespread banking failures. (If a country's financial system is disrupted, its firms in all other industries will be severely hampered in trying to complete financial transactions.)

Nevertheless, there is still considerable debate about whether deposit insurance does more harm than good for the safety and stability of the financial system. Indeed, as the mid-term review of the Bank Act approaches economists and policymakers are taking a fresh look at deposit insurance.

### MORAL HAZARD AND ADVERSE SELECTION

The need for insurance arises because uncertainty exists about future prospects, whether for our lives or our wealth. But the kind of risk-avoidance that is insurance always raises difficulties of moral hazard and risk avoidance. Sometimes they seem especially problematic in the forms of deposit insurance used today in North America. The concern here is about how banks and depositors react to the existence of deposit insurance.

15 Indeed, one view is that US legislators consider deposit insurance to be a kind of social or entitlement program. See "Won't Banking Be Splendid When Risk Is Whisked Away," *Los Angeles Times*, 3 April 1991, p. B9.

16 Some have argued that the introduction of deposit insurance in Canada was motivated by the need to increase competition between the chartered banks and near-banks.

17 In Canada, legislators were prompted by the recommendations of the Royal Commission on Banking and Finance (the Porter Commission) released in 1964 and some failures among near-banks.

## Moral Hazard

At the root of all problems with insurance is the fact of *asymmetric information*: one group, the insurers, have relatively less relevant information than those who are being insured.[18] One consequence of this problem is called moral hazard.

**Moral hazard** refers to the tendency of people who have insurance to take on, perhaps unwittingly, more risks than they would in its absence. For example, the more heavily deposits are insured, the less likely people are to worry about the safety of the bank that holds those deposits.[19] If individuals act in this fashion, there will be a tendency to bank not where it is safest to hold deposits but where interest rates are highest or where the other perks of banking are most generous. Would-be depositors will turn to banks offering free VCRs or TVs, instead of those offering the best return in relation to risk.

We can illustrate the moral hazard problem with the help of a simple diagram. Suppose that a typical investor's demand for bank deposits at a particular interest rate is shown in Figure 20.1 and is inversely related to the "price" of (premiums for) deposit insurance: in other words, the cheaper it is to purchase insurance, the more coverage will be purchased. If insurance protected against specified losses and the price of insurance would be perceived to be zero, quantity $Q_0$ will be demanded. In fact, since no bank communicates the costs of deposit insurance, the public treats this service as a free good with a zero price.

The marginal cost should lead to a demand for coverage equivalent to $Q_1$. Ideally, in fact, the government should pay for $Q_1$ conditional on a bank's failure for a reason beyond its control. Instead, all depositors receive $Q_0$ regardless of the behaviour of the bank that holds their deposits. Consequently, there is overconsumption of deposit insurance in the sense that the insurance protection is too generous. It leads banks and individuals to worry too little about where they place their funds and the relation between risk and return.

There are ways to mitigate the moral hazard problem. One is **co-insurance**, whereby the injured party pays a fraction of any loss. More common is the device of a **deductible**: the insured party is covered (up to some maximum) for any loss *beyond* some fixed sum. But despite a variety of proposals,[20] policymakers have not, as yet, eased the moral hazard problem for deposit insurance. So we

18 The information relevant here is the degree of risk aversion on the part of depositors, as well as the abilities (and honesty) of the banks that manage the depositors' funds.

19 A recent study reveals that in the 1920s in the state of Kansas, institutions that voluntarily joined an existing deposit insurance scheme were more likely to fail than uninsured banks. This illustrates the practical importance of the moral hazard problem. See D.C. Wheelock, "Deposit Insurance and Bank Failures: New Evidence from the 1920s," *Economic Inquiry* 30 (July 1992): 530–43.

20 See, for example, J.L. Carr, G.F. Mathewson and N.C. Quigley, *Ensuring Failure: Financial System Stability and Deposit Insurance in Canada* (Toronto: C.D. Howe Institute, 1994).

**FIGURE 20.1** The Problem of Moral Hazard

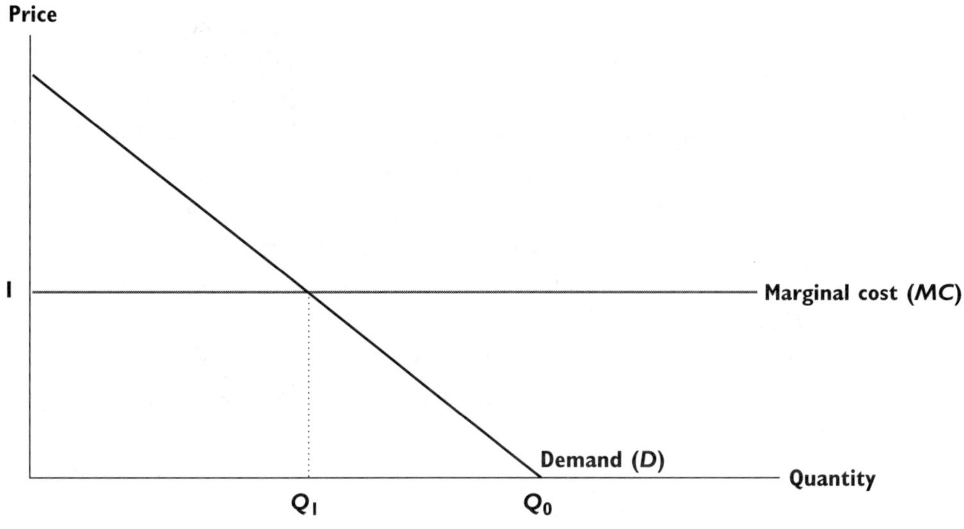


The price of deposit insurance is measured on the vertical axis and the quantity (the size of the deposit covered by insurance) on the horizontal axis. When deposit insurance is effectively free, $Q_0$ is demanded. If the marginal cost is I, $Q_1$ is demanded. Thus, the moral hazard problem leads to excess consumption of insurance.

are left with a system in which somewhere between $Q_1$ and $Q_0$ of insurance is demanded, instead of exactly $Q_1$.

## Adverse Selection

So far we have assumed that the probability of the event insured against is unaffected by the availability of insurance. But is it? Although few would argue that individuals will deliberately become seriously ill if they have health insurance, there is definitely room to believe that their vigilance against minor accidents will be adversely affected. Most forms of insurance are affected by this problem, which is known as the problem of **adverse selection**: the mere existence of insurance increases the probability that the particular event will take place.

In the case of bank deposits the existence of adverse selection implies less concern over the riskiness of particular investments on the part of depositors as well as on the part of bank managers, who will focus on return alone. Banks that emphasize the maximization of return irrespective of risk considerations are called *risk neutral.*

Why do some banks react in this fashion? Because the deposit insurance is currently administered so that all participating deposit-taking institutions pay a flat premium. An institution's record on risk management and its consequences is effectively ignored. This, of course, means that banks that are relatively cautious about how much risk they are willing to expose themselves to pay premiums that are too high in relation to the risk they face. By contrast, banks that seek the highest return no matter what the associated risks pay premiums that are too low, again relative to the risks faced. Consequently, low-risk banks are subsidizing part of the insurance premiums of the high-risk banks. Conversely, the high-risk banks are receiving insurance at a cost lower than it would be if the premium reflected their default risk. This adverse selection arises because the banks know their own default risk but the insuring agency does not know or does not bother to measure the default-risk probabilities. As we know from our discussion of moral hazard, however, deposit insurance will prompt high-risk banks to become more reckless in their borrowing and lending behaviour and, in a market in which depositors do not or cannot distinguish between the two groups of banks, the low-risk banks will become tempted to act more like high-risk banks. A simple solution appears at first glance: let premiums reflect risk. But, as we will see, such a solution raises other problems.

### THE ROLE OF GOVERNMENT IN DEPOSIT INSURANCE: IS THERE A POLITICAL MOTIVE?

Is it appropriate for government to offer deposit insurance? Its involvement is often justified on the grounds of the presence of market failure—that is, there are externalities that may prevent private markets from offering certain forms of insurance. Nevertheless, it is appropriate to question whether state intervention will result in a better allocation of resources than private markets. As we have seen, deposit insurance in other countries is not always state run, and it is unclear, based on the historical record, that private deposit insurance performs much worse than the public variety. The political motive for deposit insurance appears to be an important one. Thus, deposit insurance is created because it is a popular entitlement program, much like unemployment insurance or health insurance. Like other entitlement programs, membership is compulsory, risk considerations are ignored and the regulators are appointed by the government.

## HOW COULD DEPOSIT INSURANCE BE IMPROVED?

As we have seen, Canada's deposit insurance scheme is one of the most generous in the world. Although the country has not faced the same problems that led to the S&L fiasco in the United States, it is nevertheless proper to ask whether Canada's current deposit insurance scheme is too generous, particularly since some recent bank failures have severely strained the CDIC's reserves. More broadly, what kinds of reforms would best serve the nation?

In a financial world in which the distinctions among financial institutions are blurring, it is relevant to ask why banks and trusts are insured against losses but other institutions, such as insurance companies, are not. Guaranteeing equal competition in the marketplace would mean insuring either all types of financial institutions or none at all. Alternatively, Nobel Laureate James Tobin has suggested that only a nation's transactions balances—that is, its pure chequing account balances—be insured against losses; other bank liabilities, he says, should be backed by high-quality assets, such as Treasury bills or other government bonds.[21]

A simpler but obvious reform would be to let premiums on deposit insurance reflect the risks undertaken by the depository institutions. The only way to reduce the moral hazard problem is to assess premiums on the basis of the composition of an institution's balance sheet. Unfortunately, such a proposal presents several practical difficulties.[22] First, balance sheets show book values instead of market values, so an institution's true financial position is not always clear.[23] Second, it would be difficult to gain the necessary agreement across financial institutions about how risk levels and premiums should be related to each other. Third, as the US savings and loan fiasco has shown, regulators would have to be prepared to act on their expectations of the implications of current bank behaviour. (Otherwise, they would end up, as they often do now, reacting to events beyond even the government's control.) Fourth, the cost of policing such a scheme would be very high. Regulators would have to update balance sheets constantly, estimating the market values of vastly different assets. And they could not simply average the default risk of assets in a portfolio since what matters is the correlation of returns in a given portfolio. Moreover, obtaining a really useful picture would

---

21 James Tobin, "Financial Innovation and Deregulation in Perspective," *Bank of Japan Monetary and Economic Studies* (September 1985): 19–29.

22 The CDIC has had the power to charge risk-based premiums since 1987, but it has never exercised it, in large part because of the difficulties discussed here. The Wyman Report referred to previously also concluded that it was not possible to establish risk-related premiums. The report did, however, advocate co-insurance whereby 90% of individual deposits up to $100,000 would be insured. In its 1994–95 *Annual Report* (page 32) the CDIC explained that it was in the process of studying this issue once again.

23 Balance sheets' use of historical costs, although required by generally accepted accounting principles in most countries, creates problems that go beyond deposit insurance premiums. Reporting assets and liabilities at their historical cost, not the market values on which decision makers presumably act, can delay public detection of a risky or insolvent institution. Even regulators can be misled. Had different accounting rules been used, the insolvency of the Canadian Commercial Bank would have been evident much sooner than it was and US regulators would have known about the looming S&L scandal much earlier than they did.

## FINANCIAL FOCUS 20.1 The Savings and Loan Fiasco in the United States

US banking failures arising out of the depression of the 1930s led to the introduction of competition-stifling banking reforms, most notably ceilings on interest rates placed on deposits and on the commercial loans of savings and loan (S&L) institutions, which are equivalent to Canadian trust companies.

The rise in market interest rates during the late 1970s and 1980s led to severe distortions in the US financial system. The interest rate ceiling was eventually repealed, but it was too late for the S&Ls, which, at the end of the 1970s, found themselves with short-term deposits open to market interest rates and long-term loans that had been made at low interest rates.

By the early 1980s, most of the S&Ls became technically *insolvent*: their liabilities exceeded their assets As the crisis deepened, many became more and more inclined to invest in risky propositions, such as junk bonds, futures, and options, thereby compounding the problem facing the industry. Aided by the forbearance of regulators, who tended to react only after the problem was out of control, several S&Ls were emboldened to engage in fraudulent activities. And many simply collapsed.

These actions by the S&Ls perfectly illustrate the consequences of moral hazard. No one is sure of the total cost of bailing out the industry, but some estimates are as high as $300 billion US!

---

require regulators to consider other types of risk, such as inflation and interest rate risk, that are often not mentioned in the current debate. (Treating government bonds as riskless may be all right for making a point in a textbook, but it is hardly true of the real world.)[24]

Are there other routes to improving the system? Since the moral hazard problem is the greatest one, anything that raised the stakes for the owners of a financial institution in the event of a failure would reduce their temptation to recklessness in managing their portfolio. One device would be to raise the capital requirement. In other words, if the proportion of equity to total assets were raised, failure would become more costly to the owners (see Chapter 10). Another would be to change the governance of the CDIC to make it more accountable to the institutions who pay the premiums and who are best able to assess risk. Moreover, it may be helpful to make membership in the CDIC voluntary.[25] Combined with a more independent organizational structure, such a reform might encourage better risk management by firms joining the CDIC while it would be easy to identify those institutions which chose not to.

One difficulty with all reform proposals is that banks and near-banks are increasingly acting as brokers or intermediaries in transactions that appear only

24 For more details on this and related issues, written in an easy-to-understand fashion, see F.F. Cargill and T. Mayer, "U.S. Deposit Insurance Reform," *Contemporary Policy Issues* 10 (July 1992): 95–103.

25 Indeed, this proposal has found its way into the Federal government's review of the financial sector. See *1997 Review of Financial Sector Legislation: Proposals for Change* (Ottawa: Department of Finance, June 1996).

as off-balance-sheet items. Involvement in interest rate swaps, futures, and options, to name but a few examples, do not appear directly in their balance sheets, although these activities expose them to default risk.

All the previous suggestions have relied on the protection of deposits at face value. But what if deposits, instead of being protected in this fashion, were backed by the value of the assets of the deposit-taking institution. How would such a scheme work? Consider the development of chequable money-market mutual funds (MMMF) in the United States. Deposits would have a claim, in the form of shares, on the market value of the assets of the bank, instead of on their face value. As the value of the assets changed, so would the value of the shares. A fall in the value (price) of the shares, rather than causing a run on deposits, would mean a higher current yield (since the return produced by the assets is, at least for some time, fixed). This advantage would attract new depositors and thus prevent a loss of liquidity.

As you no doubt realize by now, the topic of deposit insurance is both interesting and controversial. There exist several proposals that address many of the existing problems with current arrangements. Indeed, the difficulties surrounding the question of whether there is too much deposit insurance have even led to the suggestion that banks should be allowed to do as few things as possible with as little risk as possible, thereby effectively eliminating the need for deposit insurance. As attractive as this idea may sound to some, it is unlikely to receive serious consideration.

## SUMMARY

- Insurance against losses in deposit-taking institutions is known as deposit insurance.

- Deposit insurance in Canada is run by the Canada Deposit Insurance Corporation, a Crown corporation. In some other countries, deposit insurance is privately run.

- Deposit insurance is thought to be necessary because the failure of a bank or other depository institution can lead to fears that all other banks will fail, thus creating bank runs. Fear is contagious.

- Deposit insurance is afflicted with two problems: moral hazard and adverse selection. Moral hazard refers to the fact that depositors and banks take advantage of insurance to take more risks. Adverse selection arises because insurance may increase the probability of failure.

- There exist many proposals to improve the current deposit insurance scheme. They include risk-based premiums and higher capital standards. But each of these solutions could create new problems.

## IMPORTANT TERMS

adverse selection (p. 459)
Canada Deposit Insurance Corporation (CDIC) (p. 451)
co-insurance (p. 458)
deductible (p. 458)
deposit insurance (p. 451)
moral hazard (p. 458)

## EXERCISES

1. During the 1980s what do you think drove deposit-taking institutions to take more risks? Explain.
2. Why did the CDIC or the government not discipline banks and near-banks more effectively in the wake of failures during the 1980s?
3. Suppose after reading this chapter you find out exactly how much protection you can obtain under deposit insurance. If a sufficiently large number of people made the same discovery, what would happen to the demand for deposit insurance in a framework such as the one illustrated in Figure 20.1? Explain.
4. Which do you think is the most important drawback to the current deposit insurance scheme: adverse selection or moral hazard? Explain your answer.
5. Assume you agree with the discussion about deposit insurance issues outlined in this chapter. Why haven't the politicians made appropriate changes? Explain your answer.
6. Why is the political motive for introducing deposit insurance possibly an important one?
7. Why has the Canadian Bankers Association routinely opposed the current structure of premiums?
8. What are some of the advantages and drawbacks of risk-based premiums?
9. Why has the independence of the CDIC from government interference possibly been an important policy issue?
10. What is the rationale for deposit insurance?

# REFERENCES


Binhammer, H., and J. Boulakia, "Deposit Insurance in Canada," *Canadian Banker*, vol. 75, 38–44.

Calomiris, C. "Is Deposit Insurance Necessary?" *Journal of Economic History* (June 1990): 283–96.

*Canada Deposit Insurance Corporation Act.* Ottawa: Ministry of Supply and Services, May 1989.

Cargill, F.F., and T. Mayer. "U.S. Deposit Insurance Reform." *Contemporary Policy Issues* 10 (July 1992): 95–103.

Carr, J.L., G.F. Mathewson, and N.C. Quigley, *Ensuring Failure: Financial System Stability and Deposit Insurance in Canada.* Toronto: C.D. Howe Institute, 1994.

Chernow, R. *The House of Morgan.* New York: Simon and Schuster, 1990.

Demsetz, H. "Information and Efficiency: Another Viewpoint." *Journal of Law and Economics* 12 (April 1969): 1–22.

Kindleberger, C.P. *Manias, Panics, and Crashes: A History of Financial Crises.* New York: Basic Books, 1989.

MacIntosh, R. *Different Drummers: Banking and Politics in Canada.* Toronto: Macmillan Canada, 1991, 214–19.

Shearer, R.A., J.F. Chant, and D.E. Bond, *Economics of the Canadian Financial System*, Third Edition. Toronto: Prentice-Hall, 1995.

Smith, B., and R.W. White. "The Deposit Insurance System in Canada: Problems and Proposals for Change." *Canadian Public Policy* 14 (December 1988): 331–46.

Tobin, James. "Financial Innovation and Deregulation in Perspective." *Bank of Japan Monetary and Economic Studies* (September 1985): 19–29.

Waterhouse, J., and D. Tims. "The GAAP in Bank Regulation." *Canadian Public Policy* 14 (June 1988): 151–61.

Wheelock, D.C. "Deposit Insurance and Bank Failures: New Evidence from the 1920s." *Economic Inquiry* 30 (July 1992): 530–43.

White, L. *The S&L Debacle.* New York: Oxford University Press, 1991, 211.

Wyman, W. Robert. *Final Report of the Working Committee on the Canada Deposit Insurance Corporation.* Ottawa: Minister of Supply and Services, 24 April 1985.

**PART IV**

# INTERNATIONAL FINANCE

CHAPTER 21

# International Banking

One cannot study the financial system of one's own country in isolation from the financial activities of the rest of the world. It is essential to know about the financial systems of other major countries, about globalized financial markets and the kinds of problems that arise there, and about some of the international finance institutions at work in the world. International banking can mean two things. It can refer to Canadian banks operating abroad or to foreign banks operating in Canada. Since regulations and risk considerations are influenced by where the banking is conducted, both forms of international banking are interesting subjects.

In this chapter, we examine a group of varied topics: the growth of international banking and financial centres; how the balance of payments is calculated and its effect on exchange rates; the Eurodollar market; the international debt crisis and the growing importance of country risk; and the absence of a global system of financial regulations.

This disparate information will provide a good background for the following chapters in this part, which discuss four quite different national financial systems and several institutional approaches to international financial co-operation.

## INTERNATIONAL BANKS AND FINANCIAL CENTRES

International trade has grown tremendously, especially since the end of World War II. Since traded goods and services must be paid for, there is a need for facilities and institutions that can handle international transactions. They are also needed to handle capital flows, which have exploded as *capital controls* (barriers to international capital investments) have been removed worldwide.

To the extent that banks[1] have international sections, operate offices in other countries, or have branches or subsidiaries outside their home country, they can

1 Unless otherwise stated, we deal in this chapter with banks, not with other financial institutions with an international dimension, such as those that assist export financing or are creatures of international gov-

be considered international banks. The internationalization of the world's banking sector is considerable.

Table 21.1 lists the 14 largest banks in the world. Swiss, Japanese, and British banks dominate. Much international banking—international lending and borrowing, interbanking operations, and foreign currency transactions—is conducted in **international financial centres**, cities that have become convergence points for such activity. Historically, such centres possess advantages such as geographical location, an expert labour force to draw upon, and a stable political and economic environment. One recent study also suggests that banking centres persist or are successful the lower the inflation rate in that country, the more financially developed it is, and the fewer the restrictions on reserve requirements.[2] Government encouragement is also now a consideration.

London, New York, and Tokyo are the prime international banking centres: London because it has long been a centre for the gold market and because it is where the Euromarket was born; New York because it is the financial capital of the United States, the dominant economic power since the end of World War II. Recently, they have been challenged by Frankfurt, the banking centre of a reunified country at the heart of a united Europe,[3] and Paris, which is seeking a greater role in international finance in part as a counterweight to the increasingly dominant German position in the European Community (EC). Zurich is also important because of Swiss expertise in banking matters. Overall, however, German and Japanese banks are the largest lenders. Banks headquartered in these two countries account for almost 42% of international bank assets in 1993, the latest year for which there is complete information. Much of this lending originates in London which continues to retain its status as the world's largest banking centre.

Much of the growth of these centres has been at the expense of New York and London. New (*and* in some cases very small) countries have also been entering the game, in large part because US financial regulations have not kept pace with international financial developments. Thus, several hundred banks have offices in the Cayman Islands, where there are no taxes, no reserve requirements, and no waiting periods before corporations can issue bonds, as well as secrecy pro-

---

ernment actions (for example, the International Monetary Fund and the International Bank for Reconstruction and Development, which are described in Chapter 23). For Canada, this approach means focusing on the chartered banks since the trust companies generally do not operate abroad (although some large ones, such as Canada Trust, do have overseas holdings).

2 See J. Eaton, "Cross-Border Banking," NBER working paper 4686 (March 1994).

3 And a city in which the cost of living is relatively low.

**Table 21.1** THE WORLD'S LARGEST BANKS, 1995

| Rank[a] | Name | Country |
|---|---|---|
| 1 | Sanwa Bank | Japan |
| 2 | Dai-Ichi Kangyo Bank | Japan |
| 3 | Fuji Bank | Japan |
| 4 | Sumitomo Bank | Japan |
| 5 | Sakura | Japan |
| 6 | Mitsubishi Bank | Japan |
| 7 | HSBC Holdings | United Kingdom |
| 8 | Crédit Agricole | France |
| 9 | Citicorp | United States |
| 10 | Union Bank of Switzerland | Switzerland |
| 11 | Industrial Bank of Japan | Japan |
| 12 | Bank America Corp | United States |
| 13 | Deutsche Bank | Germany |
| 14 | Bank of Tokyo | Japan |

According to the size of shareholders' equity. Ranking is based on capital in millions of US dollars.
Source: *The Banker* (July 1995), and the *Financial Times of London World Economy and Finance* (1996), p. 17.
Note that the data do not reflect the merger of the Bank of Tokyo (#14) and Mitsubishi Bank (#6) concluded 1 April 1996.

visions, which, like those of Switzerland, protect clients from indirect supervision of their activities by other countries.

It comes as no surprise that many governments give cities preferential treatment[4] for organizing **offshore banking centres**—international banking facilities that cater to non-residents. Indeed, countries such as the Cayman Islands, Luxembourg, Hong Kong, and the Bahamas are perhaps best known as tax and regulatory havens for banks.

Canadian chartered banks have long had an international presence. By the late nineteenth century, they had operations in various cities in the United States, Great Britain, and the Caribbean. In addition, Canadian banks have a wide net-

4 In the 1980s, Canada was tempted to develop an international banking centre. It was originally intended to be located in Montreal, but political considerations led to Toronto's and Vancouver's being awarded rights to develop such centres too. Historical precedent and the comparative advantage of the existing centres make it unlikely that any Canadian centre will receive a significant share of the international banking market, however. Indeed, after an initial bout of enthusiasm, the desire for international centres in Canada faded by the late 1980s. This despite the fact that the Canadian banking system is a net recipient of deposits from abroad, as we shall see when we discuss Canada's balance of payments.

work of correspondent arrangements in countries or cities where they have no other official representation. (A *correspondent bank* handles another bank's affairs in a jurisdiction where the latter has no legal standing.) And since the proclamation of the 1980 Bank Act, various foreign banks have opened chartered banks in Canada.

We have already discussed (Chapter 7) the fact that prices in different countries can be understood only with the help of the concept of the exchange rate. Here we consider how international transactions, which give rise to exchange rates, are summarized in countries' balance of payments records. That accomplished, we can go on to consider the balance of payments implications of different exchange rates as well as why a country benefits from trading with other countries.[5]

## THE BASICS OF THE BALANCE OF PAYMENTS

A country's **balance of payments (BOP)** records its foreign trade in goods, services, and financial instruments. For example, Canada's BOP records all receipts Canadian residents take in from foreigners and all payments they make to foreigners. A positive entry signifies that foreign exchange enters Canada and a negative entry that foreign exchange is lost. If receipts are greater than the payments, the BOP is said to be in surplus; when payments exceed receipts, the BOP is in deficit.

Table 21.2 shows Canada's BOP. Notice that it is divided into two principal categories, the current account and the capital account. The **current account** records trade between Canada and the rest of the world in merchandise, in services, and in investment income, as well as in transfers (payments made or received in government debt at all levels). Historically, the Canadian balance in merchandise trade has typically been positive, but the balances in services and investment income have generally been negative.

The **capital account** reflects flows of money for investment and government grants and loans. For simplicity, items are classified according to whether Canadians have claims on non-residents or whether they have liabilities toward non-residents. These arise because Canadians invest directly abroad or hold foreign securities. Similarly, claims on Canadians arise because, for example, non-residents

5 We do not, however, develop a full-fledged framework for the analysis of an open economy at the macroeconomic level, a task better suited for a course in international economics or in intermediate macroeconomics. Interested students may see, for example, R. Dornbusch, S. Fischer, and G. Sparks, *Macroeconomics*, 4th Cdn ed. (Toronto: McGraw-Hill Ryerson, 1993); and R.J. Barro, *Macroeconomics*, 3d ed. (New York: John Wiley and Sons, 1990). It is worth noting that several Canadians, such as Robert Mundell and Harry Johnson, have made prominent contributions in this area. Some excellent references include R. Mundell, *Monetary Theory: Inflation, Interest and Growth in the World Economy* (Pacific Palisades, Calif.: Goodyear, 1971); and J.A. Frenkel and H.G. Johnson, eds., *The Monetary Approach to the Balance of Payments* (Toronto: University of Toronto Press, 1976).

**Table 21.2** CANADA'S BALANCE OF PAYMENTS, 1994 (millions of dollars)

| | |
|---|---|
| **Current Account** | |
| 1. Merchandise trade | 15,046 |
| 2. Services | −9,430 |
| 3. Investment income | −28,895 |
| 4. Transfers | 979 |
| 5. Balance (1 + 2 + 3 + 4) | −22,299 |
| **Capital Account** | |
| 6. Canadian claims on non-residents | −12,787 |
| 7. Canadian liabilities to non-residents | 31,128 |
| 8. Net capital flows (6 + 7) | 18,341 |
| 9. Statistical discrepancy | 3,958 |
| 10. Balance of payments (5 + 8 + 9 + 10) | NIL |

Source: *Bank of Canada Review* (Winter 1995–96): Table J1, J2.

invest in Canada or hold Canadian stocks or bonds. Figure 21.1(A) records Canada's current and capital accounts since the mid-1970s. A current account that is in a deficit needs to be financed. Thus, a deficit in the current account implies a surplus in the capital account.

## EXPLAINING THE BALANCE OF PAYMENTS

In principle, one would expect the deficit in the current account to be financed by a surplus in the capital account so that the BOP should be zero. Yet the two do no offset each other exactly for two reasons. One is the difficulties of recording international transactions (stemming only in part from tax evasion and other illegal activities). The resulting statistical discrepancy is often very large as can be seen in Figure 21.1(B). Thus, while the current account had a deficit of $22,299 million there were only $18,341 million in net capital *inflows*. Since the two do not offset each other, as required, the resulting difference is referred to as the "statistical discrepancy" ($22,299 − $18,341).

### FOREIGN EXCHANGE INTERVENTION

The Bank of Canada intervenes in the market for foreign exchange either to moderate fluctuations in the exchange rate or its capacity as the manager of the country's foreign exchange reserves. As shown in Figure 21.1(C), these have changed considerably through the years.

If the exchange rate floats freely then, as we saw in Chapter 7, the market for foreign exchange will clear. However, we also saw that a country's exchange rate can either be overvalued or undervalued for some time. This could occur because

**FIGURE 21.1** The Canadian Balance of Payments, 1974–95

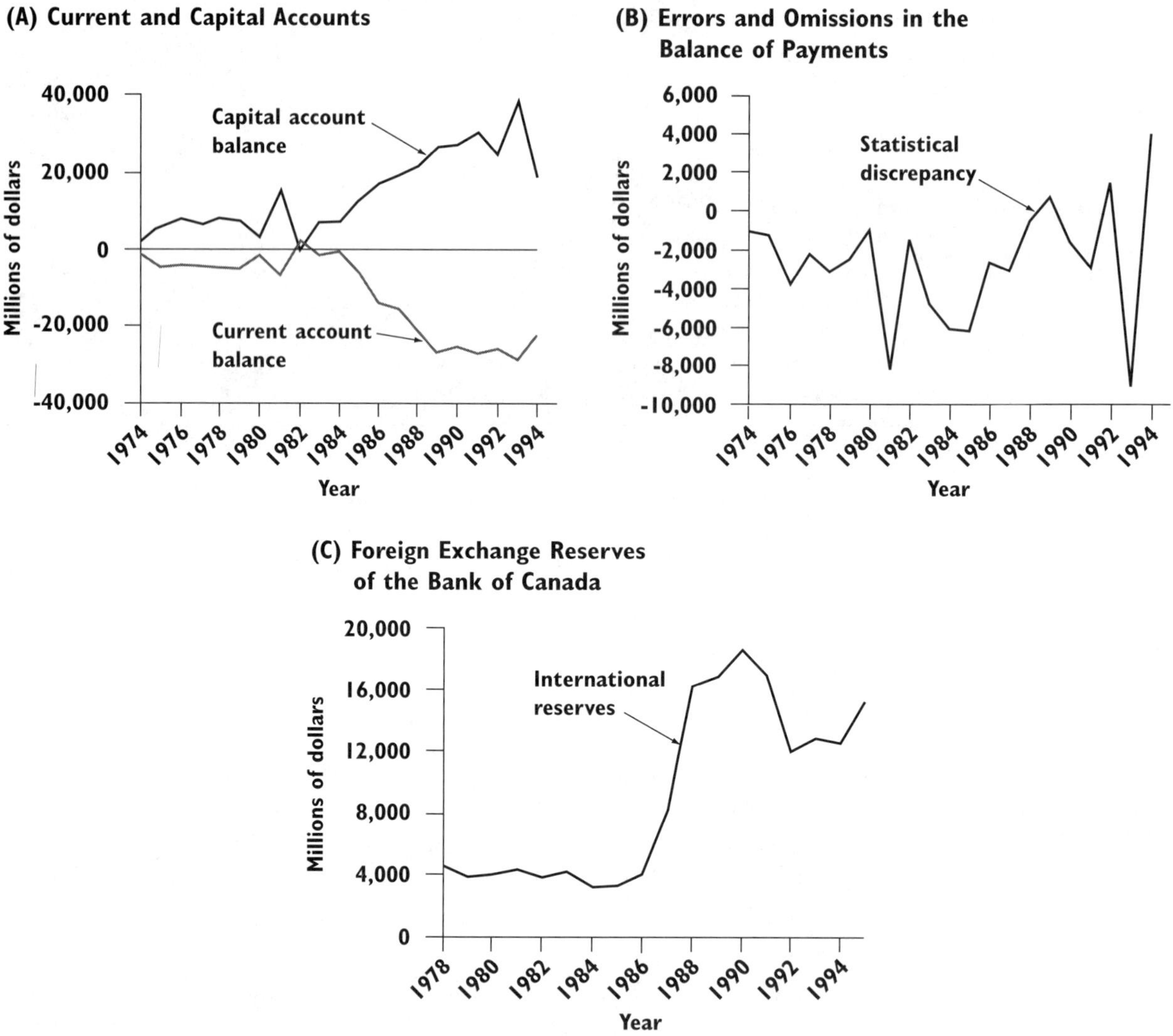


Source: *Bank of Canada Review* (Winter 1995–96): Tables 12, J1 and T2. International Reserves include US dollars and other currencies, gold and Special Drawing Rights (see chapter 23).

the central bank deliberately intervenes in the foreign exchange market to artificially influence the exchange rate. Foreign market intervention is common in many countries with Canada among the least interventionist countries in this regard. Since changes in the foreign exchange reserves have been important through the years it is worth illustrating the connection between the exchange rate and change in foreign exchange reserves.

Consider Figure 21.2. In the absence of any intervention by the Bank of Canada, the market for foreign exchange would clear at an exchange rate of $1.20 per US dollar. At this price, the quantity of US dollars demanded would be exactly $Q^*$, equal to the quantity supplied and the BOP should be zero. Suppose, however, that the current exchange rate was $1.15. This implies that the Canadian dollar is overvalued. The price of overvaluation, however, is an excess demand for US dollars. To maintain the exchange rate, the Bank of Canada must sell US dollars and thus reduce its foreign reserves.

Recall from Chapter 7 that the theory of purchasing power parity led us to conclude that the Canadian dollar has been undervalued recently. Foreign exchange reserves thus should have risen, other things being equal which is exactly what Figure 21.1(C) shows.

Many analysts believe that this situation explains why the current account balance has worsened in recent years—that balance of payments difficulties can be explained in monetary terms, a concept known as the *monetary approach to the balance of payments.*[6] Thus, in a world in which exchange rates were fixed, one would expect a balance of payments deficit to be cancelled through flows of money. The act of buying and selling foreign exchange reserves has an impact on the Canadian money supply. When the Bank of Canada sells US dollars, it buys Canadian dollars. Normally, the result is a fall in the Canadian money supply, but the Bank of Canada can offset this tendency by **sterilizing** (offsetting) the flow of foreign exchange: rather than allowing the money supply to fall, it purchases bonds in the open market. Since *open market purchases* increase the Canadian money supply (see Chapter 6), use of this sterilization device can offset the pressure of a falling money supply caused by the fixed exchange rate set at a disequilibrium level. But a central bank can only go so far in draining its reserves of foreign exchange. Eventually, it will be unable or unwilling to defend a particular exchange, a situation that will force a devaluation of the country's currency. Under flexible exchange rates, the monetary approach suggests, the exchange rate itself is the device that produces the necessary adjustments in the balance of trade, instead of the domestic money supply, by ensuring that the exchange rate is in equilibrium. Thus a country can control the domestic money supply independently. An alternative view of the balance of payments, called the *absorption approach*, views surpluses or deficits in the balance of trade as resulting from the difference between what an economy produces and what it consumes domestically (that is, what it absorbs).

---

6 This is an old idea, brilliantly first explained in D. Hume's classic work "Of the Balance of Trade," in *Essays, Literary, Moral, and Political*, vol. I (London: Longmans Green, 1898). Hume's basic ideas have since been rejuvenated and extended in, for example, H.G. Johnson's work cited in footnote 5.

**FIGURE 21.2** Balance of Payments Disequilibrium

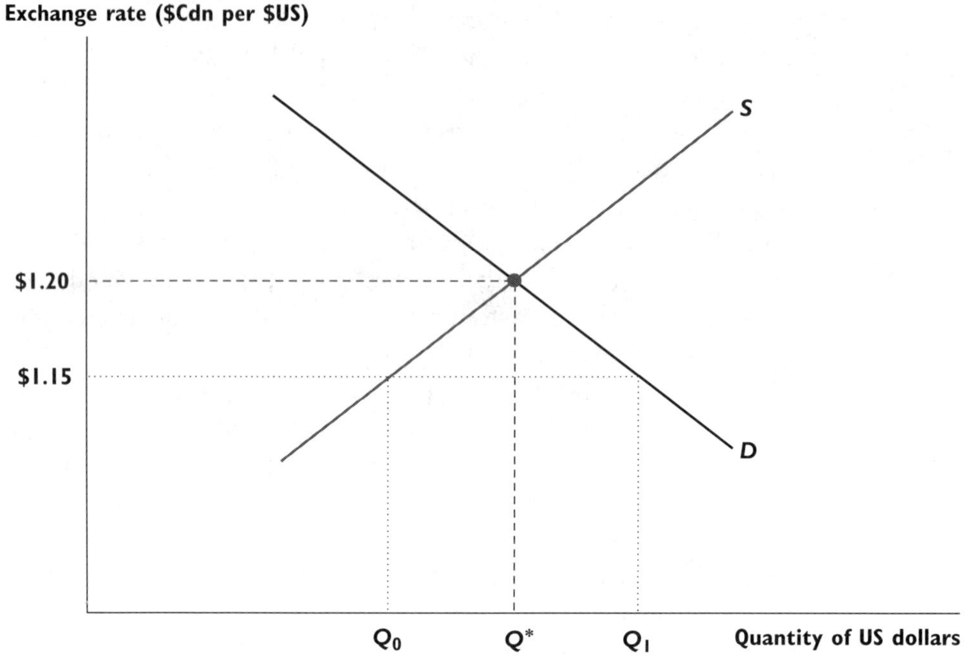


Initially, the foreign exchange market is in equilibrium at an exchange rate of $1.20 Cdn per $1 US. If the authorities push the exchange rate to $1.15 instead, the Canadian dollar is overvalued. The resulting disequilibrium in the market for foreign exchange leads the Bank of Canada to sell US dollars, reducing its reserves of foreign exchange.

## BENEFITS FROM TRADE

But does a chronic deficit in the current account imply that trading is bad? The answer is no. Figure 21.3 illustrates.[7] An individual in a country that trades with no other country faces a liquidity constraint, so point *O* is the optimal level of consumption. Trading eases the liquidity constraint because it becomes possible to borrow from abroad (at an interest rate given by the slope of the budget constraint). The result is that the individual can now select point *O** along a higher indifference curve. World trade can, therefore, improve welfare. Indeed, if the additional $c_1$ is invested, future income will increase, thereby expanding future consumption possibilities.

7 Students may find it helpful to go back to Chapter 9 for the derivation of indifference curves and budget constraints.

**FIGURE 21.3** How International Trade Can Improve Welfare

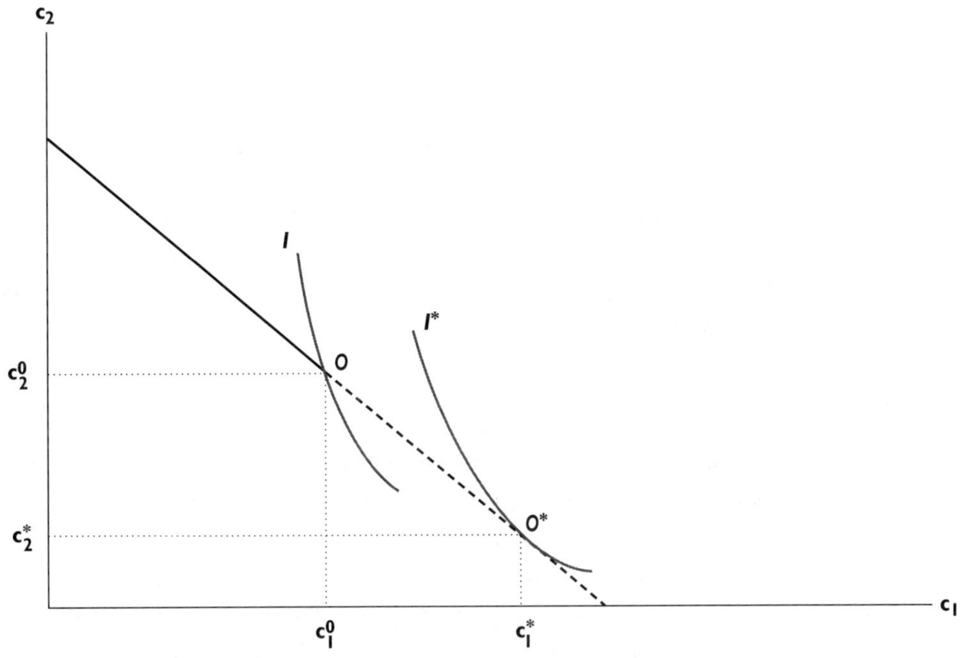


Without international trade, the optimal consumption levels are $c_1^0$ and $c_2^0$ at point *O* along indifference curve *I*. When there is international trade, individuals in one country can borrow from other countries and thereby raise total utility to $I^*$ and attain point $O^*$.

## THE TWIN DEFICITS

We have already seen that Canadian governments have for years been running deficits (see Chapter 8). Figure 21.1(A) suggests that Canada has been running another kind of deficit, namely a current account deficit. This has given rise to the concept of the **twin deficits**. What is the connection between these two deficits?

Recall from your principles of economics course that an economy's output can be divided into consumption ($c$), investment ($i$), government expenditures ($g$) and the difference between exports and imports ($x-im$). Algebraically, we can write

$$y = c + i + g + (x - im) \tag{21.1}$$

But output is also a country's income or GDP, which can be divided into a portion consumed, saved ($s$), and the amounts paid to governments in taxes ($t$).

Again, algebraically we can write

$$y = c + s + t \qquad (21.2)$$

Subtracting c from both sides of equations (21.1) and (21.2) and equating them both, we obtain

$$i + g + (x - im) = s + t \qquad (21.3)$$

Now, we know from the analysis in this text (see Chapter 3) that there is a connection between $i$ and $s$. After all, the principal function of intermediaries is to channel savings into investment. Similarly, we can summarize the government's budget as the difference between $g$ and $t$. So, rearranging (21.3), we get

$$s + (t - g) = i + (x - im) \qquad (21.4)$$

Therefore, if $(x - im)$ is negative, as is clear from Figure 21.1(A), then the current account deficit takes away from savings. Similarly, since $(t - g)$ is also negative, government deficits take away from $i$. Financing these deficits requires an inflow of loanable funds, as we saw in Chapter 7 with potential consequences for the interest rate. One can see more clearly the connection between $(t - g)$ and $(x - im)$ by assuming that $i$ and $s$ are constant. Taking changes on both sides of equation (21.4), we get (since $\Delta i = \Delta s = 0$)

$$\Delta(t - g) = \Delta(x - im)$$

In other words, the two "deficits" (when both sides of the above equation are negative) move together. Of course, $s$ and $i$ are not likely to be constant over long periods of time so that current account deficits will also be due in part to changes in investment. Empirical evidence on the connection between the "twin deficits" is mixed.[8]

## THE EUROCURRENCY MARKET

Eurocurrencies are an excellent example of the way international banking has been innovative to meet the explosive growth of international transactions and to avoid the domestic banking regulations of many countries.

8 See, for example, J.M. Rock (ed.), *Debt and the Twin Deficits Debate* (Mountain View Calif.: Mayfield and Bristlecone Books, 1991); and K. Kasa, "Finite Horizons and Twin Deficits," Federal Reserve Bank of San Francisco, *Economic Review* 1994 (3): 19–28.

## SOME HISTORY

The word *Eurocurrency* is a generic term, denoting a financial instrument deposited or traded in a currency other than the domestic currency of the country in which the transaction takes place. As noted in Chapter 4, a common synonym is *Eurodollar*, a term that goes back to the origin of the market shortly after World War II.[9] World trade was resuming, but the Cold War was setting in. The countries of the Soviet bloc, fearing that the United States would freeze-in its assets in that country, deposited their US dollars in London. It quickly became apparent that these deposits, which were not subject to legal restrictions or reserve requirements, were a ready source of the world's foremost currency. The initial growth of Eurodollars was great, and it was then much assisted by special taxes introduced in the United States during the 1960s. First, in 1963, US purchases of foreign securities were taxed. Next, the tax was extended in 1965 to loans made by US banks and foreign financial institutions to foreign borrowers. Finally, a quota-type system was instituted in 1965 to control bank loans to multinational corporations. Not surprisingly, all these moves gave financial institutions a great incentive to operate outside the United States but to continue to transact in US funds. The number and size of Eurodollars exploded. There soon also emerged similar foreign deposits in many of the major currencies, with the most prominent being Euromarks, Euroswiss francs, Europounds, and, more recently, Euroyen.

By 1991, some 15 Eurocurrencies were traded, and *Eurobanks*—foreign branches of US and other countries' banks—had appeared throughout the world. So had various financial instruments denominated in Eurocurrencies, such as Euro-CDs, Eurobonds, Euro-commercial paper, and Euromarket futures and options.

The main centre for Euromarket trading continues to be London (there is also significant activity in New York and Tokyo), and the basic interest rate is the **London interbank offer rate (LIBOR)**, which is the interest rate large commercial banks charge each other for loans in the United Kingdom. Departures from it are a function of the riskiness and liquidity of the instrument in question. Because of the uncertainty associated with whether the host country will act as a lender of last resort in Eurocurrencies, the rates tend to be slightly higher than for instruments issued domestically by a particular bank.

Actually, there exist many different LIBORs depending on the currency one is dealing with and the maturity of the instrument in question. Rates are published daily in the *Financial Times* of London. LIBOR is generally the term used to refer

---

9 The practice of borrowing and lending in the foreign-denominated currency did exist earlier in the century, but it was considered a temporary device to, say, help local businesses build their international trading activities.

to the interest rate on Eurocurrencies regardless of whether or not the market in question is in London.

### THE CREATION OF EUROCURRENCY

The size of the Euromarket, although exceedingly difficult to estimate with precision, is believed to exceed several trillion $US. Its mere existence enhances worldwide liquidity.

To see how a unit of Eurocurrency is created, consider the T-accounts in Table 21.3. Suppose the client of a Canadian bank transfers $100 million from its branch in Halifax to a Eurobank (which could be a subsidiary of the Canadian chartered bank or some unaffiliated institution). The liabilities of the Canadian bank are not altered; it records a drop of $100 million in Canadian-dollar deposits but a $100 million rise in its Eurodeposits. If the same reserves hold against both types of deposits, there will be no repercussions in the Canadian financial system. But the Eurobank has experienced an increase of $100 million in Canadian currency, which is now available to be loaned out to borrowers interested in obtaining Canadian dollars. Moreover, since no country imposes reserve requirements on Eurocurrency deposits, the Eurobank is free to create additional deposits through *multiple expansion* (see Chapter 16).

### A THOUGHT

Despite the liquidity Eurocurrencies have introduced to worldwide financial markets, they are not without danger, at least in theory. All those units of currency that exist abroad have the potential to be returned if foreigners who hold them decide to exchange them for their home currency or some other preferred currency. Just imagine what billions of US dollars returned to the United States would do to the US inflation rate! Canada could face a similar problem. But so far such worries have proved unfounded as trading in different currencies is vital in the carrying out of international trade and finance.

## INTERNATIONAL BANKING REGULATIONS

As the growth of the Eurocurrencies suggests, borrowing and lending, which used to be primarily domestic matters, have become more international in nature. Unfortunately, international banking offers not only great benefits but also the possibility of great losses and scandal. And unlike other economic endeavours, banking is solely regulated at the domestic level. There is no international supervision.[10]

10 The only possible exception is the capital standards of the Bank for International Settlements (see Chapters

**Table 21.3** THE CREATION OF EUROCURRENCY (millions of Canadian dollars)

| Canadian Bank | | Eurobank | |
|---|---|---|---|
| Assets | Liabilities | Assets | Liabilities |
| | −$100 Cdn. deposit | $100 reserves in $Cdn | +$100 deposit from Canadian bank |
| | +$100 Eurodeposit | ↓ Can be loaned out | |

The client of a Canadian chartered bank transfers $100 million from an account in Canada to a Eurobank. The liabilities of the Canadian bank are unaffected, but $100 million in Euro-Canadian dollars has now been created.

At the centre of this difficulty is the problem called **national treatment**, which means that an organization (or individual) is subject to the laws of whatever country it is in. A bank branch or subsidiary located in, say, Canada, is regulated under Canadian law, although the parent is regulated by the laws of the home country. Similarly, a Canadian bank abroad must obey the banking laws that prevail in the country in which it operates. This system has enabled banks to exploit weaknesses in the regulations of a foreign country and to play the laws of one country against another. Thus, a bank can avoid national supervision in the United States by registering so that it is regulated by one or several states instead of by the Federal Reserve System. (But manipulation of regulatory structures have also enabled the banks to open up new markets, as in the development of the Eurocurrencies.)

Another problem is what one might call the structural changes in the financial industry since the 1970s. Thirty years ago international lending was the almost exclusive preserve of banks, in part because domestic laws protected and favoured them. Today a myriad of international agencies and investment bankers act as agents or intermediaries, forming syndicates that arrange international loans. Combined with the removal of capital controls in all western industrialized countries by the end of the 1980s, the concept of an international money market permits the transfer of surplus funds from a country with surplus funds to one with a deficit. The banks no longer possess comparative advantage, natural or regulatory, over other financial market participants.

Yet the wave of deregulation that has swept the financial world over the last two decades has created problems because it has been neither co-ordinated nor consistent across jurisdiction. For example, while restrictions on financial services

10 and 23), but adherence to them is voluntary. In 1996, the BIS revised its capital adequacy standards to include market risk for "internationally active" banks. See *Federal Reserve Bulletin* (March 1996), p. 220.

## FINANCIAL FOCUS 21.1 The Bank of Crooks and Criminals International

The Bank of Credit and Commerce International (BCCI) did business in seven countries. Although supervisory agencies in at least a half dozen of them suspected fraud, there was little indication of its international scale until July 1991. One of the reasons for the delay in co-ordinated international legal action against BCCI is the absence of effective international supervision.

There is now considerable evidence that a combination of bad management and fraud originated in BCCI's home base in Abu Dhabi. Illegal activities ranged from manipulating accounts to covering losses in stock trading to acting as a conduit for illegal payments by intelligence agencies such as the US Central Intelligence Agency.

BCCI is not the first bank to exploit regulatory gaps arising out of the national treatment principle. In the 1980s the Vatican's banker, Banco Ambrosiano, was charged with fraud and illegal activities.

In every banking scandal of international scale, the common element has been the absence of international enforcement mechanisms and regulatory inconsistencies across countries. Thus, when BCCI engaged in an activity that one country found distasteful, little could be done because each country jealously guards its national sovereignty over financial regulatory matters.

---

practically disappeared in Britain and were substantially reduced in Canada during the 1980s, change lagged considerably in Japan and especially in the United States. Moreover, the world still has more than one model of a banking system. There is the **universal banking model**, in which underwriting is not a barrier to lending activities, unlike the model used in Canada and the United States in which it is presumed that a bank's holding an equity interest in firms to which it is making loans signals a conflict of interest. Some countries, even some federal countries, have a unitary system, in which all financial institutions are regulated by a single jurisdiction,[11] other countries have a **dual banking system** in which two jurisdictions have authority over the banking system. A variety of other differences in banking regulations create even more discrepancies.

Not surprisingly, many interested parties propose international regulation of banking. But that prospect raises almost as many questions as answers. Who would provide deposit insurance against a failure involving an international bank? Indeed, who would dispose of the assets of a failed international bank? Who would ensure that the goal of competition in the financial markets be achieved? Finally, given the variety of ways in which banks are regulated in different countries, how would an international harmonization of sorts take place?

Unfortunately, this section must remain incomplete; the field of international banking regulations is a nascent one and what international co-operative efforts already exist show signs of falling apart. Moreover, although one presumes the

11 These basic differences are illustrated in Chapter 22, which describes the banking structures of several major countries.

current sweeping changes in domestic regulatory practices will abate somewhat in the near future, the existing negative externalities inherent in the current standard practice of national treatment will continue to pose problems for would-be international regulators.

## THE INTERNATIONAL DEBT CRISIS

The consequences of unregulated banking activities in international lending can be disastrous for entire nations. One example is the international debt crisis. It has been going on since the early 1980s when several countries could not afford to repay the interest and/or principal on their foreign debt obligations.[12] The best-known cases were in Central and South America, though loans made to several other countries also became "non-performing."

The international debt crisis had its origins in the oil price shocks of the 1970s.[13] Countries that were net importers of oil had to either reduce citizens' standard of living or maintain aggregate via the accumulation of debt. The dramatic rise in foreign debt was assisted, at first, by low real interest rates. Indeed, we have already seen in Chapter 5, that ex post real interest rates were sometimes negative! No wonder banks like to lend to developing countries. First, as the saying goes, countries never go bankrupt. Second, there was the prospect of economic growth, which, combined with low interest rates, meant favourable conditions for borrowing. Few developing countries avoided the attractive temptation of debt. Even oil-exporting countries, such as Mexico, were not entirely spared, particularly those that wished to raise their standard of living quickly. Despite the bonanza of increasing revenues from oil exports, the costs of raising the standard of living eventually led to the accumulation of foreign debt. The situation worsened when oil prices began to fall sharply in the latter part of the 1980s; these countries were now saddled with high debt and lowered revenues from their oil exports.

Some people believe that the banks of the Western industrialized world pushed the Third World nations at this time, encouraging them to take on foreign debt.[14] Others think they were simply behaving in a normal, profit-seeking manner.

---

12 International debt crisis is not a new phenomenon. Indeed, the crisis that began in the 1980s and continues today has striking parallels with experiences during last century and the first half of this one. Moreover, the concept of a grandiose plan to rescue overindebted countries (see below) is not new. (Indeed, some of the international institutions we examine in Chapter 23 were created to manage global debt problems of the past.) Many of these plans, like those of today, experienced relatively few successes.

13 Indeed, the true origins may have been in the inflation of the late 1960s. The monetary expansion that preceded that inflation meant that a considerable amount of liquidity was available for international lending by Western banks.

14 Certainly even countries that had previously defaulted on loans were able to borrow fairly easily during the 1970s and 1980s. This granting of credit may not, however, have been greediness or myopia on the

Certainly the banks of the West either ignored or did not foresee the potential credit risk in loans to developing nations. And few warnings were sounded, even when real interest rates began to rise sharply in the industrialized world as these countries, including Canada, pursued a high interest rate policy designed to eliminate inflation. Thus, the crisis erupted suddenly in 1980 and 1981. The high real interest rates of the time were simply too great to be financed by developing countries' economic growth. Hence, countries such as Argentina, Bolivia, Brazil, Mexico, and the Philippines, and Turkey, among others, could not maintain their payments.

By the mid-1980s, some had negotiated with the banks and international agencies for debt-rescheduling arrangements, which often included stringent conditions for revamping their economies.

One result of the crisis was that Western banks began swapping the debt of one country for that of another. Bankers differed in their perceptions of the likelihood of payment, so, for example, a bank with Mexican debt on its books would trade with a bank that held Chilean debt. By the mid-1980s, there existed a secondary market for developing countries' debt. Interestingly, the creation of this market permitted a country to back its own debt at a substantial discount.[15]

That prices for debt in secondary markets began to rise quickly by early 1990 was in part a measure of how much lower interest rates and the worldwide economic boom of the 1980s helped countries service their debt.[16]

Fears of another international debt crisis emerged during the winter of 1994 when the Mexican peso devaluation led to massive outflows of capital from that country (see Chapter 7). An international consortium of central banks and international cooperation among several governments, including Canada, was formed to prevent another crisis from taking place in 1995.

---

part of bankers but rather a recognition of the fact that the likelihood of defaulting on a loan is determined primarily by current creditworthiness, not past behaviour. Moreover it appears that the previously defaulting countries could borrow only at relatively high rates. See S. Osler, "Have Commercial Banks Ignored History?" NBER working paper 3959 (January 1992).

15 By the end of 1990, prices in the secondary market for debt ranged from 10% to 70% of face value. It appears that the size of the discount is a negative function of the size of the debt outstanding and that this is a byproduct of deposit insurance and its attendant problems. See S. Osler and H. Huizinga, "Bank Finance, Capital and Secondary Market Discounts on Developing Country Debt," NBER working paper 3961 (January 1992).

16 Some people think a rising price in secondary markets signals the economic prospects of the country in question. Unfortunately, research suggests that this may not be the case. Instead, it may be that some banks benefit at the expense of others when secondary market prices change. On this and related issues, see the articles in the *Journal of Economic Perspectives* (Winter 1990).

## HOW A DEBT CRISIS CAN AFFECT A BANK

So far we have concentrated on the impact of the debt crisis on borrowing countries. But most of the lenders were the commercial banks of industrialized countries, and they too faced disaster; several Canadian banks were, at one time, exposed to significant losses from loans to developing countries.

The impact of a default on a loan made to a country is similar to the impact of a loan default by an individual or private institution and indeed similar to the impact of any loss experienced by a bank (perhaps because of rising interest rates or a fall in real estate values). Table 21.4 sets out an example, using T-accounts. The opening balance sheet shows a Canadian bank with \$1,000 in loans and \$200 in capital. (Remember that banks are required to show only the book value of their assets and liabilities.) Suppose that \$200 of the loans are to some developing country that suddenly announces it will default on both principal and interest payments. A not-uncommon step at this point is for the bank to write off, say, half the loan (on the assumption that payments will resume someday in the future). This approach leaves \$100 in capital, thereby wiping out half the shareholders' equity. Alternatively, if the loan is never expected to be repaid, then the entire amount should be written off thereby wiping out shareholders' equity entirely.

Now, these scenarios may reflect the reality of the situation, but banks, thanks to the way they are regulated, can simply pretend nothing is wrong by, for example, listing the defaulting loan as "non-performing" but nevertheless reporting assets and shareholders' equity as they were before. Of course, if the loan is indeed never repaid, the bank faces eventual insolvency since it cannot continue to pay shareholders' dividends or even its depositors when its capital is non-existent.

No wonder then that the industrialized world's financial system was threatened with collapse in the early 1980s when the international debt crisis reached its peak.

## APPROACHES TO THE DEBT CRISIS

In March 1990, the *Brady Plan*, a plan to solve the international debt crisis named after Nicholas Brady, Secretary of the US Treasury at the time, proposed a buyback of debt from secondary markets as a way of alleviating the debt burden for some countries. Mexico, Costa Rica, Chile, the Philippines, Venezuela, Bolivia, and Uruguay all took advantage of this scheme. Such a scheme, however, gives rise to a potential moral hazard problem. A secondary market that sells debt at a considerable discount may create an incentive for a country to become heavily indebted, default, and buy back its debt relatively cheaply. It is fear of this situation that has led many governments to impose strict and far-reaching economic re-

**Table 21.4** HOW THE DEBT CRISIS CAN AFFECT A BANK

**Before the Debt Crisis**

| Assets | Liabilities | |
|---|---|---|
| Loans, $1,000 | Deposits | $800 |
| | Capital | $200 |

**Default on $200 in Loans: One-half Written Off**

| Assets | Liabilities | |
|---|---|---|
| Loans $900 | Deposits | $800 |
| | Capital | $100 |

**Default on $200 in Loans: Entire Amount Written Off**

| Assets | Liabilities | |
|---|---|---|
| Loans $800 | Deposits | $800 |
| | Capital | $ 0 |

forms on the overly indebted countries.[17] (This insistence was the essence of the *Baker Plan*, named after James Baker, Brady's predecessor in the US Treasury Department. The same point had been an integral part of the Brady Plan.)

Two other solutions to the debt crisis have received some attention. One is the idea of converting debt into equity in developing countries' institutions. Although some examples of these **debt–equity swaps** exist, they have not proved attractive to banks because they involve both selling debt at a substantial discount and investing in regions or firms that are not desirable from a bank's perspective.

Another approach is **debt forgiveness**, which means effectively cancelling part of a country's indebtedness. Canada, among other countries, has implemented such a policy in a few circumstances. The difficulty is that unless governments bail out the banks involved, writing off worthless assets affects the latter's capital–asset ratios. In addition, the moral hazard problem is magnified; a country may indebt itself freely when it perceives debt relief in the future.[18]

However imperfect these solutions are, they do represent attempts to recover some of the debt. By contrast, default means no recovery of debts at all. Moreover, history offers precedents of occasions when even fairly modest debt relief has made both debtors and lenders better off eventually. Germany, for example, could

17 One of the problems with these efforts has been how to apply more or less common standards to reform packages imposed on the diverse countries involved. Experience suggests, however, that resolution to debt problems has to be addressed on a country-by-country basis.

18 Not surprisingly, perhaps, the extent to which some debts have been forgiven has raised the price of developing countries' debt in secondary markets.

not service its foreign debt after World War II. In hindsight, the fairly modest debt relief effort was quite successful.[19]

The international debt situation is of some interest to Canadians. Canada makes large loans to the Third World, and it also borrows extensively from other nations. By 1996, Canada had one of the highest debt–GDP ratio of any of the OECD countries.[20] As Canadian foreign debt accumulates, it becomes increasingly difficult to finance its cost from surpluses in the balance of merchandise trade. Alternatively, one can look at the government's net worth (see Chapter 8)—a measure of financial health—to see that Canada's ability to finance its debt deteriorated significantly during the 1980s.

## ASSESSING COUNTRY RISK

For reasons that should be clear from the previous section, banks and other institutions invest resources in assessing not only the riskiness of a loan to a particular firm abroad but also the inherent riskiness of the other country, which is called **country risk**. Countries have unique features and histories that influence their economic fortunes over time. Hence, investing in Canada implies different risks than investing in, say, Mexico.

Country risk has essentially two components: transfer risk, which is the possibility that a borrower may not be able to convert the currency in which the loan was made into the lender's currency; and sovereign risk, which is the possibility of the borrower's inability or unwillingness to repay principal and/or interest.

Assessing the level of country risk requires judicious assessment of social, political, historical, and economic factors. Perhaps the most common indicator is the **debt-service ratio**: the payments needed to service the country's foreign debt as a percentage of some average value of its exports. Recall that exports provide foreign exchange earnings and thus the ability to finance foreign debt. Even

---

19 Debt relief for Germany after World War II consisted of interest rate reductions on outstanding debts, a delay in the repayment of principal, and repayment in dollars of debts that had been denominated in gold.

20 Recent research suggests that debt–GDP ratios in highly indebted developing countries are not far apart from those in industrialized countries. Why then is a debt crisis not perceived as existing for the latter group of countries? Perhaps it is the ability of countries such as Canada to easily generate the necessary revenues to prevent a debt crisis from occurring. Also, the fact that industrialized countries grow substantially faster than developing countries mean that ability to pay is unlikely to be impaired in the long run. See P.E. Guidotti and M.S. Kumar, "Domestic Public Debt of Externally Indebted Countries," International Monetary Fund Occasional Paper 80 (June 1991); and *1991 International Monetary Fund: Annual Report* (Washington, D.C.: International Monetary Fund, 1991), 42–43.

exports as a percentage of GDP can be used as a simple measure of ability to pay.

In addition to quantitative measures of risk, potential lenders also consider qualitative characteristics, such as political risks (often determined by whether governments are democratically elected and whether they are "left-wing" or "right-wing."[21] Some combination of these characteristics can be used to generate a composite index. *The Economist* (actually its Economist Intelligence Unit branch), for example, produces just such an index for over eighty countries and it is published on a quarterly basis. Not surprisingly, countries such as Russia and Iraq are believed to have the highest country risk in 1996 while Canada, despite the threat of Quebec separation, is thought to have low country risk (although it is slightly higher than for, say, the US or Japan). Investors are keen on this type of information because it will influence the risk premium they demand on investments in particular countries.

## SUMMARY

- This chapter considers a variety of different topics that come under the heading of international banking.
- Many of the transactions involving transfers of funds from one country to another are conducted via international financial centres. London is probably the biggest such centre.
- A driving force in the international flow of funds is the Eurocurrency market. This market represents funds traded in a currency other than the one used in the country where the transaction takes place.
- The consequences of international trading in goods and money become clear in a nation's balance of payments, which consist of a current account and capital account. Both accounts record the value of movements of goods, services, and money between that country and the rest of the world.
- The chapter describes two other issues of recent interest in the field of international banking: the international debt crisis, and the problem of the lack of uniform international banking regulations.

21 Left-wing governments are sometimes referred to as "liberal," which means that they favour a relatively high degree of government intervention. By contrast, right-wing governments are often called "conservative" because they prefer little government intervention.

## IMPORTANT TERMS

balance of payments (BOP) (p. 472)
capital account (p. 472)
country risk (p. 487)
current account (p. 472)
debt–equity swaps (p. 486)
debt forgiveness (p. 486)
debt-service ratio (p. 487)
dual banking system (p. 482)
international financial centres (p. 470)
London interbank offer rate (LIBOR) (p. 479)
national treatment (p. 481)
offshore banking centres (p. 473)
sterilization (p. 475)
twin deficits (p. 477)
universal banking model (p. 482)

## EXERCISES

1. Why is the overvaluation of the Canadian dollar linked to the attractiveness of Euro-Canadian-dollar bonds from the foreign investor's perspective? Explain your answer.

2. Explain the moral hazard problem created when a country is able to repurchase its debt in a secondary market.

3. Why do secondary debt markets have prices that are always at a discount? Explain.

4. Explain why debt forgiveness in the absence of a government bailout has negative consequences for a bank's balance sheet.

5. Explain how the Eurocurrency transaction described in this chapter can have consequences for the Canadian money supply when the funds are transferred from demand deposits to foreign currency deposits.

6. What caused the international debt crisis? Explain your answer.

7. If a country has a current account deficit, is it a net lender or borrower to the rest of the world? Should a country be concerned if it runs such a deficit? Explain your answer.

8. Explain how a balance-of-payments disequilibrium can be self-correcting.

9. Suppose that the Bank of Canada and the US Federal Reserve peg their currencies against each other such that the Canadian dollar is undervalued

relative to the US dollar. Which central bank will gain foreign exchange reserves? Which bank will lose reserves? Explain your answer.

10. Suppose the Bank of Canada intervenes in the foreign exchange market and sells Canadian dollars. How does this action affect Canada's monetary base? Use T-accounts for your answer.

11. Explain why speculative attacks on a currency—this occurs when foreign exchange market participants bet that a currency will have to devalue or revalue in the near future—are more prevalent under a fixed exchange rate system than under a managed float.

12. How can a current account surplus contribute to generating inflation? Explain your answer.

13. Under flexible exchange rates, foreign exchange transactions have no direct effects on the domestic money supply. Explain why or why not.

14. Under flexible exchange rates, countries are able to pursue more independent monetary policies. Comment.

15. In 1989, the current account balance was −$26,948 million in Canada and the capital account balance was $26,318 million. What was the statistical discrepancy?

16. In 1988, the current account balance was −$21,114 million and the statistical discrepancy was −$586 million. What was the capital account balance?

17. Suppose that in the situation illustrated in Figure 21.2 the Bank of Canada pegged the exchange rate at $1.25. Would the currency be undervalued or overvalued? Why? Explain.

18. Suppose that in Figure 21.2, Canadian trading shifted toward the purchase of more US-made goods. Would the Canadian dollar appreciate or depreciate? If the Bank of Canada pegged the exchange rate at $1.20 would the resulting exchange rate be over- or undervalued?

19. What are some of the determinants of successful international banking centres?

20. Why should the balance of payments be zero?

21. What is sterilization?

22. What is the twin deficit and why is it a policy concern?

# REFERENCES


Copeland, L.S., *Exchange Rates and International Finance*, Second Edition. Wokingham, England: Addison-Wesley, 1994.

Eichengreen, B., and P.H. Lindert, eds. *The International Debt Crisis in Historical Perspective.* Cambridge, Mass.: The MIT Press, 1989.

Eng, M.V., F.A. Lees, and L.J. Mauer. *Global Finance.* New York: Harper-Collins College Publishers, 1995.

Faber, M. "Renegotiating Official Debts." *Finance and Development* (December 1990): 19–21.

Frankel, A.B., and J.D. Montgomery. "Financial Structure: An International Perspective." Brookings Papers on Economic Activity 1 (1991): 257–310.

Grabbe, J. Orlin, *International Financial Markets*, 2d ed. New York: Elsevier, 1991.

Hawawini, G., and E. Rajendra. "The Transfor1mation of the European Financial Services Industry: From Fragmentation to Integration." Solomon Brothers Center for the Study of Financial Institutions Monograph, 1989–4.

Krueger, A.O. "Resolving the Debt Crisis and Restoring Developing Countries' Credit Worthiness." In *International Debt, Federal Reserve Operations and Other Essays*, edited by K. Brunner and A.H. Meltzer, 75–114. Carnegie-Rochester Conference Series on Public Policy, vol. 30. Amsterdam: North-Holland, 1989.

Lissakers, K. *Banks, Borrowers and The Establishment.* New York: Basic Books, 1992.

Melik, A.L., and S.E. Plant, "The Short-Term Eurocredit Market." New York University Solomon Center Monograph Series in Finance and Economics, 1991-1.

O'Brien, T.J. *Global Financial Management.* New York: John Wiley and Sons, 1996.

Osler, S. "Have Commercial Banks Ignored History?" NBER working paper 3959 (January 1992).

Osler, S., and H. Huizinga. "Bank Finance, Capital and Secondary Market Discounts on Developing Country Debt." NBER working paper 3961 (January 1992).

Sachs, J.D., ed. *Developing Country Debt and the World Economy.* Chicago and London: University of Chicago Press, 1989.

CHAPTER 22

# The Financial Systems of the United States, the United Kingdom, Japan, and Germany

Although the growing volume and importance of international banking and the forces of globalization are encouraging similarities in financial behaviour and regulations around the world, each country retains important idiosyncrasies in how its financial institutions are organized and regulated. Many are rooted in history. This chapter offers a glimpse of these differences by relating some basic facts about four other major financial systems: those of the United States, the United Kingdom, Japan, and Germany. An advantage of studying experiences in other countries is that we can better understand how economic development and political considerations together have shaped other countries' financial systems. Moreover, we can better appreciate how regulatory structures are influenced by the objectives and the financial needs of the public.

Although these few pages cannot possibly do justice to the subject—entire texts are often devoted to a description of a single country's financial system—this chapter, plus the information here and there throughout the textbook about how banks and other financial institutions are organized elsewhere, should give you an appreciation of the similarities and differences between Canada and other countries of the industrialized Western world.[1] (See Table 22.7 at the end of the chapter.)

## THE UNITED STATES

What distinguishes the US financial system from that of many other countries is its dual (federal and state) control, which is reflected in the structure and organization of both its financial institutions and its central banking function.

1 The industrialized world as defined by the International Monetary Fund in 1996 consists of 23 countries: essentially all European countries, the United States, Canada, Japan, Australia, and New Zealand are included in this definition.

## HISTORICAL BACKGROUND

The peculiar structure of the US financial system is largely the result of political pressures familiar to Canadians: centralization versus regionalism. Soon after the United States was formed, opinion makers divided between those who wished to see a strong federal system and those who favoured relatively strong states rights.

The then-new constitution was ambiguous on whether the states or the federal government had jurisdiction over financial institutions.[2] Thus, even as the colonists moved westward and small, local banks were established, Federalists staked their claim. Under their influence, the Congress chartered the First and the Second Bank of the United States (1791 and 1816, respectively) and endowed them with the *exclusive* right to open branches nationally. Neither lasted long, and both were political disasters—they were accused of redistributing credit to urban centres from rural areas (the United States was largely rural at the time) as well as lending exclusively to pro-Federalists.

The result was the virtual abolition of nationwide banking. The states took over jurisdiction and each made its own rules. Some permitted only **unit banking**—no branches at all. Others allowed limited branching—say, within a designated locality or country. Still others eventually went so far as to permit branching throughout the state.

With the trend to small, local banks, it is not surprising that *free banking* became the rule in the nineteenth-century United States; anyone who could meet quite minimal requirements could open a bank. It is also not surprising that scandals and bank failures were frequent. Approximately one-third of the US banking system was wiped out in the Great Depression.

One of the political responses to that tragedy was the introduction of deposit insurance (a US invention), which also gave the federal government a way to extend its control over the banking system. To join the insurance scheme, which was a popular success, a bank had to meet stringent criteria for its assets and open its books and management techniques to inspection by federal examiners. Thus, the Federal Deposit Insurance Corporation (FDIC) helped to stabilize the system, although critics[3] believe the coverage is far too generous. Today deposits are insured up to $100,000 US, but, as in Canada, a variety of devices can be used to raise the effective limit many times over.[4] Moreover, bank regulators and

2 In fact, although it specifies that the federal government has jurisdiction over "coin[ing] money and regulat[ing] its value," it makes no assignment of the regulation of banking.

3 See, for example, L. White, *The S&L Debacle* (New York: Oxford University Press, 1991).

4 One such device is to rely on brokered deposits. Money brokers take large sums of money and break them up into segments of $100,000. Thus, several millions can be insured even though the spirit of deposit insurance was to offer protection up to $100,000 only.

politicians have acted over the years on what is called the "too-big-to-fail" doctrine. If a large institution has failed, all its depositors have been reimbursed, even if their accounts exceeded the current limit on deposit insurance. Such a policy is unfair to small and conservative institutions; it can also encourage larger ones to recklessness in the knowledge that the default risk to depositors is effectively zero.

## US FINANCIAL INTERMEDIARIES

Given the United States' legacy of state and federal jurisdictions in the area of banking, there evolved a *dual banking system*. Among the depository institutions, in order of relative importance, are[5]

1. *Commercial banks*, which, as their name implies, are primarily in the business of making commercial loans and taking chequable and savings deposits; especially since the early 1980s, mortgage lending has increasingly become a focus of activity. The commercial banks can be likened to Canadian chartered banks but because of US legal restrictions on branch banking, there are vastly more of them. Most are state chartered and largely state regulated.
2. **Savings and loan associations (S&Ls)**, which resemble Canadian mortgage loan companies and until recently were essentially restricted to mortgage lending. With the post–World War II boom in housing, S&Ls grew rapidly. But they experienced considerable difficulties during the 1970s and 1980s when market interest rates rose sharply but the S&Ls faced a legal ceiling on the rate they could pay on deposits.
3. *Mutual savings banks*, which are similar to S&Ls except they are owned by their depositors.
4. *Credit unions*, which are like Canadian credit unions and organized along the same lines, such as by region or type of employment.

## FINANCIAL REGULATORY PRACTICE AND FINANCIAL INNOVATIONS

One can argue that the variety of legal restrictions imposed on the US banking system has made it an innovative financial system in some respects and laggard in others.

For example, the Edge Act of 1919 permitted the federal chartering of banks for the sole purpose of engaging in international banking. Edge Act corporations

5 Ranked on the basis of the relative size of the institutions under each category. See, for example, F.S. Mishkin, *The Economics of Money, Banking, and Financial Markets*, Fourth Edition (New York: HarperCollins, 1995), p. 39.

may take deposits from foreigners but not from US residents. Since these situations are exempt from the severe restrictions on interstate banking, it is not surprising that Edge Act subsidiaries are a feature of most large US banks today.

Another important reform was the McFadden Act of 1927, amended in 1933, which cleared up the legal status of branching and effectively barred it across state lines. Getting around this regulation has proved easy, however. A would-be financier simply sets up a bank holding company, which becomes the legal owner of separate banks in various states. Not being itself a bank, the holding company is not subject to the interstate banking restrictions. Legislation was passed to prevent further erosion of the McFadden Act and to limit these companies' potential to engage in non-bank activities, but a grandfather clause protected existing bank holding companies, and others quickly developed new variations to undermine the intent of the McFadden Act.[6] Moreover, the recent introduction of automated teller machines (ATMs) has led to the creation of networks, permitting a form of nation-wide banking. The popularity of ATMs makes it unlikely that politicians will put a stop to such a use.

The Great Depression of the 1930s[7] eventually brought sweeping legislative changes to the US financial industry. One, as we have seen, was the introduction of deposit insurance. Another (discussed in more detail later in this section) was a mandate to the Federal Reserve System, which acts as a central bank in the United States, to become more active in supervising banks and managing the nation's financial affairs.

A third set of 1930s regulations actually originated in 1920s scandals that involved the same person's owning and managing a commercial bank and an **investment bank** (the latter is much like a Canadian *investment dealer*, purchasing new issues of securities and selling them in smaller parcels to investors). The investment branch of such an institution could, for example, sell debt with a high default risk to the commercial banking arm, thereby raising the risk to depositors. The uncovering of several such schemes prompted public outrage. The political result was passage of the **Glass–Stegall Act** of 1933, which prohibited commercial banks from selling or dealing in (that is, underwriting) corporate securities. The Act did not extend to government securities in part because they are considered default risk free and in part because Congress sought to create the widest possible market for them. It also did not extend to the foreign operations of US banks, a fact that many institutions take advantage of. This re-

---

6 For details, see M. Kohn, *Money, Banking, and Financial Markets* (Chicago: The Dryden Press, 1991), chapter 8.

7 For a lively account of the economic and social consequences of the Great Depression in the US, see J. Garraty, *The Great Depression* (New York: Harper & Row, 1987).

striction did not exist in countries such as Germany and Japan that have not experienced widespread banking failures.

The tremendous impact of the banking crisis during the Great Depression left the impression among many people, including legislators, that market competition in which one firm can undercut another could be ruinous for the banking sector. Consequently, the Glass-Stegall Act gave the Federal Reserve authority to regulate interest on bank accounts. The result was regulation Q, which placed a ceiling on deposit interest rates (but none on lending rates). At the time the regulation was put into effect, interest rates on Treasury bills were well below the ceiling, so no one was much upset. But during the 1970s, market rates rose substantially above what the banks could offer. Although the ceiling was gradually raised, it remained low enough to drive depositors to seek a better return elsewhere. The result was, for a time, considerable *disintermediation.* Banks, therefore, searched extensively for a way to avoid the restrictions of regulation Q. Some New England savings banks discovered a loophole allowing the payment of interest on chequable deposits. By calling an account a **negotiable order of withdrawal (NOW)**, savings banks, which were barred from accepting demand deposits, could effectively offer chequable savings accounts. Since the deposit was a savings account, interest could be paid. But commercial banks could not offer similar accounts because they were prohibited from effecting what were technically third-party transfers of funds from savings. NOW accounts proved popular, and eventually legislation was passed permitting all depository institutions to offer them. Banks were also able to entice corporate accounts to return, avoiding the regulation Q restrictions, by, for example, offering *overnight bank repurchase agreements (repos).*[8]

During the 1980s, the number of bank failures rose again, under the influence of high and rising and interest rates. And the S&L scandal loomed. One response to this situation was the implementation of two major pieces of financial legislation. The first, the Depository Institutions Deregulation and Monetary Control Act of 1980, had three important objectives: (1) to phase out regulation Q, (2) to relax restrictions on the types of loans savings banks could offer, so they could tap the lucrative area of commercial lending and otherwise increase portfolio diversification, and (3) to impose uniform reserve requirements on all depository institutions and to allow them access to borrowing funds from the Federal Reserve System. Unlike Canada, however, reserve requirements persist and are not likely to be eliminated any time soon.

The 1982 Depository Institutions Act further relaxed the differences between commercial banks, savings banks, and other financial institutions. Thus, savings banks were permitted to issue *money market accounts* (which operate like mutual

---

8 An alternative term for what Canadians call purchase and resale agreements (PRAs).

funds but enable the depositor to redeem "shares" by writing cheques). The maximum for commercial loans as a percentage of a savings bank's total assets was also raised. Finally, the Act gave emergency powers to the deposit-insuring agencies to facilitate mergers between ailing or failing financial institutions and solvent ones.

In 1991, reforms to the FDIC, called the FDIC Improvements Act, limited the scope of deposit insurance in the case of brokered deposits and reduced the possibility or invoking the "too-big-to-fail" doctrine by permitting earlier intervention by the FDIC in a bank suspected of being in financial difficulty.

Perhaps the biggest development in the US banking industry during the late 1980s and early 1990s was the dramatic drop in the number of banks (a 25% drop between 1988 and 1994). At the same time, Congress finally approved legislation in 1995 to deregulate the financial system to permit more widespread branch banking across states as well as relaxing some of the provisions of the Glass-Stegall Act.[9] Americans' deep desire to diffuse power as much as possible has resulted in an extremely complex web of regulatory agencies that defies easy categorization (see Table 22.1) and protects their bureaucracies well. A more comprehensive bill to reform the banking sector is still delayed, as of early 1996, because of a court case arguing what powers banks should have to sell insurance.[10]

## THE FEDERAL RESERVE SYSTEM

The tension in the United States between Federalists and advocates of states' rights, as well as the considerable influence of the rural and regional populations, delayed the founding of any central bank until the early part of this century and then produced one unlike any other in the world. The **Federal Reserve (the Fed)**, created by federal law in 1913, was not a single bank but a whole decentralized central banking system, comprising 12 banks, each the centre of a region and owned by its members. Membership was—and still is—voluntary. Each Federal Reserve Bank had sufficient autonomy to regulate the financial system in its own district. Each issued its own currency,[11] so interest rates and thus monetary policy

9 Full implementation of what has been called the Riegle-Neal Interstate Banking and Branching Efficiency Act of 1994 will not take place until June 1997. See D.F. Amel, "Trends in the Structure of Federally Insured Depository Institutions 1984–1994," *Federal Reserve Bulletin* 82 (January 1996): 1–15.

10 This is also one of the hotly debated issues in Canada. In March 1996, the US Supreme Court ruled that banks cannot be barred from selling insurance. See R. Wells, "High Court Rules Banks Can Sell Insurance," San Diego *Union-Tribune*, 27 March 1996, p. A17.

11 To this day, the front of a US note (the side on which appears a portrait of a past president) shows the name of the issuing Federal Reserve Bank on the left-hand side. However, the new notes, which will eventually replace the old ones, no longer identify the Federal Reserve City. As of 1996 only the $100 bill was replaced.

**Table 22.1** US DEPOSITORY INSTITUTIONS AND THEIR REGULATORS: A SIMPLIFIED SKETCH

| Type of Bank | Chartering or Licensing Authority | Branching Authority Supervision Intrastate | Interstate | Insured By |
|---|---|---|---|---|
| National banks | Dept. of Treasury[a] | Dept. of Treasury[a] | Prohibited[b] | FDIC |
| State banks | State | Federal Reserve | Prohibited[b] | FDIC |
| Savings banks | | | | |
| Federal | OTS | OTS | OTS | FDIC |
| State | State | FDIC[d] & state | FDIC[d] & state | FDIC |
| Savings and loans | | | | |
| Federal | OTS | OTS | OTS | FDIC |
| State | State | OTS[c] & state | OTS[c] & state | FDIC |
| Credit Unions | | | | |
| Federal | NCUAB[e] | [f] | [f] | NCUSIF |
| State | State | State | State | NCUSIF[g] |

[a] Office of the Comptroller of the Currency, a division of the US Department of the Treasury

[b] By the McFadden Act

[c] Office of Thrift Supervision

[d] Federal Deposit Insurance Corporation

[e] National Credit Union Association Board

[f] No NCUAB approval required to open a branch

[g] National Credit Union Share Insurance Funds or State Authorities

Sources: L. White, *The S&L Debacle* (New York: Oxford University Press, 1991), 26–31, Table 3-1; Ann-Marie Meulendyke, *U.S. Monetary Policy and Financial Markets* (New York: Federal Reserve Bank of New York, 1989); and *The Economist*, 10 August 1991, and Federal Reserve *Annual Reports* (various years).

were largely regionally determined. Nominally, a central agency in Washington, called the Board of Governors, co-ordinated national monetary and financial regulatory policies, but power was meant to come from below and not from above, consistent with a decentralized process.

Major reforms in the way the Fed operates occurred in the aftermath of the Great Depression. Henceforth, the seven-member Board of Governors would be responsible for determining the discount rate (that is, the rate at which the Fed lends to member banks), for setting reserve requirements (within limits), and for providing certain kinds of regulation. The Board plus the presidents of five Federal Reserve Banks form the Federal Open Market Committee (FOMC), which directs open market operations and, therefore, national monetary policy.[12] As a result,

12 The group always includes the president of the New York Fed, where open market operations are

the current Federal Reserve System operates much like any other modern central bank though vestiges of the decentralized structure persist. The FOMC meets several times a year to gauge the appropriateness of the current stance of monetary policy. Regional Feds and the Board of Governors provide economic information, analyses and forecasts to the FOMC to assist in their decision-making and deliberations.

Unlike many other central banks, however, the Fed is relatively independent of the government. Several reasons are usually cited. First, members of Board of Governors are chosen for rotating 14-year terms that do not overlap those of the presidency.[13] Second, the Fed does not receive any appropriations from the Congress; rather, it operates on the profits from its holdings of government securities and its loans to banks,[14] as well as the seigniorage earned from the issue of currency. Third, like many other central banks, the Fed conducts its operations in secrecy. Although the Congress has recently forced it to announce in public the results of FOMC meetings (with a lag) as well as to provide money-growth forecasts and information on how the money supply will facilitate the economic policies of the president, such reforms have not adversely affected the Fed's independence.

US monetary aggregates are defined in Table 22.2. Perhaps the most important monetary policy tool is the Federal Funds Rate (FFR). Federal funds are entitlements to balances at the regional Fed banks. The FFR is roughly equivalent to the overnight rate in Canada. Virtually all depository institutions have access to these funds which helps ensure the liquidity of the banking system.[15]

## FEDERAL RESERVE OPERATIONS

The Federal Reserve was not originally created to actively intervene in the economy. The Great Depression changed all that. The structure of the Fed was centralized and it was recognized that open market operations in particular represented an important instrument to control interest rates and therefore inflation. The advent of World War II effectively took away the interest rate instrument from the Fed and, consequently, some of its independence. The *Fed-Treasury*

---

conducted. Note that since the Board can always outvote the other members, ultimate control over monetary policy rests with that institution.

13 The exception is the Federal Reserve chair, who is appointed for a four-year term that can coincide with that of the president. The rationale is that the US president ought to be able to select (with the advice and consent of the Senate) the person who will head the fed and with whom the administration must work.

14 This facility used to be limited to Fed members. Since 1982, however, it has been extended to all banks.

15 For greater details on the operations of this market, see J.S.G. Wilson, *Money Markets: The International Perspective* (London: Routledge, 1993), pp. 118–23.

**Table 22.2** MONETARY AGGREGATES IN THE UNITED STATES, 1995

| | Details | Billions of $US |
|---|---|---|
| M1 | Currency outside Federal Reserve Banks; demand deposits in commercial banks; traveller's cheques of non-bank issuers; NOW and ATS (automatic transfer service) accounts; less float | 1,122.9 |
| M2 | M1 **plus** savings deposits and small-denomination time deposits (less than $100,000); overnight Eurodollar deposits of US residents; repos issued by commercial banks; and money market deposit accounts | 3,780.6 |
| M3 | M2 **plus** large-denomination time deposits and repos; term Eurodollars of US residents held worldwide; balances in both taxable and tax-exempt money market funds | 4,563.5 |
| L | M3 **plus** non-bank holdings of US savings bonds; short-term Treasury securities; and bankers' acceptances | 5,648.3 |
| Debt | L **plus** outstanding debt of federal, state, and local governments, and private non-financial sector (corporate bonds, mortgages, consumer credit, commercial paper, etc.) | 13,804.2 |

Note: The figures for L and Debt are for November 1995. The other information is for the end of the same year.

Source: *Federal Reserve Bulletin* (Washington, D.C.: Board of Governors of the Federal Reserve, March 1996, Table 1.21.

*Accord* returned interest rate control to the Fed. Until the early 1960s, however, the Fed relied mainly on the manipulation of reserves to implement monetary policy. The pace of financial innovations during the 1960s made it more difficult for the Fed to rely on money stock instruments of monetary policy and so the interest rate instrument remained the principal tool of monetary policy. The ascent of monetarism (see Chapter 26) led to the formulation of explicit monetary targets during the 1970s in the United States and elsewhere. Part of the shift is also explained by the attempt by congress to make the Fed more accountable to the public. The inflation and subsequent stagflation in the 1970s pointed the way to the need for a dramatic change. This was accomplished by Paul Volcker, soon after his appointment by President Carter, who instituted a policy of strict monetary targeting. This led in the United States and the rest of the industrialized world to dramatic increases in both the level and volatility of interest rates, as we have already seen (for example, Chapter 6). The Volcker experiment continued until approximately 1982 when targeting reserves of the banking system as well as interest rate control have to this day served as instruments of monetary policy.

Congress also intervened again in monetary policy affairs by requiring that the Fed chairperson periodically report to Congress in person as well as by way of a monetary policy report. This device has since been introduced in several other countries, including, very recently, Canada.

# THE UNITED KINGDOM

The financial system of the United Kingdom is particularly interesting to Canadians because it was the historical source of our own system. It is also of special interest to analysts the world over because it underwent fundamental changes in its regulatory structure during the 1980s.

## HISTORICAL BACKGROUND

Any historical description of the UK financial system must begin with the **Bank of England**, the country's central bank, which was founded in 1694. It was not then a central bank in the modern sense. Rather, it was one of the earliest chartered banks, privately owned and organized to accept deposits and make loans to the private sector. It did, however, have a close connection with public finance. Early on a large share of its assets was in government securities, and it held the nation's specie. It became known as a solid institution, and its notes were widely accepted as a means of payment, first in London and then throughout the widening British empire. Thus its becoming, in 1833, Britain's monopoly supplier of currency (while still a private bank) is not surprising.

During the eighteenth century and the first half of the nineteenth century, other private banks opened in London, institutions that were increasingly needed because of the growth of commerce and the effects of industrialization. Meanwhile, outside the country's main city, the growing centralization of government finance in London, the need for payments and remittances for taxes, and expanding financial wealth from the industrial revolution resulted in the founding of *country banks* (private banks outside London).

Another feature of nineteenth-century Great Britain, which was to be emulated in Canada, was the creation of **building societies** (savings banks), vehicles to permit individuals or families with modest incomes to enjoy benefits from pooling their financial resources and to profit from being able to obtain financial services they would not have had access to in the London banks.

Also developed in Great Britain at this time was the concept of the *clearinghouse*, a place and system for settling interbank claims that would grow into the cheque-clearing systems we know today.

These developments, as well as the Scottish experiments with free banking, meant that Great Britain matured financially faster than other industrializing countries. London became the centre of the domestic financial industry—and eventually the leading international financial centre, thanks to its role in the gold market and in the development of the Eurodollar market.

## FINANCIAL INTERMEDIARIES

Until 1979, the United Kingdom had no legal definition of a bank. The criteria, which were revised in 1987, now distinguish among types of deposit-taking institutions and thus influence the measurement of aggregates such as the money supply (see Table 22.3).

The UK bank financial intermediaries include.

1. Retail banks, which provide services much like those of the Canadian chartered banks. Like them, retail banks offer both time deposits and *sight* (demand) *deposits.*

2. Trusteed savings banks (TSB), originally set up in 1861 as the Post Office Savings Bank, are the forerunners of the deposit-taking side of the Canadian trust companies. They were created at a time when minimum deposit requirements barred many households from using city banks.

3. The National Savings Bank, a government-sponsored savings bank administered by a department of the Treasury and operated through the post office system. (It used to be called the Post Office Savings Bank.)

4. The National Girobank, which is operated through the post offices. It is an association of savings banks organized to facilitate the sharing of payments in an alternative to the chequing system so prevalent in North America. With a **giro system**, an individual gives a written order to his or her bank to transfer funds to the account of the payee. There is no credit risk since the funds must be in the payor's bank to begin with. The giro system has been emulated in Japan and in several European countries including Germany.

5. Secondary banks, which are depository institutions that have relatively few branches in the United Kingdom and are therefore not highly visible to the public. They include *merchant banks*, various consortiums, and especially foreign banks, which are present in the United Kingdom in large numbers. Of course many of these institutions do not compete for the country's domestic business but, rather, carry out business related to international finance in London, which has a long-held competitive advantage in this field. Nevertheless, few other countries have banking systems as open to foreign banks. By the late 1980s, foreign banks accounted for more than 50% of the assets of all the UK bank financial intermediaries.

**Table 22.3** MONETARY AGGREGATES IN THE UNITED KINGDOM, 1995

| | Details | £ Millions |
|---|---|---|
| MO | Monetary base (notes, coins, bankers' till money, balances at the Bank of England) | 22,817 |
| M4 | MO **plus** all sterling deposits, commercial paper, bonds, and other instruments of up to and including five years to maturity. | 608,140 |

Source: Bank of England *Quarterly Bulletin* 35 (November 1995), Tables 2 and 6.2, and Bank of England *Statistical Abstract*, part 2.

**6.** Discount houses, which deal in short-term securities (sold at a discount, of course). They resemble Canadian investment dealers.

The remainder of the financial system is classified as non-bank financial intermediaries: building societies, finance houses (which Canadians would call finance companies), insurance and pension funds, and investment and unit trusts. As all these institutions have functions similar to those they have in Canada, nothing more need be said about them. While deregulation has allowed building societies to tap the wholesale money market to increase their lending activities, this segment of the market has experienced a great deal of consolidation. There are fewer than 100 such societies in the UK, although they have maintained their share of the mortgage lending market.[16]

UK banks are required to hold a small fraction of their liabilities at the Bank of England in the form of non-interest-bearing deposits. The can (and do) also hold excess reserves. The reserve requirements used to be much stricter; they were, in effect, phased out in extensive reforms in 1981.[17]

In 1986 came another major reform, often called the **Big Bang.** Following legal proceedings in which it was contended that the Stock Exchange engaged in what amounted to restrictive trade practices, the rules were changed to eliminate the division between deposit-taking institutions and securities underwriters. The number of firms that could deal in government securities was enlarged from a handful to almost 30.

Building societies were allowed to offer a wide range of banking and financial services (banks had been permitted to offer mortgages since 1982). Thus, a considerable blurring of the differentiation between banks and near-banks was ini-

16 See "The Changing Mortgage Market," *Financial Times*, 22 April 1994, p. 23.

17 The building societies do not face formal reserve requirements. They also benefit from tax advantages stemming from their non-profit status.

tiated. Indeed, the Big Bang changed the whole competitive structure of the UK banking industry.

UK banks are now supervised by the Securities and Investment Board, a private sector organization with regulatory power delegated by the government. The very name reflects the elimination of barriers between banks, securities dealers, and the Bank of England. The diffusion of regulatory responsibilities has, however, proved problematic, and there have been several financial scandals. One problem seems to be that with deregulation, some institutions have become financial conglomerates, with one division in banking, and thus difficult to supervise, especially in a country that has a long history of a stable system with strict controls demarcating banking from other forms of intermediation.

## FINANCIAL INSTRUMENTS

The basic operations of financial markets in the United Kingdom are similar to those in Canada. Only some distinctive features need be described here.

### Government-Backed Instruments

Because banks and money market dealers hold large quantities of government financial instruments, the Bank of England buys and sells them in the money market. Unlike the case in Canada, the central bank can specify the maturities of bills acceptable for purchase.[18] These activities can take place on a daily basis.

A distinctive group of financial instruments is **gilt-edged securities (gilts)**, which are fixed-rate securities issued by the government and traded on the London Stock Exchange. (Securities are often referred to as stocks in the United Kingdom.) They are known as gilts because of the zero probability of default inherent in government financial instruments. These instruments are redeemed on set dates,[19] and since 1981, some have been indexed to inflation.[20]

As elsewhere in the industrialized world, a significant portion of UK government debt outstanding has become short term in nature. Nevertheless, the Treasury bill market is relative to that for other government bonds. Indeed, T-bills account for only 1% to 2% of the outstanding national debt.

Another small but noticeable fraction of public debt is in non-marketable instruments. They include national savings, essentially the equivalent of Canada Savings Bonds, as well as tax instruments, which are created in anticipation of some future tax liability.

---

18 They are specified as *bands* since they refer to the number of remaining days left until maturity. For example, Band 1 bills mature in between 1 and 14 days, and Band 4 signifies a maturity in 64 to 91 days.

19 Before World War II most of these societies were *consols*—the UK term for *perpetuities*—instruments with no redemption dates.

20 The recently introduced Canadian government real return bonds were patterned after this UK instrument.

In 1989, three-quarters of the public debt was held outside the public sector, and 15% of it by foreigners, percentages that had been fairly stable throughout the late 1970s and the 1980s. From 1987 through 1991, the central government was actually reducing the national debt, using accumulated surpluses. This five-year trend was reversed in 1992, however, when the central government, on the eve of national elections, projected a large deficit.

Another characteristic of the UK money market is that since the Big Bang the once-pivotal position held by the discount house has disappeared. So long as a firm is willing to participate in the weekly Treasury bill tender[21] and the Bank of England's money market operations, among other requirements, it can gain access to money market funds.

In 1994, the sale of repos for government bonds (see Chapter 4 for the Canadian case) were introduced in the UK. In January 1996, the gilt market was further deregulated when all restrictions on repos were removed. This means that anyone can repo, lend or borrow gilts for any purpose, whether or not this is accomplished via an intermediary.[22]

## Other Money Market Instruments

The UK money markets issue a variety of instruments of the kind familiar to Canadians. Thus, for example, banks borrow from each other in the interbank market, where the base rate is the *LIBOR (London interbank offer rate)*—an interest rate we encountered earlier—since it is a key to international rates on assets such as Eurocurrency CDs.

*Commercial paper*, a short-term financial instrument maturing in seven days to three months, also exists, but until recently, it was only issued in a foreign currency. Finally, there is the Eurocurrency market, which, as we have already seen, originated in London. In recent years, *Floating Rate Notes (FRNs)* have grown in popularity. These are bonds whose interest income varies in line with changes in money-market rates. FRNs are issued in sizes ranging from £20 to £500 million.

It is worth noting that the advances in achieving European monetary union (see Chapter 23) as well as the growing integration of financial markets will doubtless have additional influences on the UK money market. Treasury bills denominated in Ecu have already been issued. Yet there remain some important differences compared with other European banking systems, particularly in how

---

21 The offering of Treasury bills takes place each Friday. If the entire issue is not sold, the remainder can be sold on demand at the stock exchange. It then becomes known as *tap stock* because the bills are now available "on tap" as it were.

22 See "The Gilt Repo Market," Bank of England *Quarterly Bulletin* 35 (November 1995): 325–30; and N. Elliott "UK Gilt Money Traders Brace for New Era in Repos," *Wall Street Journal Europe*, 1 March 1994, pp. 1–2.

bank failures are treated and in the extent of the relationship between a bank and a firm in which a bank has a financial stake. In the United Kingdom, as in the United States, this relationship is supposed to be somewhat arm's length while the opposite is true in countries such as Germany.

## BANK OF ENGLAND OPERATIONS

The Bank of England performs all the customary roles of a modern central bank. Thus, it acts as a lender of last resort, is the government's banker, and collects and disseminates financial data. But unlike the German and US central banks, the Bank of England has always had a close relationship with the central government and has never been viewed as being independent in the sense of being able to impose views on monetary policy that might contradict those of the government in office. The Treasury can direct it to change its policies—for example, through a change in the bank rate. Indeed, the Bank has no explicit statutory policies of its own, except for a supervisory role in the banking system.

The Bank of England is headed by a governor, who is appointed by the government for a period of five years but cannot be dismissed in midterm.

The recent history of the Bank's monetary policy can be subdivided into several periods. During the 1960s, it used a variety of *credit controls*—effective ceilings on the amounts that could be borrowed from the banking system. The methods used were high cash reserve ratios and moral suasion, rather than interest rate control, but they were not especially effective because of the absence of restrictions on foreign banks in the country. As a result, a greater reliance on interest rates was put into effect during the 1970s by linking the bank rate—renamed the **minimum lending rate**—to the rate on Treasury bills. Later, at the end of 1973, an implicit tax, called the **corset**, was introduced on wholesale deposits; banks were required to deposit interest-free a fraction of wholesale deposits in excess of some preannounced figure.

New monetary policy procedures were introduced following the election of the Conservatives led by Margaret Thatcher in 1981. Reserve ratios were effectively phased out; the Bank published and sought to monitor broader monetary aggregates; interest rates were set primarily by purchases and sales of bills in the money market. Today the Bank of England, like the Bank of Canada, influences interest rates by monitoring and controlling liquidity in the financial sector. The Bank's minimum lending rate, which influences other interest rates, is set daily in response to the market.

A significant change in monetary policy operations took place in October 1992 when the Chancellor of the Exchequer announced that inflation targets would henceforth guide Bank of England policies. The current inflation target is a maximum of 2 1/2% inflation in the CPI with mortgage payments excluded from the calculations. We discuss inflation targeting in Canada in more detail in Chapter 25.

# JAPAN

Japan is often considered a modern economic miracle, having transformed itself from a ruined, defeated country at the end of World War II to a financial superpower today. Its financial system is a hybrid of endemic features and the US system imposed after the war. In general, its banking structure now lies somewhere between the fractured US system and the relatively concentrated Canadian system. Nevertheless, in the last few years the Japanese banking system has been under great financial stress due to the huge volume of bad real estate loans in particular. The central bank, the **Bank of Japan**, is considered one of the world's most independent central banks based on the inflation performance of the Japanese economy. Yet, this situation is surprising, given the Bank's administrative structure, which ties it to the government. Indeed, the Ministry of Finance influences the Bank's activities and also regulates all the country's financial institutions and sets all aspects of the government budget. Such a concentration of power is unlike that of any of the other countries mentioned in the text.

## HISTORICAL BACKGROUND

That Japan's financial system reflects both local and Western concepts is not surprising. Since the two societies began to come into regular contact with each other in the nineteenth century, Japan has sometimes scorned what it saw but more often emulated it, often with its own twists.

## THE MEIJI RESTORATION

Although historical records show that money lenders and other merchant financiers of the diamyo (feudal lords) existed in Japan as early as the seventeenth century (transactions tended to be in cash), most financial histories of Japan began with the Meiji restoration in 1868, the first period to see anything like a modern financial system under some kind of unified state. Industrial growth, which necessitated large amounts of financial capital, originated with a small group of conglomerates, such as the **zaibatsu** ("financial cliques").

Among the rapidly growing institutions were those that did not perform a large variety of functions, such as trade, production, and finance, but rather became increasingly like the commercial banks of the European or North American variety. (This development is not surprising as the central government's view of what the Japanese financial system should look like consisted of a mixture of existing European financial arrangements.) By the late nineteenth century the country had three types of banks:

1. National banks, which were broadly modelled on the US national banks of the eighteenth century and had the privileged status of being allowed to issue notes. Because the Japanese government wished to adopt a competitive laissez-faire banking system, there were more than 150 such banks at their peak. Initially, the fact that their notes were convertible only into specie potentially limited their growth to the availability of gold.[23] Later, bank notes became somewhat convertible into the unbacked paper money issued by the government, an approach that produced strong growth in the issue of notes and eventually led to the imposition of a ceiling on it. National banks were also distinct from other types of banks because a large portion of their deposits (about 25% to 35%) was in the form of government deposits. Private deposits were accepted, but the national banks were created primarily to stimulate business loans and deposits.

2. Private banks, which developed largely in urban areas as commercial interests obtained the right to use the word **ginko** ("bank") to identify their financial operations. There was little to distinguish these banks from the national banks apart from the lack of note-issuing privileges.

3. Quasi-banks, which could perform a wide variety of financial functions. They mainly served the rural areas.

At the end of the nineteenth century, the privileges of the national banks were revoked, and private and quasi-banks were transformed into "ordinary banks." The Japanese financial system would henceforth be based on a single type of commercial bank, a move meant to unify banking activities and allow them to be regulated in a similar fashion.

By this time, the Japanese financial system also featured a number of other types of financial institutions, all modelled to some extent on European counterparts. Thus, a variety of "special" banks facilitated the availability of funds for specific sectors and industries, and several kinds of savings banks—including postal savings banks, resembling the British version—encouraged small deposits by individuals.

Perhaps the most important difference between the early development of Japanese financial institutions and that of many other countries was the prominent role played by government and by conglomerates. Thus, Japanese finance was

23 Before the Meiji restoration, parts of the country were on a silver standard while Tokyo (or Edo as it was known then), the administrative capital, was on a gold standard. Gold later became the standard in the country.

structured to foster industrialization as quickly as possible. Since the newly created (1882) and generally accommodating central bank prevented major liquidity crises, the close ties between banking and industry acted as a spur and not a deterrent to economic development.

These close links continued through World War I and during the interwar period. Large firms in the steel and chemical industries, for example, benefited from long-term loans from the zaibatsu banks. Familiar names such as Mitsubishi and Sumimoto were among the groups in which commercial and banking concerns were strongly interconnected.

The relatively high concentration of commercial banks was further facilitated by laws enacted during the 1920s. They served Japan well as it prepared itself for a period of war finance. So did the Bank of Japan, which was already financing budget deficits that followed from the Japanese invasion of Manchuria in the early 1930s. A special institution, the Wartime Finance Bank, was created in 1942 to raise and co-ordinate funding to assist war-related production. In general, all banks were reorganized to some extent to facilitate war finance. In addition, as in other economies geared to war finance, interest rates were pegged at artificially low rates, to allow the government and the financial institutions to borrow cheaply.

## The Early Postwar Period

Japan surrendered to the Allies in August 1945. Its financial system would henceforth strongly parallel that of the United States, which was the dominant occupying power.

Defeat produced high inflation, as in other war-ravaged economies, and it was fuelled by the willingness of the Bank of Japan to print currency. The financial situation changed for the better in 1947, when the United States decided to aid Japan in its recovery. Other financial reforms, such as sound government budget financing and a convertible currency, set the stage for postwar economic growth. Among the most important changes were the abolition of the zaibatsus and the dissolution of the special banks. The aim, in line with US practice, was to reorganize the financial system to ensure a degree of concentration far lower than had previously prevailed. A further import from the United States was the separation of commercial lending and securities-underwriting activities.

The Japanese Ministry of Finance and Ministry of International Trade and Industry (MITI) were to have far more influence on reconstruction and economic growth than their equivalents in many other countries, especially the United States. The forging of close ties between government and industry and the re-emergence of conglomerates are today important irritants in the trading relationships between Japan and the Western industrialized countries.

## FINANCIAL INSTITUTIONS AND FINANCIAL INSTRUMENTS

The particular characteristics of the Japanese banking system include the policies known as overloan and overborrowing, and an imbalance in the liquidity positions of large and small banks.

The overloan policy is one that maintains net bank reserves—that is, cash in the banks and reserves at the central bank—in a negative position by making loans or investments funded from sources other than deposits or equity. To put the point differently, Japanese banks are essentially in debt to the central bank; unlike the case in other industrialized countries, its loans to financial institutions are larger than the reserves they hold with it. Borrowing from the central bank is routine, a policy that stems from the Bank of Japan's lack of open market operations (until fairly recently) and from regulations fixing the quantity of new loans and the rates on consumer deposits, thereby limiting the new liquidity in the system.[24]

Until the 1980s, overlending used to be a phenomenon of city banks (large banks that control a significant market share), while other financial institutions had positive net reserves. This imbalance can be partially explained by the relatively favourable position of city banks in their access and ability to borrow from the central bank and by the relatively greater demand for credit from them. A city bank is usually the main bank for some large industrial enterprise.

A second distinguishing characteristic of the Japanese financial system is called overborrowing,[25] by which is meant the corporate sector's reliance on bank loans instead of equity to raise funds. The reasons for this feature of the Japanese financial system have to do with the historically close ties between commercial and banking concerns as well as with the prohibitions of stock market operations imposed by the Americans for a short time after World War II. The result is little effective competition between the banking and non-banking sectors. In addition, the latter tends to lend to high-risk enterprises. The implication is that the non-banking sector faces a high degree of credit risk; only government assistance prevents large-scale failures.

### Types of Financial Institutions

Table 22.4 provides some summary statistics about the Japanese banking industry. As already noted, the Japanese banking system has two kinds of commercial

24 Apparently, overlending by the central bank can be traced to the Meiji era, when it was a means of ensuring the liquidity necessary to advance Japanese industrialization.

25 For no apparently good reason except as a (confusing) way of distinguishing Japanese finance from Western finance. A more apt description would be that indirect lending dominates direct lending in the flow of funds in Japan.

**Table 22.4** BANKING ACTIVITY IN JAPAN, 1995

| | |
|---|---|
| **Number of Banks** | |
| City banks | 10 |
| Regional banks | 64 |
| Regional banks II | 65 |
| Long-term credit banks | 3 |
| Trust banks | 8 |
| Total | 150 |
| **Size of Different Types of Banks (assets in 100 million ¥)** | |
| City banks | 3,399,414 |
| Regional banks | 1,950,278 |
| Regional banks II | 721,979 |
| Long-term credit banks | 749,380 |
| Trust banks | 585,629 |
| Total | 7,406,680 |

Note: Percentages of assets and liabilities do not add to 100 because of omission of small items.

Sources: Economic Statistics Monthly (Bank of Japan), January 1996; and *Japanese Banks '94* (Federation of Bankers Assoc. of Japan) (*Zenginkyo*).

banks. **City banks** operate in large urban areas but have nationwide branching.[26] They tend to be the main banks for industrial conglomerates and are likely to have an international finance division. City banks are also by far the dominant commercial lenders, and because of their links with industrial groups, a significant portion of their loans are long term. They take deposits from individuals as well as commercial enterprises; the latter deposits tend to be large—exceeding ¥10 million or more.[27]

Regional banks are the other type of commercial bank. Each operates much like a city bank except its financial base is restricted to a city or a prefecture (roughly equivalent to a province). Because of their relatively strong local presence, these banks are akin to North American or European savings banks. Since the early 1990s, two types of regional banks have coexisted. Regional banks II, as they are called by the Bank of Japan, are members of the Second Association of regional banks.

Apart from the commercial banks, the Japanese banking system includes specialized institutions called long-term credit banks. The assets and liabilities of such institutions are long term in their maturity structure. Other types of spe-

26 There are no nationwide branching restrictions, although approval for new branches must be obtained from the Ministry of Finance.

27 Approximately $124,000 at 1996 exchange rates.

cialized financial institutions include the *Shinkin* banks (credit association), *Shoko Chukin* bank (central co-operative bank for commerce and industry), *Norinchukin* bank (central co-operative for agriculture and forestry) and so-called labour banks.

There are also trusts, which do not have to conduct their operations separately from commercial banking activities. An important function of Japanese trusts in the management of pension funds and mutual funds; they also act as investment counsellors.

The Japanese banking industry is rounded out with a variety of other depository institutions, such as the postal savings banks,[28] which are similar in nature and scope to Canadian credit unions, and government depository institutions. (Table 22.4 does not list these institutions because they are not officially known as "banks," even though they perform banking-type services.)[29]

Japanese banking law governs banks and defines what they can do. Since 1982 reforms, they have been able to underwrite some types of securities, such as government-backed securities. Further reforms in 1994 permitted select commercial banks to move into the securities market. Nevertheless, the division between commercial lending and securities underwriting still exists, although institutions find ways around it. For example, the pertinent article of the Act was written to regulate domestic institutions. But by the 1980s, foreign institutions were beginning to appear in the Japanese market and to underwrite corporate securities. Japanese banks expanded overseas and began to engage in underwriting activities. The combination of a regulatory loophole and the desire to treat foreign and domestic financial institutions on an equal footing is eroding the barrier between commercial lending and underwriting activities. In 1992, when the Japanese Diet (Parliament) approved the Financial System Reform Bill, this led to the formation of subsidiaries of trust banks and of commercial banks in 1993 and 1994 whose function was to underwrite securities. Moreover, many of the restrictions governing interest rates were abolished as well.

An unhappy distinguishing characteristic of the Japanese financial system has been the unusually large number of financial scandals involving banks and securities companies.[30] Securities companies have been found to be covering the

---

28 The postal savings banks play a role in the flow of funds since almost one-third of households hold deposits in such institutions.

29 There is insufficient space here to deal with financial institutions such as securities, underwriters, and insurance companies. Good sources on these topics include T.F.M. Adams and I. Hoshi, *A Financial History of the New Japan* (Tokyo: Kadansho International Ltd., 1972), Part II, chapters 2, 4; L.S. Presnell, ed., *Money and Banking in Japan* (New York: St. Martin's Press, 1973), chapters 18, 20; and A. Viner, *Inside Japanese Financial Markets* (Homewood, Ill.: Dow Jones-Irwin, 1988).

30 In particular, (now defunct) home-mortgage companies (called *Jusen*) who could not or would not pay back interest and principal on loans from the main banks. See J. Sapsford "Don't Be Fooled: Japan's Banks Are Still in Trouble," *Wall Street Journal*, 3 May 1996, p. A6.

losses of large clients in the stock exchange. Banks have been caught making a substantial number of illegal loans. It is noteworthy, however, that no commercial bank has failed in the postwar period although their high degree of leverage, the scandals, and the burst real estate bubble have placed many of them on shaky financial ground. As a result, postal banks, that is, banks operated through the post office, experienced dramatic growth because accounts are guaranteed, interest rates are favourable, terms are flexible, and minimum deposits are smaller than at commercial banks.[31]

After the scandals, Japanese banks seemed to experience a recovery of sorts but it was a false recovery as many banks underestimated, often deliberately so, their bad loans problems stemming from the real estate price bubble which burst in the early 1990s. The bad loans themselves were facilitated by bankers, many of whom at one time were regulators themselves or worked for the Finance Ministry and had thus "descended from heaven" (*amakudari* in Japanese). Eventually, not only did government bureaucrats advise the Finance Ministry not to prosecute the fraudulent activities of bankers but, with the effective failure of seven out of eight *jusen* or mortgage lending companies, the government opted for a massive bailout in 1995 and 1996 at taxpayers expense.[32]

## TYPES OF FINANCIAL ASSETS

In Japan, unlike in North America, the market for corporate bonds or commercial paper is fairly small. Regulatory impediments, particularly collateral requirements, used to be severe enough to prevent a large market from emerging in such instruments. Although deregulation has eased restrictions, growth in the domestic market has been very slow because borrowing from abroad has been either cheaper or easier to obtain. Therefore, there is a large market for European paper.

In general, financial innovations have been hampered by strict Ministry of Finance regulations. There are restrictions on the interest paid on deposits, personal cheques are not widely used, and many government bonds are issued at negotiated rates, rather than in an auction setting. Treasury bills are comparatively rarely used since the Bank of Japan, as noted earlier, does not rely on open market operations to influence interest rates, which are highly regulated. Since the 1970s, however, there has been a significant amount of deregulation. Capital flow restrictions were dropped; so were restrictions on interest rates on large time de-

31 See "Japan's Banks Find Tough Rival in Aggressive Postal System," *Wall Street Journal*, 29 October 1992, p. A3; and "Japan's Ambitious Postal Bank," *The Economist*, 29 October 1994, pp. 89–90.

32 For a description of the events, see M. Williams, "Many Japanese Banks Run Amok while Run by Former Regulators," *Wall Street Journal*, 19 January 1996, p. A1; and J. Sapsford, "Japanese Banks Bracing for a Bitter Pill," *Wall Street Journal*, 21 February 1996, p. A11.

posits. There are no interest rate ceilings on CDs, which accounts for their important role in the measurement of the domestic money supply. Since 1985 especially, money market certificates have grown in popularity as the minimum deposits were reduced to levels within the range of households. And negotiable CDs and large-denomination time deposits have become important financial instruments. (Indeed, when interest rates were decontrolled, these markets grew so quickly that the Bank of Japan had to alter somewhat its monetary policy operations.)

Nevertheless, financial deregulation has been slower in Japan than elsewhere in the industrialized world. Nevertheless, by 1995 most interest rates were deregulated.

In the money market or short-term wholesale end of the financial market, which is free from interest rate or other issue regulations, there are two important financial instruments: the *tegata*, which are discounted bills issued for terms of two weeks to six months; and the gensaki.

The **gensaki market**, which trades repurchase agreements, negotiable certificates of deposit, money market certificates, and bankers' acceptances, is the most important market for finding out the market-clearing short-term interest rate. Its basis is long-term government bonds to which are attached a condition that the seller will repurchase them at a date agreed upon in advance.[33] Thus, a long-term instrument is effectively converted into a short-term instrument.[34] (Most of these repurchase agreements mature in three months, and since the Bank of Japan guarantees government bonds, the gensaki market is in essence the counterpart to the Canadian Treasury bill market.) The gensaki market is the repository of short-term cash and is thus influential in the short-term liquidity of the Japanese financial markets.

The Japanese call market (interbank market) is less competitive than those of other countries. Neither corporations nor individuals are permitted to engage in call or discounted bill transactions in the money market, and call money rates cannot fall below the Bank of Japan's discount rate. But only since November 1988 can the call money rate be said to be an important indicator of monetary policy. Since that time the central bank has used the call money market as the federal funds market is used in the United States. Generally, city banks borrow in the call money market and lend in the discounted bills market but, beginning in the 1970s, regional banks also became participants in the interbank market.[35]

---

33 Tax considerations have an important impact on the term to maturity of repurchase agreements in Japan. Since the tax is not dependent on the maturity it is relatively more costly to hold, say, 1-month repurchases than ones with a longer term to maturity.

34 The term *gensaki* is a composite of *gen* ("the present") and *saki* ("the future").

35 One of the reasons for the imbalance of funds in the Japanese financial markets referred to earlier is that,

The interbank network also operates the clearinghouse for the financial system. All financial institutions participate in it directly or indirectly. Settlement of net balances is done, as in most other industrialized countries, with transfers in the accounts the financial institutions hold with the Bank of Japan. Transactions between banks and non-banking institutions are handled through a computerized network called the **zengin system**. It permits funds to be available simultaneously, even if they have not been officially released with the transfer guaranteed by the Bank of Japan.

The retail level of the Japanese financial system has a narrow range of bank deposits with interest-earning or chequing features. Essentially, there exist *current deposits*, which earn no interest whatsoever, and *ordinary deposits*, which are like current deposits except they are not chequable. Some ordinary accounts can be combined with other types of deposits that yield interest, such as government-backed funds or time deposits. In one such arrangement, funds are transferred from a time deposit to an ordinary deposit as required (subject to some limitations).

## BANK OF JAPAN OPERATIONS

Like all modern banks, the Bank of Japan assists the financial system by acting as a clearinghouse for banks, by discounting bills, and by purchasing and selling government securities. Its lending rate for rediscounted commercial bills is the official discount rate. In addition, of course, the Bank of Japan acts as a central banker for the government, regulates the banking sectors, and implements policy on monetary growth and exchange rates.

Until fairly recently, the Bank of Japan made extensive use of a technique called window guidance: that is, instructing financial institutions to increase or to reduce loans. With deregulation, the Bank will increasingly rely on short-term instruments, such as discounted bills, to influence interest rates. Since 1975, the Bank's policy has been a mixture of monetary growth rules and interventions in the market for foreign exchange to ensure that the yen stays within desired levels.

The conversion to *monetarism* was, in part, a reflection of similar changes taking place elsewhere in the industrialized world and in part a recoil from the disastrous inflation consequences of the policies of the early 1970s. Under those policies, which included fixed exchange rates, Japanese inflation was consistently higher than that of Germany, the United States, and Canada, especially during

---

until 1985, institutions with excess funds could only lend them. Institutions that chronically experienced shortages of funds could only issue bills. Thus, banks could not simultaneously supply funds in the interbank market and issue bills. The major reason for the change was that accumulated trade surpluses meant that most banks became suppliers of funds and the market for the issue of bills threatened to disappear.

the oil price shock of 1973–74. Since the country switched to a flexible exchange rate régime and introduced other market-driven policies, its inflation record has been one of the best in the world, making it appear a good example of the successful implementations of monetarism.

Because of the importance of the money supply in Japanese monetary policy, it is instructive to consider how the country's monetary aggregates are compiled (see Table 22.5). The definitions of M1, M2 + CD are roughly comparable to Canadian equivalents.

Because of the way the Bank of Japan is organized, there is considerable discussion about its independence. On paper, it has always been under the firm control of the government. Indeed, the enabling act states:

> The Government shall control all the operations of the Bank of Japan, and shall prevent not only any operation which is contrary to the Act or Bylaws, but also any measure that the Government may deem disadvantageous for the State.

As a result, the Minister of Finance can dismiss any officer of the Bank and issue orders relating to all aspects of its business.

The Bank's governor, who has less individual influence than the Canadian or US counterparts, is appointed by the government, often from within the Bank or the Ministry of Finance, for a five-year term. The governor is a member of the executive board that actually formulates monetary policy. The decisions of the executive are executed by a policy board that consists of the governor, non-voting representatives from the Ministry of Finance and the Economic Planning Agency, and four representatives from various sectors of the economy.

Although the day-to-day management of monetary policy instruments is today largely left in the hands of the Bank, the Ministry of Finance still plays a major role in significant policy questions. Nevertheless it is generally conceded that, since the mid-1970s the Bank has increasingly exercised considerable independence in monetary policy. It also has independent influence in financial affairs by virtue of setting ceilings on deposit rates and running the interbank market. And execution of the window guidance policy is mostly under its control. In brief, although the Bank is legally dependent on the government, it is apparently more independent in substance.

## GERMANY

Three outstanding events mark the financial history of Germany in this century. The first is the hyperinflation of the 1920s, which may have been a cause of World War II and certainly led to today's near-universal dislike of inflation in Germany. The second is the "economic miracle" of a post-World War II trans-

**Table 22.5** MONETARY AGGREGATES IN JAPAN, 1995

| | Details | Billions of Yen ('000s) |
|---|---|---|
| — | Currency in circulation | 417,275 |
| M1 | Currency **plus** demand deposits | 1,621,550 |
| M2 + CD | M2 plus certificates of deposit | 5,496,389 |
| Broadly defined liquidity | | 11,017,182 |

Because the Japanese banking system is not of a dual nature, as it is in Canada and the United States, the definitions of the money supply need reflect no distinction between, say, chartered banks and near-banks.

Source: *Economic Statistics Monthly* (January 1996), p. 14. The data are for the month of December, not seasonally adjusted.

formation from a war-ravaged country to an economy so strong that it has become a leader in the emerging European Community (EC). The third event is the reunification of Germany, which has had some important financial consequences although it is too early to draw conclusions about their exact dimensions.

## HISTORICAL BACKGROUND

For a country that did not even exist as a unified nation until 1871, Germany has undergone a remarkable number of historic events, many of them affecting and affected by its financial history.

### The Pre-World War I Period

For the first three-quarters of the nineteenth century, Germany was a collection of states, some with more independence than others. Consequently, the financial system was made up of a collection of different issuers of notes and coins and, perhaps as a consequence, Germany was thought to be less financially sophisticated than nations such as Great Britain.

In 1834, the states formed a customs union, called the Zollverein. Its elimination of tariff barriers spurred economic and financial growth.

A distinguishing characteristic of German financial development was the combination of commercial lending and investment or *merchant banking* activities, including the acceptance of discounted bills and the placing of loans and securities. These early activities were successful at stimulating industrialization. The separation of commercial lending and securities-underwriting activities never became a feature of the German financial system.

Until German unification in 1871, several states issued their own coins or bank notes, and private bankers provided most of the payments mechanism. Modern central banking was introduced with the formation of the Reichsbank in 1876.

## FINANCIAL FOCUS 22.1 Merging Two Different Economic and Financial Systems: German Reunification

Spring 1990 marked the beginning of negotiations for the reunification of West Germany and East Germany. In economic terms, reunification meant the lifting of all trade and tax barriers, as well as the free flow of capital and labour. It also represented the advent of a common currency and exchange rate, which required setting an exchange rate between the West German deutschmark and the former East German ostmark. (See **Exchange Rates and Politics**, the **FINANCIAL FOCUS** in Chapter 7.)

The lack of knowledge about the true state of the East German economy meant that the room for error in setting the exchange rate and other policies was very large. An especially difficult aspect of reunification was wage policy. Practically overnight former East German residents faced West German prices with East German wages. Moreover, the plants and equipment in the old East Germany could not hope to be competitive with those of the highly industrialized West Germany. The outcome was a state in which the real wage—the purchasing power of wages—was low in the East relative to the West. That fact combined with the East's low productivity set the stage for a rapid decline of production in the former East Germany. By the end of 1990, it was less than half its 1989 value. Not surprisingly, the East suffered an economic depression of sorts throughout 1991.

Meanwhile there was the problem of integrating the two financial systems. Banks in centrally planned economies do not operate as they do in industrialized economies. East Germany had had only one main bank, the State Bank of the German Democratic Republic, plus a few specialized institutions that funnelled funds for, say, trade or agriculture. Individuals could open certain types of savings accounts but had little incentive to do so since the interest they received was relatively low. Moreover, individuals and small enterprises were essentially unable to borrow from the State Bank, so it never really functioned as an intermediary in the conventional sense. Financial transactions were generally cash-based.

With reunification, West German banks began to expand into the East. During the transition period, the German Credit Bank took over the activities of the former State Bank.

Meanwhile, reunification proved enormously more difficult and more costly than originally hoped. The Bundesbank looked on in dismay. It had opposed the conversion rates for the mark, saying that they were too high, and it had pleaded for less rapid reunification. When it lost both battles on political grounds, its credibility was eroded. The president resigned before his term was over. It did, however, win back some of its reputation for independence by sharply raising interest rates in 1990 and 1991. And it generally managed to maintain the foreign exchange rates of the deutschmark.

**Sources:**

G.A. Akerloff, A.K. Rose, J.L. Yellen, and H. Hessenius, "East Germany in from the Cold: The Economic Aftermath of Currency Union," *Brookings Papers on Economic Activity I* (1991): 1–106.

"The Monetary Union with the German Democratic Republic," *Monthly Report of the Bundesbank*, July 1990, 13–28.

J. Von Hagen, "Monetary Policy and Monetary Union: Germany 1990–92," in *Varieties of Monetary Reforms: Lessons and Experiences on the Road to Monetary Union*, ed. P.L. Siklos (Dordrecht: Kluwer Academic Publishers, 1994), pp. 219–46.

Until 1870, the **kreditbanken** (credit bank) played a vital role in financing industrial expansion. Initially operating in Prussia (the dominant German state), it had expanded into other states by the middle of the nineteenth century. It was the only bank of its kind at the time, and Prussia did not charter any other such institutions until 1870.

In any event, the growth of credit was largely determined by the ability of private bankers to create it. Generally, they issued *bills of exchange*. Unlike those of other countries, German bills were not rediscounted. Rather, borrowers used these bills much as individuals today use cheques to draw funds from the bank (except, of course, bills carried an interest payment). Nevertheless, bills could be passed on to other parties, thus facilitating the growth of credit, which was typically short term.

## The German Hyperinflation

After Germany became unified in 1871, both its economy and its financial system developed quickly until World War I. The financial aftermath of that conflict began with the Treaty of Versailles, by which the victors, who were in no mood to let bygones be bygones, imposed enormous reparations payments on Germany and the countries of the former Austro-Hungarian Empire.

Germany faced the necessity of making these huge payments in gold and foreign currencies. It also faced a war-ravaged economy unable to generate tax revenues sufficient to cover government expenditures. And it clung to a policy that, in effect, permitted private industry to borrow unlimited amounts from the central government. Its answer was to issue—and overissue—currency, and the result was a devastating *hyperinflation* that began in 1921 and did not end until late 1923.[36]

The socioeconomic consequences (most notably, a sharp rise in unemployment and the almost complete devaluation of investments) combined with the humiliation of the war reparations themselves ensured that fear of high inflation would henceforth become the dominant theme of German monetary policy. To this day, Germany has consistently produced some of the lowest inflation rates among the Western industrialized countries.

Price stability came during the National Socialist (Nazi) era, largely as the result of heavy regulation imposed on the entire economy, affecting both prices and wages. In addition, as Germany increased its sphere of influence and control over neighbouring countries to the east and south, it began to export its debt, thus reducing the need to resort to inflation-fuelling monetization. Part of this policy was the arrangement known as the clearing account system: international payments were not to be made in currency; rather, positive and negative balances

36 The German hyperinflation is undoubtedly the episode of high inflation most analysed by economists. See, for example, P.L. Siklos, "Hyperinflations: Their Origin, Development and Termination," *Journal of Economic Surveys* 4 (1990): 225–48.

would be recorded with the stated intention that continued trading of goods and services would eventually produce balanced trade. Instead, however, Germany utilized the arrangement to accumulate a large indebtedness with Hungary and other countries.

### World War II and Its Aftermath

During World War II, the German government borrowed mainly by issuing discounted bills, suspending normal credit operations to the public, and rationing consumer goods to facilitate military and related production. It used these methods, rather than borrowing from the Reichsbank, precisely because of fears of igniting a new round of hyperinflation.

After the war, the authorities introduced a currency reform meant to ensure that, given the country's then dire economic straits, inflation would not reappear. Thus, the conversion factor for old reichsmarks into deutschmarks was important, as were controls on credit. In general, the transition was successful; only a small slump in economic activity followed the war. With loans from the United States through the Marshall Plan, Germany was set for its postwar miracle. By 1960, its economic activity, measured by industrial production, compared favourably with that of the United States, and in the 1980s its economic growth often exceeded that country's. Germany had gained a place as one of the largest economies of the industrialized world with one of the steadiest currencies, a leader in the European Community and in the possible European Monetary Union.

## FINANCIAL INTERMEDIARIES

Banks in Germany, as in Japan, grew rapidly, especially during the 1980s, in relation to the economy as a whole as well as in relation to banks in the United States and the United Kingdom. Their importance is also reflected in the fact that more than 50% of the funds borrowed by the business sector is obtained via bank loans. In addition, banks play a dominant role in the stock exchanges since only they can act as brokers for the public.

Of all the banking systems analyzed in this text, that of Germany is the least regulated.[37] The model is that of *universal banking*: banks are permitted to engage in all forms of intermediation, including insurance and the underwriting of securities.[38] (The German term used to describe this arrangement is **allfinanz**, which means roughly that the banks behave like financial supermarkets.) Despite this ability to engage in a wide variety of financial transactions, and despite the his-

---

37 Though the differences with the recently reformed system of the United Kingdom are comparatively small.

38 Until recently, however, the banks have tended to avoid insurance and the home-loan savings sector.

torical predominance of large banks, the assets of Germany's largest banks do not represent a larger fraction of the total assets of the banking sector than those of the largest institutions in either the United Kingdom or the United States.[39]

Given the modicum of regulation, it is not surprising that German banks hold sizeable equity interests in non-financial corporations. Moreover, a bank typically has a seat on the supervisory board (board of directors) of corporations.[40]

The system includes

1. Large banks, which have nationwide branch networks. Some also have overseas branches.

2. Regional banks, which are full-service banks but lack a nationwide network of branches. They are relatively more involved in mortgage lending than the large banks.

3. **Private banks** which are owned by sole proprietors or partnerships. These are among the oldest banks in Germany; in early German financial history they financed the establishment of joint-stock banks, and today they continue to specialize in the funding of industrial investment projects. (They resemble Canada's merchant banks.)

4. Foreign banks, which are not restricted to the activities they may engage in.

5. Banks said to be *incorporated under public law*. They include savings banks, which originally took in only savings deposits and made loans only for real estate purposes, and giro institutions. The growth of the latter was facilitated after World War I by the formation of the **girozentralen** (the central giro organization), which let these locally based savings organizations take advantage of the efficiencies of a large organization.

6. Co-operatives, the largest group in terms of the total number of branches. Their numbers have, however, fallen significantly from their 1960s peak of more than 11,000. (The drop was the result of a merger policy designed to make co-ops more efficient and, therefore, more competitive relative to the other financial institutions.) The principles behind the creation of German co-ops differed little from those that led to Canadian credit unions, except

---

39 One area banks have been slow to move into is in insurance. In 1994, however, price deregulation in this market has led several of the larger German banks to move into the insurance sector. See "All Aboard for Allfinanz," *The Economist*, 25 September 1993, p. 85–6.

40 This custom might suggest that German banks have some comparative advantage about the state of the companies they are involved with. Supervisory boards meet infrequently, however, and may not have superior financial information. Moreover, the banks' seats do not appear to permit them to tell company managers what to do.

the founders of the co-op movement began by providing intermediary services to small industries and the agricultural sector. By the 1980s, however, more than over half the membership consisted of wage- and salary-earners and civil servants.

7. Specialist banks, which are banks that fulfil special functions. Some of these institutions finance the development of exports, loans to developing countries that trade with Germany, improvement projects, and so on. Others are mortgage banks, which lend primarily to public agencies, including the federal government, the states, and municipalities. Mortgage banks "incorporated under public law" provide loans to landowners and, in urban areas, to individuals with modest incomes. The institutions that most closely resemble the Canadian mortgage loan companies are the home-loan societies, which are effectively terminating societies. (The private banks are close to being specialist banks, but the official statistics report the former separately.)

Much commercial banking is concentrated in Frankfurt, one of the cities vying for status as the largest international financial centre; the other contenders are Düsseldorf, Hamburg, and Munich.

German banks are supervised under a banking law; problems and disputes are handled by the Federal Supervisory Office, an independent agency under the federal Minister of Finance.

## FINANCIAL INSTRUMENTS

Because of the universal banking nature of the German financial system, a large fraction of financial transactions are done via bank intermediaries. As in many countries, globalization is eliminating the differences in the types of instruments from those offered worldwide. For example, the German system had lagged in futures and options markets. But on 1 January 1991 a futures and options exchange, called the **Deutsche Terminbörse**, was introduced.

The bond market is dominated by fixed-interest securities. Some of these bonds are issued by the public sector, which includes, among others, the federal, state, and local governments.[41] Banks issue other bonds, which are used, in part, to finance loans made to the public sector. The majority of the bonds issued are, however, corporate bonds; they are generally taken up by the banks, which then make a secondary market in these instruments.

---

41 Governments' issues of bonds are, however, a smaller proportion of total issues in Germany than in most other countries of the European Community. This statement continues to be true despite the recent increase in public borrowing necessitated by the costs of reunification.

The money markets in Germany deal in instruments traded among credit institutions as well as between those same institutions and the Bundesbank. The Bundesbank plays a central role in these markets; purchase and resale agreements, foreign exchange swaps, and transactions that affect the banks' deposits at the central bank (that is, the reserves of the banking system) are among the instruments at its disposal in influencing short-term liquidity and thereby short-term interest rates. Since these assets are similar to their Canadian equivalents, there is no need to describe their operation here. One unusual device is **Lombard credit**: the Bundesbank lends against the pledge of securities (relatively high-quality collateral). The Lombard rate is thus a key indicator of the stance of monetary policy. In 1993 the Bundesbank began to offer discounted bills (that is, Treasury bills) sold by auction and nicknamed "Bubills." All interest and redemption commitments are to be met by the Bundesbank. The minimum denomination is DM100,000 with maturities of three, six, and nine months. The first issue is for DM25 billion. One explanation given for the introduction of this money market instrument is that it was created to soak up funds in the economy that might otherwise fuel inflation. However, as the bonds are available to foreigners as well, it is not immediately clear how this device will contribute to helping the fight against inflation.[42]

Like Japan, Germany considers its balance of payments position of central importance to its economy. Consequently, the Bundesbank is especially concerned with the exchange rate of the deutschmark in relation to other major currencies, such as the Japanese yen and the US dollar. (The importance of the exchange rate is further evidenced by the central role played by the deutschmark in the European Monetary System.) Thus, the Bundesbank has actively engaged in foreign exchange swap transactions since 1958. Since 1979, it has also relied on purchase and resale agreements in foreign exchange to supplement its influence on assets denominated in foreign currencies. These activities have become especially important as the EC moves toward complete financial integration.

Day-to-day loans, interbank loans and deposits, and acceptances are among the other important instruments of the German financial system. All are essentially the same as those of Canada.

Like Canada, Germany has moved to an electronic clearing system which began operation in early 1996. The Frankfurt Electronic Clearing System is meant to facilitate same-day clearing with sixty-seven institutions participating in the system, at least initially.

---

42 See "Bundesbank Has Reason to Cheer," *The European* (11–14 February 1993): 37; "Buba Shortcuts the Market," *The European* (25–28 February 1993): 36; *Deutsche Bundesbank Monthly Report* (February 1993): 15–16.

Reforms in 1994 led to new regulations to prevent a recurrence of the scandals in 1992, when some prominent Germans were accused of insider trading, and led to the introduction of money-market funds popular in the UK, United States and Canada.

## BUNDESBANK OPERATIONS

The **Bundesbank**, the German central bank, enjoys a reputation as a guarantor of price stability. Its success is thought to come from the lessons of history, its statutory independence from the absence of government interference, and the fact that it is one of the world's few central banks with a specific mandate that, translated, is meant to ensure price stability. In other respects, it performs the same functions as the other central banks we have discussed; acting as government banker and banker of last resort, guiding interest rates, implementing monetary and exchange rate policy, and so on.

The Bundesbank is a post-World War II institution, but it is descended from the prewar Reichsbank, which itself was reorganized a number of times because of wars, changes in government, and hyperinflation. After World War II, Germany was divided into four zones of occupation, each under the control of one of the victorious Allied powers. They differed considerably on how to reorganize the German financial system. The United States was first among the four equals, and initially its experience influenced the overall regulation. But disagreements about the degree of autonomy to be enjoyed by the new central bank, as well as the Marshall Plan for the economic recovery of Europe, delayed the founding of the Bundesbank until the late 1950s.

Although endowed with a large degree of legal independence, the Bundesbank is formally owned by the federal government. It is managed by a council, which is headed by a president and which consists of a board of directors and the presidents of the land (state) central banks. (The latter are a relic of the immediate postwar era when each of the country's zones of occupation possessed a central bank of sorts, though all operated under one currency.) With German reunification, the number of land banks has increased slightly, although not all land banks formerly in East Germany have their own central bank. Notice the overall resemblance of the structure of the council to that of the US Federal Reserve System. Moreover, the president of the Bundesbank, like the chair of the Fed, wields considerable power in dictating the stance of monetary policy. Although the president is appointed by the federal government, the president's eight-year term is not concurrent with the normal life of the government, and the federal government is unable to exert any immediate impact on the overall composition of the council.

**Table 22.6** MONETARY AGGREGATES IN GERMANY, 1995

| | Details | Billions DM |
|---|---|---|
| M1 | Notes and coins **plus** domestic sight deposits | 736.3 |
| M2 | M1 **plus** time deposits maturing in less than 4 years | 1,186.9 |
| M3 | M2 **plus** savings deposits subject to withdrawal notice | 1,894.6 |
| M3 extended | M3 **plus** money market funds | 2,195.8 |

Note: Does not include data from the former East Germany.

Source: *Deutsche Bundesbank Monthly Report* 48 (January 1996), p. 10. The data are for October and include two from East German territory.

Because of the autonomy of the central bank, there have occasionally been conflicts with the federal government over monetary policy. But it has usually managed to act independently.

We have already described the principal instruments of monetary policy used by the Bundesbank to set interest rates. In addition, like the US Federal Reserve System and some other central banks, the Bundesbank announces target ranges for the growth rate in the broad money stock called M3 (see Table 22.6). Indeed, it is one of the last remaining industrial countries to announce targets for money growth despite its overall lack of success at meeting them.[43]

Table 22.7 compares the five major banking systems discussed in this chapter.

## SUMMARY


- Financial systems in other countries differ significantly in some respects from the Canadian system. In this chapter, we briefly survey financial systems in the United States, the United Kingdom, Japan, and Germany.

- The US model is distinct in that banks have limited opportunities to develop nationwide branching. Moreover, US banks have tended to fail far more frequently, and in far greater numbers, than Canadian banks. Not surprisingly, the UK model is closest to the Canadian one.

- The German model is distinguished by the fact that banks are permitted to engage in all forms of financing including the sale of stocks and the underwriting of securities. The German financial performance since the end of World War II, as measured by inflation, is also greatly affected by that country's experience with hyperinflation during the 1920s.


43 Since 1975, the Bundesbank has failed to reach its target about half the time. See "Bundesbank's Guessing Game," *The European*, 10–16 December 1993, p. 18–19.

**Table 22.7** FIVE MAJOR BANKING SYSTEMS COMPARED

| | Canada | United States | United Kingdom | Japan | Germany |
|---|---|---|---|---|---|
| Regulators | Bank of Canada and provincial governments | Variety of federal and state agencies (see Table 22.1) | Bank of England and the Treasury | Ministry of Finance and Bank of Japan | Bundesbank, with role for Länder (states) |
| Branching restrictions | None | Yes, depending on the state | None | None | None |
| Deposit insurance | Since 1967; publicly funded | Since the 1930s; publicly funded; one of most generous in world | Since 1982, public | Since 1971, private | Privately funded |
| Bank failures | Very few | Many | Few | None | Few |
| Reserve requirements | None | Yes; uniform across types of financial institutions since 1980 | None | Yes | Yes |
| Concentration | Relatively few large banks but considerably more competitors since 1980 Bank Act | Many small banks, few large ones; competition somewhat restricted by regulatory agencies | Highly competitive since the 1980s | High, but changing | Highly competitive |
| Central banking | Bank of Canada. Some autonomy from federal government in fact but not in law. Statutory objectives not clear. Little effective regional voice, and policy conducted in relative secrecy | Federal Reserve. Considered independent of federal government. Power is centralized but regions have a say in monetary policy | Bank of England. Not seen as independent since ultimate authority rests with the Treasury | Bank of Japan. Relatively independent in substance not in law; close ties with Ministry of Finance | Bundesbank. Great autonomy. Regions have a voice. Statutory mandate for price stability |
| Central bank borrowing | Discouraged but possible | Readily available | Readily available | Common practice | Readily available |
| Commercial lending and securities underwriting separated? | Yes, but has begun to change | Yes, but likely to change substantially | No longer effectively | No; rule relaxed | No; universal banking model |

- The Japanese financial system, until recently, was largely modelled after the post-World War II US system. The success of Japan as an exporter has meant that large pools of funds need to be allocated in a fairly regulated financial system. Also, Japanese banks have been encouraged to engage in considerably more leverage than banks in other industrialized countries. Consequently, the recent sharp fall in asset prices has meant that significant portions of the financial system have technically become insolvent.
- Throughout the chapter the historical development of the financial system, the basic operations of monetary policy, and the principal financial instruments are discussed for each country.

## IMPORTANT TERMS

allfinanz (p. 521)
Bank of England (p. 502)
Bank of Japan (p. 508)
Big Bang (p. 504)
building societies (p. 502)
Bundesbank (p. 525)
city banks (p. 512)
corset (p. 507)
Deutsche Terminbörse (p. 523)
the Federal Reserve (the Fed) (p. 498)
gensaki market (p. 515)
gilt-edged securities (gilts) (p. 505)
ginko (p. 509)
giro system (p. 503)
girozentralen (p. 522)
Glass–Stegall Act (p. 496)
investment bank (p. 496)
kreditbanken (p. 519)
Lombard credit (p. 524)
minimum lending rate (p. 507)
negotiable order of withdrawal (NOW) (p. 497)
private banks (p. 522)
savings and loan associations (S&Ls) (p. 495)
unit banking (p. 515)
zaibatsu (p. 508)
zengin system (p. 516)

## EXERCISES

1. The United States' financial system is often referred to as a dual banking system. Why?
2. Almost 70% of mortgages issued by the United States' S&Ls in 1984 had adjustable rates. By 1986, approximately 70% of mortgages had fixed rates. In retrospect, why did S&Ls wish they had issued fixed-rate mortgages in 1984 and adjustable-rate ones in 1986? Explain.
3. S&Ls borrow short term and lend long term. What is the problem with such

a strategy when there is an unexpected increase in all interest rates? Why is it necessary that the increases be unexpected?

4. What arguments would you marshall for the policy that advocates the separation of commercial lending and securities-underwriting activities? Explain.
5. When the United States finally removed interest rate restrictions, its banks limited cheque-writing privileges on money-market deposit accounts in particular. Why? Explain.
6. What are some of the similarities and differences in the operation of UK and Canadian monetary policy? Explain.
7. Why was the Big Bang such an important event in the United Kingdom's financial history? Explain your answer.
8. Are regional differences in the UK financial sector as important or as apparent as those that prevail in Canada? Explain your answer.
9. Why were the UK credit controls of the 1960s largely ineffective in controlling access to liquidity? Explain your answer.
10. Some analysts think that the significant change in Japan's net capital flows in 1991 had the effect of raising interest rates in the United States (and, by implication, Canada). Can the loanable funds model (see Chapter 6) help us understand how this might happen? Explain your answer.
11. Explain how regulations that severely limit the size of the Japanese money market have led to a situation in which Japanese non-bank institutions lend to borrowers with a high credit risk.
12. Why is the debate about the substance versus the laws governing central bank behaviour particularly important in the Japanese case? Explain your answer.
13. Explain, in terms of the leverage discussion of Chapter 10, why the 1991 bursting of the real estate bubble in Japan placed its financial system at risk.
14. Explain, in economic terms, why the Nazis were afraid of inflation in designing their wartime economic policies.
15. Can the loanable funds model (see Chapter 6) explain the sharp rise in the German interest rate in 1990 apparently caused by the monetary consequences of German reunification? Use a diagram and explain your answer.
16. Since the Bundesbank directly controls Germany's central bank money, why does it set targets for a broad aggregate such as M3?
17. Outline the principal differences between the four banking systems considered in this chapter.
18. Why did the close connection between Finance Ministry officials and the banking system create problems for Japanese banks in the early 1990s?

# REFERENCES

*Banking and Monetary Statistics, 1941–1970.* Washington, D.C.: Board of Governors of the Federal Reserve System, 1976, Table 7.1.

Bordo, M.D., and L.P. Jonung. *The Long-Run Behaviour of Velocity.* New York: Cambridge University Press, 1988.

Cargill, T.F., and S. Royama, "The Evolution of Japanese Banking and Finance," in G.G. Kaufman (ed.), *Banking Structure in Major Countries.* Boston: Kluwer Academic Publishers, 1992. pp. 333–88.

Chernow, R. *The House of Morgan.* New York: Simon and Schuster, 1990.

*Federal Reserve Bulletin.* Washington, D.C.: Board of Governors, 1991.

Friedman, M., and A.J. Schwartz. *A Monetary History of the United States, 1864–1960.* Princeton: Princeton University Press, 1963.

Garber, P.M., and S.R. Weisbrod. *The Economics of Banking, Liquidity, and Money.* Lexington, Mass.: D.C. Heath and Co., 1992.

Garraty, J.A. *The Great Depression.* New York: Harper & Row, 1987.

Greider, W. *Secrets of the Temple.* New York: Simon and Schuster, 1988.

Havrilesky, T. "Monetary Policy Signalling from the Administration to the Federal Reserve." *Journal of Money, Credit and Banking* 20 (February 1988): 83–101.

Hubbard, R.G. *Money, The Financial System and the Economy*, updated edition (Reading, Mass.: Addison-Wesley, 1995).

Kohn, M. *Money, Banking, and Financial Markets.* Chicago: The Dryden Press, 1991.

Llewellyn, D.T. "Competition, Diversification, and Structural Change in the British Financial System," in G.G. Kaufman (ed.), *Banking Structure in Major Countries.* Boston: Kluwer Academic Publishers, 1992, pp. 429–68.

Meulendyke, Ann-Marie. *U.S. Monetary Policy and Financial Markets.* New York: Federal Reserve Bank of New York, 1989.

———. "A Review of Federal Reserve Policy Targets and Operating Guides in Recent Decades," in *Intermediate Targets and Indicators for Monetary Policy: A Critical Survey.* New York: Federal Reserve Bank of New York, 1990, pp. 452–73.

Mishkin, F.S. *The Economics of Money, Banking, and Financial Markets.* 4th ed. New York: Harper Collins, 1995.

Mullineux, A.W. "Financial Innovation, Banking and Monetary Aggregation in the UK," University of Birmingham, #93-06.

Pozdena, R.J., and V. Alexander, "Bank Structure in West Germany," in G.G. Kaufman (ed.), *Banking Structure in Major Countries.* Boston: Kluwer Academic Publishers, 1992, pp. 555–90.

Siklos, P.L. (ed.), *Great Inflation of the Twentieth Century.* London: Edward Elgar, 1995.

Temin, P. *Did Monetary Forces Cause the Great Depression?* New York: Norton, 1976.

White, L. *The S&L Debacle.* New York: Oxford University Press, 1991.

Wilson, J.S.G. *Money Markets: The International Perspective.* London: Routledge, 1993.

# CHAPTER 23

# International Financial Institutions

Although serious international co-operation began after World War I, it produced few mechanisms in the financial sphere.[1] The need for international trade to rebuild war-ravaged economies after World War II did, however, lead to some international financial institutions, as well as to the widespread existence of international markets for foreign exchange and bonds.

Of the many monetary, trade, and development agencies that now exist, we examine three: the Bank for International Settlements, the International Monetary Fund, and the World Bank. We also consider the Bretton Woods system of fixed exchange rates, now aborted but in place for almost a quarter century after World War II, and the European Monetary System, the precursor of the now hoped-for monetary unification of Europe.

## SOME INTRODUCTORY THOUGHTS

Why was there a flurry of new international co-operative ventures after World War II? It has been suggested that problems inherent in the operations of the gold standard, the inter-war propensity for countries to engage in beggar-thy-neighbour policies (one country attempts to artificially depreciate its currency in order to induce a favourable balance of payments outcome), and the destruction created by two world wars combined to foster a new mood of international co-operation. The resulting institutions (some of whose origins pre-date 1945) provided countries with rules of co-operation, financial resources that permitted the rules to be obeyed, and institutions that enabled the monitoring of the degree of international co-operation achieved.

Their success was not unqualified. Each of the institutions considered in this chapter failed in some sense to achieve its original lofty objectives. Yet all sur-

1 The League of Nations was the first international agency to have some responsibilities over financial matters. However, as the United States never formally joined, it was not viewed as a particularly effective international financial agency.

vived—in part because the costs of not co-operating usually seemed greater than the benefits of breaking the rules. When co-operation failed, it was because the relevant rules were not deemed credible. As noted at the beginning of this book the notion of credibility is central to the understanding of all financial systems.

Indeed, it is the flexibility of existing arrangements that has led to the suggestion that there is a sort of cycle in countries' preferences for fixed versus flexible exchange rates. Thus, the 1970s and much of the 1980s were the heyday of flexible exchange rates; in the 1990s, a preference for fixed exchange rates has emerged in some quarters.

## THE BANK FOR INTERNATIONAL SETTLEMENTS

The war reparations imposed on Germany and the former Austro-Hungarian Empire after World War I had disastrous economic consequences for those countries and many others, such as the emergence of hyperinflations and several central banks failing. One response was the formation of the **Bank for International Settlements (BIS)** to serve and foster co-operation among central banks. Founded by the central banks of the United States, Great Britain, France, Germany, Italy, Belgium, and Japan in 1930, it has today expanded to more than 25 members, including Canada.

The BIS is owned by its shareholders, the central banks, and is run by a president and a board of governors that include representatives of the central banks of the founding members and a few other countries, as well as representatives from finance, industry, and commerce appointed by the founding members. At least one general meeting is held each year. Decisions are carried out by the president and an administrative staff from headquarters in Basle, Switzerland.

In particular, the BIS serves as a forum where central banks can discuss and co-ordinate their respective monetary policies. It can also

1. Buy and sell gold and foreign exchange.
2. Make advances or borrow from its member central banks.
3. Buy, sell, or discount bills such as Treasury bills or other marketable securities.
4. Act as an agent or a correspondent for any central bank.
5. Compile data relative to the performance of the international financial system.

Its borrowing and lending activities are principally in the form of swaps against gold or foreign currencies.

The BIS played an important role during the debt crisis of the early 1980s when it granted credits to non-member central banks, such as those of Mexico and Argentina, until these countries could make loan arrangements with other international agencies. The BIS also played a co-ordinating role in halting the Mexican peso crisis of 1994–95.

The BIS is, however, best known in its capacity as a forum for international monetary co-operation. This function has become especially crucial at a time when interest rate differentials—for example, between Germany and the United States—have been a source of conflict about how monetary policies are being carried out by member countries. The collapse of the former Communist bloc and the need for those countries to develop central banks modelled along the lines of those in Canada and other Western industrialized countries also enabled the BIS to fulfil its role as an advisor to central banks and thus as a central bank for central banks.

## THE BRETTON WOODS CONFERENCE

As the end of World War II came into sight, the victors were planning the postwar financial system. In July 1944, representatives of more than 40 nations met at the International Monetary and Financial Conference in Bretton Woods, New Hampshire. Led by US and UK delegates,[2] they agreed that the financial structures of the post-World War I era had been largely a failure, that the mistakes of the past should not be repeated, and that the primary objective of the postwar order should be the creation of an international financial system that was multilateral and stable.

One of the ingredients of that stability would be freer trade than the world had ever known.[3] Another was a system of fixed exchange rates and **convertible** (tradeable) **currencies**.

In order to manage the new international order, the group, eventually working through the United Nations, created two institutions with an international mem-

---

2 The two most influential figures at Bretton Woods were Harry Dexter White, of the United States, and John Maynard Keynes, of the United Kingdom. Keynes had also been a UK delegate to the Peace Conference of Versailles after World War I. When that group demanded harsh reparations from Germany, he resigned in protest, arguing that the European economies needed stabilization, not revenge, and he criticized the aftermath throughout the interwar years. See D.E. Moggridge, *Maynard Keynes: An Economist's Biography* (New York: Routledge, 1992) for a description of Keynes' role at the Bretton Woods Conference.

3 To this end, they created the *General Agreement on Tariffs and Trade (GATT)*, an institution that continues to work to reduce trade barriers under the name of the World Trade Organization. Many Bretton Woods participants also went on to help found other multilateral organizations, including what would become the Organization for Economic Co-operation and Development (OECD) and the precursors of the European Community.

bership (though dominated by the United States): the International Monetary Fund and the International Bank for Reconstruction and Development (also known as the World Bank). We will look more closely at these institutions after we consider the exchange rate system.

## THE BRETTON WOODS ADJUSTABLE PEG EXCHANGE RATE SYSTEM

The architects of Bretton Woods wanted the advantages of the gold standard but not at the cost of forcing all countries to pursue similar monetary policies. Thus, they fixed exchange rates but allowed them to fluctuate freely within a narrowly defined band. Moreover, a mechanism would be set up to allow the fixed exchange rate to be adjusted in the event of need.

Therefore, each member of the IMF agreed to the following, which became known as the **Bretton Woods system** of *fixed exchange rates*:

1. Establish a *par value*, for its currency and maintain the exchange rate within 1% of par.
2. Change that par value only upon approval of the IMF, which the IMF would grant only if a member's balance of payments was in "fundamental disequilibrium."

In effect, the member nations pegged their exchange rates to the US dollar.[4]

This par value system meant that IMF members had to fix the value of their currencies. Against what? The natural starting place was the price of gold.

As the dominant economic power of the immediate postwar era, the United States agreed to fix the price of gold at $35 US per ounce.[5] It could defend that price because it had a large supply of gold and of dollars. If the price went up it could release gold to the market, driving down its price. If the price went down, it could use its dollars to purchase gold and raise the price back to $35 an ounce.

The other countries then pegged their exchange rates to the US dollar. If the rates were properly set and if the price of gold was held fixed, prices worldwide would be fixed. Thus, the architects envisaged there could be no sustained price level changes or inflation in the Bretton Woods system.

The system attempted to circumvent the automatic adjustment of the balance of payments. Recall that a loss of reserves stems from a balance of payments

---

4 Doing so required that currencies be convertible. That is, someone wishing to buy Swedish kroner with US dollars had to be able to do so. If there is no trading, currencies are not convertible. Some IMF members could not satisfy this condition until the late 1950s. As a consequence of World War II, many countries had no significant foreign exchange reserves or gold.

5 Since London was the centre of gold trading, it was the Bank of England that performed the transactions required to ensure that the fixed price was maintained.

deficit and a rise of reserves from a balance of payments surplus. Now consider the following illustration.[6] Suppose a country pegs its exchange rate too low. Say the country is Canada, and the rate chosen is \$1 Cdn = \$1 US, although the market-clearing rate is closer to \$1.40 Cdn = \$1 US. With the overvalued Canadian dollar, there is soon excess demand for foreign exchange. To hold the rate fixed, the central bank must make its dollars more expensive by selling some of its reserves of gold or foreign currency. The system also works in the opposite direction. An exchange rate set higher than the market-clearing rate can be defended by purchasing reserves (usually, US dollars).

But such transactions cannot go on forever. If the country is selling reserves, it will eventually run out of them. If it is buying foreign currency, it will eventually find the purchases strain its economy. Even more quickly, it will encounter the problems of changes in its money supply; enhanced by the multiplier effect, they can quickly mean inflation (from the increase in the money supply occasioned by buying reserves) or deflation (from the decrease in the money supply occasioned by selling reserves). Now a *sterilization* (offset) technique can be and often is used to prevent changes in the money supply resulting from foreign exchange transactions. If the central bank purchases foreign currency, it can sell an equivalent amount of domestic financial assets (say, bonds to the banks). The two transactions' effects on the money supply (which need not be simultaneous) offset each other, in theory at least. But sterilization in one direction cannot go on indefinitely either.

The creators of the system realized that its ideals could not be maintained at all times.[7] For this reason, they allowed some flexibility in exchange rate movements, they endowed the IMF with a pool of foreign reserves on which members could draw, they provided would-be borrowers advice (accompanied by considerable moral suasion) on the management of their economics, and they provided a mechanism for changing par value if a country's balance of payments was in "fundamental disequilibrium."[8]

An illustration of some of the difficulties encountered by the Bretton Woods system early in its history comes from the actions taken by Canada in late 1950. The Canadian dollar's par was originally set at \$1 and then devalued in 1949 to 90.9¢. Fearing that the currency was undervalued, the Bank of Canada decided in 1950 to abandon the fixed exchange rate system inherent in the Bretton Woods agreement and allow the dollar to float. Despite criticisms from the IMF, it

---

6 For the background material necessary to understand this illustration see Chapters 7 and 21.

7 That the IMF survived is remarkable in view of the very strict rules it imposed on its members.

8 The term was never defined. It seems to have been used to mean chronic balance of payments deficits that could not be reversed without considerable inflation or deflation.

continued to float until 1961, when it was pegged at 92.5¢ to the US dollar. (Since that rate was not far from the one at which it was floating, it is not clear that the Canadian decision much undermined the Bretton Woods arrangement.)

The system also had its share of successes since there is strong evidence that economic growth and inflation were relatively high and low, respectively throughout much of the Bretton Woods era.

## THE END OF THE BRETTON WOODS SYSTEM

Despite various crises and the inability of the IMF to enforce the Bretton Woods arrangements at all times (see Table 23.1), the IMF's record was one of considerable price stability during the 1950s and 1960s. But that was a period when a few international economic incidents provided major price shocks. Economics worldwide grew at a healthy rate, and the United States stood ready and able to sustain the system. That situation was coming to an end by the close of the 1960s. The Bretton Woods system did not survive much longer.

Two continuing, related problems with the system were its lack of a formal mechanism to generate exchange rate adjustments and countries' reluctance to change par values, even when it became clear that a major currency was out of line. Who would do the adjusting? When? By how much? The adjustment costs inherent in making a change provided good incentive for one country to wait until another moved.

By the end of the 1960s, the currencies of West Germany and Japan were clearly undervalued vis-à-vis the US dollar. To describe the problem another way, the US dollar was overvalued. The US balance of payments deficit had grown tremendously, the supply of dollars outside the United States was many times larger than its gold reserves, and the demand for gold was soaring.

For a time, Germany (and a few other countries) kept buying US dollars—several billion within the space of days in spring 1971—to defend its par value. Then Germany finally allowed the deutschmark to float. And in August 1971, the United States announced it would no longer permit convertibility of its dollars to gold at $35 per ounce. Although the US measure was announced as temporary, it effectively ended the Bretton Woods system of fixed exchange rates.

Although an attempt was made to patch up Bretton Woods in December 1971, through the *Smithsonian Agreement*—the price of gold would rise to $38 per ounce and exchange rates would be permitted to fluctuate in a wider band (2.25% instead of 1%)—by 1973 the major economic powers were on a de facto flexible exchange rate system that has persisted to this day.

Many people believe that the collapse of the Bretton Woods system was due to the unwillingness of Germany, Japan, and some of the other industrialized

**TABLE 23.1** A BRIEF CHRONOLOGY OF IMF CRISES UNTIL THE END OF THE BRETTON WOODS AGREEMENT

| | |
|---|---|
| December 1945 | Bretton Woods Agreement enters into force. |
| May 1947 | France is the first country to draw funds from the IMF. |
| January 1948 | Crises of the franc and subsequent ruling of France's ineligibility to use IMF resources. |
| September 1949 | First major par value adjustment. Canada is among the participants as it devalues its currency. |
| February 1952 | IMF inaugurates standby arrangement (a device to provide credit to member countries). |
| December 1958 | Most western European currencies achieve convertability. |
| November 1967 | Severe balance of payments problems for the United Kingdom leads to a major devaluation of the pound (14.3% in terms of the dollar). |
| March 1968 | $35/oz. price for gold no longer sustainable. |
| June 1968 | France and the United Kingdom draw large amounts from the IMF ($745 million US and $1.4 billion US, respectively). |
| August 1969 | France devalues the franc against gold (by reducing gold content of the franc). |
| September 1969 | West Germany lets the deutschmark float after pressure from persistent balance of payments surpluses. One month later the rate is fixed at a revalued rate. |
| May 1970 | Canada lets the dollar float after several capital outflows to the United States. |
| August 1971 | United States suspends the use of gold to settle international transactions. In effect, the announcement marked the end of the Bretton Woods Agreement. |
| December 1971 | Smithsonian Agreement resulting in a realignment of currencies. |

Source: M.G. de Vries, *The IMF in a Changing World: 1945–85* (Washington, D.C.: International Monetary Fund, 1986).

countries to defend the overvalued US currency by continually absorbing excess supplies of dollars.[9]

An alternative view[10] is that since the Bretton Woods system effectively placed the world on a US-dollar standard, US monetary policy dictated world inflation rates. In this *monetarist* view (monetarism is defined more precisely in Chapter 26), if the US money stock grew too quickly, the resulting inflation would be transmitted to the other countries in the fixed exchange rate system. Thus, the other countries in the system simply refused to support US inflationary policies by 1970. In addition, the growing freedom of capital movements, as country after

9 The fact that these countries felt strong enough to confront the United States may also be explained by the loss of US hegemony in world economic affairs, particularly as the costs of the war in Vietnam were rising.

10 But not antithetical, as we will see below.

## FINANCIAL FOCUS 23.1 Currency Unions

In a *currency union*, two or more jurisdictions share a single currency. The European Monetary System is the latest stage in the move toward a European currency union. Canada has a currency union among its provinces, although some analysts question its efficiency.

The traditional criterion of a successful currency union is factor mobility: that is, the freedom of capital and labour to move across regions and a minimum of barriers to trade. The federal government's constitutional proposals of 1991 echoed these arguments. The dispersion of unemployment rates in Canada suggests that it has serious barriers to labour mobility at least. For example, Newfoundland traditionally has far higher unemployment rates than, say, Ontario. Moreover, the financial resources of the country are also regionally concentrated. The mobility of physical capital is also limited: some plants find it economically advantageous to locate outside Atlantic Canada, for example. Similar barriers exist in the United States and the European Community.

The interest in currency unions and how to organize them most efficiently has been heightened by the demise of the Soviet Union, and the breaking up of Czechoslovakia into the Czech and Slovak Republics. Although a currency union currently exists by default, most of the successor states, ended this arrangement. Nevertheless, the notion of a currency union organized along the same lines as the Bretton Wood arrangement does appeal to some.

The principal problem with the currency union in the former Soviet Union is the lack of credibility of the Russian-dominated central bank. Since inflation cannot be contained within parts of a currency union, many of the successor states claim that Russia is inflating its economy at the expense of the other republics. This is yet another example of the problem of externalities in financial systems. What do economists think are the essential ingredients of an "optimum currency area"? Any such list would include the following:

1. *Labour mobility.* The freer the movement of labour, the fewer the regional disparities in unemployment rates.
2. *Capital mobility.* Capital should be mobile so that savings and investment can seek out the most profitable opportunities. Barriers to capital movements would prevent this from happening.
3. *Openness and regional interdependence.* It makes sense to use the same currency if goods move freely between the regions and a significant portion of trade is done within a specific region.
4. *Industrial and portfolio diversification.* Economic shocks can be devastating to an economy but these can be mitigated if there is sufficient diversification within the currency area. (We examine the benefits of diversification in Chapter 13.)
5. *Wage and price flexibility.* Because within a currency area the exchange rate is fixed, resources can only be allocated to their best uses if wages and prices are sufficiently flexible; otherwise the exchange rate has to perform this function.

**Sources:**

J.A. Frenkel and H.G. Johnson, eds., *The Monetary Approach to the Balance of Payments* (Toronto: University of Toronto Press, 1976).

R.I. McKinnon, "Optimum Currency Areas," *American Economic Review* 53 (September 1963): 717–25.

R.A. Mundell, "A Theory of Optimum Currency Areas," *American Economic Review* (September 1961): 657–65.

P.R. Masson and M.P. Taylor, "Some Issues Concerning the Successful Establishment and Operation of Currency Unions," in *Varieties of Monetary Reforms: Lessons and Experiences on the Road to Monetary Union*, ed. P.L. Siklos (Dordrecht: Kluwer Academic Publishers, 1994), pp. 23–44.

J. Shelton, "A Bretton Woods System for Ex-Soviets," *Wall Street Journal*, 4 September 1991.

country dropped capital controls, meant growing pressures on exchange rates that central banks could not (or no longer wished to) contain. The inevitable outcome of these pressures was to allow exchange rates to fluctuate freely.

Long after the end of the Bretton Woods system the major economic powers attempted to influence the value of the most important currencies. One such example was the so-called *Plaza Accord* of 22 September 1985 when the G-5 countries agreed to arrange to reduce the value of the US dollar. The accord was largely unsuccessful as was the *Louvre Accord* of 22 February 1987 when finance ministers of the G-3 attempted to target the US dollar vis-à-vis the deutschmark and the yen. These targets were effectively abandoned after the stock market crash later the same year.

Ironically, the world's subsequent experience with floating—and volatile—exchange rates has proved to be an unsatisfactory one. Hence, many people would like to return to some sort of a régime with exchange rate stability. One manifestation of this desire is the European Monetary System, which we discuss later in this chapter.

## THE INTERNATIONAL MONETARY FUND TODAY

The **International Monetary Fund (IMF)** was founded to promote international co-operation in economic matters, to provide a forum in which members could agree on a common code of conduct in their financial affairs, and to aid nations in solving balance of payments problems. This broad mandate means that one of its original purposes—the maintenance and enforcement of the Bretton Woods system of exchange rates—no longer exists. Indeed, some have argued the IMF should be dissolved since it cannot carry out its original mandate. However, it seems to have taken on a new role, along with the BIS which was discussed earlier, of coordinating lending and borrowing functions, especially in crisis situations and of helping emerging economies develop sound policies.

### ORGANIZATION AND STRUCTURE

More than 100 countries are now members of the IMF. It is headed by a managing director (by custom, a European national), who chairs a board of governors that holds most of the organization's powers and usually meets once a year.

Each member's voting rights and borrowing rights are a function of its *quota*, a kind of subscription fee whose amount reflects relative economic position.[11]

11 The quotas are denominated in special drawing rights (SDRs), an accounting unit devised by the IMF and

The quotas provide the financial resources that the IMF can use to assist member countries with particular economic difficulties. A member can borrow quite easily against the first 25% of its quota, which is called the first *tranche*.[12] Borrowing against additional tranches is progressively more difficult. In some circumstances, the IMF practises conditionality—that is, it denies access to its funds (and thus indirectly to international financial markets) until it is satisfied that the domestic monetary authorities are putting adequate adjustment policies in place.

This ability to impose stringent economic discipline on loan recipients gave the IMF a crucial—and some think successful—role during the international debt crisis of the early 1980s (see Chapter 21), and in managing the transition to a market economy in the former Socialist bloc countries.[13]

## SDRs

One of the early difficulties the IMF faced was the shortage of gold and US dollars in the world trading system. Many countries had political reasons for not liking the fact that the US dollar was the dominant world currency, and many viewed the supply of gold as potentially unreliable, again for political reasons, because South Africa and the then-Soviet Union were two of the largest producers of gold.

Ironically, the importance of the US dollar to the world economy meant that to supply a constant flow of reserves to the rest of the world, the United States would have to maintain a balance of payments deficit which, as we saw in Chapter 21, is not a desirable thing to do so in the long-run. Moreover, to do so would undermine the value of the US dollar relative to gold, the other major reserve asset. So there was an inconsistency in the Bretton Woods system, called the *Triffin paradox.*

One response to this problem was the creation in 1969 of the **special drawing right** (**SDR**), a new international reserve asset, to supplement existing world

---

explained later in this section. The quotas reflect the political influence of a country as well as its economic influence. Although Japan has now secured a greater voice in the affairs of the IMF, the US role remains a dominant one.

12 From the French term for "slice."

13 According to one first-hand account, the IMF generally attempted to reach a consensus with countries experiencing financial difficulties and not to impose ideologically motivated solutions. The fact that it played hardball on occasion may actually have had beneficial effects for some countries. For a markedly different view, which argues, among other things, that the focus on balance of payments problems is a far too narrow one, see J. Spraos, "IMF Conditionality: Ineffectual, Inefficient, and Mistargeted," *Essays in International Finance*, no. 166 (December 1986), Princeton University.

reserves of currency. The SDR was initially defined in terms of a gold content but was redefined in 1974 as a weighted average of a basket of currencies; the weights are revised every five years.[14]

Although giving countries access to a new source of liquidity, such as the SDR, has distinct advantages, there is the danger that one country will overuse it at the expense of other countries. However, obtaining financial resources in SDRs is costly since borrowers are charged a competitive rate.[15] Therefore, even if a member borrows in SDRs for a prolonged period of time, it is not obvious that the borrower is benefiting at the expense of lenders (the other members of the IMF) unless the loan has a high default risk.

That the SDR has not become a more important international currency may, in part, be explained by the fact that since its introduction, financial markets in the Western industrialized countries have managed to create a host of new financial instruments that have effectively eliminated the worldwide shortage of liquidity of the earlier years of the IMF. Concerns have also been expressed by some influential Fund members, such as Germany, that a new allocation of SDRs, blocked in 1995, could potentially have been inflationary.[16]

Nevertheless, SDRs have proved important to the developing nations and it is they who have pushed hardest to increase the availability of this financial instrument.[17] The extent to which SDRs have provided additional financial resources is evident by the fact that in the 1985–89 period 81% of net-debtor developing countries that experienced problems with servicing their debt used 70% to 100% of their SDR allocations. Also, 56% of developing countries without debt-servicing problems have used the same fraction (that is, 70% to 100%) of their SDR allocation during the same period. By contrast, net-creditor countries rarely use any of their SDR allocations.[18] Clearly, the SDR can serve as an instrument of transfer of financial resources from the developed countries to the developing countries.

---

14 An intellectual antecedent for the SDR was a plan put forth by Keynes at the Breton Woods Conference. Keynes wanted to create a new international currency unit called the "bancor." Its value would be fixed in terms of gold, and every country would then set the par value of its currency in terms of the bancor.

15 The rate charged on SDR loans is a weighted average of the yields on 3-month Treasury bills in the United States, the United Kingdom, and France, the 3-month interbank deposit rate in Germany, and the 3-month CD rate in Japan.

16 An IMF Conference in early 1996 did nothing to resolve the issue. The last allocation of fresh SDR credits was made in 1981.

17 See P. Norman, "Spanner in the Rolls-Royce Engine," *Financial Times* of London, 4 October 1994, p. 17.

18 See W.L. Coats Jr., R.W. Furstenberg, and P. Isard, "The SDR System and the Issue of Resource Transfers," *Essays in International Finance*, no. 180 (December 1990), Princeton University.

# THE WORLD BANK

The **International Bank for Reconstruction and Development (IBRD)**, but more often the **World Bank**), a United Nations affiliate, aids developing countries by

1. Assisting in reconstruction and development.
2. Promoting private foreign investment.
3. Making loans from its own funds and channelling aid from the developed countries.
4. Guaranteeing loans made to members.
5. Promoting the growth of international trade.

With about 150 current members, the World Bank is run by a president (by custom a US citizen), who chairs a board of governors.

The World Bank was conceived at the Bretton Woods Conference as an institution to help finance the reconstruction of Europe after World War II and began operations in 1946. Soon after, the advent of the United States' Marshall Plan[19] relegated the World Bank's role in Europe to a secondary one, so it sought to justify its existence through loans to developing countries.

The funds loaned out by the Bank are raised through members' subscriptions, through the retention of earnings on previous loans, and through the sale of bonds in international financial markets. The Bank also engages extensively in currency swaps. Because of the nature of the loans their term is often for periods of 15 to 20 years. In addition, there is a grace period of up to 5 years should a member prove unable to repay the loan at maturity.

In the later 1970s, the Bank began to move away from loans aimed at specific reconstruction projects toward helping countries restructure their entire economies or some of their vital sectors.

For certain specialized purposes the World Bank acts through a number of affiliates. The *International Development Association (IDA)*, for example, works

19 In 1947, US Secretary of State George Marshall, realizing that previous reconstruction plans had badly underestimated the need, offered a massive aid program to the countries of Europe provided they would work together for economic recovery. Sixteen countries of western Europe accepted, forming the Organization for Economic Co-operation and Development, which set priorities for and administered what proved to be nearly $13 billion of assistance. Canada, which was experiencing severe balance of payments problems, also benefited since the Americans agreed that Marshall Plan purchases could be made here, as well as in the United States.

for development in the poorest nations of the world, making very long-term loans that are often interest-free (though they carry some service charges). And the *International Finance Corporation (IFC)* makes loans for the express purpose of aiding the growth of the private sector.

The IMF and the World Bank are sister institutions, and they attempt to co-ordinate their work. The international debt crisis fostered more co-operation as the World Bank began to require that a borrower meet conditions at the time a loan was made. Indeed, its conditionality often goes beyond any macroeconomic adjustments the IMF may require to policies that deregulate markets, thus promoting microeconomic efficiency, reducing or eliminating protectionism in trade, and promoting improvements and maintenance of a country's infrastructure (education, health, roads, and so on).

# THE EUROPEAN BANK FOR RECONSTRUCTION AND DEVELOPMENT

The **European Bank for Reconstruction and Development** was set up in 1990 to help the former Communist countries of Europe to privatize public assets and make the transition to capitalism. In a sense, this new institution is superseding the IMF and the World Bank as the international institution responsible for advising and implementing transitional policies in an important segment of emerging market economies.

# THE EUROPEAN MONETARY SYSTEM

The **European Monetary System (EMS)** is an ambitious attempt to integrate the currencies of the European Community (EC). It currently involves exchange rates that are fixed but fluctuate within a target zone; it is planned to include eventually the use of the Euro as a common currency and significant integration of monetary and fiscal policies by the EC countries.

## SOME HISTORY

Even before the collapse of the Bretton Woods system, six European countries—Belgium, France, West Germany, Italy, Luxembourg, and the Netherlands—signed the Treaty of Rome (1957), which led to the formation of the European Community (EC), and agreed to take steps to integrate their monetary policies (1968).

The plan was to set up a pool of reserves to help members maintain a fixed exchange rate and prevent speculative attacks against their currencies. By 1971,

## ECONOMICS FOCUS 23.1 How Countries Restrict Trade

There is virtually no limit to the devices countries may use to restrict trade. Here is a glossary of some of the principal means currently used.

**Tariffs** By imposing fees of various kinds, governments effectively raise the domestic price of foreign goods. In general, tariffs have fallen substantially since the end of World War II, thanks to the General Agreement on Tariffs and Trade (GATT) and to various free trade agreements and the growth of the European Common Market.

**Quotas, Bans, Voluntary Restraints** Limits or outright prohibitions may be set on imports. All sorts of limits of these kinds exist for a variety of products ranging from shoes to cars.

**"Buy Canadian"** Government programs to exhort citizens to buy products made domestically (and often labelled as such).

**Subsidies** Government may help certain industries, thereby influencing the ability to export goods. Canadian examples range from the Export Development Corporation to outright tax breaks.

**Rules and Regulations.** Products sold in a country must satisfy government-set criteria for emissions, quality, labelling, and so on. Countries can use such regulations to influence imports.

**Price Fixing** Goods are sometimes "dumped" in another country at an artificially low price.

**Limits on Foreign Investment** Governmental agencies are set up to review applications by foreigners who wish to invest in the country. They can be a barrier to trade, especially if there are limits on how much of a local business can be owned by foreigners.

**Piracy** Governments that turn a blind eye on companies that produce copies of foreign goods without enforcing payment of, say, royalties also influence the balance of trade.

---

the political leadership of the EC member countries formally adopted a plan to achieve economic and monetary union within 10 years.

Almost immediately it was agreed that exchange rate fluctuations within the EC would be narrowed to a *band* (target range) smaller than that the IMF allowed at the time.[20] This arrangement was called the "snake within the IMF tunnel."[21] In other words, the European system was a miniature version of the Bretton Woods arrangement.

The snake never functioned smoothly—West Germany and the Netherlands allowed their currencies to float temporarily—and was abandoned in 1973, when a devaluation of the US dollar led the EC to float all of its currencies for a time. Nevertheless, EC members kept reaffirming their intention of achieving monetary and economic union.

In 1974, the second stage of the proposed union began with a pooling of EC members' foreign exchange reserves and gold, an increase in the EC's short-term credit facilities, and an agreement to intensify co-ordination of members' economic and monetary policies. Despite a variety of setbacks and delays, the EMS

20 Essentially, the rates were linked to the deutschmark.

21 The United Kingdom, which was experiencing balance of payments difficulties, was excepted.

began to operate in March 1979.[22] The system's monetary unit would be called the **Ecu (European currency unit)**.[23] Representing a weighted basket of European currencies, it is planned to someday become the common currency of the EC. Meanwhile it would serve as the *numéraire* (unit of account) for the exchange rate mechanism. The EMS also stipulated movements—2.25% (6% for Spain and the United Kingdom) in either direction of each other's currency values—and provided a mechanism to support economically the relatively less prosperous members of the EC.

The EMS can *realign* (revalue) the currencies if the exchange rates cannot be sustained within the zone, and despite the agreement to fix exchange rates rigorously, there were 27 realignments of the currency relationships between 1979 and 1983, and 12 more during the 1984–87 period.[24] After that, however, no further realignments were made until September 1992, when the United Kingdom and Italy left the EMS. Also, Ireland, Spain, and Portugal all devalued their currencies against the deutschmark. In August 1993, the bands were widened to ±15 percent (except for the Netherlands).

This apparent stability in exchange rates between 1987 and 1992 puzzles economists since the European countries showed considerable unwillingness to adhere to any of the fixed exchange rate régimes introduced in the past. Moreover, as is illustrated by the plot of the real effective exchange rates in Figure 23.1, several of the major currencies are incorrectly valued, at least in theory. Presumably, the longer a currency is overvalued or undervalued, the more likely a realignment. Why had none occurred prior to September 1992? Of the many possible explanations, a likely one is that the current behaviour of EMS participants reflects a jockeying of positions prior to the possible **European Monetary Union (EMU)**, a full monetary union within the EC.

It is also unclear whether the EMS has worked the way its framers had intended. For example, the bands within which exchange rates are permitted to fluctuate are wide enough to leave enough room for individual countries to choose their own inflation and interest rates. Only when a single currency is adopted will the European Community have achieved a truly fixed exchange rate system.

---

22 Initially, there were only six members—the original signators of the Treaty of Rome, but eventually they were joined by most EC members, including Italy and Ireland in 1978, Greece in 1981, and Spain and Portugal in 1986. The last holdout was the United Kingdom, which joined the EMS exchange rate mechanism in 1990, although it dropped out in September 1992 along with Italy. Meanwhile even several non-member countries, such as Sweden, in effect, adhered to the EMS system.

23 The "Ecu" was also the name of an ancient currency used in many countries, especially France, at various times over the centuries.

24 See *European Economy*, no. 44 (October 1990): 42.

**FIGURE 23.1** Real Effective Exchange Rates in Five EMS Countries

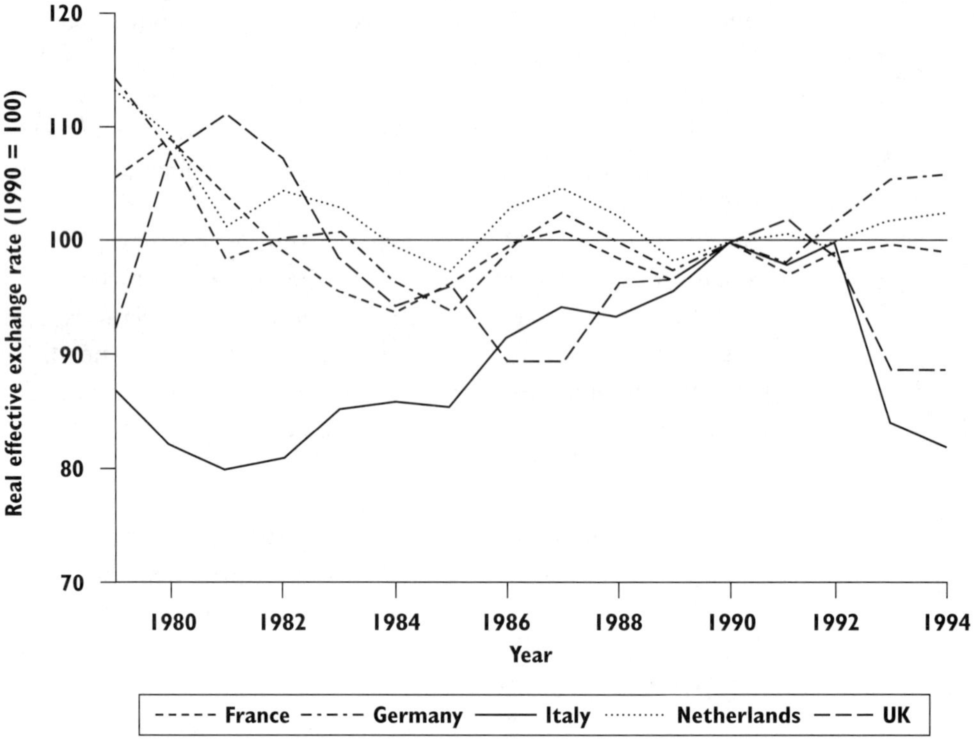


Source: *International Financial Statistics* CD-ROM (Washington, D.C.: International Monetary Fund). The real exchange rate measure is based on relative CPI calculations. Note that Italy and the UK left the ERM in September 1992. The UK joined the ERM only in October 1990.

## THE TARGET ZONE SYSTEM IN ACTION

Consider Figure 23.2 which shows a hypothetical **target zone** for a currency. The exchange rate is allowed to fluctuate anywhere within the band defined by the lines *UB* and *LB*. The line in the middle is the *central parity* or the mid-point between *UB* and *LB* around which the exchange rate can fluctuate without necessarily producing an intervention in foreign exchange markets by central banks. The objective of the system is to narrow fluctuations in the exchange rate which might possibly enhance international trade. If a currency's exchange rate approaches either the top of the band or the bottom of the band central banks are supposed to intervene to force the exchange rate to return within the band.[25]

25 Under the Basle-Nyborg Accord of September 1987, central banks in the EMS can jointly co-ordinate their activities to ensure the successful operation of the band.

**FIGURE 23.2** The Target Zone Model: Hypothetical Illustration

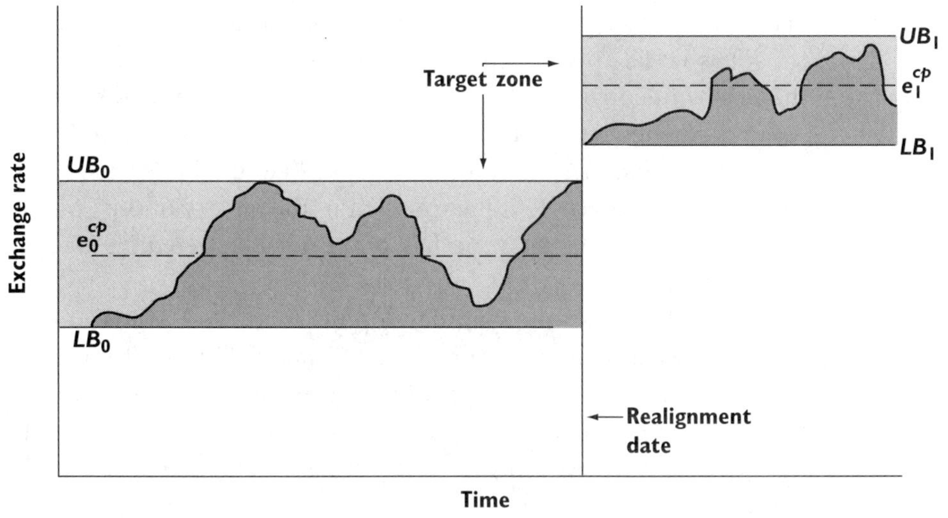


The vertical axis measures the hypothetical exchange rate level for a country. Time is measured on the horizontal axis. The lines *UB* and *LB* are the upper and lower bounds, respectively, of the target zone; $e^{cp}$ is the central parity rate. The thick line inside the bands represents hypothetical fluctuations of the exchange rate. The vertical line illustrates the effect of a realignment. Here the exchange rate band shifts up to indicate a *devaluation* of the currency.

But what happens if markets do not believe that central banks will defend the currency or view the economic policies of the participants as so divergent that the current parities are not credible? Then, as we have seen under the Bretton Woods period, sufficient pressure can be brought to bear or reserves of foreign exchange can be exhausted which would result in a **realignment**.[26] One such realignment is illustrated in Figure 23.2. In the EMS, unanimous consent of all participating members is required in order to change the central parity.

A simple way of testing the credibility of a target zone[27] is to use the theory of uncovered interest rate parity. From Chapter 15 we know, reproducing equation (15.9) below for convenience, that

26 In the crisis of 1992 the then-president of the Bundesbank, Helmut Schlesinger, claimed that it had spent 92 billion DM to defend the British pound and the Italian lira. See *Financial Times*, 4 October 1992, p.1.

27 The target zone literature has exploded in recent years with increasingly complex models developed because the simplest ones, such as the one described below, are unable to explain all exchange rate movements. For a literature review, see P.M. Garber and L.E.O. Svensson, "The Operation and Collapse of Fixed Exchange Rate Regimes," in G. Grossman and K. Rogoff (eds.), *Handbook of International Economics*, vol. III (Amsterdam: Elsevier Science, 1995), pp. 1865–1911. For more recent empirical evidence, see P.L. Siklos and R. Tarajos, "Fundamentals and Devaluation Expectations in Target Zones: Some New Evidence from the ERM," *Open Economies Review* 7 (January 1996): 33–59.

$$R - R^f = (e^{exp} - e^s) / e^s \tag{23.9}$$

The above equation states that the interest differential between two countries ($R - R^f$) is equal to the expected depreciation of the exchange rate. If the right-hand side of equation (23.9) fluctuates within the defined bands, then the current central parities are credible; otherwise they are not. Figure 23.3 shows what the right-hand side of equation (23.9) looks like for the French franc until the crisis of 1992 which was a defining moment in the history of the EMS. It is immediately obvious that the target zone has often not been credible necessitating frequent realignments.

Another way of following developments in the EMS is to examine published exchange rates as in, for example, the *Financial Times*. Table 23.2 illustrates how such data are reported. The "divergence" indicator is simply the ratio of the spread between the current exchange rate and the central parity to the maximum spread permitted within the band (usually 15%, except for the Netherlands and Austria).

## EUROPEAN MONETARY UNION

In 1989, the EC issued the Delors Report, which laid out the ground rules leading up to EMU and the introduction of a single currency. A plan agreed to in December 1991 at Maastricht, the Netherlands, now calls for full EMU by 1999. At the end of 1995, leaders of the EU announced that the planned single currency would be called the **Euro** and they reaffirmed the launch date of 1 January 1999.[28]

In the current phase of the transition, begun in 1992 and expected to take four or five years, EC member countries are to achieve convergence in (coming together of) monetary and fiscal policies and thus, in effect, convergence in inflation rates. Essentially, the criteria are that member states are permitted.

1. A maximum of 1.5 percentage points above the average of the three lowest national inflation rates.

2. A maximum of 2 percentage points above the average of the three lowest national long-term interest rates.

3. Budget deficits up to a maximum of 3% of GDP.

4. Accumulated public (government) debt of up to 60% of GDP.

---

28 L. Barber and D. White, "Euro Chosen as name for EU Single Currency," *Financial Times of London* 16/17 December 1995, p.1.

**FIGURE 23.3** Franc/Deutschmark Exchange Rates, 1979–92

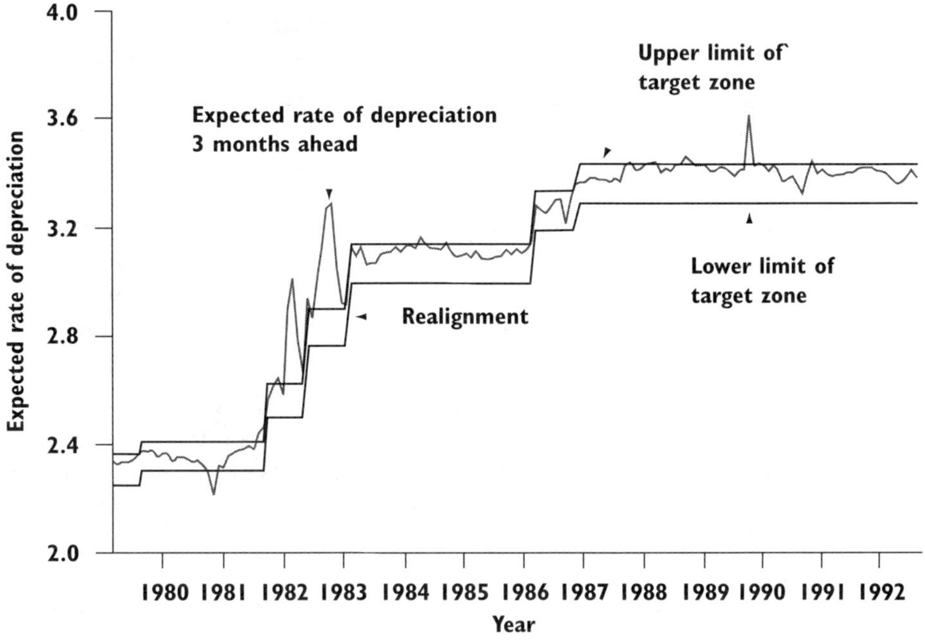


The vertical axis measures the right hand of equation (15.9), where $e^{exp}$ is the 3-month forward exchange rate for the French franc vis-à-vis the deutschmark. The bands are the horizontal lines which shift up (meaning a devaluation against the deutschmark) every time a realignment takes place.

Source: P.L. Siklos and R. Tarajos, "Fundamentals and Devaluation Expectations in Target Zones: Some New Evidence from the ERM," *Open Economies Review* 7 (January 1996): 33–59.

**5.** Maintenance of stable exchange rates for at least two years.[29]

As of 1996, most EU countries are failing some or several of these criteria. This has led to the suggestion that the transition to EMU should follow a multi-speed approach with only those countries who meet convergence criteria by a certain date entering the union first. Others would join as they fulfil all the criteria.

When full EMU is achieved, every member's debt and currency will thereafter be denominated in Euros. EMU will also imply convergence of some kind in financial markets.

Paralleling these broad developments toward monetary union is the "single market program" ("1992," as it is almost universally called), which (in theory,

29 See European Monetary Institute *Annual Report 1994* (April 1995), Frankfort, Germany.

**TABLE 23.2** EMS EXCHANGE RATES

| Currency | ECU Central Parity | Current Exchange Rate | Deviation from Central Parity (%) | Divergence Indicator |
|---|---|---|---|---|
| Spain | 162.493 | 159.063 | −2.11 | 15 |
| Netherlands | 2.15214 | 2.1176 | −1.60 | 12 |
| Belgium | 39.396 | 38.8908 | −1.28 | 9 |
| Austria | 13.4383 | 13.3087 | −0.96 | 7 |
| Germany | 1.91007 | 1.89245 | −0.92 | 9 |
| Portugal | 195.792 | 195.476 | −0.16 | 1 |
| Denmark | 7.2858 | 7.30824 | 0.31 | −2 |
| France | 6.40608 | 6.48062 | 1.16 | −10 |
| Ireland | 0.792214 | 0.816031 | 3.01 | −20 |

Note: The exchange is the amount of domestic currency required to "purchase" one Ecu. The % deviation is approximately the percent difference between the first two columns (example: $[(159.063 - 162.493)/162.493] \times 100 = -2.11$). The divergence indicator is the ratio of the third column to the maximum permissible deviation from the central parity (example: $(2.11/15) \times 100 \approx 15$ in the case of Spain). The currencies are ordered from strongest to weakest.

Source: *Financial Times of London*, 27 March 1996.

but not in practice) eliminated all intra-EC barriers by the end of 1992. The legislation is important for the market for financial services because it removes all exchange controls. This, in effect, means the removal of all barriers limiting the movement of capital within the EC.

What is the significance of such a move? Consider that just before the United Kingdom removed its exchange controls the average or spread between the LIBOR and the rate on 3-month bank loans was roughly 1.5 percentage points; within months, the spread was nearly zero! Thus, the removal of such regulations has a significant impact on a key variable we have been discussing throughout the text.

For banks in Europe, the 1992 legislation means that any depository institution in one EC country can establish branches in any other member country. Each branch must, however, conform to local laws, an arrangement that can give rise to complications. For example, if a British bank establishes a subsidiary in France on the basis of its British banking licence, it must now meet the reporting requirements of two countries, which is clearly more costly than reporting to a single country. In addition, regulatory costs will increase because should the bank or its subsidiary fail both the British and the French authorities will have to coordinate their activities.

The plans for EMU combined with the single market program imply a significant reduction, if not the elimination, of sovereignty in monetary and fiscal matters for the EC member states. Together with a planned *European Central Bank (ECB)*, EMU, if achieved, and the institutions created to support it will be among the international monetary system's most important institutions.

In anticipation of the opening of the ECB, the **European Monetary Institute (EMI)** opened its doors in Frankfurt, Germany, in January 1994. Its main task is to prepare the technical needs of a switch to a single currency as well as report to the EU on the progress towards convergence by individual member states. Consequently, the EMI has no responsibility for monetary policy. The organization of the EMI consists of a council headed by a president, appointed for three years, and governors from the central banks of the member states. The president of the EU and a representative of the European Commission are ex officio members.[30] By the end of 1995 the member governments approved a "changeover scenario" which focuses on the need for the rigorous acceptance of the convergence criteria and that a legal basis be guaranteed so that all who use the *Euro* can be safe in the knowledge that it is a means of payment. In addition, the goals of monetary policy in the Euro and conversion of accounting standards must be implemented by 1999. The end of 2001 is viewed as the target date for introducing the Euro with completion no later than June 30, 2002.[31]

## SUMMARY

- This chapter surveys the institutions of and developments in the international monetary system.
- The principal organizations in the international financial system are the International Monetary Fund (IMF), the World Bank, and the Bank for International Settlements (BIS).
- The history of exchange rate arrangements in the post-World War II period can be divided into two parts. Exchange rates were largely fixed in the Bretton Woods period, which lasted until the early 1970s. Since then exchange rates have been flexible and generally market-determined.
- The European Monetary System is an attempt to fix exchange rates among its members. It is planned that a full-fledged monetary union will eventually take place, perhaps as early as the end of this century.

30 See the European Monetary Institute *Annual Report 1994* (April 1995), Frankfurt, Germany; and European Monetary Institute *Information Bulletin*, October 1994, Frankfurt, Germany.

31 See "Scenario for the Changeover to the Single Euro Currency," Deutsche Bundesbank *Monthly Report* 48 (January 1996): p. 53–60.

## IMPORTANT TERMS

Bank for International Settlements (BIS) (p. 532)
Bretton Woods system (p. 534)
convertible currencies (p. 533)
Ecu (European currency unit) (p. 545)
Euro (p. 548)
European Bank for Reconstruction and Development (p. 543)
European Monetary Institute (EMI) (p. 551)
European Monetary System (EMS) (p. 543)
European Monetary Union (EMU) (p. 545)
International Bank for Reconstruction and Development (IBRD) (or World Bank) (p. 542)
International Monetary Fund (IMF) (p. 539)
realignment (p. 547)
special drawing right (SDR) (p. 540)
target zone (p. 546)

## EXERCISES

1. Explain why a nation in debt would prefer to borrow from a bank rather than the IMF (other things being equal).
2. Explain how the establishment of the Ecu reduces transactions costs within the EC.
3. Explain how the creation of SDRs increases liquidity in the world financial system.
4. Why did central banks want to have an international body to co-ordinate some of their activities?
5. Explain why the currencies whose real effective exchange rates are plotted in Figure 23.1 are over- or undervalued and why this creates pressures for a realignment of the currencies.
6. What are the principal functions of the BIS?
7. What is the Triffin paradox?
8. The Bretton Woods system collapsed in the early to mid-1970s. Why? What other major events not specifically mentioned in the text may also have indirectly contributed to the end of Bretton Woods?
9. What are the determinants of an optimum currency area?
10. How does the target zone exchange rate system work and what can determine a realignment of the exchange rate within such a system?
11. What are the convergence criteria for EMU and why are they important?
12. In Table 23.2 why is the Spanish currency the strongest and the Irish currency the weakest?

# REFERENCES


Bordo, M. "The Bretton Woods International Monetary System: An Historical Overview." In *A Retrospective on the Bretton Woods System: Lessons for International Monetary Reform*, edited by M.D. Bordo and B. Eichengreen, Chicago: University of Chicago Press for NBER, 1993.

Coates, W.L., Jr., R.W. Furstenberg, and P. Isard. "The SDR System and the Issue of Resource Transfers," *Essays in International Finance* (Princeton University) no. 180 (December 1990).

Colchester, N., and D. Buchan. *Europower.* New York: Random House, 1990, chapter 8.

Copeland, L.S., *Exchange Rates and International Finance*, Second Edition. Wokingham, England: Addison-Wesley, 1994.

De Cecco, M., and A. Giovannini. *A European Central Bank?* Cambridge: Cambridge University Press, 1989.

de Grauwe, P. *The Economics of Monetary Integration*, Second Revised Edition. Oxford: Oxford University Press, 1994.

de Vries, M.G. *Balance of Payments Adjustment, 1945 to 1986: The IMF Experience.* Washington, D.C.: International Monetary Fund, 1987.

———. *The IMF in a Changing World; 1945–85.* Washington, D.C.: International Monetary Fund, 1986.

Dominquez, K.M. "The Role of International Organizations in the Bretton Woods System." In *A Retrospective on the Bretton Woods System: Lessons for International Monetary Reform*, edited by M.D. Bordo and B. Eichengreen, 357–97. Chicago: University of Chicago Press for NBER, 1993.

Eichengreen, B. *Elusive Stability.* Cambridge; Cambridge University Press, 1990.

Eng., M.V., F.A. Lees, and L.J. Mauer, *Global Finance.* New York: Harper Collins, 1995.

Finch, C.D. "The IMF: The Record and the Prospect." *Essays in International Finance* (Princeton University) no. 175 (September 1989).

Flanders, M. June. *International Monetary Economics, 1870–1960.* Cambridge: Cambridge University Press, 1989.

Fraser, R. *The World Financial System.* Harlow, Essex, U.K.: Longman, 1987.

Froot, K.A., and K. Rogoff. "The EMS, the EMU, and the Transition to a Common Currency." *1991." Macroeconomics Annual.* Cambridge, Mass.: The MIT Press, 1991, 269–316.

Giavazzi, F., and A. Giovannini. *Limiting Exchange Rate Stability: The European Monetary System.* Cambridge, Mass.: The MIT Press, 1989.

Giovannini, A. "Bretton Woods and Its Precursors: Rules Versus Discretion in the History of International Monetary Regimes." In *A Retrospective on the Bretton Woods System: Lessons for International Monetary Reform*, edited by M.D. Bordo and B. Eichengreen, 109–47. Chicago: University of Chicago Press for NBER, 1993.

———. "The Currency Reform as the Last Stage of Economic and Monetary Union: Some Policy Questions." NBER working paper no. 3917 (November 1991).

———. "European Monetary Reform: Progress and Prospects." Brookings Papers on Economic Activity 2 (1990): 217–92.

Grabbe, J. Orlin. *International Financial Markets.* New York: Elsevier, 1991.

IMF *International Financial Statistics* (various issues).

*International Monetary Fund: Annual Report.* Washington, D.C.: International Monetary Fund, various years.

Keynes, J.M. *The Economic Consequences of the Peace.* London: Macmillan, 1919.

———. *A Tract on Monetary Reform.* London: Macmillan, 1923.

McCallum, B.T. *International Monetary Economics* (Oxford: Oxford University Press, 1996).

Mussa, M. "Monetary and Fiscal Policy in an Economically Unified Europe." In Carnegie-Rochester Conference Series on Public Policy, edited by A.H. Meltzer and C.I. Plosser, vol. 35, 223–60. Amsterdam: North-Holland, 1991.

Spraos, J. "IMF Conditionality: Ineffectual, Inefficient, and Mistargeted." *Essays in International Finance* (Princeton University) no. 166 (December 1986).

Swoboda, A.K. *The Road to Monetary Union: Lessons from the Bretton Woods Regime.* Per Jacobsson Lecture, Basle, Switzerland, June 1991.

Unguer, H. "Europe—The Quest for Monetary Integration." *Finance and Development* (December 1990): 14–18.

Walter, I. "European Financial Integration and Its Implications for the United States." Solomon Brothers Center for the Study of Financial Institutions working paper S-90-1 (1990).

*World Bank Annual Report*, various years.

PART V

# CENTRAL BANKING AND THE ROLE OF MONEY

CHAPTER 24

# Central Banking and the Tools of Monetary Policy

By the early twentieth century most Western industrialized countries had adopted a banking system headed by a central bank entirely owned by the state. Thus was abandoned the notion of free banking; the state gradually exercised complete control over the issue of currency, and following World War II, central banks were called on to control monetary policy and eventually to ensure price stability. These new roles were in line with an increasingly popular way of understanding economies: *monetarism*, which emphasizes the relationship between the money supply and inflation.[1]

Accordingly, the last part of this textbook explores some of the issues of modern central banking and monetarism. This chapter considers the tools of monetary policy that central banks have available, focusing on the way they are used by the Bank of Canada. We also consider some of the other functions of Canada's central bank (serving as a lender of last resort, acting as banker for the federal government, and managing the government's foreign exchange reserves) and briefly sketch monetary policy in Canada before and since the formation of the Bank of Canada.

Chapter 25 takes up the instruments and targets of monetary policy in more detail and considers the issue of central bank independence from the political authorities. Chapter 26 closes the book with an examination of possible links between monetary policy, the price level and output.

## THE FOUNDING OF CENTRAL BANKS

Many countries established central banks decades, even centuries, earlier than Canada (see Table 24.1).

1 This statement should not be taken as a definition of monetarism. Even attempting an adequate definition will take us a significant portion of Chapter 26 to outline.

**Table 24.1** YEAR WHEN SELECTED CENTRAL BANKS WERE ESTABLISHED

| Country | Year Established |
|---|---|
| Belgium | 1850 |
| Canada | 1935 |
| France | 1800 |
| Germany | 1875 |
| Italy | 1893 |
| Japan | 1882 |
| Sweden | 1656 |
| Switzerland | 1905 |
| United Kingdom | 1694 |
| United States | 1913 |

Source: F.H. Capie, T.C. Mills, and G.E. Wood, "Central Bank Dependence and Inflation Performance: An Exploratory Data Analysis," in *Varieties of Monetary Reform: Lessons and Experiences on the Road to Monetary Union*, ed. P.L. Siklos (Dordrecht, The Netherlands: Kluwer Academic Publishers, 1994), pp. 95–132.

In many cases, the primary reason was the need for a *lender of last resort.* Recall that under a fractional reserve system, banks maintain only a small percentage of their deposits in the form of reserves. If one bank experiences a run, it will likely find itself short of cash. Worse, the run can easily spread to other banks.[2] Such runs may be averted by the action of a lender of last resort—a strong bank ready to meet other banks' liquidity needs. Thus, the emergence of central banking was a natural evolution of the financial industry. Indeed, in countries such as England, central banks were created from existing private banks that had a solid reputation for managing their finances plus the financial needs and gold reserves of the government. This sort of bank was naturally called on to aid in resolving liquidity crises. Such a role was strengthened if the central bank issued its own, well-received notes. Indeed, the momentum for establishing central banks was probably increased by the realization that they enabled governments to monopolize the issue of currency and thus extract additional revenues for themselves in the form of *seigniorage.*

## THE ORIGINS OF THE BANK OF CANADA

The Bank of Canada was formed in 1935. Did it emerge because of some inherent weaknesses of the Canadian banking system? Or was its creation a purely political phenomenon?

2 As we saw in Chapters 20 and 22, such an outcome was not unusual in the United States, at least before World War II.

Two historical events of the 1930s were influential. The first was the Great Depression. The simultaneous contraction of the money supply (instead of the expansion that would have been necessary for the economy to expand) was viewed as a failure of the existing arrangements for monetary policy. The second event was the effective end of the gold standard, which, as we have seen, had prevented excessive monetary expansion and, therefore, inflation. Yet, unlike the United States and many other countries that had a central bank and still experienced the Depression, Canada saw no bank failures during the 1930s. Neither did it experience explosive inflation between December 1928, when the country withdrew from the gold standard, and the opening of the Bank of Canada.

So perhaps the impetus was largely political. One factor was simply the uneasiness of hard times combined with Canadian regionalism. The MacMillan Commission, a royal commission struck in 1933 to investigate the possibility of establishing a central bank in Canada, returned a favourable majority report after conducting hearings nationwide. As two economic historians have noted:

> Domestically, in an environment where traditional trust in the beneficial nature of the market system was eroding and a spirit of nationalism was rising, political pressure was mounting to halt the deflation which was frequently blamed on the concentrated banking industry.[3]

Deflation was especially hurting farmers, who blamed the banks for creating it and for colluding to close branches in western Canada. Simultaneously, populist sentiment was rising in the West.

Other political forces also led to the creation of the Bank of Canada. One was the need for Canada to co-ordinate its increasingly international economic policies with those of other countries. Without a central bank, it lacked an effective institution for accomplishing the task. Another factor was Canada's evolution toward becoming a fully sovereign state after World War I. Establishing a central bank was simply another manifestation of its growing independence from Britain. Thus, when the Bank of Canada Act was passed by Parliament in 1934, it was probably enacted more for political reasons than for economic ones.

At first, the Bank was a private institution with stock issued—no one directly linked to a chartered bank could own any of it—and dividends to be paid out to shareholders up to a stated maximum; any additional profits were to accrue to the federal government. After the election of a Liberal government, in 1936, however, the Bank was completely nationalized and by 1938 the government had acquired all of the shares.

---

3 M.D. Bordo and A. Redish, "Why Did the Bank of Canada Emerge in 1935?" *Journal of Economic History* 47 (June 1987): 415.

## THE RESPONSIBILITIES OF THE BANK OF CANADA

Broadly speaking, the Bank of Canada is responsible for the conduct of Canada's monetary policy and for facilitating the growth of economic activity and the attainment of low levels of unemployment. Indeed, the preamble to the **Bank of Canada Act** specifies the following objectives:

> To regulate credit and currency in the best interests of the economic life of the nation, to control and protect the external value of the national monetary unit and to mitigate by its influence fluctuations in the general level of production, trade, prices, and unemployment, so far as may be possible within the scope of monetary action, and generally to promote the economic and financial welfare of the Dominion.

In addition to those sonorous long-term goals, the Bank must also meet a number of shorter-term objectives. In its day-to-day operations, its functions include:

1. Conducting open market operations.
2. Controlling monetary policy through interest rate control and monetary base management.
3. Acting as the federal government's fiscal agent.
4. Acting as a lender of last resort.
5. Conducting a number of other operations, such as foreign reserves management.

Since we have already considered in earlier chapters how central bank operations can influence interest rates we do not further examine this issue here. Rather we concentrate on the impact of the Bank's operations on its balance sheet. A condensed version of that sheet appears in Table 24.2.

Notice that the table reveals that in 1995 more than three quarters of the Bank's assets consisted of government debt of various types and maturities and over 95% of its liabilities were in notes in circulation. Although the percentages fluctuate somewhat over the years (see Table 24.3), these two items accounted for the lion's share of assets and liabilities. Also noticeable in Table 24.3 is the rising share of notes in circulation in the Bank of Canada's total liabilities. This, in great measure, is due to the diminished role played by reserves of the banking system, which were phased out under the most recent Bank Act.

We begin by considering open market operations, which represent the process of acquisition and disposition of government debt. Next, we examine the process of money supply control, which involves changes in the Bank's liabilities. In

**Table 24.2** A CONDENSED BALANCE SHEET OF THE BANK OF CANADA (year ending 1995, in millions of dollars)

| Assets | | Liabilities | |
|---|---|---|---|
| Government of Canada Direct and | | Notes in circulation[b] | 28,777.7 |
| Guaranteed Securities | | Deposits | |
| Treasury bills | 18,072.0 | Government of Canada | 17.6 |
| Government bonds maturing in | | Chartered banks | 478.8 |
| ≤ 3 years and under | 1,523.9 | Other Canadian Payments | |
| > 3 years | 3,767.9 | Association members | 38.9 |
| Bank of Canada advances[a] | 545.4 | Foreign central banks & others | 629.2 |
| Other investments | 5,293.0 | Foreign currency liabilities | 185.4 |
| Foreign currency deposits | 548.5 | Other liabilities | 73.0 |
| Other assets | 449.9 | Total | 30,200.6 |
| Total | 30,200.6 | | |

[a] To members of the Canadian Payments Association.
[b] Of which $4,972 is held by the chartered banks.
Source: *Bank of Canada Annual Report 1995*, pp. 32–33.

particular, we examine an especially powerful tool of money supply control called the drawdown and redeposit technique, which involves the management of government accounts with the Bank of Canada and the chartered banks. Finally, we briefly consider a few other tools at the Bank's disposal, such as the management of deposits and foreign currency operations.

## OPEN MARKET OPERATIONS AND BANKING RESERVES

The buying and selling of government securities in the open market has direct effects on interest rates, as we have discovered. Thus, these *open market operations (OMO)* of the Bank of Canada can be seen as a method of intervention in the market for loanable funds. The objective is to influence interest rates in ways compatible with its overall monetary policies.

Most OMOs tend to rely on the sale of Treasury bills, because they are auctioned every week. In order to influence the demand for loanable funds, the Bank must decide whether to add more T-bills to its portfolio (buy more than those that mature during the week) or let the portfolio go down (sell more bills than those that mature).

The simplified balance sheet in Table 24.4 illustrates.[4] Suppose the Bank of Canada decides to purchase from the chartered banks $100 million more T-bills

4 Notice that the balance sheet assumes that the chartered banks hold some reserves at all times. Even with zero reserve requirements, this situation is likely (although the amounts they wish to hold may be kept to

**Table 24.3** GOVERNMENT DEBT HELD BY THE BANK OF CANADA

| | **Government Debt** | | **Notes in Circulation** | |
|---|---|---|---|---|
| | Amount[a] (billions) | As % of total assets | Amount (billions) | As % of total liabilities |
| 1977 | 10.225 | 76.2 | 8.639 | 64.4 |
| 1978 | 11.924 | 78.9 | 9.540 | 63.2 |
| 1979 | 13.551 | 86.1 | 10.315 | 65.5 |
| 1980 | 15.794 | 91.2 | 11.108 | 64.2 |
| 1981 | 16.915 | 88.3 | 11.636 | 60.7 |
| 1982 | 15.371 | 79.1 | 12.719 | 65.5 |
| 1983 | 17.026 | 82.3 | 14.163 | 68.5 |
| 1984 | 17.152 | 90.6 | 15.236 | 80.5 |
| 1985 | 15.667 | 74.1 | 16.672 | 78.9 |
| 1986 | 18.211 | 86.9 | 17.911 | 85.5 |
| 1987 | 20.195 | 87.7 | 19.947 | 86.6 |
| 1988 | 20.346 | 83.7 | 21.032 | 86.5 |
| 1989 | 20.825 | 84.0 | 22.093 | 89.2 |
| 1990 | 19.998 | 79.1 | 22.970 | 90.9 |
| 1991 | 22.096 | 81.7 | 24.481 | 90.5 |
| 1992 | 22.367 | 81.5 | 25.609 | 93.3 |
| 1993 | 23.437 | 80.7 | 27.237 | 95.5 |
| 1994 | 25.076 | 83.4 | 28.329 | 94.3 |
| 1995 | 23.364 | 77.4 | 28.778 | 95.3 |

[a] Treasury bills and government bonds of other maturities.
Source: *Bank of Canada Review* (Winter 1995–96): Table B1.

than those that are maturing that week. Its assets rise by that amount. If the chartered banks are the institutions that simultaneously decide to reduce their holdings of T-bills,[5] the net effect of the OMO is to raise their reserve deposits by $100 million. It is equivalent to a portfolio reallocation away from T-bills toward more reserves. Note, however, that the effect on the chartered banks is entirely on their assets. Their liabilities are unaffected because the entire amount of the increase is initially in *excess reserves*.[6] As discussed in Chapter 16, excess reserves can generate a multiple expansion of bank deposits and thus the money

a minimum through sophisticated cash management techniques, such as the use of the overnight market or special purchase and resale agreements). That decision would not matter to the situation analysed here. A look at Table 24.2 confirms this to be true.

5 The transaction could have involved investment dealers. We choose the banks for our example because the effect of an OMO on their excess reserves is immediate and drives the money supply.

6 Excess to its originally desired position, since reserve requirements have been phased out.

**Table 24.4** AN OPEN MARKET OPERATION AND ITS CONSEQUENCES (millions of dollars)

**Bank of Canada**

| Assets | Liabilities |
|---|---|
| Treasury bills + 100 | Deposits |
| | Chartered banks + 100 |

**Chartered Banks**

| Assets | Liabilities |
|---|---|
| Reserves | No change |
| At Bank of Canada + 100 | |
| Treasury bills − 100 | |

"Excess" reserves ↑

↓

Multiple expansion of deposits

↓

Expansion of the money supply

Note: "Excess" here is used in the sense that current reserves are not at levels desired by banks.

supply. (We return to this point a little later when we formally model the money supply process.)

Needless to say, the OMO is a powerful tool because its effect on excess reserves is immediate. The Bank of Canada relies on it, as do the central banks of Japan, France, Italy, Australia, and, most recently, Germany. OMOs are not as widely used in the United States, however, probably because its banking system is relatively more fragmented. One difficulty with OMOs is that they are apparently costly to undertake and with capital mobility nearly perfect central banks need other tools to influence interest rates more quickly.

## Other Direct Influences on Reserves

Central banks possess a variety of other instruments to influence the reserves of the banking system. One such tool is the *special purchase and resale agreement* (SPRA) described in Chapter 4.

Another is the drawdown and redeposit technique, which is available to the Bank of Canada because it is the fiscal agent of the federal government. It holds some government funds itself, while other government funds are held in the banking system. By shifting amounts between the two, it can immediately influence the cash reserves of the banking system in a manner similar to an OMO. This **drawdown and redeposit technique** is illustrated in Table 24.5. Suppose government deposits at the chartered banks rise by \$100 million—say, because tax receipts come in or Canada Savings Bonds with an attractive yield go on sale.[7] Initially, the government accounts will show an increase of \$100 million at the Bank of Canada. The Bank of Canada deducts the same amount in chartered bank deposits held at the Bank of Canada. The public, having paid for the CSBs or their taxes by writing cheques, will reduce its deposits at the chartered banks by \$100 million. Thus, chartered banks reserves will also fall by \$100 million. The latter transaction affects both the chartered banks' balance sheet and the balance sheet of the Bank of Canada. If the Bank wishes to avoid the multiple contraction of deposits and the money supply that would follow, it need only redeposit into the government's banking system deposits by an amount equivalent to the original increase, leaving the system's cash reserves unchanged. Any other policy would affect cash reserves and thus leave open the possibility of deposit contraction. The opposite scenario would take place if the government disbursed cash from the accounts to pay for its purchases. In that case, the Bank of Canada would draw down or withdraw funds from government accounts at the chartered banks. This would be necessary to prevent the swelling of chartered bank reserves.

Clearly, drawdowns and redeposits can influence the banking system even more quickly than OMOs, although the size of changes in its cash position is relatively small.[8]

The Bank of Canada makes regular use of its ability to switch government deposits to and from the banking sector. Germany and Switzerland also use this technique extensively. However, this technique is considered to be expensive. A recent report suggests that there is a substantial net cost to holding government balances.[9] As a result, cash management bills (see Chapter 4) are being used more extensively.

---

7 When the government announced a 1-year rate of 19.5% in 1981, it was flooded with several billion dollars more in CSB sales than it expected. Despite the reduced popularity of CSBs the government announced measures to make them once again more attractive to hold. See Chapter 4.

8 For other technical details about the drawdown and redeposit technique, see P. Martin, *Inside the Bank of Canada's Weekly Financial Statistics: A Technical Guide*, 2d ed. (Vancouver: The Fraser Institute, 1989): 35–36. Also, with the introduction of the LVTS tool of monetary policy (see Chapter 4) a modification was introduced in this policy due to the removal of required reserves. The Bank must make an additional calculation to ensure that settlement or clearing balances are zero on a daily basis.

9 See "Managing the Federal Government's Cash Balances: A Technical Note," *Bank of Canada Review* (Spring 1995): 55–69.

**Table 24.5** THE DRAWDOWN AND REDEPOSIT TECHNIQUE
(millions of dollars)

**Initial Situation**
**Bank of Canada**

| Assets | Liabilities |
|---|---|
| No change | Deposits |
| | Chartered banks −100 |
| | Government of Canada +100 |

**Chartered Banks**

| Assets | Liabilities |
|---|---|
| Reserves | Deposits |
| At Bank of Canada −100 | Public −100 |

**Redposit**
**Bank of Canada**

| Assets | Liabilities |
|---|---|
| No change | Deposits |
| | Chartered banks + 100 |
| | Government of Canada −100 |

**Chartered Banks**

| Assets | Liabilities |
|---|---|
| Reserves | Deposits |
| At Bank of Canada + 100 | Government of Canada +100 |

Net Effect
Reserves of the banking system are unchanged

## BASE CONTROL

By far the largest liability item in the Bank of Canada's balance sheet is notes in circulation. A distant second are deposits of the chartered banks and other members of the Canadian Payments Association, which represent the reserves of the banking system. Together they account for approximately 97% of all of the Bank's liabilities (see Table 24.2). Recall that the sum of these two items is known as the *monetary base* or *high-powered money*. So we can write

$$CUR + RES = \text{Monetary Base} \qquad (24.1)$$

where

$CUR$ = currency (held by chartered banks and the public)
$RES$ = reserves of the banking system held at the Bank of Canada

To the extent that the Bank of Canada issues currency and manages and supervises the need for banks to maintain sufficient reserves it has **base control**—control over the monetary base—and thus over the size and growth of the money supply. Its control is by no means total, however. It cannot dictate the currency requirements of the public nor the size of the variations in the chartered banks' reserves. And it cannot control transfers to and from various classes of deposits, even though these moves influence cash reserves.

Another source of uncontrollable growth in the money supply stems from the process of **debt monetization**, which means issuing money to support government spending. As we are all keenly aware, the federal government has persistently run deficits for years. The primary form of finance has been through the sale of bonds to the public and to foreigners, but the Bank of Canada always has the option of purchasing the bonds outright from the government, simply issuing a quantity of notes sufficient to complete the transaction. Table 24.6 illustrates. Suppose the federal government issues $100 million of government bonds, all of which are purchased by the Bank of Canada, which then issues $100 million in notes. If the government wishes, it may deposit the proceeds at chartered banks, which now experience a sudden rise in reserves. And an increase in reserves has the potential to lead to a multiple expansion of deposits and of the money supply, with consequences for inflation, as we know all too well.

Remember, however, that the Bank of Canada can offset any imminent rise in the money supply through OMOs or drawdowns. In any event, debt monetization has represented only a minor source of Canadian government finance, except during the war years. This is not the case in many other countries.

## OTHER CENTRAL BANK TOOLS

The Bank of Canada has at its disposal a variety of other tools with which it can influence its balance sheet and potentially the financial position of the federal government or the cash reserve position of the banking sector. We briefly consider four such tools: foreign exchange operations, the reserve requirements, the bank rate, and moral suasion.

### Foreign Exchange Operations

One of the functions of the Bank of Canada is to manage the country's foreign exchange reserves, which it holds in what is called the **Exchange Fund Account (EFA)**. By managing this account (under the authority of the Ministry of Finance), the Bank of Canada can influence the reserves of the banking system and thus

**Table 24.6** MONETIZING THE DEBT AND THE POSSIBLE CONSEQUENCES

**Bank of Canada**

| Assets | Liabilities |
|---|---|
| Government securities + 100 | Bank of Canada notes +100 |

↓

**Chartered Banks**

| Assets | Liabilities |
|---|---|
| Reserves | Deposits |
| At Bank of Canada +100 | Government of Canada +100 |

↓

Multiple expansion of deposits
Multiple expansion of the money supply

finance the temporary cash requirements of the government without having to resort to, say, a new bond issue. Table 24.7 illustrates the result of what is called a **foreign exchange swap**. The Bank of Canada reduces the EFA by $100 million through the sale of foreign exchange and uses the proceeds to increase government deposits. It can redeposit the proceeds with the chartered banks, which then experience a rise in reserves with consequences that should be clear by now. Of course, these swaps are temporary; the drawing down of foreign reserves is accomplished by a futures contract to replenish EFA at some future date.[10]

A different kind of swap was introduced in 1991. Rather than swap foreign exchange with the EFA, the Bank of Canada began to swap foreign currencies for Canadian currency. In this kind of arrangement, foreign currencies are sold to buy Canadian dollars; at a future date, the transaction is reversed with the foreign currencies being brought back for Canadian dollars. The government uses these swaps, which are short term, to obtain Canadian dollars without having to borrow in the domestic market. The costs of such swaps depend on the relative

10 If the central bank's objective is simply to effect a portfolio reallocation, it can use an OMO to *sterilize* the impact of a foreign exchange transaction immediately, rather than in the future. The extent of central banks' use of these techniques as a deliberate tool of monetary policy is open to debate. For other technical details about the swap example considered in Table 24.7, see P. Martin, *Inside the Bank of Canada's Weekly Financial Statistics: A Technical Guide*, 2d ed. (Vancouver: The Fraser Institute, 1989): 38–39.

**Table 24.7** A FOREIGN EXCHANGE SWAP

**Initial Situation**
**Bank of Canada**

| Assets | Liabilities |
|---|---|
| Foreign currency assets + 100[a] | Deposits |
| ↑ | Government of Canada +100 |
| From the Exchange Fund Account | |

**After Redeposit**
**Bank of Canada**

| Assets | Liabilities |
|---|---|
| No change | Deposits |
| | Government of Canada −100 |
| | Chartered banks +100 |

**Charter Banks**

| Assets | Liabilities |
|---|---|
| Reserves | Deposits |
| At Bank of Canada +100 | Government of Canada +100 |

[a] This actually comes under the heading "Other Investments" but the meaning is clearer with the above definitions. The amount shown is the Canadian-dollar equivalent at the spot rate.

interest rates in the different currencies, as well as the relationship between spot and forward exchange rates.[11]

## Reserve Requirements

The manipulation of reserve requirements is a tool available to the central banks in several countries. Reserve requirements were phased out in Canada to be replaced by greater reliance on more sophisticated cash management techniques. Members of the Canadian Payments Association[12] are required to maintain at least a zero balance at the Bank of Canada daily as well as over a "calculation period" (a period from the middle of one month to the middle of the next).

11 In 1995, the Bank reported foreign currency contract purchases of 64.2 million and sales of 5,646.2 million. See Bank of Canada *Annual Report 1995*, p. 37.

12 Membership in the CPA is mandatory for chartered banks and voluntary (but common) for non-bank financial intermediaries. Some CPA members are *clearers*, institutions that are permitted to settle indebtedness between a number of depository institutions. Not every bank can be a clearer. To qualify, a clearer must be responsible for at least 0.5% of transactions. Currently there are 8 banks and 4 non-bank financial institutions in this group. See *Bank of Canada Review* (Spring 1995), p. 5129.

## ECONOMICS FOCUS 24.1 To Tax or To Print

Why do some countries finance almost all their spending by taxing the income or purchases of their citizens while others resort more to the printing press—that is, to seigniorage and inflation?

Cukierman, Edwards, and Tabellini argue that the type of political system combined with the relative costs of administering and enforcing a tax system versus reliance on the printing press explains why some countries rely on inflation while others do not.

Consider the wide difference in inflation rates. In some South American countries, such as Chile, Brazil, and Argentina, triple-digit inflation has not been unheard of. By contrast, Germany and Switzerland have experienced inflation rates of less than 5% during much of the last 30 years. One reason for the difference is that low-inflation-rate countries tend to have developed efficient systems of tax collection and enforcement. This is not the case in many South American countries, where, in part because the agricultural sector is large, tax collection and enforcement are relatively costly. It is also the case that Germany and Switzerland have stable democratic institutions with independent central banks, while South American countries generally do not.

**Source:**

A. Cukierman, S. Edwards, and G. Tabellini, "Seigniorage and Political Instability," *American Economic Review* 82 (June 1992): 537–55.

Should a negative balance occur, the institution will have to take out a loan to cover the overdraft at some published lending rate. Otherwise banks need no longer maintain any required reserves.

Table 24.8 illustrates how the new zero-reserve requirement system operated in its initial phase. The calculation period here is assumed to run from the 16th (or next closest business day) of one month to the 15th of the next month.[13] Suppose that on Thursday, August 22, the hypothetical bank in question has a zero balance at the Bank of Canada. Now suppose the same bank ends up at the end of the next day with a negative balance. It would have to borrow \$25 million to maintain a minimum zero balance. However, August 23 is a Friday, when reserves are weighted more heavily than other days (because it is the last day before the weekend), so its settlement balance must be \$25 million $\times$ 3 = \$75 million. The bank can reduce its settlement balance whenever it experiences a positive end-of-day balance (as it does in the table on August 27). The example proceeds in the same fashion throughout the remainder of the settlement period, which in this example, ends on September 18.

Members of the Canadian Payments Association complained in 1995 that the averaging system portrayed in Table 24.8 was cumbersome and that a daily settlement system would be simpler. So, in early 1996, the Bank agreed to change

13 The calculation period originally ended the third Thursday of a calendar month.

**Table 24.8** ZERO REQUIRED RESERVE REQUIREMENT SYSTEM: AN EXAMPLE

| Date (weight) | End-of-Day Balance[a] | Loan[b] (millions of dollars) | Cumulative Settlement Balance |
|---|---|---|---|
| Th. Aug. 22 | 0 | | 0 |
| Fr. Aug. 23 (×3) | −25 | 25 | −25 × 3 = − 75 |
| Mo. Aug. 26 | 0 | | −75 |
| Tu. Aug. 27 | 25 | | −50 |
| We. Aug. 28 | 0 | | −50 |
| Th. Aug. 29 | −25 | 25 | −25 − 50 = −75 |
| Fr. Aug. 30 (×4) | 0 | | −75 |
| Tu. Sept. 3[c] | 25 | | −50 |
| We. Sept. 4 | −25 | 25 | −75 |
| Th. Sept. 5 | 0 | | −75 |
| Fr. Sept. 6 (×3) | 25 | | −75 + (25 × 3) = 0 |
| Mo. Sept. 9 | 0 | | 0 |
| Tu. Sept. 10 | −50 | 50 | −50 |
| We. Sept. 11 | 50 | | 0 |
| Th. Sept. 12 | 25 | | −25 |
| Fr. Sept. 13 (×3) | −25 | 25 | +25 − (25 × 3) = −50 |
| Mo. Sept. 16 | 0 | | −50 |
| Tu. Sept. 17 | 0 | | −50 |
| We. Sept. 18 | 0 | | −50 |

[a] At the Bank of Canada.

[b] Must be taken out whenever an end-of-day balance is negative.

[c] Monday, Sept. 2, in this example, is Labour Day, a holiday.

The above example shows that, in a world of zero reserve requirements, banks must ensure that there is no overdraft by the end of the calculation period. Therefore, some banks will occasionally have a positive balance at the Bank of Canada (earning interest), while at other times banks will be in an overdraft position. In the latter case, the Bank of Canada will supply the necessary liquidity at a penalty interest rate to discourage such behaviour on a regular basis. In any event, the minimum balance at the end of each day is zero and some days (Fridays or holidays) are weighted more heavily than others to cover cash demand over weekends and holidays.

Source: "The Implementation of Monetary Policy in a System with Zero Reserve Requirements," Bank of Canada Discussion Paper No. 3 (6 September 1991).

whereby it would charge a penalty rate on negative clearing balances equal to the bank rate and pay a rate equivalent to the bottom of the band for the overnight rate (see Chapter 4) when balances were positive.[14]

14 See "A Proposed Framework for the Implementation of Monetary Policy in the Large Value Transfer System Environment," Discussion Paper 2, *Bank of Canada Review* (Spring 1996): 53–66.

Other countries that have moved away from the imposition of cash ratios have different rules. Switzerland, for example, outlaws overdrafts, requiring that clearing banks ensure a positive balance with the Swiss National Bank before transactions can be completed. In addition, Switzerland, as well as Australia, requires banks to keep some liquid assets for precautionary purposes. In Sweden, alternatively, a bank whose clearings normally result in a negative balance with the central bank may be required by the latter to borrow to meet cash reserve needs. UK banks have not been required to hold reserves against deposits since 1971, but neither can they borrow directly from the Bank of England. Instead, money market dealers are used as a source of cash reserve financing.

## The Bank Rate

As one would expect from a lender of last resort, central banks lend directly to banks. In Canada, the means used are called Bank of Canada advances. The interest rate is the *bank rate.*

Until March 1980, the Bank of Canada set the bank rate independently, and so it signalled the direction the Bank wished interest rates to take. Then the bank rate has floated with the Treasury bill rate, losing much of its significance as a distinct tool of monetary policy. Recognizing this the Bank began in 1996 to tie the bank rate to changes in the overnight rate (see Chapter 4).

## Moral Suasion

Central banks sometimes resort to **moral suasion**—making suggestions, in private or in public, to influence people or institutions. The Bank of Canada may, for example, ask the system's banks to co-operate in observing some ceiling on interest rates[15] or in easing credit allocation voluntarily. A harsher view of what moral suasion stands for was made by Thomas Courchene: "Moral suasion . . . gives the Bank of Canada the freedom to revise the Bank Act between decennial revisions."[16]

Although the Bank of Canada has often resorted to moral suasion, it has probably been practised more extensively by the governments of the day. (Consider the recurring parliamentary discussions about the interest rates charged on credit card debt.) Moreover, deregulation and globalization are probably making moral suasion a rather ineffective tool of monetary policy. It is presumably easier

---

15 For example, in establishing the Winnipeg Agreement, in effect from 1972 to 1975, the Bank of Canada asked the banks to hold a ceiling on interest rates on term deposits.

16 T.J. Courchene, *Money, Inflation, and the Bank of Canada: An Analysis of Canadian Monetary Policy from 1970 to Early 1975* (Montreal: C.D. Howe Institute, 1976), 124–27.

to use, the smaller the number of banks and the more closed the financial system is to international influences.

## A SIMPLE MONEY MULTIPLIER MODEL

In Chapter 16, we outlined a simple money multiplier process. We are now ready to demonstrate more formally the links between central bank actions and the money supply. In doing so, we assume that the monetary aggregate of interest is M1, the narrow definition of the money supply.[17]

Recall the definition of the M1 money supply: the currency in circulation plus demand deposits. In equation form, we write

$$\text{M1} = CUR + DEP \tag{24.3}$$

where $DEP$ = demand deposits (at chartered banks) and $CUR$ is as previously defined.

The public determines the currency component of M1, and the banking sector creates demand deposits. Clearly, it makes a great deal of difference how the public chooses the proportions of currency and deposits for, as we have seen, currency injections or withdrawals from banks have multiplicative effects on the money supply. For this reason, economists have long been interested in the currency–deposit ratio, $cr$, which is

$$cr = \frac{CUR}{DEP} \tag{24.4}$$

Strictly speaking, the public determines $cr$, so it cannot be directly controlled by central bank actions. But for the moment, let us take $cr$ as given.

We have already seen a link between M1 and central bank actions in equation (24.1). For convenience, we repeat it:

$$\text{Base} = CUR + RES$$

where

Base = the monetary base or high-powered money

$RES$ = target reserves of the banking system

Now we express M1 and Base in terms of $DEP$ with the help of some simple algebra. Dividing both sides of equation (24.3) by $DEP$ yields

---

17 This simplification is sufficient to illustrate the relevant issues and problems, even though the Bank of Canada itself prefers to monitor broader aggregates, such as M2+.

$$\frac{\text{M1}}{DEP} = \frac{CUR}{DEP} + \frac{DEP}{DEP} = cr + 1 \tag{24.5}$$

Similarly, for high-powered money, dividing by *DEP* gives us

$$\frac{\text{Base}}{DEP} = \frac{CUR}{DEP} + \frac{RES}{DEP} = cr + rr \tag{24.6}$$

where $rr = RES/DEP$ represents the reserve ratio discussed previously. Then we rewrite equations (24.5) and (24.6) as

$$\text{M1} = (cr + 1)DEP$$
$$\text{Base} = (cr + rr)DEP$$

Finally, if we evaluate

$$\frac{\text{M1}}{\text{Base}} = \frac{(cr + 1)}{(cr + rr)} \tag{24.7}$$

we obtain an expression for the proportion by which M1 exceeds Base.

Equation (24.7) is the expression for the **money multiplier**. It is fundamentally determined by two variables: *cr* and *rr*. The latter is currently set by the banking sector.

Why is *cr* potentially an important variable? Consider the example of an open market operation. When the Bank of Canada purchases bonds from chartered banks, the proceeds create excess reserves that set in motion the money multiplier process. Thus, holding *R* constant, *rr* rises, which produces the increase in the money supply that an OMO policy is supposed to produce, in the process, reducing *cr*. But suppose that the public is satisfied with the level of *cr* attained prior to the open market operation. If it shifts funds from deposits to currency, in order to restore *cr* to its original and presumably "optimal" level, then the money multiplier is affected. Thus, we must not assume that central bank policies that influence the reserves of the banking system are independent of the behaviour of the public. (Unfortunately, this fact makes it even more difficult to gauge the significance of high-powered money changes on the money supply.)

## THE PERFORMANCE OF THE BANK OF CANADA

Entire volumes are written about the Bank of Canada and its performance,[18] and the record of its monetary policy has been mentioned in various places throughout this text. Here we outline only some of the most salient features of its history.

18 A partial list includes E.P. Neufeld, *Bank of Canada Operations and Policy* (Toronto): University of Toronto

## PRE-WAR ERA

The earliest days of the Bank of Canada were marked by its working to smooth seasonal variation in interest rates and to make a market for government debt.

Its greatest early contribution lay in its role as a provider and regulator of cash in the economy. In the mid-1930s, Canada was still a rural-based economy, experiencing considerable seasonal fluctuation in the demand for currency and thus in interest rates. A perceived advantage of creating a central monetary authority was that it could manage the money supply in such a way as to smooth out seasonal variation in interest rates. The Bank was successful in this effort. Ever since, it has been the money supply that has experienced seasonality in its movements.[19]

When the Bank of Canada began operations at the end of the Great Depression, it was under political pressure to somehow use monetary policy to manage the economy in the face of worldwide confusion. Thus, it is not surprising that its stated objectives were on a grand scale nor that it did not meet all of them. It did, however, quickly create a market for government debt instruments (particularly but not only T-bills). This development was vital, given the contemporary world's trend toward great involvement (that is, greater spending) by government in the economy. This active market would prove especially useful during the war years, when government deficit spending soared.

Another important feature of early Bank of Canada history was its fairly frequent resorting to moral suasion. This tendency was not surprising, given the highly concentrated nature of the Canadian banking system during the 1930s. After all, in 1935, when the Bank opened its doors to the public, the country had only 10 chartered banks.

## POSTWAR PERIOD

The early part of the postwar period was marked by high government debt, the need to reintermediate the Canadian economy following wartime controls, and

---

Press, 1958); R.A. Shearer, J.F. Chant, and D.E. Bond, *The Economics of the Canadian Financial System: Theory, Policy and Institutions*, 3rd ed., (Scarborough, Ont.: Prentice-Hall, 1995), especially Chapters 12 and 24; T.J. Courchene, *Monetarism and Controls: The Inflation Fighters* (Toronto: C.D. Howe Institute, 1976); T.J. Courchene, *No Place to Stand?* (Toronto: C.D. Howe Institute, 1983); P.W. Howitt, *Monetary Policy in Transition: A Study of Bank of Canada Policy, 1982–1985* (Toronto: C.D. Howe Research Institute, 1986); T.J. Courchene, *Money, Inflation, and the Bank of Canada: An Analysis of Monetary Gradualism, 1975–1980* (Montreal: C.D. Howe Institute, 1981); G.S. Watts, *The Bank of Canada Origins and Early History* (ed. by T.K. Rymes), (Ottawa: Carleton University Press, 1993); and P. Howitt, *Monetary Policy in Transition: A Study of Bank of Canada Policy, 1982–85* (Toronto: C.D. Howe Institute, 1986).

19 Recall from Chapter 2 that seasonality is an issue only for narrow aggregates, such as M1; broader monetary aggregates display little seasonality.

the great demands from reconstruction and industrialization. Still in vogue was the Keynesian prescription of government spending to ensure high employment, which translated into a policy of "cheap money"—that is, relatively low interest rates. Indeed, interest rates were artificially low since they were essentially pegged at the government's behest.[20]

In 1953, following the Korean War, the Bank of Canada faced its first major recession. It responded, exactly as it should have, by easing monetary policy and assisting the financing of government deficits.

## THE COYNE AFFAIR

The latter 1950s were marked by controversies on topics that sound very familiar today: high interest rates, particularly in a time of recession; the Canadian–US exchange rate; and the control of inflation.

During 1955 and 1956, the economy was booming, and the dangers of inflation lurked. The Bank of Canada encouraged the development of the money market (often using it itself for OMOs) and generally followed a restrictive monetary policy. But market interest rates were rising, and in late 1956, after raising the bank rate several times, the Bank allowed it to float by tying its movement to the T-bill rate, a significant policy change that is still in effect today.

By the end of the 1950s, the economy had softened, unemployment was high, the exchange rate was fairly high,[21] and interest rates were climbing, creating, among other things, a considerable differential with those current in the United States and other world capital markets. The Bank also had to find large amounts for government financing (a new phenomenon for it in peacetime—in 1956, for example, monetary policy had been assisted by a large government surplus). And it faced the approaching maturity of the wartime Victory Bonds. Partly as an anti-inflation measure, the debt was rolled over into long-term bonds. One consequence of this action was a sharp increase in the average maturity of government debt (from approximately 8 years to 15 years); another was the necessity of a temporary expansionary policy. But it was soon reversed. The Bank of Canada again began to restrict the money supply. The policy worked in that little inflation occurred. But interest rates were driven up, the difficulties of exporters increased, US capital poured into the country—and unemployment soared. The culmination of these events was Canada's best-known policy conflict between the Bank and the government: the **Coyne affair**.

---

20 Because the Bank was still supporting the war debt. We have already seen the distortions in the financial system that are created when interest rates are pegged at some value inconsistent with market equilibrium. But a similar policy was in place in the United States at the time.

21 Canada was then on a floating exchange rate régime, having left the Bretton Woods Agreements in 1950. It would return to that fixed-rate system from 1962 to 1970.

James Coyne, who had become the second governor of the Bank of Canada in 1955, believed strongly that the Bank needed to be rather interventionist, in particular to control inflation and the growth of credit in the economy.[22] His policy of high interest rates at a time of rising unemployment produced severe tension with the federal government of the day, which was led by John Diefenbaker, and the Minister of Finance Donald Fleming. By 1960, politicians, bankers, and even the academic community complained that the Bank appeared obsessed with the control of inflation at the expense of everything else.

> It has its eye firmly fixed on the moral wickedness of the slightest changes of inflation and is unmoved by the patent facts of growing unemployment and stagnating national income.[23]

The controversy reached a climax in mid-1961, although the battle was fought out not on its true grounds—the independence of the Bank—but on the details of Coyne's pension. When the board of the Bank asked Coyne to resign, he refused. As a result, the government introduced a motion in Parliament declaring an expansionary fiscal policy and a vacancy in the post of governor. The Commons passed the bill, but the opposition-controlled Senate defeated it. Following another public display in which Coyne attacked the government, he did resign, and the motion was passed.

Not surprisingly, the Coyne affair produced a revision in the government–Bank of Canada relationship. Louis Rasminsky, the incoming governor, agreed that the government has the ultimate responsibility for monetary policy. But he insisted that any disagreement between the government and the Bank must be followed by a written directive from the Minister of Finance, requiring the Bank to change its policy to conform with the government's wishes. He also stated that should a disagreement of this kind take place, he would implement the government's wishes and immediately thereafter resign his post. This relationship continues to this day, although no directive has ever been issued.[24]

---

22 Coyne's many other ideas included requiring chartered banks to hold secondary reserves and bringing the banking system into more conformity with the UK and US models to permit more long-term lending to consumers (to finance housing purchases, for example). And it was Coyne who initiated the floating bank rate and oversaw the conversion of the Victory Bonds.

23 H. Scott Gordon, *The Economists versus the Bank of Canada* (Toronto: The Ryerson Press, 1961): 15.

24 Indeed, some people theorize that the system reduces overt argument between the Bank and the government. Disagreement might force the issuance of a directive, which no Minister of Finance wants to do. See T.K. Rymes, "On the Coyne–Rasminsky Directive and Responsibility for Monetary Policy in Canada," in P.L. Siklos (ed.), *Varieties of Monetary Reforms: Lessons and Experiences on the Road to Monetary Union* (Boston: Kluwer Academic Publishers, 1994), pp. 351–66.

## THE 1960s AND BEYOND

The 1962–70 period was a time of fixed exchange rates. Many of the Bank's activities were concerned with maintaining the Canadian dollar at 92.5¢ US. Both the economy and inflation were relatively less important problems.

This relatively peaceful period came to an end with the oil price shocks of the 1970s. The resulting *stagflation*—the unusual combination of a stagnating economy and high inflation—led to the abandonment of the Keynesian prescription and stimulated renewed interest in money control as advocated by monetarists.[25] This culminated in the 1975 Saskatoon Monetary Manifesto in which the governor of the Bank of Canada, Gerald Bouey, announced that the Bank would practise **monetary targeting**—work to hold the growth of the money supply to an explicit range—rather than interest rate control.[26] In particular, the governor stated:

> Whatever else may need to be done to bring inflation under control, it is absolutely essential to keep the rate of monetary expansion within reasonable limits. Any programme that did not include this policy would be doomed to failure. There is no way of preserving its value if money is created on an excessive scale.[27]

Termed the Strategy of Gradualism (since the object was to reduce over time target growth rates in M1 from an initial range of 10% to 15% per annum), the policy encountered the difficulties inherent in monetary control. Suffice it to say for now that, partly as a result of the second oil price shock of 1979, it was deemed a failure as inflation once again began to rise toward double-digit levels. Perhaps more important, the policy led to considerably more volatile interest rates and thus magnified the problem of interest rate risk. Some critics suggested that the policy was too gradual;[28] others that the Bank should not have focused on the M1 aggregate.[29]

The recession of 1981–82 led to the next phase of monetary policy. The Bank of Canada would tolerate or even encourage high interest rates if they were necessary to stem inflation. This policy resulted from a growing focus on the primary role of the central bank as a guarantor of price stability. Indeed, as the

---

25 Monetarism is described in Chapter 26.

26 The economic implications of this choice are considered in Chapter 25.

27 T.J. Courchene, *Monetarism and Controls: The Inflation Fighters* (Montreal: C.D. Howe Institute, 1976): 25.

28 It is interesting to note that the United States also eventually abandoned a money control rule, even though its policy was anything but gradual. Unexpected changes in the relationship between money, income, and prices also doomed the money targeting experiment.

29 Our earlier discussion of money multipliers could certainly lead one to conclude that had the Bank focused on M2, it might have acceded to the wishes of those who favoured greater monetary restraint.

decade of the 1990s began proposals appeared to enshrine the goal of price stability into the Bank of Canada Act.

The ongoing recession of 1991–93 did not alter this view. In fact, John Crow, the previous governor, stated that the current excessively broad mandate of the Bank of Canada "muddies the accountability of the institution."[30] It is somewhat surprising that the governor would ask that the central bank be more accountable; traditionally, central banks seem to prefer that their actions and motives be secret. But the lesson learned from the stagflation of the 1970s is that high inflation and cheap money eventually create the need for a correction of some kind, which tends to produce large economic costs in the form of lost output and high unemployment rates. Nevertheless, it is also important to point out that monetary policy can do no more than assist economic activity. Economic growth or the lack thereof requires policies other than purely monetary ones, especially if monetary policy is viewed as being neutral in the long run.[31]

## A MANDATE FOR PRICE STABILITY

Not long after John Crow became governor of the Bank of Canada in 1987, he laid out a specific agenda for disinflation. The first statement to this effect was made in the course of the Hanson Lecture at the University of Alberta in January 1988. In the course of this lecture he argued that "monetary policy should be conducted so as to achieve a pace of monetary expansion that promotes price stability in the value of money. This means pursuing a policy aimed at achieving and maintaining stable prices."[32] But it was not until February 1991, just one month after the GST was introduced, that the federal government sealed its approval of the **inflation-targeting** approach when the then Finance Minister Michael Wilson, in presenting his budget, announced formal inflation targets.[33] The initial targets were as follows:

1. 3% inflation by December 1992
2. 2% thereafter by December 1995
3. Price stability defined as less than 2% by the second half of the 1990s[34]

---

30 "Bank of Canada Not a One-Man Show: Crow," *The Financial Post*, 17 January 1992, p. 5.

31 We consider the question of monetary neutrality in Chapter 26.

32 J.W. Crow, "The Work of Monetary Policy," *Bank of Canada Review* (February 1988), p. 4.

33 For a description of this period in the history of the Bank of Canada, see D.E.W. Laidler and W.B.P. Robson, *The Great Canadian Disinflation: The Economics and Politics of Monetary Policy in Canada, 1988–93* (Toronto: C.D. Howe Institute, 1993).

34 See W.B.P. Robson, "Canada's New Inflation Targets," C.D. Howe Institute Commentary no. 31 (May 1991), and "Targets for Reducing Inflation: Further Operational and Measurement Considerations" *Bank of Canada Review* (September 1991): 3–23.

During the federal election campaign in the fall of 1993, there was much discussion about whether the incoming Liberal government, which was about to replace the Conservatives, would share the same commitment to low inflation. In the event, Governor Crow was not reappointed for a second term but was replaced, as has been the custom at the Bank, by his senior deputy-governor, Gordon Thiessen. The target bands were extended to the end of 1998 but were redefined as consisting of a range of 1 to 3% inflation with the mid-point of 2% regarded as the most desirable outcome. A decision about the specific meaning of the term "price stability" was deferred until 1998. Nevertheless, the Bank of Canada has made it clear that while the target was in terms of overall CPI, exceptions or adjustments were to be made for changes in food and energy prices. Significantly, however, the Bank stressed that only the immediate effects of shocks to inflation would be accommodated; second round effects, such as those which might affect wages, were not to be validated by monetary policy. Figure 24.1 shows the evolution of the CPI since 1986, as well as the target bands and their midpoints. It is immediately clear that inflation in the CPI and CPI excluding food, energy, and the effect of indirect taxes, also referred to as "core inflation" display quite different behaviour.

Another major development in the area of monetary policy was the drive to increase the Bank's accountability and transparency of its operation. As noted earlier, central banks have often been surrounded by a certain aura of mystery because they kept their operations and objectives relatively sheltered from public scrutiny. In 1995, however, the Bank of Canada released its first *Monetary Policy Report*,[35] a semiannual document created to enhance the Bank's ability to communicate publicly its operations and objectives. Indeed, the inaugural issue stressed that greater accountability implied meeting the following criteria:

1. A clear policy objective, . . .
2. A medium-term perspective (given the long lags for the full impact of monetary policy actions on the economy), . . .
3. Recognition that monetary policy works through both the interest rate and the exchange rate.

Moreover, satisfying 1 to 3 required a policy which aimed for price stability, as currently defined by the inflation-control targets. Assisting the development of a new effective mandate was the *Manley Report*[36] which was virtually ignored, no doubt due to the arrival of an imminent election as well as the heat emanating

35 See Bank of Canada *Monetary Policy Report* (May 1995).

36 See First Report of the Sub-Committee on the Bank of Canada / Eighth report of the Standing Committee on Finance "The Mandate and Governance of the Bank of Canada" (February 1992).

**FIGURE 24.1** Canada's Inflation Target

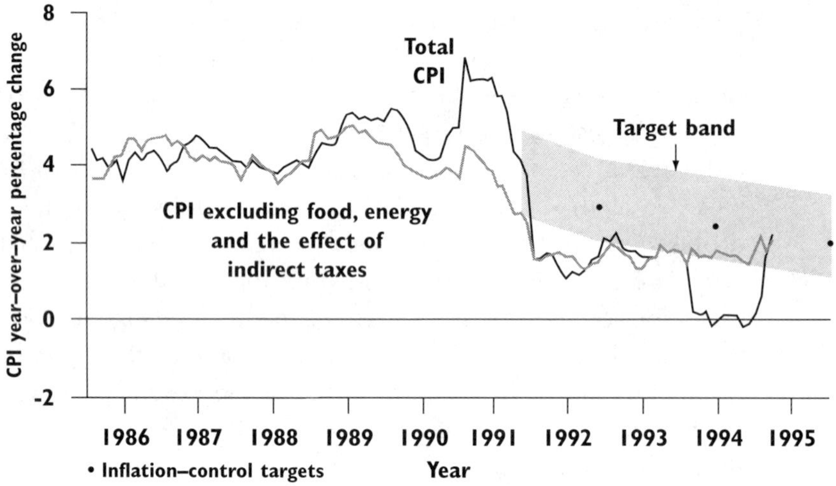


The vertical axis represents the percent change, on an annual basis, of the CPI and the CPI excluding food, energy, and indirect taxes. The dots inside the target band represent the midpoint of the band.

Source: Bank of Canada *Monetary Policy Report* (May 1995), p. 5.

from the Constitutional debate. The report called for a clearer mandate for the Bank, with price stability as the overall objective, as well as greater accountability. Otherwise, the committee which prepared the report did not go very far in suggesting any major redesign of the governance of the Bank.[37]

Was the Bank of Canada ahead of its time in committing itself to price stability? Not exactly. The lessons from the stagflation of the 1970s and 1980s taught governments and central banks that inflation is not conducive to economic growth. The first country to take major steps in using inflation targets to achieve disinflation was New Zealand which announced its Policy Targets Agreement in 1990. The New Zealand example has served as a model for several countries. Canada was second and, as Table 24.9 shows, several countries have followed suit. Unlike New Zealand, however, most countries' inflation targets are agreements between the central bank and the government and do not represent statutory requirements. However, these targets have been successfully met in most cases although this took place in a period of recession and weak aggregate demand. The real test for these targets is yet to come.

37 See D.E.W. Laidler, *How Shall We Govern the Governor?* (Toronto: C.D. Howe Institute, 1991).

**Table 24.9** INFLATION TARGETING IN A VARIETY OF COUNTRIES

| Country | Price Index | Annual Target Band or Range | Defined Horizon for Objective? | Exceptions or Caveats |
|---|---|---|---|---|
| Australia | CPI | Average of 2%–3% | No | Mortgage interest, government controlled prices and energy |
| Canada | CPI | 1%–3% between 1995–98 | Yes | Indirect taxes, food and energy; first-round effect only |
| Finland | CPI | 2% from 1995 | No | Housing capital costs, indirect taxes and government subsidies |
| Israel | CPI | 8%–11% for 1995 | Yes, annual update | none |
| New Zealand | CPI | 0%–2% | Yes, updated periodically | Commodity prices, government-controlled prices, interest and credit charges |
| Spain | CPI | Less than 3% by 1997 | Yes | Mortgage interest payments |
| Sweden | CPI | + or – 1% around 2% from 1995 | No | none |
| United Kingdom | Retail Price Index | 2 1/2% or less | No | Mortgage interest payments |

Sources: A. Haldane, "Inflation Targets," *Bank of England Quarterly Bulletin* 35 (November 1995), pp. 250–59; Bank of Canada, *Monetary Policy Report* (May 1995); Reserve Bank of New Zealand *Bulletin* (various issues); K. Andersson and C. Berg, "The Inflation Target in Sweden."

## SUMMARY

- Canada's central bank is called the Bank of Canada. It was founded in the 1930s, much later than the founding date of central banks in many other countries.

- The Bank of Canada is responsible for the management of the country's monetary policy; it is also the banker for the banking system and the federal government.

- This chapter considers a number of Bank of Canada transactions such as open market operations, drawdown and redeposit, monetizing the debt, and a foreign exchange swap.

- It also briefly reviews the history and performance of the Bank of Canada and monetary policy in Canada during this century.

## IMPORTANT TERMS

Bank of Canada Act (p. 560)
base control (p. 566)
Coyne affair (p. 575)
debt monetization (p. 566)
drawdown and redeposit technique (p. 564)
Exchange Fund Account (EFA) (p. 566)
foreign exchange swap (p. 567)
inflation targeting (p. 578)
monetary targeting (p. 577)
money multiplier (p. 573)
moral suasion (p. 571)

## EXERCISES

1. Rank the functions of the Bank of Canada in the order of their importance. Explain why you have chosen this ranking.
2. Using balance sheet accounts for the Bank of Canada and the chartered banks, illustrate an open market sale of $100 million to the chartered banks. What happens to the monetary base?
3. Why might a commercial bank borrow from another commercial bank, at a relatively high rate, instead of from the Bank of Canada at the bank rate?

4. Using balance sheet accounts for the Bank of Canada and the chartered banks, illustrate the effect of a transfer of $50 million from government deposits at the Bank of Canada to government deposits at the chartered banks. What happens to the monetary base?
5. What kind of policy action by the Bank of Canada would sterilize the foreign exchange swap considered in Table 24.7?
6. Why can moral suasion be useful, under certain circumstances, in the conduct of monetary policy? What are some of the difficulties in relying on moral suasion in the present banking environment? Explain your answer.
7. What will happen to M1 if
   (a) $cr$ increases
   (b) $k$ decreases
   (c) $rr$ increases
   (d) $R$ decreases

   (Assume that when one variable changes, all the others are held constant.) Explain your answer.
8. Suppose chartered banks borrow $100 million from the Bank of Canada. As a result, excess reserves are reduced by the same amount. What happens to M1? Explain your answer.
9. Explain how the monetary base is affected by each one of the following economic events and how the Bank of Canada can offset them:
   (a) Income tax payments are received by April 30
   (b) Christmas shopping in December
   (c) A postal strike
10. True, false, or uncertain: Whenever the government incurs a deficit, it requires the Bank of Canada to print the necessary notes. Explain your answer.
11. Why was the Coyne affair a defining moment in the history of the Bank of Canada?
12. What are inflation targets and why does inflation targeting represent an important policy change?
13. In what sense were the origins of the Bank of Canada largely political?
14. Why are OMOs less useful than they were, say, 30 years ago?
15. Many central banks abandoned monetary targeting during the 1980s. Why do you think this is the case?
16. What is moral suasion and when can such a policy be useful?
17. Why do you think inflation targets are defined in terms of a band instead of a single point?

# REFERENCES

Bordo, M.D. "The Lender of Last Resort: Alternative Views and Historical Experience." Federal Reserve Bank of Richmond *Economic Review* (January/February 1990): 18–28.

Bordo, M.D., and A. Redish. "Credible Commitment and Exchange Rate Stability: Canada's Interwar Experience." *Canadian Journal of Economics* 23 (May 1990): 357–80.

———. "Why Did the Bank of Canada Emerge in 1935?" *Journal of Economic History* 47 (June 1987): 405–18.

Cagan, P. "The Demand for Currency Relative to the Total Money Supply." *Journal of Political Economy* (August 1958): 303–28.

Courchene, T.J. *Monetarism and Controls: The Inflation Fighters.* Montreal: C.D. Howe Research Institute, 1976.

———. *Monetarism and Controls: The Inflation Fighters.* Toronto: C.D. Howe Institute, 1983.

———. *Money, Inflation, and the Bank of Canada: An Analysis of Monetary Gradualism, 1975–80.* Montreal: C.D. Howe Institute, 1981.

De Cecco, M., and Alberto Giovannini, eds. *A European Central Bank?* New York: Cambridge University Press, 1989.

"Exchange Fund Account Cash Management Swaps: A Technical Note." *Bank of Canada Review* (May 1992): 3–10.

Friedman, B.M. "The Rise and Fall of Money Growth Targets as Guidelines for US Monetary Policy," NBER working paper 5465 (February 1996).

Friedman, M., and A.J. Schwartz. "Has Government Any Role in Money?" *Journal of Monetary Economics* 17 (January 1986): 37–62.

Garfinkel, M.R., and D.L. Thornton. "The Multiplier Approach to the Money Supply Process: A Precautionary Note." *Review of the Federal Reserve Bank of St. Louis* 73 (July/August 1991): 47–64.

Goodhart, C. *The Evolution of Central Banks.* Cambridge, Mass.: The MIT Press, 1988.

Gordon, H. Scott. *The Economists versus the Bank of Canada.* Toronto: The Ryerson Press, 1961.

Haldane, A.G. (ed.). *Targeting Inflation.* London: Bank of England, 1995.

Howitt, P.W. *Monetary Policy in Transition: A Study of Bank of Canada Policy, 1982–85.* Toronto: C.D. Howe Research Institute, 1986.

Humpage, O.F. "Central Bank Intervention: Recent Literature, Continuing Controversy." Federal Bank of Cleveland *Economic Review* 27 (Quarter 2, 1991): 12–26.

"The Implementation of Monetary Policy in a System with Zero Reserve Requirements." Bank of Canada Discussion Paper No. 3 (6 September 1991).

Laidler, D.E.W., and W.B.P. Robson, *The Great Canadian Disinflation* (Toronto: C.D. Howe Institute, 1993).

Leiderman, L. and L.E.O. Svensson (eds.). *Inflation Targets.* London: CEPR, 1995.

Lipsey, R.G. *Zero Inflation: The Goal of Price Stability.* Toronto: C.D. Howe Institute, 1990.

Longworth, D., and P. Muller. "Implementation of Monetary Policy in Canada with Same-Day Settlement: Issues and Alternatives." Bank of Canada working paper 91-3 (August 1991).

MacIntosh, R. *Different Drummers: Banking and Politics in Canada.* Toronto: Macmillan Canada, 1991.

Neufeld, E.P. *Bank of Canada Operations and Policy.* Toronto: University of Toronto Press, 1958.

Rich, G. *The Cross of Gold: Money and the Canadian Business Cycle, 1867–1913.* Ottawa: Carleton University Press, 1988.

Shearer, R.A., J.F. Chant, and D.E. Bond. *The Economics of the Canadian Financial System: Theory, Policy and Institutions*, 2d ed. Scarborough, Ont.: Prentice-Hall, 1984.

Watts, G.S. *The Bank of Canada: Origins and Early History* (ed. by T.K. Rymes), Ottawa: Carleton University Press, 1993.

CHAPTER 25

# The Art of Central Banking[1]

Since central banks are generally responsible for matters of monetary policy, their actions influence or are influenced by movements in interest rates, monetary aggregates, and exchange rates. We have already described various empirical features and theories relative to these three variables, ignoring the special role of the central bank. Having described such an institution in the previous chapter, it now seems appropriate to discuss the place of the central monetary authority in the financial system.

In doing so, we focus on principles applicable to all (or most) industrialized countries. We might have chosen otherwise. The art of central banking is sometimes considered to be specific to the particular financial institutions of an economy and thus to vary greatly from country to country. However, globalization and increasing agreement that central banks should be independent of the fiscal authorities have reduced differences among financial systems. As a result, this chapter concentrates on general principles.

We begin with a discussion of the targets and instruments of monetary policy. The instruments are the variables that can be influenced directly by central bank action, and they are well known. There is somewhat more controversy about the targets of monetary policy, especially as the role of central banks has evolved over the last decade or so. Should a central bank try to reach its goals by affecting the money supply or by controlling interest rates?

Next, we consider the advantages and the disadvantages of monetary control and of interest rate control. Even if neither approach is inherently superior, perhaps one is easier to follow or has fewer harmful side-effects.

The chapter concludes by considering central bank independence. What does independence mean? What are the economic consequences of ignoring it? What is the evidence on the relationship between central bank independence and economic performance?

1 This chapter title is from a book with the same title by R.G. Hawtrey. In that book, Hawtrey describes the various links between central bank actions and economic activity in general, as well as the design of central bank institutions. See R.G. Hawtrey, *The Art of Central Banking*, 2d ed. (New York: Kelley, 1970).

# TARGETS AND INSTRUMENTS OF MONETARY POLICY

All monetary authorities face problems of choosing and meeting final goals. We can illustrate the inherent difficulties with the help of a diagram such as the one in Figure 25.1 Central banks possess **operating instruments**—tools with which they can do their work, such as manipulating the monetary base, manipulating government deposits, conducting open market operations (OMOs), and so on.[2] Changes in these operating instruments more or less directly influence **intermediate targets**, which are usually some measure of the money supply and/or some key interest rate (one that is related to most other interest rates in the economy). The point of central bank action is not only what actually happens to these intermediate targets (the size of the money supply, for example, is not very interesting per se) but also (and just as important) the performance in the economy of various **final targets**, such as inflation, unemployment, and exchange rates, individually or in some combination.

The difficulty of achieving some final target[3] in this two-stage process is partly posed by the uncontrollables of monetary policy. For example, the influence of operating instruments on intermediate targets is largely determined by the size and stability of the money multipliers. But which money multiplier is to be selected from among the long list of potential candidates? The issue is no different from the question of which monetary aggregate is the best indicator of the money multiplier over time, and choosing M2 or M2+ leads to a dramatically different picture. Moreover, how stable is the money multiplier chosen? If it is predictable, the monetary authorities will have a fairly good idea of the link between the operating instrument and the intermediate target. Otherwise their actions will have a significant measure of uncertainty.

Even if intermediate targeting is well within the reach of central banks, there remain the questions of specifying the final target and of predicting its course. Thus, the two problems that plague the relationship between operating instruments and intermediate targets remain. The behaviour of the velocity of circulation can, for example, sever the link between a monetary aggregate and inflation.

2 These tools are discussed in Chapter 24 and elsewhere, so we do no more than list them here.

3 The following discussion neglects the possibility that the central bank has an exchange rate target. Dwelling on this target would complicate the explanation. Moreover, it is an unlikely one for the Bank of Canada. That is not to say that the Bank of Canada does not intervene in the market for foreign exchange. But rather than having a specific target in mind, the Bank would argue, it attempts to smooth the volatility of exchange rate movements.

**FIGURE 25.1** Instruments and Targets of Monetary Policy

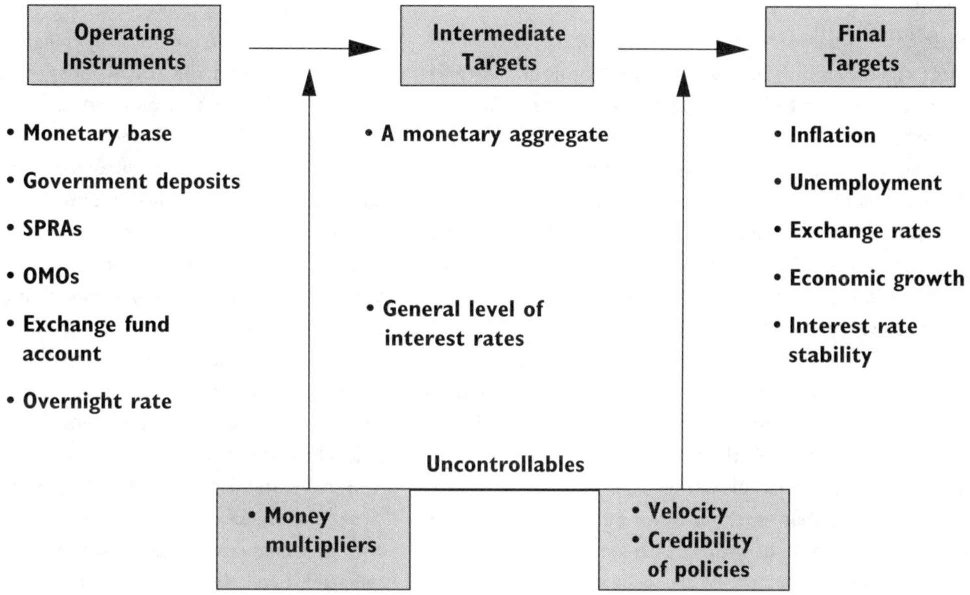


The lists here are by no means exhaustive. Final targets, for example, might also include stability in financial markets and/or full employment.

And unless monetary policies as practised by the central bank are believed by the public—that is, unless they are credible—the final target may not be attained.

Another question is whether a central bank should be committed to a single target, such as **price stability**, or seek to achieve multiple objectives, such as a combination of inflation, unemployment, and economic growth. The difficulty in specifying multiple final targets is that they often conflict with each other. For example, inflation and unemployment targets may not be compatible goals. Add to this the complications that arise because of the relationship between exchange rates and interest rates, and an optimal policy mix becomes more difficult still to attain.

Finally, policymakers' goals may conflict with those of the central bank and/or with those of the public. And someone has to decide for which group in society the policy mix should be optimal.

## ECONOMICS FOCUS 25.1 Out of Control?

Most central banks have a long-term objective (sometimes vaguely stated) of promoting economic growth and achieving price stability (low or zero inflation). Meeting the latter goal can impart an inflationary spin to an economy. Moreover, some analysts suggest that recent changes in financial systems have undercut the efficacy of some of the central banks' tools. Deregulation—the removal of capital controls, interest rate ceilings, and credit-rationing, to name but a few examples—may have reduced central banks' ability to influence the growth of credit, with the loss of control meaning higher inflation in the future. An OECD study suggested that central banks now need to practise interest rate "overkill" to achieve credit control. (In other words, interest rates have to rise by a larger percentage and for a longer period of time than in the past to achieve a reduction in credit demand. In economic terms, this translates into a lower interest elasticity of credit demand with respect to the interest rate.) All this is a reaction to the belief that bond and foreign exchange markets drive monetary policy rather than the other way around. The reaction of Mexico's government in the wake of the 1994 devaluation of the peso and pleas by presidents of such countries as Argentina and Peru to foreign investors not to take their billions out of their economies are examples of this phenomenon.

Ironically, when the Eurodollar market experienced meteoric growth during the 1960s and 1970s, similar concerns were expressed. The US Federal Reserve had no direct control over this market. The worry then was, what would happen if all Eurodollars were repatriated to the United States? Clearly, the resulting expansion in credit would be tremendously inflationary. The fears proved unfounded for today most Eurodollars remain offshore to finance trade and other financial needs abroad. Nevertheless, there is always the potential for financial innovations to reduce the efficacy of domestic central banks' control over monetary policy.

A further reason for the concern expressed about the ability of the regulators and the monetary authorities to control the financial system stems from the plethora of scandals that have plagued financial markets over the last few years. The Japanese brokerage scandal, in which large firms were compensated for losses incurred at the hands of brokerage firms, the fraudulent activities of the Bank of Credit and Commerce International (BCCI), and the attempt by Solomon Brothers to corner the market for US securities, to name but three examples, suggest to some that financial practices can no longer be effectively regulated. Even the *Wall Street Journal* says, "Regulation is a lagging indicator" (28 August 1991): that is, financial innovations that overcome some existing regulatory obstacle occur at a far faster rate than the ability to legislate their uses.

**Sources:**

"The Bank of Canada and the Money Market," *Bank of Canada Review* (May 1989): 17–33.

"Out of Greenspan's Hand," *The Economist*, 27 October 1990, 81.

D. Sanger, "Do Fickle Markets Now Make Policy?" *New York Times*, 19 November 1995, p. 3.

# *MONETARY VERSUS INTEREST RATE CONTROL: A SIMPLE CHARACTERIZATION

Despite the room for error, central banks do take action in financial markets. We can use a simplified supply–demand diagram to explore the consequences for interest rate stability of a policy for which the intermediate target is **monetary control**—controlling the money supply—versus one that aims at **interest rate control**. This is, of course, a significant simplification of the problems apparent from Figure 25.1,[4] but it will clearly illustrate the dilemmas and difficulties faced by central banks in conducting monetary policy.

We start with a familiar framework. Figure 25.2(A) shows various representations of the demand for money, which we first encountered in Chapter 6. Recall that this demand is positively related to the price level, *P* and to real income, *y*, and negatively to the nominal interest rate, *R*. The black downward-sloping line shows one such demand for money curve drawn for a particular level of real income, nominal interest rate, and the price level. Because of changes in other, unpredictable factors, the curve shifts over time. Suppose these unpredictable factors, which we'll summarize by the term *u*, influence money demand in a fashion that is random but averages to zero.

Figure 25.2(B) shows the money supply function, which we also encountered in Chapter 6. The quantity of money supplied is positively related to the nominal interest rate. But, as we saw in Chapter 24, the money supply is influenced by other factors that are not under the direct control of the monetary authorities: namely, the currency–deposit ratio and the reserves of the banking system. Here we lump together the effects of these uncontrollables in the term *v*. Once again, we assume that although *v* shifts the money supply function in an unpredictable fashion, it averages zero.

## MONEY SUPPLY CONTROL

Let us now consider the implications of monetary and interest rate control, starting with the former. We stressed in the last chapter that money supply cannot be perfectly controlled through manipulations of high-powered money. Thus, a central bank that uses control of some monetary aggregate as an intermediate target is bound to face randomly fluctuating money supply and demand functions. The resulting range of equilibrium positions is shown in Figure 25.3. The money supply values range between $M_{min}$ and $M_{max}$, and equilibrium interest rates under monetary control between $R_{min}$ and $R_{max}$. Note, however, that the range of values depends critically on the slopes of the demand and supply curves as well as on the size of the uncontrollable terms *u* and *v*. (The latter are represented by the distance between the minimum and maximum curves.)

Suppose that a central bank, before embarking on a policy of targeting the money supply, was able to implement better money-supply control procedures.

4 We do not, for example, consider other possible final targets. Neither do we discuss the choice of an appropriate monetary aggregate or which operating instruments are used.

**FIGURE 25.2** Instruments Control: The Basic Relationships

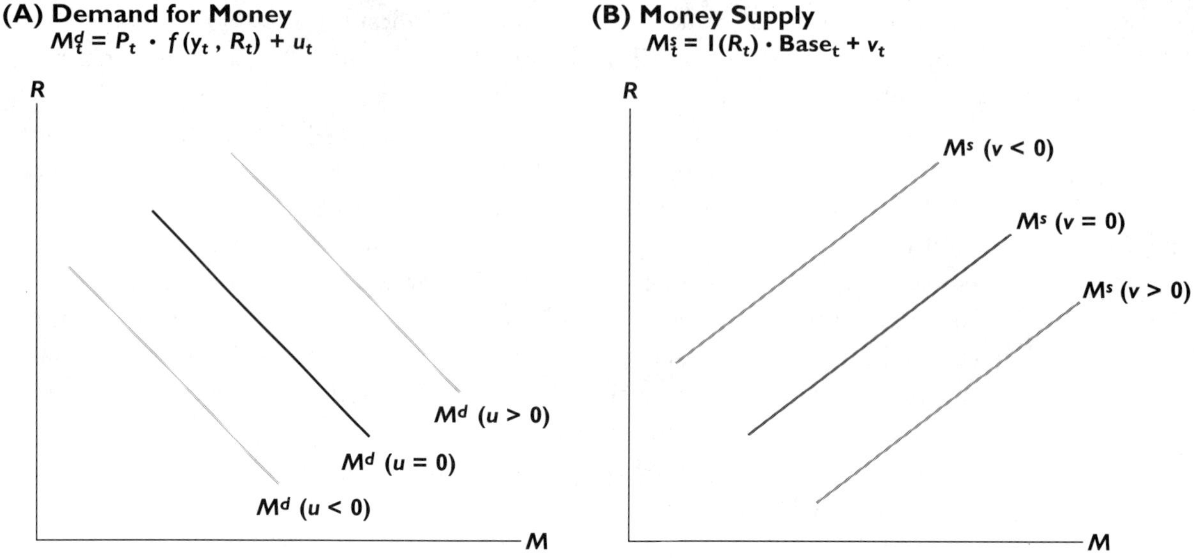


The demand for money curve is downward sloping but shifts randomly over time because of *u*, whose mean is zero. The black line in panel (A) is the demand curve when *u* is at its mean of zero; the gray lines are the demand curves when *u* is less than or greater than zero. The supply of money curve in panel (B) shifts randomly with *v* because the monetary authorities do not exercise perfect control over the money supply. *v* also may be negative or positive but its mean is zero. (For more on the demand for money curve, see Chapters 6 and 11; for more on the supply of money curve, see Chapters 6 and 24.)

Such an improvement could conceivably narrow the range of money supply values from ($M^s_{min}$, $M^s_{max}$) to ($M^s_0$, $M^s_1$). The consequences would be a reduction in the variability of both the equilibrium money supply and the equilibrium interest rate. The range of values for interest rates in equilibrium would fall from *BD* (or $R_{min}$ $R_{max}$) to *B'D'* (or $R_1$ $R_0$), and the range for the equilibrium money supply from *AC* (or $M_{min}$ $M_{max}$) to *A'C'* (or $M_1$ $M_0$).

## INTEREST RATE PEGGING

Suppose that instead of trying to control the money supply, a central bank decided to peg interest rates. In the extreme, it might simply decree that the interest rate be set at $R^*$ in Figure 25.4. Equilibrium money supply values would range between $M_{min}$ and $M_{max}$. More realistically (because no central bank completely controls the money supply), it might allow interest rates to fluctuate freely within a band, denoted as in the figure as $R_{min}$ to $R_{max}$. Then the equilibrium money supply values would range between $M_0$ and $M_1$. Notice that the effect of pegging the

**FIGURE 25.3** Money Supply Control

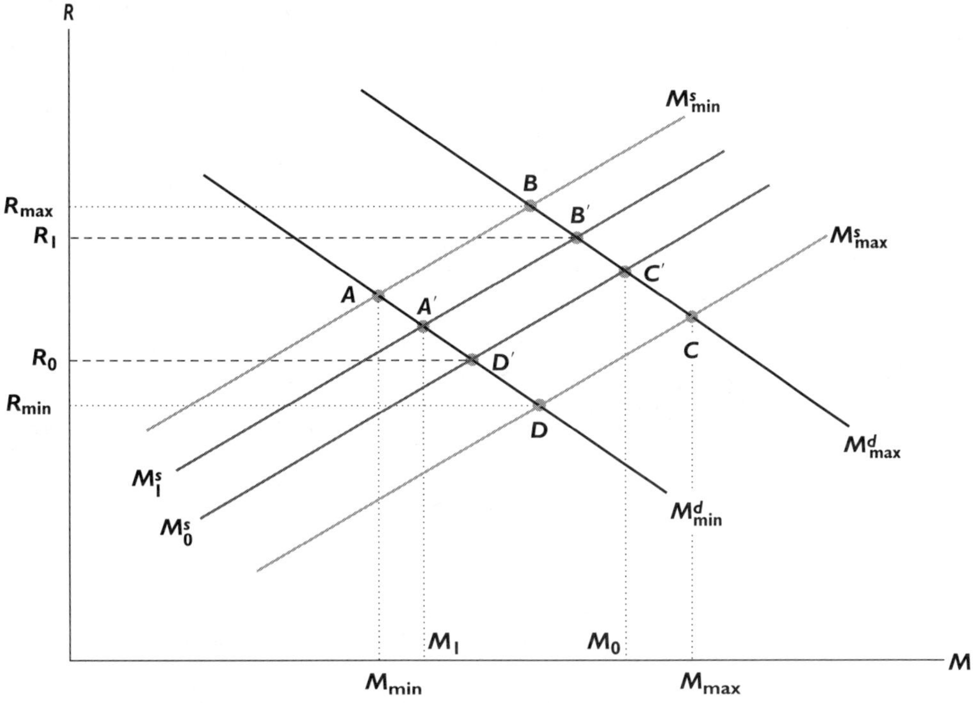


Because $M^d$ and $M^s$ fluctuate randomly within a range – $M^d_{min}$ to $M^d_{max}$ and $M^s_{min}$ to $M^s_{max}$, respectively – equilibrium money supply changes will vary between $M_{min}$ and $M_{max}$, consistent with equilibrium points *A* and *C*. Consequently, interest rates will also fluctuate, ranging from $R_{min}$ to $R_{max}$. The volatility of these variables will, in equilibrium, depend on the slope of $M^d$ and $M^s$. The distance between $M^d_{min}$ and $M^d_{max}$ represents *u*; the distance between $M^s_{min}$ and $M^s_{max}$ represents *v*.

interest rate is to render the money supply curve perfectly elastic.[5] The reason is that a central bank that is pegging interest rates has undertaken to supply quantities of money sufficient to ensure that the interest rate stays within the designated bands. Indeed the Bank of Canada officially announces a target band for overnight interest rates, one of its main tools of monetary policy (see Chapter 4).

## CONTROLLING THE MONEY SUPPLY OR INTEREST RATES?

Which of the two control techniques is superior? Is it preferable to minimize fluctuations in the money supply over time, or would the Bank be better off

5 Except within the interest rate target zone, if such a zone exists.

**FIGURE 25.4** Interest Rate Pegging

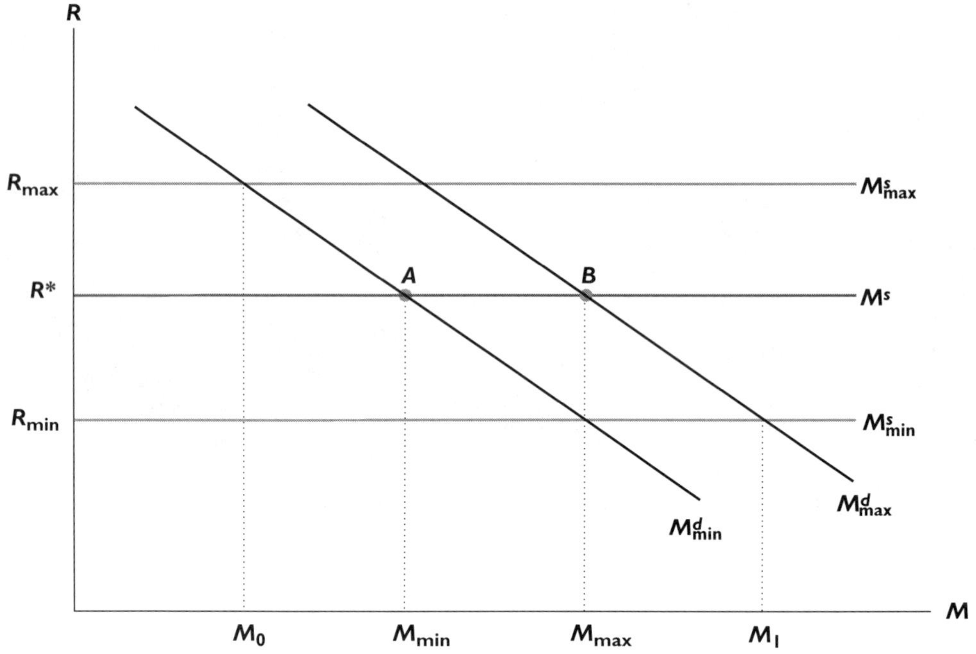


If the central bank pegs the interest rate at $R^*$, the equilibrium money supply will fluctuate between $M_{min}$ and $M_{max}$, consistent with equilibrium points *A* and *B*. In other words, the money supply function becomes perfectly elastic. Alternatively, the central bank may intervene only if there are indications that the interest rate will rise above $R_{max}$ or fall below $R_{min}$. The variation of the equilibrium money supply is held to $M_0$ to $M_I$.

pegging interest rates? The first solution means allowing interest rates to fluctuate, while the second option implies volatility—possibly considerable volatility—in the money supply. Because money supply variations have implications for the economy as a whole and for inflation and economic growth in particular, it is assumed that minimizing them is the most desirable intermediate target for achieving some final target.

We can illustrate the situation with Figure 25.5, which essentially combines Figures 25.3 and 25.4 into a single diagram. Given the slopes of the money supply and demand for money curves, interest rate control results in a smaller range for the money supply ($M_2M_3$) than does money supply control ($M_0$ $M_1$). Nevertheless, note that interest rates vary more when they are controlled ($R_{min}$ $R_{max}$) than under

**FIGURE 25.5** Selecting the Best Operating Instrument

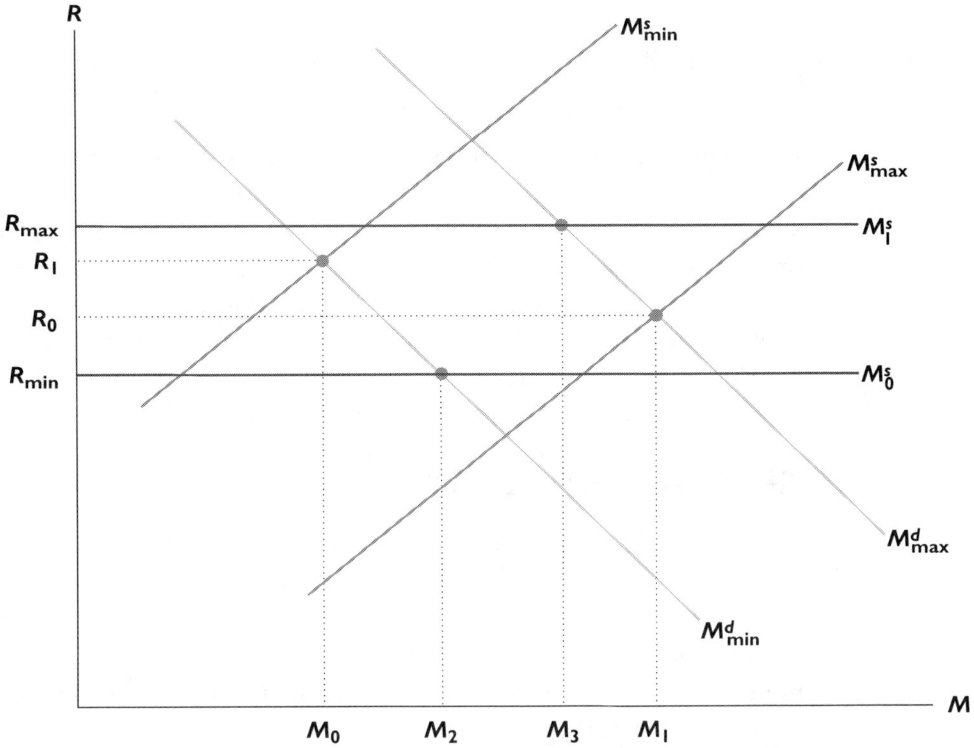


This figure combines Figures 25.3 and 25.4. Under interest rate control, the equilibrium money supply varies between $M_2$ and $M_3$; under monetary control, it ranges between $M_0$ and $M_1$. If minimizing money supply variation is the most desirable intermediate target, then interest rate control is the best operating instrument.

high-powered money control ($R_1$ $R_0$). In other words, the "price" of money supply stability is less stable interest rates.[6]

It is also important to note, however, that a result opposite to that shown in Figure 25.5 could be reached either by allowing the demand or supply curves to be more variable—that is, by widening the bands around which they fluctuate—or

6 As we have noted previously, this is precisely what happened in the early 1980s when the Canadian and US central banks adopted money-supply control procedures and perhaps this also helps explain why most industrial countries, except perhaps Germany, abandoned outright money supply control. See B. Bernanke and F.S. Mishkin, "Central Bank Behavior and the Strategy of Monetary Policy: Observation from Six Industrialized Countries," *NBER Macroeconomics Annual 1992* (Cambridge, Mass.: The MIT Press), pp. 183–227.

by changing the slopes of either of them. We leave working out the details as exercises.

## CENTRAL BANK INDEPENDENCE AND INFLATION

If it is one of the central bank's responsibilities to achieve some final target such as price stability, it must be permitted to do so without political interference. However, one can never entirely omit a role for politicians. After all, their electoral fortunes will be influenced by prevailing economic conditions, which are at least partly the fruit of the central bank's actions, and politicians directly control the tools of fiscal policy, which also influences the economy. In this section, we look at each of these temptations to interfere with the central bank. Finally, we consider the evidence on **central bank autonomy or independence** and inflation control.

### THE POLITICAL BUSINESS CYCLE

An only slightly cynical view of the inherent tension between a government and a central bank is that is produces cycles in economic activity that can be linked to election dates. This **political business cycle** argument presumes that politicians can and ultimately will resort to policies that will ensure re-election, possibly influencing much-publicized economic aggregates, such as inflation, unemployment, and economic growth.

The United States, where elections are held on a regular schedule, provided the early testing ground for this theory. Critics objected that politicians could not possibly fool voters all of the time, and the political business cycle concept fell out of favour in economic circles for a time. Recently, however, there has been a resurgence of interest in the notion. Analysts realize that voters cannot easily distinguish political actions introduced solely for electoral purposes from those that are likely to remain permanent. Moreover, political parties are ideologically motivated, so economic cycles are likely to reflect partisan preferences over time; for example, "conservative" governments may gear their policies so as to achieve a relatively low rate of inflation while their "liberal" counterparts may prefer to focus on reducing unemployment. In addition, the timing of elections in many countries, including Canada, is uncertain. Governments in such countries may try to select an election date prior to any anticipated recession.

Much of the work on political business cycles assumes that governments tend to resort to monetary policy to generate the outcomes favourable to re-election. The reason is that, unlike fiscal policies, whose implementation can involve considerable delays (legislative, among others), monetary policies can be put in place fairly quickly. But this view presumes that government directly controls monetary policy—in other words, that central banks have no possibility of independent action. Thus, say proponents of the theory, if a central bank is pursuing a policy of price stability in the midst of a recession and an election looms, that bank will likely have to abandon its action at the behest of its political masters.

Is there empirical evidence favouring the political business cycle theory? The very nature of the argument makes it difficult to prove. (After all, some ballots may go to a candidate because the economy is prospering under the party to which the candidate belongs, some because the voters approve of the party's or individual's philosophical stance, and some because the voters perceive the candidate as someone who handled constituents' problems deftly or is simply "a nice person.")

Yet the swings in some major economic indicators seem correlated to election cycles more closely than coincidence would permit. Figure 25.6 plots Canadian data for four aggregates that might be influenced by political considerations; the time of federal elections are also marked. The graphs show that the unemployment rate has tended to fall just before an election. By contrast, the bank rate rose before at least half the elections. More often than not, the exchange rate also rose (meaning a more expensive US dollar in Canadian terms).[7] Finally, average real GDP growth has tended to peak prior to an election (though the timing has been variable). Thus, there is, at least superficially, some evidence that economic cycles are influenced by electoral events.

## COMPATIBLE FISCAL POLICY

Even if the political business cycle is not operating and a country otherwise wishes its central bank to be independent, the institution can be severely hampered if its monetary policy is inconsistent with the government's **fiscal policy** (that is, its use of its taxing and spending powers). Thus, fiscal policy can result in inflation even if monetary policy is geared to prevent it. The conflict between the two sets of policies is one reason economies show a distinct bias toward some inflation. (We explore this point and other issues in the debate about the importance of money in Chapter 26.)

## THE RECORD ON INFLATION CONTROL

Clearly, a central bank in a democracy cannot be entirely independent of the political system since the voters invest in their elected officials ultimate respon-

---

7 Recall that Canada was on a fixed exchange rate régime during the 1963, 1965, and 1968 elections. Some people argue that the use of monetary policy to achieve political ends is more likely under flexible exchange rates than under fixed exchange rates.

**FIGURE 25.6** Elections and Macroeconomic Aggregates in Canada

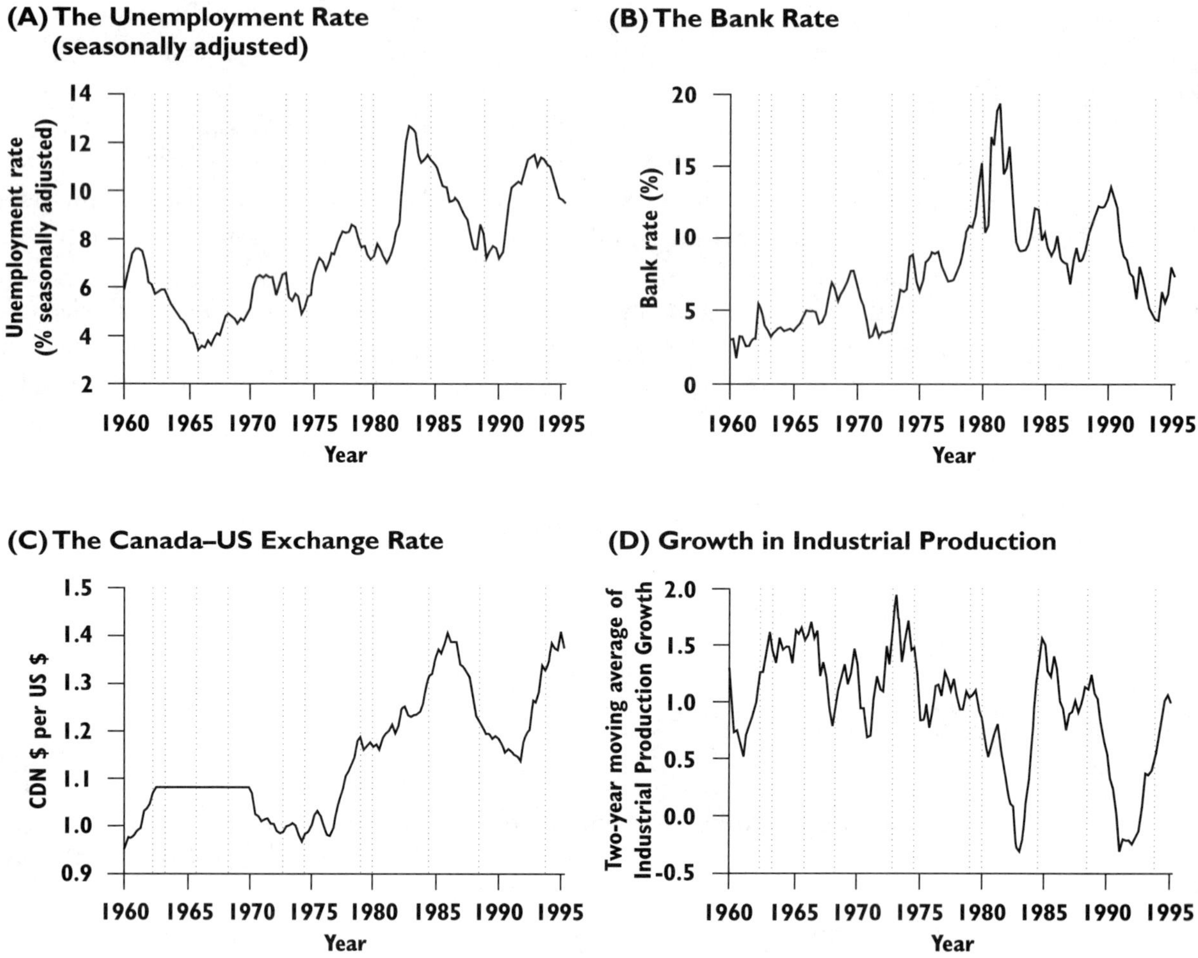


The vertical rules here mark federal elections. The Conservatives won in 1979, 1984, and 1988, and the period of their rule is outlined. After the other elections, the Liberals formed the government, not always with a majority of seats in the House of Commons.

Sources: D.R. Johnson and P.L. Siklos, "Political Effects on Central Bank Behaviour: Some International Evidence," in *Varieties of Monetary Reform: Lessons and Experiences on the Road to Monetary Union* (Dordrecht, The Netherlands: Kluwer Academic Publishers, 1994), pp. 133–64, and "Political and Economic Determinents of Interest Rate Behavior: Are Central Banks Different?" *Economic Inquiry* (October 1996).

sibility for economic performance. Moreover, the well-known tendency of central banks to shroud their actions in secrecy (a feature that is disappearing) makes it even more difficult to ascertain what they actually do and how much their actions differ from those of the political authorities.[8] Yet, it is now generally recognized that maintaining accountability is simplified by permitting central banks to focus on the goal of price stability, rather than selecting some other variable from the available "menu" (see Figure 25.1).[9] Furthermore, a positive byproduct of price stability is increased stability in economic performance with all its attendant benefits for unemployment rates.

There is increasing recognition that countries with low inflation tend to outperform other countries in terms of economic growth (see Table 25.1—but notice that the correlation is far from perfect). Perhaps for this reason, many countries are now trying to stabilize prices. Figure 25.7 shows the evolution of inflation rates in seven countries over 30 years. In the early 1970s, their inflation rates diverged considerably. But stagflation taught even politicians to dislike inflation, and by the 1980s the rates were beginning to converge.

All this evidence on the desirability of price stability is leading policymakers to favour making it the primary goal of central banks and enshrining some form of autonomy for these institutions to counter the political temptation to inflate the economy before an election. Germany, Austria, Switzerland, and, more recently, New Zealand, Canada, and a few other countries (see Chapter 24) now require their central banks to maintain some form of price stability.[10] A legislated goal of price stability is proposed for the central banks of Canada and of the United Kingdom as well as for the yet-to-be-established European Central Bank of the European Union (see Chapter 23).

## EVALUATING CENTRAL BANK INDEPENDENCE

How convincing is the evidence linking, in particular, inflation and the degree to which a central bank is autonomous or independent? First, there is the problem of defining what is meant by independence. It surely does not mean that a central bank can do whatever it pleases. Rather the term independence or autonomy refers to whether a central bank has instrument versus goal independence.[11] That

8 Indeed the "bureaucratic theory" of central bank actions argues that the Bank of Canada acts in its own self-interest as opposed to some economic objectives.

9 The governor of the New Zealand central bank must achieve precise price stability objectives or else face dismissal.

10 Many economic studies find that a central bank's *statutory* independence is of considerable importance in determining its inflation performance. Yet the record of countries where such independence exists suggests otherwise in several instances. For an alternative view, see D.R. Johnson and P.L. Siklos, "Political and Economic Determinants of Interest Rate Behaviour: International Evidence," *Economic Inquiry* (October 1996), for empirical evidence which suggests that statutory independence, while important, is not a sufficient condition for achieving low inflation. This paper also provides a survey of the relevant literature. One can say only that the available evidence is inconclusive.

11 See S. Fisher, "Modern Central Banking," in *The Future of Central Banking*, ed. By F. Capie, C. Goodhart, S. Fischer, and N. Schnadt (Cambridge: Cambridge University Press, 1994).

**TABLE 25.1** RANKING CENTRAL BANK INDEPENDENCE BY INFLATION PERFORMANCE AND ECONOMIC GROWTH

| | Inflation (rank) | Economic Growth (rank) |
|---|---|---|
| Germany | 1 | 5 |
| Switzerland | | 9 |
| United States | 2 | 4 |
| Japan | | |
| Netherlands | 3 | 8 |
| Canada | | 3 |
| France | | 2 |
| Denmark | 4 | 7 |
| United Kingdom | | 1 |
| Italy | 5 | 6 |
| New Zealand | 6 | 10 |

Note: The figures used for economic growth were GNP growth variances over the 1951–88 period. The figures used for inflation were averages for the 1973–88 period, but the rankings would have been largely unaffected if the 1951–88 period had been used.

Sources: A. Alesina and L.H. Summers, "Central Bank Independence and Macroeconomic Performance: Some Comparative Evidence" *Journal of Money, Credit and Banking* 25 (May 1993): 151–62; L.H. Summers, "How Should Long Term Monetary Policy Be Determined?" *Journal of Money, Credit and Banking* 23 (August 1991, Part 2): 625–31.

is, can the central bank choose the instruments of monetary policy (see Table 25.1) freely? Or are the goals of monetary policy specifically mandated? In countries such as New Zealand there is no goal independence because the central bank is mandated to achieve a specific inflation target. By contrast, there is instrument independence because the Reserve Bank of New Zealand can use whatever means it has at its disposal to achieve the stated inflation target. In Canada's case the inflation targets are not mandated by legislation but rather by mutual agreement between the finance minister and the governor of the Bank of Canada. As we have seen, however, the Bank of Canada's mandate is currently very broad so that it has both goal independence and instrument independence.

How is independence measured? Economists have generally adopted two approaches. One, very popular of late, is to rank central banks according to some interpretation of their statutes.[12] One such exercise divides central bank laws into the following categories (the list below is a partial one):

12 See A. Cukierman, *Central Bank Strategy, Credibility and Independence* (Cambridge, Mass: The MIT Press, 1992).

## ECONOMICS FOCUS 25.2 Why Zero Inflation?

In 1988, the then new governor of the Bank of Canada, John Crow, proposed that the Bank's goal be zero inflation. "Monetary policy should be conducted as to achieve a pace of monetary expansion that promotes stability in the value of money. This means pursuing a policy aimed at achieving and maintaining stable prices," he said (*Bank of Canada Review* [February 1988]: 4).

The policy of zero inflation raised considerable comment both in the press and among academics. What are the benefits of zero inflation? Some academics contend that the certainty of future price level stability would be beneficial to the economy. Others have argued that the biases in the measurement of prices (see Chapter 6) precludes zero inflation as a practical target. For Canada, estimates suggest that actual CPI inflation overstates the "true" inflation rate by a maximum of 0.5%. One recent estimate for the US economy estimates the net benefits from a zero inflation environment to be positive. Much of the debate centred not on whether zero inflation was desirable but whether it was feasible. Lucas explained that regional diversity would make the zero inflation goal difficult to achieve in Canada. Moreover, he points out that the Bank of Canada has little credibility in reaching its stated goal. Johnson pointed out that there were fundamental inconsistencies between the federal government's fiscal policy, with its distinct bias toward inflation, and the Bank of Canada's professed desire to eliminate inflation entirely. So much debate was sparked by the Bank of Canada's objective that the C.D. Howe Institute sponsored a conference and a volume summarizing the various views on the subject.

By the time former Finance Minister Michael Wilson brought down his budget in February 1991, however, the government had formally abandoned any pretence of wanting zero inflation, announcing objectives of 3% by the end of 1992 and 2% by 1995 in the core rate of inflation.

The core *rate* of inflation measures the rate of change in consumer price *excluding* food and energy costs. One argument for this omission in evaluating the severity of inflation is that food and energy prices are significantly determined by aggregate supply considerations, which are determined by events such as bad weather, wars, or oil price policies of OPEC (Organization of Petroleum Exporting Countries). Such costs cannot be influenced directly by the government's fiscal and monetary policies, which act on the aggregate demand side of the economy. The Bank of Canada argues, however, that the omission is because of "the volatile nature of food and energy prices" (*Bank of Canada Review* [September 1991]: 3). Yet it also suggests that "since 1979 they [food and energy prices] have exhibited no pronounced tendency to rise or fall on a sustained basis relative to prices of other goods and services" (*Bank of Canada Review* [September 1991]: 4).

**Sources:**

Bank of Canada, "Targets for Reducing Inflation: Further Operational and Measurement Considerations," *Bank of Canada Review* (September 1991): 3–23.

J.W. Crow, "The Work of Canadian Monetary Policy," *Bank of Canada Review* (February 1988): 3–17.

M. Feldstein "The Costs and Benefits of Going from Low Inflation to Price Stability" NBER working paper 5469 (February 1996).

D.R. Johnson, "An Evaluation of the Bank of Canada's Zero Inflation Target: Do Michael Wilson and John Crow Agree?" *Canadian Public Policy* 16 (December 1990): 308–25.

J. Konieczny, "The Optional Rate of Inflation: Competing Theories and Their Relevance to Canada," in *Economic Behaviour Policy Choice Under Price Stability* (Ottawa: Bank of Canada, 1993), pp. 1–40.

R.G. Lipsey, *Zero Inflation: The Goal of Price Stability* (Toronto: C.D. Howe Institute, 1990).

R.F. Lucas, " A Zero Inflation Target," *Canadian Public Policy* 15 (March 1990): 84–93.

**FIGURE 25.7** Inflation Rates over Time in Industrialized Countries

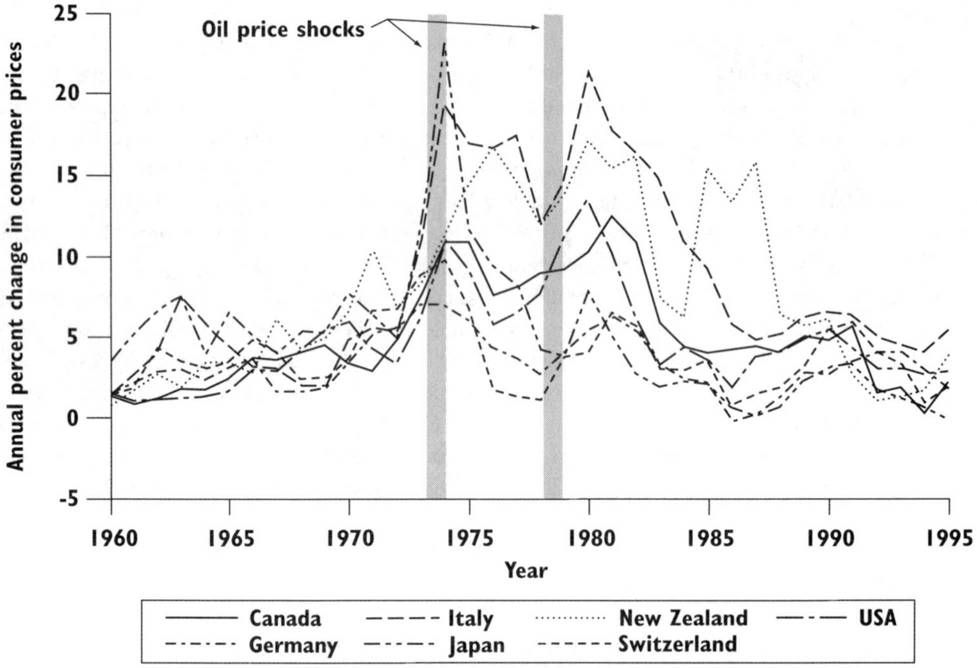


Source: International Financial Statistics CD-ROM. The shaded area represents the two oil price shocks.

1. *Monetary policy formulation.* Here the object is to determine who decides the formulation of monetary policy: the central bank or the governor.

2. *Conflict resolution.* Here the issue is how are disagreements between the government and the central bank resolved. Does the governor have to resign? As we have seen in the Canadian case, this proved to be an important question in connection with the so-called Coyne Affair.

3. *Central bank objectives.* How precisely defined are the objectives of the central bank? In other words, how much goal independence is there?

4. *Term of office.* For how long is the Governor appointed? Does it coincide with or overlap the term of the politicians who head the government?

5. *Limitations on lending to government.* How difficult is it to borrow from the central bank, that is, to effectively monetize the debt (see Chapter 24)?

Table 25.2 shows four such rankings. It is immediately clear that Germany, Switzerland, and the United States generally lead the pack and, as Figure 25.1 also

**TABLE 25.2** QUALITATIVE RANKINGS OF CENTRAL BANK INDEPENDENCE

| Cukierman | Grilli et al. | Burdekin and Willett | Parkin |
|---|---|---|---|
| Switzerland | Germany | Germany | Germany |
| Germany | Switzerland | Switzerland | Switzerland |
| Austria | United States | Austria | United States |
| United States | Netherlands | United States | Japan |
| Denmark | Canada | Canada | Denmark |
| Canada | Italy | Netherlands | Canada |
| Netherlands | Austria | United Kingdom | Netherlands |
| Ireland | Denmark | Australia | United Kingdom |
| Luxembourg | Ireland | France | France |
| Iceland | Australia | New Zealand | Sweden |
| Britain | New Zealand | Sweden | Italy |
| Australia | France | Italy | Belgium |
| France | United Kingdom | Belgium | Australia |
| Sweden | Belgium | Japan | New Zealand |
| Finland | Japan | Denmark | Austria |
| New Zealand | Sweden | Ireland | Ireland |
| Italy | Norway | Norway | Norway |

Note: The rankings were generated before recent changes in the legislation governing the Reserve Bank of New Zealand (it would now rank at the top or near the top) and France.

Source: A. Cukierman *Central Bank Strategy, Credibility, and Independence* (Cambridge, Mass: The MIT Press, 1992), Table 19.4; V. Grilli, D. Masciandaro and G. Tabellini "Political and Monetary Institutions and Public Financial Policies in Industrial Countries," *Economic Policy* (October 1991): 342–92; R.C.K. Burdekin and T. D. Willett, "Central Bank Reform: The Federal Reserve in International Perspective," *Public Budgeting and Financial Management* (1991): 619–50; M. Parkin, "Domestic Monetary Institutions and Deficits," in *Deficits*, ed. by M.G. Porter (Clayton, Australia: Monash University, 1986): 24–39.

reveals, these same countries have the lowest inflation rates. However, there are two major criticisms levelled at this approach. First, how is it that the same piece of legislation leads to such different rankings? A good example is the Bank of Japan. Its inflation performance is among the best but it ranks near the bottom in three of the four rankings and near the top in only one. Why? Because, in legal terms the Bank of Japan is subservient to the Finance Ministry. What makes it effectively independent is the autonomy of the Finance Ministry from the rest of government. A second problem is that legislation governing central banks changes very infrequently. By contrast, as is clear from Figure 25.1, inflation performance over the last 30 years has changed rather dramatically. One reason is the exchange rate régime. As we have seen (see Chapters 7 and 21) a country's inflation rate is dependent on whether the exchange rate is fixed or not. The reason, therefore, that inflation rates were comparable in the 1960s was that exchange rates were more or less tied to the US dollar. After the oil shock of

1973–74, exchange rates became flexible and inflation rates between countries began to differ considerably. Although exchange rates remained flexible into the 1990s more and more central banks began to view inflation as an evil and all began to aim for lower inflation which explains the convergence in inflation in the early 1990s.

A second approach to the analysis of central bank behaviour consists in estimating what are called *reaction functions.* These are basically equations which are supposed to model what central banks actually do. To take a simple example, let's assume that the central bank conducts policy by changing the interest rate. One way we can distinguish between central banks then is to examine how they might react to inflation, unemployment, or electoral pressures. A central bank that cares only about inflation would attach a zero coefficient to increases in unemployment. By contrast, a central bank could choose to respond only to unemployment changes and not at all to inflation. Of course, an intermediate case is when the central bank responds to both inflation and unemployment changes. In addition, a politically motivated central bank would also respond to political pressure in the form of elections and partisan changes in government (i.e., from Liberal to Conservative). Finally, in the global economy of today, a central bank such as the Bank of Canada can ill afford to conduct a "made in Canada" interest rate policy (look back at the Mexican peso case considered in Chapter 7 to see why). Therefore, domestic interest rate changes will also be influenced by foreign interest rate developments. A simple way to summarize the above relationships is with the help of the following equation:

$$\Delta R_t = a_0 + a_1\, \Delta U_{t-1} + a_2\, \Delta \pi_{t-1} + a_3\, POL_t + a_4\, \Delta R_{t-1}{}^{US} \qquad (25.1)$$

Equation (25.1) says that a change in the interest rate (say the Treasury bill rate) is a function of the previous experience with unemployment, measured as a change in the unemployment rate from last period (usually a month because unemployment data are released on a monthly basis), last period's inflation rate, a "political variable" (for example, whether there was an election or a change in government that month), and whether there was a change in interest rates in the United States. The relative importance of each of these considerations is evaluated by estimating the size of the coefficients $a_0$ to $a_4$. This approach to measuring what central banks do comes to a different conclusion than the approach which focuses on the legislative mandate of a central bank. In particular, it appears that central banks are more alike than they appear based on measures of statutory independence. Certainly, a look at the inflation performance of several countries reveals this to be a definite possibility (see Figure 25.1). Second, central banks behave quite differently according to whether exchange rates are pegged or not.[13]

## THE MONETARY CONDITIONS INDEX

Trying to divine what a central bank does preoccupies economists and financial market participants. Any piece of financial or economic news which might impact the interest rate setting behaviour of the central bank is the subject of intense scrutiny and analysis. This is particularly true, say, in the United States where the regular meetings of the Federal Reserve Open Market Committee (FOMC) has the media guessing about the direction of interest rates. Of course, given our economic and financial ties to the United States, the Bank of Canada is not immune to Fed moves.

However, because Canada is a small open economy, interest rate movements may not always clearly signal the present stance of monetary policy. In part for this reason, the Bank of Canada has developed what it calls the *Monetary Conditions Index (MCI)*. Although the technical details are beyond the scope of this text.[14] the MCI is best thought of as a judicious combination of interest rate movements and exchange rate movements. Recall from Chapter 15 that the two variables are linked to each other via the interest rate and purchasing power parity theories. In the current set-up, interest rate movements account for approximately two-thirds of movements in the MCI. By following movements in the MCI, together with other pertinent information such as Bank of Canada analyses of various scenarios for the Canadian economy based on assumptions about its future prospects, and other projections of the future path for domestic economic conditions, the Bank attempts to create monetary conditions which follow as closely as possible a path consistent with its inflation target objective

Other central banks, such as New Zealand's Reserve Bank, prefer a "checklist" approach in which several economic variables, including interest rates and exchange rates, are examined independently as well as jointly, to evaluate what the appropriate stance of monetary policy should be. Still other monetary authorities, like the German Bundesbank, place a great deal of emphasis on the growth of the money supply in relations to their stated growth targets.

---

13 See D.R. Johnson and P.L. Siklos, "Political and Economic Determinants of Central Bank Behaviour: Are Central Banks Different?" *Economic Inquiry* (October 1996).

14 For more details about the MCI, see C. Freedman "The Role of Monetary Conditions and the Monetary Conditions Index in the Conduct of Policy," *Bank of Canada Review* (Autumn 1995): 53–60, and C. Freedman, "The Use of Indicators and of the Monetary Conditions Index in Canada," in T.J.T. Baliño and C. Cottarelli (eds.), *Frameworks for Monetary Stability: Policy Issues and Country Experiences* (Washington, D.C.: International Monetary Fund, 1994).

## SUMMARY


- Central banking is an "art" because it requires the manipulation of instruments to achieve multiple and sometimes conflicting targets, as well as because it requires central bankers to fend off interference from politicians and the public.
- Central banks can choose from a "menu" of instruments, such as open market operations, SPRAs, and the manipulation of the bank rate. The aim is to achieve an intermediate target, such as steady interest rates, that is closely related to some final target, such as low inflation and unemployment.
- This chapter presents a simple model in which the central bank must choose manipulation of either a monetary aggregate or an interest rate as its instrument. The one that is not the tool becomes the intermediate target. The best instrument depends on whether the central bank prefers interest rate variability over money supply variability.
- A topic of considerable interest and importance is how much independent action a central bank should be permitted. There appears to be a connection among inflation, economic performance, and the degree to which a central bank is statutorily independent.


## IMPORTANT TERMS

central bank autonomy of independence (p. 596)
final targets (p. 588)
fiscal policy (p. 597)
interest rate control (p. 591)
intermediate targets (p. 588)
monetary control (p. 591)
operating instruments (p. 588)
political business cycle (p. 596)
price stability (p. 589)

## EXERCISES

1. Give an example and explain why there may be conflict among
   (a) Intermediate targets
   (b) Final targets

2. Do you think that the financial innovations of the last decade have made monetary policy more or less controllable by the Bank of Canada? Explain your answer. (Hint: See Chapter 4.)

3. What are the disadvantages of having a central bank satisfy multiple final targets? To whom are they disadvantages? Could these disadvantages be advantages to others? Explain your answer.

4. Discuss the pros and cons of achieving monetary stability and interest rate stability.

5. Assume that the money supply curve is perfectly inelastic and subject to complete control by the central bank. Draw the appropriate liquidity preference diagram. Would interest rate stability disappear? What about money supply instability? Why?

6. True, false, or uncertain: The more elastic the demand for money, the greater the variability of equilibrium money supply fluctuations when interest rate pegging is in effect. Illustrate, using a liquidity preference diagram, and explain your answer.

7. Figure 25.4 illustrates a case in which interest rate control is the best instrument. Use a similar diagram to illustrate a case in which the best instrument is one that relies on money supply control.

8. Suppose the Bank of Canada wants to minimize interest rate variability. What is the best instrument of monetary policy? Illustrate, using a diagram, and explain.

9. Given the evidence of Figure 25.6, do you detect any partisan business cycles in Canada? Explain your answer.

10. Why do you think politicians would rely less on monetary policy under fixed exchange rates than under flexible exchange rates? (Hint: See Chapter 7.)

11. What is meant by the term *central bank independence*?

12. Is the connection between inflation in the countries depicted in Figure 25.7 and the rankings in Table 25.2 a close one? Why or why not?

13. What is the difference between goal independence and instrument independence?

14. Why have several countries come to conclude that central banks should target inflation?

15. Central banks have come to fear a loss of control over monetary policy in recent years. Why?

# REFERENCES

Acheson, K., and J.F. Chant. "Bureaucratic Theory and the Choice of Central Bank Goals." *Journal of Money, Credit and Banking* 5 (May 1973): 637–55.

———. "The Choice of Monetary Instruments and the Theory of Bureaucracy." *Public Choice* 2 (1992): 13–33.

———. "Mythology and Central Banking." *Kyklos* 36 (1973): 362–79.

Crow, J.W. "The Economy and Canadian Monetary Policy." *Bank of Canada Review* (July 1992): 15–20.

Cukierman, A., *Central Bank Strategy, Credibility and Independence* (Cambridge, Mass.: The MIT Press, 1992).

Grabbe, J. Orlin. *International Financial Markets,* 2d ed. New York: Elsevier, 1991, 215–18.

Siklos, P.L. "Establishing Central Bank Independence: Recent Experiences in Developing Countries," *Journal of International Trade and Economic Development* (November 1995): 351–84.

CHAPTER 26

# The Debate over the Importance of Money

Disagreements among economists sometimes arise because of differences in focus. Some prefer to concentrate on long-run problems while others are more interested in short-run problems. Alternatively, some concern themselves with how best to measure some economic variable while others are more interested in exploring conditions under which one can evaluate the economic effects of certain government policies. In many cases, however, debates persist because no single ideology prevails. Perhaps the best-known and most publicized of these arguments is about whether the monetary sector influences the real sector of an economy. The debate has ebbed and flowed from the late eighteenth century to this day. Its importance cannot be underestimated; although the question is theoretical, the answers influence government policymakers, the relative emphasis on monetary and fiscal policy, and thus real economies.

The school of thought most associated with these views is called *monetarism*,[1] and we devote a sizeable portion of this chapter to discussing its essentials and considering how well its propositions accord with the facts, at least in the Canadian context. Along the way we consider a variety of related issues.

Two words of warning are in order. First, since the subject of this chapter involves the breadth and scope of macroeconomic analysis, these few pages cannot do justice to all the issues involved in the question of the importance of money. Many volumes are written about narrow facets of it. All we can do is to provide the briefest glimpse of the components of the debate.

Second, people do not agree on even nomenclature and definitions. What some refer to as "monetarism" or "Keynesianism" may not be what others call by the same name. We have tried to rely on definitions that are most generally accepted.

1 The success of monetarism has not been unchallenged. For example, there has been a resurgence of classical views of the economy and the role of money. A recent approach, called *real business cycle analysis*, begins by showing that money does not matter in determining real business cycles. Instead, monetary policy is believed to react to real factors operating in the economy. Space precludes any discussion of these theories here; interested students need to consult a fairly advanced macroeconomics textbook. For example, see D. Romer, *Advanced Macroeconomics* (New York: McGraw-Hill, 1996), Chapter 4.

# MONETARISM

As the science of economics developed in the late eighteenth and the nineteenth century, its leading practitioners—Adam Smith, David Ricardo, John Stuart Mill, Jean-Baptiste Say, and many others—worked out a self-correcting model of a free-market economy. The laws of supply and demand would produce a vigorous and growing economy with full employment so long as government did not fetter the mechanisms with regulations or income redistributions. Changes in the money supply directly influence prices (and nothing else).

This **classical economics** predominated until the 1930s, when it was superseded by the school founded by John Maynard Keynes, whose major work, *The General Theory of Employment, Interest and Money*, was published in 1936, much influenced by the experience of the Great Depression. He and his followers believed that equilibrium in the economy might involve considerable unemployment. To avoid that outcome, they said, the government should use regulation and fiscal policy (including deficit spending). Money was not very important.[2]

For a time, it seemed that **Keynesianism** would rule forever. By the mid-1950s, however, there arose in the United States an increasingly influential group of economists who would eventually be responsible for a renaissance in the study of the importance of money. These monetarists would turn the debate in their favour, especially after the 1970s, when the Keynesians failed to account for some of the ills troubling the economy, such as persistent and rising inflation. Policymakers in the United Kingdom, the United States, Canada, and elsewhere began to adopt what they believed to be a monetarist stance.

What then is **monetarism**? The question itself has spawned considerable literature. To our minds, the following are the essential, defining tenets.

1. In the long run, money is neutral.
2. The price level and inflation are monetary phenomena.
3. Business cycle movements are caused by monetary policy.
4. Money is an exogenous variable in a model of an economy.

2 Indeed in the early stages of the Keynesian era, the *General Theory* was often portrayed as saying that money did not matter at all. As Meltzer contends, this gross exaggeration arose in part because Keynes seemed preoccupied with policy issues, such as high unemployment, so monetary problems at least appeared to take a back seat.

For most of the rest of this chapter we'll consider and discuss these propositions.

## THE NEUTRALITY OF MONEY

When monetarists speak of the **neutrality of money**, they mean that monetary policy cannot affect the unemployment rate or the price level in the long run. Let's explore that concept and its implications. A **Phillips curve** plots the usually inverse relationship between inflation and unemployment. There appears to be a tradeoff between the two. Thus, society can obtain lower inflation only by accepting higher unemployment (or lower output), and vice versa. Clearly, to the extent that monetary policy can influence prices, money cannot be neutral. This understanding was the strict Keynesian view of the world until the 1960s and could be used to justify, for example, state intervention to help an economy out of a slump. Keynesians are often referred to as interventionists: they favour policies aimed at fine-tuning the economy to achieve a presumably socially desirable goal such as low unemployment.[3]

The monetarist view, by contrast, is that choosing a particular combination of inflation and unemployment creates forces that defeat the policymakers' attempt to reach a particular unemployment rate. For example, higher inflation eventually brings about changes in individuals' expectations of inflation. We know, however, from the Fisher effect that any effect on the real interest rate will be temporary. Since only changes in the real interest rate can have real economic effects once the new equilibrium is attained, a monetary policy aimed at permanently lowering unemployment cannot have any lasting economic effects. In other words, unemployment can deviate only for a short time from its long-run value, which is primarily affected by technological change and policies that favour or discourage labour-force mobility from one region or occupation to another. Thus the Keynesian tradeoff disappears in the long run (the Phillips curve becomes vertical[4]), though it may exist in the short run.

---

3 For a time at least, Keynesians believed that by properly estimating a Phillips curve, the political authorities could literally pick a point on it that coincided with their philosophy. (This flirting with social engineering was to be short-lived.)

4 Indeed, in his 1977 Nobel lecture, Milton Friedman proposed that the inflation and unemployment rates could be *positively* related to each other—that the Phillips curve could actually be upward sloping. Friedman explained this possibility as arising from the fact that as inflation goes up, so does its volatility. Since greater volatility implies more uncertainty, one result is less efficiency in the economy as a whole, which translates into a higher unemployment rate. The likelihood of this situation occurring has been greatly reduced by the last few years of relatively low inflation, but that was certainly not the case in the late 1970s, when Friedman prepared his lecture.

# EXPECTATIONS OF INFLATION IN THE SHORT RUN

How long is the short run? The answer depends on one's view of how individuals form their expectations of future prices (that is, their *expectations of inflation*).

## Adaptive Expectations

Monetarists of several generations, including Irving Fisher, claim that the effects of monetary policy occur with lags that are long and variable and, therefore, uncertain. This result hinges critically on the **adaptive expectations hypothesis**, the theory that people form their expectations of inflation by extrapolating from ("adapting to") the past behaviour of prices and continually revising their forecasts on the basis of their previous errors.

Although the idea that people learn from their past mistakes is intuitively appealing, it is suspect. Why? In a world in which inflation was more or less stable, one would surely expect individuals eventually to learn enough from their past mistakes to avoid making them in the future. But, as we have seen, inflation tends to rise or fall persistently. Suppose it rises over a considerable period. Then, an individual who uses a forecast mechanism that looks only at the past will never catch up to actual inflation rates. Similarly, in an era of falling inflation, individuals will persistently overestimate actual inflation.

## *An Algebraic Model of Adaptive Expectations

An adaptive expectations model can be defined as follows:

$$P_t^f = P_{t-1}^f + b(P_{t-1} - P_{t-1}^f) \qquad (26.1)$$

where

$P_t^f$ = the forecast for the price level at time $t$ (today)
$P_{t-1}^f$ = the forecast for the price level at time $t - 1$ (last period)
$P_{t-1}$ = the actual value of the price level at time $t - 1$
$(P_{t-1} - P_{t-1}^f)$ = the last period's forecast error

Equation (26.1) says simply that the current forecast of the price level is based on last period's or yesterday's forecast of the same price level, plus an adjustment factor that recognizes the error made in that previous forecast. The extent to which past mistakes are important in adapting the forecast is summarized in the coefficient $b$. If $b = 0$, the current forecast is unaffected by past forecast errors. Therefore, equation (26.1) becomes

$$P_t^f = P_{t-1}^f \qquad (26.2)$$

## ECONOMICS FOCUS 26.1 The Changing Phillips Curve

The 1960s data do produce a Phillips curve, as shown by the downward-sloping best-fit line, but the inflation–unemployment combinations for the 1970s and 1980s show no obvious tradeoff. During the 1970s, inflation hovered around unemployment rates of 5% to 8.5%, an indication of why the natural rate hypothesis emerged to replace the Phillips curve.

By the 1980s, we see a lot of variation in the unemployment rate relative to inflation rates, a finding that led researchers to wonder why high rates of unemployment could persist with average inflation. The result was Blanchard and Summers' hysteresis theory of unemployment. Under this view, countries with a substantial unionized labour force experience persistent unemployment because the "insiders"—the unionized workers—negotiate wages that can keep the "outsiders" out of work for long periods of time.

Comparing the experience of the 1960s with the 1970s and 1980s, one can imagine a short-run Phillips curve shifting up because expected inflation is higher. Milton Friedman suggested, however, that the Phillips curve might be positively sloped. Notice that inflation was more variable during the 1970s than during the 1960s. Since more variability means more uncertainty, Friedman reasoned that inflation variability might also have an independent and positive influence on inflation.

**(A) 1960–95**

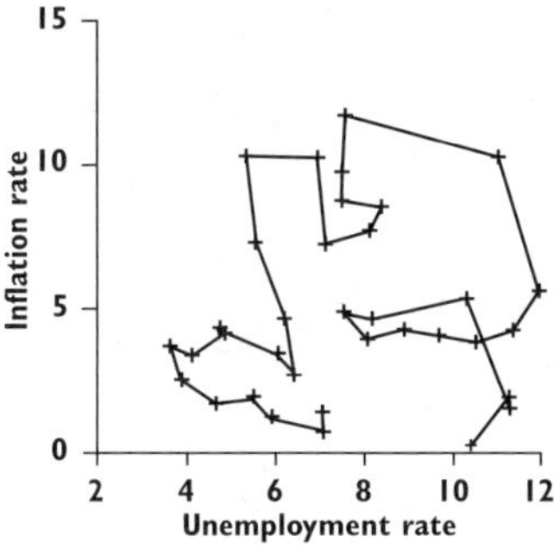


**(B) 1960s**

**(C) 1970s**

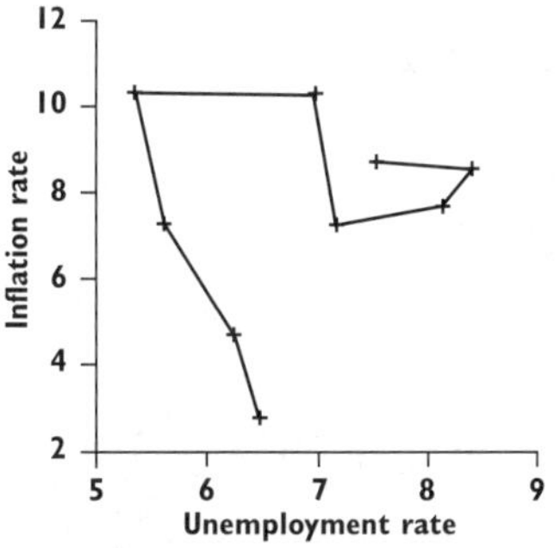


**(D) 1980s**

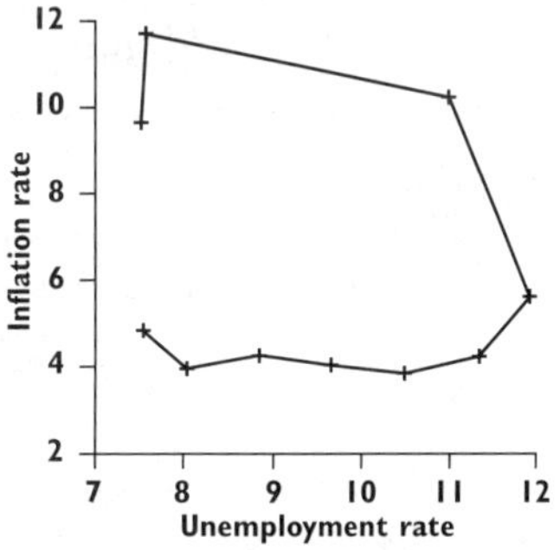


### Sources:

O.J. Blanchard and L.H. Summers, "Hysteresis and the European Unemployment Problem," in *NBER Macroeconomics Annual* 1986, ed. S. Fischer (Cambridge, Mass.: The MIT Press, 1986), 15–78.

M. Friedman, "Nobel Lecture: Inflation and Unemployment," *Journal of Political Economy* 85 (June 1977); 451–72.

A.W. Phillips, "The Relation Between Unemployment and the Rate of Change of Money Wage Rates in the United Kingdom 1861–1957," *Economica* 25 (1958): 283–99.

Note: In each case, the unemployment rate (horizontal axis) is seasonally adjusted and the inflation rate (vertical axis) is the percentage change in the CPI.

The current forecast is the same as last period's forecast; in other words the individual's expectations remain unchanged.

At the other extreme, if $b = 1$, equation (26.1) becomes

$$P^f_t = P^f_{t-1} + P_{t-1} - P^f_{t-1} \text{ or } P^f_t = P_{t-1} \qquad (26.3)$$

The current forecast is equivalent to the last period's actual value for the price level. (This forecast is often referred to as "naive" because it suggests that the individual believes that the immediate past will simply be repeated.)

In reality, people expect the value of $b$ to lie somewhere between 0 and 1.[5] Suppose that $b = 0.5$ and that an individual's 1996 expectations were correct. Then,

$$P_{1996} = P^f_{1996} = 100$$

where 100 refers to the value of, say, the consumer price index for that year. Using these 1996 values, we applied equation (26.1) for four more years. Table 26.1 shows the results. Notice how badly the adaptive expectations framework performed. The forecast errors rise over time, rather than fall as one would expect if individuals were learning from the history of the price level.

## Rational Expectations

Given that the adaptive expectations hypothesis involves individuals' being prone to overestimating or underestimating inflation, it is not surprising that monetarists believe in long and variable lags for the effects of monetary policy. It is also not surprising that economists long sought to model the way individuals actually form expectations rather than to resort to some mechanical, "black box" approach that ignores the tools of economic analysis. Monetarist ideas can be recast by substantially changing the understanding of how individuals form expectations.

The basic tenet of the **rational expectations hypothesis**, which has revolutionized economic analysis, was advanced as early as 1961 by John Muth. Specifically, he suggested that

> Expectations, since they are informed predictions of future events, are essentially the same as the predictions of the relevant economic theory . . . The hypothesis asserts three things: (i) information is scarce, and the economic system does not generally waste it; (ii) the way expectations are formed depends specifically on

---

5 There is, however, no *economic* justification for any chosen weight. Indeed, it can be shown that equation (26.1) is equivalent to a distributed lag with declining weights like this: $P^f_t = w_0P_t + w_1P_{t-1} + w_2P_{t-2} + \ldots$, where $w_0 > w_1 > w_2 > \ldots$, are the weights, which decline over time. Thus, the recent history of prices is relatively more important than the distant history of the same prices.

**TABLE 26.1** A NUMERICAL EXAMPLE OF ADAPTIVE EXPECTATIONS

| | $P_t$ | $P^f_t$ | Forecast Error $(P_{t-1} - P^f_{t-1})$ |
|---|---|---|---|
| 1996 | 100 | 100 | 0 |
| 1997 | 110 | 100 | 10 |
| 1998 | 115 | 105 | 10 |
| 1999 | 125 | 110 | 15 |
| 2000 | 140 | 117.5 | 22.5 |

Initially, the forecast is correct: $P_{1996} = P^f_{1996} = 100$. Subsequently, equation (26.1) is applied. For example,

$$\begin{aligned} P^f_{1997} &= P^f_{1996} + 0.5\,(P_{1996} - P^f_{1996}) \\ &= 100 + 0.5\,(100 - 100) \\ &= 100 \\ P^f_{1998} &= P^f_{1997} + 0.5(P_{1997} - P^f_{1997}) \\ &= 100 + 0.5(100 - 100) \\ &= 100 + 0.5(10) \\ &= 105 \end{aligned}$$

> the structure of the relevant system describing the economy; (iii) a "public prediction" . . . will have no substantial effect on the operation of the economic system (unless it is based on inside information).[6]

In other words, when individuals make a forecast, they have, in effect, some economic model in mind, and any errors in that forecast are irrelevant in future forecasts. Bygones are bygones. Only the current structure of the economy is relevant in generating price-level forecasts.[7]

## *An Algebraic Model of Rational Expectations

A simple example will illustrate the idea of rational expectations. Suppose that the public believes the price level is determined by the past behaviour of the money supply. Specifically, let

$$P_t = aM_{t-1} + v_t \tag{26.4}$$

so that the current price level is a fraction, $a$, of the last period's money supply,

6 J. Muth, "Rational Expectations and the Theory of Price Movements," *Econometrica* 29 (1961): 315–25.

7 If the structure of the economy changes, so does the model or the nature of the relationship in an existing model. This idea implies that the large-scale models of the economy popular in the 1960s are inadequate as tools for the analysis of policies for they ignore changes in economic structure. This is the central idea of the *Lucas critique*, which has had far-reaching implications in the economics profession. Indeed, Robert Lucas of the University of Chicago was awarded the Nobel Prize for his work in this area. However, the topic is beyond the scope of this text.

$M_{t-1}$, plus some unpredictable component, $v_t$. This last component has the same properties as the unpredictable term, introduced in Chapter 12, that explains why stock prices follow a random walk. Thus,

$$E(v_t) = 0 \tag{26.5}$$

so the public expects deviations from the rule to average zero.[8] The rational expectations hypothesis says that individuals base their forecasts on the expected value of the economic model they have in mind. In other words,

$$P_t^f = E(P_t) = aM_{t-1} \tag{26.6}$$

Since the expected value of $v_t$ is zero by equation (26.5), the current forecast of the price level is a function only of the value of last period's money supply.

Notice also what the rational expectations hypothesis says about the forecast errors made by individuals:

$$P_t - P_t^f = aM_{t-1} + v_t - aM_{t-1} = v_t$$

and

$$E(P_t - P_t^f) = E(v_t) = 0$$

In other words, forecasts are, on average, correct since forecast errors are expected to be zero on average. Therefore, in contrast to the adaptive expectations approach, the rational expectations hypothesis does not permit individuals to make systematic forecast errors.

## WHAT DOES IT ALL MEAN?

The implications of rational expectations for the neutrality of money centre, therefore, on the speed with which the Phillips curve tradeoff disappears. The reason that lags are long and variable in the monetarist view stems largely from the assumption of adaptive expectations. With rational expectations, there is no tradeoff worth considering.[9] The public knows the structure of the economy and cannot, therefore, be systematically fooled by policymakers if the policymakers follow some fixed rule for money supply growth. But is the solution that simple? Unfortunately, no, as we will see in the following section.

One final point. Notice that the neutrality of money issue revolves around whether monetary policy has *real* effects on unemployment or output. No one

---

8 $E(\cdot)$ is the expectations operator introduced in Chapters 12 and 13.

9 If there are no systematic forecast errors, $(P_t - P_t^f)$—that is, $v_t$—is uncorrelated through time. Unfortunately, this is not the case. For this reason, the Phillips curve theory assuming rational expectations has had a distinctly mixed reaction.

disputes the impact of monetary policy on *nominal* variables such as nominal output.[10]

# RULES VERSUS DISCRETION IN THE CONDUCT OF MONETARY POLICY

The implication of the foregoing ideas is striking. Since monetary policy cannot have long-lasting real effects on the economy, it is better for the authorities to follow a rule — such as the simple one of fixing the money supply so that $P_t = aM_{t-1}$, which was assumed in equation (26.4) — rather than discretion in formulating and implementing monetary policy. But will the authorities do any such thing? And will the "rule" they choose be a useful one? Let's further explore what we have discovered about monetary policy.

## THE POLITICAL TEMPTATION OF SHORT-RUN TRADEOFFS

Few economists consider monetary fluctuations neutral, *at least in the short run.* The reason is, in large part, errors in forecasting the future—that is, expectational errors.[11] If we assume, however, that expectations are rational—that individuals do not systematically make mistakes in forecasting the future course of the economy—then monetary policy cannot systematically influence unemployment or output.

The logic of the previous paragraph can be summarized in a single proposition: inflation and unemployment have a short-run tradeoff but no long-run tradeoff. Figure 26.1 graphically displays this concept. The long-run Phillips curve is vertical, embodying the idea that the economy tends toward $u^*$, the economy's **natural rate of unemployment**, which is the unemployment rate that would be obtained if expectional errors disappeared.[12] (The phrase "natural rate of unemployment" is unfortunate, implying that some fraction of the work force is

10 There is, however, disagreement about whether fiscal policy has any effect. The monetarist manifestation of this idea is summarized in what is known as the St. Louis model (because it was developed at the US Federal Reserve Bank of St. Louis). It contends that fiscal policy has no impact on nominal GDP. Although the evidence is almost overwhelming, there is a flaw in the St. Louis model because it assumes that fiscal policy must *cause* changes in nominal GDP and not be caused by it. Although many of the issues are beyond the scope of this text, we briefly address the causality issue later in this chapter.

11 The sources of these errors are undoubtedly varied. Individuals may confuse price changes of the commodities they happen to buy with changes in the overall consumer price index. Workers sign contracts that commit them to wage increases before they know actual price increases. Alternatively, since there are costs to changing prices (called "menu" costs) this too will imply lags in the adjustment of prices. A detailed discussion of these issues is impossible here.

12 "Natural" unemployment should not be confused with *structural unemployment*, which arises because of normal frictions in the labour market, such as changes in the demographic characteristics of the population.

**FIGURE 26.1** Phillips Curves in the Short Run and the Long Run

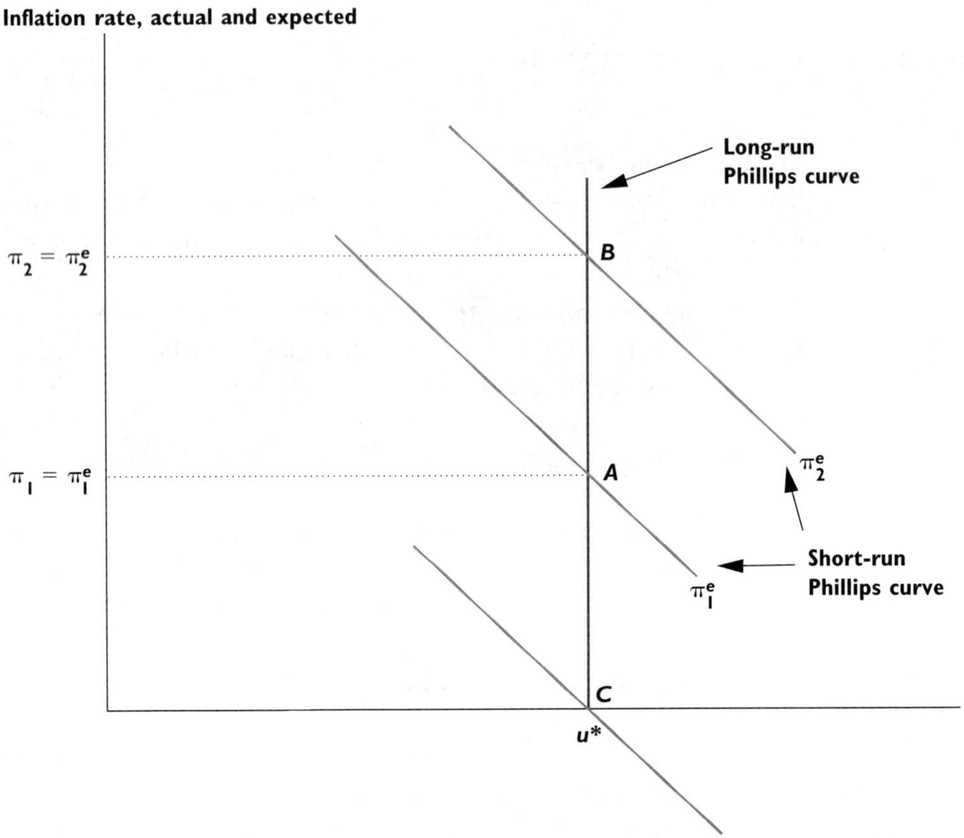


The vertical Phillips curve reflects the neutrality of monetary policy in the long run; there is no inflation–unemployment tradeoff. The downward-sloping curves describe a short-run tradeoff between the same two variables. Each time there is a change in the expected rate of inflation, the tradeoff curve shifts. The time-inconsistency problem arises because even though society prefers point *C*, policymakers generate a result such as *A* or even *B* as they continually attempt to exploit the short-run tradeoff.

eternally condemned to being out of work. An alternative phrase, the **non-accelerating inflation rate of unemployment** (NAIRU), is perhaps both more tactful and more adequately descriptive of $u^*$.)

Two NAIRU positions are displayed in Figure 26.1. If inflation is $\pi_1$ and expected inflation is $\pi_1^e$, the economy settles at point *A*. Monetary policy may cause deviations from *A* along the short-run Phillips curve, but all that can be gained from a policy aimed at reducing the unemployment rate is both higher actual and expected inflation, such as at point *B*.[13]

Now if we add the assumptions that politicians prefer lower unemployment (to enhance their chances for re-election) and that voters dislike inflation, what happens to the tradeoffs depicted in Figure 26.1? Suppose the monetary authorities declare that they will ensure a zero rate of inflation—in other words, that they guarantee the economy will end up at a point such as *C* in Figure 26.1.[14] The difficulty is that the electorate, being rational, realizes that a short-run tradeoff exists between $\pi$ and $u$. The political authorities also realize this, but they have an incentive, especially if an election is approaching, to try to generate, even temporarily, an unemployment rate lower than $u^*$.

The outcome of such an action is that the economy will eventually reach a point such as *A* or *B*. But the temptation to obtain a "short-term gain" is almost irresistible; therefore, even though everyone agrees that point *C* is best for society, the actual outcome will be less good. In other words, economics will always display a positive inflation bias unless policymakers' hands can be tied to deliver a zero inflation rate.[15]

## THE TIME-INCONSISTENCY PROBLEM

The problem just stated has been labelled the **time-inconsistency problem of monetary policy**. The phrase captures the notion that policymakers have an incentive to deviate from their promise if individuals commit themselves to act as if the announcement were to be believed. It is partly for this reason that the question of policymakers' credibility in making economic promises has proved important in economic analysis of late.[16] In a sense, policymakers are continually playing monetary policy games with the public that produce the positive bias in inflation.

### *An Algebraic Model of the Credibility Problem

The foregoing result can be demonstrated more formally. Suppose a government wishes to reach zero inflation, but it also desires an unemployment rate of less

13 The path from *A* to *B* need not, of course, be smooth, and the diagram gives no hint about how long it would take to travel it.

14 Ideally, the political authorities might also want to ensure a zero unemployment rate, but we assume doing so is not feasible. The arguments here are not materially affected by this assumption.

15 This raises the issue of the autonomy of the monetary authorities, which is discussed in Chapter 25.

16 It might be argued that policymakers with a reputation for promising and delivering low inflation may be relatively successful in avoiding the time-inconsistency problem. Unfortunately, even these policymakers have a distinct bias toward positive inflation.

than $u^*$. As depicted in Figure 26.1, it can reduce unemployment only so long as $\pi > \pi^e$—that is, so long as actual inflation is greater than expected inflation—for then a short-run Phillips curve goes into operation.

To the extent that the government achieves such an outcome, it benefits politically and its loss is reduced. But since the public dislikes inflation, there is also a political price to be paid for the relatively high inflation rate. We can summarize these two effects by writing a *loss function* as follows:

$$L = -a(\pi - \pi^e) + \frac{b}{2}(\pi - \pi^*)^2 \tag{26.7}$$

The first term describes the government's gain (or reduction in its loss) from generating a higher-than-expected rate of inflation, $\pi - \pi^e$, that translates into an unemployment rate lower than $u^*$. The coefficient $a$ is an arbitrary constant describing the size of the effect in economic terms. (This coefficient could perhaps be translated into a measure indicating the number of votes in the next election or the probability of re-election.)[17]

The second term in equation (26.7) represents the political costs of deviating from a stated inflation target, $\pi^*$, which could be zero. Here the weight attached to this element is $b/2$.

The government wishes to minimize $L$ for a given $\pi^e$, which is determined by the public. The solution to this loss-minimization problem is that inflation will be[18]

$$\pi = \frac{b}{a} \tag{26.8}$$

which clearly differs from zero.

Now, suppose that individuals, because they are rational, come to expect $b/a$—that is, $\pi^e = b/a$—even though the target inflation rate is zero ($\pi^* = 0$). If this expectation occurs, equation (26.7) becomes

---

17 Note that no time subscript is added. By assuming that this year's tradeoff can be treated independently of next year's tradeoff, we can analyse the problem abstracting from the time element. Clearly, this assumption is unrealistic, but its absence would add considerably to the mathematical difficulty of the analysis.

18 To minimize $L$ with respect to $\pi$, find

$$\left(\frac{\partial L}{\partial \pi}\right) = 0 = -a + \frac{2b\pi}{2} = -a + b\pi \text{ or } \pi = \frac{b}{a}$$

where ($\partial L/\partial \pi = 0$) is the minimization condition expressed as the first derivative of $L$ with respect to $\pi$.

$$L = -a\left(\frac{b}{a} - \frac{b}{a}\right) + \frac{b}{2}\left(\frac{b}{a}\right)^2 = \frac{b}{2}\left(\frac{b}{a}\right)^2$$

The government thus ends up with a positive loss, which translates into fewer votes and possibly a loss in upcoming elections.

## Monetary Policy Games

Another way of illustrating the time-inconsistency problem with monetary policy is to think of the policymakers and the public as being caught in a dilemma about what to believe about monetary policy and how it is being conducted. To see the implications of this approach, we need to specify some relationships.

$$U = U_n - (\dot{M} - \dot{M}^e) \tag{26.9}$$
$$W = -\dot{M}^2 + 2(U_n - U) \tag{26.10}$$
$$W = -\dot{M}^2 + 2(\dot{M} - \dot{M}^e) \tag{26.11}$$
$$U = -(\dot{M} - \dot{M}^e)^2 \tag{26.12}$$

where

$U$ = the actual unemployment rate
$U_n$ = the natural rate of unemployment
$W$ = social welfare
$\dot{M}$ = money growth
$\dot{M}^e$ = expected money growth

Equation (26.9) describes the natural rate hypothesis: when money growth is equal to its expected value, the actual unemployment rate will exactly equal its natural rate. Therefore, departures from the natural rate of unemployment can occur only when actual money growth differs from its expected value.

Equation (26.10) describes the welfare function of the policymakers. Excess money growth reduces welfare, accounting for the negative sign in front of $\dot{M}^2$. (The money growth term is squared because we wish the penalty for higher money growth rates to rise quickly.) The second term in this equation expresses the fact that policymakers obtain positive welfare whenever the actual unemployment rate is less than the natural rate. Positive welfare may translate into more votes and a greater probability of re-election.

Equation (26.11) is the policymakers' welfare function in terms of money growth. Welfare is reduced by excessive money growth, presumably because it means inflation, which voters dislike. But money growth in excess of the public's expectation ($\dot{M} > \dot{M}^e$) enhances the policymakers' welfare function for it translates into a temporary lower unemployment rate according to the short-term Phillips curve.

Equation (26.12) describes the public's utility function. The public dislikes excessive money because it is inflationary.

Now, let's consider some scenarios, assuming the policymakers can choose $\dot{M} = 0$ or $\dot{M} = 1$. Table 26.2 gives payoff tables for both the policymakers and the politicians. If the policymakers set $\dot{M} = 0$ and the public expects that move, both social welfare ($W$) and the unemployment rate ($U$) will be zero. But if the policymakers set $\dot{M} = 1$ when the public expects $\dot{M} = 0$, the politicians are the winners, at the expense of the public. And if the public expects $\dot{M} = 1$ and gets it, society as a whole loses.

Even though everyone knows that $\dot{M} = M = 0$ would leave policymakers and the public better off, the monetary game forces policymakers to prefer $\dot{M} = 1$ and society is the loser.

## THE BASE DRIFT PROBLEM

Presumably, the simpler the rule for the conduct of monetary policy, the easier for the public to forecast the future course of the price level. The difficulty is in establishing a rule that guarantees commitment. Otherwise no rule will produce zero or even low inflation.

During the 1980s, many governments announced their plans for money supply growth to build their credibility as inflation-fighters. Unfortunately, the way in which they have actually implemented their monetary policy has made it even more difficult to forecast future prices.

As we have seen, money supply control stems from the monetary base. Knowing control is not perfect, the monetary authorities stipulate a target range of money growth rates. So far so good: individuals can presumably measure the performance of the monetary authorities by examining the difference between actual and targeted growth rates. But if the target is revised every so often in terms of actual performance, rather than the previously announced target, then the target is allowed to drift over time. What happens is the **base drift** problem, which has considerable consequences for forecasting the behaviour of the monetary authorities.

For example, suppose that the government announces a policy of targeting the level of the money supply so as to achieve a 3% growth rate per year.[19] Starting

19 In actuality, the growth rate would be given as a range, rather than a specific point. The essence of the argument is not affected by our simplification.

**TABLE 26.2** PAYOFF TABLES

**Policymakers**

| | | $\dot{M}^e$ | |
|---|---|---|---|
| | | 0 | 1 |
| $\dot{M}$ | 0 | 0 | −2 |
| | 1 | 1 | −1 |

**Public**

| | | $\dot{M}^e$ | |
|---|---|---|---|
| | | 0 | 1 |
| $\dot{M}$ | 0 | 0 | −1 |
| | 1 | −1 | 0 |

The payoffs are based on the value of $W$ for policymakers and $U$ for the public. If the policymakers set $\dot{M} = 0$, then by equation (26.11), $W = 0$. And by equation (26.12), if $\dot{M} = \dot{M}^e = 0$, $U = 0$. If, however, the policymakers set $\dot{M} = 1$, believing that the public expects $\dot{M}^e = 0$, then equation (26.11) becomes $W = -1^2 + 2(1 - 0) = 1$. Thus it is beneficial for the policymakers to "surprise" the public and set $\dot{M} > \dot{M}^e$. The public loses, however, since, by equation (26.12), $U = -(1 - 0)^2 = -1$.

Clearly, the public realizes this outcome is possible, so it would like $\dot{M}^e = 1$. If the policymakers set $\dot{M} = 1$, there is no loss of utility as far as the public is concerned since $U = 0$. But, according to equation (26.11), $W$ becomes $-1^2 + 2(1 - 1) = -1$ so society as a whole loses because policymakers have the incentive to generate $\dot{M} = 1$.

Note: The overall conclusion holds even when various extensions are considered.

Source: A. Cukierman, "Central Bank Behaviour and Credibility; Some Recent Theoretical Developments," *Review of the Federal Reserve Bank of St. Louis* 68 (May 1986): 5–17.

from a level of 100, the money supply target would be 100(1.03) = 103 for the end of the first year, 100(1.03)(1.03) = 106.1 for the end of the second year, and so on (see the first column of Table 26.3). Suppose the money supply actually grows at a 4% annual rate, the target growth rate is kept constant, but the base used to calculate the target money supply level is revised by using the *actual* value. In other words, the base is allowed to drift. For example, instead of a target money supply of 106.1 in the second year, the revised target is 104(1.03) = 107.1 (see column 4 of Table 26.3). As the final column in the table shows, the difference between the revised target and the original target can grow over time. Hence, a new type of uncertainty is introduced in predicting the money supply and presumably the price level, thereby making monetary policy more difficult still to decipher.

**TABLE 26.3** A MOVING TARGET: BASE DRIFT

| Year | Target | Actual | Revised Target | Revised Less Original Target |
|---|---|---|---|---|
| 1 | 103.0 | 104.0 | — | — |
| 2 | 106.1 | 108.2 | 107.1 | 1.0 |
| 3 | 109.3 | 112.5 | 111.4 | 2.1 |
| 4 | 112.6 | 117.0 | 115.9 | 3.3 |
| 5 | 116.0 | 121.7 | 120.5 | 4.5 |

The money supply is originally 100 and is targeted for a 3% growth rate. Then for year 1, the target is 100(1.03) = 103, and for year 5, the target is 100(1.03)5 = 116. (Note that compounding is permitted.) Suppose, however, that the money supply actually grows by 4% per year. The result produces the "actual" column. Rather than continuing with the original target, the authorities announce revised targets, reflecting 3% growth based on actual estimates of the previous year. For example, in year 2, the revised target is 104(1.03) = 107.1, and so on.

Not surprisingly then, most countries abandoned formal money growth targets by the early 1990s. One notable exception to this rule is Germany which continues to stick by its money growth targets despite embarrassing misses of late.[20]

## TWO THEORIES OF MONEY

Much of the preceding discussion has centred around the view that the key to inflation lies in the conduct of monetary policy. What is the presumed connection between the two? We address two theories in this section.

Perhaps the most venerable theory linking monetary policy and the price level is the equilibrium relationship summarized in the *quantity theory of money.* Its central feature—a tenet central to monetarist thought—is that "inflation is always and everywhere a monetary phenomenon."[21] By contrast, the recently rejuvenated *real bills doctrine* takes exception to the strict monetarist view of inflation but sees a connection between inflation and printing money to cover government debt. We briefly explore both views.[22]

20 See C. Parkes, "If Not Vindicated, Certainly a Little Wiser," *Financial Times*, 21 July 1994, p. 2; and "Monetary Target for 1996 and Lowering of Central Bank Rates," Deutsche Bundesbank *Monthly Report* (January 1996): 19.28.

21 M. Desai, *Testing Monetarism* (London: Frances Pinter, 1981), chapter 1.

22 Space does not permit an analysis of the origins and development of either theory. See, however, M. Friedman, "Quantity Theory of Money," in *the New Palgrave: Money*, ed. J. Satwell, M. Milgate, and P. Newman (New York: W.W. Norton, 1989): 1–40; and T.J. Sargent, *Rational Expectations and Inflation* (New York: Harper & Row, 1986): chapter 1.

## ECONOMICS FOCUS 26.2 Taking Out a Contract on a Central Banker

It was pointed out in this chapter and the previous one that governments have been searching for ways to ensure low inflation performance and to avoid the temptations of using the central bank to exploit the short-run Phillips curve. One solution that has received considerable attention among economists is to have the central bank governor's contract tied to inflation performance. The New Zealand case comes to mind, of course, since the central bank's budget is nominally fixed while the governor can be dismissed if inflation exceeds the agreed upper portion of the target band. Yet, it seems impractical to follow up on such a suggestion if only because, even in the private sector, contracts tied to performance alone are extremely rare. Nevertheless, it is interesting to consider why such contracts might help solve the time-inconsistency problem discussed in this chapter. Consider a variant of the monetary policy game discussed in this chapter.

$$U = U_n + (\pi - \pi^e) \quad [a]$$

$$W^{SOC} = (U_n - U) - b\pi \quad [b]$$

$$W^{CB} = \text{sal} + (U_n - [U + k])^2 - b\pi^2 \quad [c]$$

Equation [a] describes the natural rate hypothesis in terms of inflation. Thus, if inflation is higher than expected then, other things equal, actual unemployment is lower than the natural rate. Equation [b] is society's welfare function (soc). Again, any inflation reduces social welfare. Finally, equation [c] is the welfare function of the central bank (CB) which is partly a function of the salary of the governor (sal). Notice that the central bank can tolerate a different level of unemployment than society (by an amount $k$ assumed to be constant). The solution to the problem of maximizing welfare, when $k$ cannot be zero, is the following (we leave the details as an exercise)

$$\pi = k/b \text{ and } U = U_n$$

which is simply the inflation bias result that was derived earlier (see equation (26.8)). Suppose, however, that in order to avoid the inflation bias, the governor of the central bank signs a performance contract that looks like the following:

$$\text{sal} = \text{sal}_o - \lambda\pi \quad [d]$$

where $\text{sal}_0$ is a base salary and $\lambda$ is some fraction of inflation performance which reduces the governor's salary. The maximization problem in this case reduces to (again leaving the problem as an exercise)

$$\pi = (k - \lambda)/b,\ U = U_n \quad [e]$$

Notice from equation [e] that as long as $\lambda$ is greater than zero, inflation with a performance contract will be *lower* than without a contract while the unemployment rate will not be the same. This is the essence of the proposal that central bank governors sign performance contracts.

**Sources:**

C. Waller, "Performance Contracts for Central Bankers," *Review* of the Federal Reserve Bank of Saint Louis 77 (Sept/Oct 1995): 3–14.

C. Walsh, "Recent Central Bank Reforms and the Role of Price Stability as the Sole Objective of Monetary Policy," *NBER Macroeconomics Annual 1995* (Cambridge, Mass: The MIT Press, 1995), pp. 237–52.

# THE QUANTITY THEORY

Although the quantity theory has evolved through several versions, it is perhaps best known in its current form as the relationship between the nominal quantity of money in circulation and the nominal income it generates. More formally, a given money stock, $M$, in equilibrium explains a fraction of nominal aggregate income, $Y$, so we can write

$$M = k \cdot Y \tag{26.13}$$

As we know, $Y$ can also be written as the product of the price level and real income (more precisely, income in constant dollars), $Py$. Equation (26.13) thus becomes

$$M = k \cdot Py \tag{26.14}$$

where $k$ is the fraction stipulating that the money stock is proportional to income. In particular, this fraction captures the fact that a given money stock will circulate or turn over several times during a given period—most often, one year—to generate a given level of nominal income. In other words, if we rewrite equation (26.14) as

$$M\frac{1}{k} = Py \tag{26.15}$$

then $(1/k)$ represents the *velocity of circulation*: a given money stock multiplied by its velocity will produce a certain level of income in a given period. For example, if the money stock is \$5 billion and each dollar generates \$2 worth of spending—which is income to someone—so that velocity is 2, then the quantity theory predicts that nominal income will be \$10 billion, which is simply \$5 billion × 2. Letting $V$ represent velocity, we can finally write the quantity theory equation:

$$MV = Py \tag{26.16}$$

Moving from equation (26.16) to a theory of the price level is now but a short step. First, assume that velocity is constant.[23] Next, by invoking the natural rate of unemployment hypothesis examined earlier, we can also take the level of output as given.

Now let us copy equation (26.16) placing a bar over the variables we have just assumed to be constants:

$$M\bar{V} = P\bar{y} \tag{26.17}$$

With $V$ and $y$ fixed, fluctuations in $P$ can be explained only by changes in $M$. It is in this sense that inflation is a monetary phenomenon.

Despite proponents' controversies about how to measure money and about whether monetary changes cause price changes, the quantity theory has endured as a theory of the price level for at least two reasons. First, because quantity theorists have, for the most part, not taken a firm stand about what constitutes money, the theory has proved fairly flexible, even as financial innovations have

23 Since only long-run factors influence it. Alternatively, one can simply assume that velocity is a *random walk*, so that it is essentially an unpredictable element.

forced changes in the monetary measures used to proxy *M* over time. Second, the theory has generally proved a reliable tool for predicting the price level. This is not to say that there have been no episodes in which the quantity theory has failed. Indeed, as we will see below, it was its perceived lack of generality that stimulated the search for an alternative view of price level determination.

## THE REJUVENATED REAL BILLS DOCTRINE

The 1980s saw a re-emergence in a new form of an old idea called the real bills doctrine. In essence, the doctrine argues that the value of money and therefore its purchasing power can be explained by the value of the assets that back it.

Suppose we consider a nation's central bank like any other financial intermediary. It possesses assets and has liabilities and thus engages in leverage. Its liabilities are, however, "money" and are backed by assets purchased via money. Therefore, if the quantity of money is increased and assets, such as Treasury bills or other forms of government debt, are received in exchange for the money printed, there is no reason to expect this increase in the quantity of money to be inflationary. After all, the central bank's assets rise by the amount as its liabilities. Or do they? If a central bank is called upon to purchase increasing quantities of government debt that cannot be financed either through future issues or through taxation, the value of these assets will presumably fall. Consequently, the value of money will fall, which is to say that the price level will rise. But so long as money is backed by assets that have value, there is no need to link a particular money stock with a particular price level.[24] Unless individuals perceive that the government's debt will eventually be financed by printing increasing quantities of money, there is no need for money supply changes to create price level changes.

This view is the essence of a rejuvenated version of the real bills doctrine—a view that is strikingly different from the quantity theory. Indeed, it has been termed an example of some unpleasant monetarist arithmetic.

When would the public fear printing money as a way of financing government debt? The example that comes most readily to mind is the case of a deficit's running out of control.

A simply way of writing the government's deficit is

$$\Delta B_t = G_t - T_t \tag{26.18}$$

where

24 A quantity theory framework offers another way in which current money supply increases need not translate immediately into price level changes: money supply changes can take time to influence prices. This is the essence of the idea of important "long and variable lags in the effect of monetary policy," expounded by Milton Friedman.

## FINANCIAL FOCUS 26.1 P*—The Holy Grail of Inflation Forecasts?

If the velocity of circulation $V$ is relatively stable, we can write the quantity theory as

$$P^* = \frac{(M \times V^*)}{Y^*}$$

If $V^*$ and $Y^*$ are the long-run values for $V$ and $Y$ and, therefore, stable, then the long-run value of $P$, denoted by $P^*$ and called $P$-star, will be determined by the money supply, $M$.

Hence, if actual prices are lower than $P^*$, they will rise until $P^*$ is attained. Therefore, there will be inflation. The opposite holds, of course, when current prices exceed the $P^*$ value. Hallman, Porter, and Small, using research based on US data, contend that the best proxy for $M$ is the M2 measure.

To take a numerical example, suppose that $V$ is 1.432, which is approximately its average value since 1971, potential GNP is approximately $418,134 million (in 1986 dollars) and M2 is $252,872 million. Then $P^*$ is

$$P^* = \frac{(252{,}872 \times 1.432)}{418{,}134} = 0.87$$

Thus, if the actual price level was 1, the fact that $P^*$ was less than $P$ would mean that inflation would be predicted to fall. The opposite would hold when $P^*$ was greater than $P$.

The figures below show what actual and potential output for Canada look like since the 1960s as well as the CPI versus $P^*$ based on the money stock measure M1. The effect of the recessions of the early 1980s and 1990s is quite evident as actual GDP is below its potential value. In the same vein, we see that the CPI was persistently above $P^*$ in the mid-1980s, precisely when inflation began to fall sharply (in 1983 CPI inflation was 5.7% while by 1985 it had fallen to 3.5%). The reverse takes place in the late 1980s when actual inflation jumped to 5.0% in 1989 from 4.0% the year before. During the 1990s the CPI and $P^*$ are very close together but with the CPI above $P^*$ this means falling inflation, which again turned out to be the case (inflation fell from 5.6% in 1991 to 0.2% by 1994).

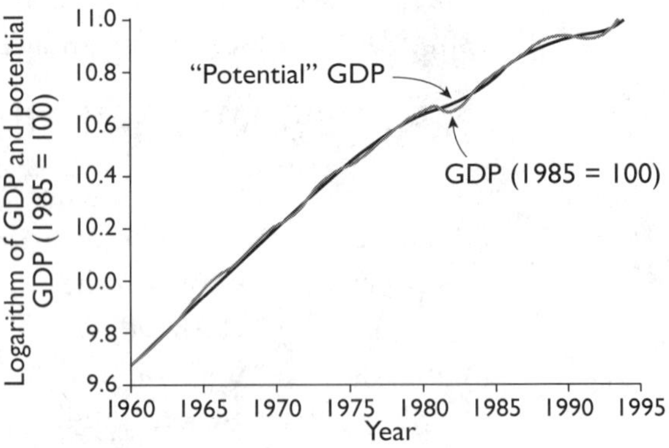


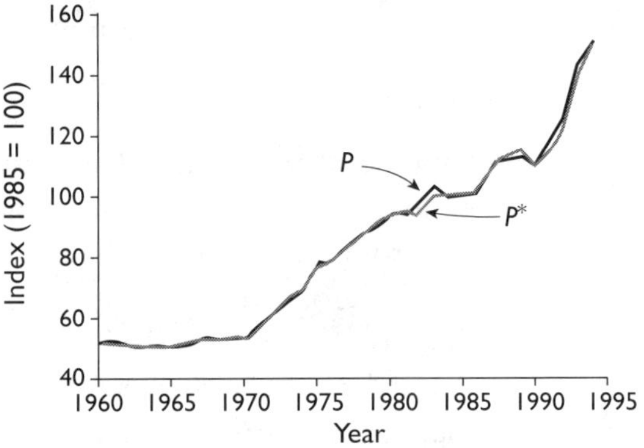


Given the crucial nature of the assumptions of a stable velocity and an output level that oscillates around its potential level, it is not surprising that critics have focused on this issue as a potentially weak element in the theory.

**Sources:**

L.J. Christiano, "P*: Not the Inflation Forecaster's Holy Grail," Federal Reserve Bank of Minneapolis, *Quarterly Review* 13 (Fall 1989): 3–18.

J. Hallman, R. Porter, and D. Small, "Is the Price Level Tied to the M2 Monetary Aggregate in the Long Run?" *American Economic Review* 81 (September 1991).

R.A. Pechemino and R.H. Rasche, "P* Type Models: Evaluation and Forecasts," NBER working paper no. 3406 (August 1990).

$\Delta B_t =$ change in government bonds outstanding at time $t$
$G_t =$ government spending at time $t$
$T_t =$ tax revenue at time $t$

Equation (26.18) stipulates that if government expenditures exceed tax revenues, the resulting deficit will be financed through the sale of bonds. The transaction could be with the public. But if the deficit becomes "too large," the public may be unwilling to purchase these bonds in sufficient quantities to finance it. Then the government can instruct the central bank to issue enough money to meet the financing needs. On the central bank's balance sheet, the result will appear as

$$\Delta B_t = \Delta M_t \tag{26.19}$$

where $\Delta B_t$ is an addition to its assets, and $\Delta M_t$, which represents the change in the money supply, is an addition to its liabilities. In the extreme, the market will value $\Delta B_t$ at zero. Such a valuation can take place only through inflation since the value of money is measured by its purchasing power.

## *The Algebra of the Difference between the Quantity Theory and the Real Bills Doctrine

A more formal illustration of the difference between the quantity theory and the real bills doctrine proceeds as follows.

Suppose that individuals' demand for money function[25] is written as

$$\frac{M_t}{P_t} = a - bE\pi_t \tag{26.20}$$

Equation (26.20) says that the demand for money or real balances, $M_t/P_t$, at time $t$ is negatively related to the expected rate of inflation at the same time, $E\pi_t$. (Assuming the real interest rate is constant, the equation amounts to saying that the demand for money is negatively related to the interest rate.[26]) Suppose now that expected inflation depends on individuals' belief about the future course of monetary policy. But that belief depends on how the government finances its deficit. To see why, write the government's budget constraint as

$$D_t + \rho B_t = (\pi + g)M_t + gB_t \tag{26.21}$$

---

25 See Chapter 11.

26 The Fisher equation (see Chapter 5) states that $R = \rho + \pi^e$, where $R =$ nominal rate of interest and $\rho =$ real rate of interest. If $\rho$ is constant, then $\Delta R = \Delta\pi^e$, so changes in the nominal rate of interest are fully explained by changes in expected inflation.

The left-hand side of equation (26.21) is the government deficit net of interest payments, measured in real terms, plus the real interest payments for the stock of government bonds outstanding. (Thus, $D_t$ is equivalent to $G_t - T_t$ of equation (26.18).) The right-hand side explains how the deficit is to be financed: through increasing the money supply or through issuing bonds. A rise in the money supply comes from: (1) inflation, $\pi$, because (holding other factors constant) it reduces the purchasing power of money and so more money has to be created in order to maintain the same level of government spending in real terms, and/or (2) economic growth because, as the quantity theory (equation (26.16)) stipulates, more real income necessitates a higher money stock (again all other factors held constant). Alternatively, the deficit can be financed by issuing more bonds to be sold to the public. It is assumed that the quantity of bonds grows at the same rate as the economy's growth rate.

Thus, deficits need not be inflationary. The money supply may be completely unaffected by deficit spending over time so long as the economy grows fast enough to offset the real interest cost of the debt (that is, so long as $g$ is greater that $\rho$).[27] But if the economy grows less quickly than the real cost of its debt, the debt can be financed only via increasing the money supply. In other words, $\pi$ becomes positive, and, as the real cost of the debt continues to exceed economic growth, could become explosive. Thus, inflation depends ultimately on *how* a government deficit is financed, not on some rigid link between the money supply and the price level, and in turn is influenced by individuals' expectations of the future course of monetary policy. Therefore, it can be shown that

$$P_t = \frac{1}{a}\sum_{j=0}^{\infty}\left(\frac{b}{a}\right)^j EM_{t+j} \qquad (26.22)$$

where $a$ and $b$ are from equation (26.20) and $\Sigma$ is a summation sign[28] so that

$$\sum_{j=0}^{\infty}\left(\frac{b}{a}\right)^j EM_{t+j} = EM_t + \left(\frac{b}{a}\right)EM_{t+1} + \ldots$$

Equation (26.22) simply says that the price level and thus inflation are determined by the current and future path of the money supply. And, as we have seen, this path need not be rigidly linked to the government deficit.

---

27 For proof, rewrite equation (26.21) as $D_t = \pi M_t + (g - \rho)B_t$. If $g > \rho$, one can set $\pi M_t = 0$ to get $D_t = (g - \rho)B_t$.

28 Equation 26.20 is a difference equation since $E\pi_t = P_{t+1}/P_t$—that is, expected inflation is the proportional change of next period's price level relative to the current period price level. The solution method is beyond the scope of this book.

## TWO THEORIES OF MONEY: CONCLUSION

The stimulus for exploring the real bills doctrine was the empirical observation that during many historical periods the money supply has grown rapidly without any corresponding increase in prices. To the extent that the version of the real bills doctrine that we have considered is more general than the quantity theory because it can explain both high and low inflation episodes, it represents an improvement over the latter. However, to the extent that the episodes in which the quantity theory appears not to work well are the exception rather than the rule,[29] it will remain a prominent explanation of price level movements.

# WHAT TRANSMISSION MECHANISM?[30]

Having discussed at some length the likelihood that monetary policy does influence output or unemployment in the short-run, it is worth pausing to ask exactly how this might take place. This involves a discussion of the **transmission mechanism** of monetary policy, a topic in vogue during the 1960s and 1970s and lately revived as central banks and governments focus on combining low inflation with healthy economic growth.

The current debate centres around four different "channels" through which monetary policy might work. Obviously, researchers have generated empirical results favourable to all four points of view which means that there is a grain of truth to each hypothesis or, to put it differently, none of the explanations summarized below has been able to dominate the others.

The four views of the transmission mechanism are as follows:

1. The interest rate channel
2. The exchange rate channel
3. The impact of asset prices more generally
4. The credit channel

The interest rate channel is simply the liquidity effect first encountered in Chapter 6. Less money in the economy drives up interest rates, because there is

29 We say "appears" because proponents of the quantity theory argue that episodes in which $g < \rho$ are rare. They also argue that the connection between money and prices will be weaker if we allow velocity to change over time.

30 This section relies on a large number of concepts and definitions covered throughout this text.

less liquidity, and therefore has a negative impact on output. The exchange rate channel adds another element to the interest rate channel, namely that the exchange rate will *appreciate* because a higher domestic interest rate attracts capital inflows which will *reduce* exports and increase imports thus lowering output. The other asset prices channel argues that a lower money supply will make stocks *less* attractive to hold and, via the impact that lower stock prices have on Tobin's $q$, will lead to lower investment spending and thus to lower economy-wide output. Finally, the credit channel emphasizes the role of financial intermediaries in the transmission mechanism. Under this scenario, a lower money supply implies fewer bank deposits and fewer loans, via the multiplier process, which combined will translate into lower investment spending as well as lower output.

One reason that empirical studies are unable to deliver decisive evidence for one of the above hypotheses is that, while the end result of monetary policy actions are the same in all cases, the intermediate steps need not be mutually exclusive. Thus, for example, hypotheses 3 and 4 both conclude that output falls because investment falls.

## THE CAUSALITY AND EXOGENEITY OF MONEY

Much of the discussion so far has presumed that monetary policy acts first and other variables, such as unemployment, real income, and/or inflation, react afterward. In other words, the chain of causality proceeds from monetary changes to changes in other economic aggregates. Is this understanding of the direction of causality accurate? Few areas of economics have created as much controversy.

### GRANGER CAUSALITY

A major problem in discussions of causality is the difficulty of defining it, much less proving any statement about it.[31] Thus, although economists are often asked to explain what "caused" a recession or an inflation and although statements about cause and effect are vital to understanding economic phenomena, analysts' ideas are difficult to formalize because cause and effect statements can rarely be proved true in any sense.

A much narrower approach to defining causality is therefore widely applied in economics. Known as **Granger causality**[32] it amounts to making a statement about causal relations based on an analysis of the properties of two or more time

31 Students interested in the philosophy and methodology of science will find a voluminous literature on the meaning and interpretation of causality.

32 Named after Professor Clive Granger of the University of California, San Diego.

series. The basic idea is as follows. Suppose we wish to examine the relationship between the money supply and the price level. We can say the money supply causes the price level in a statistical sense if the history of the money supply can "explain" the price level but the history of the price level does not "explain" movements in the money supply.

How does something "explain" the movement in a variable? The term refers to a mathematical relationship between economic time series.[33]

More formally, assume a researcher has available two time series: data on $X_t$ and on $Y_t$. Granger causality stipulates that $X$ causes $Y$ if $Y$ is better explained by using past observations of $X$ than by ignoring them. For example, suppose we write the relationship between $X$ and $Y$ as

$$Y_t = a + b_1 X_{t-1} + b_2 X_{t-2} + e_t \tag{26.23}$$

Equation (26.23) describes the relationship between $X$ and $Y$ where past observations of $X$—namely, $X_{t-1}$ and $X_{t-2}$—are presumed to explain a current value of $Y$, which is $Y_t$. The last term in the equation, $e_t$, captures all the other factors that might also explain $Y$. If $X_{t-1}$ and $X_{t-2}$ are jointly found to explain $Y_t$ statistically, $X_t$ is said to "Granger-cause" $Y$.[34]

Sometimes $X$ is found to cause $Y$ *and* $Y$ is found to cause $X$, a situation in which there is said to be *feedback*. Thus our researcher may wish to examine the following relationship:

$$X_t = a^* + b_1^* Y_{t-1} + b_2^* Y_{t-2} + e_t^* \tag{26.24}$$

Equation (26.24) is almost the same as (26.23) but asks instead whether $Y$ Granger-causes $X$. If the answer is negative, $Y_{t-1}$ and $Y_{t-2}$ do not help to explain $X_t$, and so the researcher concludes that only $X$ Granger-causes $Y$.[35]

Granger causality tests help analysts to decide the adequacy of the presumed direction of statistical causation. Thus, if the money supply Granger-causes the price level but not vice versa, we can conclude that the money supply is an

---

33 A crucial notion here is that of *regression analysis*, which is a mathematical technique for producing a statistical description of the relationship between economic time series. Interested students may wish to consult an introductory econometric textbook for more details. See D. Gujarati, *Basic Econometrics*, 2d ed. (New York: McGraw-Hill, 1988) or E. Berndt, *The Practice of Econometrics: Classic and Contemporary* (Reading, Mass.: Addison-Wesley, 1989).

34 The statistical procedure used to decide whether this relationship is correct is called an F-test. See references cited in footnote 33 for the details.

35 It should be pointed out that while most tests of Granger causality follow the logic discussed above, the original article by Professor Granger actually argues that for X to "Granger-cause" Y, equation (26.24) has to perform relatively better in a forecasting sense. Unfortunately, the technical details are beyond the scope of this text.

*exogenous* variable.[36] Such a conclusion is consistent with the monetarist view that money supply changes produce inflationary and other economic consequences.

## MONEY AND GROWTH

The quantity theory tells us that inflation is purely a monetary phenomenon. Nevertheless, we also know that, in the short-run at least, inflation, and thus money growth, have some influence on output. As economies around the world began to slow down in the 1980s and into the 1990s, economists began to turn their attention to problems of what determines economic growth. Much of the attention has centred on the role of technical innovations and how well a country is endowed with natural resources,[37] but there was general agreement that inflation was a detriment to economic growth. Yet, some also argued that the drive to zero inflation was extreme. After all, according to the Fisher hypothesis, if inflation is zero then real interest rates will be positive. By contrast, with some inflation, real interest rates can be negative (as we saw in Chapter 5) which could be a spur to economic growth.[38] This argument does not seem very convincing in light of our discussion, early in this text, about the costs of inflation. After all, even a little inflation, say 2% a year over 20 years still implies an almost 50% rise in the price level which is hardly conducive to efficiency.[39] Figure 26.2 shows very clearly the connection between inflation and economic growth. Before the oil shock of 1973–74, that is in a period of relatively low inflation (see Chapter 25), there is a definite positive relationship between economic performance and inflation. Turning to the post-oil-shock period the outcomes are quite different. This is a period of relatively high inflation and stagnant economic growth. It is experiences such as these that led policymakers to advocate that central banks focus on inflation as the goal of monetary policy. It is too early to tell, however, whether a return to low and stable inflation will augur the high growth rates achieved during the 1960s.[40]

36 In a sense, Granger causality and exogeneity are similar concepts. The relationship between the two is ambiguous, but since the details are somewhat technical, they are not pursued here.

37 See R. J. Barro and X. Sala-I-Martin, *Economic Growth* (New York: McGraw-Hill, 1995), and "Ungenerous Endowments," *The Economist*, 23 December 1995 – 5 January 1996, p. 87–89.

38 This is known as the "Summers" effect named after an economist at Harvard University.

39 For the argument that zero inflation is, in some sense, "optimal," see J. Konieczny, "The Optimal Rate of Inflation: Competing Theories and their Relevance to Canada," in *Economic Behaviour and Policy Choice Under Price Stability* (Ottawa, ON: Bank of Canada, 1993).

40 Also recall that the 1960s were a period of relatively stable exchange rates, an important consideration in explaining economic performance.

**FIGURE 26.2**

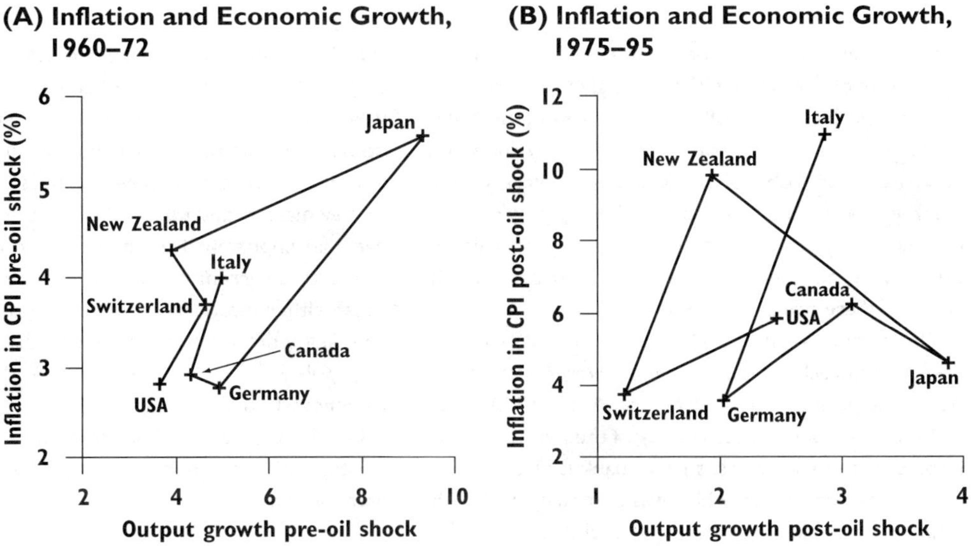


Source: International Financial Statistics CD-ROM

Note: Inflation is the percent change in the consumer price index. Output growth is the percent change in GDP. Simple averages were calculated for each country for the periods indicated.

# SUMMARY

- The debate about the importance of money centres on how important money supply changes are in explaining business cycle fluctuations.
- Monetarists place the money supply at the centre of their models because they believe inflation is entirely a monetary phenomenon. In the short run, monetary policy can influence real economic activity, but in the long run, money is neutral.
- Understanding the role of money in the economy requires that we model the formation of inflationary expectations. Expectations may be understood as adaptive—individuals learn from their past mistakes—or rational—individuals use their forecasts of inflation on an economic model that can change over time.
- Analysing the role of money can be facilitated by looking at a Phillips curve, which summarizes the relationship between the monetary side of an econ-

## ECONOMICS FOCUS 26.3 Post Hoc Ergo Propter Hoc?

"Post hoc ergo propter hoc" (Latin for "After the fact so because of the fact") is the name given to a common flaw in logic: because B follows A, B is caused by A. The phrase was used in a famous 1970 article by the Nobel Laureate James Tobin to argue that just because monetary policy actions (as measured by changes in the money supply) precede changes in prices or real income does not mean that monetary policy is necessarily the cause of these price or income changes.

The fallacy is surprisingly common. For example, Friedman and Schwartz argue persuasively that monetary policy caused the Great Depression of the 1930s in the United States. But a closer reading of their work suggests instead that other factors, such as bank failures, created an economic downturn, which was then magnified by the inappropriate response of the US central bank, the Federal Reserve. Monetary policy did not cause the Great Depression; it only enhanced and prolonged its effects.

Another example comes from the monetarist argument that monetary policy is the prime determinant of nominal income, to the exclusion of fiscal policy. This notion was translated into a model (called the St. Louis model because it was developed by researchers at the US Federal Reserve Bank of St. Louis). Essentially, the model assumes that nominal income is caused by past observations of some money supply measure and of some measure of fiscal policy, such as government spending. The theory behind the model in part stems from the view of money as Granger-causing real income. The empirical evidence is overwhelmingly favourable to the view that past observations of the money supply explain nominal income movements but past fiscal policy effects have no influence whatsoever on the same variable. Thus, money matters and fiscal policy does not. There is, however, an important flaw in the St. Louis analysis. It assumes that current nominal income could not Granger-cause either future monetary policy or fiscal policy. Raj and Siklos demonstrate, however, that although monetary policy causes nominal income, the same variable influences future and perhaps expected fiscal policy. In other words, policymakers react to the joint effects of inflation and real income changes by modifying future fiscal policy.

**Sources:**

M. Friedman and A.J. Schwartz, *A Monetary History of the United States* (Princeton: Princeton University Press, 1963).

B. Raj and P.L. Siklos, "The Role of Fiscal Policy in the St. Louis Model: An Evaluation and Some New Evidence." *Journal of Applied Econometrics* 1 (July 1986): 287–94.

J. Tobin, "Money and Income: Post Hoc Ergo Propter Hoc?" *Quarterly Journal of Economics* 84 (May 1970): 301–17.

omy—and thus, inflation—and the real side, as measured by unemployment. Differences between monetarists and others can be described by Phillips curves.

- Because monetary policy is so important, economists debate whether policymakers should be allowed discretion in conducting monetary policy or should rather be tied to fixed rules known to the public.
- Not everyone agrees that money supply changes automatically lead to proportionate changes in the price level (as in the quantity theory of money). One theory, called the real bills doctrine, concentrates on the role of government deficits and the point at which they can become inflationary.

- Which comes first: a money supply change or a change in inflation or real economic activity? No one is certain but there are tests, called Granger causality tests, that can reveal which variable causes another variable in a statistical sense.

# IMPORTANT TERMS

adaptive expectations hypothesis (p. 612)
base drift (p. 622)
classical economics (p. 610)
Granger causality (p. 632)
Keynesianism (p. 610)
monetarism (p. 610)
natural rate of unemployment (p. 617)
neutrality of money (p. 611)
non-accelerating inflation rate of unemployment (NAIRU) (p. 618)
Phillips curve (p. 611)
rational expectations hypothesis (p. 614)
time-inconsistency problem of monetary policy (p. 619)
transmission mechanism (p. 631)

# EXERCISES

1. Evaluate the statement: "Countercyclical monetary policy is still effective if money is neutral in the long run."

2. Evaluate the statement: "The stability of velocity is important for the monetarist philosophy."

3. **ECONOMICS FOCUS 26.1: The Changing Phillips Curve** alludes to the possibility of a positively sloping Phillips curve relationship. Can you explain how this is possible? (Hint: Think of the risk–return relationship described in Chapter 13; recall footnote 4 this chapter.)

4. One reason given for the existence of a short-run Phillips curve is wage contracts. Explain how labour contracts permit the existence of a short-run inflation–unemployment tradeoff.

5. In constructing Table 26.1, we assumed an adjustment coefficient of 0.5. Reproduce the table assuming an adjustment coefficient of 0.2 and of 0.9. Which coefficient produces the fastest adjustment of expectations? In what sense is the adjustment coefficient a "black box"?

6. In constructing Table 26.3, we assumed that actual money growth was 4% per year. Suppose instead that actual money growth was

| Year | Actual Money Growth |
|---|---|
| 1 | 4% |
| 2 | 1% |
| 3 | −2% |
| 4 | 6% |
| 5 | 3% |

Calculate the actual money stock levels, revised target levels, and the difference between the revised and original target values. What conclusions do you draw?

7. The figures below give the annual unemployment and inflation rates for France and the United Kingdom. Plot a separate Phillips curve for each country for 1961–69 and another one for 1970–90. Discuss the results in light of the issues considered in this chapter. Also compare the results to the Canadian experience.

| | France | | United Kingdom | |
|---|---|---|---|---|
| | Inflation[a] | Unemployment percent | Inflation[a] | Unemployment percent |
| 1961 | 2.3 | 0.6 | 3.4 | 1.6 |
| 1962 | 4.9 | 0.6 | 4.3 | 1.5 |
| 1963 | 4.8 | 0.5 | 1.9 | 1.9 |
| 1964 | 3.4 | 0.5 | 3.2 | 2.3 |
| 1965 | 2.5 | 0.5 | 4.8 | 1.7 |
| 1966 | 2.7 | 0.6 | 3.9 | 1.4 |
| 1967 | 2.6 | 0.7 | 2.5 | 1.5 |
| 1968 | 4.6 | 0.9 | 4.7 | 2.3 |
| 1969 | 6.4 | 2.3 | 5.4 | 2.4 |
| 1970 | 5.4 | 2.5 | 6.5 | 2.6 |
| 1971 | 5.6 | 2.7 | 9.2 | 2.8 |
| 1972 | 6.0 | 2.8 | 7.5 | 3.1 |
| 1973 | 7.4 | 2.7 | 9.1 | 2.1 |
| 1974 | 13.5 | 3.0 | 15.9 | 2.1 |
| 1975 | 11.9 | 4.3 | 24.1 | 3.3 |
| 1976 | 9.6 | 4.5 | 16.6 | 4.5 |
| 1977 | 9.2 | 5.0 | 15.9 | 4.8 |
| 1978 | 9.1 | 5.4 | 8.2 | 4.7 |
| 1979 | 10.7 | 6.0 | 13.4 | 4.3 |
| 1980 | 13.6 | 6.4 | 18.0 | 5.4 |
| 1981 | 13.4 | 7.6 | 11.9 | 8.5 |
| 1982 | 11.8 | 8.2 | 8.7 | 9.9 |
| 1983 | 9.6 | 8.4 | 4.5 | 10.7 |
| 1984 | 7.4 | 9.9 | 5.0 | 11.1 |
| 1985 | 5.8 | 10.2 | 6.0 | 11.3 |
| 1986 | 2.7 | 10.4 | 3.4 | 11.4 |
| 1987 | 3.1 | 10.5 | 4.2 | 10.0 |
| 1988 | 2.6 | 9.9 | 4.9 | 8.0 |
| 1989 | 3.6 | 9.4 | 8.0 | 5.8 |
| 1990 | 3.6 | 9.0 | 9.4 | 6.2 |

[a] Year-to-year percentage change in consumer prices.

Sources: OECD, *Historical Statistics*, 1960–79 and 1969–88; and OECD, *Main Economic Indicators*.

8. What is monetarism?

9. What is meant by the term "neutrality of money"?

10. Describe, in flowchart form, the four transmission mechanisms described in this chapter.

11. What is the difference between adaptive and rational expectations?

12. Is there a connection between the "shape" of the Phillips curve over time and economists' ideas about the tradeoffs between inflation and unemployment?

13. Describe the time-inconsistency problem.

14. What is a performance contract for a central banker meant to accomplish? Why is such a thing perhaps impractical?

15. What is the base drift problem and why did it lead most central banks to abandon monetary targeting?

16. What are the two theories of money?

17. What is $P^*$ and why might it be a useful inflation forecasting tool?

18. What is Granger causality and why is it an important concept in the study of the role of monetary policy?

## REFERENCES

Bain, A. *The Economics of the Financial System.* Oxford: Martin Robertson, 1981.

Barro, R.J., and D.B. Gordon. "A Positive Theory of Monetary Policy in a Natural Rate Model." *Journal of Political Economy* 91 (August 1983): 589–610.

———. "Rules, Discretion and Reputation in a Model of Monetary Policy." *Journal of Monetary Economics* 12 (January 1983): 101–22.

Batten, D.S., and D.L. Thornton. "The Monetary-Fiscal Policy Debate and the Andersen-Jordon Equation." *Review of the Federal Reserve Bank of St. Louis* 68 (October 1986): 9–17.

Bean, C., and J. Symons. "Ten Years of Mrs. T." In *NBER Macroeconomics Annual 1989*, edited by O.J. Blanchard and S. Fischer, 13–72. Cambridge, Mass.: The MIT Press, 1989.

Berndt, E. *The Practice of Econometrics: Classic and Contemporary.* Reading, Mass.: Addison-Wesley, 1991.

Blanchard, O. "Why Does Money Affect Output? A Survey." In *Handbook of Monetary Economics*, Volume II, edited by B.M. Friedman and F. Hahn, Amsterdam: North-Holland, 1990.

Bordo, M.D., E.V. Choudhri, and A.J. Schwartz. "Money Stock Targeting, Base Drift, and Price-Level Predictability: Lessons from the U.K. Experience." *Journal of Monetary Economics* 25 (April 1990): 253–72.

Cagan, P. "The Monetary Dynamics of Hyperinflation." In *Studies in the Quantity Theory of Money*, edited by M. Friedman, 25–117. Chicago: University of Chicago Press, 1956.

Christiano, L., and L. Ljungqvist. "Money Does Granger-Cause Output in the Bivariate Money-Output Relation." *Journal of Monetary Economics* 22 (October 1988): 217–35.

Clarke, W.M. *How the City of London Works.* London: Waterloo Publishers, 1988.

Cuthbertson, K. *The Supply and Demand for Money.* Oxford: Basil Blackwell, 1988.

Desai, M. *Testing Monetarism.* London: Frances Pinter, 1981.

Engle, R.F., D.F. Hendry, and J.F. Richard. "Exogeneity." *Econometrica* 51 (March 1983): 277–304.

Fairbanks, D., and J. Ireland. *Savings and Co-operative Banking.* London: Financial Times Business Publishing Ltd., 1981.

Frankel, A.G., and J.D. Montgomery. "Financial Structure: An International Perspective." Brookings Papers on Economic Activity 1 (1991): 257–310.

Fraser, R. *The World Financial System.* Harlow, Essex: Longman, 1987.

Friedman, M. "Inflation and Unemployment Nobel Lecture." *Journal of Political Economy* 85 (June 1977): 451–72.

———. "Quantity Theory of Money." In *The New Palgrave: Money*, edited by J. Eatwell, M. Milgate, and P. Newman. New York: W.W. Norton, 1989.

Granger, C.W.J. "Investigating Causal Relations by Econometric Models and Cross-Spectral Methods." *Econometrica* 37 (3, 1969): 424–38.

Granger, C.W.J., and M. Hatanaka. *Spectral Analysis of Economic Time Series.* Princeton: Princeton University Press, 1963.

Gujarati, D. *Basic Econometrics*, 2d ed. New York: McGraw-Hill, 1988.

Hall, R.E., J.B. Taylor, and J. Rudin. *Macroeconomics: The Canadian Economy.* New York: W.W. Norton, 1990, chapter 16.

Kydland, F.E., and E.C. Prescott. "Rule Rather than Discretion. The Inconsistency of Optimal Flows." *Journal of Political Economy* 85 (June 1977): 473–91.

Laidler, D. *Monetarist Perspectives.* Cambridge, Mass.: Harvard University Press, 1982.

———. "The Quantity Theory is Always and Everywhere Controversial—Why?" Centre for International Economic Studies, University of Adelaide, Australia, seminar paper 89-03 (July 1989).

Lucas, R.E., Jr. "Econometric Policy Evaluations: A Critique." In Carnegie-Rochester Conference Series on Public Policy 1, edited by K. Brunner and A. Meltzer, 19–76. Amsterdam; North-Holland, 1976.

Mayer, T., ed. *The Structure of Monetarism.* New York: Norton, 1978.

Meltzer, A.H. *Keynes's Monetary Theory: A Different Interpretation.* Cambridge: Cambridge University Press, 1988.

Muth, J. "Rational Expectations and the Theory of Price Movements." *Econometrica* 29 (3, 1961): 315–35.

OECD. *Historical Statistics*, various issues.

———. *Main Economic Indicators.* (various issues).

Partington, I. *Applied Economics in Banking and Finance.* Oxford: Oxford University Press, 1989.

Raj, B., and P.L. Siklos. "The Role of Fiscal Policy in the St. Louis Model: An Evaluation and Some New Evidence." *Journal of Applied Econometrics* 1 (July 1986): 287–94.

Sargent, T.J. *Rational Expectations and Inflation.* New York: Harper & Row, 1986.

Sargent, T.J., and N. Wallace. "The Real Bills Doctrine Versus the Quantity Theory: A Reconsideration." *Journal of Political Economy* 90 (December 1982): 1212–36.

———. "Some Unpleasant Monetarist Arithmetic." Federal Reserve Bank of Minneapolis, *Quarterly Review* (Fall 1981): 1–17.

Sims, G. "Money, Income, and Causality." *American Economic Review* 62 (1972): 540–52.

Stock, J., and M. Watson. "Interpreting the Evidence on Money-Income Causality." *Journal of Econometrics* 40 (1989): 161–81.

# GLOSSARY

**Adaptive Expectations Hypothesis:** the theory that individuals adjust their forecast of inflation gradually, partly from learning from the mistakes (or forecast errors) of the past. (p. 612)

**Adverse Selection:** decision making that results from the incentive for some people to engage in a transaction that is undesirable to everyone else. This problem exists because of asymmetric information. See also **moral hazard**. (p. 46)

**Allfinanz:** the name used to describe the universal banking model of the German financial system. (p. 521)

**Annuity:** an instrument that converts a lump sum amount into annual instalments over a specified period. (p. 440)

**Appreciation:** the increase in the value of one currency in terms of another. The opposite of **depreciation**. (p. 147)

**Arbitrage Pricing Theory:** A model which suggests that there are several factors which can explain the links between market return and the return on a particular asset or portfolio of assets. See also **capital-asset pricing model**. (p. 296)

**Asymmetric Information:** when one party to a transaction has relatively more information than another. (p. 46)

**Balance of Payments (BOP):** a record of international transactions between countries. (p. 472)

**Balance Sheet:** an accounting format that describes the activities of a firm in financial terms. (p. 172)

**Bank Act:** the federal piece of legislation that now regulates most deposit-taking and other financial institutions in Canada. The Act is revised approximately every 10 years. (p. 394)

**Bank for International Settlements (BIS):** acts as a central bank for central banks, originally created to co-ordinate German war reparations payments after World War I. The BIS is based in Basel, Switzerland. (p. 532)

**Bank of Canada:** the central bank of Canada. Is responsible for the conduct of monetary policy and acts as a banker for the federal government. (p. 27)

**Bank of Canada Advances:** loans made by the Bank of Canada to members of the Canadian Payments Association. (p. 70)

**Bank of England:** the central bank of the United Kingdom. (p. 502)

**Bank of Japan:** the central bank of Japan. (p. 508)

**Bank Rate:** the rate of interest charged by the Bank of Canada on loans made to members of the Canadian Payments Association. Now tied to the overnight rate. (p. 65)

**Banker's Acceptance:** a document that serves as a promise to pay where the bank has undertaken to guarantee payment when the debt is due. (p. 73)

**Barter:** an exchange of commodities without money. Transactions of this kind are inconvenient because of the problem of the "double coincidence of wants." (p. 19)

**Base Control:** the means by which a central bank controls movements in the monetary base. (p. 566)

**Base Drift:** the (upward) revision of the base from which monetary growth targets are adjusted. (p. 622)

**Basis:** the futures price less spot price. (p. 310)

**Basis Point:** one-hundredth of one percentage point. (p. 66)

**Big Bang:** the term used to describe the October 1987 changes in the United Kingdom that deregulated the securities market. This allowed, for example, banks to acquire companies that dealt in stocks. (p. 504)

**Bimetallism:** a monetary system based on the value of two precious metals, usually gold and silver. (p. 25)

**Bond:** a debt instrument that promises to pay interest on a regular basis and principal at maturity. (p. 78)

**Bond Rating:** an evaluation by some agency of the risk of default by the issuer of a particular bond. (p. 276)

**Bretton Woods System:** the adjustable pegged exchange rate system negotiated at the end of World War II at Bretton Woods, New Hampshire. Ended in the early 1970s. (p. 534)

**Brokers:** individuals who bring together a buyer and a seller and assist in the completion of a financial transaction between them. (p. 46)

**Budget Constraint:** the limits, usually dictated by income, within which consumers must decide how to allocate their consumption. (p. 185)

**Building Societies:** UK financial institutions that provide mortgages. These are non-profit bodies, somewhat like the credit unions and caisses populaires in Canada. (p. 502)

**Bundesbank:** the German central bank. (p. 525)

**Caisses Populaires:** co-operative non-profit deposit-taking institutions that offer a large variety of services, including non-financial services to individuals at the local or parish level. Caisses populaires operate in Quebec only. See also **credit unions** (p. 427)

**Call Option:** the right, but not the obligation to buy an asset at a particular price during a stipulated period. (p. 318)

**Canada Deposit Insurance Corporation (CDIC):** the agency in Canada that is responsible for the operation and supervision of the deposit insurance system. (p. 451)

**Canadian Dealing Network:** a system that provides electronic quotations of over-the-counter stocks in Canada. Previously referred to as Canadian Over-the-Counter Automated Trading System (COATS). (p. 250)

**Canadian Payments Association:** the association, responsible for cheque-clearing for all financial institutions in Canada. Membership is mandatory for all chartered banks and the Bank of Canada, but many near-banks are also members. (p. 30)

**Capital Account:** the part of the balance of payments that records net changes in domestic versus foreign holdings of financial assets. (p. 472)

**Capital-Asset Pricing Model:** A simple relationship which links the return on a particular stock with the return on a portfolio made up of the entire market or some proxy. (p. 295)

**Capital-Asset Ratio:** some measure of a firm's capital, such as shareholders' equity, divided by the assets of a firm. (p. 210)

**Capital Gain/Loss Rate of Return:** the profit or loss, in percent, from a change in the price of a financial asset. (p. 101)

**Capital Gain or Loss:** the gain or loss incurred by an investor who sells a financial instrument at a price other than the purchase price. If the selling price is higher (lower) than the purchase price the investor is said to make a capital gain (loss). (p. 100)

**Capital Market:** the market for financial instruments that mature in more than one year. (p. 52)

**Capital Mobility:** the ability to shift funds between countries easily. If there are no impediments at all and costs are minimal, capital is used to be perfectly mobile. (p. 347)

**Central Bank:** the financial institution responsible for the conduct of a country's monetary policy. Often, a central bank also acts as the banker for the central government. (p. 27)

**Central Bank Autonomy or Independence:** the degree to which the central bank of a country is able to work toward its objectives without intervention from politicians. (p. 596)

**Certificate of Deposit (CD):** a type of bank deposit that usually promises a fixed return on a large sum of money for a specified maturity. Penalties may be imposed if the funds are withdrawn before maturity. (p. 76)

**Chartered Bank:** a bank that obtains a charter from the federal government and is federally regulated under the Bank Act. (p. 389)

**City Banks:** commercial banks with nationwide branching that are located in large urban areas in Japan. (p. 512)

**Classical Economics:** the body of economic theory that believes that a model of a competitive economy is appropriate and that market forces can be relied upon to produce full employment. (p. 610)

**Co-Insurance:** a form of insurance where the insured is responsible for some of the losses covered by the insurance. (p. 458)

**Consumption Function:** a functional relationship that describes the economic variables, such as income and the interest rate, that determine consumption spending over time. (p. 194)

**Consumption Possibilities:** the opportunities available to consumers, with a given income, to consume goods and services today versus in the future. (p. 185)

**Contractionary Monetary Policy:** monetary policy aimed at reducing the level or growth rate of the money supply (the opposite of an **expansionary** monetary policy). (p. 135)

**Convertible Currencies:** currencies that can be freely exchanged against one another. (p. 533)

**Corporate Paper:** a form of corporate debt that typically matures in 90 days but can mature from 30 to 365 days. (p. 77)

**Correlation Statistic:** a statistical measure of the strength of the linear relationship between two or more variables. (p. 281)

**Corset:** a percentage of wholesale deposits held by banks that was required to be deposited at the Bank of England to stem credit growth. It was abandoned permanently in June 1980. It is also known as the supplementary special deposit. (p. 507)

**Cost-of-Carry:** the costs associated with carrying an asset, such as financing, storage, and insurance costs. (p. 314)

**Country Risk:** the risk that a national government will default on its debt. (p. 487)

**Coupon Rate:** the stipulated return, typically on a bond, expressed as a percentage of the principal. (p. 97)

**Covariance:** a statistical measure of the relationship between two or more returns across time or across states of the world. (p. 281)

**Covered Interest Arbitrage:** the use of a forward foreign exchange contract to hedge against foreign exchange risk as it affects the yield on foreign assets. (p. 350)

**Coyne Affair:** the controversy of the late 1950s that ended with the resignation of James Coyne, governor of the Bank of Canada. Originated with a monetary policy dispute between the federal government and the Bank of Canada. (p. 575)

**Credit Unions:** co-operative non-profit deposit-taking institutions that offer a variety of services, including non-financial services, to individuals at a local level. Credit unions operate in all provinces except Quebec. See also **caisses populaires**. (p. 426)

**Cross-Rate:** the exchange rate between two currencies calculated via a third currency. (p. 147)

**Current Account:** the part of the balance of payments that records the net change in exports and imports of goods and services. (p. 472)

**Current Yield:** the yield on a financial asset if it is sold in the current period. (p. 98)

**Debt:** an obligation to repay principal and interest. (p. 486)

**Debt–Equity Swap:** the exchange of a debt issued via the bond market for an issue of shares. (p. 486)

**Debt Forgiveness:** a program to eliminate a debt liability as a write-off to the lender. (p. 486)

**Debt Monetization:** the issue of money by the central bank to support government spending. (p. 566)

**Debt-Service Ratio:** the measure of a nation's ability to repay a debt. Calculated as interest and principal over some period as a percentage of exports. (p. 486)

**Deductible:** a fixed amount that is deducted from a loss claim against insurance. (p. 458)

**Default Risk:** the likelihood that a debtor will cease paying interest and/or principal. (p. 276)

**Demand Deposit:** a deposit (at a chartered bank) available on demand without notice. (p. 29)

**Demand for Money:** the desire to hold some form of money. Usually represented as a **function** of income and a proxy for the opportunity cost of holding money. (p. 131)

**Deposit Insurance:** a form of insurance against losses from the failure of a financial institution. (p. 451)

**Deposit Multiplier:** the multiple by which deposits in the banking system can increase or decrease given an increase or decrease in the banking system's cash reserves. (p. 367)

**Deposit-Taking Institutions:** institutions that accept deposits and make loans. (p. 47)

**Depreciation:** the decrease in the value of one currency in terms of another. The opposite of **appreciation**. (p. 147)

**Deregulation:** the process by which legislation imposes fewer restrictions on the activities of an institution or industry. (p. 11)

**Derivative Products:** financial instruments derived from financial products bought and sold in the spot market. They include, for example, options and futures. (p. 82)

**Deutsche Terminbörse:** the futures and options exchange that opened in 1991 in Germany, bringing it up to international norms. (p. 523)

**Devaluation:** an arbitrary decrease in the value of a currency that had previously been fixed in value. The opposite of a revaluation. (p. 148)

**Diminishing Marginal Returns:** a description for the principle that increases in an input, other inputs held fixed, produce successively smaller increases in output. (p. 215)

**Discounted Bond:** a financial instrument that is sold at a price below its face value. (p. 98)

**Diversification:** the inclusion of more than one asset in a portfolio in order to reduce portfolio risk. (p. 285)

**Drawdown and Redeposit Technique:** the technique of shifting deposits between Government of Canada accounts and those of the members of the Canadian Payments Association. (p. 564)

**Dual Banking System:** a financial system where there are two classes of banks, each supervised and regulated by different levels of government or agencies. (p. 482)

**Duration Analysis:** Same as GAP analysis, but assets and liabilities are arranged according to when they mature. (p. 382)

**Duration Gap:** same as gap analysis except that calculations are adjusted for the fact that assets and liabilities mature at different times. (p. 382)

**Ecu (European Currency Unit):** a weighted average of the currencies of the members of the Exchange Rate Mechanism, which links several European currencies. The Ecu is a possible candidate for the planned single European currency. (p. 545)

**Efficient Frontier:** those portfolios that provide the highest yield for any given level of risk. (p. 283)

**Efficient Markets Hypothesis:** the theory that individuals make informed forecasts of the future based on all available information. (p. 248)

**Equilibrium Interest Rate:** the market-clearing interest rate. (p. 116)

**Equity Premium Puzzle:** Describes the empirical feature whereby stocks tend to outperform other financial assets in rate of return. (p. 266)

**Estate, Trust, and Agency (ETA) Business:** the primary function, also known as a fiduciary function, of trust companies. This function involves the management of funds left in trust by an estate or individuals where the trust company acts as an agent. (p. 422)

**EURO:** the name for the eventual European currency. (p. 548)

**Eurocurrency:** the market for deposits, loans, or bonds deposited or traded in a currency other than the one in which the instrument is bought or sold. (p. 77)

**European Bank for Reconstruction and Development:** the financial institution created by the United States and the European countries to facilitate lending and other financial needs of the former centrally planned economies. (p. 543)

**European Monetary Institute:** the precursor of the proposed European Central Bank is responsible for planning eventual monetary union in Europe. (p. 551)

**European Monetary System (EMS):** the target zone exchange rate system that fixes exchange rates within a defined bank. Member countries agree to ensure, via central bank intervention, that the EMS target zone will be maintained. (p. 543)

**European Monetary Union (EMU):** the plan, as contained in the Maastricht Treaty, to replace the existing currencies of the members of the European Community with a single currency. (p. 545)

**Excess Reserves:** reserves held by banks over and above required reserves. These required reserves were phased out in Canada by 1994. (p. 363)

**Exchange Fund Account (EFA):** foreign exchange funds of the Canadian government. The EFA is managed by the Bank of Canada. (p. 566)

**Exchange Rate:** the price of one currency in terms of another. (p. 146)

**Exercise (Strike) Price:** the price at which options are set. (p. 318)

**Expansionary Monetary Policy:** a policy aimed at increasing the level or growth in the money supply. (p. 135)

**Expectations Hypothesis:** the theory that states that future interest rates can be forecasted by looking at the term structure because the return on a long-term bond is essentially the average return on short-term bonds over the same period. (p. 338)

**Expectations of Inflation:** a forecast of future inflation. The forecast can be extrapolated from past inflation alone, among many alternatives of generating such forecasts. (p. 8)

**Expected Return:** the weighted average of returns anticipated over time, where the weights are given by the probabilities of various states of the world. (p. 278)

**Externality:** a phenomenon whereby individual action produces costs (or benefits) to other individuals over and above private costs or benefits. (p. 47)

**Federal Reserve (the Fed):** the US central bank. (p. 498)

**Final Targets:** generally, a measure of aggregate economic performance such as inflation or GDP growth. (p. 588)

**Financial Assets:** that part of the national balance sheet that shows bank deposits, loans to various enterprises, and the public debt. (p. 173)

**Financial Flow Accounts:** reports how funds are used nationally in borrowing and lending activities. (p. 171)

**Financial Intermediary:** an institution that channels funds between borrowers and lenders. (p. 47)

**Financial Leasing Corporations:** a company that specializes in contracts to lease an asset over the anticipated term or life of the asset. (p. 434)

**Fiscal Policy:** the policy by which a government resorts to expenditures or taxes to influence the economy as a whole. (p. 597)

**Fisher Equation:** formula which states that nominal interest rate is the sum of the real interest rate plus an expected inflation rate component. (p. 104)

**Fixed Exchange Rate System:** an exchange rate system that pegs an exchange rate at a particular value. (p. 149)

**Flexible Exchange Rate System:** an exchange rate system that allows the marketplace to determine the exchange rate independently. Also called a **floating system**. (p. 149)

**Flow Measures:** measures flow of funds activity over time. (p. 174)

**Flow of Funds:** changes in asset and liability holdings during a given period. (p. 175)

**Foreign Exchange Risk:** the risk that the exchange rate between one currency and another may fluctuate in a direction or to a degree unanticipated by investors dealing in assets denominated in a foreign currency. (p. 276)

**Foreign Exchange Swap:** similar to an ordinary swap, except it involves the exchange of foreign currencies. See **swaps**. (p. 567)

**Forward Contract:** a contract in which a seller undertakes to provide a buyer with an amount of an asset at some future date at a price agreed to in advance. (p. 567)

**Forward Exchange Rate:** the exchange rate on a contract to deliver foreign exchange at some future date at a price negotiated today. (p. 347)

**Four Pillars:** the term used to describe the specialized functions of the four different sectors of the Canadian financial system: chartered banks, trusts, insurance companies, and investment dealers. With the passage of the 1992 Bank Act, these divisions are no longer formally in place. (p. 50)

**Free Banking:** the doctrine that permits banks to issue their own currency and that there be a minimum of government regulation in the banking industry. (p. 390)

**Fundamentalist Approach:** the position that states that the price of a stock is determined by fundamentals of a company's performance, such as the flow of anticipated dividends. (p. 257)

**Futures Contract:** a contract to buy and sell an asset at a specified future date. (p. 304)

**Gap Analysis:** the subdividing of a bank's assets and liabilities into components that are rate sensitive and those that are not. The gap is the difference between the rate-sensitive assets and liabilities. (p. 381)

**Gensaki Market:** the Japanese financial market in which are traded repurchase agreements, negotiable certificates of deposit, money market certificates, and bankers' acceptances. (p. 515)

**Gilt-Edged Securities (Gilts):** a fixed-interest government security issued in the United Kingdom and traded on the London Stock Exchange. Called gilt-edged because they are considered to be default-risk free. (p. 505)

**Ginko:** "bank" in Japanese. (p. 509)

**Giro System:** a service permitting the direct transfer of funds among current account holders. (p. 503)

**Girozentralen:** the German name given to the giro system of funds transfers between chequing accounts. (p. 522)

**Glass–Stegall Act:** a piece of US legislation, passed in 1933, that prevented commercial banks from engaging in underwriting and dealing in securities. (p. 496)

**Globalization:** an expression for the growing integration of financial markets worldwide. (p. 12)

**Gold Standard:** a monetary system wherein the exchange rate is fixed to the price of gold. (p. 24)

**Granger Causality:** a statistical definition of causality which says that *X* causes *Y* only if the past history of *X* predicts *Y* but the past history of *Y* does not predict *X*. (p. 632)

**Gresham's Law:** the dictum that bad money drives out good. If two currencies exist in an economy, the one that is least valuable will tend to circulate while the more valuable currency will be hoarded. (p. 26)

**Hedge Ratio:** the number of futures contracts bought or sold per unit of the asset in the spot market. (p. 315)

**Hedging:** the process of using one transaction to offset the effect of another transaction with the objective of reducing or eliminating risk entirely. (p. 304)

**Holding Period Yield:** the return on a financial instrument during the period it is held, which is less than the period to maturity. (p. 100)

**Hyperinflation:** inflation where prices rise faster than 50% per month. (p. 236)

**Income Statement:** statement that shows the difference between generated revenue and expenses incurred during a given period of time for an economic sector. (p. 172)

**Income Risk:** the risk associated with fluctuations in income over time. (p. 276)

**Inflation:** the rate of change in an aggregate price index such as the consumer price index (CPI). (p. 7)

**Inflation Risk:** the risk stemming from the effect of inflation on the real and nominal return on assets. (p. 277)

**Inside Money:** Money created inside the banking system via the process of intermediation or asset transformation. (p. 36)

**Inflation Targets:** Several countries have redefined the objectives that their central banks have to meet in terms of a target for inflation. Usually such targets are defined as ranges within which the rate of change in the CPI is expected to fluctuate (p. 578)

**Insurance:** a contract that protects individuals against unforeseen events that can have negative financial (or physical) consequences. (p. 438)

**Interbank Deposits:** bank funds deposited by one bank in another with which the depositing bank usually does business. (p. 77)

**Interest Rate:** the price of renting money. (p. 90)

**Interest Rate Control:** the intermediate target of a central bank policy to maintain interest rate stability. See also **monetary control**. (p. 591)

**Interest Rate Parity:** the condition that the differential between domestic and foreign interest rates reflects the forward premium or discount between currencies. (p. 350)

**Inter-listing of Stocks:** stocks for a company listed on several stock exchanges at once. (p. 265)

**Intermediary:** the act of transforming assets and liabilities which results in the creation of new assets and liabilities. (p. 43)

**Intermediate Target:** an economic variable, which is only indirectly under the control of a policymaker, that the policymaker analyses to determine whether a particular policy is having the anticipated effects on the economy as a whole. (p. 588)

**Intermediation:** the function of transforming assets into other assets. This is the principal activity of most financial institutions. (p. 44)

**International Bank for Reconstruction and Development (IBRD or World Bank):** the financial institution created after World War II to facilitate lending and other financial needs of developing countries. (p. 542)

**International Financial Centres:** typically large cities, such as London or New York, that, because of location or government subsidies, offer a variety of specialized financial services in close proximity to each other. (p. 470)

**International Monetary Fund (IMF):** an international organization created after World War II to manage the international financial system. (p. 539)

**Investment Bank:** an intermediary that purchases new financial instruments and sells them in smaller amounts to investors. Also advises clients on mergers and acquisitions. Also known as a merchant bank. (p. 496)

**Investment Company:** an intermediary that specializes in placing funds for its clients. (p. 442)

**Investment Dealer:** a specialist who buys, sells, and advises in the market for securities. (p. 436)

**Keynesianism:** the theories associated with the work of John Maynard Keynes. This includes the belief that government action may be necessary when an economy is at less than full employment conditions. (p. 610)

**Kreditbanken:** German credit bank. (p. 519)

**Large Value Transfer System (LVTS):** a new system for influencing liquidity in the financial system introduced by the Bank of Canada in 1996 and used to affect the overnight interest rate which it targets. (p. 69)

**Law of One Price:** a law stating that, under certain assumptions, the domestic and foreign price of a tradeable good should be equal. (p. 149)

**Lender of Last Resort:** usually, a central bank that can advance credit to a failing financial institution when no other sources of funds are available. (p. 70)

**Letter of Credit:** a draft authorizing funds when certain conditions have been met. (p. 74)

**Leverage:** the activity of investing with borrowed funds. (p. 28)

**Leveraged Ratio:** a measure of the debts of a firm divided by shareholders' equity. (p. 208)

**Lifecycle Hypothesis:** a theory stating that consumption spending is a function of an individual's age. Thus, individuals accumulate wealth during their working years and consume their wealth following retirement, thus maintaining relatively stable consumption spending. (p. 198)

**Liquidity:** the availability of funds to meet claims or the ease with which an asset can be sold. (p. 21)

**Liquidity Preference:** the desire to hold cash in preference to an alternative financial asset, such as a bond. (p. 127)

**Liquidity Premium:** the extra yield that must be paid to entice investors to hold long-term instead of short-term investments. (p. 345)

**Liquidity Risk:** the risk associated with a shortfall in the availability of funds. (p. 276)

**Loanable Funds:** funds that are available to be borrowed for investment. (p. 115)

**Lombard Credit:** a generic term to describe loans by the Bundesbank to commercial banks, secured against a financial instrument. The rate on such loans is the Lombard rate. (p. 524)

**London Interbank Offer Rate (LIBOR):** the rate of interest charged on bank funds in the London market to the "best" banks for a specified but short period of time. (p. 479)

**Long Position:** the purchase of an asset that is to be held until it matures or must be sold. (p. 310)

**M1:** currency outside banks plus chartered banks' demand deposits. (p. 30)

**M2:** M1 plus non-personal notice deposits and personal savings deposits at chartered banks. (p. 31)

**M2+:** M2 plus notice and term deposits at near-banks, generally, trust and mortgage loan companies. (p. 32)

**M3:** M2 plus non-personal fixed-term deposits at chartered banks plus foreign currency deposits of residents booked in Canada. (p. 32)

**Managed ("Dirty") Float System:** a system of flexible exchange rates where the central bank intervenes from time to time to influence exchange rates. (p. 149)

**Margin:** usually, a deposit placed as security against the purchase of an asset or used to ensure that a particular contract is fulfilled. (p. 304)

**Marginal Propensity to Consume (MPC):** a measure of the increase in consumption spending due to an increase in disposable income. (p. 194)

**Market Concentration:** the degree to which only a few firms account for most of the sales or output in a market. The more concentration the less competitive a market is said to be. (p. 405)

**Market Risk:** the likelihood of changes in the future price of an asset. (p. 276)

**Market Segmentation:** the theory that markets for long-term and short-term assets are distinct. Only the demand of and supply for funds in these markets determines relative interest rates between short-term and long-term assets. (p. 345)

**Market-to-Market:** the settlement of an account done on a daily basis to reflect price changes at the close of trading each day. (p. 310)

**Medium of Account:** something that circulates and that provides a standardized means of evaluating the relative price of goods and services. (p. 21)

**Medium of Exchange:** something that is generally acceptable in exchange for goods and services. (p. 21)

**Merchant Bank:** See **investment bank**. (p. 435)

**Minimum Lending Rate:** the interest rate at which the Bank of England lends to the money market. (p. 507)

**Modigliani–Miller Theorem:** the theory stating that, under specific conditions, a firm will be indifferent between borrowing via bonds versus equity. (p. 220)

**Monetarism:** the theory that inflation can largely be explained by monetary policy. Monetarism is also critical of an activist monetary policy. (p. 610)

**Monetary Control:** the intermediate target of a central bank policy to maintain interest rate stability. See also **interest rate control**. (p. 591)

**Monetary Policy:** the policy enacted by a government or a central bank that affects the money supply, interest rates, and exchange rate. (p. 135)

**Monetary Targeting:** the attempt by central banks to control the growth of selected monetary aggregates. (p. 577)

**Monetization:** situation where the use of cash and cheques has become increasingly common. (p. 243)

**Money:** a commodity or device of some kind used for the purposes of completing transactions in goods and services; a medium of exchange. (p. 4)

**Money Illusion:** the belief that nominal values are the same as real values. The individual does not understand that a price level change implies a change in the purchasing power of a given stock of money. (p. 230)

**Money Market:** the market for financial assets that mature in one year or less. (p. 52)

**Money Multiplier:** the multiple by which the money supply changes in response to a change in the monetary base. (p. 573)

**Money Supply (Money Stock):** some measure of aggregate liquidity in the economy. Includes definitions such as M1 or M2. (p. 28)

**Moral Hazard:** the chance that an individual may have an incentive to act in such a way as to put that individual at greater risk. The individual perceives to be beneficial a course of action that is deemed to be undesirable by another. See also **adverse selection**. (p. 458)

**Moral Suasion:** a technique used by a central bank to persuade financial institutions to change their behaviour voluntarily. (p. 571)

**Mortgage Loan Companies (MLCs):** financial institutions that specialize in mortgage loans. (p. 422)

**Mutual Fund:** a pool of funds from a large number of individuals, invested in a variety of assets, thereby permitting economies of scale, risk sharing, and risk reduction in investments. (p. 442)

**National Accounts, System of:** description of economic activity and its components at an economy-wide level. (p. 171)

**National Balance Sheet Accounts:** set of balance sheets prepared for each group in the economy and for the economy as a whole. (p. 171)

**National Treatment:** the fact that an organization in another country is subject to that country's laws. A branch of a Canadian bank in a foreign country is subject to that country's banking rules and regulations. (p. 481)

**Natural Rate of Unemployment:** the rate of unemployment that arises because of normal frictions in the labour market and not because of monetary policy. Alternatively, it can refer to the unemployment rate when inflation is zero. Also known as the **non-accelerating inflation rate of unemployment (NAIRU).** (p. 617)

**Negotiable Order of Withdrawal (NOW):** a US financial instrument created to circumvent a ceiling on interest rates (Regulation Q). By calling a cheque a negotiable order of withdrawal, the account from which the funds are withdrawn is not legally called a chequing account, and so such an account can pay market interest rates. (p. 497)

**Net Worth (Net Wealth):** total assets less total liabilities. (p. 172, p. 174)

**Neutrality of Money:** the theory that a change in the money supply produces a proportional change in prices, leaving the real side of the economy unaffected. (p. 611)

**Nominal Income:** income measured in current dollars. (p. 131)

**Nominal Interest Rate:** the total return on a financial asset including compensation for inflation. (p. 103)

**Non-Accelerating Inflation Rate of Unemployment (NAIRU):** See **natural rate of unemployment.** (p. 618)

**Non-Financial Assets:** physical holdings of a sector, such as land or machinery. (p. 173)

**Offset Transaction:** a transaction in which the purchase of one asset is offset by the sale of another asset; two opposite positions are taken in the spot and futures markets. (p. 305)

**Offshore Banking Centres:** financial centres that are also tax havens, and that perhaps offer secrecy in financial dealings. (p. 473)

**Open Market Operations:** the purchase or sale of government bonds in the open market. (p. 68)

**Operating Instruments:** the policy tools used by a central bank, for example, to achieve specific monetary policy targets. (p. 588)

**Opportunity Cost:** the cost of something measured as the value of the next best available alternative; the cost of forgone actions. (p. 130)

**Optimal Cash Management Approach:** the attempt by an individual to minimize the costs of holding a given stock of cash. (p. 231)

**Outside Money:** Money created outside the banking system such as by the central bank. (p. 36)

**Overnight Rate:** The rate of interest charged on loans made overnight. Large corporations use the overnight market to earn interest on funds which would otherwise be idle. The Bank of Canada sets an overnight rate to conduct monetary policy. (p. 66)

**Over-the-Counter (OTC) Trading:** the trading of stocks outside stock exchanges. (p. 249)

**Par Value:** the value of a financial instrument, typically a bond, that is equivalent to its maturity value. (p. 64)

**Pension Fund:** a device to accumulate assets for retirement to which employees and/or employers can contribute; usually offers tax-shelter benefits. (p. 443)

**Permanent Income Hypothesis:** the theory that permanent income (that is, annual income based on expected lifetime earnings) determines actual consumption spending. Since permanent income is stable, actual consumption spending is also stable. (p. 198)

**Peso Problem:** Named after the Mexican peso. Describes a phenomenon in which the economic fundamentals predict a devaluation which almost never actually takes place. (p. 153)

**Phillips Curve:** a function that relates the tradeoff between inflation in consumer prices or wages, and the rate of unemployment or output. (p. 611)

**Political Business Cycle:** a cycle in which economic activity is linked to election dates as politicians resort to policies to ensure their re-election. (p. 596)

**Portfolio:** a collection of financial assets. (p. 44)

**Precautionary Motive:** the demand for money that results from the desire to prepare for unforeseen expenditures. (p. 130)

**Preferred Habitat:** the particular term to maturity for which an investor has a distinct preference. (p. 346)

**Present Value:** the current value of a stream of future payments. (p. 91)

**Price Index:** an aggregate measure of current prices in relation to prices in a selected base year. (p. 6)

**Price Stability:** measured in terms of the consumer price index (CPI). There is no universally agreed-upon definition of what constitutes price stability but it is generally believed to be a rate of inflation in the CPI of between 0 and 3%. (p. 589)

**Primary Market:** the market for newly issued financial instruments. (p. 51)

**Private Banks:** institutions that have a long history in Germany; today these banks specialize in funding industrial investment projects. They resemble Canadian merchant banks. (p. 522)

**Production Possibilities:** the opportunities available to a firm, with a given set of labour and capital, to produce today versus in the future. (p. 215)

**Purchasing Power:** the ability, usually of one unit of currency, to buy goods and services. Can be measured as $1/P$ where $P$ is the price level measured, say, by the consumer price index. (p. 158)

**Purchasing Power Parity (PPP):** the situation that exists when the exchange rate between two currencies is such that the domestic purchasing power of those currencies is equivalent. Two forms exist: absolute (in terms of price levels) and relative (in terms of inflation rates). (p. 158)

**Put Option:** the right, but not the obligation, to sell an asset at a particular price during a stipulated period. (p. 318)

**Quantity Theory:** the theory that there is a direct relationship between the quantity of money in circulation and the price level: an increase in the quantity of money leads to a proportional increase in the price level. This relationship is summarized in the formula $MV = Py$, where $M$ = stock of money, $V$ = velocity of circulation, $P$ = price index, $y$ = measure of aggregate income. (p. 237)

**Random Walk:** in its simplest version, the notion that the best forecast of next period's value for an economic variable, such as stock prices, is its current value. (p. 253)

**Rational Expectations Hypothesis:** the theory that market participants use economic information rationally. Consequently, unexploited profitable opportunities do not occur in a persistent fashion. (p. 614)

**Real Balance:** a measure of the money stock divided by a price index; the purchasing power of a stock of money. (p. 228)

**Real Bills Doctrine:** the view that any increase in the money supply should be fully backed (by tax revenues or bonds), otherwise money supply increases will be inflationary. (p. 390)

**Real Estate Investment Trusts (REITs):** mortgage finance companies under the direction of an "advisor" or trust corporation. (p. 424)

**Real Exchange Rate:** the exchange rate adjusted for changes in relative price levels in different countries. (p. 162)

**Real Income:** income measured in constant dollars. This measure incorporates the effect of a loss of purchasing power due to inflation. (p. 131)

**Realignment:** the act of changing the value of a fixed exchange rate (also see **central parity**). (p. 547)

**Real Interest Rate:** the return or yield on a financial asset excluding compensation for inflation. (p. 103)

**Real Return Bond:** A Canadian government bond which specifies a return adjusted for inflation. Is used as a gauge for future inflation developments. (p. 108)

**Registered Retirement Income Fund (RRIF):** an annuity, pioneered by the insurance industry, to channel retirement funds that must be withdrawn from tax-sheltered instruments. (p. 440)

**Registered Retirement Savings Plan (RRSP):** a tax-shelter that permits taxpayers to accumulate savings toward their retirement. (p. 446)

**Reinsurance:** insurance that is sold in the resale market. (p. 439)

**Reserves:** a portion of assets set aside by banks to provide for payments to be made, although generally, reserves now serve as a means of enhancing depositor confidence. Required reserves were phased out by 1994. (p. 363)

**Revaluation:** an arbitrary increase in the value of a currency that had previously been fixed in value. The opposite of a devaluation. (p. 148)

**Ricardian Equivalence Theorem:** A theory, attributed mistakenly to the great classical economist David Ricardo, which predicts that a tax cut will lead individuals to increase their savings to take account of the higher future tax burden. Also used to describe why there need not be a direct positive relationship between interest rates and government deficits. (p. 201)

**Risk:** the likelihood that an investment may prove to be unprofitable. (p. 275)

**Risk Averse:** the condition describing an individual who is willing to give up return in order to reduce risk. (p. 286)

**Risk Neutrality:** the situation in which an individual is concerned only with maximizing return irrespective of the level of risk. (p. 286)

**Risk-Seeking:** the condition describing an individual who actually is willing to give up return to increase risk. (p. 286)

**Risk Structure of Interest Rates:** the structure of interest rates such that the greater the risk of default of an underlying asset, the greater the yield to maturity for that asset. (p. 331)

**Savings & Loan Associations (S & L):** the US equivalent of the Canadian credit union or caisses populaires. (p. 495)

**Savings Deposit:** a bank deposit that typically earns a rate of interest and is highly liquid. (p. 29)

**Secondary Market:** the market for previously issued financial instruments. (p. 51)

**Sectors of the Economy:** the different groups that participate in the national economy. (p. 172)

**Securitization:** Describes the phenomenon whereby an asset which is normally not liquid, such as mortgages, are made liquid by pooling them and reselling the combined amount as short-term assets. Credit card debt as well as other types of assets normally illiquid are also securitized. (p. 84)

**Segregated Funds:** a portion of the insurance business that invests in mutual funds. These assets are kept separate from the rest of the insurance firm's activities, hence the term segregated. (p. 439)

**Seigniorage:** the profit made by printing money. (p. 37)

**Short Position:** the sale and delivery in the future of an asset, with the intent to buy it back at a lower price. Often the seller does not own the asset, but has borrowed it from a broker's inventory of assets. (p. 310)

**Special Drawing Right (SDR):** a unit of account created by the International Monetary Fund. It represents a weighted average of the exchange rates of a select group of industrialized countries. (p. 540)

**Special Purchase and Resale Agreement (SPRA):** an agreement made by the Bank of Canada to purchase a financial instrument and resell it to the vendor at a different price sometime in the near future (usually overnight). To achieve certain goals, the Bank may sometimes reverse the procedure and sell securities one day and repurchase them the next. (p. 71)

**Speculative Motive:** the demand for money that results from the existence of the opportunity cost of holding money. (p. 130)

**Speculator:** an individual who undertakes a transaction with a view to profit from a price change in the assets in question. (p. 304)

**Spot Market:** the market in which price and delivery of an asset are determined simultaneously. Also called the cash market. (p. 304)

**Spot Rate:** the rate for immediate delivery of an asset, usually of a currency. (p. 149)

**Spread:** the difference between borrowing and lending rates. (p. 208)

**Standard Deviation of Returns:** the square root of the variance of returns. (p. 280)

**Sterilization:** the actions taken by a central bank typically to offset a potential change in the domestic money supply due to a foreign exchange transaction. (p. 475)

**Stock Exchange:** the market where stock issues are traded. (p. 250)

**Stock Measures:** measures flow of funds activity at a particular moment in time. (p. 174)

**Stock Price Index:** an aggregate measure of the value of several stocks. Examples include the TSE 300 and the Dow Jones Industrial Average. (p. 250)

**Stocks:** shares of ownership that are sold by private corporations to raise funds. (p. 82)

**Store of Value:** the ability of money to command purchasing power in the future; considered to be one of the functions of money. (p. 21)

**Swaps:** exchanges of interest payments between two debtors or exchanges of foreign exchange. (p. 303)

**Systematic Risk:** the risk associated with the fact that changes in the price of an asset change systematically with the prices of other assets. (p. 276)

**Target Reserves:** when required reserves were eliminated in Canada the amount of reserves held were a function of cash management practices of individual banks necessary for day-to-day operations. (p. 363)

**Target Zone:** Describes an exchange rate system in which the exchange rate for the participating country is permitted to fluctuate in a specified range. The European Monetary System is the archetypical example of such an arrangement. (p. 546)

**Tax Risk:** The risk which arises when there is a change in the tax system which affects the return on a financial instrument. (p. 277)

**T-Bill Auction:** refers to the market in which Government of Canada Treasury bills are sold. The actual market is today an electronic one. (p. 66)

**Term Deposits:** a bank deposit paying a market rate of interest with limited liquidity. (p. 29)

**Term Insurance:** a type of insurance policy for a specified amount for a specified duration. (p. 440)

**Term Structure of Interest Rates:** the structure of interest rates on instruments that differ only by term to maturity but are otherwise the same. (p. 333)

**Time-Inconsistency Problem of Monetary Policy:** the theory which argues that the policymakers' commitment to a given rate of inflation is not a credible one because policymakers always have an incentive to deviate from their promise and implement inflationary monetary policy. (p. 619)

**Tobin's *q*:** the market value of a firm's capital divided by the replacement cost of a firm's capital. (p. 222)

**Transactions Costs:** the costs, financial and nonfinancial, of completing some economic transaction. Does not include the purchase price of the item in question. (p. 22)

**Transactions Motive:** the demand for money brought about by its use as a means of buying and selling goods and services. (p. 130)

**Transmission Mechanism:** the manner in which the monetary side of the economy can influence the real side of the economy. (p. 631)

**Treasury Bills (T-Bills):** short-term financial instruments sold at a discount, and issued by various levels of government. (p. 64)

**Trust Companies:** deposit-taking institutions that also specialize in the estate, trust, and agency business. (p. 422)

**Twin Deficits:** Describes the phenomenon of a deficit in the balance of payments which occurs simultaneously with a deficit in the government's budget. (p. 477)

**Underwriter:** investment dealer that helps governments and corporations raise capital by buying new securities from an issuer at a discount and reselling them to investors. (p. 81)

**Unit Banking:** single-bank banking operations as opposed to a banking operation with several branches. (p. 494)

**Universal Banking Model:** a banking model in which there are no restrictions on the types of financial activities that a bank can engage in. (p. 482)

**Utility Maximization:** the principle in economics that consumers are assumed to attempt to reach the highest level of satisfaction that can be enjoyed in the consumption of goods and services, that is, the highest or maximum level of utility. (p. 184)

**Variance of Returns:** the weighted average of the squared deviations of asset prices or yields. (p. 278)

**Velocity of Circulation:** the turnover rate of money. Usually measured as aggregate income (GDP) divided by a money stock measure. (p. 237)

**Volatility:** a measure of size of changes; for example, changes in price of bonds. (p. 102)

**When-issued T-Bill:** a Treasury bill which will be made available for purchase before it is actually issued. Yields on when-issued T-bills are viewed by some as a barometer of future interest rates. (p. 83)

**Yield Curve:** the curve of the yields to maturity of assets of different maturities. Essentially, the yield curve describes the relationship between short-term and long-term interest rates. (p. 334)

**Yield to Maturity:** the return of a financial asset if it is held until maturity. (p. 92)

**Zaibatsu:** the Japanese name for "financial cliques" of the late nineteenth and early twentieth centuries, which were conglomerates that carried out a number of functions, among which was that of financial intermediation similar to that of European and North American commercial banks. (p. 508)

**Zengin System:** the Japanese computerized network that handles transactions between banks and non-banks. (p. 516)

# INDEX